Alexander Hamilton

Alexander Hamilton

A BIOGRAPHY

Forrest McDonald

W·W·Norton & Company

NEW YORK

Library of Congress Cataloging in Publication Data
McDonald, Forrest.
Alexander Hamilton: a biography.
Includes bibliographical references and index.
1. Hamilton, Alexander, 1757–1804.
2. United States—Politics and government—1783–1809.
3. United States—Economic conditions—To 1865.
4. Statesmen—United States—Biography.
E302.6.H2M32   1979   973.4'092'4 [B]   78–26554
ISBN 0–393–01218–2

1 2 3 4 5 6 7 8 9 0

For Eliza—His and Mine

Contents

Preface

The founders of the American republic were ardently concerned with the judgment of posterity. Had they known what a fickle muse Clio would prove to be, they might have been more anxious. The making of myths and legends, complete with a hagiology and a demonology, is inherent in the process of evolution toward nationhood. Consequently, individual actors in the original drama have often been consigned by History to roles they did not actually play, and the most important of them have played shifting roles, being heroes in one generation and villains in the next. It is therefore not surprising that Alexander Hamilton—along with Washington, Jefferson, Adams, and Madison—has had his ups and downs at the hands of historians.

There are, however, two surprising things about the way Hamilton has been treated. First, much of the literature about him has been written by people who professed neither expertise nor interest in the areas of his greatest contributions: economics, finance, and the law. It is as if study of Napoleon be done by people with no knowledge of military affairs, or of Bach by people with no interest in music. I undertook the writing of this book for just that reason—Hamilton's fields of special prowess were not difficult for me. Two of them coincided with my own special fields of interest: having studied his fiscal policies and the eighteenth-century economy for thirty years, I believed I could make those matters intelligible to the general reader. The law was less familiar, but study of the great commentators (particularly Blackstone) and the great natural-law theorists (particularly Vattel) helped fill the gap. Two modern works, Julius Goebel's edition of Hamilton's legal papers and Morton Horwitz's excellent book *The Transformation of American Law*, informed and tempered my understanding of the subject.

Equally surprising is that few historians, and no biographers,

Preface

have sought to reconstruct Hamilton's world view by analyzing his writings in the context of his personal intellectual milieu—despite the obvious advantages of doing so. Valuable insights into Hamilton's psyche are available by that means; in Carl Becker's words, "Generally speaking, men are influenced by books which clarify their own thought, which express their own notions well, or which suggest to them ideas which their minds are already predisposed to accept." Moreover, isolating the particular intellectual milieu that Hamilton selected from the many that were available would necessarily clarify the meaning of his words and actions.

At first, believing I could build on previous scholarship, I thought this task would not be formidable. I was mistaken. For one thing, such writers as Thomas Hobbes, whose works have long been assumed to have influenced Hamilton, turned out upon careful study to have thought in patterns so different from Hamilton's mode of thinking as to rule out the likelihood of influence. For another, students of Hamilton's intellectual development have tended, misleadingly, to treat Hamilton as if he never grew—to ignore the striking differences between his writings before the age of twenty-five and the ideas he expressed in maturity. There was nothing for it, then, but to wade through the works of everyone who might conceivably have shaped Hamilton's thinking at the various stages of his life.

A lot of wasted motion accompanied the undertaking. It seemed improbable that Hamilton devoted much time to the works of the English Oppositionists (Davenant, Trenchard and Gordon, Bolingbroke, Burgh) who so profoundly influenced his political enemies; and yet, in his early political tracts he spouted Oppositionist clichés with ease and abandon, so it was necessary to study Oppositionist writings and compare them with Hamilton's. It was almost certain that in college Hamilton read the works of the Scottish moral philosophers Francis Hutcheson and Thomas Reid; and then and later he read and quoted from the works of other Scots, including David Hume, Adam Smith, and James Steuart. Study of the entire Scottish Enlightenment thus became necessary. In time, I thereby learned that it was the likes of Hutcheson and Reid whom Hamilton had in mind when he referred contemptuously to "speculative philosophers" who devised systems that were "geometrically true" though false in fact. I was also enabled to discern which ideas of

Preface

Hume and Smith he accepted and which he rejected. In similar fashion, I made my way through the works of other writers, including those of the English, French, and German Enlightenments.

Nuggets of gold gradually began to emerge from mountains of dross: besides Blackstone and Hume—to whom Hamilton's debt was obvious at the outset—there were Plutarch and Pope, Shaftesbury and Smith, Vattel and Beawes, Postlethwayt and Necker. Then, slowly, tediously, I began to reconstruct my understanding of what Hamilton did with his life, to reconcile my view of Hamilton with Hamilton's view of Hamilton. I do not claim that I have in every way succeeded. I do believe I have come closer than anyone has come before.

My labors were facilitated by many people. In particular, I am grateful to Mr. Richard Ware and the Earhart Foundation for financial support. I am obliged to Professor Kathryn T. Preyer, who offered valuable suggestions regarding legal history. I am deeply in debt to Professor Thomas P. Govan, the best scholar I have ever known, who has supplied me with ideas and information over the course of a long friendship and who read and criticized the manuscript with the loving care and critical faculty that he brings to every historical subject. Finally, there is one other person whom I might mention. With Hamiltonian gallantry I offered to put her name on the title page as co-author. With Hamiltonian propriety, she declined.

Forrest McDonald

Coker, Alabama
October 25, 1978

Alexander Hamilton

❦ I ❦

Young Man Hamilton

Ask of thy mother earth, why oaks are made

Taller or stronger than the weeds they shade? [1]

Until he was in his twenties, Alexander Hamilton dreamed of winning glory on the fields of battle. By the time he was twenty-five that adolescent yearning had been replaced by a craving for Fame, the secular equivalent of Christian immortality, and this craving never left him. Before he was thirty he had figured out how to reach his goal, and he spent the rest of his short life pursuing it.

Fame was the province of demigods, of mortals whose heroic deeds win them eternal and grateful remembrance in the hearts of posterity. In the ancient pantheon of demigods, as resurrected in the eighteenth century, the highest place was reserved for the Lawgiver, who "transmits a system of laws and institutions to secure the peace, happiness, and liberty of future generations." Hamilton was by no means alone among founders of the American Republic who aspired to that role, but he viewed it differently from the others. Their vision was grand: they sought to transform the nature of government by binding it with a fundamental law, a written constitution that would govern the exercise of power. His vision was grander: he sought to transform the American people into free, opulent, and law-abiding citizens, through the instrumentality of a limited republican government, on the basis of consent, and in the face of powerful vested interests in the status quo. The others were content merely to effect a political revolution. He set out to effect what amounted to a social revolution. [2]

As Hamilton saw the people of his adopted country, they were kept from being a great nation, indeed kept from being a nation at all, by the inertia of a social order whose pervasive attributes were

[3]

provincialism and lassitude. Provincialism was reinforced by habit, by opinion, by familiarity, by interests; but in every state and every region its main prop, as well as its main beneficiary, was an oligarchy, great or small. That scheme of things discouraged industry by failing to reward it. Status derived not from the marketplace, where deeds and goods and virtues could be impartially valued, but from birthright. More precisely, status rested upon personal relations which rested upon family connections which in turn rested upon ownership of the land. In the few, this social order bred the habit of arbitrary command or rule by cabal, in defiance of law; in the many it bred the habit of deference and, because a tolerable subsistence was easy to come by, it bred laziness as well. To be sure, the work ethic and opportunity for advancement energized the people in the larger port towns and in those parts of New England nearest the seaports, and the German-Americans in and southward of Pennsylvania were likewise diligent. But otherwise energy and persistent application were scarcely to be found. His countrymen, Hamilton said, had "the passiveness of the sheep in their compositions"; it was almost impossible to rouse them from "the lethargy of voluptuous indolence." To him all this was anathema because it was alien to his own nature, because it was inherently unjust, and because, in his eyes, it made the nation weak and despicable.[3]

Hamilton's audacious mission in life was to remake American society in accordance with his own values; and by 1787 he had conceived a means of accomplishing that revolutionary change. What distinguished the industrious minority from other Americans was that they measured worth and achievement in terms of money and worked to obtain money, whereas the others disdained to work for money (though they were willing to connive for it) and made do with a cumbersome system of personal obligations, barter, and fiat credit. To transform the established order, to make society fluid and open to merit, to make industry both rewarding and necessary, all that needed to be done was to monetize the whole—to rig the rules of the game so that money would become the universal measure of the value of things. For money is oblivious to class, status, color, and inherited social position; money is the ultimate, neutral, impersonal arbiter. Infused into an oligarchical, agrarian social order, money would be the leaven, the fermenting yeast, that would stimulate growth, change, prosperity, and national strength.[4]

A passion for immortal Fame is characteristic of the romantic, and Hamilton was a romantic to the core of his being. (Hamilton to a boyhood friend, at the age of twelve: "I . . . would willingly risk my life tho' not my Character to exalt my Station. . . . I wish there was a War." To the people of New York, at eighteen: "The arms of Britain, . . . discipline and military skill are certainly matters of great importance, [but] natural intrepidity, and that animation, which is inspired by a desire of freedom, and a love of one's country, may very well overballance those advantages." To a young lady, at twenty: "ALL FOR LOVE is my motto." To another young lady, at twenty-two: "I should have thought myself bound to have set prudence and policy at defiance, and even to have attacked *windmills* in your Ladyship's service . . . to have fancied New York an *inchanted castle* . . . and myself a valorous knight." To a comrade in arms, at twenty-two: "I wish . . . it might be in my power, by action rather than words, to convince you that I love you. I shall only tell you that 'till you bade us Adieu, I hardly knew the value you had taught my heart to set upon you." To his fiancée, at twenty-three: *"I would this moment give the world to be near you only to kiss your sweet hand."* To fellow delegates in the Constitutional Convention, at thirty: "Mr. Hamilton . . . professed himself to be as zealous an advocate for liberty as any man whatever, and trusted he should be as willing a martyr to it." To a friend, at thirty-eight: "The game to be played . . . may be for nothing less than true liberty, property, order, religion and of course *heads*.")[5]

Romanticism, perhaps the most sublime of afflictions, is a congenital psychic disorder whose symptoms are evident throughout life. In childhood the romantic writes poetry and dreams of grand and noble exploits. As a youth he embraces causes and fights for them with reckless bravery—which is easy enough for him to do, since he is unable to imagine that failure or defeat is possible. He falls in love once, passionately, and for life, though he is capable of additional *affaires d'amour* that imperil everything. He is spirited, gallant, and bold and sees high drama where others see blandness. He inspires admiration and loyalty in some, envy and hatred in others; he can be charming and witty but not genuinely humorous, for though life to him is always a joyful affirmation, it is never funny. Like the sentimentalist, the dreamer, and the do-gooder, the romantic is ruled by his heart rather than his head. Unlike them, he is also tough-minded and realistic, and that creates within him a turbulence they never know: he drives himself to excel, requires discipline of himself far beyond that of other men, is ever concerned with honor, sometimes obsessively.

One more thing. Romanticism is a malady suitable only to the young: at best it can sustain a man half a lifetime. The lucky ones die in the summer of their years, for autumn brings the news that they are mortal as the vulgar herd, and the chilling hint that the cosmos is indifferent to man's pathetic doings. Facing the long winter of old age and then extinction, the romantic, like other men, is forced to make the awesome choice between cynicism and belief.

That was Hamilton, start to finish. He shared the world stage with George III, Louis XVI, Napoleon, Talleyrand, Pitt, Fox; in America his co-actors were Washington, Jefferson, Madison, Adams, Burr. But these were merely contemporaries. His true kin were the likes of Byron and Beethoven.

It is easier to describe the romantic personality than to account for it, but surely that and much else in Hamilton's makeup derived from his parents and his childhood. His mother, Rachel Faucett Lavien, was of a respectable family of French Huguenots who unfortunately lacked the knack of establishing stable marriages. Her father was John Faucett, a physician, man of letters, and planter on the British West Indies island of Nevis. In 1740 her parents were legally separated. Five years later she went with her mother, Mary Faucett, to visit her older sister, who was married to a prosperous planter on the Danish island of St. Croix. There she met a planter and merchant named Johan Michael Lavien, whose peacock wardrobe suggested falsely that he was a man of great wealth. Though Rachel was only in her teens, her mother forced her into a marriage with Lavien, and she had by him a son named Peter. The marriage was a wretched one, however, and Rachel—described as "a woman of great beauty, brilliancy, and accomplishments"—apparently found it impossible to perform her wifely duties. In 1750 Lavien had her imprisoned for "indecent and very suspicious" behavior, thinking that incarceration in the miserable island prison would stimulate her to change "her ungodly mode of life" and that upon her release she "would live with him as was meet and fitting." Instead, she fled the island and made her way back to Nevis.[6]

Hamilton's father, James Hamilton, was of noble lineage. He was the fourth son of a Scottish laird, descended from a ducal line, who had married the daughter of an "ancient Baronet," Sir Robert Pollock. Such a bloodline, as Hamilton remarked late in life, gave him "better pretensions than most of those who in this Country plume themselves on Ancestry." It did not, however, give him material well-being. James Hamilton went to the West Indies as a merchant but gradually succumbed to the languors of the islands; easy-going, lazy, excessively generous, and no doubt regularly drinking to excess, he went bankrupt and began a long career as a ne'er-do-well and drifter. Nonetheless, he instilled in Hamilton a pride of ancestry and, as a man of fine Celtic imagination who dreamed and planned even if he failed to execute, he doubtless aroused in his son a high level of expectations.[7]

Hamilton's parents met on Nevis after Rachel's return and began a cohabitation that lasted more than fifteen years. They had two sons; James was born about 1753 and Alexander on January 11, 1757. When Hamilton was two, Lavien obtained a divorce from Rachel, and it seems likely that James and Rachel then went through a marriage ceremony. If so, they were in for a surprise, for the terms of the divorce precluded Rachel from ever remarrying. They may not have learned this until 1765, when the family went to St. Croix, James Hamilton having been sent by his mercantile employer to collect a debt there. Possibly that explains what he did next: he remained a few months, collected the debt, then sailed for the island of St. Kitts, leaving the family behind. He stayed in touch for a while, but he never got around to returning.[8]

Rachel managed. She rented a house from the merchant Thomas Dipnall and in it opened a retail store, selling food and other imported items to local plantations. She bought her goods on credit from Dipnall and from David Beckman & Nicholas Cruger, a wholesale import-export firm recently established in Christiansted by two young New Yorkers; she kept her books in good order and made her payments punctually. The boys also went to work, Alexander for Beckman & Cruger. No doubt he served only as an all-purpose flunky at first, but it is safe to assume that he rapidly acquired a solid grounding in the rudiments of wholesale and retail trade, both foreign and domestic. Thus Hamilton's personal indifference to property was tempered by a hard-nosed realism about credit and accounts. Rachel also saw to more bookish training. She had Alexander at an early age in a school run by a Jewish lady, and he could repeat the decalogue in Hebrew when so small that he gave his recitations "standing by her side on a table." Rachel apparently loved books, for she acquired thirty-four of those rare treasures herself; and though young James was not especially interested, Alexander probably read them avidly. He also became reasonably fluent in French.[9]

Then the world of childhood suddenly came crumbling down. In February 1768, Rachel died of a tropical fever. Peter Lavien claimed and obtained her estate, leaving his half-brothers penniless; and it became clear that Hamilton's father, gone two years now, was not coming back to take care of his sons. They became the ward of Peter Lytton, Rachel's nephew, but in 1769, grieved over the death of his own wife, Lytton committed suicide. The others of Rachel's relatives went broke or left St. Croix. Young James was apprenticed to a carpenter and moved in with his master. Alex is said to have been taken in by Thomas Stevens, father of his boyhood chum Edward Stevens.[10]

At the age of nine Hamilton's prospects had surely seemed boundless, for one can imagine the fanciful future James Hamilton painted for his precocious son. At the age of twelve he had no apparent future at all, and from then onward he had no one on whom he had a right to rely but himself.

He was, it is true, remarkably self-reliant. He continued to work for Beckman & Cruger and was increasingly trusted with managerial as well as clerical functions. When Alex was fourteen Cruger took a trip to New York for his health and left Hamilton in charge for several months; the boy bought and sold cargoes and gave orders to sea captains with the authority of a seasoned merchant. Meanwhile, his circumstances afforded time for reading as well as access to books, and he read whatever he could lay his hands on. His reading reflected his parental mix: his favorites were Pope (he wrote idyllic poetry himself) and Plutarch's *Lives of the Noble Grecians and Romans,* which he devoured along with the firm's accounts and treatises on mathematics and chemistry. As he read, he improved upon a capacity for total concentration and an ability to master complex subjects rapidly. [11]

But it is not easy being a frail little boy, having nobody, in a world in which the privileged few live in idle luxury from the labor of Negro slaves who outnumber them more than ten to one; and the difficulty is not lessened when one believes that, by right of birth and talent, one deserves a better lot. Possibly Hamilton felt betrayed and deserted by his parents, but there is no evidence that he did so. There is abundant evidence that he resented his fate, that he attributed it to the injustices of the socio-legal system that ordained it, and that he was fiercely determined to overcome it.

The most revealing of his early letters is the first that is known to exist. On November 11, 1769, he wrote to Edward Stevens, who had been sent to New York to attend King's College. "To confess my weakness," the twelve-year-old wrote, "my Ambition is [so] prevalent that I contemn the grov'ling and condition of a Clerk or the like, to which my Fortune &c. condemns me and would willingly risk my life tho' not my Character to exalt my Station. Im confident, Ned that my Youth excludes me from any hopes of immediate Preferment nor do I desire it, but I mean to prepare the way for futurity. Im no Philosopher you see and may be jusly said to Build Castles in the Air. My Folly makes me ashamd and beg youll Conceal it, yet Neddy we have seen such Schemes successfull when the Projector is Constant I shall Conclude saying I wish there was a War." [12]

His "weakness" was that he was unable to accept his lot like a "Philosopher," and was "ambitious" enough to risk his life, though not his good reputation, to improve his station. He did not desire "Preferment"—special or unearned favors—but would welcome a war, for war would provide a quick means of earning advancement on his own merits. The propensity to "Build Castles in the Air" surely came from his father; the phrases "prepare the way for futurity" and "the Projector is Constant" as surely reflect the influence of his mother. The other key passage bespeaks his reaction to what had happened: "I contemn the grov'ling . . . to which my Fortune &c. condemns me." The archaic word "contemn," like "despise," indicated "the judging of a thing as mean, petty, worthless, or repulsive, and a consequent, often derisive, looking down upon it"; but "contemn" went further, suggesting an even "harsher though more intellectual judgment." The word "groveling" would disappear from Hamilton's vocabulary, but he never outgrew his hatred of dependency.[13]

And thus, with a sense of otherness that attends the truly gifted, the boy knew he was destined for greater things. He never ceased to dream of grand and heroic accomplishments, but he tempered his dreams with regular habits, reliable behavior, systematic and persistent application, and constant attention to self-improvement. He despised laziness, disorderliness, unpredictability, impropriety, procrastination, drunkenness, sloth—the ways of the islands and, as he would come to believe by 1779, the ways of most Americans as well. His own moral code became the opposite of all those characteristics; and in that sense, though Hamilton was by no means a prude, he was emphatically a puritan. Indeed, when he found his life's calling, it would be to refashion his countrymen into moral beings, as he understood morality.

What the teen-aged Hamilton needed was some formal education, a larger arena, and a cause. He got all three through the agency of the Reverend Hugh Knox, who showed up on St. Croix in the spring of 1772, "discovered" Hamilton, and (probably in collaboration with Cruger and others) organized plans to provide for his education. Knox was an Ulster Scot, a Princeton-educated Presbyterian minister who also practiced medicine, wrote theological tracts, and considered it a high calling to serve as a "patron who draws genius out of obscurity." His influence upon Hamilton, during the few months he had him under his direct tutelage, was considerable, especially in focusing and reinforcing his moral sense. Knox inspired Hamilton with a religious piety that lasted for some time, impressed upon him the dangers of drinking to excess, and taught him to abhor slavery as the wellspring of many other evils. Most immediately important, however, was the orientation of Knox's faction of the Kirk: in a manner of speaking, the fifteen-year-old Hamilton fell in with a group of revolutionaries.[14]

The Presbyterian Church, the Kirk of Scotland, was one of several Calvinist sects that had numerous adherents in British America, even though the Church of England was established by law in most of the colonies south of New England. Hamilton had been exposed to three varieties of Calvinism—the Scottish through his father, the French through his mother, and the Dutch through Henry Cruger—before coming under Knox's influence, and two cardinal tenets of the Calvinist persuasion, those extolling the virtues of education and hard work, had been instilled into his makeup. But Calvinism had been radically altered in recent years by a religious revival movement known as the Great Awakening, which split most of the sects into opposing theological groups called (among the Presbyterians) New Sides and Old Sides. In addition to the rigid, authoritarian, and predestinarian doctrines of traditional Calvinism, the New Sides preached an evangelical theology of moral regeneration and individual responsibility. In other words, they were a disruptive dissenting group within a dissenting church. By the 1760s they had gained control of Presbyterianism in America and had established a college at Princeton. Hugh Knox, Hamilton's counselor, was a thoroughgoing New Sides man, and so were the friends in New Jersey into whose care he proposed to entrust Hamilton. Hamilton's college, of course, was to be Princeton.[15]

There was also a political dimension to American Presbyterianism. In the Middle Colonies, Scottish and Scotch-Irish Presbyterians were political radicals, leaders (in alliance with Dutch Calvinists and transplanted New England Congregationalists) of the resistance against the mother country in the impending revolutionary struggle; when the showdown over independence came, the Calvinist coalition seized control of New York, New Jersey, and Pennsylvania by ousting the Anglican and Quaker Tories. Knox's New Jersey friends—especially William Livingston and Elias Boudinot, with whom Hamilton would live while preparing himself for Princeton—had already distinguished themselves as American Patriot leaders. Livingston's son-in-law, John Jay, would be an even more influential Revolutionary figure.[16]

Things did not work out as Knox had planned them, however, though the first year went better than anyone but Hamilton himself might have predicted. When Hamilton arrived in New Jersey in the fall of 1772, he was placed in Francis Barber's Elizabethtown Academy to prepare for Princeton's entrance requirements. Two years, even three, would have been a short time for the task: Hamilton had had little formal schooling, and Princeton required for admission—besides the "common branches" of English literature and composition, elocution, mathematics, and geography—"the ability to write Latin prose, translate Vergil, Cicero, and the Greek gospels, and a commensurate knowledge of Latin and Greek grammar." But Hamilton was allowed to work at his own pace, which was brisk: he completed his preparations in less than a year.[17]

Then he ran into a snag. Accompanied by his friend Hercules Mulligan, Hamilton called upon the Rev. Dr. John Witherspoon, the Scots-born, Edinburgh-educated Presbyterian divine who presided over the College of New Jersey at Princeton. Witherspoon examined "the young gentleman . . . to his entire satisfaction," but Hamilton came up with a surprising proposal—that he be admitted among Princeton's eighty-five students in whatever "of the classes to which his attainments would entitle him but with the understanding that he should be permitted to advance from Class to Class with as much rapidity as his exertions would enable him to do." Witherspoon discussed the request with his trustees, then rejected it. Undeterred, Hamilton took his proposal to President Myles Cooper of King's College in New York (Columbia University), who accepted the audacious young man on his own terms. King's was Anglican and Tory, but Cooper, in time, would be grateful that he had admitted the radical Scots Presbyterian.[18]

Despite differences in theological and political orientation, the curriculum at King's was roughly that of any other American college. The environment, however, was another matter, for New York was politically more volatile than Princeton and most other college towns, and the ferment that soon erupted into revolution was beginning to brew. The Boston Tea Party came two months after Hamilton entered King's, Britain's retaliatory Coercive Acts came five months later, and the First Continental Congress was meeting before the end of Hamilton's first year. The temptation to take part in the revolutionary movement was irresistible.

Not that Hamilton neglected his studies. Until early 1776, when he began to devote his full time to military activities, he devoured King's curriculum in huge gulps. Satisfying requirements through private tutoring as well as in formal classes, he virtually completed the course of instruction in less than two and a half years, though he never took a degree. (Besides learning fast and working long hours, he developed a peculiar study habit that he continued to follow throughout his life: when walking alone he talked to himself

continuously, rehearsing lessons, working out problems, or compos-
ing papers or political tracts.)[19]

But the arena beckoned. As early as mid-1774 he was speaking at
patriotic rallies, swaying crowds with argument despite his delicate,
boyish appearance (he was seventeen and looked even younger). In
the winter of 1774–75 he published two major political tracts, *A Full
Vindication of the Measures of the Congress* and *The Farmer Refuted,* in a polemical battle with the Anglican minister and Tory
Samuel Seabury. Hamilton's pair of articles, totaling around 60,000
words, were dashed off in about two weeks apiece and published
anonymously; when their authorship became known, there was
general astonishment that one so young could have written them.
In truth, though they were as sophisticated as the celebrated tracts
of the thirty-one-year-old Thomas Jefferson and the thirty-nine-
year-old John Adams, they did not measure up to Hamilton's later,
more mature standards.[20]

Meanwhile, unlike either Jefferson or Adams, Hamilton was also
preparing himself for the fighting. Together with Robert Troup and
other classmates and friends, he formed a volunteer drill company
and learned the manual of arms and rudiments of soldiery from a retired officer, Major Edward Fleming. On the night of August 23,
1775, under fire for the first time, he coolly helped remove two
dozen cannon from the Battery, beneath the blazing guns of H.M.S.
Asia. In the ensuing weeks he began to study artillery, probably
under the tutorship of his mathematics professor. By midwinter he
had formed an artillery company and was commissioned a captain,
with sixty-eight officers and men under his command.[21]

Personal ambition and ardor for the cause of American independence had become one. The fusion would be permanent, but the
quality of the parts would change. In 1775–76 Hamilton saw fighting as his contribution to the cause and military glory as the only
reward he coveted from it. He thought the justness of the cause
beyond question, and enthusiastically assumed that most of his
countrymen shared his devotion. The assumption is inherent in the
initial embracing of a cause. The measure of the strength of one's
ideals comes later, when one is forced to see that good men stand on
the other side, and that one's own ranks are riddled with knaves and
fools. Hamilton's idealism survived the challenge: what changed
were his ideals.

His naïve faith in the virtue of American Patriots was subjected to strain even before the war started. On the evening of May 10, 1775, a "murderous band" of about four hundred men had gathered to attack the home of the King's College president. To Hamilton that was simply not acceptable: preparing to fight a war for American liberty was one thing, wantonly destroying the property and imperiling the life of a defenseless individual, however odious his opinions, was quite another. Upon hearing the din, Hamilton and Troup hastened to the scene and interrupted the angry mob. Hamilton delayed its progress with a political harangue while the sleeping Cooper was roused and led from his house. Then Hamilton, just as the "ferocious throng" broke down the college gates, escorted Cooper through back streets to the banks of the Hudson, where he found refuge in the home of a friend.[22]

Hamilton made the transition from boy to man in the army, serving from a month after his nineteenth birthday until two months before his twenty-fifth. The first year of his service was with his artillery company, which he commanded with both zeal and thoroughness. In his prewar polemics he had written, "There is a certain enthusiasm in liberty, that makes human nature rise above itself, in acts of bravery and heroism" and predicted that such "animation" would be enough to overcome Britain's advantage of having a professional army. He built upon that enthusiasm, inspiring his men by his own example and by ensuring that their achievements were recognized and rewarded. At the same time, he disciplined them and, through assiduous administrative labors, saw to their being splendidly uniformed, well provisioned, and regularly paid. Hamilton's company fought with distinction in the defense of New York and during the seven-weeks' retreat across New Jersey. If Hamilton showed a fault during this first year of the war, it was that he was bold to the point of recklessness.[23]

He came to the attention of his superiors. Two major generals sought his services as aide-de-camp, but he turned them down because the office had in it "a kind of personal dependance." Then General George Washington, the commander-in-chief himself, invited Hamilton to join his "family" as an aide, with a double promotion to lieutenant colonel. Hamilton accepted in February 1777 and worked intimately with Washington for four years. He managed the general's administrative affairs, wrote much of his correspondence, and carried out a variety of special assignments. Indeed, his services were almost those of a modern chief of staff. The experience taught him something about himself, which rankled even as it contributed to his maturity. Much as he yearned to prove his worth on the battlefield, he was forced to recognize that he could contribute far more as an administrator—for he was a man who could run things, and that talent was in great demand and short supply.[24]

There were compensations. Though he had no field command and thus no opportunity to win glory, he repeatedly knew the thrill and danger of combat. And there was the joy of comradeship: he developed a strong sense of brotherhood with all the officers who served with honor in the Continental line, and he retained that feeling throughout his life, even toward those who became his political opponents. His feelings were strongest for Lafayette, Nathanael Greene, Baron von Steuben, and the fellow aides who constituted Washington's military family. Among the aides—Tench Tilghman, Robert Hanson Harrison, James McHenry, Richard Kidder Meade, John Laurens, and a dozen others who served at one time or another—mutual affection was apparently unmarred by jealousy, despite differences in talent. Hamilton's feelings toward Laurens, for whom he openly avowed his "love" and whom he called "my dear," were especially intense.[25]

And then there were the ladies. During the long intervals between fighting, young ladies of quality often visited army headquarters to flirt and exchange patriotic sentiments with the dashing young officers. In youth and maturity Hamilton loved the ladies, and they him; there was scarce a one he could not charm, and none who could not deceive him. They were susceptible to him because of his attentiveness and flirtatious pleasantries, his polished manners, his gracefulness as a dancer, his wit, and his good looks. He was, in the phrase of the time, a very pretty fellow. He had auburn hair, "deep blue—almost violet" eyes, fair skin, and rosy red cheeks. His male friends called him "little Hammy" or the "little lion"—not because he was short, since at five feet seven inches he was of average height or perhaps an inch taller, but because he was light of frame in an age of fat people. Women doubtless called him little things more intimate, and were smitten with his slender elegance and boyish appearance. As for his gullibility in dealing with women, it derived from his romantic exaltation of them and from his belief that they found him irresistible.[26]

Hamilton once wrote a playful letter to Laurens, specifying his requirements for a wife: "She must be young, handsome (I lay most stress on a good shape) sensible (a little learning will do), well bred ... chaste and tender (I am an enthusiast in my notions of fidelity and fondness) of some good nature, a great deal of generosity (she must neither love money nor scolding, for I dislike equally a termagent and an oeconomist). In politics, I am indifferent what side she may be of; I think I have arguments that will easily convert her to mine. As to religion a moderate stock will satisfy me. She must believe in god and hate a saint. But as to fortune, the larger stock of that the better." At the same time, however, Hamilton was asserting that he would never marry, since the burden of a wife would interfere with his ambition.[27]

Having made that adolescent claim, he fell hopelessly in love, and in December of 1780 he was married. The lady was Elizabeth Schuyler, a shy, sweet-tempered, "nut brown maid," not especially attractive by the standards of the time except for hauntingly lovely black eyes and a small body that precisely fit Hamilton's specifications. She fit them in another way, too, for her father was General Philip Schuyler, a wealthy Hudson River patroon. Some have suggested that the family connection was the most appealing thing to Hamilton about Betsey, and that he cynically subordinated love to ambition in making his choice. Doubtless he would never have considered a lowborn woman for a wife, but otherwise the suggestion is nonsense. His devotion to her was passionate and constant; moreover, though he and his father-in-law became intimate friends as well as political allies, and the connection served him well, he scrupulously avoided taking money from Schuyler even when he and Betsey had to live in strained circumstances.[28]

Despite his love and marriage, however, he remained susceptible to female wiles. Sometimes he was blameless, as with respect to Mrs. Benedict Arnold. That lady, having been privy to and at least partly the instigator of her husband's treason, was left alone at the headquarters house when Arnold, detected, fled to board H.M.S. *Vulture*. She put on a convincing act, pretending to be deranged by distress at the conduct of her husband, screaming that Washington was at the head of a plot to murder her child, and indulging in other histrionics. Next morning she had calmed but continued the act, aiming to win the Americans' sympathy so they would give her safe conduct to join her husband. Hamilton was totally gulled by the performance. "Her sufferings," he wrote Betsey, "were so eloquent that I wished myself her brother, to have a right to become her defender. As it is, I have entreated her to enable me to give her proofs of my friendship." He could sooner forgive Arnold "for sacrificing his honor reputation and duty," Hamilton went on, than "forgive him for acting a part that must have forfeited the esteem of so fine a woman." In Hamilton's defense, it must be admitted that Peggy Shippen Arnold was no tyro.[29]

At other times he was less innocently seduced. His meeting with Angelica Schuyler Church, Betsey's beautiful, vivacious, worldly sister, was the beginning of a lifelong flirtation that some have judged adulterous. That judgment is unsubstantiated; but he would have one extramarital affair, and it would be costly.[30]

But in the main the years with Washington were a time of frustration and disillusionment, of the shattering of naïve beliefs about his country and its leaders. He expressed his idealism when penning three newspaper articles denouncing a corrupt member of the Continental Congress. The station of a member of Congress, Hamilton declared, "is the most illustrious and important of any I am able to conceive. He is to be regarded not only as a legislator, but as the founder of an empire. A man of virtue and ability, dignified with so precious a trust, would rejoice that fortune had given him birth at a time, and placed him in circumstances so favourable for promoting human happiness." He spelled out the way a man of virtue and ability would behave in those circumstances. The "generous objects of his care" would be to form useful foreign alliances, to establish a wise government, and to improve the finances and internal relations of his country. "Anxious for the permanent power and prosperity of the State, he would labour to perpetuate the union and harmony of the several parts." In council or debate he would show the "candor of a statesman, zealous for truth, and the integrity of a patriot studious of the public welfare; not the cavilling petulance of an attorney, contending for the triumph of an opinion, nor the perverse duplicity of a partisan." He would show his superior wisdom not by an affectation of learning but "by foreseeing evils, and contriving expedients to prevent or remedy them. . . . In his transactions with individuals, whether foreigners or countrymen, his conduct would be guided by the sincerity of a man, and the politeness of a gentleman." At first, Hamilton devoutly believed the nation was led by such men.[31]

Disillusionment began with a rush late in 1777. In October General Horatio Gates won a crucial victory over the British at Saratoga, though the success had nothing to do with his leadership or valor. Washington, seeing an opportunity to bring the war to a speedy end, dispatched Hamilton to Gates's headquarters to borrow a sizable body of troops for a decisive attack upon British forces in New York or Philadelphia. The mission was an exercise in futility, for Gates refused to cooperate. Instead, he became involved in a "cabal" with Thomas Conway, an Irishman and former officer in the French army who was now a brigadier general in the American army, to have Washington deprived of his command and replaced by Gates. That plot collapsed, but Gates was lionized at Washington's expense in the press, and Congress created a new Board of War and placed Gates at its head. Hamilton, who at that time idolized Washington, understandably suspected that Congress might not be so wise and virtuous after all.[32]

Suspicion soon turned into hostility. After the unsuccessful mission Hamilton was stricken with a near-fatal illness, involving fever and rheumatic pains, which kept him abed for three weeks; then he rejoined the army at its winter quarters in Valley Forge. When he arrived there in January he found his comrades hungry, half-frozen, and in rags. Like most officers, he attributed the sufferings of the army to corruption and incompetence on the part of Congress.[33]

His disenchantment was doubtless increased by the presence at Valley Forge of a small committee of congressmen which included Gouverneur Morris. That young New York aristocrat, who would be an intimate social and political friend the rest of Hamilton's life, was outspoken in his contempt for the people at large, for most politicians, and for what he called the "set of scoundrels" who dominated Congress. His devotion to the cause of American liberty was as unreserved as his skepticism of popular government, and Hamilton found him personally irresistible. His wit was biting, his power of ridicule devastating; so infectuous was his personality that Hamilton, when dealing with him, unconsciously imitated his style. If the doings of Congress that winter—Congress came within one vote of replacing Washington with Gates—and what Hamilton saw around him were not enough to shake his political beliefs, the presence of Gouverneur Morris surely was.[34]

When he first revealed his skepticism to an important official—in a letter to Governor George Clinton of New York—Hamilton pointed the way his thinking would move for some time. He lambasted Congress for its "folly, caprice [and] a want of foresight," for its "ductility and inconstancy," and for its "feeble indecisive and improvident" treatment of the army. "These things," he said, "wound my feelings as a republican more than I can express." He confided a suspicion that much of the evil was attributable to Gates and Conway, who had become inspector general when Gates became head of the Board of War; Conway, he said, was a "vermin" and a "villainous calumniator and incendiary." But the heart of the problem, he believed, was a degeneration of the quality of members of Congress (which, he insisted, had earlier been such as "would do honor to any age or nation"). The reason for the decline was that the best people, out of "local attachment, falsely operating," had forsaken Congress for service in state governments. Unless this "pernicious mistake" were corrected, the common cause of the union would end in ruin.[35]

That line of thinking—a belief that attachment to the interests of states, rather than to the nation, would undermine the American cause—would grow in Hamilton's mind. So would a more personal feeling that Hamilton revealed in his letter to Clinton: that the irresponsible actions of "the great council of America," the Congress, "in some degree make me contemptible in my own eyes." His identification of the nation's honor with his own would, in time, become total.

Meanwhile, Americans on all levels, not just in Congress, were disregarding honor, and even decency, in their actions. Merchants were profiteering through price-gouging and manipulation of markets; they preyed upon the very troops defending them, and soon that practice would spread until it became what Hamilton called an *"epidemical spirit of extortion."* ("I hate money making men," he said to Laurens.) Bands of thugs roamed the countryside, pillaging private property under the pretense of combatting traitors. In New England state politicians played loose with the war effort in order to facilitate private speculations. South of Virginia, as General Greene wrote Hamilton, there was "no such thing as National character or National Sentiment." In Virginia as well as North Carolina, law and political liberty disappeared, victims of the fiat rule of rival groups of plantation oligarchs. Perhaps worst of all, state governments and Congress alike were engaging in an orgy of expropriation, ostensibly to finance the war but in actuality to enrich some individuals at the expense of others. Hamilton commented early in 1778, "we have gotten into the spirit of making *ex post facto laws,* or rather violating all law." That spirit was soon running berserk, and Hamilton's sense of shame in his country grew apace.[36]

His disenchantment was evident in his personal behavior. He had always comported himself with a good deal of pride, a touch of hauteur, and as much frankness as the code of gentlemen allowed; those habits now became exaggerated, sometimes to the point of short-tempered contempt for others. He regaled General Charles Lee with insults when, at the battle of Monmouth, Lee behaved in a way that Hamilton thought disgraceful and cowardly; the aftermath of that episode might have led to a duel between the two except that Laurens beat Hamilton to it. Hamilton also thought about challenging a clergyman named William Gordon. Gordon had circulated a rumor that Hamilton, while on a mission to Congress in the winter of 1778–79, "had declared in a public coffee house in Philadelphia, that it was high time for the people to rise, join General Washington, and turn Congress out of doors." Hamilton not only denied the rumor but traced it to its source and then flooded Gordon with a torrent of abuse. Nonetheless, his criticism of Congress, voiced to friends in private, was outspoken. To Laurens, he declared that three-fourths of the members of Congress were mortal enemies to talent and that three-fourths of the remainder were contemptuous of integrity.[37]

Hamilton's romantic conception of warfare disappeared along with his trust in politicians. His original notions were in keeping with an idea, then fashionable in some circles, of war as more than a mere instrument of statecraft. To those who took part in it as officers, it was also a polite game, as gracefully stylized as a minuet and as formal and rule-bound as a duel. Its function was that of a proving ground for gentlemen. The measure of a true gentleman was virtue, in the original Latin sense of the term, meaning manhood. The marks of virtue were sense of duty, responsibility, courage, and coolness in time of danger, along with propriety, candor, gallantry, magnanimity, self-discipline, and above all honor. It may have been true, as Blackstone said, that in ordinary circumstances a gentleman was anybody who could pass himself off for one; but on the battlefield the imposter was unmasked.[38]

Some aspects of the gentlemanly approach to war are illustrated by the case of Hamilton's friend Laurens. Hamilton and Laurens were fellow aides-de-camp for about two years, then Laurens resigned and returned to South Carolina. His purpose was to organize four battalions of Negro troops, who would be freed in exchange for military service—a scheme that Hamilton heartily supported. When the plan was rejected by the South Carolina legislature, Laurens rejoined the army, only to be captured by the British upon the fall of Charleston in May 1780. In accordance with military convention, he was "paroled" and sent to Pennsylvania on his promise as an officer and gentleman that he would neither rejoin the fighting nor leave the state unless and until he were exchanged for a British officer of equal rank captured by the Americans. His "prison," in other words, was the state of Pennsylvania, which was entirely in American hands and which he was free to roam at will; all that bound him was his word of honor, but that was as restrictive as walls of steel. Hamilton made repeated efforts to negotiate an exchange that would release his friend, but that was difficult because propriety ruled out giving Laurens preferential treatment. As his attempts ran into snags, he commiserated with Laurens, urging him to "play the Philosopher," to bear his fate "like a man," and have recourse "neither to the dagger, nor to the poisoned bowl, nor to the rope." These melodramatic references to suicide were doubtless romantic hyperbole, but romantic hyperbole was as familiar as death to both young men, and each was capable of entertaining the idea.[39]

In his letters to his absent friend—and to him alone—Hamilton recorded his growing disenchantment with the American people, the American cause, and the military life. In September of 1779 he predicted failure for Laurens's plan to raise the slave battalions: "Even the animated and persuasive eloquence of my young Demosthenes will not be able to rouse his countrymen from the lethargy of voluptuous indolence, or dissolve the fascinating character of self interest, to inspire them with the _____ and wisdom of legislators and with the natural enthusiasm of republicans. . . . The birth and education of these states has fitted their inhabitants for the chain, and . . . the only condition they sincerely desire is that it may be a golden one." In January 1780: "I am a stranger in this country. I have no property here, no connexions. If I have talents and integrity, (as you say I have) these are justly deemed very spurious titles in these enlightened days, when unsupported by others more solid." He had been seeking a field command, Hamilton went on, but others had dissuaded him. "I am chagrined and unhappy but I submit. In short Laurens I am disgusted with every thing in this world but yourself and *very* few more honest fellows and I have no other wish than as soon as possible to make a brilliant exit." In June: "Our countrymen have all the folly of the ass and all the passiveness of the sheep in their compositions. They are determined not to be free and they can neither be frightened, discouraged nor persuaded to change their resolution. If we are saved France and Spain must save us. I have the most pigmy-feelings at the idea." And in September: "The officers are out of humour, and the *worst* of evils seems to be coming upon us—*a loss of our virtue.* . . . I hate Congress—I hate the army—I hate the world—I hate myself. The whole is a mass of fools and knaves; I could almost except you and Meade."[40]

Disillusionment with the military was completed a month later, in the aftermath of Benedict Arnold's treason. The occasion was the execution of Major John André, the British officer directly involved in Arnold's betrayal. André had been sent by his superior, General Sir Henry Clinton, to treat with Arnold in uniform, under a flag of truce, and with a pass made out by Arnold in the name of John Anderson. Dirty as the business was, those precautions ensured that André, if caught, would be treated as a soldier; but after the conference Arnold became rattled and insisted that André return in civilian disguise. André, knowing the danger involved, chose to risk his own life rather than antagonize Arnold and jeopardize a mission possibly fatal to the American cause. He was caught, brought before a board of American officers, and—since he was in civilian clothes—sentenced to be hanged as a spy.[41]

Hamilton visited André several times during his brief confinement and was deeply impressed by the doomed man's qualities—his "candor and firmness," his "excellent understanding," his "peculiar elegance of mind and manners." André's main concern was that Clinton might reproach himself or be reproached by others, "on the supposition of my having conceived myself obliged by his instructions to run the risk I did. I would not for the world leave a sting in his mind, that should embitter his future days." With Hamilton's intervention, he was allowed to send a letter to Clinton absolving the general of responsibility.

Touched as Hamilton was at the spectacle of a young man "in the height of his career . . . precipitated from the summit of prosperity . . . all the expectations of his ambition blasted and himself ruined"—Hamilton could readily imagine being in such a position—he did not question the necessity of André's execution. He did, however, strongly support André's request "to be indulged with a professional death"—by a firing squad rather than by hanging. The request was denied. In his moving description of the execution, Hamilton recorded that André, when asked whether he had any last words, replied, "nothing, but to request you will witness to the world, that I die like a brave man." Said Hamilton: "Never perhaps did any man suffer death with more justice, or deserve it less."

Hamilton admitted to Laurens that he was judging André under the best of circumstances, since "a man of real merit is never seen in so favourable a light, as through the medium of adversity." He also admitted that André had flaws: it was "a blemish on his fame, that he once intended to prostitute a flag" of truce. Nonetheless, Hamilton could not hide his bitterness and disgust. "The authorised maxims and practices of war," he said, "are the satire of human nature. They countenance almost every species of seduction as well as violence; and the General that can make most traitors in the army of his adversary is frequently most applauded."

This loss of faith was apparent in the last episode but one in Hamilton's career as a soldier. In February 1781, just over four months after André was executed, Hamilton resigned as Washington's aide-de-camp. The precipitating incident would seem trivial but for the intensity of Hamilton's feelings about honor and propriety. One day at headquarters, Washington passed him on the stairs and said he wanted to see him. Hamilton said he would wait upon him immediately after delivering an important message downstairs, but then he was delayed possibly two minutes by Lafayette. When he returned he found Washington waiting angrily at the head of the stairs. "Col. Hamilton (said he) you have kept me waiting at the head of the stairs these ten minutes. I must tell you Sir you treat me with disrespect." That, of course, was a gross affront, an accusation that gentlemen did not make toward one another, and adequate in some circumstances to provoke a duel. Hamilton replied, "without petulancy but with decision 'I am not conscious of it Sir, but since you have thought it necessary to tell me so we part.'" Within an hour Washington had cooled down, realized that his temper had cost him his most valued aide, and sent another aide in an attempt to effect a reconciliation. Hamilton refused and would not be dissuaded by subsequent pleas from others.[42]

There was more to it than that. Hamilton had never overcome his dislike for the personal dependency of the office of aide, and though he knew his work was important, he had long resented being deprived of the opportunity for advancement (as well as for glory) that service in the line would have given him. Beyond that, Washington was especially difficult to live with. Though the general's public demeanor was always circumspect, in private he could explode in fits of rage and was a "most horrid swearer and blasphemer." He was also, by Hamilton's fastidious standards, not especially elegant. After all, he had learned his soldiering by fighting Indians in the wilderness; and when frustrations and the pressure of responsibilities overwhelmed him he was capable of almost savage response. Hamilton served him because "his popularity has often been essential to the safety of America, and is still of great importance to it." But Hamilton, in a letter to his father-in-law, maintained that "for three years past I have felt no friendship for him and have professed none." He had long expected the break to come and had been coldly resolved that when it did, he would not be in the wrong, lest Washington's "self-love would never forgive me for what it would regard as a humiliation." In fact, Hamilton misjudged Washington: the general wanted him not merely out of self-interest but also because of sincere affection. Washington was genuinely sorry about the resignation, the more so because he realized that he was at fault.[43]

Hamilton stayed with Washington a few weeks longer, until suitable replacements were on hand, then left headquarters. For another three months he tried in vain to obtain a field command, meanwhile writing political tracts. Finally, on July 31, after offering to resign his commission, he was given command of a New York battalion of light infantry.

The assignment came just in time to provide him a chance at his long-coveted military glory. Lord Cornwallis had invaded Virginia—sending Governor Thomas Jefferson and the legislature fleeing for safety in the back country—and a combined American and French force, Hamilton's battalion included, gathered to besiege the British at Yorktown. The siege began on October 6; Cornwallis's outlying batteries were steadily reduced until, on the 14th, his main body was defended from infantry assault only by a pair of powerful artillery emplacements, dug in the earth and protected by piles of felled trees, the sharpened limbs pointed toward attackers. That afternoon the French and American engineers thought these redoubts ready for storming. One redoubt was assigned to French troops under Rochambeau, the other to American forces under Lafayette. Despite his friendship for Hamilton, Lafayette gave the command to his own former aide, Lt. Col. Louis Gimat. His heart sinking, Hamilton pleaded with Lafayette, who laid his request before the commander-in-chief. After a fervent appeal to Washington in his tent, Hamilton emerged, embraced his friend Major Nicholas Fish, and shouted, "We have it! We have it!"[44]

Hamilton was to lead 320 men frontally, and Laurens was given 80 men for a simultaneous attack upon the rear. When night fell, the signal was given: for silence and surprise, Hamilton ordered his men to advance with arms unloaded and rely on the bayonet. Under heavy fire from above, Hamilton leaped to the parapet, shouted for his men to follow, and sprang into the works. The enemy was taken within minutes. The French attack on the other redoubt was likewise successful, though with more casualties. Cornwallis's position was now hopeless, and two days later he surrendered. For all practical purposes, the war for American independence was over at long last; and at long last Hamilton had won his taste of glory.

But glory, though sweet, was not enough. Already, Fame was calling.

II

Education in the Political Arts: 1775–1783

'Tis Education forms the common mind,

Just as the Twig is bent, the Tree's inclined.

Battlefield heroics come easily to those who have a youthful indifference to death. The thirst to do grander things is less readily slaked. To conceive the plan Hamilton had conceived by 1787 required creative powers of imagination, tempered by far more knowledge than he had possessed a dozen or even a half-dozen years earlier. The requisite imagination was inborn, a gift. The requisite knowledge could come only from experience and study.

His education in the arts of politics had begun erratically. Partly temperament stood in his way. An ardent disposition, accentuated by precocious self-confidence, led him to form, hold, and act upon his opinions with more assurance than his understanding justified, and a tactless compulsion for candor led him to assert them more readily than was prudent. Throughout his young manhood his tendency was therefore to move swiftly and too far in one direction, overreact when he learned the error of his ways, then gradually find a path back to a firmer position.

Another barrier to his development was a distrust of theory, of the speculative thinking of what he derisively called "empirics," meaning quacks. It is true that to an extent this skepticism reflected a wholesome capacity to learn from experience. He attributed the failure to endow Congress with adequate powers, for instance, to the atmosphere of "chimerical projects and utopian speculations," his own included, which had marked "the spirit of the times" early in the Revolution. To persist in such "fatal mistakes" in the face of sobering experience, he said, would be "disgraceful and even criminal." But his antipathy to theory extended beyond approving the corrective of experience. "A great source of error," he wrote in a typical passage, "is the judging of events by abstract calculations, which though geometrically true are false as they relate to the concerns of beings governed more by passion and prejudice than by an enlightened sense of their interests." The difficulty with that attitude was that study of the works of empirics and abstract calculators was necessary to his political education, if only to arm him with the tools of debate.[1]

He struggled through them, and even found some to his liking, and in time emerged as a profound political and constitutional theorist in his own right. But the whole subject was alien to his true genius, which was for running things, for organizing and regularizing human activity and establishing procedures whereby work could most effectively be done. This talent was reinforced by an intense concern for proper forms of personal behavior. Accordingly, though his political education was more or less complete by the early 1780s, it was irrelevant until he had gone through two other chapters in his education—one legal, the other social and institutional. What would be involved was a simple but gigantic intellectual leap: he came to understand that procedures determine actions, that rules of conduct govern what can and will be done. Understanding that, when others did not, he could set out to make the rules, and succeed.

Hamilton's earliest political writings were his 1775 pamphlets defending the actions of the First Continental Congress and hurling polemical shafts against Samuel Seabury. His positions were generally those of the radical wing of the Patriot movement, except that in his naïveté and enthusiasm he went further on almost every point. He wrote in the Patriots' ready-made language of protest, original with earlier English Oppositionists, which the colonists had been imbibing and employing for half a century. One central cliché of the Opposition and the radical Patriots, for example, was that Great Britain's public debt was an oppressive and corrupting burden. It was in fact the source of unprecedented national prosperity and growth, as Hamilton would ultimately learn; but in 1775 he declared it to be "a debt unparalelled, in the annals of any country," that as a consequence of the taxes necessary to support it "the common people are extremely impoverished," and that given one more war "Great Britain, already tottering under her burthens, will be obliged to increase them, 'till they become altogether insupportable; and she must sink under the weight of them." Another humbug of the Oppositionists (and of the Congress) was "standing armies." Hamilton would soon champion a military establishment as necessary for the defense of freedom, but in 1775 he warned against "a large standing army, maintained out of our own pockets to be at the devotion of our oppressors. This would be introduced under pretence of defending us; but in fact to make our bondage and misery complete." Again, Oppositionists and radical Patriots feared a conspiracy against liberty by government ministers and their lackeys. Hamilton would ultimately seek to establish his version of ministerial government as the instrument of a better America, but in 1775 he warned of "ministry, ministerial tools, placemen, pensioners, parasites" who, impelled by "a wicked thirst of domination and disregard to justice," had fabricated a "system of slavery" against America that could not be regarded "as the effect of inconsideration and rashness. It is the offspring of mature deliberation."[2]

In dealing with political philosophy, Hamilton likewise embraced conventional doctrines and went overboard with them. Political thinkers in the English-speaking world were generally agreed that the primary object of government should be the protection of liberty. No "pure" form of government, they believed, whether monarchical, aristocratic, or democratic, could long serve that end. Each pure form had its inevitable course of degeneration into tyranny; that of democracy invariably proceeded "through licentiousness, demagoguery, and egalitarian delusion, back to despotism." Englishmen and British Americans shared the assumption that they had solved the problem by developing a mixed form of government, one that so combined the three pure forms as to preserve the best features of each. In Britain, according to this model, the Crown represented the monarchical principle, the House of Lords the aristocratic, the House of Commons the democratic; and government in the colonies was similarly arranged through governors, councils, and assemblies.[3]

When the imperial crisis arose in the 1760s, however, British Americans came to realize that the model was unsuited to the governance of the empire, for it had to do with the distribution of power along a horizontal axis, on a single level of government, and imperial questions turned on the distribution of power along a vertical axis, among different levels of government. Technically speaking, the point at issue between colonies and mother country was whether the sovereignty of Crown-in-Parliament extended to the colonies. The British maintained that it did; those in the resistance movement in America maintained that it did not, and that each of the colonial assemblies bore the same relationship to the Crown, in respect to the individual colony, that Parliament did in respect to Britain. In theory, each position was entirely logical because sovereignty, defined by Blackstone as the *supreme* law-making power, was logically indivisible: Parliament either had absolute power to legislate for the colonies or it had none at all. In practice, the empire had functioned as a federal system, but the *concept* of federalism had not been developed, and thus thinking in terms of it was impossible for disputants on both sides. For want of an idea, an empire collapsed.[4]

Hamilton groped his way toward a workable concept of federalism and came surprisingly close to finding one. Other American efforts to prove that the colonies owed allegience to the Crown but not to Parliament had failed logically because, among other reasons, the king himself was a part of Parliament. Hamilton worked his way around that obstacle by distinguishing the king's several capacities, physical and political, from one another. In his political capacity as a part of Parliament, Hamilton argued, the king had no authority over the colony of New York; nor was New York beholden to him as a physical person. Rather, it was in his political capacity as part of the legislature of New York that his authority was to be acknowledged. This, Hamilton said, was "an obvious distinction, and cannot be contested without an affront to common sense." It was in fact an extremely subtle distinction, and the notion of an empire held together by nothing more than a politically plural but physically single king who wore a multiplicity of abstract crowns implied a decentralization that would have meant no empire at all. Nearly a century later such thinking would provide the basis for the British Commonwealth system; in 1775 it was inopportune, and Hamilton himself did not pursue the argument.[5]

In the impasse Hamilton, along with other American radicals, fell back upon the natural-rights doctrines associated with John Locke and others. Locke, though better known at the time for his *Essay on Understanding,* had also written a pair of treatises which, after the fact, had served as a theoretical justification for the deposing of James II in England's Glorious Revolution of 1688. Simply put, Locke's argument ran as follows. In some distant past, man had existed in a state of nature, wherein he had been endowed by God with inalienable rights to life, liberty, and property. Because men are imperfect creatures, however, some violated the rights of others. For their mutual defense, men banded together and formed governments, whose sole function was the protection of individuals in their natural rights. As long as a government rested upon consent and performed its function, it was legitimate and must be obeyed; if it ceased to do so, those living under it had the right to abolish it and erect a new government that was more likely to do its proper job.[6]

Natural-rights theory could be employed to justify a wide range of behavior, depending upon the way it was interpreted. In its more conservative reading (that used in the Declaration of Independence, for example), resistance to measures of government was warranted only as a last resort in extreme cases—only when those in government, through a long course of consistently illegal actions, displayed an unmistakable intention to yoke the people under an absolute despotism. In its more radical reading, the doctrine justified civil disobedience whenever, in the judgment of people affected by particular laws, government trespassed upon the natural rights of any body of citizens or subjects. Though Hamilton maintained that the British ministry was following a systematic design to enslave the colonists, he also struck the more radical stance. "When the first principles of civil society are violated," he asserted, "and the rights of a whole people are invaded, the common forms of municipal law [meaning legislative enactments and judicial decisions] are not to be regarded. Men may then betake themselves to the law of nature." Of the four major Patriot propaganda writers of the 1774–75 resistance season—the other three being Jefferson, John Adams, and James Wilson—Hamilton was the only one to interpret natural rights in that extreme fashion.[7]

Hamilton also gave the doctrine a special emphasis and a peculiar twist that propelled him into maintaining that democracy was indispensable to liberty—at a time when none but a handful of extremists believed the two were even compatible. He explicitly rejected the conventional idea that only a mixed government could be free. "It is not," he said, "the supreme power being placed in one, instead of many, that discriminates an arbitrary from a free government." The distinction "between freedom and slavery consists in this: In the former state, a man is governed by the laws to which he has given his consent, either in person, or by his representative: In the latter, he is governed by the will of another. In the one case his life and property are his own, in the other, they depend upon the pleasure of a master." Unless laws are enacted by the people's representatives, periodically elected by themselves, "no laws have any validity, or binding force." In sum, "the democratical part of the government" was what made the difference between freedom and slavery.[8]

It can be argued that Hamilton did not intend to go to that extreme; after all, he was young to be swimming in such deep and murky metaphysical waters and might have been swept away by the current of his own rhetoric. Moreover, his polemics were dashed off hurriedly, and they dealt with a number of other subjects in addition to natural-rights theory. But the argument is spurious, for Hamilton made his position explicit in a private letter to Gouverneur Morris in 1777. In an exchange concerning the recently adopted New York constitution, Hamilton said he saw in that conservative instrument only one major danger: that the state senate, "from the mere circumstance of its being a separate member of the legislature, will be liable to degenerate into a body purely aristocratical." In answer to Morris's comment that popular governments were inherently unstable, Hamilton declared that that hackneyed notion was unfounded; historically, he said, they had proved unstable only when mixed with, and thus corrupted by, monarchical or aristocratic principles. A government consisting of the whole "collective body of the people" would, of course, be unworkable. "But a representative democracy, where the right of election is well secured and regulated & the exercise of the legislative, executive and judiciary authorities, is vested in select persons, chosen *really* and not *nominally* by the people, will in my opinion be most likely to be happy, regular and durable."[9]

In truth, Hamilton's early political thinking, though sometimes showing flashes of his later brilliance and depth, was longer on passionate idealism than upon reasoned analysis; his positions were often muddled and self-contradictory. Until 1777 he explicitly or implicitly endorsed decentralization, representative democracy, and civil disobedience as efficacious means of securing liberty. Decentralization was implicit in his theorizing about Parliament's lack of power over the colonies, and yet he championed the centralized power of Congress. His attitude toward Congress also ran counter to his advocacy of representative democracy, for that body was by no means elected by the people, really or nominally, but by parts of legislatures and by self-appointed extralegal assemblies. As for civil disobedience, even Hamilton's feelings on the matter were contradictory.

On the one hand, civil disobedience implied mob action, which offended both his sense of justice and his sense of order. His protection of the Tory Myles Cooper against the mob at King's College was a clear indication of this attitude. Clearer yet were his remarks in a private letter to John Jay. "The same state of the passions which fits the multitude . . . for opposition to tyranny and oppression," he wrote, "very naturally leads them to a contempt and disregard of all authority," since they "have not a sufficient stock of reason and knowledge to guide them." When the minds of the unthinking populace are "loosened from their attachment to ancient establishments and courses, they seem to grow giddy and are apt more or less to run into anarchy. . . . In such tempestuous times, it requires the greatest skill in the political pilots to keep men steady and within proper bounds, on which account I am always more or less alarmed at every thing which is done of mere will and pleasure, without any proper authority."[10]

On the other hand, the young revolutionary went to considerable lengths in his pamphlets to justify specific examples of mob action. While admitting "that there have been some irregularities committed in America," he excused the excesses on the ground that "it would be miraculous, and inconsistent with human nature, for a people in such critical and trying circumstances to act perfectly right." He dismissed the actions of the mobs in Boston as the work of "a small number of people, provoked by an open and dangerous attack upon their liberties"; all they had done under such extreme provocation, he said, was destroy "a parcel of Tea" that was merely the private property of a gigantic and monopolistic corporation, the East India Company.[11]

On the whole, the Hamilton of 1775 often sounded rather like his opponents in maturity. In one crucial respect, however, his attitude never changed: he always championed liberty and abhorred slavery. Much of what he said about slavery at first was patriotic hyperbole, but beneath the talk about evil ministerial designs lay an intense hostility toward slavery in the more conventional sense. In support of Laurens's plan to recruit several battalions from the slave population in South Carolina, Hamilton wrote a strong letter to Jay, then president of the Continental Congress. Renouncing the bigotry that prevailed in regard to blacks, which "makes us fancy many things that are founded neither in reason nor experience," he argued the egalitarian position that "their natural faculties are probably as good as ours" and the culturally deterministic position that their intellectual shortcomings stemmed only from a "want of cultivation." It was an essential part of Laurens's scheme, he said, "to give them their freedom with their muskets. This will secure their fidelity, animate their courage, and I believe will have a good influence upon those who remain, by opening a door to their emancipation." Thus from "dictates of humanity and true policy equally," Hamilton was an abolitionist, and on that subject he never wavered.[12]

Hamilton had neither occasion nor inclination to reexamine his political thinking until the winter of 1777–78. Then, as he began his fulminations against the corruption and incompetence of Congress and the imbecility and want of patriotism in the state governments, he came to realize that he had shown poor judgment in underrating the strength of Great Britain and in overrating the efficacy of citizen-soldiers. Recognition of the immaturity of his earlier thinking took the most sincere of forms: he plunged anew into study.[13]

He made notes on the unused pages of the pay book for his New

York artillery company. Much of what he recorded was factual information, mainly economic and financial, taken from Malachy Postlethwayt's *Universal Dictionary of Trade and Commerce;* Hamilton would draw heavily from that reference book a year or two later when he essayed his first, tentative pieces on public finance. In the pay book, too, he took down a number of random scraps, "selected more for their singularity than use," from Plutarch's *Lives* and other ancient sources. One passage recorded from Demosthenes' Orations pointedly summed up Hamilton's attitude about leadership. "As a general marches at the head of his troops," Demosthenes said, "so ought wise politicians, if I dare to use the expression, to march at the head of affairs; insomuch that they ought not to wait the *event*, to know what measures to take; but the measures which they have taken, ought to produce the *event*."[14]

He also studied writers, both practical and theoretical, who might offer insights into the problems besetting the American cause. In immediate practical terms, the most pressing problem was the financial one of supplying the army; and to inform himself on matters economic and financial Hamilton studied, besides Postlethwayt, Wyndham Beawes's *Lex Mercatoria,* Richard Price's recent treatise on *Schemes for raising Money by Public Loans,* and possibly Adam Smith's *Wealth of Nations*. In broader terms the problems were governmental, and here Hamilton's master was David Hume. Hume's skepticism fit precisely Hamilton's mood during and after Valley Forge, and the Scotsman's sophisticated, appreciative analysis of the English Constitution squared with what was happening during the war far better than did Hamilton's earlier, simplistic, Oppositionist-derived misunderstanding of it. Even if Hamilton had not specifically acknowledged his admiration of Hume ("the cautious and accurate *Hume,*" "The Judicious *Hume*") in his writings, the influence of the great philosopher and historian would be evident, for Hamilton repeatedly expressed Hume's thoughts as his own.[15]

Early on, he had struck upon a proposition of Hume's that he quoted at length in his 1775 *The Farmer Refuted*—though he misread or misused it at the time. "Political writers," he said, citing Hume's essay "On the Independency of Parliament," "have established it as a maxim, that, in contriving any system of government, and fixing the several checks and controuls of the constitution, *every man* ought to be supposed a *knave;* and to have no other end in all his actions, but *private interest.* By this interest, we must govern him, and by means of it, *make him co-operate to public good,* notwithstanding his insatiable avarice and ambition. . . . It is therefore a just *political* maxim, that *every man must be supposed a knave.* Though, at the same time, it appears somewhat strange, that a maxim should be true in politics, which is false in fact." Developing this proposition, Hume conceded that "honour is a great check upon mankind. But, where a considerable body of men act together, this check is in a great measure removed." In a court or legislative body, Hume added, this principle is so potent that the whole body "acts as if it contained not one member, who had any regard to public interest and liberty."[16]

Hamilton first used the quotation as a justification for resisting measures of Parliament—which, to say the least, was far from what Hume was talking about. Hume meant, and Hamilton now embraced the idea as a cardinal tenet of his political faith, that one must suppose men to be inherently corrupted by their lust for power and property and design governmental institutions to harness those passions and make them "subservient to the public good." To put it differently, people would act in the public interest if government made it advantageous for them to do so, and constitutions and laws should recognize that fact.[17]

Underlying this political observation was Hume's conception of the nature of man. The "age of reason," in Great Britain, did not deify reason, nor did it even postulate that man is a rational creature. Quite the contrary: Hume and many of his contemporaries maintained that all human action springs from desire for pleasure and aversion to pain, which meant that truly disinterested action was impossible and that reason is "the slave of the passions, and can never pretend to any other office than to serve and obey them." The idea of the passions, or drives for self-gratification, was central. Hume divided them into two categories: the direct passions such as "desire and aversion, grief and joy, hope and fear"; and the indirect, such as pride or humility, and love or hatred. On this foundation he and others erected an enormous superstructure to explain human behavior.[18]

Every person was supposed to have a "ruling" passion, which most regularly inspired his conduct. Ambition and avarice were generally regarded as the most common ruling passions. Curiously, Hume's friend Adam Smith, whose reputation was to rest mainly upon a treatise on economics, believed that ambition was the more powerful of the two. "That passion," he declared, "when once it has got entire possession of the breast, will admit neither a rival nor a successor. To those who have been accustomed to the possession, or even to the hope, of public admiration, all other pleasures sicken and decay." Hume, though he wrote less about economics than about politics, ranked the love of possessions first. In any event, Hamilton readily accepted, as a psychological and philosophical principle, the proposition that ambition and avarice were the most common wellsprings of human activity.[19]

Another aspect of the theory of the passions related to Hamilton's desire to do great deeds in service of his country. The passions were ranked in many gradations from the basest to the noblest, and classified according to relative good or evil at each level. Ambition, for instance, was of neutral morality in itself. When directed toward mere popularity, toward winning the acclaim of the vulgar multitudes, it was not necessarily reprehensible, but it was more laudable if directed toward gaining the esteem of the virtuous, the knowledgeable, and the wise. When directed only toward the acquisition of power and unchecked by principle, it led to the blackest villainy, to infamy. In its highest form, when ambition was directed toward winning the approbation of the wise and the just not only in one's own lifetime but through immortal posterity, it was transformed into the noblest passion of all, the love of Fame. Hume, though ever skeptical of the possibility of unselfish action, nonetheless believed that the love of Fame was the most praiseworthy of the drives for self-gratification, for in practice it almost amounted to "the love of laudable actions for their own sake." That sentiment was widely shared; Alexander Pope expressed an attitude common throughout the English-speaking world when he said that "passion for fame" was the "instinct of all great souls."[20]

Hamilton had encountered elsewhere the notion that men could achieve immortality through heroic deeds. In his pay book he summarized the ancient idea of a progression of "virtuous souls," whereby men become heroes, heroes become demigods, and demigods "are raised to consummate felicity and enrolled amongst the gods." The scheme, Hamilton commented, was "as inconsistent with fact as sublime in theory." Its appeal to him lay in the tension between his inherent self-confidence and optimism and the skeptical and pessimistic mood he was in during the most trying years of the war. Temperamentally, Hamilton shared Shaftesbury's view that virtuous men desire to act in the public good simply because they are virtuous. But in his period of disillusionment, when "disgusted with every thing in this world" and seeing the whole as "a mass of fools and knaves," Hume's explanation of the rare man of virtue was considerably more comforting.[21]

At first blush, the proposals Hamilton was soon to make would seem contrary to his new-found Humean perspective. Hume's system of thought, as applied to America's problems, had two sets of implications: to induce Americans to support the cause, it should be made in their selfish, immediate, individual interests to do so; and government should be reorganized to provide the necessary checks and controls. What Hamilton advocated was compatible with the first; but it seemingly contradicted the second, for he proposed that Congress begin to exercise a host of new powers without first being refashioned to provide checks upon their abuse.

The contradiction is only apparent, not real. Hamilton was primarily concerned, then and later, with the distribution of power on the vertical axis, not the horizontal. He perceived, accurately, that the failure of Congress to provide adequately for the conduct of the war was only partly owing to the shortcomings of some congressmen. More fundamentally, it was due to the narrow and niggardly provincialism of their constituents, the state governments. Checks and controls were wanted to restrain the powerful and often lawless actions of the latter—which themselves were unchecked by an effective separation of powers—and the states could be restrained only by a vast increase in the powers of Congress. To burden the central authority with an internal set of checks and balances would be to prevent it from holding its own against the states.[22]

The primary source of the existing imbalance was the states' refusal to grant Congress the power to tax. They left Congress dependent upon requisitions, then proved unwilling or unable to contribute their quotas. In the circumstances Congress had had to make do. It borrowed at home and abroad until its credit ran out, it resorted to expropriation and confiscation, it printed and circulated enormous quantities of unsecured paper money. Continental bills of credit, as the paper money was called, served well in moderate quantity early in the war, but $76 million issued in 1777 and 1778 yielded goods worth only about $16 million, and $125 million issued in 1779 bought less than $6 million in supplies. The nation's urgent need was to end the nightmare of frenzied finance and come up with a coherent, regular, and adequate system in its stead.[23]

Hamilton addressed the first of his treatises on the labyrinthine subject of public finance to this problem. He did so in a letter written late in 1779 to a member of Congress, identity unknown but possibly Hamilton's future father-in-law, Philip Schuyler. The root cause of the nation's financial mess, Hamilton figured, was that there was simply not enough money in the country to pay for the war, no matter how effective the system of taxation. The remedy was to create more money by establishing a national bank (there were, at the time, no banks of any kind in the country). He proposed that half the capital be raised by a foreign loan, the other half by private subscriptions payable in continental bills of credit at a depreciated ratio—which would give the bills a new life by making it profitable for merchants and other monied men to accept them. Congress would own half the stock of the bank, that acquired with the proceeds of the foreign loan, and the bank would help finance government both by making direct loans and by facilitating taxation through an increase in the circulating medium, which would come about in the ordinary course of financing business activity. All in all the scheme was a clever one; indeed, it contained many of the principles that would later underlie Hamilton's workable plan for a national bank. But there was little art in the way Hamilton proposed to employ those principles in 1779, and art was the essence of his later system. He assumed that monied men would support government if it were in their interest, but he could think of nothing to offer them that was half so attractive as profiteering in army supplies or even engaging in legitimate wartime trade. He recognized, shrewdly, that establishing public credit is partly a matter of creating illusions, but he had an inadequate understanding of the hard realities that must support the illusions. He perceived that, in establishing a radically unorthodox financial plan, the employment of symbols of fiscal orthodoxy was crucial, but his proposed means were clumsy: for instance, he would reissue the public paper in pounds sterling instead of dollars, so that "the currency having changed its name will seem to have changed its nature." In other words, the plan was unworkable because Hamilton did not yet know enough to devise a system that would work.[24]

The proposal was also premature, for in the winter of 1779–80 few men in Congress except Schuyler would have considered resorting to such a drastic experiment. As the nation's financial plight worsened, however, more and more state legislatures sent able and national-minded men to Congress, and by the fall of 1780 the complexion of the body had changed considerably. One of the new men, the New York Patriot leader James Duane, asked Hamilton for his ideas on what should be done in the deepening emergency, and Hamilton responded with a long set of proposals. It was essential, Hamilton told Duane, that Congress have more power, which it ought simply to assume but doubtless would not; accordingly, a constitutional convention should be called forthwith. Meanwhile, Hamilton recommended a series of specific actions, including an overhaul of Congress (to make it more efficient, not to check it), a reorganization of administration, and new financial measures. Several months of reflection had ripened and refined Hamilton's thinking on finances somewhat, and in reiterating his proposal for a national bank he dropped the far-fetched idea of using Continental paper money as part of the capital, since Congress had now substantially repudiated that paper by devaluing it at a ratio of forty for one. But Hamilton also introduced some new unsound principles into his plan, particularly the idea of allowing up to three-quarters of the bank's stock to be subscribed in real estate, the least liquid form of capital. Even so, he was showing signs of growth as a budding financial expert, and quite as importantly, among influential nationalists he was gaining a reputation for fiscal expertise.[25]

That reputation was soon to be enhanced and made consequential. Early in 1781 the Congress, now fully under the control of ardent nationalists, began to act with the vigor that the times demanded. On February 3 it approved, as an amendment to the Articles of Confederation (the loose national constitution drafted in 1777 and just then being finally approved by the states), a request that the states vest Congress with a permanent independent source of revenue in the form of an impost—a 5 percent tax on all imports. Two

weeks later it voted to reorganize and centralize its several administrative departments, placing each under the direction of a single
head, and to ask the Philadelphia merchant Robert Morris to take
over the crucial office of superintendent of finance. These were precisely the administrative reforms Hamilton had recommended to
Duane, and thus he was emboldened to write a long, unsolicited letter of advice to the Financier.[26]

In some respects this third financial essay had the shortcomings
of the other two. Hamilton lacked some elementary information; he
did not consider that Congress had a huge public debt in addition to
its devalued bills of credit; and he relied upon ingenious but inaccurate calculations to arrive at an estimate of the nation's revenues
and expenditures. His plan for a bank still contained unsound principles, including the use of land in the capital, and its means for
combining public and private credit were ineffective. His proposal
was also financially impractical, since it called for considerably
more capital than could actually be raised; indeed, when Morris did
create a bank, on his own principles, he found it necessary to provide most of the capital by using the proceeds from a foreign loan,
since almost no private subscribers came forward.[27]

Above all, Hamilton's recommendations were politically unrealistic. Congress lacked the authority to do what Hamilton proposed,
but Congress, he asserted, "must deal plainly with their constituents. They must tell them, that power without revenue is a bubble,"
that unless the states gave Congress ample sources of revenue it
would become necessary, "in justice to the public and to their own
honor," to "renounce the vain attempt of carrying on the war." Having given their constituents that stern lecture, Congress must then
"demand an instant, positive and perpetual investiture of an impost
on trade, a land tax and a poll-tax to be collected by their own
agents." Such a course would collide with the hard realities of popular politics, but Hamilton waved that aside. Like Demosthenes, he
would "produce the event." (To Laurens's objection that Hamilton's
"remedies" were good but "would not go down at this time," Hamilton had replied "I tell you necessity must force them down; and that
if they are not speedily taken the patient will die.")[28]

Yet despite its flaws this long letter—it ran about 15,000 words—
was a virtuoso performance. Glimpses of the mature Hamilton in-
terlace the manuscript. His understanding of the interconnections

of military strategy, finance, and politics was profound. Prudent maxims, both derivative and original, appear repeatedly. "No wise statesman," he said, "will reject the good from an apprehension of the ill. The truth is in human affairs, there is no good, pure and un-mixed; every advantage has two sides, and wisdom consists in avail-ing ourselves of the good, and guarding as much as possible against the bad." Again, speaking of the danger that reaction against the ex-cesses of paper money might incite people to turn to the "visionary" and "chimerical" extreme of attempting to use only gold and silver as money: "Nothing is more common than for men to pass from the abuse of a good thing to the disuse of it." Yet again, forecasting the revolution he would one day attempt to effect in American society: "A national debt if it is not excessive will be to us a national bless-ing; it will be powerfull cement of our union. It will also create a necessity for keeping up taxation to a degree which without being oppressive, will be a spur to industry; remote as we are from Europe and shall be from danger, it were otherwise to be feard our popular maxims would incline us to too great parsimony and indulgence. We labour less now than any civilized nation of Europe, and a habit of labour in the people is as essential to the health and vigor of their minds and bodies as it is conducive to the welfare of the State. We ought not to Suffer our self-love to deceive us in a comparrison, upon these points."[29]

Hamilton also attempted, during the interim between his resigna-tion as Washington's aide and his obtaining a field command, to in-fluence policy through public opinion. In a series of four articles published in July and August 1781 and collectively titled "The Con-tinentalist," he repeated many of the suggestions he had made pri-vately and tried to persuade his countrymen that his "remedies" must "go down." The effort had an ambiguity about it that would mark Hamilton's public behavior the rest of his life. He had come to profess the "pessimistic" view of man, maintaining that people are governed by "passion and prejudice" rather than by "an enlightened sense of their interests"; and yet throughout his career he expended more energy and talent in appeals to the intelligence and virtue of common citizens than did any other American in public life. So much stronger was his natural optimism than his acquired pes-simism.[30]

The essence of the Continentalist essays was a plea for greater powers for Congress. They reek of Humean moral philosophy as well as Humean politics. Their most striking features are an implicit concept of divided sovereignty and an explicit statement of Hamilton's idea of establishing checks on power along a vertical axis. Regarding the first, Hamilton admitted that each state had "a distinct sovereignty," as the Articles of Confederation provided, but casually spoke also of Congress as "the common sovereign." Regarding the second, he asserted that "the security . . . of the public liberty, must consist in such a distribution of the sovereign power, as will make it morally impossible for one part to gain an ascendency over the others, or for the whole to unite in a scheme of usurpation."[31]

All this served as prelude and preparation for Hamilton's first venture into government. After Yorktown he resigned from active duty, joined Betsey in Albany, and commenced the study of law. At that point Robert Morris offered him a job as Receiver of Continental Taxes for New York, which provided a remuneration of one-fourth of one percent of all moneys collected. At first Hamilton declined, partly because he could not spare the time from his studies and partly because New York—its countryside devastated by war, its economy disjointed, its principal city and five of its fourteen counties still occupied by the British—could not afford to pay enough taxes to make Hamilton's commission more than about £100, New York currency, or $250. But Morris told Hamilton his commission would be figured on the basis of what was due from New York to the continental treasury, not what was collected, which meant that Hamilton would be paid nearly a thousand dollars. He could, moreover, delay performing his duties until his studies were done. Hamilton accepted the offer.[32]

A principal part of the job involved lobbying, coaxing the legislature to vote the funds and improve the means of collecting them. Hamilton was not particularly successful in that regard but, characteristically, he sought on the occasion to bring about something far larger. In July 1782, through the influence of Philip Schuyler, the New York legislature passed a series of resolutions, apparently drafted by Hamilton, calling for a general convention to augment the powers of Congress through amendments to the Articles of Confederation. Two days later the legislature appointed Hamilton as a member of its congressional delegation for the next session. Nothing came of the call for a convention, but Hamilton took his seat in Congress on November 25.[33]

He arrived just in time to play a role in the climactic act of the politics of the Revolution. The 1781 impost amendment had been thwarted by Rhode Island's refusal to ratify it (amendments to the Articles required the approval of all thirteen legislatures) and then irrevocably killed when Virginia rescinded its earlier ratification. The rejection did not affect the outcome of the war, for the negotiators in London had already agreed upon preliminary articles of peace recognizing American independence, though the news would not arrive in the United States until March 1783. In longer-range terms, however, the failure of the impost amendment made a great deal of difference, for without funds Congress would not be able to honor the debts it had accumulated to help finance the war. What was more, it would be doomed to remain impotent, and thus the United States, instead of being a nation of potential consequence, was likely to degenerate into thirteen petty, bickering, and loosely allied republics, ripe for partition by the greedy powers of Europe.[34]

All hopes of creating a real and respectable national government through ordinary means having apparently failed, Robert Morris and his circle, with some support from Hamilton, prepared a daring maneuver. Their aim was to obtain for Congress authority to service all the continental debts, assume responsibility for the war debts of the states, and establish permanent revenues adequate to support both sets of obligations. Since the war debts were enormous, amounting to something like twenty times the amount of all the gold and silver in circulation in the country, the creation of the necessary financial machinery would ensure that the central government would play a leading role in the peacetime affairs of the nation. Their method was to combine the efforts of two powerful interest groups, the major public creditors and the army, to move Congress to propose and the states to ratify the necessary amendments to the Articles of Confederation. Some months earlier Morris had seen to the organization of the public creditors in the Middle States into a coordinated pressure group, and Hamilton himself had helped organize those in New York. The idea of employing the army in the scheme arose about a month after Hamilton entered Congress.[35]

Despite the skill with which Morris had managed congressional finances, the army had received virtually no pay in hard money in years. As long as the fighting had continued, stern discipline had been sufficient to contain the complaints of enlisted men, and Congress had mollified the officers by promising them a postwar bonus of half-pay for life. But the army was now encamped, idly, at Newburgh, New York, and peace appeared imminent. With peace soldiers would face the prospect of returning home and losing their relative immunity from long-neglected private obligations. Many officers, in particular, had allowed their personal affairs to fall into disarray, and as Washington pointed out, unless they received either the promised bonus or substantial payments of back wages, many of them had nothing to look forward to except being jailed for nonpayment of accumulated debts.[36]

The defeat of the impost amendment made the officers' prospects dimmer, and during the next month (December 1782) grumbling grew rife and informal protest gatherings of officers became common. They considered resigning in a body, then decided instead to draft a memorial to Congress. On the 29th, a deputation consisting of General Alexander McDougall and Colonels Matthias Ogden and John Brooks arrived in Philadelphia with the memorial, which they formally presented on January 6. In form and tone the document was a reserved and respectful plea for "justice," much as a demand for "explanations" prior to a challenge for a duel would be worded; but the officers included the ominous suggestion, again reminiscent of such a demand, that "any further experiments on their patience may have fatal effects."[37]

Where most members of Congress saw peril Morris and his inner circle saw opportunity. To seize it would require boldness, art, and luck, and failure could be calamitous. But the men in the inner circle were, if nothing else, bold. They included the sometimes extravagantly daring and imaginative Gouverneur Morris, now employed as Robert Morris's associate; Richard Peters, the active head of the Board of War; James Wilson, a Scots-born Philadelphia lawyer and congressman; and a handful of others. For a week or two they conferred with the McDougall committee and thrashed out a nebulous plan for coordinating the power of the army with the influence of the organized public creditors. They did not intend actually to employ the force of a rebellious army, for the practical reason that it was not likely to work. Instead they proposed to keep the army continuously threatening without exploding into outright violence, and thereby nudge both Congress and the state legislatures, with more individualized pressures from the public creditors, into granting quick approval of their plan. Thus by playing upon "the terror of a mutinying army," as Arthur Lee wrote to Sam Adams, they sought to effect radical changes within the framework of the existing governmental system.[38]

The stage was set on January 24, when Robert Morris suddenly issued an ultimatum to Congress. Declaring his despair that public credit would ever be established and that he could "never be the minister of injustice," he informed Congress that unless his system were enacted by the end of May he would quit his office and let Congress shift for itself. McDougall and Ogden were then sent back to army headquarters with a message well calculated to leave everything hanging in air: Morris would pay the army "as soon as the state of public finances will admit." Next day, Wilson proposed that Congress drop its other business and concentrate upon establishing a financial system. He and Hamilton led the way, with support from three new congressmen who were not privy to the inner plan—Thomas Fitzsimons of Pennsylvania, James Madison of Virginia, and Hugh Williamson of North Carolina. Within a few days, despite some resistance from state particularists, they succeeded in tying the parts of the program together so that Congress had to consider them all as a piece.[39]

Meanwhile, Hamilton and Gouverneur Morris were pushing forward with efforts to bring greater pressure to bear from the army. For ten days after the other two army delegates had returned to headquarters, Colonel Brooks (an intimate friend of Hamilton's) remained in Philadelphia for consultation. Then he returned to Newburgh to prepare the junior officers for "manly, Vigorous Association with the other public Creditors." He also delivered a message to Henry Knox, one of the two influential generals on whom Hamilton and Morris could rely. In a persuasive letter outlining the whole plan, Morris told Knox that "after you have carried the post the public creditors will garrison it for you." A week later Morris sent a similar letter to the other trusted general, Nathanael Greene. Less extravagantly, Hamilton wrote to Washington. Sketching a picture of a severe crisis in congressional finance, Hamilton pleaded with Washington to use his great prestige to harness the army's demands for justice, and particularly to ensure that the pressure would be utilized not merely for temporary relief but for the establishment of a permanent national system of finance. At the same time, Hamilton urged caution, so as "to keep a *complaining* and *suffering army* within the bounds of moderation." He added a postscript suggesting that it might be wise to consult General Knox, whom Hamilton knew Washington trusted.[40]

But the scheme was soon to collapse, for the two groups being manipulated suddenly got out of hand. At the beginning of March Colonel Walter Stewart, holder of a huge amount of public securities and former aide-de-camp of General Gates, spent a week in Philadelphia. He used a large part of his time in conference with the leading members of Philadelphia's public creditors committee, most of whom were intimate friends of his and enemies of Robert Morris. The plan they hatched is unknown, but on March 8 Stewart returned to Newburgh and proceeded directly to the tent of his former chief. Gates, bitterly hostile toward both Washington and Morris, had for some time flirted with the audacious idea of increasing the agitation in the army and using it to overthrow Washington. From Gates's tent began to emanate a word-of-mouth campaign, rumors that Congress was going to do nothing for the officers and that the officers were gathering to take drastic action. From the same tent came two written addresses, the unsigned work of Gates's aide John Armstrong, Jr. The first called for a meeting to discuss the relations between the army and Congress; since such a call without permission of the commander-in-chief was in violation of regulations, it amounted to a call for mutiny. The second address called for the officers to declare publicly, in defiance of orders from Washington or Congress if need be, that they would not disband until they had obtained "justice."[41]

Washington was able to quell the budding insurrection, but the very threat of it crushed the prospect of using the army to bring Morris's long-range plan to fruition. Thenceforth the two problems, paying and demobilizing the army and making provision for the public debts, had to be considered separately, and only the first had emergency priority. Moreover, just as Newburgh was exploding, the other last hope of the archnationalists was vanishing. They had hoped that even if their plan failed, the fear of a resumption of hostilities might perpetuate the atmosphere of crisis and stimulate nationalistic measures. But on March 12 came news of the conclusion of a provisional peace treaty with Britain, and on the 24th came news of the conclusion of a general peace.[42]

A three-stage anticlimax followed. Congress did pass a diluted revenue plan on April 18, 1783, but it was poorly designed and unlikely to be ratified by the states. The army received some back pay in the form of personal notes from Morris (who did not have access to enough funds to cover them); that satisfied some, and others went home on furlough, never to return, and the victorious army of the republic simply melted away. A few mutinous enlisted men remained together, marched to Philadelphia, got drunk there, and threatened Congress for several hours by milling about Independence Hall and periodically poking bayonets through the windows. Congress prudently adjourned to Princeton, but few members actually made the trip; and in effect the national government, such as it was, melted away also.[43]

Thus Hamilton's first, limited participation in an attempt to manipulate private interests to make them serve the public interest ended in failure. He may have thought that the failure was due to bad luck, or he may have recognized that the moment was not ripe. He did not realize, however, that in embracing Humean "realism" he had overreacted in disillusionment to his earlier idealism. By the time a new opportunity for statecraft arose six years later, he would understand that Hume, for all his subtlety, had erected a model too crude to be useful. Remembering Hume, Hamilton would ponder seriously the idea of strengthening the nation by tying private interests to the fate of public measures. "Yet upon the whole," he would write afterward, that "was the consideration upon which I relied least of all. . . . Such means are not to be resorted to but the good sense & virtue of the people."[44]

~§ III §~

Education in the Legal Arts: *1782–1784*

ORDER *is Heaven's first law; and this confest,*
Some are, and must be, greater than the rest.

The next chapter in Hamilton's education for statesmanship was his training in the law, which began in 1782. When he took it up, he was far from excited by its allurements. He spoke contemptuously of its practitioners (the "cavilling petulance of an attorney") and was skeptical of its intellectual merits. Remarking upon the common practice of filing contradictory pleas on a single case, he said that that was "among the Absurdities with which the Law abounds." One kind of legal process, he noted, "subsists Chiefly upon Fiction"; of another he said "there is the usual Confusion in this Doctrine." As for courts, they had only recently acquired "some faint Idea that the end of Suits at Law is to Investigate the Merits of the Cause, and not to entangle in the Nets of technical Terms."[1]

But he proved to have a strong natural affinity for the subject, and necessity forced him to plow through its maze of absurdities and abstractions. Some vital lessons for his career as a public man and nation-builder resulted. He learned that liberty and compliance with prescribed rules of behavior are not opposites that must somehow be balanced, as they had seemed earlier, but are complementary and inseparable. He learned to temper his Humean skepticism with principles of natural law, and thus to reconcile political theory with practical experience and to reconcile both with his deepest-rooted feelings.

Most importantly, he learned an elementary fact about the law which, applied on a larger scale, would constitute a new idea in the art of government. Blackstone had defined the law as "a rule of civil conduct prescribed by the supreme power in a state, commanding what is right and prohibiting what is wrong"; but every practicing attorney knew that in operation the law was less a matter of commands and prohibitions than of procedures. Hamilton was the first statesman to perceive that this characteristic of the law could be consciously applied not merely to bringing government under law through a constitution but to the grander goal of transforming society. He saw that one could best combine freedom and energy in a people, and infuse them with industry and love of country, by establishing the *ways* that things be done rather than trying to order *what* was to be done.[2]

Aproblem arose at the outset. There were no law schools in those days; a young man prepared himself for the bar by "reading law" in the office of an established attorney while serving as his clerk, copyist, and general flunky—and paying for the privilege. In New York, the period of apprenticeship was required to be at least three years. Hamilton could not afford such a wait, even had he had the patience for it, for he had a wife and child to support. His son Philip, the first of eight children, had recently been born.[3]

There was a loophole, a miniscule one: in January 1782, the state supreme court suspended the three-year requirement "in favor of such young Gentlemen who had directed their Studies to the profession of the Law, but upon the breaking out of the present war had entered into the Army in defence of their Country," provided that such gentlemen pass a rigorous bar examination by the end of the court's April term. Technically Hamilton qualified for the exemption, for he had, while at King's, done some reading (possibly wide but far from deep) in the works of various legal authorities. In his 1775 pamphlet, "The Farmer Refuted," he had referred his readers to various theorists of natural law and specifically cited Sir William Blackstone and Sir Edward Coke. But he had mentioned none of these in his earlier piece, "A Full Vindication," which suggests that he may have merely skimmed through them during the six or eight weeks between his writing of the two tracts. Moreover, since he did not refer to Coke's magnum opus, the four-volume *Institutes*, but only quoted one of Coke's better-known pronouncements, it seems likely that he was simply using the citation as window-dressing and had at most scanned Coke's work. His references to Blackstone, considered in the context of the argument Hamilton was making, suggest that he had actually studied only the early parts of the first of the four volumes. On the other hand, he had studied Beawes's *Lex Mercatoria*.[4]

That brush with the law had been as much as seven years earlier, and in January 1782 it was quite impossible for Hamilton to make the deadline. He set about the task anyway, and in April he appeared before the supreme court in Albany to ask for a special dispensation, an extension until October. The extension was granted, and it proved to be more than enough: in July he was admitted as an attorney qualified to practice before the supreme court, and on October 26 he was admitted to practice as counsel before the supreme court. (New York, unlike the other states, followed the English practice of separating the office lawyer, who prepares cases and documents, from the courtroom practitioner, who argues cases; in nine months, starting essentially from scratch, Hamilton had qualified himself for both roles.)[5]

The feat was impressive, and it is revealing to examine the way he went about performing it. Hamilton had unrestricted access to James Duane's good private law library. In addition to the works of the great commentators and the theorists of natural law, Duane's books included a fairly full collection of reports of English judicial decisions and such reference works as Robert Richardson's *The Attorney's Practice in the Court of King's Bench, with Precedents*, Giles Jacob's *A New Law Dictionary*, Matthew Bacon's *A New Abridgment of the Law*, Henry Bathurst's *An Introduction to the Law Relative to Trials at Nisi Prius*, and Sir Geoffrey Gilbert's *The History and Practice of Civil Actions, Particularly in the Court of Common Pleas*. These were treatises on the laws of England, not of New York, but New York followed English law more closely than did perhaps any other state; and Duane's library contained the New York statutes that prescribed variations from English practice. Two other students, John Lansing and Hamilton's friend Robert Troup, were also using Duane's books during the first portion of Hamilton's study. That was an advantage, for they could coach him on the kinds of questions asked at the bar examinations after they passed them in April.[6]

The most difficult part of the task was reducing the enormous mass of diffuse material to some kind of system that might be committed to memory. The expedient Hamilton hit upon was to write a book—that is, to compose a practice manual summarizing proper procedures and the essential substance of the laws under major headings, such as Damages, Process, Joint Actions, Judgment & Execution, Pleas, Venue, and so on. The order of Hamilton's headings was random, but he was both thorough and accurate in his research. The best modern legal historians have been able to find only eight minor mistakes in Hamilton's work, though a good deal of it was based upon inference and conjecture. The manual, running to 177 manuscript pages and about 40,000 words, was subsequently copied by many other law students and in the 1790s formed the basis of a published work that became the standard manual for New York lawyers.[7]

Having composed the manual, Hamilton now memorized it in his usual manner, pacing to and fro and reciting aloud to himself. How well he performed on his examinations is not knowable, since they were given orally, but it is known that the examinations were stiff. James Kent, who studied law in New York shortly after Hamilton did and later became chancellor of the state and the author of the American counterpart of Blackstone's *Commentaries,* wrote in 1786, "I believe there never was a Commonwealth before this of New York under the Sun whose Municipal Laws required an Examination so various so extensive & so profound, & which involved in them so much splendid & useful as well as so much tedious & antiquated Learning."[8]

Two of the authorities Hamilton studied, Vattel and Blackstone, significantly reshaped his thinking. Emmerich de Vattel was one of several theorists of international law ("natural law" and the "law of nations") whom Hamilton first read in 1782. The pioneer in the field was Hugo Grotius, who had been a professor of law at the University of Groningen, the Netherlands, when his book, *The*

Rights of War and Peace, was first published in 1625. James Duane, expressing opinions obviously shared by Hamilton, said that "tho' this celebrated work contains many excellent precepts, it is neither methodical nor comprehensive." Next came Samuel F. Pufendorf, a German whose *Law of Nature and Nations* (1703) had "more order, and great erudition," but was "not free from error" and misunderstood the relationship between natural and civil society. A Saxon philosopher, Christian Wolff, attempted to clarify the relationship in a diffuse tome that neither Hamilton nor Duane read; then a professor of civil and natural law in Geneva, Jean Jacques Burlamaqui, repeated the effort in briefer compass in *Principles of Natural and Politic Law* (1747–51), a work that both studied. Duane characterized Burlamaqui's effort as "rather an *introduction* than a *system*" which "served only to excite a desire to see it continued with equal perspicuity and elegance. The honor of this task was reserved for the great Vattel," whose classic *The Law of Nations* was published in 1758.[9]

Vattel's work was truly Hamilton's kind of book: its logic was forceful, its style terse and clear, its coverage thorough. Its impact upon him, however, was mainly corroborative. By giving him a thorough grounding in the principles of natural law, it enriched, supplemented, or corrected ideas he had acquired from other writers, including Hume, and provided a respectable rationale for ideas Hamilton sensed in his bones but had found nowhere else. Earlier Hamilton had read natural-rights theory, and his opponents later in life would continue to draw on that theory; but, while natural law and natural rights were related concepts, they were far from identical—the one being tough-minded, the other soft. Vattel dramatically illustrated the difference in his introductory essay. Rights, he declared, "being nothing more than the power of doing what is morally possible, that is to say, what is proper and consistent with duty,—it is evident that right is derived from duty, or passive obligation."[10]

Vattel went on in a fascinatingly reasoned passage to a succint summary of the "science of the laws of nature." The first principle, he said, was an "axiom of incontestible truth," namely, that "the great end of every being endowed with intellect and sentiment, is happiness." Only by harnessing the natural desire for happiness can we "bind a creature possessed of the faculty of thought, and form the ties of that obligation which shall make him submit to any rule." By studying the nature of things, man in particular, it was possible to discover the rules of behavior that lead to happiness, and those rules constituted natural law. Natural law was ordained by God, was unalterable, and was universally binding. The penalty for violating it was, quite logically, unhappiness. "Now, one of the first truths which the study of man reveals to us, and which is a necessary consequence of his nature, is, that, in a state of lonely separation from the rest of his species, he cannot attain his great end—happiness: and the reason is, that he was intended to live in society with his fellow creatures. Nature herself, therefore, has established that society, whose great end is the common advantage of all its members; and the means of attaining that end constitute the rules that each individual is bound to observe in his whole conduct."[11]

That line of reasoning provided Hamilton with a view of morality quite different from the one he had found in the works of Hume. Hume believed that men behaved morally because it was socially useful for them to do so. Vattel insisted that they did because they were required to by natural law. Vattel, it is true, said only that men "ought" to behave morally, but to him there was no tension between what ought to be and what is: he used "ought" not to mean "should" but to mean obliged to, commanded to by the laws of nature. Hamilton could see the matter both ways—he recognized the social utility of morality but also felt a powerful natural obligation to act morally—and thus he acquired a broader basis of understanding than either Vattel or Hume had. A keen awareness of the distinction between what was right and what was expedient marked his appraisal of all questions of public concern; his warmest endorsement of any course of conduct was that it was both intrinsically proper and good policy.

Another of Vattel's teachings that was valuable to Hamilton concerned the motives of men in government. Montesquieu, whom Hamilton (along with nearly every other literate American) had read and sworn by, had taught that the actuating principle of a republic, without which it could not survive, was virtue—in the people and in their chosen leaders. Hume taught, on the contrary, that when one is contriving a government one must suppose every man to be a knave. Vattel had still another suggestion. Choosing virtuous men as rulers was inadequate, he said, for the obsequious flattery that attends people in positions of power personally corrupts all but the very purest. That was compatible with Hume's view, but Vattel made the additional observation that the personal corruption of rulers was of little consequence if, *in the performance of their public duties,* they used "the public power only with a view to the public welfare." Private morality and private behavior, in other words, were no reliable measure of performance in office. Men were in fact likely to behave more morally when acting in a public capacity than when acting privately. (The founding generation of Americans abounded with personally corrupt men who nonetheless, out of a sense of duty and love of country, served the nation well.) Hamilton availed himself of this insight when seeking support for his measures.[12]

Vattel also altered Hamilton's conception of the proper functions of government—or, rather, provided him a system of ideas more congruent with his instincts than was the Lockean doctrine that government existed only to preserve natural rights to life, liberty, and property. Vattel described the "principal objects of a good government" under three main heads: to provide for the nation's necessities, to "procure the true happiness" of the nation, and to "fortify itself against external attacks." The first of these squared with Hamilton's activist nature and his activist notions about the role of government in the economy. Taking issue specifically with Hume's contention that trade must be left free to regulate itself, Hamilton argued (in a tract published while he was studying for the bar) that government should intercede with its authority as well as its revenues when "the avarice of individuals" threw trade in channels inimical to the public interest, when desirable enterprises might otherwise not be undertaken for want of sufficient private capital, or when unexpected causes thwarted a prosperous flow of commerce. In keeping with a natural-law view, Hamilton agreed that trade had its "fundamental laws . . . and that any violent attempts in opposition to these would commonly miscarry"; but he firmly shared Vattel's belief that government should play a positive role in what Vattel termed providing for the necessities of the nation. (Incidentally, Hamilton accepted Vattel's belief that private ownership of property was a civil right, derived from society, and not a natural right antecedent to society, as Locke and other natural-rights theorists had maintained.)[13]

The second object of good government, "to procure the true happiness of the Nation," bore no relation to the selfish concept of "doing one's own thing" that unthinking moderns might regard as the meaning of the phrase "pursuit of happiness" in the Declaration of Independence. Indeed, it was the antithesis of such a concept. On the part of the state, it entailed rigorous instruction of the people in good citizenship and the arts and sciences, both practical and "polite," and the cultivation of religious piety within the limits of the right to liberty of conscience. On the part of the individual, it entailed love of country and rigorous attention to the duty of making oneself as virtuous, moral, and useful a member of society as possible. The matter provided "an infallible criterion, by which the nation may judge of the intentions of those who govern it. If they endeavour to render the great and the common people virtuous, their views are pure and upright; and you may rest assured that they solely aim at the great end of government, the happiness and glory of the nation." On the other hand, if they corrupted the morals of the common people with permissiveness, thus spreading "a taste for luxury, effeminacy, a rage for licentious pleasures, . . . beware, citizens! beware of those corruptors! they only aim at purchasing slaves in order to exercise over them an arbitrary sway." Hamilton's public life and the way he reared his children demonstrated that he shared Vattel's view of what constituted "true" happiness.[14]

The third object, in Vattel's judgment, was to fortify the nation against external attack. Self-evident as that idea might seem, Hamilton was one of the few Americans taught by experience to believe in it. Despite the lessons of the war, the popular view continued to be that peacetime military establishments, "standing armies," were incompatible with public safety and popular liberty. Rejecting that dogma, Vattel maintained that the only way to ensure peace was to keep the nation well prepared for war. He went further, advancing a proposition that Hamilton ardently embraced and was anathema to his enemies: that a nation ought to strive "to establish its reputation and glory."[15]

Finally, Hamilton might have obtained from Vattel the germ of a doctrine that became a keystone of the American constitutional system—namely, the judicial review of the constitutionality of government actions. Vattel maintained that the citizens must obey their sovereign so long as his orders did not violate natural law or the constitution; and he declared that "in all well-regulated states, in countries that are really states, and not the dominions of a despot," an independent judiciary decides disputes between the sovereign and private citizens. Reasoning from those premises, and seizing upon a dictum of Montesquieu's and a pronouncement made by Sir Edward Coke (which Coke, however, had subsequently recanted), Hamilton advocated judicial review in the first significant case in which he was involved. He continued to champion the doctrine, and, just before his death, it became an established principle of American jurisprudence.[16]

Blackstone's influence upon Hamilton was more subtle. Blackstone's *Commentaries* were studied by virtually every American lawyer, and by many nonlawyers as well; the number of copies sold in America was several times the number of lawyers, and James Madison could refer to the work as "a book which is in every man's hand." Consequently, and because the Founding Fathers were accustomed to overpraising the *Commentaries*, extravagant claims have been made about his influence in America. Blackstone has been called not only the paramount influence upon Hamilton but also the intellectual wellspring of both the Declaration of Independence and the Constitution.[17]

There are many things, however, that Hamilton did *not* learn from Blackstone. One of them was how to be a practicing attorney, for the necessary information is simply not there. Because the *Commentaries* are a majestic and massive survey of the law rather than a guide to practice, they were far too general for Hamilton's purposes. A single example will illustrate the point. In assembling his practice manual, Hamilton needed to learn the details of the writ of *scire facias*, which was an order to show cause why a court judgment should not be executed. Blackstone mentions the writ in seven different places, and Hamilton's brief general description of it could be a paraphrase of Blackstone's; but Blackstone never explained just how to use it. For that kind of practical information, Hamilton had to study Jacob's *Law Dictionary*, Crompton's *Practice in the Courts*, and Sir John Strange's *Reports of Adjudged Cases*.[18]

Nor did Hamilton derive his understanding of natural law from Blackstone: that came principally from Vattel. True, Blackstone devoted a little space to the law of nature and nations in his introduction to the "Nature of Laws in General," but it was not among his major concerns; and besides, Blackstone relied mainly upon outdated authorities, especially Grotius and Pufendorf, and showed no indications of having studied Vattel. Moreover, though he paid lip service to the supremacy of natural law over man-made law, he went on to negate his endorsement. In a celebrated passage (which Hamilton had quoted in "The Farmer Refuted"), Blackstone declared that the "law of nature, being coeval with mankind and dictated by God himself, is of course superior in obligation to any other. It is binding over all the globe in all countries, and at all times: no human laws are of any validity, if contrary to this." No sooner had he moved on to his introduction to the laws of England, however, then he demonstrated that the laws were in fact whatever they were declared to be "by the king's majesty, by and with the advice and consent of the lords spiritual and temporal and commons in parliament assembled," anything in the common law or natural law to the contrary notwithstanding. Returning, in his book IV, to the subject of natural law in a short chapter on the law of nations, Blackstone again made a strong statement only to back away from it. The law of nations, he said there, was adopted in England in its "full extent by the common law, and is held to be part of the law of the land." Parliament, he conceded, had in fact periodically changed the law; but, said Blackstone, such changes "are not to be considered as introductive of any new rule, but merely as declaratory of the old fundamental constitutions of the kingdom." That was pure sophistry, for Blackstone had earlier declared unequivocally that Parliament could "do every thing that is not naturally impossible." Blackstone explicitly rejected Locke's doctrine that there was a point beyond which Parliament must not go, lest power revert to the people. "No human laws," he said, will "suppose a case, which at once must destroy all law, and compel men to build afresh upon a new foundation. . . . So long therefore as the English constitution lasts, we may venture to affirm, that the power of parliament is absolute and without control."[19]

Blackstone disposed of the doctrine of judicial review in similar fashion. The courts could, he said, disregard portions of statutes if they were so "manifestly absurd or unjust" that it could not be reasonably assumed that Parliament meant literally what it said when enacting a law. But, he added, "if the parliament will positively enact a thing to be done which is unreasonable, I know of no power in the ordinary forms of the constitution, that is vested with authority to control it." Should a court overstep its power and declare an act of Parliament unconstitutional, it would be to no avail; for Parliament, in addition to being the supreme legislative power, was also the supreme court of appeals in the kingdom.[20]

To appreciate what Blackstone did contribute to Hamilton's mature thinking, one must first understand why the *Commentaries* appealed to Hamilton. To any reader having a keen mind and a love of intellectual adventure, as Hamilton surely had, Blackstone is well-nigh irresistible. His style is elegant; his methods of reasoning are varied and ever-persuasive; by turns, he is charming and concise, seductive and sarcastic, witty and sober, anecdotal and crisply logical.[21]

Blackstone often employed a delightful, Alice-in-Wonderland kind of closed logical system to justify his proposition that English law as a whole was perfect (though steadily improving). For instance, there is his explanation of the reasonableness and necessity of the tenet of English law which held that the king could do no wrong. The law could not express distrust of those whom it vested with any part of supreme power, he said, for when it anticipates the abuse of power "it always vests a superior coercive authority in some other hand to correct it." Since there can be no power superior to the supreme power, and since in a perfect system of law there can be no wrong for which there is no remedy, the law must suppose not only that the king can do no wrong but that he is incapable even of thinking wrong. If the king should *appear* to have done a wrong, the law assumed either that he had been deceived or that his ministers were at fault, in which case the wrong could be redressed. In the event of an extreme abuse of power, it would have to be assumed that the king had abdicated the throne—but Blackstone thought it best not to dwell upon that. Hamilton could appreciate such a closed system of logic, for he had the subtlety of mind to understand that what seemed contradictions were actually ambiguities, and that ambiguity inheres in government and law as it does in life.[22]

Blackstone also appealed to Hamilton and influenced him so powerfully because the *Commentaries* are studded with gems of pure wisdom. For example, in discussing equity courts (those that judge disputes in which no formal law seems to apply, or in which strict application of the law in a special case would effect an injustice), Blackstone praises them as indispensable and invaluable. On the other hand, he declares that "the liberty of considering all cases in an equitable light must not be indulged too far, lest thereby we destroy all law, and leave the decision of every question entirely in the breast of the judge. And law, without equity, though hard and disagreeable, is much more desirable for the public good, than equity without law: which would make every judge a legislator, and introduce most infinite confusion."[23]

As to Blackstone's substantive contributions to Hamilton's maturation, at least three can be isolated. The first is the most obvious: Blackstone taught Hamilton a reverential enthusiasm for the law itself. The lesson was not, however, easily learned. On superficial reading the *Commentaries* seem to justify Hamilton's initial reaction that the law abounds in absurdities; they appear to contain one contradiction after another, one exception after another, one catch after another. In his book I, entitled "Of the Rights of Persons," Blackstone declares that the "first and primary end of human laws" is to protect individuals "in the enjoyment of those absolute rights, which were vested in them by the immutable laws of nature"—and then demonstrates that all personal rights are relative, limited, derived not from nature but from society, and subject to cancellation at the whim of Crown in Parliament. At the beginning of his book II, entitled "Of the Rights of Things," he defines property as "that sole and despotic dominion which one man claims and exercises over the external things of the world, in total exclusion of the right of any other individual in the universe"—and then devotes the remaining 518 pages of the volume to qualifying and specifying the exceptions to his definition. He says the common law is immutable and then cites a thousand instances of change; he says precedent is absolutely binding and then offers repeated instances of deviation from precedent.[24]

Yet upon close study of the *Commentaries* the law emerges as a beautiful, symmetrical whole—a set of fundamental and simple principles, within each of which the variations are endlessly complex but logically consistent, like the variations on a simple theme in a fugue by Johann Sebastian Bach. Moreover, the law as Blackstone spelled it out resolved once and for all the tension Hamilton had felt between liberty and law. Mankind had a natural right to freedom, Blackstone said, that being "one of the gifts of God to man at his creation, when he endued him with the faculty of free-will." But upon entering organized society man gives up "part of his natural liberty, as the price of so valuable a purchase," thereby obliging himself "to conform to those laws, which the community has thought proper to establish. And this species of legal obedience and conformity is infinitely more desirable than that wild and savage liberty which is sacrificed to obtain it." No person who gave the matter a moment's thought "would wish to retain the absolute and uncontrolled power of doing whatever he pleases: the consequence of which is, that every other man would also have the same power; and then there would be no security to individuals in any of the enjoyments of life." In sum, "laws, when prudently framed, are by no means subversive but rather introductive of liberty," for as even Locke had seen, "where there is no law there is no freedom."[25]

Secondly, Blackstone contributed a great deal, albeit obliquely, to Hamilton's development of a workable theory of federalism. Blackstone insisted that sovereignty was indivisible, that there could be no law unless there was a single supreme power to formulate it; but that unqualified pronouncement he in fact subjected to endless qualifications. The governmental and legal system of England as he described it was hierarchical: the power of Crown in Parliament was absolute at the top of the pyramid, but so was that of each part of the system on its own level, down to the lowly justiceships of the peace. Upon that model, it was possible to conceive of the American national government as sovereign yet leave room for the continued existence of the several states to have sole authority in those areas exclusively of concern to themselves. That dual authority had been implicit in Hamilton's "Continentalist" essays in 1781, and by early 1784 he was arguing explicitly that "portions" of sovereignty inhered in the Congress, other shares were delegated to it by the states, and still another share remained in the people. Various American lawyers nourished on Blackstone—including James Wilson, Rufus King, and Oliver Ellsworth, all of whom would sit with Hamilton in the Constitutional Convention of 1787—developed such a concept of sovereignty about the time Hamilton did.[26]

Thirdly, it may have been Blackstone who wooed Hamilton back into a belief in the desirability of mixing governmental powers on the horizontal axis. Hamilton had abandoned the idea earlier but embraced it anew after studying Blackstone's persuasive rationalization. Blackstone maintained that the principal ingredients of good polity are power or energy, wisdom, and concern for the good of the people. The Crown could supply the power, and the Lords could supply the wisdom; but only the Commons, representing the people, could be counted on to look after the interests of the people, for those were their own interests. Put that way, the notion of a mixture of monarchy, aristocracy, and democracy would appeal to a man of Hamilton's bent—though when he finally formulated his ideas on the subject, he would add a fourth ingredient to the mix, an independent judiciary.[27]

For all the speed with which he prepared himself for the bar, Hamilton took his time about commencing his practice. In part the delay was occasioned by his service in Congress, which extended from early December 1782—five weeks after he had qualified as counsel—until the following July. More importantly, there was no occasion for haste, since he intended to practice and live in New York City, which the British, whose evacuation was delayed for various reasons, continued to occupy until November 1783. That month he established his home and office there, at 57 Wall Street.

Once Hamilton got under way, he was immediately successful. Connections helped. His wartime services had won him considerable renown and facilitated the making of contacts with eminent people. His political activities had established him a reputation for ability and integrity and led to firm personal relations with Duane, Jay, Morris, and other influential and wealthy men. Early in 1784 he became a founder and director of the Bank of New York, which continuously gave him business. Above all there was the Schuyler connection, which among other things made him a brother-in-law to Stephen Van Rensselaer and to John B. Church, a wealthy British businessman who had played an important part in the Revolution by helping supply the American and French armies. Church returned to England just after the war, leaving Hamilton not only as his legal representative but also as his business agent. That alone would have been enough to spare Hamilton the shilling-and-pence work that might otherwise have made up the main business of a young and inexperienced attorney—though Hamilton handled a great deal of that, too.[28]

But Hamilton rose to the top rank among the two or three dozen lawyers in New York City primarily because he was better than they were. Judge Ambrose Spencer, whose career spanned many years and gave him occasion to hear two generations of the greatest American lawyers, once compared Hamilton with Daniel Webster. "In power of reasoning," he said, "Hamilton was the equal of Webster; and more than this can be said of no man. In creative power Hamilton was infinitely Webster's superior." Chancellor Kent, discussing in 1832 the greatest New York lawyers who had practiced during his lifetime, ranked Hamilton first and attributed Hamilton's greatness to "his profound penetration, his power of analysis, the comprehensive grasp and strength of his understanding," and his firmness and frankness of character. These were not idly chosen words: Kent was attempting a careful analysis of Hamilton's distinctive characteristics. Troup had an explanation for those qualities. Hamilton was always so busy with politics, said Troup, that he never became "a learned Case Lawyer" but instead concentrated on "elementary books," whereby he became extremely "well grounded in first principles." He applied those principles "with wonderful facility, to every question he argued. But if you stated a Case to him, and allowed him time to examine the Reporters, he would propound the law respecting it, and give an opinion that would bear the test of the severest discussion."[29]

These contemporary evaluations are substantiated, with modifications and additions, by study of Hamilton's arguments, briefs, and notes. Troup's analysis was in a sense accurate; for Hamilton did not like arguing the facts or merits of a cause nearly so much as he enjoyed doing battle on grounds of the law, and he became a master of the kind of special pleas that made argument on the latter grounds possible. Troup was wrong, however, in thinking that Hamilton devoted little time to study. His finished products—his arguments, interrogations, and final briefs—often seemed to be merely the results of native brilliance and intensive reflection, but in fact Hamilton put endless hours of "hard, grinding work" into his preparation of a case. This was especially true when he prepared for a courtroom duel on points of law.[30]

Troup was readily deceived on this count, for Hamilton had a natural gift (which he carefully cultivated) for making things look easier than they were; indeed, he had a virtual compulsion for doing so, even among his intimate friends. Another of his characteristics as a lawyer, again partly a personal attribute and partly a tactic, was also missed by most contemporaries. In the courtroom as in his mature political polemics, he rarely engaged in direct rebuttal but instead preferred to build a progression of positive propositions which came together into an unassailable structure of argument. "His habit of thought even when acting for the defense was affirmative," say the editors of his law papers; "in other words, he was always carrying the war to the enemy." That, together with "an intuitive sense of where lay the vitals of a cause," forced his adversaries to argue on his terms—and usually to come out second best.[31]

From the outset, however, Hamilton's success as a lawyer was attended by controversy and public hostility because of his defense of unpopular causes in general and Loyalists and British subjects in particular. Feelings against such persons were especially intense in New York, and during and immediately after the war the state legislature enacted a number of harsh measures against them. In the ensuing litigation, three major statutes were involved: the Confiscation Act (1779), whose essence is evident from its title; the Citation Act (1782), which stayed execution on debts due Loyalists by Patriots and permitted the debtors to pay their obligations in depreciated paper currency; and the Trespass Act (1783), which offered relief to Patriots who had escaped the city when the British captured it by enabling them to recover damages from persons who had occupied their premises during the war.[32]

The Trespass Act was a classic and dramatic illustration of the inherent difference between democracy and law: it was immensely popular, having virtually unanimous approval of the citizenry, and yet it flouted fundamental principles of law. Contrary to the common law, under which trespass actions must be tried where the property was located, the act allowed Patriots to sue in any court where the defendant could be found. Contrary to the laws of war, it prohibited defendants from pleading that they had acted under orders of the occupying British army. Contrary to established legal tradition, it denied defendants the right of appeal to a higher court. The act overtly violated the law of nations, the treaty of peace that recognized American independence, and a mandate from Congress to the several states—whatever those might be worth in the state of New York. Hamilton and a handful of others determined to challenge the act in the courts.[33]

By agreement of attorneys on both sides, the suit of Mrs. Elizabeth Rutgers against Joshua Waddington was decided upon as a test case. From the point of view of counsel for the plaintiff the choice was ideal. Mrs. Rutgers was a widow in her seventies who had fled the British army in 1776, abandoning substantial property to them. She also happened to be the aunt of Egbert Benson, the state's attorney general. Waddington was agent for his uncle Benjamin Waddington and the latter's partner Evelyn Pierrepont. Waddington and Pierrepont had, in 1778, occupied a large brewery and alehouse owned by Mrs. Rutgers, run it at a whopping profit throughout the war, then returned to England, taking their profits with them. The brewery, ravaged by a fire of mysterious origins, lay in ashes when she returned to the city. Under the Trespass Act, the widow sued for £8,000 in damages.[34]

From Hamilton's point of view as counsel for the defendant, the choice of cases was likewise a good one. Waddington and Pierrepont were not nearly so culpable as popular opinion made them out to be: they had paid substantial rent to British authorities for the use of the property; the brewery had actually been a shambles when they took it over and they had invested £700 in rebuilding it; and they had suffered a £4,000 loss in goods when it burned. None of these facts, however, was relevant unless Hamilton chose to remove the case to chancery court for hearing in equity—a course he considered but rejected. In a direct challenge to the statute, such as Hamilton planned, the central fact of the case was that the defendants had occupied the brewery under authority of the British army. Under the laws of war, as Vattel made clear, an occupying army had the right to the full use of all property in enemy territory it held, and the owners had no claim to compensation afterward. (The precise nature of the military authorization to Waddington and Pierrepont also turned out to be important. For the first two years, 1778 to 1780, they had used the property rent-free with permission of the commissary general; thereafter, under an order of the commander-in-chief, they occupied the premises upon payment of £150 annual rent to the Vestry for the Poor.)[35]

Even before argument was heard, Hamilton managed to outmaneuver his opposition. In April 1784, when he filed his formal plea, he said more than he needed to say, thereby tipping his hand to counsel for the plaintiff; clearly, if between the lines, he let it be known in general what his defense would be. In anonymous pamphlets (which the opposing lawyers knew he had written) he went further and more or less specified his argument in detail. So notified, plaintiff's counsel armed themselves by preparing a point-by-point rebuttal. That meant their case would be a counterattack on Hamilton's own grounds, which was advantageous enough for him. But he did more: he prepared an alternate line of reasoning to use as a surprise weapon in the field.[36]

The case was argued on June 29 before the Mayor's Court of New York City, comprising the mayor, the recorder, and the five aldermen. The first two, Hamilton's friend and erstwhile patron Mayor James Duane and Recorder Richard Varick, were sympathetic toward Hamilton's cause; less so were the aldermen, including one who had himself filed a suit under the Trespass Act (again Hamilton for the defense). Representing the plaintiff were Attorney General Benson (acting in a private capacity on behalf of his aunt, but also unofficially representing the state), along with William Wilcox, John Lawrence, and Robert Troup. Co-counsel with Hamilton for the defendant were Morgan Lewis and Brockholst Livingston.[37]

After an opening statement by the plaintiff, Hamilton presented his case, making three major arguments. First, he said the Trespass Act violated the laws of war. Hamilton pointed out that the state constitution expressly incorporated the common law as part of the law of New York, that the common law included the law of nations, and that the law of nations included the laws of war. Waddington was within those laws in using the Rutgers premises under British military authority; and thus to award damages to Mrs. Rutgers would be to violate the law of nations, the common law, and therefore the law of New York.

Hamilton's second argument involved the Treaty of Peace. By the Articles of Confederation, Congress had been vested with exclusive power to conclude treaties of peace, which implied the power to include all reasonable conditions within such treaties. The law of nations implied a general amnesty in all final treaties of peace, Hamilton maintained, and thus Congress, in approving the treaty, must have consented to a general amnesty. Moreover, the treaty, in its sixth article, specifically forbade further confiscations and prose-cutions for the part anyone on either side had played during the war; and Congress, when proclaiming the treaty, explicitly declared that that and other clauses meant nobody on either side was entitled "to any compensation, recompence, retribution, or indemnity what-ever, for or by reason of any injury whatsoever whether to the public or to individuals relating to the war."

Third, Hamilton argued that the court, in hearing the present case as in hearing any other, was obliged to consider whether the statute involved was incompatible with any kind of higher law; if it found the statute to be so, the court was obliged to declare the statute null and void. Since the Trespass Act violated the law of nations as well as the peace treaty and direct commands of Congress, he con-tended, the court must hold the act invalid.

Counsel for plaintiff had prepared a clever rebuttal. Pointing out that the Articles of Confederation, which gave the Congress its legal existence, expressly reserved to the several states their "freedom, sovereignty, and independence," counsel argued that resolutions of Congress could not be of binding force in regard to the internal af-fairs of the sovereign state of New York. As to the treaty, it did not affect the validity of the Trespass Act because it was not ratified until after the act was passed. Those contentions, though tech-nically defensible, were not especially appealing to a judge of Duane's predilections, but plaintiff's next line of argument was more persuasive. It was true, plaintiff conceded, that the state con-stitution had incorporated the common law, but that by no means warranted the use of the law of nations to invalidate a statute. The state constitution itself had been essentially no more than a legisla-tive act, for it had been proclaimed by an ad hoc legislature, the Provincial Congress, and had never been ratified by the people. Ap-proval of the Articles of Confederation had been another legislative act, never ratified by the people. The Trespass Act was yet a third act of the legislature, and even if it contravened the earlier acts when it barred defendants from pleading military authorization—a contention that plaintiff denied—it took precedence by virtue of being the latest legislation. What was most telling of all, plaintiff argued that the Mayor's Court, being a creature of the same legisla-ture, had no authority whatever to overrule a legislative enactment or to set aside legislatively prescribed rules of evidence.

It was there that Hamilton sprang his surprise. Plaintiff's counsel had anticipated that he would seek judicial review of the statute on grounds of incompatibility with higher law, and he did so; but in his argument he developed another and more effective ground. Courts were regularly called upon, Hamilton said, to construe the meaning of the law as it applied to particular cases. The rules of construction were clear and well known. One of these was the supposition that the legislature is wise and honest; and thus if a narrowly literal reading of the language of a statute leads to an absurd, contradictory, or unjust application, it must be assumed that the legislature had not intended for the act to be read that way. Similarly, if the general language of one statute, read literally and without reference to circumstances, resulted in a conflict with the specific language of another statute or with the common law, it must be supposed that the legislature intended no such conflict.

Hamilton recited a series of real and hypothetical examples to illustrate his point, then came to focus on the present case. The defendant was a foreigner; to make a British alien subject to suit under the Trespass Act would violate the common law, the peace treaty, the law of nations, the honor of the United States, and a number of established legal principles. Since the statute did not declare that the legislature intended to do all that, Hamilton concluded, it must be held that the act did not apply to the defendant, even if it be held that the statute itself were valid.

By stressing that line of reasoning, Hamilton undermined the ground on which plaintiff's case had been built. Counsel for Mrs. Rutgers had argued for legislative supremacy over court decisions; and though Hamilton disagreed, he emphasized the question of presumed legislative intent, not judicial review, as the basis for a decision in favor of his client. That enabled the court to affirm plaintiff's position and disavow any power to overrule a statute ("for this were to set the *judicial* above the legislative"), and yet at the same time do just that by ruling for Waddington.

That was the way the court ruled, though the decision was ambiguous. Duane, in his opinion, accepted Hamilton's entire argument in regard to the law of nations and the authority of the treaty and of Congress, yet he shied away from endorsing judicial review as such. Nor was the judgment itself unmixed. In regard to the first period of Waddington's occupancy of the Rutgers premises (1778–80), Duane held that protection of the law of nations did not apply since authorization was from a subordinate army official. In regard to the later period (1780–83), when authorization was by the commander-in-chief, Duane ruled that the law of nations did apply and that any person who is *"clearly exempted* from the operation of this statute by the law of nations, this Court must take it for granted, could never have been *intended* to be comprehended within it by the Legislature." The damages for the first period of occupancy, when finally settled, amounted to about £800 instead of the £8,000 claimed by Mrs. Rutgers.[38]

But if Hamilton's victory was not total, it was a victory nonetheless, and a sweet one.

This small triumph of law over popular passions was not greeted by huzzahs from the multitudes. The decision was condemned in public gatherings and in petitions to the legislature. The legislature adopted a resolution denouncing the decision and entertained but defeated a resolution calling for the removal of Mayor Duane and Recorder Varick. Hamilton was personally castigated in the newspapers, and the condemnations grew stronger when he went on to defend (sometimes successfully) other British subjects and Loyalists in forty-four more actions under the Trespass Act and twenty or so under the Confiscation and Citation acts. Only his outstanding war record prevented the attacks from becoming more than verbal.

Hamilton was not fazed by the outcry, for he had sworn to defend the law, not the people, and had learned to believe that the people could be happy only when they obeyed the law rather than their impulses. Besides, he had long since observed that there were "men in all respects qualified for conducting the public affairs, with skill and advantage," but that "their influence was too commonly borne down by the prevailing torrent of ignorance and prejudice," by "the passions of the vulgar." This is not to suggest that he advocated government by "the rich and well born"; he never did that. But it was obvious that some were better qualified for leadership than others, and he would have been less than human had he not expected to find most of the leaders among, say, the officers with whom he had served and the members of the social class into which he had married. In his natural optimism, he probably assumed that such people would soon or late make and enforce the law as well as tend to the needs of the nation.[39]

But he was about to undergo, once again, a round of experiences that would be simultaneously disillusioning and enlightening. When he had assimilated those lessons, Hamilton would be prepared to serve as his country's Lawgiver.

IV

Completion of an Education:
1784–1787

And hence one MASTER PASSION *in the breast,*
Like Aaron's serpent, swallows up the rest.

During the first four years of peace, when he was in his late twenties, everything that made Hamilton what he was—his romanticism, his compulsion to excel, his contempt for dependency, his hostility toward the provincial social systems that nourished what he deplored, his religious training, his military career, his strong sense of propriety, his gifts as administrator and lawyer, his blend of skepticism and faith, his years of experience and study—all coalesced. The crystallizing agents were two ideas Hamilton learned, or rather unlearned, in postwar economic and political life.

The first had to do with his assessment of the political complexion of the nation. In 1783 he wrote Washington, "There are two classes of men Sir in Congress of very Different views—one attached to state, the other to Continental politics." The latter he characterized as "the most sensible the most liberal, the most independent and the most respectable characters in our body." To Robert Morris, he had earlier said that the nation needed as leaders "individuals of established reputation and conspicuous for probity, abilities and fortune." What he had to unlearn was a tendency to overrate the numbers, talents, integrity, and nationalism of such men, and to underrate their opposites.[1]

This habit of thought was born of inexperience as well as temperament. Hamilton's personal knowledge of the United States was confined to the small area bounded by Albany, Boston, and Yorktown, and he was really familiar only with the area between Albany and Philadelphia. During the war that area had been the most consistently nationalistic part of the country. Off and on, it is true, the government of Pennsylvania had been in the hands of radicals, but even they normally gave Congress solid support; and the governments of New York and New Jersey were conservative as well as committed to the national cause. Virtually everyone Hamilton knew intimately shared his views about national honor, or seemed to, and virtually all were persons of gentility and means. Moreover, his wife's kin and connections, his fellows at the bar, his friends among former army officers (with whom he remained in contact through the Society of the Cincinnati), and the extensive and powerful mercantile network that radiated outward from Robert Morris were interconnected through marital, economic, and sentimental ties. Together, throughout the war, they had constituted a solid phalanx of nationalism against state particularism and of conservativism against democratic excess. But with the coming of peace, governments in the Middle States developed a localism as narrow as that in isolated North Carolina and New Hampshire, and members of the propertied nationalist connection turned out to be as principled and cooperative as a pack of sharks.

Hamilton also had to unlearn, or at least to rethink, his belief that, because of the potency of self-interest, the "national debt if it is not excessive will be to us a national blessing; it will be a powerfull cement of our union." State-oriented politicians proved masterful at the art of manipulating ambition and avarice to the disadvantage of the union, and their most efficacious instrument was the public debt. That was instructive to Hamilton in more ways than one—not least in causing him to question whether a national system founded upon an appeal to the baser passions could endure. He came to realize that something at once stronger and more subtle would be necessary, and to know what that something was. Now he knew what he must do with his life, and he knew, in detail, how to do it.

The first apostate from the ranks of "those who think continentally," as Hamilton saw things, was Governor George Clinton.

The governor had given Hamilton cause to respect and trust him. Clinton was born into a good family, ultimately of noble lineage, and had married into a better one. He had a large and growing fortune, obtained mainly through land speculations, and a commensurately wholesome respect for property rights. He had held a field command as brigadier general early in the war, before being elected in 1777 to the first of six consecutive three-year terms as governor. In the gubernatorial office he was stronger and more consistently nationalistic than his counterpart in any other state. Hamilton had worked with him on the official level and found him nearly indispensable to the war effort. They had a number of long, serious conversations about national affairs, and once, when Hamilton fell gravely ill, it was Clinton who saw to his care. Another thing stood in Clinton's favor. Though New York was overrun with Loyalists and the governor was vigorous in the measures he took against them, he had refused to countenance lawlessness in their treatment. He was as opposed to mob action as Hamilton was; he even opposed the Confiscation Act at first. Thus, though Hamilton had some reservations about his intellectual powers ("his passions are much warmer," said Hamilton, "than his judgment is enlightened"), he nonetheless regarded Clinton as a man of honor and integrity and enough ability to pass among "his particular friends for a statesman."[2]

Clinton's first major sin, in Hamilton's eyes, was that he yielded, ultimately, to popular demands for persecution of Loyalists after the war. The intensity of public feelings on the matter is understandable, for New York had witnessed more fighting, contained more Loyalists, and had more of its territory occupied by the enemy for a longer time than had any other state, and Patriots were in no forgiving mood as the war ended. In response to popular outcry, the legislature had passed the Trespass Act and several other measures which, together, deprived Tories of both civil and property rights and disfranchised two-thirds to nine-tenths of the electorate in the lower countries.[3]

Hamilton opposed such persecution on grounds of humanity and national honor, but also on grounds of policy, and he wrote a long letter to Clinton before the evacuation urging the governor to use his influence to stem the flood of anti-Tory legislation. The British, said Hamilton, were hardly so magnanimous or dispassionate as not to respond in kind to persecutions of Loyalists in violation of the peace treaty. Indeed, they would be eager to seize upon American violations as an excuse to violate disadvantageous articles of the treaty themselves—for instance, by retaining control of their military posts in western New York, which were the keys to the lucrative fur trade with the Indians. Soon afterward, Hamilton discovered another practical reason for moderation. Tories were fleeing in droves: some 35,000, nearly a fifth of the state's prewar population, left for Britain, Nova Scotia, or Canada, draining the city of money in the doing. "Many merchants of second class, characters of no political consequence, each of whom may carry away eight or ten thousand guineas," were departing, Hamilton said. "Our state will feel for twenty years at least, the effects of the popular phrenzy."[4]

Despite Hamilton's arguments and pleas—which he reiterated in pamphlets and which were repeated by others in his circle—Clinton made no attempt to halt the persecution. True, his political future was in jeopardy. Moreover, Clinton did not, just yet, support the many popular politicians who were preaching disregard for the Congress even as they practiced disregard for the treaty. But Hamilton wrote Clinton off nonetheless; after 1783 he ceased all correspondence with him. Soon the break between the two men would widen and lead to a lifetime of enmity.

Clinton's apostasy could be shrugged off as no great loss, for he had not yet begun to demonstrate his formidability as an opponent. Less easy for Hamilton to understand or to accept was the behavior of Chancellor Robert R. Livingston.

Livingston was a pure-bred manor lord, New York variety. Born to wealth, social status, and political power (the Livingston manor had had its own hereditary seat in the colonial legislature), he took all three entirely for granted. In dealing with less privileged mortals his conduct was habitually arrogant, or so it seemed to them. On his part no offense was intended: he treated social inferiors as social inferiors. Could they be treated any other way? The Livingstons, like the Van Cortlandts, the Van Rensselaers, the Morrises, the Schuylers, and the Beekmans, had been staunch Patriots, but Patriotism did not mean the same thing to the manor lords as it did to the population at large. They resented and resisted George III for meddling in their affairs and joined in revolution against him much in the spirit of the feudal barons who had exacted Magna Carta from King John at Runnymede. In the same spirit they lamented the emergence of a popular party as a product of the Revolution. Crotchety old Robert Livingston, Jr., rather a caricature of the others, viewed the state constitution of 1777, conservative as it was, as the triumph of radical democracy and the leveling impulse. Between those born to the manor and their thousands of tenants, the gentry, and the yeomanry, stood an almost impenetrable wall of mutual suspicion, resentment, and fear.[5]

Hamilton did not comprehend a number of things about these landed aristocrats; he admitted he did not understand them. He did not fully realize that they rarely acted from a sense of class solidarity except in a direct confrontation with the lower orders, and sometimes not even then. He did not perceive that their nationalism, like their Patriotism, was a matter of convenience rooted in provincialism. Above all, he did not understand their landlord mentality: their rapacious greed notwithstanding, they were different from and contemptuous of merchants, money men, and financiers, for they reckoned ownership of the land as the legitimate source of life's bounties.[6]

Livingston's example should have taught Hamilton, if anyone's could. In 1783 Livingston resigned his position as secretary for foreign affairs (the Confederation's equivalent of secretary of state) to devote his attention to what he regarded as a more important and prestigious job as chancellor of New York. That action revealed something about his priorities; more revealing of his character was his sudden change of position regarding Loyalists. In 1779 he had written Jay, "Never was there a greater compound of folly, avarice & injustice than our confiscation bill." In mid-1783 he wrote Hamilton, "I seriously lament with you the violent spirit of persecution which prevails here and dread its consequences upon the wealth commerce & future tranquility of the state. I am the more hurt at it because it appears to me almost unmixed with pure or patriotic motives. In some few it is a blind spirit of revenge & resentment but in more it is the most sordid interest," mere covetousness for "the house of some wretched Tory." He concluded, "It is a sad misfortune that the more we know of our fellow creatures the less reason we have to esteem them." Only five months later he was again writing to Jay, piously declaring that legal distinctions should be made between the wicked Tories and the "virtuous citizens, that have at every expense and hazard fulfilled their duty," and asking Jay to arrange credit for him in Europe of £6,000 to £8,000 for use in buying confiscated estates.[7]

The occasion for his change of heart was "the most sordid interest." Livingston's property had been damaged during the war, his tenants were in arrears on their rent, and he had been unable to collect much in salary either from the state or from Congress. Vast as his landholdings were, in other words, he was strapped for cash. Along came opportunity to make a killing through speculation in confiscated estates. The property was being sold in large blocs at public auction, which preserved the field for gentlemen of substance, who could by gentlemanly arrangements keep the prices low. Moreover, the purchases could be paid for in depreciated government securities at their par value, making the prospect for profits elegantly handsome. Livingston's conversion was a simple as that.[8]

Rather more complex was the matter of finding the cash necessary for capitalizing on the opportunity. Trying local sources of credit, Livingston could come up with only £2,800 sterling (about $12,500, of which $2,000 was a loan from Governor Clinton, who kept his assets liquid and won a lot of friends that way). That was enough to buy several "good, substantial brick houses" in the city, but Livingston had his eyes on property that would require $50,000 to $60,000 more in cash. His effort to obtain credit through Jay failed, as did a similar request to the Dutch minister, P. J. Van Berckel.[9]

Then he hit upon a scheme that was in keeping with the proprietary attitudes characteristic of his class: he proposed in effect to have the government finance his purchase of government property. The idea was to have the legislature establish a bank, but not an ordinary one. Private subscribers would put up $250,000 in hard money, and the state would put up $500,000 in paper money, to be issued to stockholders against the security of mortgages on real estate and backed by the state's taxing power. Such a bank could create all the currency that Livingston and other speculators would need, and he formed a group to implement the plan. Using their influence with the governor and gaining the support of up-country legislators through cash payments or a share in the venture, they laid the foundations for a favorable reception of the scheme. Then on February 17, 1784, they presented a formal petition to the New York Assembly.[10]

Hamilton vigorously opposed the plan. Some of his reasons were disinterested: he believed that using the power of government to support private speculations was improper and immoral, and besides, New York was already flooded with public notes and bills of one sort and another, ranging from unsecured wartime paper money to the securities of both the state and the Congress. But there were also tangible private reasons for Hamilton's opposition, having to do with his brother-in-law John B. Church and Church's partner Jeremiah Wadsworth of Connecticut. The partners had large liquid resources and grand plans. Just now they were in Paris attempting to negotiate a contract that would give them a monopoly over the exportation of American tobacco to France. They also aimed to control, or at least to have an influential hand in, all the banking power in the United States. They had become the largest stockholders in the sole existing bank, Philadelphia's Bank of North America, and they had plans for establishing a bank in New York. Livingston's doings, if successful, would interfere with their own. In their absence and as their agent, Hamilton was more or less obligated to frustrate Livingston's scheme if he could.[11]

Accordingly, he approached several of Livingston's prospective investors in the city and attempted to persuade them that Livingston's plan was unsound. He succeeded, but only in part. He hoped to forestall the creation of a bank until Church and Wadsworth returned but managed only to convince the city's monied men that the state should be kept out of it and that a land bank was undesirable. To his surprise, a number of the more liquid speculators and public creditors in the city determined instead to form a private bank with an original capital of $125,000.

The new promotion killed off Livingston's plan and Church's and Wadsworth's as well. Hamilton learned of it after about a week. Finding it hopeless to try to stop it, he subscribed for his clients to as many shares of the bank as possible, took a leading part in its organization, and became a director—and, characteristically, set out to learn as much about the practical details of running a bank as he could. The organizers soon requested a charter from the legislature, which was already considering Livingston's petition. The Assembly, not knowing which way to turn, declined to approve either plan. But the directors of the Bank of New York decided to operate without a charter, and in July of 1784 they opened their doors for business.[12]

That ended that, but it did not end Livingston's high-handed dealings or his run-ins with Hamilton or Hamilton's clients. The chancellor's most brazen venture was a raid upon the property of his second cousin Robert Livingston, Jr. (known as "the manor lord" to distinguish him from Robert R., who was referred to as "the chancellor"). The manor lord's estate adjoined the chancellor's on the north and was considerably larger. The boundary between them was a stream on which were two substantial falls admirably suited for mill sites. The chancellor built a large grist mill on one of the sites and claimed the exclusive right to the other, though in law the two parties had equal rights to the falls. The old manor lord, furious, could not decide whether to sue the chancellor or to send a gang to pull down the mill and let the chancellor sue him if he chose. Lawyers advised him he could follow either course but recommended that he consult Hamilton before acting.[13]

He did so, and Hamilton's reply was artful. Hamilton told him the law was on his side but warned that juries were capricious and that a suit could be long, complicated, and expensive. He would institute proceedings if Livingston insisted, Hamilton said, but he urged a negotiated compromise, such as getting the chancellor to "content himself with one Mill, relinquish all pretensions to erecting more, and bind himself in firm covenants" not to encroach on the stream in future. Then Hamilton slyly appealed to the old man's class prejudices by switching the subject to politics. The legislature, he said, had been taken over by men of the *"leveling kind"*—New England Yankees, no less, who aimed "to subvert the constitution and destroy the rights of private property." To prevent such "despotism and iniquity," it was vital that "all men of respectibility" and the "principal people in the community" unite for their common defense. In other words, if the rich and well born did not cooperate with one another, the rabble would devour their all.[14]

But Hamilton had a lot to learn about the ways of the New York aristocracy; his effort was as futile as it was clever. The manor lord warmly endorsed Hamilton's political comments but with greater warmth rejected the idea of compromising with the chancellor, whose "pretentions are so very wild, Romantic & Extensive" that if it were in his power he would "take all & leave me none." That was the beginning of a long, bitter feud between the two branches of the Livingston clan. The chancellor, though a master of invective, was too proper to attack his cousin directly in public, but he could and did vent his spleen upon other members of the old man's family. He grew extremely cool toward his erstwhile friend Jay, who had married the manor lord's niece, and was especially vicious toward James Duane, who had married the manor lord's daughter. Hamilton tried to stay on good terms with both sides, but he faced a dilemma. Sentimentally and in principle, as well as through the connections of his friends, he sided with the manor lord; but professionally and politically it was important to get along with the chancellor. In due course Chancellor Livingston would solve Hamilton's problem for him by joining ranks with George Clinton.[15]

The moral to the story was not lost on Hamilton: where large amounts of property were concerned, principle was likely to fly out the window, even—perhaps especially—among the wealthy and the socially pretentious. A complex series of events then unfolding in Philadelphia reinforced the lesson. Again Hamilton became involved both out of conviction and out of regard for the interests of his clients.

Early in 1784 the financial situation in Philadelphia was peculiarly unhealthy. Unlike New York, the city had a great deal of liquid capital: it had long since been vacated by the British, several wealthy Tories remained after the peace, and it had the Bank of North America, newly expanded from an original capitalization of $400,000 to a whopping $1.6 million. But its monied men and institutions were working at cross-purposes. Many of the richer inhabitants were speculating heavily in continental securities, profiting from the price fluctuations that were inevitable as long as the fate of Congress's 1783 revenue plan was uncertain. The Tories, for their part, had gone into money-lending, specializing in loans to craftsmen and laborers, who normally could not get bank loans, and charging interest at the fantastic rates of 12 to 18 percent per month. ("See how good a Thing it is," commented Gouverneur Morris, "to be Merciful to the Poor.") Thomas Willing, president of the bank and partner of Robert Morris, was properly conservative in making loans to help the speculators, and he infuriated the Tory loan sharks by entering the small loan market and driving interest rates down to 2½ percent per month. These actions made the bank two powerful new sets of enemies in addition to its preexisting enemies, the radical politicians.[16]

A pair of developments in the spring made the bank even less popular. One was Willing's decision to refuse the legislature's request, inspired by speculators, to lend the state $500,000 to finance a complicated plan for servicing the state's debts and assuming payment of the continental debts owned by Pennsylvanians. The other episode was beyond the bank's control. Philadelphia merchants, anticipating a huge postwar demand for British goods, had placed unprecedentedly large orders, and when the goods began to arrive they called upon the bank to expand credit accordingly. Unhappily, with the spring imports also came news from Europe that $300,000 of Robert Morris's bills of exchange, drawn in his capacity as superintendent of finance, had been protested for nonacceptance.* Morris had expected the difficulty and had made arrangements to cover the bills through intergovernmental loans in Europe, but the Bank of North America had to stand ready to cover him in the event that the European loans fell through. Thus instead of expanding loans to meet the needs of merchants, it had to contract its loans to protect itself. Quite a few individuals were crushed in the ensuing squeeze, and overall economic activity in the city and surrounding countryside was seriously dislocated.[17]

Hamilton kept abreast of all this through John Chaloner, Church's and Wadsworth's agent in Philadelphia, and he followed the developments with appropriate concern for the interests of his clients. His concern was soon to become far greater, for the sequel brought a threat to the continued survival of Congress.

What came next was a political attack on the Bank of North America and a severance of the financial connections between Pennsylvania and the Union. A coalition of speculators, Tories, and radicals, following a plan devised by a Philadelphia merchant-

---

* A bill of exchange was a draft drawn by a merchant on a merchant in another port against goods being shipped or against credits outstanding; in effect, Morris's check had bounced.

speculator-politician named Charles Pettit, organized and conducted a vigorous campaign which, in the fall of 1784, won them
control of the state's unicameral legislature. The next year, the
legislature enacted Pettit's complex financial program. One part of
it was straightforward: the revocation of the charter of the bank. As
for the rest, though the details were intricate, the essence was simple. In brief, by the terms of the legislation Pennsylvania assumed
responsibility for servicing not only its own war debts but also that
portion of the national debt owned in the state, and issued £150,000
($400,000) in paper money. Two-thirds of the new money was ap-
propriated for the payment of back interest on the national debt.
The remainder was issued on loan against real estate mortgages of
thrice the amount of the loans.[18]

"To unravel the code of policy" in this program, as one newspaper
put it, required "no small amount of sagacity and Machiavellian
shrewdness"; but the larger implications were clear. First, speculators in Philadelphia made tidy profits from a doubling and then a
trebling of the market price of public securities. Moreover, since the
legislation provided for interest payments only on the basis of annual appropriations—rather than by establishing permanent
funds—and since a new legislature was elected every year, the market would continue to fluctuate, which meant that speculation
would continue to be profitable. It also meant that speculation
would drain liquid capital away from normal commercial activity.
Second, land speculators profited as well. As back-country legislator
William Findley explained it, a man could borrow £100 from the
state against the collateral of land he already owned, use the money
to buy public securities on the open market at a third of their face
value, turn these securities over to the state at par in exchange for
public lands, sell the land and repay his loan, and emerge with substantial profit. Third, the state government benefited. The increase
in circulating medium made it easier to service the interest on its
own and the nation's debts; and besides, following out Findley's example, by lending £100 in paper (on which it would receive £6 annual interest) the state would bring about the cancellation of £300
of its public debt (on which it had been obligated to pay £18 annual
interest).[19]

Hamilton filed in his mind, for future reference, his understanding of how people profited from the Pennsylvania program;

but in the immediate circumstances he was more concerned by its negative implications. One was that the richest state in the Union had, in effect, declared its financial independence, and to a Congress that was already virtually bankrupt that action could be fatal. Moreover, public creditors in Philadelphia, whom nationalists had counted upon for their lobbying power in efforts to strengthen Congress, were now effectively neutralized. Yet another was that the bank, for whose welfare Hamilton was concerned both as a nationalist and as a lawyer, was now on a perilous footing, for if a legislature could revoke its charter of incorporation the same legislature could entirely forbid its existence.

The reaction of stockholders to the revocation of the charter was instructive to Hamilton. The price of the bank's stock plummeted from $500 a share in 1784 to $370 when the charter was annulled in 1785, and investors were at a loss as to what to do. Hamilton's own proposal, arrived at in consultation with Wadsworth (who had returned home, leaving Church in England), was to follow the orderly procedure of instituting a test case in the Pennsylvania courts to determine whether the bank retained its corporate existence through its charter from Congress. If the courts so ruled—it was unlikely that they would, given some recent proceedings of the Pennsylvania Council of Censors, but Hamilton apparently did not know that—then there was nothing to worry about. If the courts ruled against the bank, Wadsworth and Church could, together with other stockholders, sue and force the bank to liquidate and return their investments.[20]

Others had different ideas. Congressman Arthur Lee, a Virginian whose hostility to Robert Morris bordered on paranoia, had invested in bank stock as a profitable means of spying on the doings of his favorite enemy. He proposed that stockholders take the losses involved in dumping all their holdings on the market, thereby destroying Morris and the bank in one stroke and weakening what Lee regarded as the sinister forces of nationalism. A stockholder named William Edgar talked as if he agreed with the Hamilton-Wadsworth plan but had connections that made his protestations suspect. On the one hand, he was the brother-in-law and sometime partner of William Constable, an intimate of Robert Morris. On the other, he was a full-time partner of Alexander Macomb, an intimate of Governor Clinton; and it was scarcely a secret that Clinton was willing to wreak financial havoc in Philadelphia so as to transfer financial power to New York. Then there were Walter Livingston and his partner William Duer. Livingston, a son of the manor lord, was a member of the three-man Board of the Treasury, which managed the Confederation's finances after Morris resigned as superintendent, and Duer was soon to become secretary of the board. Blithely heedless of the conflict of interests, these New Yorkers were engaged in large-scale speculations and were "anxious to have a Bank to play off their Continental paper with." They tried to get Hamilton and Wadsworth to join them in pulling out of the Bank of North America, in persuading others to do the same, and in using the proceeds to establish a new bank in New York.[21]

None of these schemes materialized, but a showdown between insiders and outsiders was soon to come. In the meantime Wadsworth inadvertently ensured that the confrontation would be rancorous. In an effort to get a reliable account of what was happening in Philadelphia, he wrote to the one man in the city with whom he had had satisfactory dealings but was not connected with the bank. That man happened to be Charles Pettit. Wadsworth, unaware of Pettit's role in bringing about the Pennsylvania financial legislation, confided to Pettit a suspicion that the directors had provided for their own escape by borrowing from the bank sums equal to their investments. Pettit showed the letter to friends in the legislature, and when the bank directors learned of this they were furious at Wadsworth. Said he, in the true spirit of class solidarity, "I am perfectly willing they should think & act as they please if I can rescue my property from their grasp."[22]

The annual meeting of stockholders in January 1786 was turbulent. It was disclosed that the bank's attorney, James Wilson, had received almost $100,000 in loans on questionable security, and it was strongly suggested that such transactions were not uncommon. Wadsworth insisted upon the court actions that Hamilton had proposed; Morris, who had originally opposed the actions, "softended down much" and "consented to our Propositions"; Willing managed to irritate Wadsworth repeatedly. At last the insiders ostensibly admitted defeat and agreed to follow Hamilton's orderly course of legal disintegration, but in fact they had no intention of doing anything of the kind. In the end Hamilton and Wadsworth trusted overmuch: they permitted the resort to the courts to be instituted by the bank itself, which gave the insiders opportunity to stall for a year and beyond. The outsiders would not soon trust the insiders again.[23]

The more Hamilton saw of these grubby people, the more clearly he perceived that he was not one of them. The game they were engaged in was exciting, challenging, and lucrative, and to them it was reality; but to him it was only a game, unworthy of his talents.

About this time he read a book that influenced him mightily: the three-volume memoirs of the celebrated Jacques Necker, who had performed heroically as France's wartime minister of finance before being ousted as a result of intrigue. The memoirs were a veritable encyclopedia of practical information on fiscal management, and in time Hamilton would find them quite useful. Just now, however, their impact upon him was emotional. In a long introduction, Necker spelled out the qualities necessary for greatness in a minister of finance, and those qualities matched Hamilton's self-image with mirrorlike precision; then Necker sketched a picture, far broader than any Hamilton had imagined, of the things an able minister could do. After warning his readers that the ministry of finance was no place for gentle and peaceful souls who hoped for serenity in their lives, Necker closed with a passage that seemed addressed directly to Hamilton. "There are men," Necker wrote, "whose zeal ought not to be cooled: such are those who being conscious that they are qualified for great things, have a noble thirst for glory; who being impelled by the force of their genius, feel themselves too confined within the narrow limits of common occupations; and those, more especially, who being early struck with the idea of the public good, meditate on it, and make it the most important business of their lives. Proceed, you, who after silencing self-love find your resemblance in this picture."[24]

Those stirring words hit home in a breast already filled with a desire for Fame, as that term was understood in the eighteenth century. Writers of the Enlightenment, in keeping with their enthusiasm for sorting and classifying and ranking everything, had devised a number of classifications of great achievements leading to Fame. Their model was classical: secular thinkers from Machiavelli through Sir Francis Bacon to Hume and beyond had been fascinated with the ancient orders of gods and demigods, and combed the pages of Plutarch's *Lives* for archetypical representatives of mortals whose achievements won them immortality. According to Bacon's system, perhaps the best known in the eighteenth century, five classes were recognized. From bottom to top, these were fathers of their country, "which reign justly, and make the times good wherein they live"; champions of empire, "such as in honorable wars enlarge their territories or make noble defence against invaders"; saviors of empire, who deliver their country from civil war or the yoke of tyrants; lawgivers, "who are also called *perpetui principes* or perpetual rulers, because they govern by their ordinances after they are gone"; and finally, at the pinnacle, "FOUNDERS OF STATES AND COMMONWEALTHS." Bacon later added a higher category, the "inventors and authors of new arts and discoveries for the service of mankind," such as Bacchus, the inventor of viniculture, or Aesculapius, the inventor of medicine. Adam Smith and David Hume expressly rejected the addition, and tended to regard the two original top roles as one. "Of all men that distinguish themselves by memorable achievements," Hume wrote, "the first place of honor seems due to LEGISLATORS and FOUNDERS OF STATES, who transmit a system of laws and institutions to secure the peace, happiness and liberty of future generations."[25]

It was in the context of this system of ideas that Hamilton's romantic compulsion, his "ruling passion," took definite shape when he read Necker's memoirs. He expressed himself as clearly on the subject as on any he ever wrote about. Ambition, he once said in regard to Aaron Burr, "unchecked by principle or the love of glory, is an unruly tyrant, which never can keep long in a course which good men will approve. . . . Ambition without principle never was long under the guidance of good sense." In the 72nd Federalist paper he spoke of the "love of fame, the ruling passion of the noblest minds, which would prompt a man to plan and undertake extensive and arduous enterprises for the public benefit." In an autobiographical fragment written after his retirement, he as much as told his uncle in Scotland that the love of Fame had been his "spring of action."[26]

He testified to his preoccupation in another way as well. Following the convention of the times, he signed his polemical articles with pseudonyms. For his major pieces he usually chose *noms de plume* from characters sketched by Plutarch and picked them carefully to suggest to his classically educated readers the role in which he conceived himself for the occasion. His pieces defending Loyalists against popular harassment in 1784, for instance, had been signed "Phocion." Phocion, an Athenian general, was celebrated for his magnanimity to vanquished enemies and his efforts to protect prisoners of war from demagogues seeking to "persuade the people in their anger into committing some act of cruelty"; and, as Hume put it, Phocion "always suspected himself of some blunder when he was attended with the applauses of the populace." Similarly, writing in 1794 in denunciation of the Whiskey Rebellion, Hamilton would use the name "Tully" to invoke "memory of Cicero's invective against the horrid conspiracy of Cataline."[27]

Twice in his life Hamilton wrote under the name "Publius," after the Roman who overthrew the last king of Rome and established "the republican foundation of the government." The first time was in 1778, when he was expressing his outrage at a member of Congress who had betrayed the revolutionary cause for the sake of private speculations. The second was a decade later, when with Jay and Madison he wrote the monumental series of essays collectively known as *The Federalist*. On the one occasion he declared that the role of legislator and founder of an empire was "the most illustrious and important of any I am able to conceive." On the other he declared the love of Fame to be the noblest of passions.[28]

Neither time did he see fit to quote Hume's gentle disclaimer, tacked on the end of a little essay on the "Idea of a Perfect Commonwealth." Noting that no government could last forever and that the "world itself" was probably not immortal, Hume said, "It is a sufficient incitement to human endeavours, that such a government would flourish for many ages; without pretending to bestow, on any work of man, that immortality, which the Almighty seems to have refused to his own productions."[29]

From his new perspective as a would-be minister of finance, Hamilton's vision for the nation came rapidly into focus; now it became easy to see how to put ideals and theory together with experience and observation. And, even as Hume was explaining his emotions to him and Necker was teaching him how to do what his passion for Fame compelled him to do, Hamilton was receiving practical lessons thick and fast. The next one was disturbing: it was that state governments could develop their own systems of harnessing private greed for public ends, and could do it as effectively as a national government could, if not more effectively. So successful were they, indeed, that by 1786 it began to appear that, unless they were stopped, there would soon be no national finances to administer.

New York took the lead. There, George Clinton and his close associates conceived the idea of New York as the Empire State and acted to implement that conception. The governor and his friends had been growing increasingly disenchanted with Congress— mainly because of its refusal to support New York's claims to the renegade state of Vermont and its inability to induce Britain to evacuate the military posts in western New York—but they had been loath to take any separatist action. Their hesitancy rested on the single assumption that New York was one of the Confederation's weakest members. War-torn and debt-ridden, its citizens incapable of paying much in the way of taxes, the state lacked the revenues necessary either to pull itself out of its economic bog or to take any measures against the Indians who controlled its whole interior west of Albany. But in 1785 New York unexpectedly experienced the most prosperous year in its history. The harvest was the greatest ever, as was the city's import and export business; and, thanks mainly to import duties, the state's revenues had burgeoned from $95,000 in 1784 to $450,000 in 1785. When Clinton and his cohorts went over the books at the end of the year, their grudging loyalty to Congress vanished forever.[30]

Under Clinton's leadership the legislature ground out, in the early months of 1786, a long-range program whereby New York effectively declared that it would be first among equals in the United States or else not be one of the States at all.[31] The most important single step toward that end was an act creating a financial system patterned after Pennsylvania's only bolder and more sophisticated by far. The particulars of the act were instructive to Hamilton even as their political implications were anathema to him.

The act provided for the issuance of £200,000 ($500,000) in paper money. Three-fourths was lent to individuals at 5 percent interest against real estate mortgages, thus satisfying the earlier advocates of a land bank and incidentally providing the state with a tidy revenue in interest. The act also provided for the consolidation of the various kinds of state debt and the assumption by New York of two portions of the national debt, Continental Loan Office Certificates and "Barber's Notes." The former were the highest-grade national securities, being a rough equivalent to United States government bonds; Barber's Notes were certificates issued by the United States for supplies furnished the continental army. The reserved £50,000 of the paper money was appropriated for immediate payment of one-fifth of the back interest due on these various securities.[32]

There were two significant differences between the New York and Pennsylvania plans. First, New York's was designed by politicians for political ends, not by financial operators for their own enrichment. The political ends, in fine, were to solidify the power of George Clinton and his adherents and to redirect the energies and resources of the state toward the welfare of New York instead of the United States. Under the terms of the financial act, some 5,000 holders of continental securities (about half the voters in a normal election) were provided for, and thus made into pensioners of the state. No provision was made for the few hundred persons in New York who held huge amounts of unassumed kinds of continental securities. As one critic charged, in a futile effort to unite public creditors in opposition to the act, the scheme was "a studied design" by "temporizing politicians" and "popularity-struck gentlemen" to "divide your interest."[33]

And it was more: it was a means of rewarding those who had been loyal to Clinton and of punishing those who had not. The rise in security prices that quickly followed the passage of the act caught speculators in confiscated estates as bears in a bull market. That is, they had contracted to purchase estates in installments payable in state securities, which they could buy at depreciated prices and deliver at par. The market price of state securities trebled, and so paying for confiscated estates cost the speculators three times what they had bargained for. Many were broken. In addition, because several were merchants who dumped goods on the market in frantic attempts to raise money to meet their maturing obligations to the state, the city had its first experience with a phenomenon that would later be common—a commercial recession born of financial panic. Those who had proved loyal and intimate friends of the governor, however, were protected from the disruptions. Being informed in advance, they could cover their positions and even profit by going long in the appropriate continental securities.[34]

The other main difference between the New York and Pennsylvania systems was that the antinationalist implications of New York's were stronger. The mechanism by which New York assumed responsibility for the continental securities was that security holders exchanged their certificates for new state bonds of the same face value. New York thereby became a creditor of the Congress, and Congress now owed it more in annual interest than it owed Congress for annual requisitions. The state could (and would) ignore congressional requisitions in future. The Clintonian legislature hampered Congress in another way as well. In a separate act, the legislature voted to grant Congress the power to collect an import duty as requested in the April 1783 revenue amendments, but the grant was not at all in accordance with what Congress had sought. Instead, New York provided that its own customs officials would collect the impost, that the duties would be payable in the state's paper money as well as in specie, and that the proceeds would be turned over only upon assurance that they would be used to pay interest on Congress's war debts—in other words, that the money would come right back into the treasury of the state of New York.[35]

New York's program was only one of several that threatened to dissolve the public debt as a potential adhesive of union. Maryland had, long since, quietly assumed a large part of the national debt owed its citizens, Pennsylvania had adopted its program, and New Jersey had worked out a similar one. In the year after New York made its move, three other states took actions similarly damaging to the union and less honorable. Rhode Island issued a huge amount of paper money on loan, watched it depreciate to a ratio of fifteen for one, then levied taxes payable in it and used the paper to pay off its creditors. Virginia and North Carolina, having made no provision for their war debts, had for some time been taxing the depreciated securities out of existence; and now they established "sinking funds" with which to buy, at depreciated market prices, the continental securities held by their citizens.[36]

The few nationalists who remained in Congress could do little to arrest this trend. Without prospects for revenue Congress was no more potent than a debating society. As it happened, Georgia had become the twelfth state to ratify the 1783 impost amendment just as New York was for practical purposes becoming the only one to reject it. Congress responded by requesting Governor Clinton to call a special session of the legislature to reconsider its action. Clinton flatly refused.

Hamilton, for his part, determined to launch a personal campaign on two fronts to save the nation. The first, which he doubtless considered a long shot at best, was to try to engineer the calling of a national convention to rewrite the Articles of Confederation entirely, to scrap the Congress and create a genuine government in its stead. The other was to have himself elected to the state legislature, where he proposed to lead a fight to save the Congress by ratifying the revenue amendment.

He moved on the two fronts almost simultaneously, though it worked out that the long shot was to be played first. In the annual elections held in April 1786, he entered as a candidate for one of the eight Assembly seats representing the City and County of New York and won a spot by gathering 332 votes, thus coming in fourth among sixteen candidates. Since Clinton refused Congress's request to call a special session, the new Assembly would not meet until the following January. Meanwhile, the old Assembly had agreed to send delegates to an interstate commercial convention scheduled to meet in Annapolis in September, and through the influence of Troup and William Duer in the Assembly and Philip Schuyler in the state Senate, Hamilton managed to be chosen as one of the delegates.[37]

The Annapolis convention was the brainchild of James Madison, who at that time was as ardently nationalistic as Hamilton was. In 1785, commissioners from Virginia and Maryland had worked out a mutually satisfactory agreement regarding navigation of the Potomac. When the Virginia legislature ratified the agreement in 1786, someone suggested another conference, this one to include Pennsylvania and Delaware and to consider commerce and navigation on Chesapeake Bay and the Susquehanna and Delaware rivers as well. The implications of such a conference were antinationalist, for the states would be bypassing the constitutional machinery of the Articles of Confederation; but Madison saw a national opportunity in the proposal, albeit a dim one. On the off-chance that something broader might come of it, he moved that the invitation be enlarged to include all the states. Hamilton, in getting himself chosen as a delegate, aimed to make sure that broader results did emerge.[38]

Hamilton did not intend to work out interstate commercial agreements or to allow the other delegates to do so. As he left for Annapolis, he told Betsey he would be gone eight or ten days, perhaps a fortnight, scarcely enough time to scratch the surface of such a complex subject. When he got there and found delegates from four other states, he offered a resolution declaring that the task of the convention was hopeless. When word arrived that delegates from two more states were on their way, requesting that the convention not break up until they arrived, Hamilton pressed his resolution the harder. In collaboration with Madison and John Dickinson of Delaware, Hamilton carried the day, and his resolution was adopted as the "report" of the convention. The report said, in effect, that the nation was in a grave crisis, that it was futile to consider commercial regulations except in the context of larger problems, and that not enough states had shown up anyway. Accordingly, the legislatures of the several states should send delegates to a general convention to meet in Philadelphia in May 1787 and devise such provisions "as shall appear to them necessary to render the constitution of the Fœderal Government adequate to the exigencies of the Union." The report was sent both to Congress and to the state governors.[39]

In the circumstances that prevailed that fall, the proposal had little chance of being acted upon. Other individuals and other conferences had proposed constitutional conventions before, and nothing had resulted. But Hamilton was impelled by a feeling of urgency which, as he approached his thirtieth year and became a father for the third time, may have been reinforced by a sense of impending loss of youth. ("Youth," Necker had said, "is the only time for an ardent desire of doing good: it is perhaps the only season, in which we believe in virtue, or at least are charmed by the magic of it.") Hamilton's sense of urgency was not widely shared, however. Congress was peopled mainly by members who mistrusted one another, despised the state governments but feared a strong central government, and jealously guarded their prerogatives even though they had no powers. Their disposition to call a convention to revise the

Articles of Confederation was nonexistent. Congress referred the proposal to a committee of three, which in turn referred it to a committee of thirteen, which Congress never appointed.[40]

Hamilton's efforts in the legislature seemed equally vain. Trying to undo the work of the 1786 legislature was not his only activity in the Assembly, and some of his contributions in regard to a general revision of New York's legal code were of lasting value. But he was in the Assembly for the purpose of correcting the damage that had been done a year earlier, and in that undertaking he failed. Ironically, the failure itself strengthened the bid for a constitutional convention.[41]

His specific aims were two: to undermine the 1786 financial program and to remove New York's unacceptable conditions from its grant of the congressional impost. He accepted the paper-money portion of the financial legislation without objection, for it was neither inflationary nor a scheme whereby debtors could defraud their creditors. Nor did he directly attack the debt-servicing features of the act. Rather, he followed the same tactic that opponents of the system had employed when the program was being enacted: to plead, in the name of justice, that the state go further and assume responsibility for all continental securities held in the state. The measure, if adopted, would have nearly trebled the burden on the state treasury and would have resulted in a collapse of the whole system. That is why Hamilton proposed it, and why the Clintonian majority rejected it.[42]

In fighting on behalf of the impost, Hamilton acted (as he would repeatedly do in future) on the same premise he followed when attempting to influence public opinion: despite his professed skepticism regarding human nature, he proceeded as if political opponents, confronted with logically irrefutable arguments, would change their positions. In a masterful speech that lasted several hours and left him doubled up in exhaustion and pain, Hamilton disposed of all the objections voiced against the impost. It had been contested on the ground that it violated the state's constitution; Hamilton demonstrated that it was constitutional. It had been objected to as a scheme whereby Congress would usurp the liberties of the states; Hamilton demonstrated that the fear was without substance. He went further. In a remarkable display of knowledge of the finances of the several states as well as the nation, he argued that the removal of financial support from Pennylvania and New York would be fatal to Congress. In regard to New York's insistence that its paper money be accepted for duties, he pointed out that other states had issued paper money that had depreciated; if all state paper issues were accepted, then New Yorkers would be paying 100 cents on the dollar while South Carolinians would be paying 75 cents, North Carolinians 50 cents, and Rhode Islanders 20 cents.[43]

Hamilton won the argument and lost the issue. When he sat down, not a single Clintonian rose to challenge him on any point. Nor did they need to challenge him: they had the votes. They stuck by their original position, and by a vote of thirty-seven to twenty-one sounded the "death knell of the Confederation."[44]

The timing was fortuitous. Congress, then sitting in New York City (as was the legislature), had learned only a week earlier that Governor James Bowdoin had issued a proclamation declaring a state of rebellion in Massachusetts. Shays' Rebellion, as it was called, had originated as a protest against the heavy taxes Massachusetts had levied in attempting to service its public debts, but that was not the impression abroad in the land. Most people had been misled by calculated misinformation spread by Hamilton's old comrade-in-arms, General Henry Knox, who was now serving as superintendent for war. Knox spread the rumor that 12,000 to 15,000 well-disciplined and well-armed men had gathered in western Massachusetts with a view toward exacting a common division of all property. If they succeeded, he said, they would be reinforced by malcontents in the other New England states and would spread anarchy and bloodshed the length of the land. In response to that horrifying prospect, seven state legislatures voted to send delegates to the proposed constitutional convention whether Congress approved or not, and Congress itself agreed to take the convention proposal off the shelf. It had just done so when New York's final decision on the impost was reached. At the end of their wits, the congressmen voted on February 21, 1787, to ask the states to send delegates to the convention.[45]

Even New York voted to send three delegates and, as a result of Schuyler's efforts in the Senate, chose Hamilton as one of them. His effectiveness, however, would be limited by the choice of John Lansing and Robert Yates as his co-delegates; both were devout

Clintonians, and voting would be by states rather than individually. Toward the end of the legislative session, when most upstate representatives had gone home, Hamilton attempted an audacious maneuver, proposing that two additional delegates, both nationalists, be added to the state's contingent. The motion actually passed the Assembly, only to be rejected in the Senate.[46]

It was a disappointment to be deprived of a vote in Philadelphia, but that was not of crucial importance. What really mattered was that Hamilton's bold move in Annapolis had paid off against the odds: there would be a convention.

V

Constitutional Revolution: A Preliminary Step

Wants, frailties, passions, closer still ally

The common int'rest, or endear the tie.

For a man who craved the Fame of a Lawgiver, after the fashion of the ancients Solon of Athens or Lycurgus of Sparta, Hamilton appears to have behaved strangely during the critical period 1787–88. He worked hard to obtain increased powers for the Congress, though he and nearly every other ardent nationalist thought Congress was established on unsound principles. He worked to bring about a constitutional convention to effect a "Revolution in government," and yet he contributed little to the deliberations of the convention and did not even bother to attend much of the time. In private he expressed sore disappointment in the finished Constitution, and yet he performed herculean labors to bring about its ratification. Most interestingly of all, he performed his greatest effort in behalf of the Constitution anonymously.

The explanation for this seemingly inconsistent conduct lies in Hamilton's unique conception of the role of the Lawgiver. Most of those who aspired to the part—including James Madison, James Wilson, and perhaps others who sat in the convention—saw it in terms of constitution making. To them the crucial task was to construct a properly balanced national government that would have adequate powers so arranged as to provide institutional safeguards for popular

[95]

liberty. Hamilton did not materially disagree with their notions about how the powers should be distributed at the national level, save that he would have preferred a more "high-toned" system (the phrase is his) than Madison and Wilson espoused. But, as he admitted, it was almost a matter of indifference to him how the national government was organized: what was important was to organize one and to endow it with as much power in relation to the powers of the states as possible.

That attitude was born of experience, study, and abiding self-confidence. Experience had convinced Hamilton that paper constitutions were, of themselves, as he later said of the United States Constitution, "frail and worthless fabrics." New York's constitution, for instance, was a conservative document, replete with checks and balances and property qualifications for voting and officeholding; yet it had produced a fiscal and administrative system quite as pernicious as that of Pennsylvania, whose radical constitution created an unchecked unicameral legislature, annually elected by universal manhood suffrage—the closest approximation to an elective democracy ever established by an American state. At the same time, reading and reflection upon human nature and study of Necker's treatise on administration had convinced Hamilton that, if a strong national government could be established on almost any plan at all, and if he could become minister of finance, he could personally activate the government to "provide for the happiness of our country."

In other words, establishing the Constitution was, for Hamilton, but a preliminary step: the work of the Lawgiver would begin afterward. Hamilton's ideas of how to perform that work, and for what ends, were well formed in 1787, and they were awesome in their scope. He aimed not just at the creation of a free government but at the creation of a great nation.

Hamilton had no occasion to specify his plans for America until he became secretary of the treasury, but his constitutional principles were clear in observations he made during and soon after the convention. His conception of the nature of government and its relation to society, greatly influenced by Hume and Vattel, was different from that of most Americans. Hume rejected Montesquieu's widely held proposition that the spirit of a people determined its government on the grounds that laws and institutions were far more important than "spirit," and that a people received its "manners" and morals and "national character" from the example of "people in authority," anyway. On much the same grounds he rejected the idea of the economic basis of politics—the dictum, associated with John Locke and fully developed by the Scottish legal philosopher and historian John Millar, that government was instituted primarily to protect property and therefore "power follows property." Power followed property, said Hume, only if a society's institutions permitted it to do so or channeled activity in that direction. Hume rejected Locke's thinking in another crucial respect. Locke insisted that the origin of all just governments was in a compact between governors and governed, and that the duty of the governed to obey the laws arose from the obligations of that contract. That was nonsense, Hume scoffed; most governments originated in force or fraud, and the reason for obeying them was *"because society could not otherwise subsist."* On all three points, the positions of Montesquieu and Locke were so generally accepted in America as to amount to clichés, if not to holy writ, and on all three points Hamilton followed Hume in rejecting them.[1]

In regard to the objectives of government, Hamilton's views were also unorthodox, paralleling as they did the ideas of Vattel. Virtually every member of the convention held that one primary end of government was the protection of liberty and agreed with Madison's Lockean statement that the other primary objects of civil society, and thus of government, "are the security of property and public safety." Hamilton took a much more positive position. Paraphrasing Vattel, he declared that the ends of government were three: (1) providing for "the great purposes of commerce, revenue, [and] agriculture"; (2) facilitating "domestic tranquility & happiness"; and (3) establishing "sufficient stability and strength to make us respectable abroad."[2]

To be sure, property and liberty were both essential in Hamilton's scheme of things. He considered an unequal distribution of property to arise inevitably from liberty in any society where industriousness was encouraged, and he believed that that inevitable tendency, in turn, was a bulwark of continued liberty. It had been pointed out by another Scotsman whose work Hamilton studied, Sir James Steuart, that modern commercial society was "a better scheme for limiting the arbitrary power of princes than all the rebellions that were ever contrived." As to liberty, that was equally essential. He "trusted he should be as willing a martyr to it," Hamilton said, "as any man whatever," and all who knew him knew he meant it. But unlike most Americans, he had ceased to regard the protection of liberty as an *end* of government. Rather, he had come to regard liberty as an indispensable *means* to the attainment of desired political ends. By turning the equation around, by making political liberty the activating principle rather than an objective of government, he would render it far more secure, for it would no longer depend upon the goodness of anyone, in government or out.[3]

That idea, inferred from but not explicit in Hume's writings, was fundamental to Hamilton's thinking. He shocked many of his colleagues in the convention by endorsing Hume's judgment that "corruption"—the king's power to influence Parliament by appointing its members to lucrative or prestigious offices—was essential to the equilibrium of the British constitution. That judgment was in keeping with Hume's notion that men in government must be supposed corrupt, that they could be counted on to act in the public interest only if doing so squared with their greed or love of power and position. Endorsing the principle was as far as Hamilton went in the convention, but he had evolved a much subtler idea than Hume's as to the way the principle could be applied. It was that a "wise government" could arrange the details of administration in such a way that, if the people at large were at liberty to follow the passions of private ambition and avarice—indeed, were expected and encouraged to do so—what they did would *necessarily* contribute to the welfare of the public. Moreover, because his system would reward people for honesty and diligence in pursuing their interests, it would in time actually make them more virtuous.[4]

That this broader idea was in his mind is evident from a few cryptic remarks and from some private notes he made during and just after the convention. In the notes for his most important speech he said that the general government must have not only a "strong soul, but *strong organs* by which that soul is to operate." Later, in the very speech in which he declared that men are ruled by ambition and avarice, he suggested that "there may be in every government a few choice spirits, who may act from more worthy motives"—that "perhaps a few men in a state, may, from patriotic motives, or to display their talents, or to reap the advantage of public applause, step forward." Still later, in some private musings about the finished constitution, he tied these two thoughts together. General Washington, he speculated, would probably be president, which would "insure a wise choice of men to administer the government. . . . A good administration will conciliate the confidence and affection of the people and perhaps enable the government to acquire more consistency than the proposed constitution seems to promise for so great a Country." Clearly, the constitution was what he meant by soul and "administration" was what he meant by organs. Equally clearly, he reckoned himself to be among those "few choice spirits" who would, from "worthy motives . . . step forward."[5]

Hamilton's understanding of man and society, however, was deeper than his talk of harnessing the baser passions might seem to indicate. With Hume, he recognized that the labor of a Lawgiver was not to be performed in a day; exploiting human knavery was an operating principle that might hasten the process, but if the structure were to last it must be erected upon firmer foundations. On June 18, 1787, he described those foundations in a single speech that took five or six hours in the delivery, occupied the convention's full day of deliberations, and contained some of the most profound observations on government ever uttered by an American.[6]

He delivered the speech by way of introduction to a constitution he proposed be substituted for the two sets of resolutions (the Randolph or Virginia Plan and the Paterson or New Jersey Plan) then before the house. As he was candid to admit, he did not expect his proposal to be accepted or even acted upon, and it was not. His objective, instead, was to raise the tone of the proceedings both in a philosophical sense and in terms of the kind of government to be created.

The philosophical content of the debates so far (they had begun on May 30) had been slight: by and large, the delegates had stuck to the individual resolutions under consideration and kept their remarks brief. Hamilton said little and tried to amuse himself, or perhaps force himself to listen, by taking notes, as others were doing in fuller fashion—but with neither much enthusiasm nor much success. His thoughts kept wandering. In the middle of one of Madison's speeches, for instance, he was struck with a notion as to why a free government was preferable to an absolute monarchy. It was not, he noted, "because of the occasional violations of *liberty* or *property*" that were experienced under a monarchy. Rather, it was because a free government tended "to interest the passions of the community in its favour," and that tendency begets "public spirit and public confidence."[7]

Only twice had a delegate ventured, tentatively, into discussing the philosophical underpinnings of his position, and both times Hamilton thought the ideas being expressed were wrong-headed. One of the confused was the aged Benjamin Franklin, who began reasonably enough by declaring that men were moved primarily by ambition or avarice, but from that premise drew what was, to Hamilton, the absurd inference that the president should be constitutionally prohibited from being paid a salary. The other was Madison, who on June 6 gave a speech that later formed the basis for a much fuller speech that in turn, ultimately evolved into his essay on factions, *Federalist* number 10. "Maddisons Theory," as Hamilton put it in his notes, was that there were two principles on which republics ought to be constructed: "I[.] that they have such extent as to render combinations on the ground of interest difficult—II By a process of election calculated to refine the representation of the People—Answer—There is truth in both these principles but they do not conclude so strongly as he supposes—The Assembly when chosen will meet in one room if they are drawn from half the globe—& will be liable to all the passions of popular assemblies."[8]

In regard to the kind of government to be created, Hamilton was "seriously and deeply distressed at the aspect of the Councils which prevailed." Fearing that the convention would lose a "golden opportunity of rescuing the American empire," he determined to propose a plan so bold that, if some delegates were shocked, others might be encouraged "to tone their Government as high as possible."[9]

In the opening part of his speech Hamilton quickly sketched the possible approaches the convention might take. It might leave things much as they were and provide for the public debt by apportioning it to the states; it might recommend addition of powers to the existing confederation; or it might propose the "forming of a new government." All the debates so far had turned upon what was to Hamilton the secondary issue of how to organize and distribute, among various branches, such powers as might be given to the national government. The primary and crucial question was the distribution of powers between the state governments and the national government. That had been Hamilton's position for some time, and now he proposed that the convention create a national government "with decisive powers in short with complete sovereignty," and reduce the states to little more than administrative units of that national government.[10]

Couching his analysis in terms of the tension between states and nation and the question whether the creation of a durable national government was possible, Hamilton proceeded to consider what he called the "principles of civil obedience." Going beyond Hume and every contemporary theorist, Hamilton classified these under five broad headings: interest, opinion, habit, force, and influence. His intention was to show that, as things stood in America, each of these basic supports of stable government was biased toward the states.[11]

By *interest* in supporting a government, Hamilton meant the short-range, narrow, "active and constant" economic or psychic rewards of doing so. He cited the example of New York and other states, where "particular plans of finance" had purchased loyalties at the expense of the requisitions and plans of Congress. In the same way, the love of power, on the part of those who had it in the states, impelled them rather "to regain the powers delegated by them than to part with more, or to give effect to what they had parted with." They had a strong "esprit de corps" (then a pejorative term), and "the ambition of their demagogues is known to hate the controul of the Genl. Government."[12]

In explaining what he meant by *opinion,* Hamilton followed Hume's observations upon the subject. Hamilton meant the general, usually unarticulated assumption that government was more or less useful and necessary; and thus defined, and the weight of opinion was solidly on the side of the state governments. If the general government were entirely dissolved, he said, nobody would miss it much, for the particular governments could still perform the functions of government to a considerable degree, and that would become truer as the states grew stronger. On the other hand, to dissolve the particular governments, in the present state of things, would be regarded as fatal.[13]

By *habit* Hamilton meant the "habitual sense of obligation" and the "habitual attachment of the people." Obviously, "the whole force of this tie," historically and currently, was on the side of the state governments. (Hamilton overrated popular loyalty to states, for he was unaware of the intense feelings of loyalty to extended families, towns, counties, or regions in the back-country of upper New England and the South, but in principle he was on sound ground.) The sovereignty of the state government, he said, "is immediately before the eyes of the people: its protection is immediately enjoyed by them. From its hand distributive justice, and all those acts which familiarize & endear Govt. to a people, are dispensed to them." Contrariwise, as Hume had pointed out, "distance has a physical effect upon mens minds," and thus when the unfamiliar, almost alien general government called upon the people with a demand for service or money, the demand was odious to them.[14]

By *force,* Hamilton explained, he meant coercion (or the threat or fear of coercion) of law and the coercion of arms, both of which were necessary. As to the coercive powers of laws, the existing Congress had virtually none, whereas those of the states was "nearly sufficient," though in most cases not entirely so because law was "inefficient unless the people have the habits of Obedience." As to force of arms, most states had been accustomed to doing without it, but the recent experience of Shays' Rebellion in Massachusetts had demonstrated that "a certain portion of military force is absolutely necessary in large communities." Congress for its part had but the shadow of a military force, and force would be useless to it anyway: since it had no power to deal with individuals, only with states, the employment of force would amount to civil war.[15]

Finally, there was *influence.* Hamilton said that by this he did not mean corruption (he had not yet dropped the bombshell of endorsing Hume's endorsement of corruption), but his clarification amounted to "corruption" as the word was then understood. His meaning would later be comprehended by the word "patronage"—those regular "honors & emoluments," such offices as judgeships and militia commissions and the like, which "produce an attachment" of the recipients.[16]

All the weight of these forces being on the side of the states, Hamilton went on, the American confederation was doomed to ultimate collapse no matter how its powers were shored up or reorganized. After buttressing his case with a survey of ancient and modern confederations to demonstrate what, on a different occasion, he had called "the natural imbecility of federal governments," he brought his argument to a focus. He almost despaired, he said, of the possibility of establishing a republican government in America. For his own part, citing Necker's observations on the subject, he frankly admitted that he thought Great Britain's limited and constitutional monarchy was the best government in the world; but he was equally frank in saying that it would be unwise to attempt to establish one like it in America. What then, he asked rhetorically, "is the inference from all these observations?" In establishing a national government, "we ought to go as far in order to attain stability and permanency, as republican principles will admit."[17]

The last is a key passage in Hamilton's argument. It was vital that the national government be republican, by which Hamilton meant simply that no person should have hereditary power, privilege, or status, and that all officers of government must be chosen "by the people, or a process of election originating with the people." But within that limitation, the principles governing the establishment of offices should be whatever was best calculated to ensure stability and permanency in the national authority—lest the state authorities, having the weight of all fundamental supports of government on their side, destroy the national. The constitution Hamilton proposed was designed to attain that stability and permanency and was not suggested out of a belief that any one way of organizing power was *intrinsically* better than another. In sum, his proposals were practical, not doctrinal or ideological.[18]

A central part of the plan was based upon Hamilton's sociological perception. As indicated, he observed that natural inequalities among men would give rise to unequal distribution of wealth in any free society in which industry was encouraged (not in every society, just in those so defined). This was already true of the United States, despite the country's newness and abundance of vacant land, and the inequality would increase with time. The rich and the poor, the few and the many, he added, were natural antagonists. If all power were given to the few, they would oppress the many; if all power were given to the many, they would oppress the few. Most "abstract political doctors" would have sought to check both the tendency and the inherent antagonism, but Hamilton, in keeping with his conviction that it was more efficient to go with nature than against it, sought to harness or channel it instead. He would institutionalize class struggle, as it were, by vesting each, the few and the many, with a separate branch of government. Neither would dare neglect to participate actively in affairs of the nation, lest its natural enemy gain exclusive control.[19]

For such a system to be efficacious, each branch must truly represent its constituency. The upper house, in his proposed constitution, would be chosen by electors chosen by property holders and would hold their seats for life unless removed by impeachment. The lower house would be elected for three-year terms by universal manhood suffrage—a considerably more democratic process than the one adopted in the finished constitution.[20]

The turbulence engendered by the rivalry between the institutionalized few and the institutionalized many would, in Hamilton's constitution, be checked by an executive who would serve for life unless impeached. The executive would be chosen by electors chosen by electors chosen by the voters. He would have an absolute veto power over congressional enactments and the power to appoint all state governors, who themselves would have authority to veto all state laws that contravened the national constitution. The national executive, in turn, would be restrained by the legislature's control over appropriations and by the Supreme Court—also chosen for life or good behavior—which, together with the chief justices of the state supreme courts, would try all cases of impeachment.[21]

It was Hamilton's proposal of a president for life that stirred up most opposition, for a lifetime president smacked of an "elective monarch." The word "monarch" was still highly charged; it had been only thirteen years since the country had echoed with denunciations of George III, and in the ensuing reaction against alleged executive tyranny the Americans had emasculated their state governors and vested the nation with no executive branch at all. But Hamilton did not shy from the word. Monarchy, he said, was a relative term: every executive partook of monarchy to some degree, and all thinking Americans now realized that government without an executive arm was no government at all. He preferred a lifetime executive because he thought it would help make national government durable, but he also offered two other justifications. If a president served for life, he argued, he would be less likely to be corrupted from abroad, for it would be in his interest (or, more properly, in accord with his ambition and desire for fame) to enhance the strength and integrity of the United States. More tellingly, Hamilton argued that a president chosen for a limited term of years would continuously be looking forward to reelection, and that even the best would be driven by their interests to abuse their power in order to be reelected.[22]

Hamilton's performance scarcely turned the convention around. Three days later a delegate from Connecticut, William Samuel Johnson, declared that the "gentleman from New-York" had "been praised by every body" but had "been supported by none." Yet the speech did have an impact, for the delegates in Philadelphia were a far cry from the yokels and disciplined party hacks in the New York Assembly who had voted Hamilton down while refusing to debate him. The tone of the proceedings was raised: Madison, Wilson, Charles Pinckney, and Gouverneur Morris especially began to dazzle the convention with orations based upon a broad knowledge of history and philosophy. Moreover, by following his customary legal technique of carrying the attack on his own terms, Hamilton repolarized the debates: questions now turned upon the federal axis, upon whether states were likely to swallow the national government or vice versa. And, finally, once the vexing issue of the basis of representation was settled in the celebrated (if misnamed) Connecticut Compromise on July 16, a clear majority of the delegations proved willing to heap great powers upon the new national government.[23]

As it happened, Hamilton was not around at the time of the compromise. He went home on some pressing legal business on June 30, expecting to return in ten or twelve days. Then he was held up by a curious development: Major William Pierce of Georgia, one of the delegates and a friendly acquaintance of Hamilton's, became involved in an affair of honor with one of Hamilton's clients in New York, John Auldjo, and Hamilton spent several days negotiating to prevent a duel. By the time that was settled the convention had recessed, turned its resolutions over to a Committee of Detail, and agreed to reconvene on August 6. Meanwhile, the other two delegates from New York, Lansing and Yates, had walked out of the convention, apparently in the hope of breaking it up, and had returned home to report to Governor Clinton that sinister developments were afoot in Philadelphia, and incidentally to misrepresent Hamilton's views. Forthwith, Clinton began to organize an opposition to whatever proposals should emanate from the convention, and Hamilton plunged into the murky jungle of New York politics with a polemic designed to nip Clinton's plans on the vine.[24]

When he returned upon the reconvening, Hamilton found himself in an awkward position. He felt free to make motions and offer suggestions but—though neither the rules of the convention nor his instructions from his state prevented it—he felt bound by propriety not to vote in behalf of New York. Besides, he was almost certain not to like what the convention did but was determined to sign the finished product nonetheless; thus there was no point in subjecting himself to several weeks of aggravation and frustration. Accordingly, he left again and was not in attendance during the crucial month when the convention worked out the necessary compromises and hammered the powers of the new government into shape. For the sake of form he wrote a letter asking Lansing and Yates to rejoin him in attendance; and to be in on the finish he asked Rufus King, a friend and delegate from Massachusetts, to inform him when the end was near.[25]

The word from King came early in September, and by September 6 Hamilton was back in Philadelphia. In the few remaining days he tried, largely in vain, to make the final form of the Constitution more to his liking. He supported the creation of the electoral college (in place of the previously agreed-upon plan to have Congress elect the president), for the adoption of that innovation brought the Constitution closer to his own proposal both by making the president more independent and by contributing structurally to the independence of the judiciary. The electoral college as adopted, however, contained serious weaknesses that his proposed system would have avoided. He persisted, unsuccessfully, in his efforts to make the House of Representatives more democratic. He did not try to change the clause that made the Senate represent the states, though he considered that a pernicious feature. In the end, on September 17, Hamilton said that "no man's ideas were more remote from the plan than his were known to be"; but he signed the Constitution and urged all others to sign on the ground that it was impossible "to deliberate between anarchy and Convulsion on one side, and the chance of good to be expected from the plan on the other."[26]

His friend Gouverneur Morris—who had intended not to support the Constitution until Hamilton convinced him it was the nation's only hope—put the matter more succinctly. "The moment this plan goes forth all other considerations will be laid aside—and the great question will be, shall there be a national Government or not?"[27]

Hamilton's best-known contribution to the making of the Constitution is his co-authorship of *The Federalist*. He conceived the project as a joint venture involving Gouverneur Morris, John Jay, James Madison, and himself, but Morris declined the invitation and Jay fell ill and was able to write only five essays, so the burden fell upon Hamilton and Madison. Despite the harried pace at which they worked—they ground out four articles nearly every week—what began as a propaganda tract, aimed only at winning the election for delegates to New York's ratifying convention, evolved into the classic commentary upon the American federal system.[28]

The essays, after an introduction by Hamilton, unfolded in five sections. Numbers 2 through 14 were designed to show the importance of union to the "political prosperity" of America; Jay handled national defense, Hamilton wrote on the maintenance of order at home and on the economic advantages of union, and Madison disposed of a theoretical stumbling block, Montesquieu's widely accepted dictum that republics could govern effectively only in small territories. Numbers 15 through 22 pointed out the inadequacy of the existing confederation—or of any confederation—for the purposes of union. Madison traced the "imbecility" of confederations throughout history, and Hamilton singled out the weaknesses inherent in the confederate form: its inability to legislate for individuals, its lack of effective sanctions upon member states, its dependence upon quotas for revenues, its inability to regulate commerce, its principle of equal representation by states, and its lack of authority to adjudicate disputes through courts of law. The third section, comprising essays 23 through 36 and treating of "the necessity of a Constitution, at least equally energetic with the one proposed," was written entirely by Hamilton. The fourth, designed to show the conformity of the Constitution to "true republican principles," included numbers 37 through 51 and was all Madison's work.

At that stage the authors departed from their original plan. The warm nationwide reception of the early essays encouraged Hamilton and Madison to broaden their sights beyond New York and to develop a veritable debater's handbook for advocates of the Constitution in all the states. Accordingly, they abandoned their original intention to compare the federal constitution with that of New York and proceeded instead to analyze the proposed new government branch by branch. Madison analyzed the House of Representatives (numbers 52–58); Hamilton followed with three essays on the regulation of elections (59–61); and then Madison did one, Jay one, and Hamilton three of the five essays on the Senate (62–66). At that point, March of 1788, Madison returned to Virginia to campaign for a seat in his state's ratifying convention, leaving Hamilton to write the remainder. Those on the executive branch (67–77) followed soon; interestingly, the essays on the judiciary (78–83), plus one on the question of a bill of rights and a concluding piece, came almost two months later, long after the New York elections were over.[29]

The collaboration was successful, and the individual contributions of the two main authors were complementary, and yet in less than three years Hamilton and Madison were to become irreconcilable antagonists. Hamilton himself was mystified and felt betrayed when the break came, and countless historical postmortems have sought to discover how a relationship that seemed so right could have gone so wrong. But the differences were there all along. In part they are visible in the division of labor, which reflected differences in temperament, talent, and preoccupations. Hamilton, for instance, did most of the writing on national defense and matters concerning the economy, Madison most of the pieces on history and political theory.[30]

Beneath the differences in areas of specialization lay more fundamental, if more subtle, disagreements. For starters, the two men did not see eye to eye either in regard to the nature of American federalism or in regard to what constituted a republic. Madison, employing the word "federal" in its traditional sense as the adjectival form of "confederation," argued that the Constitution established a government that was partly national, partly federal—depending upon whether its powers were derived from and operated on individuals or states. The creation of the Constitution was a federal act, for instance, since the document was to be ratified by state conventions. The Senate, representing states, was also erected on federal principles, whereas the House, representing people, was national, as was the provision that the new government could exert its authority directly upon individuals. Hamilton heartily disliked the federal features of the Constitution, in Madison's sense of the term, and he tended to ignore them. His own understanding of federalism was the sophisticated concept of divided sovereignty that he had evolved by 1784—the idea that each level of government in America was sovereign, but only in regard to the objects entrusted to it.[31]

As to the meaning of republicanism, Hamilton and Madison agreed that a cardinal element in a republican form of government was that all powers must be derived ultimately from the people—however "the people" might be defined—but to Hamilton there was another and more basic touchstone. As he put it elsewhere, he regarded the essence of republicanism as an *"equality* of political rights exclusive of all *hereditary* distinction." Inasmuch as Madison owned slaves, bought and sold them, and lived on the fruits of their labor, he could scarcely claim to be a republican as Hamilton defined the word, despite a professed abhorrence of slavery as an institution.[32]

Most importantly, Madison and Hamilton had different attitudes about power. In essay number 51 Madison developed the argument that "usurpations are guarded against" in the Constitution by the distribution of power both up and down the various levels of the federal system and through the various departments on each level. Hence, he said, "a double security arises to the rights of the people. The different governments will control each other, at the same time that each will be controlled by itself." Overwhelmingly, Hamilton's essays were concerned with the vertical axis, and invariably he came down on the side of a greater concentration of power at the national level to offset what he once called "the aristocracy of state pretentions." Almost as exclusively, Madison's essays dealt with the horizontal axis, and invariably he came down on the side of a diffusion of powers. Given his preoccupations and his temperament, Hamilton liked best those parts of the national government that were least fettered and provided greatest energy and durability, namely the executive and judicial branches; and his essays on those subjects are his most eloquent. Madison, given his preoccupations and his temperament, preferred those features of the Constitution that fixed and distributed powers; and his essays on those subjects are by far his best. When Madison ventured into Hamilton's territory he did so cautiously, as when he said that the more he "revolved" the subject the more persuaded he was that the balance was "much more likely to be disturbed" by the states than by the general government. By contrast, when Hamilton crossed into Madison's turf he was prone to dismiss the whole area as of no consequence. "The truth is," he said, "that the general GENIUS of a government is all that can be substantially relied upon for permanent effects. Particular provisions, though not altogether useless, have far less virtue and efficacy than are commonly ascribed to them."[33]

Related to that difference was another: Madison was far more literal-minded in his reading of the Constitution than Hamilton was. Madison believed the new government would have only such powers as were explicitly granted it or were implied by the "necessary and proper" clause; its powers, said he, are "few and defined." Hamilton believed the government would have powers inherent in sovereignty that were limited only by the ends for which it was created; it had, he said, "an unconfined authority, as to all those objects which are intrusted to its management." Madison, in dealing with the necessary and proper clause in essay number 44, was almost apologetic about its existence; Hamilton was also, in essay 33, but on the entirely different ground that there was no need for such a clause, since it was implicit in the very act of establishing a government. Madison, in essay 41, analyzed punctuation marks to refute the anti-Federalist claim that the language giving Congress the taxing power "amounts to an unlimited commission to exercise every power which may be alleged to be necessary for the common defence or general welfare." Hamilton, in essays 23, 24, and 35, declared that placing limits upon the legislative power to provide for the common defense was "unheard of" and argued that the taxing power was "indefinite." As checks against the possibility that Congress would exceed the boundaries of its authority, Madison forecast resistance by the president, the courts, the electorate, and the state governments; for Hamilton, the veto power and review by an independent judiciary, for which he provided the classical argument in number 78, were quite enough.[34]

Hamilton's eagerness to increase the powers of the national government, seen against Madison's cautious approach, brings us to the bedrock difference between them. Both men used the so-called pessimistic view of human nature as the basis of the "science of politics"; both maintained that men were governed by passion rather than by reason; both believed that a great danger to liberty and good government in America lay in an excess of unchecked power in the people, in the democracy or simple majority. But they reasoned in opposite directions from those premises. Madison's thinking was essentially negative: man is governed by his passions, and therefore the force of those passions should be checked to prevent public harm. The great difficulty in framing a government, Madison said, was that "you must first enable the government to control the governed; and in the next place oblige it to control itself." He saw only one efficacious means to that end; power must be divided, and "ambition must be made to counteract ambition." And again, "sixty or seventy men may be more properly trusted with a given degree of power than six or seven." And yet again, as he said elsewhere, "all men having power ought to be distrusted to a certain degree."[35]

Hamilton's thinking was affirmative: man is governed by his passions, and therefore the energy of those passions should be channeled for the public good. His analysis of the presidency illustrates the nature of his thinking. The president's eligibility for continuing reelections, said Hamilton, reduced "the temptation to sordid views, to peculation, and in some instances, to usurpation." For instance, an avaricious man, if he had no prospect for reelection, "might not scruple to have recourse to the most corrupt expedients to make the harvest as abundant as it was transitory"; but with the prospect of reelection he would be less willing "to risk the consequences of an abuse," and thus "his avarice might be a guard upon his avarice . . . the same man might be vain or ambitious as well as avaricious. And if he could expect to prolong his honors, by his good conduct, he might hesitate to sacrifice his appetite for them to his appetite for gain. But with the prospect before him of approaching and inevitable annihilation, his avarice would be likely to get the victory over his caution, his vanity or his ambition." Again, "a sense of national character . . . can only be found in a number so small, that a sensible degree of the praise and blame of public measures may be the portion of each individual." The "sole and undivided responsibility of one man will naturally beget a livelier sense of duty and a more exact regard to reputation"—which, after all, was one of the most potent of the passions. And yet again, as he said elsewhere, "Sir, when you have divided and nicely balanced the departments of government; When you have strongly connected the virtue of your rulers with their interest; when, in short, you have rendered your system as perfect as human forms can be; you must place confidence; you must give power."[36]

One cannot resist a conjecture that the differences between Hamilton's willingness to trust and Madison's unwillingness to do so lay even deeper, in the innermost recesses of the psyche where each man's soul resides alone. At that level, Hamilton trusted Hamilton, and Madison did not trust Madison.[37]

That aspect of Hamilton's psychological makeup—projection of self-trust—was a quality that no amount of education or experience could erase, and that was simultaneously noble and dangerous. He repeatedly trusted men who were not to be trusted, and it cost him dearly. Already the list included George Clinton, Robert R. Livingston, and the Philadelphia bankers. Misplaced trust so far, however, had been merely costly. His misplaced trust in future would be fatal, for among those from whom he would expose himself to danger by counting on honor and decency were Madison, Thomas Jefferson, James Monroe, and Aaron Burr.

That same psychic quality also introduced an element of weakness into his design for the nation. Though he labored brilliantly and diligently to build a system that was not dependent upon men's goodness, he could not avoid the consequences of an unconscious assumption that an adequate number of virtuous men would always be available to run the system. Ironically, that very faith would be perverted into a charge that he advocated the creation of an aristocracy of the privileged few. He spoke feelingly to that point during the New York ratifying convention. "What reasonable man," he asked, "for the precarious enjoyment of rank and power, would establish a system, which would reduce his nearest friends and his posterity to slavery and ruin?" Were he to do so, he must be blind to the vicissitudes of the human condition, for "if, to day, I am among the favoured few; my children, tomorrow, may be among the oppressed many: These dearest pledges of my patriotism may, at a future day, be suffering the severe distresses, to which my ambition has reduced them."[38]

The story of the ratification of the Constitution and of Hamilton's part in it can be briefly told. The way the contest unfolded confirmed and strengthened Hamilton's newly found realization that making the rules is a more efficacious means of influencing political behavior than is appealing to self-interest. Hamilton, in attempting to anticipate what the alignments would be, figured that the Constitution would be supported almost unanimously by "the commercial interest," by "most men of property in the several states," and by the public creditors, and that it would be opposed by "all men much in debt." In fact the alignments did not follow that pattern or any clearcut pattern based upon economic interests.[39]

What did determine the outcome were the rules of the contest, which Hamilton played an important part in formulating. The convention decided to disregard the amendment procedures prescribed by the Articles of Confederation and instead provided that each state should hold a special election for delegates to a ratifying convention. If and when the conventions of nine states voted to ratify, the Constitution would go into effect for those states, leaving the others free to come under the new roof or not as they pleased. Had the rules of the Articles been adhered to, the Constitution would never have been adopted.[40]

Three states ratified before the end of 1787, and two more followed in January of 1788; the vote in every instance was overwhelming, though Pennsylvania's involved a bit of trickery on the part of "Federalists," as advocates of the Constitution were calling themselves. One more easy state, Maryland, came through in the spring.[41]

Otherwise, however, the opposition stiffened formidably during the winter. The defeated "antis" in Pennsylvania mounted a strong propaganda campaign for circulation in undecided states. Rhode Island refused even to call a convention. The New Hampshire convention met, refused to ratify, and adjourned until June. Governor Clinton and his cohorts in New York organized what amounted to national campaign headquarters, which operated out of the New

York customs house and attempted to coordinate the strategy and tactics of anti-Federalists everywhere. Among those who cooperated with the New York antis were three of the most respected patriots in Virginia—Patrick Henry, Richard Henry Lee, and George Mason.

Against such powerful opposition, the *Federalist* essays were of little avail. Indeed, in a manner of speaking Hamilton's efforts were once again praised by everybody and supported by nobody: after the first five quick successes and excepting Maryland and South Carolina, the vast majority of the delegates elected in the remaining states were opposed to ratification when their conventions began. Even so, the Massachusetts convention was induced to ratify by a narrow margin, after a goodly measure of maneuvering by Federalists, and when Maryland ratified in April and South Carolina followed in May, Federalists stood within one state of their immediate goal.

The climax came in June, when New Hampshire's convention reassembled and those of Virginia and New York convened. New Hampshire, with almost no debate, approved by a margin of ten votes, thanks largely to the efforts of Hamilton's erstwhile fellow officer General John Sullivan. Then Virginia, after a long and brilliant debate, ratified by 89 votes to 79. New Hampshire's ratification officially gave life to the Constitution, and Virginia's meant not only that the reconstituted Union would contain the largest and most prestigious of the American states but also, and quite as importantly, that George Washington was eligible to become president. Without these developments it would not have been possible for Hamilton and his allies to carry the issue in New York.

The elections in New York illustrated a fact of political life that would plague Hamilton throughout his career—namely, that wisdom and sound policy are, in the arena of popular politics, no match for organization. Despite *The Federalist*, New Yorkers voted about 16,000 to 7,000 against ratification, electing forty-six anti-Federalists and only nineteen advocates of ratification. The debates in the ensuing convention—with Hamilton, Jay, and Chancellor Livingston speaking mainly for the Federalists and Melancthon Smith, Samuel Jones, and John Lansing carrying most of the argument for the opposition—were a fascinating rhetorical exercise, but they changed precious few votes, if any. Then Hamilton and Jay played upon a threat that had been circulated as a rumor for several weeks: they declared that if New York did not ratify, New York City would secede from the state and join the Union on its own. Faced with that prospect, the Clintonian majority had no choice but to capitulate. After some negotiations over proposed amendments, designed to make the pill less difficult to swallow, it did so. On July 26, 1788, enough Clintonians reversed their positions to enable the vote for ratification to carry, 30 to 27.

The stage was set: Alexander Hamilton could now take his place upon it.

VI

Hamiltonianism

For Forms of Government let fools contest;
Whate'er is best administered is best.

Hamilton's assigned duty, upon becoming minister of the nation's finances, would be to devise a way of managing the Revolutionary War debts so as to place public credit upon firm foundations. Formidable though the task was, Hamilton conceived of it not as a goal but as a vehicle for reaching a larger goal. In a sense his objective was a fairly common one in the eighteenth century, though hardly one for commoners. Like the enlightened despot Charles Frederic of Baden, Hamilton proposed to make his countrymen into "free, opulent, and law-abiding citizens, whether they liked it or not"; like the Prussian philosopher G. G. Lamprecht, who drew up a social blueprint for another benevolent despot, his master Frederic the Great, Hamilton set for himself "the task of making the citizens in every regard more well-behaved, healthier, wiser, richer, and more secure." Specifically, he proposed to use his administration of the public finances as an instrument for forging the American people into a prosperous, happy, and respected nation.[1]

Had Hamilton been a despot such an undertaking would have been arduous enough. Within the framework of a republic, wherein government rested upon the consent of the governed, the barriers were well-nigh insurmountable. The greatest general obstacle was inertia: the American people, who tended to think of themselves as God's chosen, had no urge to be remade in Alexander Hamilton's image. The greatest specific obstacle was interest: the oligarchs who dominated the American republic by the grace of the existing rules were of no mind to have those rules changed.

The existing rules defined "the people" in a fashion that excluded most of them. Of the roughly 4 million Americans, nearly 700,000 were slaves; of the remainder half were female and half were children under sixteen. Slaves, women, and children had legal rights to life, but slaves had almost no rights to liberty or property, women and children had few, and all three groups were denied a voice in politics. Nor was every white adult male allowed to participate in choosing those who governed him. Nearly half were disfranchised by property qualifications, and others were effectively disfranchised by distance from polling places, which were often located in county seats, a day's travel over primitive roads and trails. In the most important elections Americans had ever known, those for delegates to the state ratifying conventions, about 160,000 people voted—one-twenty-fifth of the population.[2]

And the limitations on rights and on voting were only the beginning. More important were the structure of power and the restrictions upon access to it. Despite the lip service paid to the theory of checks and balances, power was in fact exercised directly in most places. In state governments it resided with the legislatures, and locally it was the province of magistrates—boards of selectmen in the towns of New England and justices of the peace in the counties of the South. Pennsylvania permitted all "taxpayers" to hold such offices, but elsewhere the property restrictions were larger, ranging from twenty-five acres of improved land for eligibility for a seat in Virginia's assembly to £2,000 ($8,560) for a seat in the South Carolina senate.[3]

Thus were status and power monopolized, in most American communities, by a handful of intermarried families which, for the most part, were closed to newcomers: except through birth or marriage, precious few entered the ranks of the squirearchy that dominated rural New England, the manor-lord aristocracy of New York, or the slave-plantation gentries of Maryland, Virginia, and South Carolina. A generation or two earlier, American society had been more nearly fluid, but except in the cities the gates to wealth and power had long been closing. In Virginia, for instance, nearly all members of the richest hundred or two hundred families who dominated state and local government in 1790 bore the same names as the people in power in 1750.[4]

The key to this political situation lay in ownership of the land and in American attitudes about land. Most Americans shared Chancellor Robert R. Livingston's view that land was the legitimate source of wealth and status, and their laws and institutions reflected that view. The property qualifications for voting and officeholding were not just any property; normally what was required was "real" property, land and improvements. Moreover, the value of land, for purposes of taxation as well as politics, was not its market or appraised value but its "fair" or intrinsic value—a concept rooted in feudalism. It is true that most American families, possibly 80 percent of the nonslaves, owned their own farms. It is also true that in the United States, in contrast to Europe, land could be bought and sold as a commodity, and that during and after the Revolution many states liberalized their land laws, ridding them of feudal vestiges and making the buying and selling of land still easier. Except in parts of New England, however, most of the land belonged to the few; in the older areas of the South, 10 or 15 percent of the white families owned upwards of two-thirds of the land. As for the legal reforms designed to make a freer market in lands, those did not serve to redistribute land to smaller holders. On the contrary, they mainly helped landed people gain larger quantities of it.[5]

The methods were sometimes gross, sometimes subtle. In most states, public lands and confiscated loyalist estates were sold in large blocs, which meant that only men of means could buy. Alterations in mortgage law illustrate the subtler ways in which the legal revisions worked to the benefit of the landholding oligarchs. In colonial times mortgages had been of limited use as a source of credit because the complex body of law governing them prevented easy foreclosure and sale for nonpayment. Beginning with New York in 1774, various legislatures enacted statutes whereby the debtor agreed in advance that, in the event of default, the creditor could sell the mortgaged property without going to court. That facilitated the raising of money by small landholders as well as large ones, but it was most advantageous to the latter. When they encountered difficulties the great landholders could, through their control of the legislatures, simply pass laws staying executions for debts—as, for example, the "nabobs" of South Carolina did in 1786.[6]

That practice, setting aside contractual obligations by legislative fiat in times of trouble, was habitual among those who ruled America. The Constitution expressly stipulated that the states could no longer "impair the obligation of contracts," but the efficacy of the interdiction was limited, for contract law in America was a part of the general law of real property and like it rested on the theory that everything had an objective value and a just price. A new contract theory, in which the market was the determinant of value, had recently emerged in England—"it is the consent of parties alone, that fixes the just price of any thing, without reference to the nature of things themselves, or to their intrinsic value"—but no American state had accepted that innovation. Patrick Henry spoke for the landed gentry as a whole, Federalists as well as anti-Federalists, when he declared that "there are thousands and thousands of contracts, whereof equity forbids an exact literal performance."[7]

The arrogance of the landed oligarchs was almost unbounded, especially in the South; and the more firmly they were entrenched, the more likely they were to declaim in favor of liberty and against aristocracy and privilege. The immensely wealthy South Carolina lawyer-planter John Rutledge, who had been instrumental both in the movement to check the "tyranny" of Parliament and in the writing of the Constitution, had an innkeeper censured by the state legislature for speaking harshly to one of Rutledge's favorite house slaves: lowly innkeepers dared not speak that way to even the slaves of the nabobs. A liberty-loving Virginian, owner of vast tracts of land and many human beings, once asked his friend James Madison to acquire a black person for a visiting French lady who sought to amuse herself by breeding blacks—a request Madison cheerfully honored. Oligarchical attitudes were by no means confined exclusively to the South. In New York a wealthy alderman had two "uppity" Irish ferryboat operators jailed and publicly flogged for refusing to adapt their schedule to suit his convenience.* "Go into every village of New England," John Adams wrote in 1787, "and you will find that the office of justice of the peace, and even the place of representative, which has ever depended only on the freest election of the people, have generally descended from generation to generation, in three or four families at most." Students at Harvard were listed not alphabetically but in accordance with the prominence of their families. But the oligarchs were least bridled in the South.

---

* Hamilton deplored this *"vile affair,"* as he termed it, and joined the radical young attorney William Keteltas as co-counsel in a damage suit brought by one of the victims.

There, as Congressman Fisher Ames said, "a few gentlemen govern; the law is their coat of mail."[8]

Hamilton had nothing against a hierarchical and deferential social order. He thought such an order natural, desirable, and, in any politically free society, inevitable. Furthermore, he abhorred the leveling spirit. But his detestation of dependency and servility was stronger yet, for those were contrary to his very idea of manhood, and the American system of pluralistic local oligarchies made everyone dependent upon those born to the oligarchy. He hated the narrow provincialism that the system nourished and fed upon; and he resented, as only a natural-born outsider can, the clannishly closed quality of the system. Most objectionable of all was that the system failed to reward industry—industry in the sense of self-reliance and habitual or constant work and effort. Accordingly, though Americans everywhere were prone to praise the virtue of hard work, the fact was, as Hamilton said, they "labour less now then any civilized nation of Europe." Certainly devotion to work was not to be found among slaveowners, nor among their slaves, nor among the Scotch-Irish herdsmen who dominated the interior uplands, nor among the majority of yeoman farmers. Orderly and systematic attention to business was likewise missing among the great majority; when Hamilton attempted to gather information about the relative profitability of agriculture and manufacturing, he was able to find few farmers who knew even approximately how much they had planted, their crop yields, their revenues, or their costs.[9]

Nor, as matters stood, was any of this likely to change through the natural operation of market processes, for the market was not free. State and local regulations hampered both the production and the sale of goods. The new states continued the English practice of regulating public markets to prohibit what Blackstone called "offenses against public trade," which included forestalling ("buying or contracting for any merchandize or victual coming in the way to market"), regrating (buying a commodity "in any market, and selling it again in the same market"), and engrossing (acquiring "large quantities of corn or other dead victuals, with intent to sell them again"). Beyond that, the interest on money, the price of bread, the fees of millers and lawyers, and a host of other activities were fixed by law, and the states had enacted mercantilistic systems for the inspection of goods destined for international trade. Only in the Lex

Mercatoria—the established rules and customs governing the international exchange of commodities and of bills of exchange, notes, and other negotiable instruments—was economic activity free of government regulation.[10]

Therein lay the reason Hamilton could believe it possible to bring about fundamental change through administration of the nation's finances. The Lex Mercatoria was consistent with Hamilton's notions about liberty, industry, justice, and honor, because it was built upon free contractual relationships. It governed all commercial paper transactions, and if the public debt could be transformed into a species of paper money, Hamilton could see to it that the spirit of the Lex Mercatoria would govern that, too. Since the public debt was so large, amounting to many times more than all the "hard" money in circulation, its monetization could infuse the whole of American society with that same spirit.[11]

Hamilton's method for bringing about the monetization of American society, against its preference and yet with its approval, eluded his contemporaries: otherwise it could not have been done. To be sure, some of his techniques were fairly obvious. He solicited cooperation by appealing to self-interest, on the ground that it was easier to harness human nature than to fight it, check it, or change it. He applied the stick as well as the carrot—the people, he said, must feel the sting as well as the benefits of government—for he understood that an excess of nominal freedom in America, meaning a want of lawful government, perpetuated a social system in which most people were actually less than free. Again, he managed things through an artful mixture of action, example, and illusion. But these were only techniques. The genius of his system lay far deeper, in his idea of establishing the procedures by which people interacted, rather than attempting to ordain what they should do.

His conception was elegant in its simplicity. He would construct efficient fiscal machinery, make it beneficial to everyone, and interlock its operations into the workings of the economy. Imperceptibly, the people would come to find it a convenient, a useful, and finally a necessary part of their daily lives, and a stimulus to industry as well. That accomplished, everyone must comport himself in accordance with the rules by which the machinery of government itself functioned, and it would be almost impossible to dismantle the machinery short of dismantling the whole society.

How things are done governs what can and will be done: the rules determine the nature and outcome of the game. That was the heart of Hamiltonianism. It was a concept as essential to the art of free government as Ockham's Razor was to the philosophy of logic.

At every step along the way, Hamilton paid meticulous attention to the details of how things were done. The first step, the writing and ratification of the Constitution, had been taken. The next three were to ensure that Washington became president, for the aegis of his prestige would be essential; to see that the Treasury Department was properly constituted, for otherwise the ministerial function could not be performed; and to obtain his own appointment as head of the Treasury. Once Hamilton was in office, his real work would begin, and that, too, would unfold in three major phases. He would work out a way of servicing the public debts that would stabilize their value and thus make them liquid capital; he would use some of that capital to establish a national banking system; and he would direct the flow of the remaining capital into permanently productive channels, lest it be dissipated in the purchase of consumer goods or in land speculation.

To the unthinking there was no need for concern about Washington's election, since Washington was everybody's choice; indeed, had there been no Washington in whom to entrust it, the presidency could scarcely have been created. But there were two nice points on which serious snags could develop. The Constitution originally provided that presidential electors, instead of voting separately for president and vice-president, should cast two ballots, the candidate with the most votes becoming president and the runner-up becoming vice-president. Federalists agreed to support Washington and John Adams for the two offices, but Hamilton foresaw that if all the electors did so the result would be an awkward and embarrassing tie. The obvious solution was for a few electors to waste their second ballots by casting them for nonentities, but there was a potential danger in that tactic. It was rumored that anti-Federalists were planning to support George Clinton for the vice-presidency; if they did, and if Federalists wasted too many of their second ballots, the result could be the humiliating one of having the foremost opponent of the Constitution in a position to succeed to the presidency.

(The danger of the possibility would be dramatized when, during his first few weeks in office, Washington came close to dying from a malignant pustule in his leg, diagnosed as anthrax, and again a month or two later when he nearly died of pneumonia.) Taking no chances, Hamilton wrote to Federalist leaders in several states and helped orchestrate an appropriate distribution of the electoral votes.[12]

The other possible snag involved a matter of personal delicacy. Upon surrendering his command in 1783, Washington had declared that he was unequivocally and unalterably retiring from public life. Few men but Washington, under the new circumstances that prevailed six years later, would have given a moment's thought to the idea that his retirement had constituted an inviolable promise to the public. Hamilton, knowing his old chief, anticipated that Washington might be concerned about the matter and wrote a circumspect letter urging the general to heed the call when it came. As it turned out, Washington was grateful to Hamilton for raising the problem—which no one else had had the consideration to do. He had wanted to discuss the matter with someone, but, he said, "situated as I am, I could hardly bring the question into the slightest discussion, or ask an opinion even in the most confidential manner; without betraying, in my judgment, some impropriety of conduct, or without feeling an apprehension that a premature display of anxiety, might be construed into a vain-glorious desire of pushing myself into notice as a Candidate." After a further exchange of letters Hamilton was able to overcome Washington's scruples, partly through a challenge to hazard the glory he had already won, partly through an appeal to the duty of giving unqualified support to the Constitution he had signed. Incidentally, the exchange served the additional purpose of reestablishing the relationship between the two men on a footing of intimacy and affection.[13]

The timing of their rapprochement was important: since the national capital would temporarily be located in New York, Washington would be calling upon Hamilton for advice during the crucial early months when the president personally constituted the entire executive branch of the government. Distrusting and disliking John Adams, Washington refused from the first to consider the vice-presidency as a functional part of the executive, and the various departments were not established by Congress until five months after Washington's inauguration. In the meantime, the president relied mainly upon four men for advice: John Jay and Henry Knox, old and trusted friends who continued to serve on an interim basis in the now defunct Confederation offices of secretary for foreign affairs and secretary at war; fellow Virginian James Madison, newly elected to the first House of Representatives and its most active leader; and Hamilton. To put it another way, Washington's principal advisers were his former general of artillery and Publius.[14]

Since there were not yet any laws to execute nor any appointments to make, the first subject on which Washington needed and sought advice was purely ceremonial. Washington had a social dilemma. On the one side he was besieged by hordes of strangers who felt free to wander into his house at any hour, to meet and chat with the people's president. Upon inquiry he learned that the presidents of the old Congress had been "considered in no better light than as a maître d'hôtel . . . for their table was considered as a public one and every person who could get introduced conceived that he had a *right* to be invited to it." On the opposite side, many persons including the vice-president and most members of the Senate were insisting that the presidency should be characterized by royal pomp, ceremony, and unapproachability. Neither extreme was acceptable to Washington, and he asked Hamilton and the others for advice on rules of behavior that would strike a balance between "too free an intercourse and too much familiarity," which would reduce the dignity of the office, and an "ostentatious show" of monarchical aloofness, which would be improper in a republic.[15]

Though the matter contained a comic dimension, the problem was in fact an important one, and Hamilton treated it as such. Running through all his writings on the presidency is an implicit awareness that the presidency is inherently dual in nature, entailing two functions so different that only a rare individual could perform them both well. One is that of the head of state: the president is expected to be chief magistrate, chief administrator, and chief policy formulator. The other is ritualistic and ceremonial: the president is expected to be the symbolic incarnation of the Union. Hamilton recognized that the second function was as vital as the first, and his doubts as to the feasibility of an executive branch founded on republican principles derived from doubts as to whether an elected official could ever command the necessary respect. Knowing British history, he knew that the development of a stable executive branch had been difficult enough in the mother country, for the British had gone through centuries of civil wars and regicides and usurpations before they became able to reconcile the dual aspects of the office. Their solution, which they stumbled across during the reigns of the first two Hanoverian kings, George I and George II, had been to divide the functions. Those functions that had to do with the exercise of power—defending the nation against alien enemies, enforcing domestic order and justice, and formulating and implementing governmental policy—became the province of the ministry, headed by a "prime minister" who doubled as an active member of Parliament and as the chancellor of the exchequer. The ritualistic and ceremonial functions remained the province of the Crown. Largely removed from the actual work of government, the English Crown became the symbol of the nation—its mystical embodiment—and as such the object of reverence, awe, veneration, even love; a people formerly given to killing their kings now became willing to fight and die for them. At the same time, their government, for all its bungling and corruption, became the most effectively administered one in Europe.[16]

The American presidency lent itself to just such a division of functions. The possibilities were wide open, for the framers had been so squeamish about establishing an executive branch at all that they sketched it only in broad outlines in the Constitution, entrusting the evolution of its details to the early occupants of the office. Circumstances also favored the development of a modified ministerial system. Washington was perfect for the ceremonial role, for nearly every American revered him and already regarded him as the symbol of nationhood. Moreover, despite the Americans' fervid protestations to the contrary, they missed having a king, as was attested by their regular celebrations of the birthday of Louis XVI of France and the rituals with which they surrounded their state governors.[17]

Hamilton contemplated an American adaptation of the British scheme of things—with Washington as George II and himself as Sir Robert Walpole. But, like Washington, he had to await the event, for no overtures on his part would have been proper.[18]

Hamiltonianism

Washington clearly did not think of himself as a symbolic king. Indeed, though he always wanted the esteem of his countrymen, he thought they carried the matter too far: it made him downright uncomfortable to receive the adulation normally due to royalty. He was also genuinely afraid of such treatment, for his popularity, unlike that of a king, rested ultimately on performance, and as he took office the people were expecting miracles. If the constitutional experiment failed, extravagant praise could become equally extravagant censure. Nor was he being falsely modest when he protested, in his inaugural address, that his talents were not up to the tasks before him. Most of the problems with which he would have to deal as president were beyond his experience, and—harsh fact— many of them were beyond his ken as well. He determined that his only hope was to surround himself with able men, supervise them as closely as possible, and pray for the best.[19]

In the crucial business of making appointments, several things worked in his favor. He was a good judge of character, and the range of his acquaintances was wide, and the same was true of his principal advisers. The pool of available talent was large, for veritable hordes offered their services, and the revolutionary generation of Americans produced an astonishing number of gifted and public-spirited men. Too, recent events, particularly the war and the contest over ratification of the Constitution, had served as an effective screen whereby pretended patriots were readily separated from able and dedicated friends of the nation—or so it seemed. Finally, Washington had no political debts, and thus was free to make his appointments on the basis of ability and honesty, provided that he gave prudent regard to their geographical distribution.

Personalities, however, entered the appointment process even if political obligations did not. Chancellor Livingston, who had administered the oath of office to Washington, eagerly sought an appointment, preferably as chief justice or as head of the treasury department, but Hamilton or Jay, perhaps both, frustrated his efforts. Arthur Lee of Virginia, a longtime enemy of Madison's, wanted a district judgeship, but Madison effectively blocked that. Washington wanted Jay to be secretary of state, but Jay preferred the chief justiceship and got it. When Jay made his wishes known, Madison urged that his own particular friend Thomas Jefferson be offered the secretaryship of state, and Washington agreed.[20]

Just when Washington decided upon Hamilton for secretary of the treasury is not definitely known, but it was doubtless early. There is an old story, based on secondhand recollections, that before his inauguration Washington asked Robert Morris what was to be done about the public debts, and Morris replied, "There is but one man in the United States who can tell you; that is, Alexander Hamilton." Hamilton had been preparing himself to be the nation's financier, and he had acted as if he were confident that the appointment would be forthcoming. In 1788 he was extremely active politically but avoided running for any office. In 1789, a few days after Washington's inauguration, he told Troup that the president had asked him to accept the secretaryship, and Hamilton asked Troup to be prepared to take over his law practice. On May 27, 1789, less than four weeks after the inauguration, Madison wrote Jefferson that Hamilton would probably be appointed as soon as the office was created. Yet two months later Hamilton was apparently not sure, for in late July he accepted John Adams's son as an apprentice in his law office—which was quite incompatible with service as secretary of the treasury.[21]

His hesitancy to make a final commitment, despite his preparations and his dreams, derived from a determination that the conditions of his appointment must be compatible with the success of his grand plan. From his point of view three conditions were vital. One he took for granted: that he would have the support of his friend and erstwhile collaborator James Madison, the ablest and most powerful man in the House of Representatives. The second, of which he was less confident, was that the treasury must be under the control of a single person with ample powers—unlike, for example, the impotent three-man Treasury Board that had attempted to administer the Confederation's meager finances since 1784. The third, most important, and least certain condition was that the office must have some measure of independence from the executive and permit direct dealings with Congress. Hamilton knew from experience that Washington would supervise his administration closely, requiring of his subordinates daily written reports on every item of business they transacted, requiring frequent written opinions and compilations of information as well, and not allowing even a routine letter to go out without his having seen it. Such a system would leave Hamilton limited room for creativity and none at all for becoming a genuine minister of finance; it would have amounted to resuming a role as aide-de-camp. The system would have other shortcomings, too. Washington was seasoned and knowledgeable in areas of concern to two of the three original departments, state and war, but he knew next to nothing about fiscal management, taxation, commerce, and other subjects in the purview of the Treasury Department. Moreover, the mere administration of treasury affairs would be so complex and exacting that full compliance with Washington's procedures would have been paralytic.[22]

But the decision as to how the department would be organized was not Washington's; it was up to Congress. Debates on the makeup of the executive departments had been going on in the House intermittently for two months when Hamilton accepted young Adams as an apprentice, and had elicited a great deal of controversy. Hamilton's old friend and sponsor, Elias Boudinot of New Jersey, had opened the subject on May 19, proposing that "an officer be established for the management of the finances of the United States." Boudinot suggested that his duties be specified along lines entirely acceptable to Hamilton: in addition to superintending the national treasury and finances, he would "examine the public debts and engagements, inspect the collection and expenditure of the revenue," and, crucially, "form and digest plans" that would be submitted directly to the House. A procedural objection was immediately raised. Madison, anticipating demands for a multiple head of the treasury but general agreement upon single heads for the war and state departments, shrewdly moved that it must first be resolved that all three executive departments should be established. That done, it would be appropriate to organize all three on the same basis—with a single secretary apiece. Madison's tactical motion was accepted and formed the general framework of the debate.[23]

Three broad substantive issues came into contention. Hamilton lost the first that was settled, or rather the position he favored was defeated. At the very beginning of the debate it was routinely moved that the secretaries be appointed by the president with the advice and consent of the Senate and be removable by the president. Someone objected that the phraseology of the appointment process was unnecessary, since it merely repeated the language of the Constitution. That raised the question whether Congress must literally adhere to the Constitution's specifications in creating executive departments. If so, an interesting problem emerged, for the Constitution provided no means of removing appointive officers except the vexatious and cumbersome process of impeachment. William Loughton Smith of South Carolina, a newcomer to national politics who was soon to become one of Hamilton's staunchest supporters, took precisely that position at first. Madison, Boudinot, and Benson of New York countered with the commonsense argument that the power to appoint inherently carried with it the power of removal. Elbridge Gerry of Massachusetts, a deep-dyed curmudgeon and ideologue who had been in the Constitutional Convention but refused to sign the document on the ground that it did not perfectly accord with republican theory, agreed that the power to appoint might carry with it the power of removal; but he maintained, quite logically, that the power to remove must be assumed to lie in the same hands as the power to appoint. Removal therefore could not be made by the president alone but only with the advice and consent of the Senate. Madison and his allies replied that since the Constitution specifically authorized Congress to create offices that would be appointable only by the president, it had an equal power to vest him with exclusive removal power. Smith agreed with Gerry, as did Madison's anti-Federalist colleague from Virginia Theodorick Bland, who saw granting exclusive removal power to the president as a step toward monarchy. James Jackson of Georgia, who had come to New York with a letter of introduction to Hamilton from General Anthony Wayne, declared somewhat irrelevantly that if the House did have any voice in the removal power it must retain that power itself. Though the opposition was strong, however, it was inadequate, and at the end of the day's debate advocates of exclusive presidential removal carried the issue.[24]

The subject came up again a month later, and this time Smith hit Madison and the others with a surprise. Someone had called Smith's attention to *Federalist* number 77, and he now read a long passage of it to the House. In that essay Hamilton had said explicitly that the consent of the Senate "would be necessary to displace as well as to appoint." He treated his interpretation of that feature of the Constitution as self-evident, and went on to indicate what he thought the advantages would be. "Where a man in any station has given satisfactory evidence of his fitness for it," he wrote, "a new president would be restrained from attempting a change, in favour of a person more agreeable to him" by fear of the embarrassment of senatorial disapproval. Had Hamilton's interpretation been sustained, the door would have been opened to a permanent ministry independent of the president—or, as in the parliamentary system, one responsible to the legislative as well as the executive.[25]

Madison dealt with the awkward confrontation by ignoring it. The earlier arguments were repeated and elaborated at considerable length, and in the meantime Benson informed Smith, accurately or inaccurately, that Hamilton had changed his mind in the interest of expediency. Then the question was put on Smith's motion to require the consent of the Senate in removing appointive officials. The motion failed, 20 votes to 34. Hamilton's hope for a short cut to a ministerial system was thus frustrated.[26]

The next point to be settled was whether the department heads would be singular or plural. Disregarding the resolution to consider all departments together, Gerry delivered a long, rambling diatribe against a single head of the treasury. If he were dishonest, Gerry said, there would be no way to check his thievery; if he were honest, the job would cost him his reputation, for everyone would assume he was stealing anyway. Shifting his ground, Gerry maintained that no single person could be found with the ability to perform the wide range of functions implicit in the office. Shifting again, he argued that with a three-man board, one would be able to devote his "genius" and "fine imagination" to the task of "reducing a chaos to a beautiful system" while the other two did the routine labors "which required less elevation of thought." Along the way, Gerry made ambiguous reference to the period when Robert Morris had been superintendent of finance. That touched some raw nerves, for people were still hotly divided in their feelings about Morris's superintendency. Those who were devoted to the nation first and to republican theory only secondarily believed Morris had saved the Revolution; those who were republican ideologues first and only secondarily nationalists believed Morris had been a champion of plutocracy who had mismanaged the public accounts, fattened the purses of himself and his friends, and done little that actually furthered the Revolutionary cause.[27]

Gerry's speech provoked a defense of Morris by Jeremiah Wadsworth (who appreciated Morris's public services despite their private differences) and elicited a bitingly sarcastic counterattack by Boudinot, but it also made a number of people who had advocated a single treasury head uneasy, including Madison. It was Abraham Baldwin of Georgia who came up with a proposal that calmed the fears Gerry had fanned. Boards were worthless, said he, but Gerry was right in insisting upon "the necessity of proper checks in the department having care of the public money." The solution was to provide by law for an auditor and a comptroller to settle and keep track of public accounts, a register to record them, a treasurer to hold the money, and so on; Baldwin "would not suffer the Secretary to touch a farthing of the public money" other than his own salary. That arrangement, both safe and efficient, had the additional advantage of freeing the secretary from routine chores so that his "fine imagination" would be able to do its creative work. Baldwin's proposal was readily adopted. [28]

The third issue bore directly on the ministerial question and generated considerable acrimony. The language of the resolution included among the secretary's duties the requirement that he report directly to the House on matters concerning revenue and public credit. The purpose of the measure was to make the secretary responsible to Congress and thus, in effect, to remove control of the treasury department from the president to the House, which had exclusive power to originate money bills. Many congressmen, however, feared it would have the opposite result. John Page of Virginia, Thomas Tudor Tucker of South Carolina, and others shrilly denounced the proposal as a "dangerous innovation upon the constitutional privilege of this House." It would unite the power of the purse with the power of the sword, a combination fatal to liberty. "It would establish a precedent which might be extended, until we admitted all the ministers of the Government on the floor, to explain and support the plans they have digested and reported: thus laying a foundation for an aristocracy or a detestable monarchy." Gerry said that "if the doctrine of having prime and great ministers of state was once well established"—as he predicted would surely happen if this measure, "giving an indirect voice in legislative business to an executive officer," were adopted—"we should soon see them distinguished by a green or red ribbon, or other insignia of court favor and patronage." [29]

Sponsors of the resolution scoffed at this militant fear of aristocracy and monarchy. Requiring the secretary of the treasury to digest and report information, said Benson, was hardly the same as inviting the president to usurp the power of legislation. Benjamin Goodhue of Massachusetts sneered, "we certainly carry our dignity to the extreme, when we refuse to receive information from any but ourselves." John Lawrence of New York gibed Gerry for having first argued that no individual could be found who was capable of running the treasury alone, and now arguing that the secretary would be able not only to run the treasury but "be adequate to all purposes of legislation." Madison defended the clause solemnly and at length. After a full day of debate, it was adopted.[30]

The bill finally cleared the House late in June. It was then in the Senate for more than a month before being approved, and afterward some time was consumed in reconciling the differences between the versions adopted by the two houses. That done, it went to the president, who signed it into law on September 2. As finally passed, the act specified strict procedures to protect public funds; for example, disbursements could be made only by the treasurer upon warrants signed by the secretary, countersigned by the comptroller, and recorded by the register. Otherwise, however, the secretary was given a wide range of duties and a goodly measure of latitude in carrying them out. He was empowered to appoint his assistant, superintend the collection of the revenues, decide upon the forms of keeping accounts, and prepare and report budgetary estimates. He was also "to digest and prepare plans for the improvement and management of the revenue, and for the support of public credit." He must make reports, "and give information to either branch of the Legislature, in person or in writing (as he may be required), respecting all matters referred to him"—and then a most significant addition, "or which shall pertain to his office." Hamilton could scarcely have asked for more.[31]

Nine days after he signed the bill, Washington sent Hamilton's nomination to the Senate for confirmation, along with nominations of Nicholas Eveleigh for comptroller, Samuel Meredith for treasurer, Oliver Wolcott, Jr., for auditor, and Joseph Nourse for register. The nominations were confirmed the same day, Friday, September 11, 1789. On Sunday Hamilton went to work.[32]

Hamilton's management of the Treasury Department was subject to four kinds of checks: the law, politics, his position as a member of the executive branch, and his personal standards. The legal restraints, just mentioned, proved highly advantageous and in a way even liberating. Politics came to bear heavily a bit later on, but during his first few months in office, when he was organizing his administrative machinery and setting it in motion, political pressure was virtually nonexistent. The other two sources of restraint, Washington and himself, were much more potent.

Though Hamilton's statutory responsibility to Congress partially exempted him from the president's rigorous and time-consuming administrative methods, he remained subject to them in many respects because of the overlapping character of his functions. Treasury affairs were necessarily involved in matters of primary interest to the other departments. By law, the Treasury Department was concerned, though not directly, with supplying and paying the nation's tiny army. In the nature of things, the department was also involved in foreign affairs: inescapably, the principal objects of peacetime State Department activity, regulating and taxing international commerce and establishing credit abroad, were major concerns of Treasury as well. Moreover, Washington liked to discuss the whole range of executive questions with each of the department heads and Chief Justice Jay, and he often required written opinions on them. According to Hamilton, the president informed him of the progress of diplomatic affairs on a day-to-day basis. When dealing with interdepartmental matters, or with Treasury matters in which he was not lawfully made responsible to Congress, Hamilton was obliged to follow Washington's procedures—which, according to Jefferson, were so exacting that every letter sent or received by a department head was forwarded to the president before any action was taken.[33]

However, Hamilton exercised some discretion even in these areas. For instance, when he took office he made informal overtures, on his own initiative, to various people connected with the French government. The United States was far in arrears in payments of both principal and interest on the loans France had advanced during the Revolution, and Hamilton wanted some breathing room before committing the limited funds of the Treasury to that high-priority obligation. To seek a deferral openly and officially would defeat its own ends, for news that the United States had made such a request would have depressed American credit elsewhere in Europe, especially Holland. Accordingly, Hamilton sought by private negotiations—in conversation with the Comte de Moustier, French minister to the United States, and in a letter to Lafayette—to induce the French government to make an "unsolicited" offer, "as a fresh mark of good will," to forgo its claims for principal if arrears of interest were paid. There is no surviving evidence as to whether Hamilton made these moves known to Washington.[34]

In talking with George Beckwith, the unofficial minister of Great Britain to the United States, Hamilton likewise acted on his own as long as the conversation was unofficial—but only that long. Late in October 1789, he talked with Beckwith at length about the prospects for an American commercial treaty with Great Britain, which both Hamilton and Washington much desired, and during the course of the conversation he offered some frank opinions and picked up some useful information. There is no record whether he informed anyone of the talk, but it is unlikely that he did so, for Congress was then out of session, Washington was taking a four-week tour through New England, and Jefferson had not arrived to take up his duties in the State Department.[35]

When Beckwith approached Hamilton again the following summer, however, after returning to London and making a trip to Canada, the Englishman was seeking to conduct official business through Hamilton as an intermediary, and Hamilton would have no part of that. He promptly and properly informed Jefferson, and the two of them proceeded to inform Washington. It was agreed that Hamilton should continue private conversations with Beckwith, since he had the advantage of Beckwith's confidence and Jefferson did not; but Hamilton kept both Jefferson and Washington informed and acted directly on instructions from the president.[36]

In all other matters Hamilton was guided by Necker's advice, by his own sense of propriety, and by the ends he was seeking to accomplish. Necker had written that a great minister must have five attributes: genius, regularity, prudence, firmness, and breadth of knowledge. Administrative genius, he said, was the capacity to perceive, simultaneously, the whole of a system and the relations of all its parts to one another and to the whole, and to discern instantly the effects of a change in any of the parts. As for regularity, it was necessary not only in the distribution of a minister's time and occupations, but also in his habits of mind; "regularity is to the ideas, and to the memory, the same as discipline is to an army." Prudence, which Necker defined as knowing when to act and when to stop, was indispensable in a minister of finance, for the delicate and vulnerable nature of his position required that he "must not commit any errors"; prudence also dictated that a minister make his reforms slowly, step by step, so that they might not excite alarm and "that they may reciprocally support and strengthen each other." As for firmness, Necker maintained that flexibility, or willingness to compromise, which might be harmless or even advantageous in other ministers, was an unforgivable failing in a finance minister; a weak and compromising minister of finance was worse than a dishonest one. Finally, breadth of knowledge was imperative: a finance minister must know and understand his own country in microscopic detail and follow closely events and ways of doing things in other countries as well.[37]

Hamilton had those qualities and scrupulously tried to conduct his operations in accordance with their dictates. So, too, did he act in regard to three guiding principles that Necker recommended. First, said Necker, the minister must be attentive at all times to the interests of the people, especially the common people, and thus he must see to it that all laws concerning finance were made as simple as possible and that the main burden of new taxes should always fall upon "objects of luxury and splendor" rather than upon necessities. Second, the financier must be guided by a strict and punctual adherence to promises, for there could be neither public credit nor justice otherwise. Third, Necker insisted on "the infinite importance of making the state of the finances publicly known." Hamilton followed these dicta with exactitude—and often made enemies in the process.[38]

Otherwise, propriety was Hamilton's polestar. Characteristically, the standards he required of himself were higher than those he required of others. The nearly hysterical fears expressed during the debates over the creation of the Treasury made it clear, as Necker had repeatedly warned, that suspicions would attend his every move as secretary. His sensitivity to the problem was revealed in an exchange with his old army friend Henry Lee. After Hamilton had been in office about two months, Lee wrote him asking information about the prospects for investments in public securities, if it were proper for Hamilton to tell him. Actually, Hamilton could not have divulged information of any real value even had he wanted to. Inside information about the government's prospective financial operations was useful to speculators only if it was specific—only if, for example, a speculator could learn just what securities were to be provided for, on what terms, and when—and Hamilton did not have such information at his command: though he would make specific recommendations to Congress, he was in no better position to forecast what Congress would do with his recommendations than was Lee's brother, Congressman Richard Bland Lee.[39]

But that was not the position Hamilton took in writing his answer. "I am sure you are sincere," he wrote, "when you say, you would not subject me to an impropriety. Nor do I know that there would be any in my answering your queries. But you remember the saying with regard to Caesar's Wife. I think the spirit of it applicable to every man concerned in the administration of the finances of a Country. With respect to the Conduct of such men—*Suspicion* is ever eagle eyed, And the most innocent things are apt to be misinterpreted."[40]

Hamilton also made sure his personal finances would bear hostile scrutiny. He did retain a small investment he had made in the Ohio Company in 1787, and that organization had purchased a million acres of western lands from the Congress; but since the transaction had been completed neither he nor anyone else saw any conflict of interest in such a holding. As to public paper, he owned no securities, having long since disposed of the various certificates he had received in military pay; and he even declined to collect substantial bonuses lawfully due him. Moreover, by totally surrendering his law practice, he cut off all his private sources of income—which neither Washington nor any other man in the national government except Hamilton saw fit to do. His salary as secretary was $3,500 a year. That was a considerable sum for the times, but far less than he had been earning as a lawyer and not enough to support himself and his family in their accustomed style. In 1789 his affairs were so prosperous that he was able to make personal loans to friends in amounts as high as $2,000. When he left the treasury five years later, he was himself deep in debt.[41]

It proved impossible, however, to arrange everything as tidily as Hamilton would have liked. His father-in-law, Philip Schuyler, owned (or acquired by 1791) public securities with a face value of $67,000, and Hamilton almost certainly discussed his operations with Schuyler. That did not constitute impropriety, though perhaps it approached what Hamilton would have called delicacy. Rather stickier were the affairs of his brother-in-law John B. Church. Church planned to stay in England and was liquidating his American holdings, but Hamilton continued to act as his agent. His most important remaining investment in America was 140 shares of stock in the Bank of North America, which Hamilton was in process of selling to Robert Morris. Before becoming secretary Hamilton had arranged for the sale of the first forty shares, for which Morris gave a one-year personal note, putting up various public securities as collateral. For the purchase of the remainder Morris sought a similar arrangement; but Hamilton insisted upon real estate mortgages as security for the second transaction, so as to avoid being the holder of public paper even on that indirect trustee basis. Nonetheless, the collateral for the first forty shares did place some public securities temporarily in Hamilton's hands.[42]

Stickier yet was the problem of William Duer, an intimate friend of both Schuyler's and Hamilton's, whom Hamilton appointed as his assistant. On the face of it, the appointment appeared entirely reasonable, for Duer had been secretary of the Board of the Treasury since 1786 and was presumed to be better informed about the details of the nation's financial morass than anyone else. His social and political connections were impeccable, and his honor was reputed to be so. It may be that he was actually helpful to Hamilton. For the most part, however, he turned out to be another instance of misplaced trust on Hamilton's part, since he was secretly engaged in security speculations on a large scale and not especially scrupulous as to how he went about it. It was fortunate for Hamilton that after six months he decided to resign. Between the lines of Hamilton's letter accepting Duer's resignation is a soft sigh of relief that his friend got out before he could cause any serious mischief.[43]

Otherwise, with the possible exception of a minor clerk who was fired, there is no evidence that any officer or employee of the Treasury ever misused a farthing of the public's money during Hamilton's administration.

But it was toward the creation of smooth-working, self-regulating administrative machinery, not the mere setting of examples, that Hamilton particularly directed his labors. Given his gifts for orderly and systematic management, he could accomplish a great deal of this with minimal efforts. For routine activities that lent themselves to standardized procedures, such as the calculation and collection of customs duties, he prescribed uniform procedures and devised forms that customs officers were required to follow. To prevent standardization from degenerating into the kind of bureaucratic stupidity in which mindless form-filling is substituted for substance, he employed a number of techniques. One was to grant a measure of discretion to collectors in the larger ports, who could usually be counted on to be more intelligent and better informed than those in small outlying ports; but he did that only when he personally knew the collector to be honest and responsible. More importantly, he provided for an efficient two-way flow of information. To that end, he kept Treasury officers apprised of all developments that concerned them, required weekly reports of their collections and payments (which incidentally kept him informed of the volume of business and the movements of shipping in every American port), and invited reports on other matters. He especially solicited observations that "may serve to discover the merits or defects" of the revenue system—in other words, what worked effectively as well as what did not—so as "to point out the means of improving it." He also asked to be told of complaints of merchants, which "always merit attention" though they were by no means "infallible indications of defects."[44]

The gathering of information was crucial, for without it Hamilton's grand conception was useless. He was acutely aware that to redirect the channels through which human activities shall flow, one must first obtain an accurate and thoroughly detailed understanding of the ways in which they are already flowing. No one man had such knowledge, though many had parts of it. To gather it, Hamilton more or less invented a research technique: he conducted a large-scale socioeconomic research project using questionnaires. The first, dated October 15, 1789, was concerned with shipping and consisted of seven broad questions, each of which invited an essay as well as hard facts and figures. It went out to the customs collectors and to everyone else Hamilton had reason to believe had useful information on the subject. The replies poured in, providing him a wealth of data and practical wisdom, much of which was contrary to common assumptions. When all the returns were in and Hamilton had studied and digested them with his usual alacrity, he knew more about the ordinary business of his fellow citizens than anyone else possibly could have.[45]

There was, however, a problem inherent in being so well informed. A number of powerful, influential, and strong-willed men in government, foremost among them James Madison, failed to perceive that Hamilton's newly acquired storehouse of information placed his understanding qualitatively beyond their reach; like Hamilton's friend Troup, they underestimated his capacity for research and were therefore inclined to mistake his depth for facility. That mistake, together with Hamilton's facile manner, his unwillingness to suffer fools gladly, and his natural combativeness, was certain to generate misunderstanding and probably conflict.

An example of the potential friction is seen in the 1789 tariff act, passed about two months before Hamilton took office. The legislation, which provided the main source of the national government's revenues, was largely the work of Madison and Congressman Thomas Fitzsimons of Pennsylvania. Madison's understanding of international trade was broad but wholly theoretical. That of Fitzsimons, a Philadelphia importing merchant, was practical but narrow. Madison, deeply hostile toward Great Britain, thought the tariff should discriminate severely against British ships and goods so that Britain would be forced to relax the commercial restrictions it had imposed on Americans since independence. (Hamilton, from conversation with Beckwith, had learned that this was precisely the wrong way to get anything from the ministry of William Pitt. Pitt would meet friendly overtures with friendship, but to get tough with him was to ensure that he would get many times tougher. Madison never learned that; indeed, he tended to regard the British government as a monolith, as if it made no difference whose ministry was in power. Hamilton explained to Beckwith that Madison was uncorrupted and incorruptible but, though he was "a clever man, he is very little Acquainted with the world." He was soon to become aware that that was an understatement, that Madison's approach was unsound for a hundred additional reasons.)[46]

The House rejected Madison's proposal, only to draw upon the collective ignorance of its members and make a thorough botch of the legislation. Nearly everyone except New Englanders, for instance, thought that Yankees built the best ships in America and that their primary commercial activity was the "carrying trade," the hauling of freight. Those beliefs seemed logical, since New England had an abundance of white pine timber and skilled craftsmen and grew no staples of its own for sale in international markets. In fact, however, New Englanders built the worst ships and were rarely engaged in carrying freight, partly because their white pine was far inferior to southern live oak for ship construction and partly because their chronic shortage of capital prevented them from doing what everyone assumed they did. Thus when Madison and other non-Yankees proposed special tariff protection for American shipping interests, some congressmen from New England suggested duties lower than those advocated by southerners, leaving the non-Yankees confused and suspicious.[47]

Guided by such intelligence, Congress passed a tariff law that was a textbook example of bad legislation. As Otho H. Williams, collector of the customs at Baltimore, wrote in exasperation to Hamilton, the law was muddled, self-contradictory, and impracticable, and a rigid adherence to it "would be ruinous to individuals without the least public benefit." The system was, he declared, absolutely "the most complicated and embarrassing of anything that has employed my attention." That was the source of revenue that Hamilton would have to work with. More importantly, it was the legislature he would have to deal with.[48]

The pejorative undertone of that last statement is not entirely fair. On a constitutional, legal, and theoretical level the first session of the First Congress made some monumental achievements. The Bill of Rights, largely Madison's work, became a vital part of the Constitution, though Hamilton and even Madison had earlier thought it unnecessary. The Judiciary Act of 1789, largely the work of Senator Oliver Ellsworth of Connecticut, virtually became a part of the Constitution, for it established the court system on what proved to be its enduring basis. The executive departments, likewise virtually part of the Constitution, were erected on eminently sound principles.

But these subjects lent themselves to treatment in a different light than did practical, complex financial affairs. They aroused few passions, they pricked few interests, they required little knowledge that was not readily available to anyone versed in the law. Financial matters, by contrast, required expertise tempered by calm deliberation, but inspired the warmest feelings in the least informed souls. Under those conditions, to bring order to the nation's finances—not to mention the grander goals Hamilton had in mind—would be a huge task.

He was explicitly ordered to try. On September 21, two days before adjourning until January, the House directed him to prepare a plan for providing adequate support of the public credit, and "to Report the same to this House at its next meeting." That gave him 110 days.[49]

VII

The Financial Dilemma

Is yellow dirt the passion of thy life?

The words of Hamilton's assignment implied more than they said. He was to produce a plan for providing adequate support of the public credit. Credit means credibility or believability, as measured by that most accurate of gauges, people's willingness to entrust their money to the hands of others. In the early days of the Revolution, when patriotic enthusiasm was sufficient to sustain the cause, Congress had had credit in abundance. But the supply of public credit based upon goodwill was soon exhausted: ordinary Americans and their duly elected representatives, it turned out, loved liberty so dearly that they were willing to pay for it with anybody's dollars but their own. Consequently, the public had earned a credibility rating of nearly zero.

In those circumstances, restoring public credit entailed two separate acts of persuasion. One was to convince investors, present and prospective, that the United States had both the determination to honor its obligations and the wherewithal for doing so. The other was to convince the public, or its representatives, that it was high time to pay the price. From a disinterested point of view, neither task need have been especially arduous, except that neither set of interested parties—creditors on the one side and taxpaying public on the other—was eager to make any sacrifices. Creditors avariciously sought full and prompt compensation for all their claims, including many that were dubious and some that were fraudulent. The public, or at least a large segment of it, sought with no less avarice to renege upon all or parts of its obligations, legitimate or otherwise. Absolute compliance with the more extreme demands of the creditors would have been unjust, inexpedient, and in practical terms impossible. Absolute compliance with the more extreme demands in the name of the public would have been unfair, impolitic, and in long-range terms nationally suicidal.

Then and later, defenders and detractors alike thought Hamilton supported the claims of the first group and opposed those of the second. In fact he was one of the few in the disinterested center who sought accommodation and reconciliation between the interested extremes—for he wanted to mend the nation, not to rend it.

Almost everyone had opinions as to how the public debts should be handled, but almost no one knew just how much the debts amounted to, which governments owed what to whom, or how and to what extent the debts were currently being managed. Scores of kinds of evidences of public obligations were outstanding; scores of thousands of Americans held or had held public paper in one form or another.

When Hamilton took office, however, the largest single category of public debts was not obligations of governments to individual citizens but intergovernmental obligations and credits. In theory, the financing of the war was to have been simple—the states supplying the funds and the Continental Congress disbursing them; but in practice both the states and Congress had spent large sums directly and on their own initiative. The total amount spent by the state governments for the common defense had been something over $100 million. The Articles of Confederation and various congressional ordinances specified that the costs of the war were to have been audited, a total arrived at, and shares apportioned among the states on the basis of land values. Direct expenditures by the states were to be credited against the shares thus reckoned.[1]

The amounts at stake ensured disagreements over the ways the accounts should be audited. Each state believed or professed to believe that it had spent more than its share, and each feared that the accounting method adopted by Congress might not give it full credit. Southerners, as was their wont, had been slipshod in keeping the books on their expenditures—or, as one of them put it, they had acted "in the true Spirit of a patriot . . . without taking any heed concerning the day of retribution." Understandably, they demanded after the war that lax standards be maintained in the verification of claims and even that sworn statements be accepted in lieu of receipts and other documents. By contrast, New England Yankees, ever concerned with the day of reckoning, insisted upon receipts in writing even in emergencies. Understandably, they feared that southern demands for lax accounting masked a design to justify fraudulent claims. There was another reason for distrust as well: some states had made military expenditures in their own interests and not those of the nation. Virginia had, without congressional authorization, backed George Rogers Clark's expedition into the Ohio country in 1778 with a view toward gaining control of that area for itself; Massachusetts had sponsored a similar action for similar motives against Penobscot, Maine, in 1779; and both states insisted that the cost of those ventures should be charged to the Union.[2]

Congress had started the auditing of such accounts as early as 1782, but it changed the rules repeatedly over the next five years. Then in 1787 a compromise procedure was agreed upon. Five regional commissioners were appointed, with instructions to accept all verifiable claims as rapidly as possible and to pass questionable claims on to the General Board of the Treasury. Despite that effort to expedite the auditing, however, the process had only just begun when Hamilton became secretary.[3]

The remaining public debt was of three broad descriptions: foreign, national, and state. During the war the United States had received from abroad just over $10 million in loans. In round sums, $4.4 million had come directly from the French royal treasury, $1.8 million from Dutch bankers in a loan guaranteed by the French government, $3.6 million in direct loans from Dutch bankers, and $175,000 from the Spanish royal treasury. As of the end of 1789, the United States was $1.6 million in arrears for interest payments on these various loans and nearly $1.4 million in arrears on scheduled repayments of principal. Additional repayments of principal were falling due at a rate of $463,000 a year.[4]

Politically the foreign debt was neutral, since everyone agreed that it had priority over any domestic debts; but that very consensus posed a major problem for Hamilton. The cost of servicing the foreign debt was more than $1 million a year. Meeting those charges, if any serious effort were made to pay the overdue sums promptly, would consume virtually all the revenues that Hamilton could foresee being generated by the 1789 tariff, the national government's sole tax. Scarcely a cent, in other words, would be left over for servicing the domestic debt, not to mention meeting current expenses of government. Either some alternative way must be found to handle the foreign debt, or taxes must be increased to a dangerously high level. Resistance to taxation had torn the British Empire asunder, and Hamilton had no doubt that the same fate could befall the American Union.[5]

This situation had prompted Hamilton to seek a postponement of the debts due France. If the United States could be temporarily freed from that obligation, it could quickly bring itself up to date with its Dutch banking creditors and thus be in a position to negotiate a new loan in Holland large enough to repay all its foreign debts. That done, the annual interest would be only $500,000 to $600,000, an entirely manageable sum.[6]

But wealth and greed were already at work to frustrate Hamilton's plans. A group of Americans in Paris, led by Gouverneur Morris and the former army contractor Daniel Parker, had formed a syndicate with a group of Frenchmen, headed by Etienne Clavière and Jean Pierre Brissot de Warville, to enrich themselves by doing the governments of their countries a favor. The French government was near bankruptcy, and its bonds could be purchased at a small fraction of par. The syndicate proposed to buy the entire American debt from France, paying for it in French bonds. Jacques Necker, who had been recalled as minister of finance after a period of disfavor with the court, rejected the proposal because he needed cash; but when the syndicate offered to pay half in French bonds at par and half in cash on the same profitable scale, Necker listened, insisting only that the syndicate provide guarantees that it had ample resources for the transaction. Confidently, they assured him they could obtain abundant backing in Holland. Had they been able to do so they would have sought to have the French debt incorporated as part of the American domestic debt, thus taking pressure off the United States and making a whopping profit for themselves. The United States' bankers in Holland, however—the Amsterdam firm of Willinks, Van Staphorsts, and Hubbard—had other plans. On the professed ground that the proposal of the French-American syndicate would, if consummated, dry up American credit in Holland—Morris maintained to the contrary that they were acting to protect their own profitable speculations—they effectively thwarted the syndicate's negotiations. They went further, raising a loan on their own initiative to buy up the overdue portion of the American debt to France. That would provide Hamilton the needed relief despite the fact that France proved unable to grant the relief herself.[7]

All this took place while Hamilton was working on his report on the public credit; he did not learn of it until several months later. Meanwhile, he assumed that France could be held off one way or another, started preparing to make prompt interest payments on the loans due in Holland, and counted on being able soon or late to refinance the whole foreign debt in Amsterdam. Indeed, in his report he would budget for the foreign debt only $542,599 a year, the amount that would be necessary for interest on the consolidated loan if it could be floated.[8]

The domestic debt was in confused shape, but Hamilton was able to make some sense of it. During the war, Congress had raised funds in three main ways, not counting requisitions and foreign loans: by issuing unsecured paper money, by issuing bonds called loan office certificates, and by issuing or authorizing the issue of promissory notes for paying and supplying the army. The paper money, of a gross face value of more than $200 million, had depreciated almost to nothing and had been officially devalued at a ratio of 40 for 1. The new paper bore no interest and was regarded as virtually worthless. The loan office certificates had been adjusted on various bases to compensate for inflation and were settled at about $11 million. The army-related debts, originally a nightmare of confusion, had since 1782 mostly been scaled, audited, and "liquidated" by the issuance of new certificates.[9]

Existing arrangements for servicing these debts ranged from nearly adequate to nonexistent. In lieu of interest Congress had issued "indents," or certificates of interest, and made them receivable for portions of the annual requisitions upon the states. The states had then levied taxes payable partly in indents, and by that means about $1.5 million found their way back into the national treasury for cancellation. Similarly, several states made army certificates receivable for state taxes and subsequently paid their requisitions in them; some $10 million in Quartermaster's and Commissary's certificates were thus paid into the national treasury and cancelled. Despite such doings, about $16 million in army certificates and related securities remained outstanding in 1789. The outstanding arrears of interest on the various forms of national debt was $13 million, making a grand total (including loan office certificates) of about $40 million.[10]

But there was a complication arising from several states' adoption of fiscal systems more or less like those of New York and Pennsylvania, whereby they had assumed responsibility for servicing their citizens' national debts. By that means and by means of direct taxes payable in securities, some states had become large-scale creditors of the United States. The biggest such creditors were Pennsylvania, New York, and Maryland. All told, state governments owned about a third of the continental securities that remained outstanding in 1789—which compounded the problem of intergovernmental debts still further.[11]

Finally, there were the war debts of the several states. A large portion of the $100 million the states had spent for war purposes had been financed through inflation, confiscation, expropriation, and taxation, but around half had been covered with the various kinds of deficit means employed by Congress. As a result, the states owed enormous debts at the end of the war. Some, Massachusetts and South Carolina for instance, attempted to manage their debts honorably but proved unable to collect the high taxes they levied to service them and thus remained deeply in debt in 1789. On the other extreme, Rhode Island, Virginia, and North Carolina employed more or less fraudulent means to retire a large part of their obligations. In between were those few states that proved both able and willing to service their debts on a fair and equitable basis. Hamilton estimated that the combined debts of the several states outstanding at the end of 1789 were between $21 and $25 million.[12]

Recapitulating, the foreign debt was around $11 million, the continental debts including arrears of interest around $40 million, and the state debts around $25 million. Most of the foreign debt bore 5 percent interest, some 4 percent; Hamilton budgeted $543,000 for that interest. The continental and state debts normally bore 6 percent interest, or an annual cost of nearly $4 million. The total annual interest bill of $4.5 million was three times as much as Hamilton could foresee having at his disposal. To establish public credit he had to refinance on more favorable terms, obtain additional revenues, or both.

The Constitution defined the taxing power, but economic and political realities delimited the ways that power could be exercised. Hamilton's ability to perform his tasks would therefore depend in large measure upon his understanding of national and international economic and financial conditions and institutions, and upon his skill in turning these to the advantage of the United States.

In broad terms, three kinds of taxes were theoretically available: direct taxes, excises, and duties on imports. Direct taxes, whether levied on persons or property, were the most onerous, least productive, and most difficult to collect. Moreover, federal power to levy them was restricted by the constitutional requirement that they be apportioned by states on the basis of population rather than of property. For those and other reasons Hamilton (unlike his friend Madison) preferred that direct taxes be allowed to remain the virtually exclusive province of state governments. On the other end of the scale, customs duties were the most productive and easiest to collect and were the exclusive realm of the national government. In between was the excise, a tax on particular commodities, which both levels of government were empowered to levy. Some believed that the federal government, having the best source of revenues, should leave the second best, the excise, to the states. But there was a flaw in that thinking: if customs duties and excise taxes on the same commodities were collected by different governments, evasion on both levels was relatively easy, whereas if both were collected by different agents of the same government evasion was virtually impossible. If, however, the federal government took the excise unto itself, it followed logically and almost necessarily that it must also assume responsibility for the debts of the states. That was just what Hamilton wanted.[13]

The willingness of congressmen to approve such an arrangement depended mainly upon two variables—who would benefit and who would pay. These variables, in turn, would hinge at least partly upon the interests of members of Congress as individuals and upon the interests of states. The first was difficult to know, the second fairly easy. As to the question of which states would benefit, it was clear that Massachusetts, Connecticut, and South Carolina, owing almost half the total amount of state debts among them, might be eager to embrace assumption even though it included the excise. Similarly, New York, Pennsylvania, and Maryland had such large amounts at stake as national creditors that their interests dictated augmentation of federal revenues by any reasonable means. Only two states, Virginia and North Carolina, had little or nothing to gain from assumption and not much to gain from funding of the continental debts—but those two states had between them nearly a fourth of the seats in the House.[14]

The question of who would pay was rather more involved. The excise, being a simpler affair than the customs, may be disposed of briefly. It was generally understood that an excise would fall mainly upon spirituous liquors of domestic manufacture. American distillers were of two general kinds, large producers of rum in New England and New York and small but numerous makers of whiskey in the back country from Pennsylvania southward. The rum distillers, since most of them were also public creditors, would gain enough to compensate themselves for such of the increased tax as could not be passed along to consumers; and besides, they could expect some indirect compensation in the form of increased import duties on competing foreign spirits. The whiskey distillers, largely Scotch-Irish frontiersmen, could count on no pecuniary advantages from a national financial system. Perhaps they might support the national government in exchange for defense against the Indians, but even then they like other Americans preferred that someone else bear the cost.[15]

Customs duties meant only duties on imports, since the Constitution prohibited taxes on exports. Americans bought most of their manufactured goods from Britain, most of their wines from the Iberian Peninsula and from the Spanish and Portuguese wine islands, and all of their sugar and sugar products (much of this for reexport) from the West Indies. The largest all-purpose American ports were Philadelphia and New York, the largest in direct trade with Europe were Charleston and Norfolk, the largest in the West Indies trade were Boston and Baltimore. Most of the revenues from customs duties, upwards of 80 percent, would be collected in those six ports.[16]

That was straightforward enough; what complicated the tariff question was that various groups wanted import duties to be employed for other purposes besides raising a revenue. For example, handicraft manufacturers, who constituted a potent voting bloc in port towns from Philadelphia northward—and incidentally had been strong supporters of the Constitution—were anxious to have the tariff schedules arranged to protect them from foreign competition. Hamilton planned, in fact, that they should have the protection they sought, but only as adjustments to the tariff laws after an adequate revenue system had been established.[17]

The designs of politicians representing tobacco planters were more ambitious. During the colonial period, planters had been required by the Navigation Acts to ship all their tobacco to Britain; British merchants then profitably reexported it to the Continent, where most of it was consumed. With independence, Virginians and Marylanders visualized the dawn of a halcyon era in which the lucrative benefits of direct trade to the Continent would be theirs. When that era failed to materialize in the 1780s, and Britain continued to be their main buyer as well as supplier, they blamed monopolists, by which they meant Robert Morris. Now, upon the creation of the national government under the Constitution, they sought to use the tariff as an instrument for redirecting American trade away from Britain and toward the Continent, especially France. Toward that end Madison, as the leading congressional spokesman for the tobacco-growing region, attempted to form a coalition with others whom he thought amenable to an anti-British policy. Specifically, he was prepared to woo the handicraft manufacturers and a variety of groups in New England, mainly the fishing, whaling, and shipping interests, who were or seemed to be suffering from various postwar restrictions upon trade with the British Empire.[18]

In fact, however, American trade could not be shifted from Britain to the Continent, no matter how American commercial taxation and regulation might be manipulated. As to the Dutch, they were bankers to Europe, but they neither controlled the markets nor produced the goods necessary for handling more than a small fraction of the American trade. Neither the French nor the Spanish produced enough of what Americans wanted to buy; and quite as important, they lacked the institutional, cultural, and financial means to grant credit to American exporters and importers on terms

ar as favorable as British merchants could and cus-
provide.[19]

ost American revenues had to come from import duties,
t mainly duties on British goods, which incidentally
venues of commerce with Britain must be kept as free
from impediments as possible. The secondary revenues must come
mainly from excises, which meant mainly levies on distilled spirits,
which incidentally meant that the federal government must assume
the state debts. Policies dictated by the interests of the United
States were therefore clear; but, equally clearly, certain special and
local interests ran counter to national interest. It would ever be
thus, and the task Hamilton faced was one that would ever face
American statesmen: to reconcile and harness conflicting special
interests in behalf of the national interest.

The groups most actively and aggressively interested in the
means taken for the support of public credit were speculators. Everybody knew that speculators were busy, greedy, and to lesser and
greater degrees unscrupulous. This general awareness, however,
was inadequate for Hamilton's purposes. Several aspects of their
operations, known to few people, required particular understanding
if the activities of speculators were to be channeled in the public interest.

Speculation in and of itself was politically neutral. Individual speculators might be nationalists or state particularists, monarchists or
republicans, aristocrats or democrats, but the sole object of their
speculative activities was to make money; and from that perspective
ideology was of no consequence. Whether they made or lost money
depended upon their skill and luck, upon the vicissitudes of the
market, and upon the most important determinant of the market,
government fiscal policies. Some were winning and some were losing under the existing state fiscal systems. As both Hamilton and
the speculators were aware, however, in long-range terms the opportunities for profits were greater under the state systems than
they would be under his, for profitable speculation requires a fluctuating market—one can profit both on the decline and on the
rise—and Hamilton intended to create a stable market.

Hamilton was indifferent as to whether speculators made or lost money, but from his point of view speculation under the existing rules was highly detrimental to the public welfare. Obviously the existing systems had a centrifugal political effect, increasing the influence of the states at the expense of national authority. Less obviously but quite as detrimentally, speculation had a depressing effect upon conventional economic activity, for it drew money away from agriculture and trade, as did the heavy taxes levied by some states in their efforts to retire their war debts. Land values and commodity prices in the South had fallen steadily for three or four years, despite a growing demand for both land and commodities; commercial activity in Philadelphia and New York, thriving until the new fiscal systems were adopted, had been relatively stagnant since; the economies of Connecticut and Massachusetts, crushed under unbearable tax burdens, had all but ceased to function. Hamilton believed that a properly designed national fiscal system should reverse both these effects, simultaneously increasing national power and stimulating rather than retarding economic growth.[20]

Another important consideration was that speculators were betting both ways, as bulls and bears. Very few of the highest rollers were betting unreservedly on the rise; indeed, only three clearly bullish groups can be distinguished. First were original holders of securities, those who had received public paper for military service or for supplying money, goods, or services in the war effort. Between 25 and 40 percent of the original holders—some fifteen to twenty thousand creditors of the nation and perhaps as many more creditors of the states—still owned their securities toward the end of 1789. A second group consisted of merchants who had, since the peace, accumulated securities at discounts in payment for goods, until their holdings were quite sizable. Several hundred merchants had thus acquired securities in their normal conduct of business; their combined holdings of perhaps $2 to $3 million (face value) represented only nominal cash investments, and any appreciation in security values would bring large windfall profits to them. A third group of bulls included about 120 merchants in Boston and Providence who held well over $3 million (face value) in securities among them. These men had made large profits during the war, only to gamble nearly everything afterward on a pair of investments that had long since gone sour: they had overimported British goods on credit and had bought up immense quantities of public securities at as little as a tenth of their par value. The goods had proved unsalable, and British investors were hounding them and threatening to sue in the newly established federal courts. The suits would ruin them—unless the appreciation of their public securities was fast enough and great enough to enable them to pay their bills.[21]

The more active and daring speculators were betting the other way, at least to some extent. In part this curious state of affairs resulted from an endemic condition of American economic life. For decades, Americans had been addicted to gambling in vacant lands: the high road to wealth, they believed, was to acquire big tracts of frontier lands at a nominal cost, wait for the inevitable expansion of the population, then sell the lands in farm-sized parcels to settlers at huge profits. Though things rarely worked out that way, almost no one was immune to the lure of land speculation. Washington had acquired more than 500,000 acres of wild land, Knox devoted more attention to his land investments in Maine than to his War Department duties, Madison was forever conniving to become independently wealthy through land ventures, and even Hamilton sometimes took a plunge. Independence had expanded opportunities for land speculation, for the Congress and several state governments had acquired vast expanses of former Crown and proprietary lands as public domains. Since 1787 the biggest and boldest speculators had been buying these public lands on a basis that would be profitable only if the prices of public securities remained low. They had contracted with Congress or state governments to purchase huge tracts, the price being payable in several annual installments and in government securities at their par value. If securities could be bought on the open market for, say, fifteen cents on the dollar (as some still could even at the end of 1789), then a million acres of land at a nominal cost of a dollar an acre could be obtained for a cash outlay of only $150,000. The prospects for profits from land speculation on that basis had seemed so high, and the prospects for most kinds of securities so low, that nearly every man of means and a gambling instinct had found investment in public lands irresistible. As the market prices of securities rose, profit margins declined, and if prices rose too high too fast, land speculators would be wiped out.[22]

Hamilton had to take all this into account. He recognized that public credit could be established only in the market and, on a day-to-day basis, speculators had a large part in making the market. In broader terms, however, the market would be made elsewhere or not at all. It was a fact of life in the eighteenth century that any nation seeking to establish public credit must do so in Holland, for Amsterdam was the financial capital of the western world. Coincidentally, recent developments in Holland had made Dutch financiers amenable to investing in the United States. Historically their closest ties had been with England, and without Dutch capital the Walpolean financial system could not have succeeded; but in 1780 the British had provoked Holland into a war that lasted for four years. In 1785 the Dutch began to dump their holdings of British government securities and to look elsewhere for profitable investment outlets. Partly for political reasons, they found France and the United States especially attractive; and they made several timely loans to the United States under the Confederation. Dutch loans had helped finance the late stages of the Revolutionary War, and loans in 1784, 1787, and 1788 had made it possible for Congress to avoid total default on interest payments due France.[23]

More immediately of interest to Hamilton, the Dutch had, upon the publication of the Constitution in Europe, begun buying American domestic securities on a large scale. In March of 1788 the Dutch banker Peter Stadnitski had contracted with Daniel Parker, then residing in Paris, for the purchase of $200,000 in American securities at 37½ cents on the dollar. In August the order was increased to more than a million dollars' worth. By early 1789 Dutch investors, working mainly through the New York brokerage firm of Leroy and Bayard, had contracted to buy at least $4 million in continental securities. The aggressive buying policies of Leroy and Bayard, in tandem with a generally optimistic popular mood, sent the prices of continental securities soaring even before Hamilton took office.[24]

Few American speculators, even among those not involved in land purchases, were able to take full advantage of the rise. A number of them, hoping to acquire large quantities of securities for profitable resale in Amsterdam before Hamilton could institute a system that would drive the market still higher, began to buy frantically. That resulted in another 50 percent increase in security prices during Hamilton's first two months in office, which was to the good as far as Hamilton was concerned; but it was in the interest of the speculators to increase their profit margins by depressing the market in the United States, and many of them attempted to do so. They also, in November and December 1789, became caught in a squeeze because of tangential developments. Major crop failures in Europe had sent the demand for American staples so high that American ports were crowded with European buyers, and for the only occasion in living memory good bills of exchange on Europe were a glut on the American market. At the same time, the Bank of New York, overextended for loans for speculative purchases of securities, stopped discounting and began calling in its outstanding loans. Philadelphia's Bank of North America later did likewise. That cut the speculators' buying power drastically, and security prices stopped rising and actually began a temporary decline.[25]

It was in this heady atmosphere that Hamilton wrote his report to Congress. No small number of speculators were bursting with curiosity over what he would recommend. The great rise in prices, so far, had been in continental securities, for that was the only kind for which the Dutch had placed orders. Indents were still available at a third or less of their face value (as opposed to prices of 50 percent and more on loan office and army certificates), and some state securities were still available at less than ten cents on the dollar. How Hamilton would propose to handle the indents was unpredictable, but there was a hint that Congress contemplated assuming the state debts, for the House had instructed Hamilton to make a survey of those debts and of the existing arrangements for servicing them. One speculator, the New York merchant William Constable, assiduously tried to learn Hamilton's intentions regarding indents and state securities; as Hamilton's friendly acquaintance, erstwhile client, and occasional dinner guest, he was in a position to probe more insinuatingly than were such friends as Henry Lee. But Hamilton would talk only in generalities, and on a key point he misled Constable or allowed him to mislead himself. Hamilton let the speculator believe that indents and state debts would be ultimately provided for, but not immediately as a part of the original proposal. Constable unabashedly told correspondents in Europe that he had inside information that indents and state securities would be funded and solicited a contract for the delivery of a large amount of them. Unfortunately for him, he read Hamilton's comments to mean that he could be leisurely in starting to buy state securities. Hamilton's report, which proposed the funding of both indents and state securities, triggered a spectacular rise in their prices; and Constable, who had hoped to buy $4 million of South Carolina securities at eleven for one in cash, found his plans frustrated by a quadrupling of prices.[26]

The significance of speculative activity is easy to misunderstand. Hamilton could not leave the speculators out of his reckoning, but on the whole he found them a sorely troublesome nuisance, for their interests and his were diametrically opposed. His interest—establishing public credit on the best possible footing—was bullish: it lay in getting the market prices of securities up to par as rapidly as possible and holding them there. Their interest was bearish: it lay in getting the Dutch market as high as possible while keeping the American market low and unstable. Yet Hamilton was loath to see the bears suffer, for widespread failures among them could wreak such general financial havoc as to undermine any system he might devise. Moreover, contemplation of the extent of their avarice convinced him that speculators, far from being stable props for a national system of finance, were greedy enough to erect their own fortunes upon the ruins of public credit. Their greed could be harnessed, but only in the short run. If the report were carefully designed, they might become a powerful lobbying force and help pressure Congress to pass the legislation Hamilton desired. But if "increasing the number of ligaments between the Government and the interests of Individuals" had been "the weightiest motive to the measure," he said afterward, "it would never have received my patronage." Immediate private interest was simply too unreliable.[27]

There was one other set of factors, less tangible but not less real, that Hamilton needed to consider, and that was general popular and political attitudes toward the public debt. The most radical position was that the debts should simply be repudiated. Not many men in public life, to be sure, openly advocated repudiation, but sentiment for repudiation of all but the foreign debt was actually common. In a vague sort of way, back-country folk from New Hampshire to Georgia reckoned they were about to be taxed for the enrichment of men of wealth in the seaboard cities, and their representatives tended to share that feeling. Stephen Higginson, Hamilton's most trusted adviser in New England, warned that unless the debts or the interest on them were scaled down, dangerous popular resistance would erupt. Several members of Congress advocated repudiation of accrued interest, and at least four proposed that the principal of the debts be scaled down to its market value, which would have effectively repudiated half to three-quarters of the debt.[28]

A related and considerably more popular position was the advocacy of discrimination between original and present holders of government paper. Many believed that original holders should be compensated in full, with or without payment of accrued interest, but that all other holders were much less deserving. Various ways of giving original holders the difference between face value and market price were suggested. All such proposals rested upon the widespread and intense popular antipathy toward speculators in the public debts, or "bloodsuckers" as they were commonly called. In many instances such hostility was justified; yet discrimination as a remedy would have created more problems than it solved. Even as a matter of justice, the problem was complex. The old soldier who had sold his pay certificates to a speculator for ten cents on the dollar would be taken care of by discrimination; but the honest merchant who had accepted the soldier's certificate at little or no discount in payment for goods was surely entitled to something for his faith in the credit of the nation. More important, discrimination would be fatal to public credit. To refuse full payment to present holders would be to make government bonds nonnegotiable, and thus investors in future, faced with the inability to sell government bonds in times of personal need, would simply not buy any bonds in the first place.[29]

On the opposite extreme from the repudiators and discriminators were those who insisted that every cent of the public debt, including interest, must be paid precisely and literally on the terms of the original contracts. William Bingham, a Philadelphia merchant who offered Hamilton a long, detailed, and generally helpful set of suggestions for the management of the debt, was the leading spokesman for this school of thought. His views were shared by a large segment of the business community, and they were entirely honorable. But from Hamilton's point of view they were also impracticable, for Bingham's recommendations required much more money than would be available.[30]

And even among those who insisted on full compensation for all present holders of public paper, opinion was divided as to whether state debts should be assumed. Pocketbooks were involved, as indicated, but the issue ran deeper. Some viewed the matter simply: honor dictated that governments, like men, must pay their just debts; the state war debts were just; and that was that. Others feared the aggrandizement of national power implicit in assumption, and opposed it because it would in effect create a group of fifteen to twenty thousand pensioners of the national government. Many ardent nationalists favored assumption for exactly that reason.[31]

Finally, an emotionally laden issue overlapped and sometimes overrode all the others. Simply put, this question turned on whether the debts were to be repaid or merely "funded." Those who held the first position believed that a public debt was a public curse, a mortgage upon the future that necessitated a burden of taxation inimical to economic development and a burden of government inimical to personal freedom. The proper course of action that followed from this premise was to retire the debt as rapidly as possible by levying taxes as high as they could be equitably imposed and collected, pushing the sale of public lands for public securities, and keeping all government expenditures at a barebones minimum. Usually the advocates of such a course also favored a species of fraud: they wanted the government itself to become a speculator by buying up its debts at a discount. The opposite way of thinking was that a public debt could be a public blessing, something that, if properly managed, could facilitate both growth and stability. From this point of view the proper course was to provide permanent funds for making regular interest payments on the debt, but to leave the principal more or less intact, to be managed by sophisticated fiscal techniques so as to serve as a basis for a uniform and elastic currency. The English had adopted the latter system, and their experience had demonstrated that it was a remarkably efficacious instrument. Any attempt to emulate the British example in America, however, was sure to be unpopular. Americans had imbibed deeply of the propaganda of the reactionary English Opposition; they had taken the Opposition's shibboleths and diatribes against public debts and "money men" and corruption, along with its glorification of the gentry ethic, as unvarnished truth.[32]

It was no coincidence that the English Opposition had been led by a landed gentry that saw its power undermined by the new financial order. Nor would it be coincidental that the strongest opposition to Hamilton's program would emanate from landed oligarchs who feared the same fate.

Generations have argued the question, whether Hamilton's Reports on the Public Credit were original or imitative; the weight of opinion is that, to a lesser or greater degree, the reports were based largely upon study of the English example. It can be maintained, on the contrary, that given Hamilton's personal makeup, his view of human nature, his design for the country, his experiences in New York, and the conditions described here, he could have composed his reports without advice from anyone and without reference to any theoretical thinkers, and the end result would not have been drastically different.[33]

Nonetheless, he did seek and receive advice, and he did consult the written works of the best thinkers on the subject. Obviously he had discussed the matter with both Robert and Gouverneur Morris; he had been discussing it with them for years. Both, however, were too involved in their own schemes in 1789 to have been of much help to Hamilton, and Gouverneur was out of the country by the time Hamilton became secretary. Moreover, a system he proposed before he left was, as was not unusual with him, so excessively extravagant as to be worthless. The suggestions of William Bingham and Stephen Higginson, the one going much further and the other not nearly as far as Hamilton wanted to go, have been mentioned. Doubtless Hamilton discussed the matter with his father-in-law, who had devoted considerable study and made endless calculations in an effort to find a way of refinancing the public debts to make them manageable. In addition, Hamilton solicited and took into account suggestions from Madison, Samuel Osgood, Benjamin Walker, John Witherspoon, and Oliver Wolcott, Jr. None of these except Wolcott's was especially helpful.[34]

As to writers on economic and financial subjects, Hamilton had read relevant works by Adam Smith, Hume, Montesquieu, Necker, Blackstone, and Postlethwayt, among many others. From them one could readily derive the idea of monetizing the public debt, which was central to Hamilton's plans, and also obtain a notion of the means by which Britain had monetized its debt. For that matter, a full discussion of the British example was available in the contemporary press, both in newspapers and in such periodicals as *The American Museum,* so that any reasonably well-informed American might be familiar with the general outlines of the British system.[35]

Yet there is a curious thing about these supposed influences upon Hamilton's thinking. Every one of the writers just mentioned, while recognizing the economic advantages of monetizing a public debt, nonetheless vigorously denounced the very idea of public debts. Hume, for example, thought the British debt would surely lead to national bankruptcy; Smith devoted the entire last chapter of *The Wealth of Nations* to proving that public debts were pernicious; Postlethwayt, in article after article, lambasted the entire British fiscal system. Indeed, virtually the only part of the British system that was universally applauded was the unsoundest part—a ridiculous scheme, dreamed up by Dr. Richard Price and made national policy by Pitt, of retiring the debt "magically" through a sinking fund.[36]

There is no real mystery here, however. Hamilton did study the British example, and it did provide him with useful information regarding the workaday details of financial operations. Moreover, Hamilton's system was erected upon the same three institutions as was the British system—funding, a national bank, and a sinking fund. But the resemblance was largely superficial, for Hamilton founded the institutions on different principles and used them in different ways to obtain different ends. The British system was designed solely as a means of raising money for purposes of government; political, social, and economic by-products of the system, though profound, were incidental. Hamilton's system was designed to employ financial means to achieve political, economic, and social ends; and that made all the difference in the world.

❧ VIII ❧

Funding and Assumption

. . . Self-love, in all, becomes the cause

Of what restrains him, Government and Laws.

The difficulties inherent in any attempt to establish public credit in America were compounded by Hamilton's conception of the task. It was a central part of his plan that each of his proposals be adopted on its own merits, but each to him was but a step toward a larger goal. From the narrower first perspective it was necessary only that his recommendations for servicing the public debts be regarded as an acceptable immediate solution to an immediate problem. From the broader second perspective it was imperative that Congress act swiftly and decisively. Indeed, if he were to succeed in effecting his grand design, he must accomplish something that had never been done before—the establishment of public credit almost instantly.

Public credit, as he pointed out, was normally earned "by good faith, by a punctual performance of contracts. States, like individuals, who observe their engagements, are respected and trusted: while the reverse is the fate of those, who pursue an opposite conduct." Earning a reputation for acting in good faith, in other words, was a slow process, and Hamilton could not afford to wait. Yet the United States, having consistently violated its pledges, year in and year out, for more than a decade, had scarcely won itself any special consideration. It did have an advantage in the form of a good excuse, the inadequacy of its former government under the Articles of

Confederation, and Dutch investors were strongly disposed to give the United States a second chance after the adoption of the Constitution. The second chance, however, would not last indefinitely. Rather, it reemphasized what Hamilton already perceived as the urgency of the situation.[1]

To perform his unprecedented feat, Hamilton proposed a pair of different but interdependent courses of action. One was concerned with making solid fiscal arrangements. The system for servicing the debts must be erected upon the soundest foundations possible, given the materials at hand, but it must be so designed as to generate improved materials in the near future, which must then be used to establish even firmer foundations. Had the eighteenth century been as addicted to the use of pseudomilitary catchwords as the twentieth, this course might have been dubbed Operation Bootstrap. In the same jargon, the other requisite course might have been called Operation Mirrors, for it involved the creation of illusions. Ultimately, the only way to establish public credit was in the marketplace, and the marketplace dealt in beliefs as well as facts. As Hamilton put it, "in nothing are appearances of greater moment, than in whatever regards credit. Opinion is the soul of it, and this is affected by appearances, as well as realities." If the market prices of government securities could be raised to their par value by any means whatever, the investing public would be convinced that public credit had been established; and if and when investors believed public credit had been established, it would ipso facto be established.[2]

For these various reasons, Hamilton's Report on the Public Credit—actually the first of several such reports—was more than a simple set of recommendations. It was also an analysis of a problem, a proposed plan of action, an argument designed to induce Congress to enact the proposal, and an argument designed to convince public creditors that it was fair and would work. In the report Hamilton blended far-ranging vision with meticulous attention to detail and tempered boldness with care, imagination with discipline, creativity with craftsmanship. In sum, his report was sophisticated in the extreme.

But Hamilton's performance was marked by a curious naïveté as well, for he genuinely expected his proposals to be approved simply because they were good for the country. He was a man who understood power; and yet he had no power base in Congress, did not seek to build one, and failed entirely to anticipate the tangle of political interests that would govern the congressmen's conduct. He understood that men are governed by their baser passions; and yet he trusted the fate of his measures to the willingness of congressmen to act in the public interest.

The oversights are understandable, for Hamilton was almost alone in having no petty personal interests at stake. Driven by his lust for Fame, he failed to anticipate that most others—not only speculators and demagogues, but even the likes of Washington, Madison, and Jefferson—had special axes to grind, fortunes to make, or power to win, if not for themselves then for their constituents. It was in his nature to underrate the extent of his opposition and overrate the virtues of his supporters. Perhaps that was a defense mechanism: otherwise, the sense of isolation would hardly have been bearable.

Two value judgments, or philosophical premises, underlay Hamilton's argument for the objective of establishing public credit. The first was that the sanctity of contracts is the foundation of all private morality and the indispensable condition of every sane social order. The second was that good government—by which he meant active, affirmative government—is essential to the happiness and freedom of society. It was necessary to happiness because only such a government could provide for the safety of the citizens, stimulate their industry, and provide the conditions under which they, through their own efforts, could earn prosperity. It was necessary for freedom because only such a government could impose the restraints of lawful order, regularity, and predictability that are indispensable if freedom is not to be self-destructive.[3]

A more specific assumption underlay Hamilton's choice of specific means for establishing public credit. Rather than attempting to pay off the debts as soon as possible, he proposed to "fund" them: to provide for regular interest payments by a permanent appropriation that would have priority over all others, rather than by making annual appropriations; and to leave the question of retiring the principal—whether it should be retired soon, late, or never—to the discretion of government. The assumption underlying this decision was that the United States, as a raw and undeveloped land, was long on natural wealth but short on institutional wealth, meaning liquid capital. Any stable and orderly means of increasing the quantity and circulation of the money supply, up to though not exceeding what was necessary for the development of the natural wealth, was therefore desirable. The readiest means to that end was to transform the public debt, which under existing institutional arrangements was a heavy drain on the limited supply of money, into a form of money itself by depoliticizing and thus stabilizing public securities as a kind of annuity. "It is a well known fact," Hamilton said, "that in countries in which the national debt is properly funded, and an object of established confidence, it answers most of the purposes of money." Monetization of the public debt would be advantageous "to every class of the community"—not just to public creditors, but to merchants, planters, farmers, handicraft manufacturers, and laborers as well. These advantages, however, "are only to be looked for, when, by being well funded, [the public debt] has acquired an *adequate* and *stable* value. Till then, it has rather a contrary tendency. The fluctuation and insecurity incident to it in an unfunded state, render it a mere commodity, and a precarious one. As such, being only an object of occasional and particular speculation, all the money applied to it is so much diverted from the more useful channels of circulation, for which the thing itself affords no substitute: So that, in fact, one serious inconvenience of an unfunded debt is, that it contributes to the scarcity of money." The general decline in land values, and especially that in the South, Hamilton maintained, was a direct consequence of the money shortage created by speculation. The options facing the nation, then, were "whether the public debt, by a provision for it on true principles, shall be rendered a *substitute* for money; or whether, by being left as it is, or by being provided for in such a manner as will wound those principles, and destroy confidence, it shall be suffered to continue, as it is, a pernicious drain of our cash from the channels of productive industry."[4]

The perceptive among Hamilton's audience might have noticed, at that stage of his argument, that he had made two subtle and clever rhetorical strokes. One was to play upon the widespread hostility toward speculators: by describing their role in the depression of land values and dislocations of trade, then pointing out that the cure for the evils of speculation was to do away with the opportunity for it by removing the fluctuations on which it fed, he enlisted his audience's prejudices in the cause of funding. The other was to set up the alternatives as funding versus annual appropriations, rather than as funding versus attempting to pay off the public debt. Listeners and readers who missed the latter stroke were logically trapped, for given that premise the ensuing parts of his argument were irrefutable.[5]

Those next parts concerned the questions of discrimination, the assumption of state debts, the settlement of accounts, and back interest. Discrimination between original and present holders of public securities he disposed of as *"unjust,"* citing the wide range of circumstances that had been involved in transfers from original holders to secondary and tertiary owners; *"impolitic,"* on the crucial ground that to discriminate would be to make securities nontransferable, or only partly transferable, and thus prevent their circulation as money; *"injurious,"* even to original holders in future, because it would make it difficult or impossible for investors to sell their securities in time of need; and *"ruinous"* to public credit for these reasons. Finally, and tellingly, Hamilton quoted the congressional resolution of April 26, 1783—authored by Madison—which explicitly pledged that there would be no discrimination between original and later holders.[6]

The questions of assumption and the settlement of accounts were closely related, but Hamilton dealt with them serially rather than together. Assumption was the most convenient and economical way to provide for state creditors, he said; it was good policy, for otherwise national and state governments would be competitors for the same tax resources; it was fairer than leaving the individual states to provide for their debts, since some had better tax bases than others; it was advantageous to the nation, for it would bind the interests of the state creditors to support the national fiscal arrangements; and it was just, for state and national debts were contracted in the common cause and thus should be supported by all.[7]

In dealing with the settlement of state accounts, Hamilton proposed a method, based largely upon suggestions of Oliver Wolcott, whereby that explosive issue would be defused. Intergovernmental debts would form no part of the funding system. Instead, they would be audited and apportioned in an ingenious two-stage process. The net result of the process would be that, though not all state governments would receive funds from the general government (except indirectly by relieving them of their public debts through assumption), no state governments would be required to pay anything more into the general treasury. In effect, Hamilton was suggesting a sort of negative revenue-sharing program.[8]

On the matter of arrears of interest, Hamilton reasoned on different princples than had others before him. Since the capital of the debt had no maturity date but merely bore 6 percent interest and was redeemable at the pleasure of the government, he pointed out, certificates of that debt could properly be regarded as annuities. In other words, creditors had no right to demand the principal, and Hamilton proposed to keep things that way. Accrued interest, however, stood on a different footing: that was due and payable. Since the United States was incapable of paying, it was obliged to offer an equivalent, "and what other fair equivalent can be imagined for the detention of money, but a reasonable interest?" The only just standard of that interest was "the market rate, or the rate which the government pays in ordinary cases." Ergo, indents for arrears of interest must be funded on the same basis as the principal. Hamilton thus split the difference between partial repudiationists, who held that back interest should either be paid with no interest or funded at a reduced rate of interest, and strict advocates of creditors' rights, who could reasonably argue that back interest was entitled to compound interest since the time it fell due.[9]

Having made clear his value premises, his objectives, and his governing principles, Hamilton now laid out the pertinent facts. They were embarrassing. As indicated, the foreign debt including arrears was $11.7 million, the domestic debt including arrears $40.4 million, the state debts an estimated $25 million. In addition, Hamilton allowed $2 million for the "unliquidated" debt, mainly old Continental paper money. Leaving the state debts out of the equation for the moment, he reckoned that the annual interest on the national debt was $4,587,444. To that it was necessary to add the operating budget, for which Hamilton allowed $600,000 a year. In sum, if the national debts were funded at the interest rates they were currently bearing, expenditures would vastly exceed revenues.[10]

Now Hamilton had to do some equivocating, for his analysis so far had shown that public obligations must be met but could not be. He indulged in what seemed to be rationalization but was in fact an argument addressed to public creditors, and principally to foreign investors in the American domestic debt. He showed that interest rates could be expected to fall in the next few years to 5 percent and then to 4, at which time the government would be able to retire its 6 percent annuities by borrowing anew at the lower rate. That was of particular concern to Dutch investors, for the Dutch preferred to make permanent investments in interest-bearing annuities, and it was an inconvenience for them to have their principals redeemed. When the principal was redeemed, they simply reloaned their money at whatever interest it would now command—which meant that it would be they who would lend the lower-interest money to the United States for the later refinancing. Thus, in effect, the United States had the ethical and legal right to make mandatory reductions in the interest rates it paid, any time the market rate declined. On that ground, Hamilton proposed to cut the interest rate immediately to 4 percent, but as part of the package to offer creditors their choice of several kinds of compensations for the losses they would suffer in the interim before the market rate actually declined.[11]

Specifically, he proposed that the United States open subscriptions for a new loan in the amount of the entire domestic debt, that of the states included, the subscriptions being payable in old evidences of debt. The new loan would bear interest at an average rate of 4 percent instead of the present 6, but creditors would be given their choice of six ways of subscribing, each of the ways containing different forms of compensation for the reduction in interest. Three features of the options were especially important. First, Hamilton insisted that compliance be voluntary, though he held over the creditors a club of sorts: creditors would be allowed to insist upon the 6 percent interest to which they were entitled under their existing contracts, but those who chose to do so would have a lower priority upon the available public funds and would be dependent upon the willingness of Congress to make annual appropriations. Second, certain of the options were carefully designed as a hedge for those speculators who were bulls in regard to lands but bears in regard to securities, for they offered cheap lands as the compensation for the reduction of interest. Third, creditors had the option of taking part

[*169*]

of their new certificates in 6 percent bonds whose principal could be redeemed only at the rate of 1 percent of the original sum in any year. Since the market value of the bonds would appreciate when interest rates fell, this would afford creditors a considerable compensation.[12]

Before going on, Hamilton paused briefly to deal with a pair of loose ends. As to the foreign debt, he proposed that interest be provided for, but not principal; though the foreign debt, unlike the domestic debt, fell due and payable on specified maturity dates, Hamilton believed that maturing principal could readily be managed by floating new loans as the old ones came due. As to the state debts, they would be assumed now but interest would be allowed to accumulate on them for one more year, as additions to the principal, before revenues were provided for servicing them. The formal reason for the delay was to ascertain whether the state creditors would be willing to have their securities assumed; the real reason was to give the government time to raise taxes slowly and in steps rather than all at once.[13]

Having thus proposed to cut expenses by refinancing at lower interest rates, Hamilton now proposed to increase revenues by raising taxes. He suggested that the import duties on coffee and tea be increased, that imported alcoholic beverages be subjected to much higher duties on a scale determined by the proof or percentage of alcohol, and that an excise be laid on domestically distilled spirits. In making these proposals he indulged himself in a bit of moralizing against strong drink, which Americans consumed in prodigious quantities and which Hamilton, in keeping with his general view of American society, regarded as "a source of national extravagance and improverishment." Indeed, in the very title of the proposed legislation he declared that the purpose was as much "to discourage the excessive use of those Spirits, and promote Agriculture, as to provide for the support of the Public Credit." More to the immediate point, he estimated that these taxes would net an additional $1.7 million in revenues, bringing the total up to the amount necessary given the reduced interest on the public debts.[14]

Finally, as the touch that would make the whole system work, Hamilton proposed the creation of a "sinking fund." In this fund would be placed the surplus revenues of the post office, estimated at $100,000 a year, up to a total of $1 million. In addition, the fund would be endowed with about $5 million of the proceeds from a $12-million cash loan Hamilton proposed to float in Europe, the residue being used to refinance portions of the foreign debt at a reduced interest rate. The sinking fund would be managed by a committee made up of the secretary of the treasury, the vice-president, the speaker of the house, the chief justice, and the attorney general. It would perform its functions through a national bank, for which Hamilton indicated he would submit a plan in the near future.

The purpose of the sinking fund was not to retire the debt—the purpose of its counterpart in the British system—but rather to create the appearance that the debt was being retired. It would do this by purchasing public securities in the open market as long as they continued to circulate below their par value. Such purchases would in fact retire a portion of the debt cheaply, which Hamilton regarded as legitimate if done after the debts had been funded. But the more important purpose of the sinking fund would be what, in the twentieth century, would be known as "pegging the market" or "open market operations," designed to drive the market price of securities to par and maintain it at that level. With securities stabilized at par, speculation would be ended, public credit would be established, and the public debt would be monetized.[15]

Controversy attended the proposals from the beginning. Hamilton notified the House on January 9, 1790—two days before his thirty-third birthday—that he was prepared to report on his assigned task. A dispute immediately arose as to whether he should do so in person or in writing. Boudinot and others of Hamilton's friends advocated a personal report on the ground that Hamilton should be present to explain any points that were unclear, but archrepublicans shrilly insisted that a personal appearance would be an intrusion of the executive branch into the legislature, and they carried the point. Accordingly, the report was sent in writing and read to the House on January 14. The immediate reaction was one of utter confusion. The body of the report, running something over 20,000 words, could be read aloud in less than two hours, and its general outlines could be followed by ear, but to it were added eleven appendices consisting mainly of numbers and an itemized draft of the proposed tax revision, which was as long as the report itself. What was more, the reading was interrupted by a break for another matter of business. A long silence followed the reading, after which someone had the wits to move that the report be printed. It was duly published late in January, and soon thereafter it was printed or summarized in newspapers in all parts of the country.[16]

Reaction ranged from mixed feelings to outright disappointment. Though all conceded that the report was brilliant, many thought it went too far or not far enough in one direction or another. Owners of continental securities were less than elated by the prospect of having their interest reduced by a third—for, since no provision was proposed for repaying the principal, it could be and was argued that that amounted to repudiating a third of the debt. Moreover, many believed that burdening the national government with the state debts would make it impossible to service any of the debts on a regular and adequate basis. In Virginia, which had established its own sinking fund for buying up continental military certificates, the governor responded to Hamilton's report by dropping the market price from forty cents to thirty-three cents on the dollar; and many army veterans who had held on to their certificates for years, and even purchased others, now despaired of obtaining full recompense from the national government and decided to sell to the state at the reduced price. In New England the great merchant-speculators threatened to join forces with anti-Federalists to defeat assumption and thus make it more likely that the national government would redeem their continental paper at par. In Philadelphia, creditors who held about one-seventh of all the outstanding loan office certificates vowed not to subscribe their paper at the reduced rates.[17]

Nor were the bears happy. Those who were bearish by virtue of land speculations might have their losses minimized if Hamilton's proposals were enacted, but those who hoped to buy low in America and sell dear in Holland could visualize their prospects for profits vanishing immediately if Congress acted with anything resembling dispatch. They were in the most exasperating situation a gambler encounters. American securities in Holland had actually reached par, thanks to the diligent promotions of Stadnitski and of Willinks, Van Staphorsts, and Hubbard, though they could still be bought in the United States for prices ranging from twenty cents to fifty cents on the dollar. That made Hamilton's task easier, but to the speculators it was agonizing. Surrounded by a sea of fantastic opportunities, in a market almost certain to rise spectacularly, they lacked the money necessary for reversing their positions and capitalizing directly on the rise. Ironically, the boom in American commodities, engendered by crop failures in Europe, had diverted almost the whole of the American money supply away from speculation into legitimate avenues of commerce. Exports of flour from Philadelphia had jumped from 220,000 barrels in 1788 to 369,000 barrels in 1789, while prices were rising from $3 to $4.40 per hundredweight; and because bills on Europe were at a discount, foreign buying of securities slowed, and security prices fell. The money squeeze would be relieved with the spring importing season, when cash profits from the flour trade began to come in, and by May or June specie would be plentiful and credit easy. But that was months away, and the time to buy was now.[18]

Among the general public, opinion was divided, but a writer in the New York *Daily Gazette* was probably accurate when he asserted that, judging by the letters written to and published in newspapers, those objecting to all or parts of the report were considerably more numerous than those who approved it without reservation. Hamilton's rejection of discrimination proved to be especially unpopular. A group calling themselves "sundry officers of the late federal army" presented a petition to the House, declaring that the certificates they had received for pay had been depreciated at the time of issue and demanding full recompense now. Others took up the cry, though apparently much of the demand for "jusice" to original holders stemmed from anti-Federalists seeking to thwart the whole funding program beause of its nationalistic implications.[19]

In Congress there were two sets of ready-made enemies of Hamilton's proposals. One can be loosely described as the frontier faction, consisting of representatives from Georgia, the back country of South Carolina and Pennsylvania, and northern New Hampshire. In the Senate this group's main spokesman was William Maclay of Pennsylvania, a puritanical Scots Presbyterian uneasy with the notion that someone else might be making money or having a good time, a man whose principal pleasure in life came from sniping at persons wiser or more cultured or richer than himself. In the House, one member of the group was General Thomas Sumter of South Carolina, an anti-Federalist whose intense hatred of the nationalistic establishment derived from having been passed over for promotion during the war, despite a good combat record, solely because he had the unfortunate habit of plundering enemies and patriots with equal gusto. Others, such as Samuel Livermore of New Hampshire and Thomas Scott and Thomas Hartley of Pennsylvania, opposed Hamilton's system mainly because they could see nothing in it for their constituents except higher taxes. The most vocal leader of the group was a great bull of a man, James Jackson of Georgia, a fierce, uncouth rustic who once silenced unruly members of the gallery by pointing a brace of pistols in their direction and ordering them to begone lest he shoot them dead—"dead, Sirs, dead." Jackson did not orate, he bellowed and roared; on one occasion the Senate was forced to close its windows to shut out the sound of his voice booming in from the House chambers. Despite his rudeness of manner, however, Jackson was a formidable adversary, for he was fearless, uncompromising, and surprisingly learned.[20]

These frontier politicians had one thing in common besides their opposition to Hamilton's report, especially the provision for assuming the state debts: nearly all were engaged in trying to make a fortune through the purchase of state-owned lands with depreciated public securities, as were most of the representatives soon to arrive from North Carolina (which had only recently ratified the Constitution). Some of them, for example Hartley, Scott, Daniel Heister, and Maclay of Pennsylvania, were small fry accustomed to buying only a few hundred acres at a time. Others, including Representatives Timothy Bloodworth and Hugh Williamson of North Carolina and Jeremiah Van Rensselaer of upstate New York, operated at the level of 4,000 to 20,000 acres. Still others, including Jackson, Sumter, George Mathews of Georgia, and John Sevier of North Carolina in the House and Senators James Gunn of Georgia and Benjamin Hawkins and Samuel Johnston of North Carolina, were directly or through syndicates engaged in speculations involving hundreds of thousands of acres. Assumption of state debts, if it accomplished Hamilton's objective of raising the market price of those securities to par, would spoil these speculators' lucrative game.[21]

The other set of enemies was a faction of special-interest politicians based in the tobacco-growing regions of Maryland, Virginia, and tidewater North Carolina and led by James Madison. Most of these men recognized the need for establishing public credit. Most even believed that Hamilton's report offered an efficacious means to that end. Nonetheless, they were prepared to drive a hard bargain, to demand particular advantages for their region as the price for allowing the funding system to become law. Putting their special interests ahead of national interest was habitual with planters in the tobacco belt, and just now they had compelling reasons for doing so: early frosts had wiped out half the tobacco crop, and the bizarre money market prevented tobacco prices from rising enough to make up more than a fraction of the losses. In those circumstances, they were in no mood to pay taxes for the support of a public debt of which they held but little. They were even less eager to have the settlement of state accounts divorced from politics, for that would cost them millions. Congressmen from the area who valued their political lives were obliged to take these considerations into account. Madison himself, having learned between sessions of the angry mood of his constituents, came to the second session of the First Congress prepared to temper his nationalism with militant concern for the interests and prejudices of his constituency.[22]

And as usual with Madison there was more to his position than was readily apparent. After consultation with Washington, Madison had joined Hamilton's friend Henry Lee in a grandiose speculation to acquire lands on the falls of the Potomac and erect a manufacturing and commercial city there. If, as the speculators planned, the permanent national capital should be located on the Potomac, their £4,000 investment would be multiplied many times over, and Madison would obtain his long-cherished financial independence from his father and brother. On the face of things none of this had anything to do with Hamilton's fiscal proposals; but Madison was prepared to make the connection an intimate one. Madison—who was soon to surprise Hamilton not only with his opposition but also with his adroitness as a political manipulator—had long since determined to engineer some kind of political trade that would ensure the success of the Potomac speculation. Hamilton's funding and assumption plan was admirably suited for that purpose. The tactic Madison and his allies employed, as it gradually emerged, was to seek out the most vulnerable part of Hamilton's proposals, block the passage of that part, and hold the line there until they could negotiate a bargain favorable to their region and to themselves.[23]

But greed on the one side was met by greed on the other. Jackson,

Maclay, and a few more of their ilk charged that Hamilton's supporters in Congress stood to profit mightily from their labors (a charge that would later be blown up to an accusation that the whole business was a plot to enrich speculators); and though innuendoes were being shuffled about more assiduously than public securities were, it is true that several of Hamilton's staunchest supporters in both houses were security holders. The largest, in the House, were the erstwhile anti-Federalist Elbridge Gerry of Massachusetts (who held $32,900, face value, in continental securities and $16,180 in state securities), Roger Sherman ($7,700) and Jeremiah Wadsworth ($21,500) of Connecticut, Elias Boudinot of New Jersey ($49,500), George Clymer of Pennsylvania ($12,500), and William L. Smith of South Carolina ($11,900). Moreover, of the representatives who supported assumption, eight held more than $1,000 in state securities (the foregoing plus Theodorick Bland of Virginia and Aedanus Burke of South Carolina). Yet the two most ardent champions of assumption, Fisher Ames and Theodore Sedgwick of Massachusetts, held no state securities, and five *opponents* of assumption held more than $1,000 apiece in state securities (Nicholas Gilman of New Hampshire, George Gale of Maryland, Alexander White of Virginia, Thomas Sumter of South Carolina, and Abraham Baldwin of Georgia).[24]

In the Senate, seven members who championed Hamilton's proposals held large amounts of securities, ranging from $6,000 to more than $60,000: John Langdon of New Hampshire, Caleb Strong of Massachusetts, Oliver Ellsworth of Connecticut, Rufus King and Philip Schuyler of New York, Robert Morris of Pennsylvania, and Ralph Izard of South Carolina. Schuyler, however, would certainly have supported Hamilton whether he had anything invested in securities or not; and Morris, as a bear by virtue of enormous land speculations, worked against his personal interests in fighting to establish public credit, as he had been doing for some years. Aligned against Hamilton's proposals in the Senate were at least four security holders who had larger interests in land speculations: Maclay of Pennsylvania, Richard Henry Lee of Virginia, Samuel Johnston of North Carolina, and William Few of Georgia.[25]

In sum, there is little doubt that a number of congressmen who supported Hamilton were motivated at least in part by personal interests—probably eight or nine of the sixty-five representatives and four of the twenty-six senators. But the others took their stands on the basis of a mixture of motives that included concern for the interests of their constituents, ideology, regard for public honor, nationalism, and intelligence.

After a few days of initial skirmishing, debate on Hamilton's report began in earnest on Monday, February 8. It had scarcely started to warm up, however, before a disruptive unrelated issue arose. Fitzsimons of Pennsylvania and John Lawrence of New York presented petitions from the Quakers of their states, asking for the abolition of the slave trade, and then came a petition from the Pennsylvania Abolition Society, of which Benjamin Franklin was president, asking for an outright end to slavery. Congress was constitutionally prohibited from acting on such petitions, but they stirred anger and fear among southerners, and the raising of sectional animosity had an unfavorable bearing upon Hamilton's proposals. On the one side Fitzsimons and Lawrence were among the strongest advocates of funding, and Hamilton's own abolitionist sentiments were well known; on the other, opposition to Hamilton's measures was mainly from southern slaveholders, the only southerners who unreservedly supported him in the House being Smith and Burke of South Carolina and Bland of Virginia. Presenting petitions against slavery was scarcely the way to kindle southerners' lukewarm nationalism.[26]

That diversion waved aside but not forgotten, debate on the report resumed. For fully two weeks, the focus was upon proposals for discrimination, especially upon a shrewd motion Madison offered. He moved that present holders of securities be given new certificates equal to the highest price their old ones had reached in the market, and that original holders be given new certificates for the balance. There was a certain appeal in such an approach, but the administrative obstacles would range from formidable to insurmountable; and to adopt the proposal would have been to compromise the negotiability of securities and thus to prevent their monetization. Quite as importantly, it would also have destroyed foreign credit, since so many Dutch investors had bought securities at depreciated prices, and without the Dutch all hope of establishing public credit would have been forlorn. Supporters of the motion spoke feelingly, or mock feelingly, in behalf of widows and orphans and crippled veterans, as if all original holders who had alienated their securities were of those categories. Opponents blasted the proposal with endless variations of the arguments Hamilton had supplied in his report. On February 22 it was put to a vote, and Madison was roundly defeated, 36 to 13.[27]

Madison's motion was inspired by several considerations. He may have thought it just, despite having earlier thought otherwise; he told Jefferson that the only objections made to it were grounded in practicability, not equity. The claim was less than candid, for the proposal was patently unconstitutional, and at least two representatives pointed that out. The Constitution specified that "All Debts and Engagements entered into, before the Adoption of this Constitution, shall be as valid against the United States under this Constitution, as under the Confederation," and the congressional pledge of April 26, 1783, was clearly comprehended by that clause. In any event, Madison's primary motives were tactical: he was sounding out the resistance in the House and he was stalling for time, awaiting the belated arrival of additional supporters, the five representatives from North Carolina.[28]

Madison's delaying tactics were a godsend to speculators, and they were prompt to recognize his doubtless unintended benefactions. "Mr. Maddison has contributed not a little by his proposition," William Constable wrote. "For my own part I am not afraid but all will go right," if only the stalling would continue until the money market eased, after which he would be able to "purchase deeply." Since the debates actually did drag on until the end of July, and since, in the meantime, continental securities fell to less than fifty cents on the dollar and state securities to a range between one cent and twenty cents, many speculators were in due course enabled to reverse positions on a grand scale. Eleven New Yorkers acquired $617,185 in North Carolina securities, face value, for a cash outlay of perhaps $80,000. Eight New Yorkers acquired $606,643 in South Carolina securities, face value, for a cash outlay of perhaps $120,000. Twenty-two outsiders acquired $1,070,077 in Virginia securities, face value, for comparable outlays of cash. Before he was through Madison would put more profits into the hands of speculators than Hamilton could have done by inviting them to help themselves to the Treasury.[29]

Unburdened by concern for any special interests except his own and, as he perceived them, those of his Virginia constituents, Madison pushed on, and soon it became evident what he was seeking. Beneath the façade of pleas for suffering original holders and denunciations of speculators, beneath "the Arguments our grave politicians bring forward," as Richard Peters put it, the outcome of the debate would "be determined by local Interests which will not suffer Intrigue and Management to grow rusty for Want of Use." What Madison and his southern faction wanted, in a word, was More. To get more they would have to bargain, and in order to bargain they had first to obtain something to bargain with. That was the aim of their next series of maneuvers.[30]

They focused their efforts upon the provisions for settlement of state accounts and the assumption of state debts. They did so partly because there was room for trading between those two points, but mainly because interested support for Hamilton's recommendations was weakest there. Only three states with nineteen votes among them (Massachusetts, Connecticut, and South Carolina) were vitally interested in assumption, and only three representatives from other states (King, Bland, and Gale) personally held large amounts of state securities; and Gale perversely opposed assumption. The remaining ten or so votes necessary for approval of assumption had to come from disinterested, hard-core champions of public credit—some of whom had reservations about the wisdom of assumption, anyway. And against them, of course, were the dozen or so members of the House who, as speculators in state-owned lands, had an active interest in defeating assumption.[31]

The Madison faction's campaign was well orchestrated. On February 24 Madison moved that assumption should be coupled with "effectual provision" for settling state accounts—after Hamilton had carefully divorced the two. Then White of Virginia offered an amendment, expressing an extreme version of Madison's proposal: he moved that assumption be restricted to the amounts found to be due to creditors after the auditing of state accounts was completed. That horrified the Yankees and South Carolinians, for it would delay relief to their taxpayers and public creditors for as long as two or three years. White's motion was rejected 32 to 18, but the scare it engendered made Madison's motion seem moderate by comparison, and after a long debate Madison's proposal to connect assumption

[*179*]

with settlement of state accounts was adopted. The victory for Virginia was a hollow one, however, since the board responsible for auditing the accounts was just then preparing to issue a report containing a wholesale rejection of the claims of southern states; so Madison pressed on with another maneuver. Though he had been arguing so far that assumption prior to the settlement of state accounts would burden the nation with an unnecessarily large and insupportable load of debts, he now moved to increase the load much further, proposing that Hamilton's recommendations be broadened to include the debts of states that had already been retired. This motion was defeated, but only by a 28 to 22 vote; and, wearying of the seemingly endless wrangling, some strong supporters of funding now began to talk of abandoning assumption in order to preserve the rest of the system. [32]

And their patience was only beginning to be tired. On the same day that Madison's extravagant motion was being rejected (March 2), White moved to require of the secretary a report on what taxes could be raised to support the state debts if they were assumed. The motion carried by the narrowest of margins. Since Hamilton had pointedly avoided this question in his report, many thought the order would either catch him unprepared or uncover a design to impose highly objectionable taxes. But Hamilton, who had been following the debates closely (often as a gallery spectator), was ready. Within two days he presented the House with a crisp report suggesting ten painless and easily collected sources of taxation, which together would yield more than $1 million annually and thus service the state debts comfortably. [33]

That dispelled the fog the Virginians had created, and during the next week the House broke through to end its first round of debate on the report. On Tuesday, March 9, it approved assumption as amended by Madison's motion connecting state accounts with assumption. During the next three days Hamilton's proposed options for creditors were discussed and simplified. Specifically, the refinancing options of creditors were cut to two. They would receive two-thirds of the amounts of their old securities in new certificates bearing 6 percent interest; for the remainder, they could either receive public lands at twenty cents an acre or receive new certificates on which 6 percent would be payable after a term of years. Otherwise, by March 13 the entire report had been approved, by a margin of four or five votes on each point. [34]

The agreement, however, was only in principle, expressed in committee of the whole. Legislation had yet to be drafted and approved, and that would take time. In the interim, another rancorous debate on slavery erupted and lasted more than a week. Meanwhile, two of the five representatives from North Carolina showed up, determined to defeat both funding and assumption. As a result, when the resolutions of the committee of the whole came up for discussion on March 29, Madison and his allies were able to obtain a two-vote majority for recommitment.[35]

The next round of debates elicited no new arguments but a great deal of political maneuvering, each side hesitating to hazard a final vote on assumption. One more North Carolinian arrived; a Pennsylvania supporter of assumption went home temporarily. On April 12 Madison's forces called for the question, and assumption was rejected 31 votes to 29. During the next six weeks, as the funding bill was being hammered into shape, repeated efforts were made to reinsert assumption into the package, but to no avail. Assumptionists gained the votes of two New Jersey representatives by privately agreeing to amendments in the funding plan beneficial to their state, but lost ground by the arrival of another North Carolinian; some representatives left, others returned, one died; assumptionists fell as far behind as five votes and drew as close as a tie, but never obtained a majority. On June 2, when the House finally passed the funding bill and sent it to the Senate, the measure was essentially the same as it had been when passed in March, except that assumption of state debts was not in it. Significantly, killing assumption also threw the provision for settling state accounts back into limbo, since the passage of Madison's amendment had coupled the two subjects.[36]

The stage was now set for one of the most complex, fascinating, and controversial political deals in American history. Ironically, Hamilton and Madison, the central figures in the drama so far, were able to play only supporting roles when the plot thickened. Hamilton, for his part, was eager to strike a bargain with anybody who could deliver votes for assumption, but he had nothing to offer in a trade. Nor could he control any votes: he had neither followers nor a party, only supporters for a particular measure—which is quite a different matter. He did have one important asset: Jackson, Maclay, and others of his more vociferous enemies were convinced that he controlled a solid phalanx of congressional votes, and that supposition, together with Hamilton's equally unfounded reputation as a wily, devious manipulator, was advantageous; for in politics as in credit appearances are no less important than realities and can in fact sometimes create realities.[37]

Madison's problem was different. He did have followers and he did have something to trade—life or death power over assumption. But not everything he wanted in exchange could be overtly delivered. He wanted Virginia (and if possible Maryland and North Carolina) to have a bigger slice of the pie through an increased share of the debts assumed, an alteration in the system for settling state accounts, or both. Given the political and ideological values of the time, it was not feasible to switch sides on assumption, after such a vigorous fight against it, in exchange for more money for one's own state. Such a "corrupt bargain" would not have been tolerated; other representatives, especially New Englanders, might well have reacted by voting against assumption. On the other hand, trading votes for votes and trading bills for unrelated bills was generally acceptable among all but the most puritanical of republicans. Already in April Representative Richard Bland Lee of Virginia had dropped a broad hint that just such a trade was in the offing: Virginia would trade votes for assumption in exchange for northern votes in favor of locating the permanent national capital on the Potomac. But then the Virginians employed an adroit maneuver. On May 31, only two days before the funding bill passed the House with assumption deleted, the question of the location of the capital was under discussion. On that day, advocates of the Potomac had more than enough votes to carry the issue, but failed to do so because two Marylanders and two Virginians, *Madison and Lee,* voted instead for location on the Delaware. Since the Virginians were deeply interested in locating the capital on the Potomac, they obviously had an ulterior motive in wanting the Potomac to be defeated for the time being. That motive, however, was not yet evident; for the moment all Madison and his allies could do was wait.[38]

The hands of the principal players being temporarily tied, others attempted to work out private arrangements on their own. William L. Smith of South Carolina was the most diligent and most nearly effective of these maneuverers. It was he who won the two New Jersey representatives over to assumption, and he came close to winning three upstate New York anti-Federalists as well, or at least so he thought. They were eager that the capital remain in New York, and Smith got their conditional promise to vote for assumption if he could deliver enough New England votes for New York as the capital. But neither Smith nor anybody else could deliver New England. Fisher Ames, who with Theodore Sedgwick was the closest approximation of a "Hamiltonian" among the Massachusetts representatives, declared that he was willing to have the capital located on the wild frontier if that were ncecessary to carry assumption; but in fact the New Englanders in the House perversely and unrealistically insisted that each of the questions be decided on its own merits—that is, they refused to trade.[39]

Two powerful new characters now emerged from the wings. One was Robert Morris, intimate and peer of the president, a man with nearly as many friends and enemies as Hamilton would soon acquire. Unlike Hamilton, but like Washington, Morris was of a class and a generation that made no distinctions between private and public interest. He was like Washington in other respects as well: he was caught up in his own image as a Great Man; he was acting out a part that fate and the audience had written for him; he was embarked upon a venture from which there was no return. Unlike Washington, he would not be able to follow his destiny with fame and fortune intact. But now, in the spring of 1790, he was by dint of both reputation and ability the most powerful man in the Senate; and he was a tower of strength, of character, and of acumen, all committed in behalf of the nation.

Morris agreed with most parts of Hamilton's proposed funding and assumption scheme, though in one detail he differed sharply. But he also, in keeping with the ethic that blended private and public values, had more personal objectives in mind. At fifty-six, having served the nation well, he believed it was time for the nation to consider his convenience by establishing its temporary seat within walking distance of his home in Philadelphia, and its permanent seat on lands he owned near the falls of the Delaware. Washington, on similar grounds, entertained similar sentiments about the Potomac.[40]

Enter Thomas Jefferson, secretary of state. Contrary to his later claim, Jefferson was actively interested in all the points at issue. He desired the Potomac capital as ardently as Washington and Madison did, though unlike them he had no personal economic stake in the location. He was concerned that Virginia improve its position in the funding of the war debts, but equally concerned that Hamilton's overall plan be enacted without further delay. He told his son-in-law and Francis Eppes that if Congress would "separate without funding there is an end of the government"; he told James Monroe that compromises must be effected "for the sake of union, and to save us from the greatest of all calamities, the total extinction of our credit in Europe." There was another consideration as well, vitally affecting the affairs of the State Department. War was impending in Europe, and Jefferson was convinced that the United States could remain neutral only if it remained strong. Strength and credit were inseparable, and thus "our business is to have great credit and to use it little. Whatever enables us to go to war, secures our peace."[41]

Jefferson was incapacitated by one of his periodic migraine attacks through most of May, but when the headache began to clear in June he initiated the negotiations that would lead to the assumption of the state debts. Quite possibily he was acting informally on behalf of the president; Senator Maclay, for one, thought that was obvious. In any event, on June 15 he proposed to Robert Morris a compromise regarding the capital: after the present session of Congress, it should be moved from New York to Philadelphia, where it should remain for fifteen years before being moved permanently to the Potomac. This first compromise being agreed to (though the length of the stay in Philadelphia was subsequently cut to ten years), it was now possible to work out a second one by dealing with Hamilton.[42]

On or about June 20, Jefferson invited Hamilton and Madison to a dinner at which the Virginians offered Hamilton some proposals. For their part, they would obtain the three or four votes necessary to pass assumption in the House (Morris had already arranged two vote changes that would assure passage in the Senate). In exchange, Hamilton must do two things. First, he must help them fulfill the terms of their compromise deal with Morris. Morris did not have quite enough votes in the Senate to remove the temporary capital from New York, and Hamilton must find those votes. This he agreed to do by persuading the only two amenable New Englanders, Massachusetts Senators Tristram Dalton and Caleb Strong, that the only way to obtain assumption was for them to reverse their positions regarding the site of the capital. Second, Hamilton must help the Virginians obtain a better financial deal for their state. He must support Madison's attempt to increase the commissioners of state accounts from three members to five, the understanding being that the additional commissioners would be more receptive to allowing the claims of Virginians; that failing, he must try to induce the members of the existing board to relax their accounting methods, or to look the other way while someone else induced them. As a hedge against the failure of both these efforts, Hamilton must arrange to have the sum allotted Virginia under the assumption increased enough so that, when state accounts were settled, Virginia would have received more than she would be required to pay. Hamilton agreed, and the bargain was struck.[43]

The Virginians had been extremely artful. They used the first trade, which would give them the permanent capital, to provide a cloak of respectability for the second, which would be worth a net to their state of more than $13 million in the final settlement. Thereby, because only one trade rather than two appeared to have been made, and because the trading appeared to have involved not money but only assumption in exchange for the capital, they avoided giving the impression of having made a corrupt bargain.[44]

One more compromise needed to be worked out. Morris had a majority for assumption in the Senate, but the assumptionists were divided over the rate of interest to be paid on the entire debt. Most of them, including Morris himself, Rufus King, and Philip Schuyler, insisted on 6 percent; a minority, led by Oliver Ellsworth and Caleb Strong, were equally adamant in insisting upon 4 percent. The first position seemed impractical, the second unjust. Hamilton met with senators in both camps to try to find a way out of the dilemma, and a complex formula was worked out. The new certificates would be of three kinds, some bearing 6 percent, some bearing no interest for ten years and 6 percent thereafter, and some bearing 3 percent. Only one-fiftieth of the original principal of the 6 percents could be redeemed in a single year. Continental creditors would receive, for the principal of old securities subscribed to the new loan, two-thirds in 6 percents and one-third in deferred sixes; for indents or other evidence of arrears of interest they would receive 3 percents. As to state debts, no distinction would be made between principal and accrued interest; creditors would receive four-ninths of the total subscribed in 6 percents, two-ninths in deferred sixes, and three-ninths in 3 percents. That constituted an average interest rate of about 4 percent. If, however, the government's credit so improved in a decade that it could then command money on the open market at 4 percent, the market value of the semi-irredeemable bonds would increase accordingly. As a result, the appreciation and interest combined would work out, under the compromise formula, so that creditors would have received the equivalent of almost exactly 6 percent for the entire period.[45]

All that remained was for the parties to the agreements to fulfill their promises, and they did so. On June 29 Dalton and Strong changed positions and killed a last-ditch effort to keep the temporary capital in New York (their votes were unnecessary to placing the permanent capital on the Potomac). Two days later the Senate passed the bill putting the temporary capital in Philadelphia and the permanent one on the Potomac. On July 9 the House approved the Senate bill, the swing votes being those of Madison, Lee, Isaac Coles of Virginia, and Michael Jenifer Stone of Maryland.[46]

The path toward enacting the financial agreements was also smooth at first. The Senate again took the lead, amending the House's funding bill by reinserting a provision for assumption and by changing the interest rates in accordance with the complex formula Hamilton and Morris had agreed upon. That was on July 14; the House took up the Senate's amendments on July 22. Two days later came the crucial vote on assumption. Various shifts had left assumptionists outnumbered 29 to 33, but on July 24, four representatives who had been persuaded by Jefferson and Madison to change their votes—Daniel Carroll and George Gale of Maryland and Lee and White of Virginia—crossed over as agreed, and the measure carried. (The swing votes were scarcely disinterested. Three of them represented districts on the Potomac—Carroll, in fact, owned a large plantation in what became the District of Columbia—and the fourth, White, held nearly $2,000 in state securities. Gale also held more than $4,000 of state securities. Over in the Senate, Maclay commented sourly but revealingly, "we have ruined our land-office by the assumption. The state certificates were the materials to buy the lands with.") By July 29 all differences between the House and Senate bills had been ironed out, and the final bill was passed.[47]

But a snag developed in delivering the financial considerations Virginia had sought and Hamilton had promised. The increased allowance for assumed debt got through without difficulty, Virginia obtaining an additional $500,000. The bill for the settlement of state accounts, however, ran into trouble. Thanks largely to the efforts of William L. Smith, a bill providing for an extension of the time for the presentation of claims had been approved, and Madison worked into it a provision for increasing the number of commissioners, but the Senate refused to concur with the addition. A supplementary bill increasing the number of commissioners met the same fate. Hamilton was thus forced to resort to nonlegislative means to honor his end of the bargain. With his tacit approval, the commissioners relaxed the rules in regard to Virginia, with the result that—though Smith said "every honest man would cut off at least half their claim"—the Virginians' allowed claims were doubled from $13 to $26 million. That brought the state within $100,000 of its apportioned share of the final settlement, and that small sum was more than compensated for by Virginia's increased allowance under the revised provision for assumption.[48]

For separate statutes had been passed to give life to the proposals in Hamilton's report. One was the act providing for the settlement of state accounts. Another was the funding and assumption act, which provided for refinancing and servicing the domestic debts and also authorized a new European loan for $12 million to consolidate and refinance the foreign debt. A third established the sinking fund and authorized a separate $2 million European loan to endow the fund; the Sinking Fund Committee was constituted as Hamilton had proposed except that, as would prove to be significant, the secretary of state instead of the speaker of the house was to be a member. The fourth act increased and revised import duties along the lines Hamilton had proposed.[49]

The laws as passed were close enough to Hamilton's original proposals to be acceptable to him, though the variations from his recommendations necessitated some adjustments in his plans. He had his way in regard to discrimination, funding, assumption, and the sinking fund, all essential features. In two important particulars, however, he did not have his way. The proposed excise tax was not enacted, which meant that battle would have to be fought in the next session of Congress. The other disappointment was more complex. The interest rate had been cut by a third, as Hamilton had proposed and as was essential to the success of the whole plan; but, by adopting the Hamilton-Morris interest-rate compromise instead of Hamilton's original recommendations for compensating creditors, Congress brought about certain inconveniences. Land speculators were deprived of the protection Hamilton had sought to give them, which would soon result in serious financial dislocations. And Hamilton's plans for monetizing the public debt would have to be altered, since it would scarcely be possible to support the 3 percent securities and the deferred sixes as firmly or at the same market prices as the 6 percents.

Its work temporarily done, Congress adjourned on August 12. Once again it gave Hamilton a difficult assignment: by a resolution adopted on August 9, the House instructed him to make a further report on the public credit, by which it was understood that he would draw up plans for further taxes and for a national bank. The new report was to be ready when Congress reconvened in December. The only other tasks Hamilton faced in the meantime were managing the Treasury, implementing the revised tariff, establishing a coast guard, and supervising a financial transaction involving twenty to forty thousand people and $60 million.

Before undertaking any of those duties, however, he took time to heed Necker's advice about publicity. He published an "Address to the Public Creditors," summarizing succinctly the measures Congress had passed, informing creditors of their rights, and—to the displeasure of speculators—urging holders not to sell their securities until the market price climbed to its "true value."[50]

❦ IX ❦

The Mint, the Excise, and the Bank

'Til jarring int'rests, of themselves create

Th'according music of a well-mixed State.

Hamilton saw things differently, and from more perspectives, than other men did. Objectively speaking, the public debt had been an enormous number of pieces of paper, representing pledges of various American governments to pay various amounts to the bearers, if and when government should so decide, and to pay a stipulated rate of interest in the meantime. Until 1790 each of the governments that coped with those pieces of paper regarded them negatively and directed its efforts toward retiring them in one way or another. As a consequence, the paper was a national burden, politically divisive and economically destructive. Viewing the problem differently, Hamilton brought about funding, assumption, and the sinking fund, which transformed the paper into a form of capital. Moreover, a huge amount of new capital was created into the bargain: the market value of the paper a few months before Hamilton took office had been less than $15 million; by the end of 1790 it was about $45 million. Thus $30 million in liquid capital had been manufactured, as it were, out of thin air. Indeed, the new capital was made of stuff even more ephemeral: all that happened was that the public, instilled with illusions and expectations, changed its opinion about the value of those pieces of paper.[1]

Accordingly, the praise being heaped upon Hamilton was premature, and he knew it. Three more steps were necessary (and now possible) before public credit could be put on an enduring basis: the establishment of a mint, a revision of the tax system, and the creation of a national bank. Properly rigged, each would support the others and the funding system as well, and the funding system in turn would support them all. Opinion would remain the heart and the life's blood of the whole, but opinion would now be institutionalized; and opinion, firmly institutionalized, becomes well-nigh unalterable.

In executing these new steps Hamilton was encumbered by less political opposition than before. His new proposals met with no such array of antagonistic personal and state interest groups as had resisted funding and assumption. The popularity of his earlier measures and the obvious merit of his additional recommendations also helped make the going easier. So, too, did the euphoria born of the nation's unprecedented prosperity. To a considerable extent the boom derived from continued crop failures and political turbulence in Europe, but Americans, as would ever be their wont, tended to attribute it to the doings of the administration. More measures on the same track were therefore welcome.[2]

There was, to be sure, some dissent. For instance, when the last session of the First Congress convened in December 1790, a wealthy and influential group of public creditors in Philadelphia greeted it with a petition objecting to the reduction of the interest rate and asking for full recompense. The House ignored the petition, but a minor fracas erupted in the Senate. Robert Morris, reconciled to but not happy with the reduction of interest, wanted at least to make an apologetic gesture to the creditors; Philip Schuyler urged a vigorous resolution denouncing the very idea of revising the funding system in any way. After some rancorous discussion the Senate dropped the matter. The petitioners, for their part, refused to subscribe their securities to the new loan.[3]

Much more foreboding was a political development in New York. Chancellor Robert R. Livingston, still smarting from being passed over for federal appointment in 1789—which he attributed to Hamilton and Jay—and unhappy as well with the tenor of Hamilton's financial program, joined forces with Governor George Clinton late in 1790. Together, and with manipulative assistance from the wily state attorney general, Aaron Burr, they induced the legislature to defeat Schuyler's bid to be reelected to succeed himself when his term expired on March 3, 1791. Instead they elected Burr to his

Senate seat. It was charged that Schuyler's conduct as a senator had "not been very honourable to the State," since he was regarded as being "led by the Treasury." As Troup informed Hamilton, the formation of a Clinton-Livingston-Burr coalition and the ouster of Schuyler meant that New York was "going headlong into the bitterest opposition" to the national government.[4]

Quite as ominous were developments in Virginia, or so Hamilton believed at first. In November 1790 the Virginia House of Delegates, under the sway of the great anti-Federalist orator Patrick Henry, adopted a pair of resolutions declaring assumption unconstitutional and objecting to part of the funding system as "dangerous to the rights and subversive of the interest of the people." Hamilton, thoroughly alarmed, declared that the resolutions were "the first symptom of a spirit which must either be killed or will kill the constitution of the United States."[5]

The resolutions, however, were apparently just a charade. In Jefferson's view, they were nothing more than an elaborate subterfuge on the part of Henry and his minions (whom Jefferson and Madison despised and whose political control of their state they bitterly resented). In 1789, said Jefferson, Henry and various cohorts had, through the Virginia Yazoo Company, contracted with the state of Georgia for the purchase of a huge tract of interior lands, the price being payable in several annual installments and in certificates of the Georgia debt at par. Assumption stimulated a rapid rise in the price of the debt and frustrated the Virginians' speculation; hence the resolution. That there was nothing to fear was soon demonstrated. The Henry group had accumulated sizable holdings of Georgia securities before the rise, and early in 1791, when the certificates approached par in the market, they decided to forfeit on their land purchase and sell their securities at a whopping cash profit. (Much later Jefferson charged that, as of that moment, Henry became a Hamiltonian.)[6]

Whatever the reason, Hamilton ceased to be concerned about the Henryites; and what was more, the Virginians who had caused him such anxiety over his funding and assumption plan now appeared receptive to his additional measures. Their earlier opposition, after all, had arisen mainly from legitimate concern for the interests of their state and had in the end occasioned no mischief. Now, neither Jefferson nor Madison voiced any disapproval when Hamilton presented his reports on the excise and the bank, and Jefferson was solicitously cooperative in helping Hamilton with the report on the mint, though he disagreed with some of the details. The Virginians remained studiously wrong-headed about wanting to declare commercial warfare against England, but they were cordial about it. Indeed, for more than a month after Hamilton's reports on the excise and the bank were published, Jefferson was openly professing affection for Hamilton. Those professions were given additional credence when the select American Philosophical Society, of which Jefferson was a vice-president and possibly the most influential member, voted on January 21, 1791, to elect Hamilton a member. A more sincere mark of affection and esteem could scarcely be imagined.[7]

Even so, Hamilton took no chances. This time he consulted in advance with staunch nationalists—certainly Morris and Fitzsimons of Pennsylvania and probably Ames and Sedgwick of Massachusetts, Lawrence and Benson of New York, Boudinot of New Jersey, and Smith of South Carolina—to orchestrate plans for steering his new proposals through Congress. As an additional precaution, he declined to make more than passing comments about the social implications of his overall plans or to dwell upon the fact that the mint, the excise, and the bank, like the funding and assumption plan, were only financial means to a larger, revolutionary social end. The new measures were, in their own right, valuable contributions to the political and economic well-being of the nation, and Hamilton preferred that they be adopted on those grounds.[8]

Hamilton's new proposals, like his funding plan, were submitted to the House in the form of reports, again made in response to specific resolutions of instruction. His report on taxation, which he styled "First Report on the Further Provision Necessary for Establishing Public Credit," was sent to the House on December 13, 1790; his "Second Report" on the bank was sent the next day. The Report on the Establishment of a Mint was sent six weeks later, on January 28, 1791. The bank was by far the most important of the three interrelated proposals, and the recommendations regarding taxes, in turn, were much more important than those for the mint.[9]

Hamilton's thinking in regard to a bank had changed in recent months. His original idea had been to monetize the public debt, in the doing of which a national bank would be indispensable. Pegging the market for securities would require moderate but regular purchases through the sinking fund, whereas the flow of revenues from import duties fluctuated seasonally. A reliable source of short-term loans would therefore be necessary. Since the existing commercial banks must expand or contract their loans in accordance with their own needs and the needs of the commodity market, they simply could not be counted upon; and besides, Hamilton had had enough experience with bankers to know it was hardly safe to leave public finance at their mercy. But all such thinking became obsolete when it was decided that the new certificates of public debt would bear three different rates of interest: they obviously could not be pegged at the same price, and thus the idea of transforming them directly into money was impractical. If suitably shrewd arrangements were made, however, the capital they formed could be used as a basis for money rather than as money itself. If that were to be done, it would be advantageous to discourage their rapid circulation so as to facilitate stabilization of their market values. Hamilton signaled this change in his thinking with a quiet but important administrative decision. Instead of having the new securities issued in convenient denominations—say, of one dollar, ten, and a hundred—he ordered that they be for the full sum subscribed by the public creditor. Thus, for example, the holder of $1,000 in old state securities would be issued a 6 percent bond of $444.45, a deferred 6 of $222.22, and a 3 percent certificate of $333.33. A man could scarcely be expected to walk into an apothecary's shop and tender a $444.45 certificate in payment for medicine. Under Hamilton's administrative ruling, he could sell part of his bond (or use it in making purchases), but doing so would entail a complex process of registering the transaction with the Treasury. In those circumstances the security holder would be disposed to retain his certificates and borrow such cash as he needed, using the certificates as the basis of his credit. Hamilton proposed to do much the same thing in establishing the national bank.[10]

Hamilton recommended that Congress grant a character to a corporation to be called the Bank of the United States. Its capitalization was to be $10 million, more than four times as much as that of the three existing banks combined and far more than the amount of all the gold and silver in the country. The United States government would subscribe for $2 million of the stock, payable in cash. It did not have that much cash, so instead it would borrow the amount from the bank itself, repaying the loan in ten equal annual installments. As to the remaining $8 million of stock, that would be offered for public subscription, the purchases being payable one-fourth in gold or silver and three-fourths in 6 percent securities of the federal government. Subscribers would make their payments in four equal installments spaced six months apart.[11]

The plan was almost poetic in its beauty and symmetry. Though at the outset the bank would have only $500,000 in hard money, not counting the deposits it attracted, it could safely issue notes and take on other obligations up to $10 million, as if it had that much in cash; and it was virtually certain to earn wholesome profits, for the interest on its loans, at 6 percent, would be augmented by the additional 6 percent it received on the government bonds that formed most of its capital. Subscribers would therefore rush to invest in the bank, and their avidity would send the government's 6 percent bonds soaring. Thus government bonds, supported in the first instance by the prospect of sinking fund purchases financed by loans from the bank, would as a result of that prospect be enabled to form the capital of the bank, which in turn would make the bonds even more valuable than expectations had already made them. In that manner the very creation of the bank would establish the public credit on an enduring basis—even if the bank should never make loans to the sinking fund that started it all. Hamilton had found banking's equivalent of the philosopher's store, whereby base elements are turned into gold.[12]

He had not found it unaided, for much of his plan was closely modeled after the Bank of England, sometimes nearly copying the English institution's charter verbatim. This was advantageous, since by using the symbols of fiscal orthodoxy, Hamilton lent an aura of legitimacy to his own measures. But there was a fundamental difference between Hamilton's plan and its English predecessor, perhaps deriving from Hamilton's study of Necker's experiences in France. The Bank of England was designed solely as an instrument of public finance. Its capital consisted exclusively of public debt; its only source of specie apart from deposits was the interest it received on its holdings of public debt; and, most importantly, its conventional commercial operations, though of great consequence, were only ancillary and secondary to its functions as an instrument of government. Hamilton proposed that the Bank of the United States, by contrast, should not deal with the public debt—it was expressly forbidden to buy government bonds—except for the original transactions in which it solidified public credit. Afterward, it would continue to be of service to government by providing short-term loans, by facilitating the collection of taxes, and by serving as a depository for government funds; but its main function would be to provide a large, stable, but flexible national money supply for the financing of ordinary business and general economic development. Moreover, Hamilton insisted that it be operated for the private profit of its stockholders, thus making it in the interest of the stockholders to run it properly. If it were operated as an instrument of public policy, the temptation toward abuse through fiscally unsound practices would, soon or late, prove irresistible to people in government.[13]

The bank was not to be all-powerful: Hamilton proposed a number of restrictions upon it. Its charter would last only twenty years, and though Congress would agree to charter no competing banks during that period, the states could prevent the bank from being a monopoly by chartering as many banks as they saw fit. The Bank of the United States would be prohibited from issuing notes and incurring other obligations in excess of its capitalization; foreign stockholders would be unable to vote; a rotation of directors would be mandatory; the secretary of the treasury would be authorized to remove the government's deposits, inspect the books, and require statements of the bank's condition as frequently as once a week.[14]

Ingenious as the scheme was, it was not a perpetual motion machine: it needed fuel in the form of tax revenues to service the interest payments. Revenues from import duties had risen markedly during 1790, both because of Hamilton's improvements in the administration of the customs service and because of the commercial boom, and the prospective increase in the circulation of money would make taxes easier to collect in future. Even so, additional sources of revenue would be necessary, for interest payments on the assumed state debts would begin to fall due at the end of 1791. Hamilton estimated that those payments would require $788,333 annually, and that an additional $38,291 was needed to cover deficiencies in the funds that had been appropriated for existing commitments.[15]

As a tangible proposition, his recommended additional taxes were essentially those he had proposed a year earlier—an increased duty on imported spirits of eight to fifteen cents a gallon, depending on proof; an excise of eleven to thirty cents a gallon on rum and other liquor manufactured in the United States from imported materials; and an excise of nine to twenty-five cents a gallon on whiskey and other liquor distilled in the United States of domestic ingredients, if the still was located in a city, town, or village. Upon country stills he proposed a tax, from which producers for home consumption would be exempted, of sixty cents a year for each gallon of capacity. These taxes, he estimated, would meet the government's needs and leave some surplus for the sinking fund.[16]

But the report was more than just a reiteration of a tax proposal. Following Necker's advice as well as his own compulsion, Hamilton spelled out the principles on which he was acting, treating Congress to a small lecture on taxation. He reminded Congress that excise taxes were unpopular, the American hostility toward them being rooted in an earlier English tradition. He declined to address himself to one of the more common charges against excises—that they unduly increased executive influence by encouraging a proliferation of "placemen" in the form of excise collectors. But he proposed to defuse the issue by providing against the most odious abuses of individual rights associated with excisemen in England: he would forbid them summary jurisdiction by explicitly preserving the right to trial by jury, and he would restrict the collectors' power of arbitrary search by confining it to places designated by the dealers themselves.[17]

He did, however, argue strongly that the burden of collection should fall on the *"vigilance* of the *public officers"*—which he would ensure by making their compensation a commission of 5 percent— rather than, as was the practice with some state excise systems, "on the *integrity* of the *individuals"* charged with paying the tax. To Hamilton, any policy was bad if it depended on men's voluntarily acting in violation of their interests. Taxes laid on that basis would be unjust as well as unproductive, for they would fall disproportionately upon the honest. Moreover, they would undermine religion and morality by encouraging "frequent and familiar violations of oaths," and protecting such values was to Hamilton ever a matter of genuine concern.[18]

Most importantly, Hamilton offered the congressmen some observations on the principles that should govern taxation. One was that, while import duties were a convenient and desirable form of taxes, they should never be so high as to curtail business activity, for that would be to deprive the whole society of the engines of wealth, or to encourage smuggling. Nor should the government become excessively reliant on import duties, for the flow of international commerce was subject to interruption by the vicissitudes of international politics. Despite his advocacy of a diversified tax base, however, Hamilton would avoid levying taxes on land (which Madison, among others, preferred, though Madison indicated to Hamilton that he thought an excise on liquor would also be useful and desirable). Partly Hamilton wanted to shun taxes on houses and lands because of the constitutional inconvenience of all direct taxes; partly, too, he believed it politic to avoid levying any taxes on farmers except as consumers of luxuries, and except in emergencies such as war. Abstaining from levying property taxes, moreover, would have an additional advantage for supporting public credit: every western nation collected taxes on real property, and if the United States could manage its finances while keeping that source in reserve, the impression on European creditors would be salutary.[19]

Finally, there was the Report on the Mint. A national mint, to Hamilton, was important as another symbol of fiscal orthodoxy, but he was also concerned with the nationalistic implications of having one's own coinage. For instance, he flirted with the idea of calling the dollar by some other name—the Unit was the best he could come up with—inasmuch as the dollar, the coin in most common circulation in America, was Spanish. Otherwise, however, few of his proposals were original. Most of his recommendations followed conventional lines and grew out of earlier proposals by Gouverneur Morris and Thomas Jefferson, as well as from laborious study of standard practices as described by European authorities. These included a bimetallic currency at a ratio approximately the same as that of most European countries, except that Hamilton preferred to overprice gold slightly on the ground that the United States would always have an influx of silver from the West Indies trade. Only in regard to the denominations of coins was Hamilton particularly innovative. Most Americans who had considered the subject thought in terms of large denominations, coinage useful primarily for large transactions in international trade. Hamilton urged the minting of coins of small value as well, including a silver ten-cent piece and copper cents and half-cent pieces. Such fractional currency would reduce the cost of living for the poor; as he pointed out, the lowest price for any commodity would be a cent if that were the smallest coin, but the same commodity would often sell for half a cent if such a coin were available. His motive was not charitable. "To enable the poorer classes to procure necessaries cheap," he said, "is to enable them with more comfort to themselves to labor for less; the advantages of which need no comment." Another reason he desired small coinage was in keeping with his overall social objectives: he wanted to get everyone accustomed to handling money. In a nation in which most people rarely used money as a material object, the effects of that change could be profound.[20]

The mint was brought into being by congressional resolution and elicited no serious controversy. At first, it seemed that the excise and bank bills were also destined to pass without difficulty, for majorities of nearly two to one in the House and nearly three to one in the Senate favored Hamilton's proposals. Both bills, however, became involved in a celebrated but essentially bogus clash of constitutional interpretations. A complex web of machinations underlay that clash.

The House spent much of January intermittently debating the excise. Jackson of Georgia again took the lead in opposing Hamilton, declaring that the excise would fall particularly hard on southerners—to whom, he averred, hard liquor was a necessity of life. Other southerners joined him and recited a litany of opposition that had been formulated in England sixty years earlier and had been repeatedly employed in America: excises bred placemen and excessive power in the executive, were inimical to liberty, fell disproportionately on the poor, would proliferate until everything was taxed but air. It soon became evident that in large measure the opponents were refighting the battle over assumption, hoping to thwart it by withholding the necessary revenues—and most congressmen thought that would be dishonorable. Moreover, though the opponents included all but seven of the southern members of the House, they were hampered by Madison's support for the excise. They did manage to modify Hamilton's bill by placing a limit on the remuneration that collectors could receive. Otherwise, their objections stirred no one, and the bill passed by an overwhelming margin.[21]

Meanwhile, the Senate was passing the bank bill. Only a handful of senators, all southerners, opposed the measure, and most of the time spent on it was devoted to careful consideration of details. Hamilton's personal hand was evident in the proceedings. For example, on one occasion Robert Morris and several others suggested that the government should subscribe for its stock on the same basis that individuals did. Schuyler took the matter to Hamilton, and when he reported back that Hamilton said the change was objectionable, the idea was dropped forthwith. Unsurprisingly, the bill as passed by the Senate thus ended up, for the most part, closely resembling what Hamilton had proposed. There was one point of partial difference. Hamilton had mixed feelings about whether the bank, whose main office would be in Philadelphia, should be empowered to establish branches elsewhere. On balance, he thought it should not have the power; if branches seemed advisable in future, enabling legislation could then be passed. But the Senate voted to leave the question to the discretion of the directors. The Senate's bill to charter the bank was passed on January 20, 1791.[22]

When the two bills changed houses, complications set in. In the Senate, Hamilton's supporters rejected the House's alteration in his plans for the excise. They also, working in regular consultation with Hamilton, added a new feature that was administratively sound but was certain to arouse fierce opposition among state particularists in the House. Since the sizes of the states varied so greatly, it would have been cumbersome to use state lines as the boundaries of collection districts. Hamilton therefore wanted to disregard state boundaries and draw up more convenient and more nearly uniform districts. The idea coincided with his political views as well as his administrative perception, and the Senate concurred. As a result, the version of the excise bill passed by the Senate was markedly at variance from that of the House.[23]

Reconciling the differences between the two versions of the excise bill proved difficult, for the question became enmeshed in the far more complex question of the bank bill. Jefferson and Madison were more or less indifferent to the matter of the bank as such, but they had become alarmed over a tangential implication of its creation. When they first arrived in Philadelphia, they were shocked to hear the Pennsylvania members of Congress declare openly "that they never intended to aid in a removal" of the capital to the Potomac. As indicated, placing the permanent capital on the Potomac was an object dear to the Virginians' hearts, and Madison had had a sizable financial stake in the objective. He and Jefferson, having politicked hard to gain the capital, could scarcely view with aplomb the Pennsylvanians' threat to undermine all their efforts. The seriousness of the move was soon attested when the Pennsylvania House of Representatives voted to appropriate money to build permanent buildings for the federal government in Philadelphia.[24]

Connecting all this to the bank bill was the Virginians' fear that once the bank became firmly entrenched in Philadelphia, it would be almost impossible to move the capital a decade later. When the Senate's bank bill arrived in the House, it was subjected to two readings, during which time Madison said not a word against the bank. Instead he worked feverishly behind the scenes trying to gain support for limiting the charter to ten years, so that the bank would expire and the capital would be transferred at the same time. As a part of his maneuvering, he warned the Pennsylvanians that if they failed to cooperate, he would attack the bill in the House as unconstitutional. Given Madison's reputation as an expert on the Constitution, such a threat carried weight. The Pennsylvanians, however, were obdurate; and besides, they distrusted the Virginians, fearing that in their eagerness to prepare the permanent site they would deny Philadelphia even its agreed-upon ten years.[25]

Rebuffed, Madison made good his threat. In long speeches delivered on February 2 and 8, he maintained that Congress had no power to charter a corporation. He declared that the constitutional convention had considered a motion to give Congress that power but explicitly rejected it. He read from the published accounts of debates in the various ratifying conventions, quoting advocates of the Constitution who insisted that the powers of Congress were to be interpreted narrowly. Where in the Constitution, he asked, could the power to establish a bank be found? Not from the power to levy taxes, not from the general welfare clause, which was limited to the objects listed in the enumerated powers, and not from the power to borrow money. That left only the "implied powers" clause at the end of article I, section 8, authorizing Congress to "make all laws which shall be necessary and proper for carrying into Execution" the enumerated powers. To stretch that clause to comprehend the chartering of a bank, Madison insisted, would require the implying of power three stages removed. First, to borrow money would be the specified constitutional end, to create capital the implied means; then the creation of capital would become the end, a bank the implied means; and finally, a bank becoming the end, granting a charter would become the implied means. "If implications thus remote and thus multiplied, can be linked together," he concluded, "a chain may be formed that will reach every object of legislation, every object within the whole compass of political economy."[26]

In rising as a champion of the doctrine of strict construction, Madison contradicted himself. He had enunciated the doctrine of implied powers as early as 1781, reiterated it in *Federalist* number 44, and carefully preserved it in framing the Tenth Amendment. He had been no strict constructionist when he advocated vesting the removal power solely in the president, and he had taken a palpably unconstitutional position by favoring discrimination in funding the public debts. He had proposed to stretch the necessary and proper clause immensely in 1790, when advocating an enlargement of the powers of census takers, and had proposed an equally loose interpretation of the clause just a few days before the debate on the bank bill, in justification of a scientific expedition he favored.[27]

The majority in the House failed to be persuaded by Madison's tardy discovery of the Constitution. Vining of Delaware questioned his authority to pontificate about the intentions of the framers of the Constitution, since no fewer than eleven members of the Senate, which had passed the bank bill, had been members of the convention. Gerry, as a former member of the convention himself, asked the same question. Ames, Sedgwick, and Smith shot Madison's arguments down with full and lucid expositions of the doctrine of loose construction. The outcome of the debate was never in doubt; on February 8 the House voted to concur with the Senate, 39 to 20. Nineteen of the twenty dissenting votes were from the South, twelve of them from the two states on the Potomac. Representative Benjamin Bourne of Rhode Island wrote home that Madison had combatted the bank "both on the ground of inconstitutionality and inexpedience. But I am persuaded we would not have heard anything of either, did not the Gentleman from the Southward view the measure, as adverse to the removal of Congress, ten years hence." That, Ames said flatly, was what had influenced Madison and was influencing the secretary of state and perhaps "a still greater man."[28]

That still greater man, the president, was seriously upset by the raising of the constitutional issue. He regarded the Constitution as a cross between holy writ and a manual of instructions, and he regarded himself as the chief defender of its sanctity. He knew little of legal and constitutional theory but had outsized respect for Madison's acumen in such matters, and he trusted Madison as both adviser and friend. Thus, even before he received the engrossed bill from Congress, he sought a formal opinion from the attorney general on the constitutionality of the bill. Unsurprisingly, Attorney General Edmund Randolph, another Virginian, endorsed Madison's argument that the bill was unconstitutional. That was on Saturday, February 12. Two days later Washington handed the bill to the secretary of state for his opinion. Jefferson's opinion, though destined to become the classical statement of strict constructionism, was for the most part a shorter and less persuasive version of Madison's arguments—and it was given with approximately the same measure of consistency, since Jefferson was on record in support of loose construction almost as definitely as Madison was. Jefferson did add a touch of his own: in a masterpiece of legal obfuscation, well calculated to confuse the president, he asserted that the bank bill violated the laws of mortmain, alienage, descents, forfeiture and escheat, distribution, and monopoly. Washington, overwhelmed by the arguments from three trusted fellow Virginians, sent copies of Randolph's and Jefferson's opinions to Hamilton with a cool, formal note inviting Hamilton in effect to defend the bank if he could. Expecting that he could not, Washington asked Madison to prepare a draft of a veto message.[29]

But with Washington, too, the matter ran deeper than the issue of constitutionality. The president also wanted the capital on the Potomac and, after Congress passed the enabling legislation, he had been all too avid in setting the ball rolling. The congressional legislation provided for a three-man executive commision which was to choose a ten-mile-square site at any point along the Potomac between the Eastern Branch (Anacostia River), a few miles below the Great Falls, and Conococheague Creek, some sixty miles above the fall line. Instead, Washington chose the site himself. Moreover, though the legislation clearly contemplated a site on or above the falls, Washington decided to place it downstream, adjacent to his Mount Vernon estate. Indeed, he went further, placing it three miles downstream of the authorized southeasternmost location. Only afterward did he make a tour of the prospective upstream sites so as to give the impression that he was considering them as the act of Congress required. That entrapped him further in his little web of deception, for it made it necessary to invite proposals from the upstream inhabitants and to go through the motions of appearing to weigh them in arriving at a decision. Then, because all this looked bad—the transactions increased the value of Washington's property, as he admitted, by a considerable amount—he groped for a means of putting a face of propriety on things. He asked Congress to amend the federal district act so as to cast, retroactively, its mantle of approval over his actions. Washington wanted his every action to appear proper in the eyes of the public, and his concern for the passage of the requested amendatory legislation was far more pressing than his concern over the constitutionality of the bank.[30]

And if Washington did not connect the two issues in his thinking, others were there to make the connection for him. Madison had at least three long interviews with him regarding both the bank and the residency amendment, and Jefferson saw the president regularly and had been involved in the chicanery all along. Both men, for more than a year, had been dropping in Washington's ear bits of poison against Robert Morris, who had never ceased maneuvering to keep the capital in Philadelphia despite his bargain with Jefferson in 1790, and who, it could be fairly assumed, was instrumental in ramming Hamilton's bank bill through Congress. Several congressmen whispered that Washington connected the two for purposes of his own tactics, and the timing of his next move bore out the rumors. On February 16 he sent his note requesting Hamilton's opinion on the constitutionality of the bank and made his arrangements with Madison for the veto message. On the same day, by advance agreement with Washington and Jefferson, Senator Charles Carroll of Maryland asked leave, in violation of Senate rules, to bring in an amendatory bill regarding the capital. That was the threat: no amendatory bill, no bank. Simultaneously, the president and the secretary of state set out to woo the wayward. They courted the dour William Maclay unashamedly, though neither had paid any attention to him before, and if they could bring themselves to woo Maclay, they doubtless pressed their charms on other senators as well.[31]

But this time Hamilton outmaneuvered the Virginians. The bank bill could be held hostage to ensure passage of the amendatory bill, but the pressure could be equally applied the other way around. On Friday, February 18, the Senate considered Carroll's motion to amend the federal district act, but after some discussion it was moved to postpone consideration of it for one week. Behind that tactic were Hamilton's two staunchest supporters on the bank, Morris and Schuyler, and they carried with them two of Morris's more or less captive senators, John Langdon of New Hampshire and George Read of Delaware. The issue was carried by those four votes. "They might as well have voted against the bill," Maclay recorded in his diary, "for the postponement is equally ungrateful at court. Saturday we had communications from the President, etc." Maclay failed to observe that the week's postponement set consideration of Carroll's motion for Friday the 25th, Washington's very last day to decide whether to veto the bank bill, to sign it, or to let it become law without his signature. The waiting game, or war of nerves, had begun.[32]

On Monday Hamilton added to the suspense by sending Washington a note saying that he had been working hard on his opinion regarding the constitutionality of the bank but could not finish it until Tuesday evening or Wednesday morning. Wednesday morning, the Senate suddenly agreed to propose a conference to settle the deadlock over the excise bill, and when the House promptly agreed, named three supporters of the bank as its committee. That conference, too, was set for Friday the 25th. Just before noon on the same Wednesday, Hamilton sent his written opinion to the president. Washington, a master at the waiting game, sent a note acknowledging receipt of the opinion and asking Hamilton a pointed question regarding the bank bill: "To what precise period, by legal interpretation of the constitution, can the president retain it in his possession, before it becomes a Law by the lapse of ten days?" That was a new bluff in the game, for Hamilton obviously wanted and perhaps needed Washington's public sanction for the bank, not a mere acquiescence. With crisp formality, Hamilton responded that the president had until the close of business on Friday.[33]

While everyone in government waited anxiously for the great man's decision, Washington sat down to study Hamilton's opinion—presumably on Thursday the 24th. The president was in for a treat. He had, over the years, read notes, memoranda, reports, and letters that Hamilton had written; he had heard Hamilton's speeches in the Constitutional Convention; he had read *The Federalist;* he had read the Reports on the Public Credit; but he had never observed Hamilton in action as a lawyer. And now, in his opinion on the constitutionality of the bank, Hamilton brought his profound legal gifts to bear.

After an appropriately diffident introduction, Hamilton opened his argument by stating a self-evident proposition—"that every power vested in a Government is in its nature *sovereign,* and includes by *force* of the *term,* a right to employ all the *means* requisite, and fairly *applicable* to the attainment of the *ends* of such power; and which are not precluded by restrictions & exceptions specified in the constitution; or not immoral, or not contrary to the essential ends of political power." To disprove this premise, Hamilton said, would require showing "that a rule which in the general system of things is essential to the preservation of the social order is inapplicable to the United States." Nor did it alter the case that sovereignty in the United States was divided between the federal and state governments; that only meant "that each has sovereign power as to *certain things,* and not as to *other things.*" To deny that the national government had sovereign powers simply because its powers were limited would be also to deny that state governments had any sovereignty, since their powers were also limited. That would "furnish the singular spectacle of a *political society* without *sovereignty,* or of a people *governed* without *government.*"[34]

It was equally self-evident that sovereignty carried with it the inherent power to create corporations, for anything government could legitimately require or permit individuals to do, it could require or permit legal or artificial persons, corporations, to do. Thus it is "unquestionably incident to *sovereign power* to erect corporations, and consequently to *that* of the United States, in *relation to the objects* intrusted to the management of the government." This was so palpably obvious, Hamilton said, that he might well rest his case

[205]

against the attorney general and the secretary of state there. But he would go on.[35]

Next he disposed of two of Jefferson's and Randolph's central propositions. The first was that the Constitution was founded on the principle declared in the Tenth Amendment that "all powers not delegated to the United States by the Constitution nor prohibited to it by the States are reserved to the States or to the people." No one, Hamilton said, could quibble with the premise, for "it is nothing more than a consequence of this republican maxim, that all government is a delegation of power." But no one contended that there were not implied powers as well as expressed powers, the implied powers being the legitimate means of obtaining the expressed ends. Jefferson and Randolph had argued as if the creation of a corporation was an end rather than a mean. Nonsense, Hamilton scoffed; it was merely a way of doing things. The only point at issue was whether the corporation in question was being erected for a proper end. Thus, for example, Congress could not set up a corporation to superintend the police of Philadelphia, for it was "not authorised to *regulate* the *police* of that city"; but it could create a corporation in relation to the collection of taxes or the regulation of foreign or interstate commerce.[36]

The second central proposition to be rebutted was Jefferson's narrow interpretation of the necessary and proper clause. Jefferson had argued that it meant literally and indispensably necessary, that it restricted congressional powers "to those means, without which the grant of the power would be nugatory." Every government, Hamilton declared, was confined to passing only such laws as were necessary and proper "to accomplish the objects intrusted to it. For no government has a right to do *merely what it pleases.*" But necessary, he said, "often means no more than *needful, requisite, incidental, useful,* or *conducive to.*" Jefferson's narrow reading of the term would paralyze government, for it could rarely be said with certainty "that a measure was absolutely necessary, or one without which the exercise of a given power would be nugatory." Hamilton offered a number of examples of the proper interpretation of "necessary." No state constitution expressly authorized the creation of corporations, and it could scarcely be argued that incorporating towns was indispensably necessary; yet everyone recognized that states had the power to create them. Similarly, the congressional act establishing lighthouses, beacons, buoys, and public piers—whose constitutionality no one questioned—would have to be rejected by Jefferson's criterion, for establishing harbor facilities was only incidental to the regulation of commerce, not indispensable to it. Hitting home with Washington, Hamilton offered a third example, pointing to the acts giving the president the power to remove his appointees.[37]

Pausing to summarize, Hamilton formulated what would become the classical criterion for determining constitutionality. "If the end be clearly comprehended within any of the specified powers," he said, and "if the measure have an obvious relation to that end, and is not forbidden by any particular provision of the constitution—it may safely be deemed to come within the compass of the national authority." To be sure, lest that rule of interpretation be used to overextend the power of the national government, two further questions must be asked: "Does the proposed measure abridge a preexisting right of any State, or of any individual?" If it does, it is questionable; but if not, "there is a strong presumption in favour of its constitutionality."[38]

Now Hamilton turned to a task he obviously relished; to employ words that Henry Adams used in another connection, Hamilton was almost "shouting with a schoolboy's fun at the idea of . . . teaching the Virginia democrats some law." Hamilton destroyed Jefferson's legalistic pettifoggery on every count, showing that his arguments had been a mixture of bad law, nonlaw, and irrelevant law. He was equally merciless in dealing with Randolph, picking his logic apart point by point, as if plucking a chicken.[39]

Artfully, Hamilton paused again, interposing a brief summary of the general propositions he had established, so that Washington might not become swamped in details. The gist of his summary was that Congress incontrovertibly had power to create corporations as means of effecting constitutional ends. To underscore the message, he reminded the president that Congress had in fact passed and Washington had signed into law two earlier acts of incorporation, those providing for the government of the northwest and southwest territories.[40]

All that remained was to show that the incorporation of a bank, "*politically* speaking," was "necessary to the effectual execution of one or more" of the powers enumerated in the Constitution. Hamilton did so on five different grounds: the powers to collect taxes, borrow money, regulate trade, provide for the common defense, and regulate the government's own property.[41]

The logic with which he connected taxation with banking illustrates the subtlety of the whole. To designate the money or thing in which taxes are to be paid, he pointed out, is obviously a necessary part of the power of collecting them. Congress had declared that import duties were payable in gold or silver, but it could with equal propriety have made them payable in commodities or anything else. It could, for instance, make them payable in bills issued under the authority of the United States.[42]

"Now," he continued, "the manner of issuing these bills is again matter of discretion. The government might, doubtless, proceed in the following manner. It might provide, that they should be issued under the direction of certain officers, payable on demand; and in order to support their credit & give them a ready circulation, it might, besides giving them a currency in its taxes, set apart out of any monies in its Treasury, a given sum and appropriate it under the direction of those officers as a fund for answering the bills as presented for payment.

"The constitutionality of all this would not admit of a question. And yet it would amount to the institution of a bank, with a view to the more convenient collection of taxes. For the simplest and most precise idea of a bank, is, a deposit of coin or other property, as a fund for *circulating* a *credit* upon it, which is to answer the purpose of money. That such an arrangement would be equivalent to the establishment of a bank would become obvious, if the place where the fund to be set apart was kept should be made a receptacle of the monies of all other persons who should incline to deposit them there for safe keeping; and would become still more so, if the Officers charged with the direction of the fund were authorised to make discounts at the usual rate of interest, upon good security. To deny the power of the government to add these ingredients to the plan, would be to refine away all government."[43]

To justify incorporation of a bank as a legitimate exercise of the power to borrow money, Hamilton demonstrated that circumstances could arise in which it would be necessary to create the power to lend. He tied this example to the common defense by reminding Washington that a military expedition against the Indians, just then being prepared, would have been impossible to finance had there been no banks. It happened that there were some banks, "but if there were none, it would be indispensible to create one." Hamilton used these illustrations to reemphasize his point that "necessary" is a relative term, varying among other things with changing circumstances and thus in practice being interchangeable with "expedient." And, he stressed, "circumstances may affect the expediency of the measure, but they can neither add to, nor diminish its constitutionality."[44]

In similar fashion, Hamilton showed the constitutional justification for a bank on grounds of the powers to regulate trade and regulate the government's own property. Along the way, he also pointed out that virtually every European government had created corporations incidentally to the collection of taxes and the regulation of commerce. Then he was ready for a conclusion.[45]

Characteristically, he closed not by summing up but by adding a series of apparent afterthoughts. He went back over the briefs of Jefferson and Randolph to make sure that he had disposed of every detail. For instance, to Jefferson's irrelevant argument that the general welfare clause was not a grant of power but a restriction on the taxing power, Hamilton agreed but pointed out that the clause meant Congress could levy taxes only for general purposes, as opposed to purely or merely local purposes. He thought of more examples; he thought of more legal and logical considerations. The cumulative effect of this method of concluding was to leave the impression that, but for the sake of mercy, he might go on reciting irrefutable arguments forever.[46]

No man with a reasonably open mind, reading Hamilton's argument after reading Randolph's and Jefferson's, could fail to appreciate Hamilton's superior intellect and superior case. The only doubt was whether Washington's mind was open.

Maneuvering continued. On Thursday, February 24, the Senate received a bill passed by the House the day before, extending the time for subscribing to the stock of the bank and altering various other minor features that had occasioned discontent. Charles Carroll, sponsor of the amended federal district bill, together with two supporters of that bill, James Monroe and James

Gunn, invoked parliamentary procedures to delay passage of the House's amendment to the bank bill. In two notes that day, Hamilton informed the president of these doings, calling particular attention to the "*studied* delays on the part of the *opposers of the Bank.*" That was an adequate reminder to Washington, if he needed reminding, that the fates of the residency amendment and the bank bill were interlocked.[47]

There is no clear record as to which side capitulated first, but it was probably Washington. The Senate, on the 25th, agreed to a compromise in regard to the excise, discussed a foreign loan, became involved in a hassle over the time for convening the next session, and engaged in an acrimonious debate over a proposal to open its sessions to the public. Only as its last item of business did it take up the Potomac amendatory bill; Schuyler, Morris, Langdon, and Read reversed their votes of a week earlier, thus assuring its passage.[48]

Sometime during the course of the day, Washington had signed the bank bill into law.

X

Triumph and Trouble:

1791

But when his own great work is but begun,

What Reason weaves, by Passion is undone.

Things were working out as well as Hamilton had dared hope and better than he may have expected. Despite his dreams, plans, and self-confidence, his mixed feelings about the nature of man must have whispered to him, all along, that what he hoped to do could not be done; and yet it was happening. When the bank bill became law he knew that, given careful management and barring a cataclysm, the purely financial parts of his operations were sure to succeed. By late fall, when he was preparing the climactic effort in his series of performances—the Report on Manufactures—he believed that his work as the architect of a new and happy America was nearly complete.

In the circumstances, it is scarcely cause for wonder that he became dangerously overconfident. Natural pride moved subtly in the direction of arrogance, self-assurance toward a sense of infallibility. This is not to suggest that he became slipshod or careless. His attention to the proprieties and niceties of official conduct was never keener, his skill as an administrator never greater. But he said things that in prudence he should not have said, and he did things that in prudence he should not have done. He made powerful enemies and made himself vulnerable to them. At the same time, the irresponsibility and greed of some erstwhile supporters jeopardized the very foundations of his financial system.

All this made his thirty-fifth year, 1791, the most momentous of his life so far. It was a season of triumph, but also a season of mounting danger. And yet, underrating his enemies, overrating his friends, and contemptuous of peril from either, Hamilton threw caution to the winds and revealed the broad social design of his program. That was certain to multiply the opposition. The popularity of his measures thus far had derived to no small extent from their being nearly free: the benefits were vast and the costs nominal, or so anyway had it seemed. Now he was making it clear that the aim of his program as a whole was the abandonment of the leisurely, agrarian life-style to which Americans had long been accustomed. The ranks of his enemies would grow apace.

Before 1791, Hamilton had won himself an abundance of rivals and opponents, but only two groups—the adherents of Governor George Clinton and of Chancellor Robert R. Livingston—could properly be regarded as genuine enemies, and neither was yet in a position to cause any serious damage to his programs. That spring, however, he made an enemy of Thomas Jefferson, a man formidable enough to pose a threat not merely to his programs but even to his quest for Fame.

This turn of events is surprising only in that it took so long in coming. Jefferson, product and beneficiary of the Virginia oligarchy, loved and cherished the Virginia way of life as he viewed it. It was easy for him to idealize the serene, secure life of the plantation gentry, for in that world all things came to men of inherited power, and he was one of them. As an intellectual dilettante and frequenter of salons—which the labor of his slaves permitted him to be—he liked to talk of revolution and of the abolition of privilege so that a natural aristocracy of the virtuous and wise could govern the affairs of mankind. In fact, however, even in advocating revolution he was seeking a mechanical, mathematically definable, and predictable social order comparable to a Newtonian physical order; and the only privilege he ever seriously opposed was privilege that threatened the security of his own little world. Hamilton, having grown up as the victim of a similar world, despised it and, as a true revolutionary, devised a program that would ultimately destroy it. For him the ideal world was not a safe and comfortable one but a competitive and just one in which, contrary to the biblical order, the race went to the swift, bread to the wise, favor to men of skill. Soon or late, Jefferson must recognize that, and recognizing it must regard Hamilton as an enemy to everything he held dear.

Fisher Ames, Massachusetts congressman and the most perceptive of Hamilton's adherents, foresaw the rupture and analyzed tellingly the differences underlying it. To the northward, Ames said with characteristic Yankee self-righteousness, "we see how necessary it is to defend property by steady laws," and "the same system of strict law, which has done wonders for us," would promote the advantage of southerners as well. But in the South there was no steady law, only the commands of the gentry. Many among the gentry had favored ratification of the Constitution "because they needed some remedy to evils which they saw and felt, but mistook, in their view of it, the remedy. A debt-compelling government is no remedy to men who have lands and negroes, and debts and luxury, but neither trade nor credit, nor cash, nor the habits of industry, or of submission to a rigid execution of law." Ames's words, though harsh, accurately described Thomas Jefferson and nine-tenths of his fellow planters in Virginia and North Carolina.[1]

There were also important personal differences. The love of power for its own sake was alien to Hamilton; he sought power only as a means of effecting desired ends. To Jefferson, power for its own sake was ingrained; power went with his social status, was an indispensable condition of it, was taken for granted. On another plane, Jefferson distrusted people to whom attainments of the mind came easily, without continued and disciplined effort. Hamilton thought it in bad taste to appear to have to work hard in intellectual endeavors and devoted much effort to making his attainments seem easy and natural. And there were more specific sources of animosity. Jefferson's friends had supported a presidential succession bill that would have made the secretary of state next in line after the vice-president, and Hamilton's friends had thwarted the effort. Jefferson had lost the argument over the constitutionality of the bank, and Hamilton's overkill rebuttal could have done nothing to assuage Jefferson's vanity. And Jefferson must have expected, as others had, that the office of secretary of state would have been the most prestigious position under the president, and yet Hamilton as a mere financial minister was hogging all the glory and even playing an important role in foreign affairs. All things considered, Jefferson would have been more than human if, by the spring of 1791, he were not in search of a respectable excuse for lashing out at Hamilton.[2]

The incident that provided the excuse was so trivial and inadvertent that Hamilton never became aware that it had triggered the estrangement. About a month after Congress adjourned, Washington left on an extended tour of the southern states. In a move often regarded as the origin of the president's "cabinet," Washington authorized the secretaries of state, treasury, and war to meet in his absence, act in his behalf if necessary, and summon him if his presence became needed. Washington added that Vice-President John Adams should participate in the meetings if he happened to remain in Philadelphia during the congressional recess. Adams did remain in the city, and as a result he, Jefferson, and Hamilton were together under reasonably relaxed circumstances for the first time. That provided the occasion for a dinner party, given by Jefferson, which had fateful consequences for all three men.[3]

After dinner—this was an April evening in 1791—Jefferson and his guests discussed various items of business, and then the conversation turned to political philosophy. The pompous and porcine vice-president, as was his wont, solemnly pontificated about the virtues of the British governmental system: "Purge that constitution of its corruption," he said, "and give to its popular branch equality of representation, and it would be the most perfect constitution ever devised by the wit of man." Chagrined as he was to hear his old friend openly espouse a government consisting of "two hereditary branches and an honest elective one," Jefferson was scarcely surprised, for Adams's drift toward monarchism was well known. But Hamilton's retort shook him deeply. "Purge it of its corruption," Hamilton said rather flippantly—repeating the statement, original with Hume, that he had expressed in the constitutional convention—"and give to its popular branch equality of representation, and it would become an *impracticable* government: as it stands at present, with all its supposed defects, it is the most perfect government which ever existed." Hamilton was advocating neither monarchy nor corruption for America, he meant only what Hume had meant: that, since the House of Commons had come to control the purse strings, the balance of Britain's partly elective, partly hereditary governmental system could be preserved only if the Crown protected itself by using its patronage to influence votes in the Commons. What Jefferson (and possibly Adams, too) took Hamilton to mean was something far more sinister.[4]

Jefferson and most other Americans, especially southerners of his generation, had learned to perceive political reality through an ideological prism developed in England six decades earlier, in which the word "corruption" had a special coloration. When Parliament, under the leadership of Sir Robert Walpole, had transformed the kingdom by monetizing the public debt and thus ushering in the Financial Revolution and the ministerial system, the once-dominant English gentry class saw itself being replaced by what it contemptuously referred to as "money men." A vehement Opposition developed, first led by "real Whigs" and then by the arch-Tory Henry St. John, First Viscount Bolingbroke. Between them, the Oppositionists formulated, codified, and reduced to a veritable litany a body of thought which, among its American adherents, became an almost knee-jerk pattern of response to government policies.[5]

According to Bolingbroke's version of the ideology, the Walpolean revolution had utterly corrupted English government and society. Earlier, said he, relations had been based upon agriculture and ownership of the land, honest labor in the earth, craftsmanship in the cities, and justly regulated trade among individuals. All men revered God, respected their fellows, deferred to their betters, and knew their place. Because they were secure in their sense of place, they were also secure in their sense of values; and manly virtue, honor, and public spirit governed their conduct. Walpole's instrument of corruption was money—not "real" money, gold and silver, but artificial money in the form of public debt, banknotes, stocks, and other kinds of paper—the acquisition of which had nothing to do with either land or labor. He and subsequent ministers encouraged people to traffic in such paper and thus to pursue easy wealth. A frenzy for gambling, stock jobbing, and paper shuffling permeated the highest councils of state, enabled ministers to pervert the constitution by controlling Parliament, and spread among the people themselves. Manly virtue gave way to effeminacy and vice; public spirit succumbed to extravagance and venality.[6]

Americans swallowed Bolingbroke's message whole, pausing only to republicanize what had been formulated as Tory doctrine—which proved easy to do. Indeed, Jefferson and hordes of his countrymen came to believe that the American Revolution had been fought to prevent the invasion of the American garden by the twin serpents, money and ministers, which Bolingbroke taught them had corrupted England. Given that cast of mind and his predisposition against Hamilton, when Jefferson heard Hamilton casually endorse corruption as the indispensable ingredient in the most perfect form of government ever devised, his revulsion and fear were immediate and total. Forthwith, he became convinced that Hamilton had been "bewitched and perverted by the British example" and had formed a "mercenary phalanx" of paper men and stock jobbers in Congress in a conspiracy to poison America, even as his evil idol Walpole had poisoned England.[7]

That was a distorted view of Hamilton's goals. To be sure, Hamilton was employing monetization and the firm hand of government as means to achieve his ends, and those means were built largely on the British model; but, far from using them to reduce Americans to servility and dependence, he proposed to employ them to make the nation industrious and self-sufficient. It was true that he opposed the agrarian ideal; but, far from seeking to destroy a pastoral paradise, he was trying to liberate and energize a society that slavery and oligarchy had oppressed and rendered lethargic. It was true that he had found consistent supporters for his measures in Congress; but far from commanding a party, he deplored the very idea of parties and appealed not to the interests of the congressmen but to their sense of honor and love of country. Finally, it was true that he was skeptical of the prospects for the American experiment in republicanism and constitutional government; but, far from trying to undermine it, he had invested the immortality of his soul in his efforts to make it succeed. Jefferson, blinded by his Bolingbrokean fantasy, could see none of that. Thenceforth, he saw Hamilton's every word and deed, past and present, as confirmation of his evil designs.[8]

Thenceforth, too, Jefferson along with Madison and an ever-growing number of supporters became engaged in a "republican" conspiracy, or counterconspiracy, to thwart what they perceived as Hamilton's "monocratic" conspiracy. Their opposition was three-pronged and structurally resembled the general strategy laid out by

Bolingbroke nearly sixty years earlier. They would reveal Hamilton's monstrous designs to the president. Washington, the pure republican version of what Bolingbroke had called a "patriot king," would undo the wicked system of his unfaithful minister, provided the ministerial phalanx in Congress had not already grown so powerful as to make that impossible. Then, to destroy the hold of Hamilton upon Congress, they would make a concerted effort to overcome the money men and dissolve the connection between the legislative branch and "heads of departments"—which is to say, require Hamilton hereafter to report only to the president rather than directly to Congress. Lest their first two tactics fail, they would organize a political party. Parties were widely regarded as inimical to republican government, but theirs, Bolingbroke-style, would be an exception. It would be a party to end all parties, for it would gain control of government, oust the ministers and moneychangers from the temple, and restore the Constitution. Its goal accomplished, it would wither away, leaving the people to enjoy their liberties once again. (Said Ames, bitingly, they "generated a regular, well-disciplined opposition party, whose leaders cry 'liberty,' but mean, as all party leaders do, 'power.' ")[9]

Washington being out of town and Congress being out of session, Jefferson and Madison launched their party mission first. In May they went to New York on a "botanical expedition," during which they had conferences with Robert R. Livingston, Aaron Burr, and possibly George Clinton. Their attacks on the other two fronts would begin in November.[10]

Unaware that he had alienated Jefferson—the Bolingbrokean tradition had not been part of his ideological conditioning—Hamilton disregarded the warnings of friends that Jefferson and Madison were meeting with his enemies in New York and proceeded with the administrative implementation of his program. The way he did so was strikingly at variance from Jefferson's image of him as an arrogant agent of monarchical corruption, running roughshod over the liberties of the people. For instance, there were Hamilton's orders to the captains of the cutters in the newly founded coast guard service, established by Congress to prevent violations of the revenue laws. Hamilton informed the officers of their duties, instructed them to keep full journals and forward copies to him once a month, and requested them to gather and send in navigational information that might prove useful to the public. Then he gave them a stern admonition. They had been carefully chosen in the expectation that they would behave as good officers and good citizens, he said, but they must "always keep in mind that their Countrymen are Freemen. . . . They will therefore refrain with the most guarded circumspection from whatever has the semblance of haughtiness, rudeness or insult."[11]

Hamilton repeatedly made explicit his ideas of proper behavior for people entrusted with administrative responsibility in a republic. For example, in writing to Washington to recommend Oliver Wolcott's promotion from auditor to comptroller, he said that Wolcott "combined all the requisites that could be desired." He tempered "moderation with firmness, liberality with exactness," and "indefatigable industry" with discernment, a thorough knowledge of business, and a "spirit of order & arrangement." Hamilton set for himself the task of infusing the entire Treasury Department with such qualities. That was not easy, for the Treasury, with more than 500 employees, was a mammoth operation compared to the other executive departments. (Knox had only twelve civilian employees in the War Department and Jefferson only six in State plus two chargés d'affaires in Europe.) Moreover, the difficulties of supervising the Treasury's employees were compounded by the fact that only about an eighth of them worked directly under Hamilton's eye at the main offices in Philadelphia. Yet it was crucial to keep this far-flung apparatus functioning smoothly for, on a day-to-day basis, the Treasury Department very nearly *was* the national government.[12]

Several of Hamilton's administrative techniques are illuminating. First, he made it standard policy to handle the more vexing and delicate problems himself, which served at once to relieve his subordinates of burdens and to set an example for them. Many such problems involved the unpleasant task of saying no to supplicants, some of whose appeals were just but improper. When the Board of Assessors of the Town of Boston asked for a list of security holders so they could be taxed on their holdings, Hamilton could readily reject the request, though he was tactful in doing so because of the political implications of his refusal. When petitioners from North Carolina and Rhode Island sought special treatment or coverage under the

assumption act for state debts that had been more or less fraudu-
lently retired, Hamilton was sympathetic, especially because some
of the appeals came from staunch friends of the national government; but he unhesitatingly rejected their claims. Particularly difficult for him was the appeal from the widow of General Nathanael
Greene for reimbursement for expenditures Greene had made in
behalf of the army. Hamilton had loved and respected Greene, and
he had no doubts that the expenditures had been legitimate and
necessary—but they could not be documented. The law was plain:
no documents, no reimbursal. Hamilton refused to make an exception even for Catharine Greene. Then, having done his official duty,
he helped her obtain reimbursal through a special act of Congress.[13]

Second, Hamilton strove to build pride in the organization and to
instill all members with his own high standards of public service.
He was quick to spot excellence and generous in rewarding it, but
he discountenanced the military system of granting promotions automatically as vacancies occurred and avoided promoting men to
positions in which they would be less happy and less proficient. He
was patient with his subordinates and liberal in devoting time and
attention to them, which was doubly effective because his attention
clearly gave them a sense of sharing his glory. He listened to complaints from merchants against customs collectors, but if investigation proved the collectors to be in the right, he backed his people unequivocally. At the same time, however, he believed in working his
subordinates hard, requiring them not only to perform their statutory duties but also to gather information and make reports on
myriad matters of present or prospective interest to the department
and the public. He believed that, within reasonable limits, the more
he required of his people the better they would perform. (That attitude was in sharp contrast to Jefferson's notions of how to handle
the State Department's ministers and consuls. "The less we give
them to do," said Jefferson, "the more secure we shall be of having it
done." So lackadaisical was Jefferson, in fact, that he allowed one of
his chargés, William Carmichael at Madrid, to go two full years
without sending a single report.)[14]

Most importantly, Hamilton was at pains to ensure that collectors,
loan officers, and other supervisory personnel were fully instructed
in their duties. In the main he did this through circular letters,
which economized his own time and established uniform proce-

dures and practices. The circulars were usually general in nature, though they sometimes became meticulously detailed, as when Hamilton instructed the customs collectors on the use of Dycas's hydrometer, the device for measuring the proof of alcohol. He was well aware that not every contingency could be provided for, but he tried to lay down policy guidelines to govern subordinates in the exercise of discretionary authority, and when they reported successful innovations in the handling of unanticipated problems, he often used such reports as the basis for supplementary circulars of instruction.[15]

Some idea of the department's efficiency, and of the complexity of its tasks, may be had by considering the matter of making quarterly interest payments on the public debt. Perhaps 25,000 separate transactions were involved. Payments were made on the first days of January, April, July, and October at the Treasury and in thirteen state loan offices, scattered over a 1,000-mile area and as much as two weeks' travel time from the Treasury. There were only six banks in the country. The main source of revenue was sixty-seven customs offices, which collected widely varying, seasonally fluctuating, and often unpredictable sums. Normally Hamilton facilitated the flow of commerce by accommodating the requests of banks for drafts on collectors and (stretching the statutory requirement that duties be paid in gold or silver to include their paper equivalents) by requiring collectors to accept bank notes in payment of duties. About a month before interest payments fell due, however, he curtailed the movement of paper so that sufficient funds would be available to the loan officers. This entailed knowing just how much money was available, in what forms, and in what places—a seemingly impossible task, given the slowness of transportation and communication. Yet during Hamilton's tenure as secretary there was never once a complaint of error or delay in the making of interest payments.[16]

There was one minor flaw in Hamilton's scheme of things: some subordinates had their own notions about the concept of agency, and no amount of standardization could change their habits. The operations of the sinking fund illustrate the problem. Hamilton, upon authorization by the sinking-fund committee, designated particular individuals to make the actual purchases of public securities on the open market. When he instructed William Seton (cashier of the Bank of New York, whom Hamilton often called upon to perform functions for the Treasury) to buy $150,000 of securities and pay twenty shillings in the pound for 6 percents, twelve shillings sixpence for deferred sixes, and twelve shillings for 3 percents, he could count on Seton to do precisely as he was instructed. But when Hamilton instructed Benjamin Lincoln, collector of customs in Boston, to make sinking-fund purchases, Lincoln could not bring himself to do exactly what Hamilton told him to do—to buy at the market price, but to lean toward the upper rather than the lower side of the price range, since one object of the purchases was to raise the market. It violated Lincoln's frugal Yankee sensibilities to pay more in behalf of the public when he could pay less, and he purchased at the market, neither raising nor lowering the price. When such departures from the letter of his instructions caused no mischief, Hamilton let them pass without comment.[17]

The most important official on whose agency Hamilton had to rely was a borrowed one. In Europe the only active American officer was Jefferson's former secretary William Short, who had remained as chargé d'affaires in Paris when Jefferson returned home and who continued to be Jefferson's State Department subordinate. The interdepartmental nature of the arrangement did not in practice create any friction, for Short was charged by law to be the Treasury's agent in negotiating loans abroad. What did cause problems was the slowness of communications and Hamilton's consequent inability to respond quickly and decisively to fluctuations in the European money market. At one point, for instance, the price of American securities in Amsterdam took a sudden dive as a result of dislocations inside Holland, then promptly rose again to satisfactory levels. Two months elapsed before Hamilton heard of the downturn and anxiously wrote to Willinks, Van Staphorsts, and Hubbard for an explanation. By the time their reply could reach him the trouble had long since vanished, and his several worried months had been for nothing.[18]

Generally speaking, Short was able and effective, and he provided invaluable services for Hamilton, but once he took a step that might have occasioned serious damage. Hamilton instructed Short to study the markets and make sure the services of Willinks, Van Staphorsts, and Hubbard were the best that could be obtained, and he added that it would be desirable for the United States to have more than one market in which to borrow. But he warned against overdoing it: "Changes of public servants ought never to be made, but for cogent reasons. If lightly made, they are not only chargeable with injustice and are a symptom of fickleness in the public councils, but they destroy the motives to good conduct; and, in money concerns especially, are apt to beget a disposition to make the most of possession while it lasts." Short's tendency was to disregard that warning, and in one instance he floated a loan in Antwerp that incensed the Hollanders and jeopardized the advantages of a standing relationship. Hamilton soothed their ruffled feathers, then adroitly turned the incident to American advantage by using the hint of further operations in Antwerp to obtain lower interest rates in Amsterdam.[19]

Meanwhile, investors at home were proving to be much less tractable than those in Europe. Of all the dangers to his system, Hamilton believed, the greatest was that it would engender a speculative bubble of the kind that had destroyed John Law's French banking program, and nearly destroyed England's, seven decades earlier. Despite that concern, however, he seriously underestimated the demand for stock in the Bank of the United States, with the result that just such a bubble began to develop.[20]

Hamilton had originally proposed that subscriptions be opened in Philadelphia on the first Monday in April, 1791, that payments for the $400-par-value stock be made in four equal semiannual installments, and that the first $100 payment be due at the time of subscription. But Congress, concerned lest Philadelphians gain exclusive control of the bank, responded to prodding by William Loughton Smith and passed a supplementary act designed to facilitate a wide distribution. Opening day for subscriptions was set up to July, and the initial payment was reduced to twenty-five dollars—for which the subscribers would receive certificates, called "scrip," which entitled them to buy the stock subsequently at par. Hamilton, sharing the desire that stockholding be widespread and also seeking to ensure that the stock offering be fully subscribed, using Treasury Department machinery to facilitate subscriptions by investors in Boston, New York, Baltimore, and Charleston. That greatly augmented an already huge demand.[21]

When the stock went on sale on July 4, a mob poured in, swarmed over the clerks, and in less than an hour oversubscribed by 4,000 shares the $8 million in stock offered to the public. Overwhelmingly, the subscriptions came from non-Philadelphians who promptly took their scrip home with them. That was the beginning of a speculative orgy: in each of the major cities, people from all walks of life became engaged in buying and selling scrip. As Rufus King described the scene in New York, mechanics were deserting their shops, shopkeepers were dumping their wares at auction so as to raise funds for speculation, and respectable merchants were neglecting their business. Jefferson reported a similar situation in Philadelphia: "Ships are lying idle at the wharfs, buildings are stopped, capitals withdrawn from commerce, manufactures, arts & agriculture, to be employed in gambling." Jefferson, in keeping with his new view of Hamilton, saw the speculative mania as symptomatic of the evils that had destroyed Walpole's England. "The spirit of gaming," he wrote, "once it has seized a subject, is incurable. The taylor who has made thousands in one day, tho he has lost them the next, can never again be content with the slow & moderate earnings of his needle." Hamilton was concerned on a different account. Prices of every form of paper soared, and talk of a "new bubble" became common. Scrip, purchased for $25 on July 4, reached $325 on August 10; 6 percent government bonds, previously at 75 to 80 cents on the dollar, reached 130; and even 3 percents and deferred sixes, previously going around 40 cents on the dollar, rose nearly to par.[22]

Thoroughly alarmed, Hamilton issued a public statement that the prices of both scrip and bonds were too high. That, in conjunction with the machinations of short sellers and—according to King—of speculators who had sold scrip at $50 to $100 and were now spitefully determined to depress the market, checked the extravagant rise. But when the market broke on August 11, an equally frenzied wave of selling ensued, and the entire market structure seemed imperiled. Hamilton moved swiftly to counter the decline with judicious purchases through the sinking fund, and in a week the market began to be stabilized. He contributed to further stabilization by permitting himself to be quoted on the "real value" of securities: scrip at $195, and 6 percents at 110, and the lower-grade bonds at 60 to 65. Temporarily, the danger was over.[23]

But another disconcerting problem had begun to surface. Hamilton had opposed the opening of bank branches outside of Philadelphia, fearing that rivalries between the national and local banks would politicize all banking, feed speculation, and render the entire system unstable. To prevent that, he encouraged the existing banks to effect some kind of partnership with the new national bank. Accordingly, the Bank of Massachusetts bought 250 shares of the national bank's stock. The Bank of New York took the opposite tack, offering 300 shares of its own stock to the Bank of the United States. Hamilton soon learned, however, that the Massachusetts people aimed to have their bank absorbed and operated as a branch of the national institution. Moreover, merchants and speculators in Providence were proposing to organize a local bank for the same purpose, and the South Carolina investors' primary objective was to ensure the establishment of a Charleston branch. The matter was clinched when, after the scramble for stock among rival groups of New Yorkers, those who favored branches ended up with most of the shares. It thus came as no surprise when, less than three weeks after the organizational meeting of the bank in October, the directors voted to establish branches "in the cities of Charleston and New York, and towns of Baltimore and Boston, as soon as may be after the first Monday of January next."[24]

By and large, the men who gained control of the bank and instituted the branch system were ardent nationalists, personal and political friends of Hamilton's; they included Congressmen Fisher Ames, William Loughton Smith, Jeremiah Wadsworth, John Laurance, and Senator Rufus King. Their motives, though tempered by desire for personal and local gain, were primarily nationalistic: they viewed the establishment of branches as a powerful "Cement of the Union." In short, they shared Hamilton's goals but disagreed with him on a basic question of fiscal policy. Their success would lead to a great deal of trouble.[25]

For there was another dimension to the question: in state after state, local-minded politicians were moving to exploit the discontents and rivalries among monied men. In Massachusetts the old anti-Federalist leaders, including John Hancock, Sam Adams, Charles Jarvis, and James Sullivan, had voiced no objections as Hamilton's financial measures were being enacted; and they had generally been indifferent to the doings of the Bank of Massachusetts. Now, however, they began to realize that two could play at the game of winning loyalties through the manipulation of financial institutions. Soon a movement was under way to have the Massachusetts Bank brought under the control of the state; the movement gained popularity when the state bank's stockholders proved willing to sacrifice local interests by seeking to be absorbed by the national bank. If the state government did gain control over the Massachusetts Bank, the legislature—which had long been "liberally dispos'd to discern & oppose the power & influence of the nation" but heretofore had been unable to do so because of "their meanness & parsimony" and lack of resources—would be in a position to cause serious mischief in competition with the Bank of the United States.[26]

In New York the Clintonians and Livingstonians were more experienced in turning avarice to the account of the state and the injury of the nation. Ironically, the success of Hamilton's measures had greatly increased their capacity for doing so: because the state government was a creditor of the national government, funding and assumption had filled its treasury to the point of overflowing. Moreover, though the Clintonians commonly employed the same agrarian, Bolingbrokean rhetoric that Virginia republicans used and believed, they in fact operated an activist state government that vigorously supported and took part in capital ventures. In keeping with their activism rather than with their rhetoric, they determined not to oppose Hamilton's policies directly but to exploit them for the advantage of the state.[27]

In effect, the Clintonians set out to turn New York into a business corporation, into an entrepreneurial capitalist, with a view toward promoting and developing the state's resources and bringing profits to its citizenry. In 1791, the legislature resolved to convert a regular portion of its revenues into "productive capital." The state became a stockholder in both the Bank of New York and the Bank of the United States, became a banker itself by lending $554,000 to its citizens against land as security, began the survey that would ultimately lead to the building of the Erie Canal, proposed a road system to open its interior, and authorized a variety of related promotional activities.[28]

Two specific measures of the Clintonians boded ill for Hamilton's system. They made a calculated appeal to the big-time speculators who had lost out in the bidding for stock in the Bank of the United States. William Constable, Alexander Macomb, Daniel McCormick, and other speculators failed to obtain any stock at the initial subscription; and others, including various Livingstons and a number of William Duer's intimates, lost to Hamilton's friends in the rivalry for bank directorships. The Clintonians, blatantly attempting to seduce these disgruntled operators, arranged to sell them 3.6 million acres of state-owned frontier lands for the paltry price of $300,000. Thenceforth, these men could never be counted as reliable supporters of Hamilton's again—if, indeed, they ever could have been so counted.[29]

The Clintonians' other move was toward politicizing control over the Bank of New York. Consenting at last to the incorporation of the bank was a step in that direction (the bank had operated sine 1784 without a charter), and so was the state's investment in the bank's stock. In addition, the Clintonians encouraged increased investment in the bank by state-oriented financiers, even as the more national-minded of its stockholders were shifting their loyalty to the national bank. Hamilton, alert to the disadvantages of splitting the monied community, proposed an arrangement that would provide a measure of local control over the national bank's branches. Each branch, he suggested, should have its own board of directors, appointed and supervised by the national board. His proposal was adopted, but it came too late to forestall what Hamilton saw as the development of "political parties . . . in the monied interest" which would result from having "rival banks under Foederal & State authorities."[30]

Finally, there was a discomforting development in Pennsylvania. Many of the largest public creditors in that state had stubbornly refused to accede to the terms of the funding act and insisted upon receiving the full interest to which their original securities entitled them. Their adamance irritated and embarrassed Hamilton, and their stand was contrary to the public interest as he perceived it; but they were legally and morally within their rights, as he was painfully aware. Now, after lengthy and awkward negotiations, the state of Pennsylvania took him off the hook by making provision, in regard to its own citizens, for paying the difference between their contracted interest rates and the reduced rates specified in the funding act. On a less generous basis, New York had previously taken a similar action, and Maryland soon would follow. That creditors could obtain full contractual justice only through the actions of state governments was humiliating to Hamilton, and it did nothing to endear him to them.[31]

In sum, the "monied phalanx" of Hamiltonians that Jefferson imagined and feared simply did not exist. Nationalists among monied men refused to follow Hamilton's advice, when they bothered to ask it; state particularists among them turned his measures to state account; and the great speculators proved indifferent to the political consequences of their actions. Their attitudes would create problems in future. Fortunately, Hamilton had long since abandoned the simplistic notion that direct manipulation of self-interest could serve as a reliable means of effecting the public good.

For the conceptual center of his design for America—of his plan to make the United States a great nation despite itself—lay elsewhere. He wanted to institutionalize behavior. From that perspective, squabbling over the details of the organization of the banking system was essentially irrelevant. What was important was that there would be a banking system, and that the currency of the nation would be based upon it, not upon gold and silver. That meant the nation could be built on credit, for the crucial characteristic of banking currency is that it is money created in the present, not out of past savings but out of the expectation of future profits. Moreover, it was inherent in Hamilton's system that capital as well as currency could be formed through the institutionalization of future expectations. Finally, the system provided stimulus as well as wherewithal, for the incentive to industry is powerful indeed when the choice is between paying one's debts and failing to survive.

Even as he was managing or attempting to manage these grand undertakings, Hamilton was becoming involved in a bizarre personal adventure. He had remained in Philadelphia for the initial offering of bank stock and then, a week or two later, packed up Betsey and the children and escorted them to New York. There they were met by a member of the Schuyler household, who took them to the Schuyler estate near Albany. Going to the country for the summer was prudent and, among those who could afford it, customary, for large cities were dangerous from mid-July to mid-September, when epidemic diseases periodically ravaged the inhabitants. Besides, Betsey's health was none too good, and she needed a rest from the harassments of tending to four small children. Hamilton also needed a rest, but the demands of his job, unlike those of his cabinet colleagues and the president, precluded taking one, so he returned alone to Philadelphia.[32]

One day a lady appeared at his residence, 79 South Third Street, and asked to speak to Hamilton in private. Maria Reynolds was in fact a lady, as the term was understood in eighteenth-century America; in that deferential age no person of vulgar breeding would have presumed to call upon a man of Hamilton's status at the front door. Her pretentions to a genteel background were confirmed in the ensuing conversation: her parents were of the gentry class in Dutchess County, New York, and she was the sister-in-law of Gilbert Livingston, a nephew of the manor lord. Her story elicited Hamilton's sympathy. Her husband, she said, had deserted her for another woman, leaving her destitute and with a five-year-old child; she had come to Hamilton, as a fellow New Yorker, to ask for help in the form of funds with which to return to her family. Strangers often called upon Hamilton for assistance, since he had, as one supplicant put it, a reputation for "benevolence and Humanity to the distress'd," and he commonly helped them if he was able and they were deserving or even plausible.[33]

But if the request was not extraordinary, the lady was, and so was Hamilton's reaction to her. She was a beautiful, bold, vivacious, and sensuous woman, exuding sexuality; and between the lines of Hamilton's dispassionate description of the encounter, written six years later, the electricity of passion fairly crackles. He told her he had no money with him, which was presumably true, but that if she would give him her address he would either send or bring "a small supply of money," which was only partly true, for he had no intention of merely sending the money. That night, having obtained a thirty-dollar banknote, he called upon her at the address she had given—134 South Fourth Street, little more than a block away from his own rented house. "I inquired for Mrs. Reynolds and was shewn up stairs, at the head of which she met me and conducted me into a bed room. I took the bill out of my pocket and gave it to her. Some conversation ensued from which it was quickly apparent that other than pecuniary consolation would be acceptable." Assignations between them became regular and frequent thereafter.[34]

That Hamilton was a novice at marital infidelity is painfully evident in the clumsiness with which he handled the affair. For instance, he was torn between longing for Betsey's return and desire that his affair not be interrupted; and, as a man unaccustomed to deceit, he was as transparent and awkward as an adolescent Romeo in his letters to Betsey. "I . . . will wait with all the patience I can the time for your return. But you must not precipitate it. I am so anxious for a perfect restoration of your health that I am willing to make a great sacrifice for it." Again, "I cannot be happy without you. Yet I must not advise you to urge your return. The confirmation of your health is so essential." Yet again, fresh from a romp in the sheets with Maria, "I . . . only want you with me . . . but I charge you . . . not to precipitate your return." And yet again, chided for writing so infrequently, he was unable "to imagine what can have become of my other letters"; surely they must have been stolen by "some very foul and abominable" person. Any seasoned philanderer would have been more adroit in handling the matter.[35]

Nor was the affair a passing, if torrid, sexual dalliance between two lonely people, or even such on his side alone. Sexual ardor is a powerful force, especially in a man of great physical energy and strong creative drives, and it can be almost irresistible if the woman is, or appears to be, as aroused as the man is. But sex is not nearly so powerful in the consummation as in the pursuit, and eventually desire is sated, no matter how skilled a lover the woman may be, if it is not reinforced by something stronger. Moreover, though a touch of danger may heighten desire, genuine danger will douse its fires, especially if other, safer sexual outlets are available. Hamilton's relationship with Maria Reynolds became so dangerous as to jeopardize not only his marriage but also his life's work, and in September Betsey was home again, conceiving their fifth child two months later.[36] No mere lust could have survived those developments—and yet the affair went on.

Hamilton was suffering what, among romantics, is known as the grand passion. It is an affliction to which pure romantics are particularly susceptible, and its victims are helpless in resisting it. It is neither love (Hamilton loved Betsey) nor sexual attraction, though it resembles and partakes of both and is temporarily more powerful than either. Knowing that it is wrong, as Hamilton knew, does not mitigate its force. Quite the contrary: it can exist only if it is immoral, it feeds upon forbiddenness, it thrives upon frustration, it grows stronger in proportion as it is resisted or suppressed—and the more moral its victim, the more virulent the malady becomes.[37]

Hamilton's inability to control the passion was soon demonstrated. A short time after the affair had begun, Maria told Hamilton that her husband, James Reynolds, had returned and asked for a reconciliation. Hamilton advised her to accept it, and she did. That was reasonable enough, for when her husband is around, one's mistress may not interfere in one's own marriage. What came next, however, hinted of darker things, and Hamilton's response was far less reasonable. Maria told Hamilton that Reynolds had information concerning improprieties by a certain Treasury official. An interview ensued, during which Reynolds "confessed that he had obtained a list of claims from a person in my department which he had made use of in his speculations." These doubtless had been lists of unsuspecting veterans in back-country Virginia whose special pay claims, as was rumored at the time (the winter of 1789–90), had been bought up at bargain rates by northern speculators. Hamilton invited Reynolds, "by the expectation of my friendship and good offices, to disclose the person." Reynolds said that William Duer had given him the lists. Since Duer had long been gone from the Treasury, Hamilton considered this as no great revelation. But "it was the interest of my passions to appear to set value on it, and to continue the expectation of friendship and good offices. Mr. Reynolds told me he was going to Virginia, and on his return would point out something in which I could serve him." Possibly—Hamilton did not remember—he said "something about employment in a public office."[38]

Whatever Reynolds had in mind, the time had come for Hamilton to break off the relationship with both Reynoldses, for it was obvious that foul doings were afoot. That became clearer during the following weeks, when Hamilton learned from discreet inquiries that Reynolds had a reputation as a scurvy fellow. Hamilton began to suspect (what subsequent developments would seem to confirm) that Maria and James had been in cahoots all along, that she had seduced him solely for the purpose of making him vulnerable to Reynolds' designs. But he did not—could not—make the break.

The Reynolds affair warped Hamilton's vision only in regard to the affair itself; otherwise, Hamilton continued to be at the top of his form. His efforts during the fall of 1791 were directed mainly toward executing the third step in his plan to nationalize, monetize, and energize American society. The objective was to promote industry, both in the sense of industriousness and in the sense of large-scale manufacturing. He had two specific means in mind: to transform the paper capital created by his fiscal policies, or as much of it as possible, into productive capital, and to persuade Congress to promote manufacturing with a broad system of protective tariffs, subsidies, and similar inducements.[39]

Transforming the capital proved easy, at least at first. Believing that American businessmen were moved largely by a "spirit of imitation," he set out to provide an attractive example. With the help of Assistant Secretary Tench Coxe and the backing of several entrepreneurs in New York and Philadelphia, he proposed to create a corporation, the Society for the Encouragement of Useful Manufactures (commonly called the S.U.M. by historians and the Manufacturing Society by those involved in it). The encouragement of manufacturing in the United States had long been regarded as vital to the public interest, as Hamilton wrote in a prospectus for the corporation, but so far the dearness of labor and the want of capital had prevented it. Recent developments in the use of machinery could overcome the first obstacle, provided that British law preventing the export of machinery and the emigration of skilled workers could be circumvented. As to the second obstacle, subscriptions to capital stock could be made in certificates of the public debt which, after partial exchange for stock in the Bank of the United States, could be pledged as collateral for specie loans abroad. Once organized, Hamilton believed, the company would have "a moral certainty of success" in the production of paper, pottery, brass and iron ware, and a variety of textiles.[40]

As for obtaining the necessary corporate character, Hamilton thought almost every state would be eager to grant one, but that New Jersey would probably be the most desirable location. It had an abundance of cheap and easily tapped water power at the falls of the Passaic; it was thickly settled and had access to cheap provisions and raw materials; it had neither extensive commerce nor vacant frontier lands to be peopled and thus could feel "no supposed interest hostile to the advancement of manufactures." It was unnecessary for Hamilton to add that, being located between New York and Philadelphia, New Jersey was well situated for attracting investors in those two cities. It would have been politically imprudent to add, though Hamilton had it in mind, that a location close to New York City would help induce the Bank of New York to be generous in making accommodation loans to the Manufacturing Society.[41]

The plan met with a warm reception. Merchants, brokers, and speculators were interested from the outset, and the magic of Hamilton's name together with the effects of William Duer's salesmanship ensured that investors would be forthcoming. Hamilton proposed an initial stock offering of $500,000, to be increased ultimately to $1 milliion; when subscriptions were opened in the fall, $600,000 in stock was sold almost immediately. Moreover, the market value of the stock doubled within a month. Similarly, steering a bill of incorporation through the New Jersey legislature was a breeze, thanks partly to the efforts of Governor William Paterson, after whom the Manufacturing Society's new factory town would be named. The charter was a generous one, vesting the society with monopoly status and exemption from taxation.[42]

A weakness in the plan would soon become visible. A controlling interest in the company was bought up by a syndicate consisting of Duer, Walter Livingston, Alexander Macomb, William and J. Constable, John Dewhurst, Benjamin Walker, and Royal Flint. These respected businessmen would prove to be little better than rich and/or wellborn versions of the unsavory Mr. Reynolds.[43]

But Hamilton's model corporation seemed off to an auspicious start, and he turned his attention to his third great state paper, his Report on Manufactures. In the report Hamilton revealed at last the full range of his program for making the United States a prosperous, secure, and happy nation. Underlying the whole plan was his conviction that none of these three ends of government was obtainable unless Americans fundamentally changed their ways. He believed the country could achieve prosperity and safety only if it broadened its economic base to include manufacturing as well as agriculture and commerce, and he was "morally certain" that it could be happy only if its people were infused with the spirit of industry, regularity, order, and improvement.

The report begins with a rejection of the agrarian ideal. Knowing that he was dealing with a set of deep-rooted prejudices shared by the vast majority of Americans, Hamilton trod softly at first. Instead of considering the emotionally laden ideal directly, he started obliquely with an attack upon an economic theory that had been employed to justify it. The French physiocrats, following the lead of a doctor named François Quesnay, had developed a systematic body of thought which held that land, or agriculture, was the source of all wealth. The physiocrats maintained that only agriculture produced a net surplus over the costs of production, and that all nonfarm labor was "sterile," since it merely changed the products of the land into consumable forms and added nothing to those products except the direct value of the labor. Fanciful as the theory was, it gained wide currency and became, in agrarian dogma, the economic counterpart of the political and social doctrines of Bolingbroke. (As Hamilton learned in doing his research for the report, few American farmers knew whether farming was more or less profitable than other enterprises, for almost none kept any records. The lack of information did not, however, prevent them from having opinions.)[44]

Hamilton demolished the physiocratic theory by quoting and paraphrasing at length from Adam Smith's *Wealth of Nations*. That was a shrewd approach, for the Scots economist's free-trade doctrines were highly respected in America, appealing to agricultural and commercial interests alike. Shrewd, too, was Hamilton's reserve in drawing conclusions from Smith's arguments. He was not contending, he said, *"that manufacturing industry is more productive than that of Agriculture,"* only that both were productive, probably about equally. Having demonstrated that, he went on to show in a series of analyses and examples that the development of manufacturing would benefit the farmers themselves. Domestic manufacturing establishments would provide the farmer with cheaper goods and create a more profitable outlet for his produce. Besides, the existence of factories where cash wages could be earned would "afford occasional and extra employment to industrious individuals and families, who are willing to devote the leisure resulting from the intermissions of their ordinary pursuits to collateral labours, as a resource of multiplying their acquisitions or their enjoyments." And for the less industrious, for the husbandman who was immune to the lure of "a new source of profit and support from the encreased industry of his wife and daughters" and for "persons who would otherwise be idle," Hamilton would provide an extra incentive. He suggested that a "Motive to *greater exertion* in any occupation" could be created by raising taxes—not so high as to discourage in-

[233]

dustry by engendering despair, but high enough so that everyone would have to work in order to pay them.[45]

Having used Smith in his rejection of agrarianism, Hamilton next rejected Smith's own central argument, that economic activity is regulated by natural laws and is most beneficial when government does not interfere with its workings. Insofar as this implied free trade, or the taxation of trade only for purposes of revenue and so moderately as not to interfere with its flow, Hamilton could endorse noninterference as an ideal; but as a statesman and not a theorist he saw that it was unrealistic in practice. The nations on whom the United States depended for markets and manufactures were committed to mercantilism, and if the United States followed a free-trade policy without reciprocation abroad, she would merely increase the disadvantages under which she traded. As Necker put it, "all those hypotheses which are founded upon a general freedom of commerce, are chimerical propositions; the powers who would lose by this freedom would never adopt it, and those who would gain by it," if they should introduce it to set an example, "would imitate the folly of a private individual, who in the hope of establishing a community of effects, suffered all his neighbors to share his patrimony." Hamilton agreed entirely with Necker's view.[46]

But Hamilton also rejected Smith's doctrine of noninterference in its broader sense—that human industry, "if left to itself, will naturally find its way to the most useful and profitable employment." In doing so he was influenced by both Necker and Hume, but in the main his thinking was his own. For Hamilton perceived—as later economic theorists, befogged by Marxism, failed to see—that social values and habits normally dictate economic activity, and not the other way around. "Experience teaches," Hamilton wrote in a pellucid and persuasive passage, "that men are often so much governed by what they are accustomed to see and practice, that the simplest and most obvious improvements, in the most ordinary occupations, are adopted with hesitation, reluctance and by slow gradations." Men would resist changes so long as even "a bare support could be ensured by an adherence to ancient courses," and perhaps even longer. The natural order of things was for social habits and values to dictate economic norms and for government to reflect the interplay of the two. Hamilton saw the advantages of turning the formula around, of using government to bring about economic changes which in turn would alter society for its own benefit.[47]

While rejecting *laissez faire,* however, Hamilton was emphatic in his commitment to private enterprise and to a market economy. Primarily that commitment was moral, not economic. Hamilton believed that the greatest benefits of a system of government-encouraged private enterprise were spiritual—the enlargement of the scope of human freedom and the enrichment of the opportunities for human endeavor. "Minds of the strongest and most active powers," he wrote, "fall below mediocrity and labour without effect, if confined to uncongenial pursuits. And it is thence to be inferred, that the results of human exertion may be immensely increased by diversifying its objects." In its own right, "to cherish and stimulate the activity of the human mind" was a distinct good. Too, "even things in themselves not positively advantageous, sometimes become so, by their tendency to provoke exertion. Every new scene, which is opened to the busy nature of man to rouse and to exert itself, is the addition of a new energy to the general stock of effort. The spirit of enterprise, useful and prolific as it is, must necessarily be contracted or expanded in proportion to the simplicity or variety of the occupations and productions, which are to be found in a Society. It must be less in a nation of mere cultivators, than in a nation of cultivators and merchants; less in a nation of cultivators and merchants, than in a nation of cultivators, artificers and merchants."[48]

Hamilton spelled out what he regarded as the proper role of government in the economy of a free society. Except in the "manufactories of all the necessary weapons of war"—which the experience of the Revolution had convinced him was unreliable in private hands—the means of production should be managed privately and for profit. The function of government should be to promote a general spirit of improvement. It should reward productivity and punish dissipation, idleness, and extravagance. Taxes should be designed to encourage industry, never to impede it. Regulation of productive activity should be confined to inspection to prevent frauds and ensure the highest quality and marketability of products. If such policies were adhered to, every member of society would gain—the poor as well as the rich, the farmer as well as the manufacturer and merchant, the South as well as the North—and the gains would be justly distributed, for rewards would be proportionate to ability, integrity, and industry.[49]

There was one more function of government in the Hamiltonian scheme of things, one that Adam Smith had not even taken into account. Hamilton perceived, as Smith had not, that beyond money, land, equipment, and goods, wealth is also the industriousness of a people channeled by institutionalized social coordination; and to him the most vital task of government was to erect or foster the appropriate institutions. It had already taken large strides toward doing so with the funding and assumption and banking systems. Hamilton believed the next step was crucial. On the one hand, it must not succumb to the illusion that it could go on multiplying debt-based paper capital endlessly; there was a point beyond which paper capital and paper currency would cease to stimulate real productivity and would serve only "to pamper the dissipation of idle and dissolute individuals." On the other hand, the moment was now ripe for transforming the American stock of paper capital into permanent, tangible, productive capital, to prevent its being wasted on the consumption of foreign luxuries or upon the development of interior lands that would not become productive for many years.[50]

Hamilton proposed several specific measures, all designed to build upon such manufacturing as the country was already engaged in and to promote other industries that it needed or for which it was naturally well adapted. These measures included levying protective tariffs or prohibiting the importation of competing manufactures until American producers in a given industry were firmly established; prohibiting the exportation of raw materials; granting bounties and other direct subsidies; awarding premiums or prizes "to reward some particular excellence or superiority, some extraordinary exertion or skill"; exempting imported raw materials from duties or granting drawbacks of such duties; encouraging inventions; inspecting manufactured products; and facilitating internal commerce through an extension of the banking system and improvement of internal transportation facilities. Finally, Hamilton proposed the creation of a board to promote the useful arts, agriculture, manufactures, and commerce.[51]

It was a noble design. Unfortunately for Hamilton, a majority in Congress had other designs.

XI

Attack and Counterattack: *1791-1792*

The Dull, flat Falsehood serves for policy;

And in the Cunning, Truth itself's a lie.

In his youth, Hamilton had remarked that "a man of real merit is never seen in so favourable a light, as through the medium of adversity." By that standard he now had abundant opportunity to prove his worth. His affair with Maria Reynolds led to blackmail by her husband and then to something worse. Madison and Jefferson established a newspaper, subsidized it with government funds, and used it to vilify Hamilton personally and undermine faith in the Treasury Department. They and their friends in Congress waged a vicious succession of attacks designed to drive him out of office and to destroy him and all his works. Jefferson sought to ruin his relationship with Washington by pouring innuendoes, rumors, and lies into the president's ear. As if that were not enough, erstwhile friends initiated a speculative orgy that gave fodder to Hamilton's enemies and then, when it engendered a panic in the securities market, seemed on the verge of reducing his fiscal creations to rubble.[1]

He rose to the occasion. He handled the Reynolds situation as few men would have had the wits or the courage to do. He met the newspaper attacks with a ferocious counterattack, grinding out articles under nine different *noms de plume,* single-handedly taking on hordes of opponents with an energy and skill that inspired awe in his enemies. He met the challenges in Congress head-on and emerged not only vindicated but with his department vested with new trusts. He answered Jefferson's charges so candidly, fully, and effectively that, in time, the secretary of state had little choice but to resign himself. His fiscal machinery weathered the financial panic with a minimum of disruption.

His success, however, could not obscure one crucial fact: he was now on the defensive. His momentum was broken, and though he would regain the initiative, all chances of completing his system with the full implementation of his Report on Manufactures were dashed. His revolution would come, but it would be much longer in the making than he had hoped.

The task that Jefferson and Madison set for themselves would be no small undertaking, for Hamilton was a national hero. His doings were immensely popular in their own right, and Washington's sanction made them doubly so. Prosperity was so widespread that for the first time in memory nearly everybody except the tobacco planters was able to get out from under debt to Europe. Fresh capital was pouring in from abroad and, together with the paper capital created by Hamilton's system, it fueled an unprecedented burst of developmental energy. In New York the excess of money triggered a mania for getting rich quickly, but elsewhere the money was translated into tangible improvements. Forty corporations—as many as had been chartered in the colonial and Confederation periods combined—were chartered by state legislatures in 1791–92, nine of them for banks, the remainder for manufacturing and for canals, turnpike roads, and water works. Farmers, too, were faring well, and not just because they were getting good prices for their products. Before the Hamiltonian system was enacted, Massachusetts and Virginia had been levying a million dollars a year in direct taxes on land, Connecticut more than $200,000, Pennsylvania $600,000. Almost all these taxes were for servicing public debts, since the "civil lists" or regular expenditures in each state were nominal. After Hamilton's system was adopted, these tax burdens disappeared, and in most places ordinary landowners became as free from taxation, except for modest local needs, as in the halcyon days before 1763.[2]

Nor was there only prosperity. Washington, on his tour through the South in 1791, made a point of sounding out the popular mood, especially in areas that had opposed ratification of the Constitution, and learned that the people "appeared to be happy, contented and satisfied" with the national government. There had been some opposition to the whiskey excise, but that had subsided when the law was explained—presumably when people learned that stills for home consumption were exempt from the tax—and Washington heard no complaining about Hamilton's other measures. Significantly, he recorded in his diary that where discontentment did appear, "it was not difficult to trace the cause to some demagogue, or speculating character."[3]

But the demagogues were about to go to work in earnest. "Republicans," as Jefferson and Madison and their friends were shrewdly if misleadingly calling themselves, potentially had a fairly solid minority power base. In addition to state-oriented politicians in Boston, New York, and Philadelphia, they had prospective supporters among the lawless frontiersmen and throughout the southern tobacco-growing regions. What they lacked was propaganda machinery. Only two anti-Federalist newspapers, Thomas Greenleaf's *New York Journal* and Francis Bailey's *Freeman's Journal* in Philadelphia, had survived as antiadministration organs, and only a few others, such as Francis Childs's New York *Daily Advertiser,* printed articles opposing as well as favoring administration policies. Virtually all the rest were solid in their support of the administration, and the most influential newspaper in the country, John Fenno's *Gazette of the United States,* was explicitly dedicated to the function of endearing "The GENERAL GOVERNMENT to the PEOPLE." Fenno, who had established his daily some months before Hamilton took office, had praised all administration measures from the outset and, once Hamilton set to work, waxed almost lyrical. If the self-styled Republicans were to create the popular discontents necessary to abet their schemes, they would need a mouthpiece of their own.[4]

In 1791, for this purpose, Jefferson and Madison promoted an antiadministration newspaper. They sought out Philip Freneau, an old college friend of Madison's and Henry Lee's who had gained some renown as the "Poet of the Revolution" and, working as a journalist in recent years, had become notorious for his vituperative pen. Madison appealed to Freneau's hatred of Britain and of monarchists, who, Madison assured him, were taking over the federal government. The Virginians arranged financial backing from Francis Childs and pledged themselves to find subscribers—at which, with the help of Daniel Carroll in Maryland and Thomas Bell and Henry Lee in Virginia, they worked diligently and effectively. In addition to these private exertions, they arranged for a pair of government subsidies to help underwrite Freneau's attacks upon the government. The first was direct: Freneau would be hired as a translator in the State Department, a job that would consume little of his time and provide him a modest income. Second, they would support a cheap postage rate for newspapers, crucial for any paper that aimed at a national circulation. (The act they got through Congress established the newspaper rate at one cent for a distance up to a hundred miles and a cent and a half for farther distances—as compared with six cents for letters up to thirty miles and twelve and a half to twenty-five cents for longer distances.) Thus induced, Freneau established the *National Gazette* in October 1791.[5]

Freneau did not launch any attacks immediately. Instead, showing good business and political sense, he spent three months building a reputation for his journal as a fair and thorough purveyor of the news. When Hamilton or his measures were mentioned at all, the tone was either neutral or laudatory. The paper hailed the assumption plan, the bank, and the effort to stimulate manufacturing, and the promoters of the Manufacturing Society were singled out for praise. The only severe criticism of a federal government policy—understandably enough, considering the Virginia clientele Freneau hoped to cultivate—was an attack on the federal judiciary for opening the courts to suits by British creditors of American debtors. The paper demanded that such suits be suspended until Britain make restitution for slaves its army carried off at the end of the war. A series of essays, written but unsigned by Madison, were the only serious political opinion pieces, treating a variety of subjects in a dispassionate, somewhat turgid way.[6]

Then everything abruptly changed. Madison set the stage with three essays reminding his readers of the evils of the British system and piously declaring his hope that "a government operated by corrupt influence" would never be established in America. An unsigned piece by some other author quickly followed, tying speculation to the spirit of aristocracy, then an article by "A Farmer" denouncing the chartering of the Manufacturing Society (which Freneau had applauded ten weeks earlier) as "one of the most unjust and arbitrary laws . . . that ever disgraced the government of a free people." Then came the full treatment, from an author pointedly signing himself "Brutus" to suggest that Hamilton was a proto-Caesar. In a series of articles, each more extravagant than the last, Brutus charged that Hamilton's system had put the public wealth into the hands of rich "foreign and domestic speculators," giving them "a fee simple in the resources of the country; while the industrious mechanic, the laborious farmer, and generally the poorer class of people . . . are all made tributary" forever. With each issue, Freneau's paper grew more extreme, repeating and building upon the theme that Hamilton aspired to establish monarchy, aristocracy, plutocracy, and corruption in America, and that so far he was getting away with it. Regularly, too, Freneau coupled his shafts at Hamilton with praise of Jefferson as an "illustrious Patriot" and "Colossus of Liberty" who stood almost alone in defending America against Hamilton's cabal.[7]

The Republicans' efforts inside government were coordinated with Freneau's, or at least followed the same timetable. At first Madison and his supporters were relatively restrained, pushing favorite measures and engaging in minor obstruction but initiating nothing that could properly be called an attack. They were successful on most points of contention; Madison was on the winning side on roughly three-quarters of the roll-call votes, whereas such staunch friends of government as Fisher Ames and William Loughton Smith were on the winning side barely more than half the time. But the Republicans did not have quite enough strength to carry any major issues except their Post Office bill. They failed in a renewed attempt to place the secretary of state in the line of presidential succession; they were unsuccessful in a bid to increase Virginia's representation and to defeat a reapportionment bill that increased the representation of predominantly nationalist states; they fought in vain to defeat a Senate bill granting bounties to cod fisheries. In short, during the first four months of the long session (from early November 1791 through the following February) they simply lacked the votes to mount a serious offensive.[8]

Jefferson attributed their failure to a "monied phalanx" of Hamiltonians in Congress. He identified twenty representatives as paper men who in conjunction with "blind devotees" and the "lazy" and "ignorant" members gave Hamilton control of the House. There were in fact six additional "paper men," holders of several thousand dollars apiece in public securities, whom Jefferson missed; but the group scarcely constituted a phalanx. One of the twenty-six, Jonathan Dayton, was absent most of the session. Of the others, fourteen regularly voted with Ames and against Madison, but eleven regularly voted with Madison. And if the monied phalanx was not a phalanx, neither were the Republicans republicans—not, anyway, according to Hamilton's strict definition of republicanism as "the sublime idea of a perfect equality of rights among citizens," to the exclusion of hereditary distinctions—for most of Madison's co-partisans were slaveholders, including two erstwhile anti-Federalists from New York.[9]

Whether or not Madison and Jefferson truly believed their frustrations in Congress were owing to a corrupt Hamiltonian influence, the frustrations were real enough; perhaps for that reason, they suddenly stepped up their actions on other fronts toward the end of February. Jefferson made a bold move just as Freneau was opening his slur campaign. The recently passed Post Office act had put the postal service on a permanent basis, and Jefferson was aware of the patronage and propaganda possibilities inherent in control of the office. On February 28 he met with the president and tried to convince Washington that the terms of the act warranted transfer of the Post Office from the Treasury to the State Department. He could not be accused of making a power grab, Jefferson insisted, since he intended shortly to retire. The conversation was interrupted, and Washington invited Jefferson to resume their talk over breakfast the next day.[10]

Next morning Washington seemed favorably disposed toward the transfer but was disturbed at Jefferson's talk of retirement. Jefferson reiterated the sentiment and insidiously contrasted himself with Hamilton, whose plan "embraced years in its view." The president's reply gave Jefferson opportunity to open a tirade against Hamilton. Hamilton had contrived a plot, said Jefferson, "for deluging the States with paper money instead of gold and silver, for withdrawing our citizens from the pursuits of commerce, manufactures, buildings, and other branches of useful industry, to occupy themselves and their capitals in a species of gambling, destructive of morality, and which had introduced its poison into the government itself." Support for the system so far had come from congressmen who had "feathered their nests with paper." As for the proposed next steps in the nefarious scheme, as outlined in the Report on Manufactures, those were really a design to destroy the Constitution. Only if those proposals were defeated, Jefferson concluded, would the widespread popular discontentment with the national government begin to wane.[11]

Washington's response to this panorama of fantasies is not recorded. He must, to say the least, have been dumbfounded.

Hamilton paid little attention to any of this at first, partly because he was unaware of Jefferson's and Madison's designs, partly because he was preoccupied with more vexing concerns. In late November or early December James Reynolds had returned to Philadelphia, claiming that Hamilton had promised him a job in the Treasury Department. Hamilton put him off and resolved to end the relationship with Mrs. Reynolds, whereupon Maria, "with a most imposing art," giving "all the appearances of violent attachment, and of agonizing distress at the idea of a relinquishment . . . employed every effort to keep up my attention and visits." Helplessly, Hamilton adopted "the plan of a gradual discontinuance rather than of a sudden interruption, as least calculated to give pain."[12]

Then came a squeeze. On December 15 Maria sent Hamilton a note saying that Reynolds had found out about their relationship. That same day and again two days later came notes from Reynolds, professing to be aggrieved and asking for "satisfaction." Suspecting, at last, that he was the intended victim of a plot, Hamilton began to save every communication he received from the pair. When he met with Reynolds, however, he was relieved to learn that the wounded husband had—or seemed to have—nothing more sinister than blackmail on his mind. Hamilton had little money, but it was arranged that he pay Reynolds $1,000 in two installments.[13]

In mid-January 1792, the relationship took yet another twist. Reynolds sent a note inviting Hamilton to call on both Reynoldses socially, and Maria bombarded Hamilton with notes begging him to see her privately and hinting that she might kill herself in grief if he did not. Apparently Reynolds and his partner in various criminal activities, Jacob Clingman, hoped to have Hamilton seen calling at the Reynolds household as a means of furthering some scheme for enriching themselves. As for Maria, it is possible that she was sincere in her impassioned professions and was being used by her husband; it is equally possible that she was merely a consummate actress. In any event, Hamilton believed her and, for three or four more months, resumed their liaison. He was now extremely cautious, however, which frustrated whatever plans Reynolds and Clingman had in mind. Reynolds then forbade Hamilton to see Maria, and by that time "the interdiction was every way welcome." Maria continued to plead with Hamilton for months, and Reynolds hit him up for three small loans, but otherwise the affair was over—for the time being.[14]

The Reynolds business, trying as it was, was not Hamilton's most troublesome problem that winter. In New York, the preceding summer's near-bubble had not stopped the frenzy for speculation, and by year's end another spectacular rise seemed in the making. To profit from it, William Duer hatched a grandiose plan. On December 29 he formed a secret partnership with the wealthy land speculator Alexander Macomb, into which were soon brought most of the leading investors in the Manufacturing Society including Walter Livingston, Benjamin Walker, and William Constable. Early in January Macomb, acting for the partnership, stirred up a movement to charter a new state bank. The attending publicity set off a "bancomania" in the form of projects to create three separate banks: the "Million Bank," to be capitalized at $1 million but immediately oversubscribed by $10 million; the "Merchants Bank," also to be capitalized at $1 million; and the "Tammany Bank," to be capitalized at $2 million. After a few days the projects were combined, and a petition for a charter was submitted to the legislature. The combined corporation, known first as the Million Bank and later as the State Bank, was to be capitalized at $1.8 million.[15]

Hamilton reacted in outrage and "infinite pain." "These extravagant sallies of speculation," he said, "do injury to the Government and to the whole system of public Credit, by disgusting all sober Citizens and giving a wild air to every thing." Denouncing the Million Bank as "a dangerous tumour" and a "Monster," Hamilton said that the addition of a third bank in New York City would "raise such a mass of artificial Credit, as must endanger every one of them & do harm in every view." He also supported William Seton, cashier of the Bank of New York, in his efforts to stop the mania; Seton refused to accept deposits from the speculators, tendered mostly in bank notes and especially notes of the Bank of the United States, saying that when subscriptions to the Million Bank became payable, the speculators would cause a run by withdrawing specie. Hamilton not only approved that maneuver but pledged Treasury support to protect legitimate banks from the "attacks of a confederated host of frantic and . . . unprincipled gamblers."[16]

Had Hamilton known who the unprincipled gamblers were and the extent of their schemes, he would have been even more outraged. Macomb's promotion of the Million Bank was essentially bogus: its purpose was to depress the stock of the Bank of New York to facilitate the Duer-Macomb group's acquiring a controlling interest in it. The operation succeeded—the group acquired contracts for delivery of 290 of the Bank of New York's 700 shares and soon thereafter increased their holdings to 400 shares. Gaining control of the bank, in turn, was but a means to finance a more audacious undertaking. Duer sought nothing less than to corner the market in 6 percent government bonds before July, when the next installment on the subscriptions for stock in the Bank of the United States would become payable. If he succeeded, one of two things would happen: subscribers could be forced to pay him exorbitant prices for the 6 percents or, if they proved unable to do so, the Duer group could snap up control of the Bank of the United States. Either way, the syndicate would reap profits that staggered the imagination.[17]

But there were fatal weaknesses in the plan. One was personal: Duer, always excessively sanguine, now became so much so that he virtually lost contact with reality. (Troup wrote two months later, "This poor man is in a state of almost complete insanity.") That weakness aggravated another, the timing of the venture. By beginning at the first of the year the speculators allowed themselves the maximum possible time for effecting their corner before the next bank subscription payment, but six months was not enough. Their stock in the New York bank was not holdings in hand but contracts for future delivery two to four months hence. In the interim they could not obtain control of the bank, and thus had to rely on other sources of credit. Moreover, the magnitude of the undertaking, already straining the limits of their resources, was increased by the need for speed, which required them to buy considerably above the market to attract sellers—rather than, as is vital to would-be cornerers, at the lowest possible prices. In these circumstances Duer truly behaved like a madman. He borrowed against every scrap of collateral he had; as president of the Manufacturing Society he lent himself, on personal notes, $60,000, practically all the company's cash surplus; he borrowed the funds of a lottery of which he was trustee; he borrowed through endorsements from his associates and friends up to and sometimes beyond their abilities to repay. When he exhausted his conventional sources of credit, he turned to unconventional ones, paying usurious rates of 2 to 4 percent a month for loans from "persons of all descriptions," from "merchants, tradesmen, draymen, widows, orphans, oystermen, market-women, churches," and even a notorious madam. The proceeds were plunged into the purchase of 6 percents at prices three and four shillings above the market, for delivery two, three, or four months later.[18]

Another weakness in Duer's operation was political. Duer was connected by marriage to the manor Livingstons, and his associate Walter Livingston was of that branch of the family; the Livingstons on the chancellor's side of the family, now politically allied with Governor Clinton, were fierce enemies of both Duer and Walter Livingston. Brockholst, John R., and Edward Livingston, as short sellers, contracted to deliver most of the New York bank stock that the Duer syndicate had contracted to buy. It was therefore in their interest to keep alive the Million Bank proposal as a means of holding down the bank's stock; and Clinton, sorely needing the Livingstons' support in his reelection campaign, found it in his interest to abet them. Apparently the Livingstons also attempted simultaneously to weaken the bank and dry up Duer's credit by draining the bank of as much of its specie reserves as possible—this at a season when a large part of the city's gold and silver had, as was customary, been sent to the back country to buy produce for spring export. The pressure on the bank was doubly severe because the New York branch of the Bank of the United States was delayed until April in opening.[19]

Because "Duer kept himself, as usual, very much out of sight" and because the Million Bank was repeatedly in the news, Hamilton thought at first the greater danger was from the Livingston quarter. The impression was reinforced by the Livingstons' direct threat on the solvency of the New York bank and the attendant indirect threat on banks elsewhere. Accordingly, he directed his efforts toward ensuring the stability of the banking system. "The state of things," he advised Seton, "requires unusual circumspection. Every existing bank ought within prudent limits to abridge its operations," by which he meant tighten credit. "The superstructure of Credit is now too vast for the foundation. It must be gradually brought within more reasonable dimensions or it will tumble." The whole situation was mad, Hamilton declared, and "the enemies to Banks & Credit are in a fair way of having their utmost malignity gratified." The banks followed Hamilton's advice—though they scarcely needed it—and thus were in good condition when the inevitable collapse occurred.[20]

It was the Treasury Department that arrested the speculative orgy. On Friday, March 9, Duer found it necessary "to stop payment" of certain notes "issued by my Agent during my absence, under Circumstances which require Investigation." That started rumors, well founded or not, that Duer was in serious trouble, but was not necessarily fatal in itself. The fatal blow came on Monday. Duer, like most other former Confederation officials, had been lackadaisical in settling his accounts with the government, despite Wolcott's repeated requests. Specifically, there were $203,000 in old indents and $36,000 in old state paper money unaccounted for since 1789. On March 12 Wolcott instructed Richard Harison, federal district attorney in New York, to require Duer either to come immediately to Philadelphia and settle the accounts or post satisfactory security for them; and if Duer did not do so, to institute suit against him. Duer got wind of the impending action before Wolcott's letter was sent, and dispatched a frantic plea in the name of friendship asking Hamilton to stop the suit. Sympathetically, regretfully, but nonetheless firmly, Hamilton refused. Duer was a ruined man: news of the action destroyed his ability to raise new funds and to meet his maturing obligations.[21]

Panic swept the city. Prices of every manner of securities plummeted. Duer, besieged by angry mobs of creditors, vainly tried to fend them off and come up with an acceptable plan of payment, and on March 23 he was imprisoned for his debts. Three days later Walter Livingston fled the city, first transferring all his tangible property to his brothers to protect himself against foreclosure on $160,000 in notes he had endorsed for Duer. Several of Duer's associates absconded with funds; most stayed and were ruined. Failures multiplied daily.[22]

As always in an emergency, Hamilton was at his best. His priorities were to protect public credit and the banking system and to minimize disruptions in the flow of trade and losses suffered by the innocent. In behalf of the gamblers, including his friend Duer, he was unwilling to lift a finger, for, as he said, " 'Tis time there should be a line of separation between honest Men & knaves." His means were masterful. He kept in close touch with the banks, orchestrating their activities to obtain maximum effectiveness. He induced them to contract their outstanding paper sufficiently to ensure their own safety, then expand their loans cautiously to relieve the distressed. He urged them to favor borrowers who put up public securities as collateral, and to negotiate standstill agreements between legitimate, nonspeculative dealers in securities. He requested them to be liberal in making loans to merchants for import duties coming due and protected the banks by promising that the Treasury would not draw on those merchants' notes for ninety days. He employed publicity to calm the storm, spreading word that the Treasury had a surplus of $1 million that could potentially be used by the sinking fund, that American credit abroad had never been higher, that orders would be arriving from Amsterdam for open market purchases well above present price levels. He relieved pressure on the banks by paying as much of the quarterly interest on the public debt as possible in specie from the customs offices. In sum, he employed the machinery of all parts of the financial system to preserve the stability of the whole.[23]

One dangerous obstruction arose. Jefferson, scarcely able to suppress his glee over the catastrophe, added to it by spreading exaggerated and false accounts of the extent of the dislocation, and Freneau reached a larger audience with similar misinformation. That was only irresponsible; another of Jefferson's actions was openly malicious. The climax of the panic in New York was known to be coming on April 15; on that day Macomb had a half million dollars in security purchases falling due, and it was generally expected that he would default. It was imperative that the sinking fund be prepared to stabilize the market in the ensuing dislocations. Jefferson, however, had joined forces with Attorney General Edmund Randolph to tie up the sinking fund with a legal technicality. Hamilton and Adams were on the other side, of course; but Jay, the fifth member of the committee, was away on court duty, and so the issue was deadlocked. Jay's opinion, submitted in writing, favored the authorization. Jefferson objected to that proceeding, but Randolph went along with the majority and the authorization was approved barely in time. Macomb went under and soon joined Duer in debtors' prison, but the sinking fund, skillfully eked out over many small purchases rather than wasted in an effort to stop the blow all at once, minimized the aftereffects. By mid-May business was back to normal, despite Jefferson's negative vote on every subsequent sinking-fund authorization. Before the end of the month Hamilton was able to begin shoring up the Manufacturing Society.[24]

Only when it was over did Hamilton show any favoritism to a personal friend. Baron von Steuben, the man who had infused the Revolutionary army with discipline, had fallen into financial problems unrelated to the Duer-Macomb episode. He owed a balance of £506 and 13 shillings on a court judgment for an old debt. On May 28 Hamilton sold the one and a half shares he owned in the Bank of New York, withdrew his accumulated dividends, and used the proceeds to pay Steuben's debt. Seton urged Hamilton to borrow from the bank instead of selling his stock, for the stock had still not risen to its real value, but Hamilton chose not to be, just now, personally interested in or indebted to an institution he had aided in the public interest.[25]

Meanwhile, smelling death, the vultures had swooped in prematurely to pick the carcass from Hamilton's bones. On March 8 Madison and his minions in the House attempted to strip Hamilton of his ministerial functions. Hamilton's legislative achievements had been possible only because the organic act of the Treasury Department, authored principally by Madison in 1789, had required him to report directly to the House, and because the House had repeatedly and habitually requested specific reports. Now, when a routine proposal was made to require Hamilton to report on the necessity for additional supplies for the year, the Madison Republicans opposed the motion in an effort to force Hamilton to resign. Hamilton's "overthrow was anticipated as certain and Mr. Madison, *laying aside his wonted caution,* boldly led his troops as he imagined to a certain victory." Hamilton's friends rallied and thwarted the attempt, but only by a four-vote margin.[26]

On March 27, four days after Deur was jailed, the Madisonians tried again. An Indian expedition in the Ohio country the preceding fall had resulted in a disastrous defeat for the army under General Arthur St. Clair, and it came to light that Duer had had some of the army supply contracts. Hoping to find that Hamilton had been culpable and confident of being able to smear his reputation, House Republicans demanded that he and Secretary of War Knox be investigated, hinting darkly that impeachments would be in the offing. In actuality, the supply contracts had been Knox's responsibility; Hamilton had given advice which, if followed, might well have avoided the defeat. The hearings not only exonerated him but resulted in an increased vote of confidence, for army purchasing was transferred from the War Department to the Treasury. Hamilton did not need the harassment, however, and it was followed by still more. Toward the close of the congressional session in May, when a number of Hamilton's friends had gone home, Madison moved to amend the sinking-fund act to require that all future purchases be made at the lowest market price. In supporting the motion Madison "dealt much in *insidious insinuations,"* suggesting that Hamilton had been supporting the debt at artificially high prices for the benefit of speculators. The motion passed, 24 to 23, and was subsequently enacted into law. That portended additional harassment when Congress reconvened in fall.[27]

On another front the Republicans pressed ahead with their efforts to organize a national party of opposition. Rather, they sought to coordinate the oppositionists in enough states to accomplish two specific ends—increased representation in Congress and the replacement of Vice-President John Adams with George Clinton. The stakes in the latter effort were enormous, for Washington did not decide to serve a second term until late fall; thus had Clinton drawn more votes than Adams he might conceivably have become president.[28]

The most vital area of attack concerned Washington himself: if

Jefferson could turn the president against Hamilton, Hamilton would be driven from office. Late in May, having allowed three months of Freneau's rantings and the news of the New York debacle to register their impressions, Jefferson wrote a long letter to Washington, placing his own interpretation upon the Hamiltonian system. First, he charged, a fraudulent bookkeeping method had been used to pad the public debt, and the interest rate was set half again as high as it needed be. This, Jefferson claimed, necessitated an enormous tax burden, which "will produce evasion and war on our citizens to collect it." Next, by making the public debt "irredeemable," Hamilton made the debt attractive to foreigners, the result of which would be to drain the United States of hard money for the payment of interest. In the place of coin the Hamiltonians created, through the instrumentality of the bank, $10 million in paper on which the citizens would have to pay 10 to 12 percent "annual profit." All this engendered paper speculation and "nourishes in our citizens habits of vice and idleness, instead of industry and morality." Most importantly, it provided means for corrupting the legislature, the "ultimate object" of which was "to prepare the way for a change from the present republican form of government to that of a monarchy." Hamilton had sought to establish a monarchy on the British model in the Constitutional Convention, Jefferson charged, and failing he sought to achieve the same goal through a diabolical conspiracy. There was one hope, Jefferson concluded: the increased representation under the new apportionment law might produce a republican majority in Congress, in which case the worst of the evils could be undone. That failing, the result would be the secession of the South, for "the division of sentiment and interest happens unfortunately to be so geographical," Hamiltonian monarchists and paper men being concentrated in the North, pure republicans in the South.[29]

Six weeks later, in conversation with the president, Jefferson repeated his phantasm about Hamilton and added some fanciful embellishments. Washington believed not a line of Jefferson's remarkable tale. He knew from bitter wartime experience the desperate circumstances a loss of credit entailed, and Hamilton's achievement in restoring credit had been a marvel to him. Charges of a monarchical design he thought both nonsensical and dangerous, and he chided those who repeated them. If anybody was encouraging monarchy, he told Jefferson, it was such irresponsible newspapermen as Freneau who "seemed to have in view the exciting opposition to the government," and actually had fomented resistance to the excise law in Pennsylvania. He declared that the irresponsible charges of Freneau and his ilk (he was unaware of Jefferson's and Madison's connections with Freneau) "tended to produce a separation of the Union . . . and that whatever tended to produce anarchy, tended, of course, to produce a resort to monarchical government." He added that "he considered those papers as attacking him directly," for "in condemning the administration of the government, they condemned him." Washington also disbelieved the stories of sectional discontents and disagreements, declaring that "the people in the eastern States were as steadily for republicanism as in the southern." Having "seen and spoken with many people in Maryland and Virginia" on his recent tour, "he found the people contented and happy."[30]

That interview took place in Philadelphia. Soon after returning to Mount Vernon, Washington wrote Hamilton about the charges. He did not reveal their source; interestingly, he said they came from people who were unfriendly to the national government, such as "my neighbour, & quondom friend," the militant anti-Federalist George Mason. Clearly, though implicitly, Washington was seeking not a resolution of doubts but a point-by-point rebuttal that he could use if he encountered such charges again. (He had asked Hamilton for similar verbal ammunition concerning the Bank before going on his southern tour.) To facilitate Hamilton's efforts, he listed the charges under twenty-one headings, the language taken almost verbatim from Jefferson's May 23 letter. Washington closed his letter "with affectionate regard"—a sentiment absent just then from his correspondence with Jefferson.[31]

Hamilton's reply, a document of 14,000 words, is a classic, more persuasive than *The Federalist,* as irrefutable as his opinion on the constitutionality of the Bank. It is prefaced by an apology for the "severity" of expression that appears "here and there." He had not, Hamilton said, "fortitude enough always to hear with calmness, calumnies, which necessarily include me, as a principal Agent in the measures censured." Actually, however, the tone is crisp, businesslike, and restrained. For instance, in dealing with the charge that the debt was excessive, Hamilton answered, "the public Debt was produced by the late war. It is not the fault of the present government that it exists; unless it can be proved, that public morality and policy do not require of a Government an honest provision for its debts." The only proposition "which would truly have swelled the debt artificially," Hamilton pointed out, had been Madison's motion to assume all state debts including those that had been retired. Hamilton denied that a "corrupt squadron" of paper men in Congress existed. He said that holding of Bank stock could scarcely have influenced the vote on the charter, since congressmen could have become stockholders only after the charter was granted; and as for public creditors, "it is a strange perversion of ideas, and as novel as it is extraordinary, that men should be deemed corrupt & criminal for becoming proprietors in the funds of their Country." He did allow himself one dig at Madison and at southerners, reminding Washington that southern creditors of the states, gambling that Madison would succeed in blocking assumption, had been speculators equally with the northerners on whom they unloaded their securities; only when Madison failed had it turned out that the buyers had the better of the bargain. Otherwise, Hamilton's rebuttal was a quiet, systematic, and effective exposition of the sophistry of Jefferson's charges.[32]

In dealing with the charge of a monarchical conspiracy, Hamilton expressed the same sentiments Washington had expressed to Jefferson, but far more eloquently. "The only path to a subversion of the republican system of the Country," he wrote, "is, by flattering the prejudices of the people, and exciting their jealousies and apprehensions, to throw affairs into confusion, and bring on civil commotion. Tired at length of anarchy, or want of government, they may take shelter in the arms of monarchy for repose and security.

"Those then, who resist a confirmation of public order, are the true Artificers of monarchy. . . .

"It has aptly been observed that *Cato* was the Tory—*Caesar* the whig of his day. The former frequently resisted—the latter always flattered the follies of the people. Yet the former perished with the Republic the latter destroyed it.

"No popular Government was ever without its Catalines & its Caesars. These are its true enemies."[33]

Despite friends' warnings, Hamilton refused to recognize the enmity of Madison and Jefferson until their actions between March and May of 1792 made it unmistakable. Madison's betrayal, especially, bewildered Hamilton almost as much as it angered him. When he finally did face up to their animosity, his instinct was to lash out wildly against them, and he wrote four articles filled with invective before he checked himself. Then he scrapped those pieces without publishing them and adopted the more rational strategy of taking the case to the public as if before a court of law. Writing under a variety of pseudonyms—"T. L.," "An American," "Anti-Defamer," "Civis," "Amicus," "Fact," "Catullus," "Metellus," "A Plain Honest Man"—he set out to rebut the charges that had been made against himself and his ministry and, simultaneously, to file countercharges against the enemy.[34]

The charges repeatedly sounded in Freneau's *National Gazette* and some other newspapers were essentially the same that Jefferson had voiced to Washington, though in the press their tone was more impassioned. In his articles of rebuttal Hamilton analyzed them dispassionately, picking each count apart much as a skillful trial lawyer would do, then presented a fully documented and logical exposition of the truth. The cumulative effect was powerful, especially since the defenses were paired with attacks and since the articles appeared to be coming in from a variety of different writers. (Hamilton indulged himself in a bit of humor on this score: as "Amicus" he averred that he could speak of the secretary of the treasury "from a long, intimate, and confidential acquaintance with him, added to some other means of information.")[35]

By way of attack Hamilton disclosed four chapters of Jefferson's recent past, each disclosure being entirely true and together casting doubts upon Jefferson's loyalty to the nation's honor and to the national government. As minister to France, Hamilton revealed, Jefferson had proposed that the debt due that kingdom from the United States be sold to individuals in Holland, so that when the Confederation went bankrupt—as it then appeared on the verge of doing—the loss would fall upon private investors and no discredit would be suffered at the French court. The proposal was in keeping with the way tobacco planters customarily did business, but the old Congress, pitiful as it was in many respects, had refused to countenance so immoral and disgraceful an act and rebuked Jefferson for suggesting it. Hamilton also revealed that Jefferson, for all his declarations about the sanctity of the Constitution, had expressed strong reservations when it appeared, had at first believed that ratification should be withheld until amendments were made, and then had switched tactics and recommended that it be ratified but that four states remain out of the Union to force amendments to be adopted. Thirdly, Hamilton pointed out that Jefferson had obstructed all administration measures for restoring public credit and, in fact, nearly all measures that had not originated with himself. He had a right to disagree with the measures as they were being considered, Hamilton said, but it was a violation of public faith to attack them once they became national policy and contracts and commitments had been made on the basis of them. That point led to the fourth and most damaging of Hamilton's revelations, that Jefferson had been instrumental in the establishment of Freneau's newspaper as a party instrument, using government funds to vilify government itself and "to disturb the public peace, and corrupt the morals of the people."[36]

Conspicuous in these writings is the common eighteenth-century assumption that any effort to organize a political party was inimical to the public good, since parties or "factions" were by definition groups with interests different from those of the nation as a whole. Related to this assumption was an attitude toward opposition. Those who hold power in a popular government are often tempted to equate opposition with disloyalty, for if one represents the sovereign people, one's enemies must be enemies of the people. Along with Hamilton, Washington had that feeling, and so too would President Jefferson when his own policies were resisted.

But there was more to Hamilton's position than the mere psychology of power. The Republicans were in actuality fanning the flames of open defiance of government. Resistance to the enforcement of the whiskey excise tax had abated, but the hard-drinking backcountrymen in North Carolina and Pennsylvania responded to the provocative message that the purpose of the tax was not to defend them against Indians but to saddle them with monarchy and plutocracy. By the fall of 1792 resistance to the law became so common in those states that Washington found it necessary to issue a proclamation ordering "persons whom it may concern, to refrain and desist from all unlawful combinations and proceedings . . . having for object or tending to obstruct the operation of the laws."[37]

In fact Americans had yet to learn the habit of loyal opposition. Opposition to parliamentary taxation had led to revolution in the seventies, and opposition to state taxation had led to rebellion in the eighties. In this respect Jefferson was exceptional only in that he regularly spoke more seditiously than most. He was fond of talking of a "return to first principles" and of uttering radical epigrams: "I like a little rebellion now and then"; "God forbid we should ever be twenty years without . . . a rebellion"; "The earth belongs to the living, not to the dead, a living generation can bind itself only"; "The tree of liberty must be refreshed from time to time, with the blood of patriots and tyrants"; the "catholic principle of republicanism" is that "every people may establish what form of government they please, and change it as they please"; and, commenting on the Reign of Terror during the French Revolution, "Rather than it should have failed I would have seen half the earth desolated; were there but an Adam and Eve left in every country, and left free, it would be better than as it now is." Such talk, in the infancy of America's republican experiment, did not augur stability.[38]

Nor did Jefferson confine himself to seditious talk. On October 1, after meeting with George Mason the day before, he visited Washington at Mount Vernon and made one last effort to convince the president of Hamilton's wickedness. When Washington rejected every charge, Jefferson departed, sulking, later to claim that Washington had grown senile. Coincidentally or not, Freneau soon abandoned the restraint he had shown toward Washington personally and, starting with the suggestion that Washington was one of the "forerunners of Monarchy and Aristocracy in the United States," grew increasingly vitriolic. More immediately to the point, on the very evening of his unsuccessful attempt to pervert Washington's mind against Hamilton, Jefferson wrote a remarkable letter to Madison. There had been plans to establish a branch of the Bank of the United States in Richmond, and some Republicans had proposed to establish a state bank there as a competitor. Jefferson proposed that the assembly reject this "milk & water measure," and instead "should reason thus. The power of erecting banks & corporations was not given to the general government it remains then with the state itself. For any person to recognize a foreign legislature [i.e. the

Congress of the United States] in a case belonging to the state itself, is an act of *treason* against the state, and whosoever shall do any act under colour of the authority of a foreign legislature—whether by signing notes, issuing or passing them, acting as director, cashier or in any other office relating to it shall be adjudged guilty of high treason & suffer death accordingly."[39]

Jefferson's letter to Madison stands in striking contrast to a pair of letters Hamilton had recently written to Rufus King. In the New York gubernatorial election John Jay had defeated George Clinton— whom Republicans would support for vice-president/president come fall—but Clintonian canvassers had stolen the election by throwing out the votes of three frontier counties on a technicality. Jay's supporters howled, held popular meetings, circulated petitions, erected liberty poles, and even talked of a Lockean (of Jeffersonian) "reversion to original principles" and of preventing Clinton's reinauguration by force. Hamilton was as outraged by the perversion of the principle of free elections as anyone, but he firmly opposed a resort to "extraordinary expedients." It would not be "right or expedient," he said, "to attempt to reverse the decision by any means not known to the Constitution or Laws." The case, he insisted, would "justify neither a resort to first principles nor to violence," for it must "not be forgotten that the opposers of Clinton are the real friends to order & good Government; and that it will ill become them to give an example of the contrary."[40]

Washington's efforts to make peace between Hamilton and Jefferson were futile. Hamilton told the president he would try to be cooperative but that unless the attacks upon him ceased, Washington would have to choose between him and Jefferson. Jefferson made the choice himself: in a letter filled with self-justification and no small measure of dissimulation, he reiterated his intention to resign at the end of Washington's first term.*[41]

The feud carried over into the elections in the fall of 1792, though neither principal was especially active personally. Hamilton was most concerned with the vice-presidency. He was genuinely

---

*Actually Jefferson stayed on nine months into the second term, until the end of 1793.

alarmed when it appeared that the Republicans might support Aaron Burr, whom he considered extremely dangerous; when that threat faded, he wrote a few letters to friends urging them to support Adams against Clinton, and that was the extent of his electioneering. Jefferson, too, left the burden of the campaigning to others, but his adherents were more vigorous than were supporters of the administration. As a result, though Washington was again elected unanimously and Adams defeated Clinton by a comfortable margin, Republicans made major gains in the congressional elections. In the absence of national parties and with little formal political organization even in the states, most candidates had no party identification, but it seemed certain that Republican partisans and their sympathizers would have a decided majority in the Third Congress.[42]

In anticipation of their future majority, Republicans determined to nothing in the final, lame-duck session of the Second Congress but prevent constructive legislation and harass Hamilton. Consequently, all hope for action on the Report on Manufactures was forlorn, and the Senate defeated, after House passage, Hamilton's proposal that certain additional state debts (those of South Carolina and Massachusetts which exceeded the authorization of the 1790 act) be assumed. On the other hand, Jefferson's ambitious agenda of destruction—which included splitting the Treasury into two departments, abolishing the Bank, repealing the excise, requiring the Treasury to pay and accept only specie, and excluding "paper holders" from service in Congress—had no chance of success either.[43]

Two serious threats to Hamilton did arise. The first was in connection with the Reynolds affair. Reynolds and his partner, Clingman, had attempted to defraud the government by making themselves executors of the estate of a claimant against the United States who happened not to be dead. In mid-November Wolcott found them out and had them arrested. Reynolds appealed in vain to Hamilton for help; Clingman appealed to his former employer, Pennsylvania Representative Frederick Muhlenberg, who agreed to assist him. During the next three weeks, Clingman hinted several times to Muhlenberg "that Reynolds had it in his power, very materially to injure the secretary of the treasury, and that Reynolds knew several very improper transactions of his." Muhlenberg, an honorable and more or less nonpartisan man, was deeply concerned, and on December 12 he confided Clingman's hints to Representative Abraham Venable and Senator James Monroe of Virginia, both Republicans. The three called upon Reynolds, who repeated Clingman's statement and charged that Hamilton had been deeply involved in illegal speculations, and then questioned Maria, who corroborated her husband's story. Clingman added to the growing evidence against Hamilton by giving the congressmen several cryptic notes that Hamilton had written to Reynolds in a disguised handwriting.[44]

The three congressmen started to send their findings to Washington but decided first to confront Hamilton directly. They called on him on the morning of December 15 and informed him of the charges Clingman and Reynolds had made. He promised to prove beyond doubt that his relationship with Reynolds had in no way compromised the integrity of his official conduct, and invited them to his home that evening to examine the evidence. That night, with Wolcott present as a witness, Hamilton laid bare the full story, complete with the letters of documentation he had been prudent enough to save. He had scarcely begun his confession and submission of evidence when Muhlenberg and Venable, embarrassed no doubt by the passionate quality of Maria's letters, delicately suggested that Hamilton need say no more. He insisted upon going through the whole thing, however, and did so. Monroe was cooler than the others, but all three congressmen expressed their full satisfaction with the explanation, and Venable and Muhlenberg apologized for the awkwardness of the confrontation. Hamilton in turn assured them that he was satisfied with the "fairness and liberality" of their conduct. As they were all eighteenth-century gentlemen, it went without saying that no one would ever reveal what had happened.[45]

Monroe, however, did not believe that gentlemanly proprieties transcended the dictates of partisan politics, and he wasted no time before informing Jefferson and the Republican's chief political operator, Clerk of the House John Beckley, of the whole episode. Seeing no practical way to use the information just then, they nonetheless copied the documents for an opportune future occasion.[46]

The other threat was less readily managed. Late in November Hamilton submitted an ingenious plan for beginning to retire the public debt without any rapid increase of taxes. Part of the plan involved borrowing abroad at 5 percent or less and using the proceeds to redeem all the outstanding 6 percent domestic bonds which, under the terms of the original funding act, could annually be redeemed. Ancillary to this proposal was a recommendation that the proceeds from foreign loans also be used to repay the government's debt to the national bank for its original stock subscription. The proposals allowed the Republicans, who suspected a sinister scheme for providing the bank with more money for corrupt purposes, to push through the House a resolution calling for an accounting of the handling of previous foreign loans. Hamilton's report in response seemed to indicate that he had, contrary to the intentions of Congress, intermixed the funds from two separate loans authorized in 1790 and totaling $14 million, and that he had used some of the proceeds for purposes not authorized by Congress, though with the authorization of the president and, where relevant, of the sinking-fund committee.[47]

Those revelations were merely implicit, for the report consisted only of accounts and a brief formal note of transmission; it was Representative William B. Giles of Virginia, working closely with Jefferson, who ferreted them out. Giles eagerly sponsored five resolutions demanding a detailed accounting of the handling of all foreign loans, of all transactions between the government and the bank since its inception, of all operations of the sinking fund, and of the current state of government monies. He supported his resolutions with several charges of misconduct, including accusations that Hamilton had concealed shortages in the accounts, had unlawfully favored the Bank of the United States, and had drawn money from Europe to America for the benefit of speculators. The Republicans expected that Hamilton could not possibly prepare the necessary reports before Congress adjourned on March 3; thus Giles's charges would be generally believed and be regarded as proven fact by the time the Third Congress convened in December. The maneuver put Hamilton's friends and supporters in a bind: they did not believe the charges and did not want Hamilton subjected to the harassment, but they dared not oppose lest the charges be allowed to stand. Accordingly, with their support, the resolutions passed on January 23, 1793.[48]

By virtue of demonic labors, Hamilton was able to confound his accusers. By February 19 he had submitted the last of seven reports, totaling some 60,000 words and a large mass of figures, which amounted to a financial history of the national government. In the meantime, a special Committee of Fifteen, headed by Giles, had been conducting its own investigation of the Treasury Department, of Treasury officials, and of Hamilton's personal finances, expecting that abundant dirt would be the result; but there was no dirt to be found.[49]

Overconfidently, Jefferson had already drafted, for Giles to introduce, a series of resolutions condemning Hamilton for much the same things that Jefferson and the *National Gazette* had charged him with and demanding his removal from office. In the face of Hamilton's reports and the disappointments of his inquisition, Giles dropped the more extreme of Jefferson's resolutions. The remaining nine were considered by the House on February 28 and March 1. In a special evening session of March 1, the votes were taken. Every resolution was rejected by a large margin, and even the Virginians deserted the Republican ranks. Only five members of the House, including James Madison, voted for every resolution.[50]

⚘ XII ⚘

The Duel with
Jefferson:
1793

A kingdom of the Just then let it be:
But first consider how those Just agree.

Within a week after the House rejected Giles's resolutions, the Virginia oligarchic Republicans resumed their attack. On March 8, Senator James Monroe of Virginia—slaveowner, erstwhile anti-Federalist, and adamant defender of Bolingbrokean agrarianism—published a long, vitriolic tract repeating the charges as if they had been proved. Next day Freneau, claiming that Hamilton's speed in reporting had precluded fair and deliberate consideration of Giles's charges, published the first in a series of distorted accounts of the House's investigation. In Virginia, congressmen who had voted against Giles's resolutions were subjected to vicious campaigns when they returned home.[1]

For the most part, however, the House vote was regarded as a full exoneration of Hamilton's official conduct and an endorsement of his measures. Letters of congratulation and reports of popular approval came in from New England, New York, New Jersey, and even the lower South. Nor did Hamilton leave public opinion to chance. He protested to Jonathan Trumbull, Speaker of the House, that a number of inaccuracies had appeared in the printed version of his reports to the House, and when he was supplied with 300 copies of a corrected version he sent these and copies of the House proceedings to friends to ensure the widest possible publicity. At his request, for instance, his friend Edward Carrington saw to the publication of the House proceedings in "the most public and generally circulating paper" in Richmond and arranged for publication in Norfolk, Alexandria, Petersburg, and Winchester. William Loughton Smith also armed himself with copies of the reports and the debates for distribution on a tour through the back country of South Carolina and Georgia. The people there, Smith reported, were a wild and bizarre lot, though considerably improved from "a few years ago," when "they were such a set of bandetti that it was less safe for a Gentleman to be among them than in the midst of the Wabash Tribes"; and, as he expected, the only newspaper he encountered was the *National Gazette*. Nonetheless, Smith believed his truth-spreading work was successful.[2]

In initiating these efforts, Hamilton was continuing to follow Necker's maxim that keeping the public informed was crucial to a minister of finance; but he had another motive as well. Having endured repeated calumny as his reward for public service, and realizing that the completion of his system through the implementation of his Report on Manufactures was now politically impossible, he decided to retire at the end of the next session of Congress, early in 1794. In his letter so informing Washington, he said he would stick it out that long because there were details remaining to be perfected in his fiscal system, and because he intended to demand a "more deliberate prosecution of the Inquiry" into his conduct as secretary of the treasury. It is a measure of his consciousness of official rectitude that he insisted upon a full investigation before being willing to depart. It is a measure of his naïve faith in the fundamental honorableness of his fellow man that he entrusted such an investigation to the members of the Third Congress.[3]

Hamilton's decision to retire, however, was wishful thinking, for the United States was just then becoming caught up in the maelstrom of international politics. In theory foreign relations was none of his concern as secretary of the treasury. In reality the Treasury Department had, in the nature of things, been more active internationally than had the State Department. Hamilton's activity had derived from two inescapable facts, that the government's main source of revenue was tariffs on international trade and that its foreign debts necessitated continuous attention to the international flow of money. His increased activity from the spring of 1793 on-ward—and his bitter fight with Jefferson over the proper course of American foreign policy—derived from those two facts and from three others. The first was that he was explicitly required by the president to participate in foreign policy decisions. The other two were that he was constitutionally inacapable of remaining a passive spectator when the vital interests of his country were in jeopardy, and that he understood European affairs better than did his counterpart in the State Department.[4]

The differences that separated Hamilton and Jefferson during the French crisis of 1793 and the British crisis of 1794 stemmed from their angles of approach. Jefferson liked to talk about the force of reason in human affairs, but his political attitudes were visceral, not rational, at their base. He had what Hamilton described as *"a womanish attachment to France and a womanish resentment against Great Britain,"* and his foreign policy initiatives were always colored by those emotions. As the French Revolution moved inexorably leftward, his abstract enthusiasm for revolutions led him to favor France ever more warmly. As war between France and Britain loomed inevitable, his hostility toward Britain increased apace. This is not to suggest that he would willfully have done anything to sacrifice or jeopardize American interests out of favoritism for France or antipathy toward Britain. Rather, his favoritism and his antipathy blinded him to what America's interests were.[5]

Hamilton was the opposite: he talked of men being driven by their passions and their interests but based his politicies on reason and careful calculation. In the face of war in Europe, he saw neutrality as the great desideratum, but not because, having known war, he cherished peace. Rather, he understood that war, in the emotional and ideological climate of the United States during the 1790s, would divide the nation against itself and sap the strength of its infant national government. Every year of peace, conversely, would allow the country to grow stronger and its government to become more stable. As a matter of policy, he therefore regarded war as acceptable only if the alternative was national disgrace or the sacrifice of vital national interests, and only if the American people could be counted on to support the war with some measure of solidarity.[6]

His modus operandi for maintaining peace was likewise rational. Whenever American relations with any European power became strained, the United States must simultaneously negotiate and prepare to fight. In negotiating, it must understand its own interests, the relevant strategic considerations, and the premises on which other nations operated. Among those premises, three were crucial. First, Europeans could generally be counted on to comport themselves according to the law of nations, however much they might interpret the rules to their own advantage. Second, they would follow the dictates of their national interests as they perceived them. (Hamilton assumed that the fundamental aims of nations remained the same irrespective of changes in régimes, and that, irrespective of protestations, neither morality nor ideology had any significant influence.) Third, nations like men had feelings which, if played upon with skill or if clumsily offended, could lead them to act irrationally and contrary to both international law and national self-interest. Whether dealing with France, Britain, or Spain, Hamilton took his position in accordance with these principles.[7]

Both Hamilton and Jefferson had had occasion, some time before the wars of the French Revolution began, to reveal their diplomatic stances and styles. In 1790 Britain and Spain had almost gone to war over their American possessions, and a question involving the United States arose. If the war materialized Britain might decide to send troops overland from Canada to attack the Spanish at New Orleans, which would involve the passage of British troops through the uninhabited interior of the United States. Washington requested written opinions from his department heads as to whether right of passage should be allowed if Britain should request it. Jefferson's response was prompt and brief. He said that British seizure of Spanish Louisiana and Florida would be such a calamity that the United States should go to war if necessary to prevent it. He did not advise any preparations for war, however; expecting that war would become general and that France would enter as Spain's ally, he counseled waiting and, presumably, relying upon American militias to aid France and Spain in defending the Spanish territory. Meanwhile, he instructed the American minister in London to inform the British that the United States would demand a price for its neutrality: it would remain neutral only if Britain would cease its violations of the peace treaty of 1783 and pledge not to conquer

Louisiana and Florida. As for the request for right of passage, if it came the United States should "avoid giving any answer."[8]

Hamilton was slower, more thorough, and more cautious in formulating his reply, and used the occasion to make a general analysis, ten times as long as Jefferson's, of the considerations that should govern American conduct. After an exposition of the relevant points of international law, he turned to questions of national interest and geopolitics—couching his observations, significantly, in a military metaphor, facing Europe and referring to British Canada "on our left" and to Spanish "possessions on our right." He dismissed the idea that the United States should side with Spain and its prospective ally France out of gratitude for services those countries had rendered during the American Revolution. He agreed that British control of the Mississippi would pose a danger to the United States but reminded Washington that Spanish control was already being exercised in a hostile manner and maintained that ultimately "we ought not to leave in the possession of any foreign power, the *territories* at the mouth of the Mississippi, which are to be regarded as the key to it." Until the United States became "able to make good our pretentions," however, it would be folly to make a commitment to either side, since it was impossible to know which side would win. Backing the loser would ensure that the area would be administered unfavorably to the United States, whereas remaining strictly neutral would leave open the possibility of favorable negotiations with the victor. In conclusion, Hamilton added two specific points that were in sharp contrast to Jefferson's position. As for the idea of handling the prospective request from the British by giving no answer, Hamilton called Washington's attention to a practical detail—the United States had a military post on the Wabash River, along which any British expedition must proceed. In the absence of orders the commanding officer there would be obliged to attempt to halt the British troops by force, in which case a policy of silence would be a certain route to war. Finally, whereas Jefferson had said nothing about military preparedness, Hamilton insisted that if Washington's decision involved any prospect of fighting, the president must be prepared to support the decision "if necessary by the sword," even if that entailed calling a special session of Congress.[9]

It was in dealing with the young British minister to the United States, George Hammond, that the contrasts in style between

Hamilton and Jefferson were most pronounced. Relations between Britain and the United States were strained by both a lingering mutual ill will and some important tangible differences. Britain had substantially closed her West Indies possessions to American shipping and, like France and Spain, had imposed various restrictions upon American trade. A sorer spot, for some Americans, was that British troops had carried off about 50,000 slaves at the end of the war and the British government had, in violation of the peace treaty, persistently refused either to return the slaves to their American owners or to pay restitution for them. Sorer yet, the British, in flagrant violation of both the treaty and American sovereignty, continued to occupy seven military posts in the northern and northwestern United States and thereby retained their monopoly of the fur trade with the Indians. On the other side, Americans were guilty of serious breaches of the treaty themselves. Most states had refused to return property of British subjects they had confiscated during the war, and several imposed legal barriers to the collection of debts due from Americans to British merchants. By 1792 such debts, owed mainly by tobacco planters in Maryland, Virginia, and North Carolina, amounted with accrued interest to about £3 million sterling—more than the government's foreign debt and nearly a quarter as much as the entire public debt.[10]

From the moment Hammond arrived in November 1791, Jefferson treated him as an adversary. After several months of skirmishing and of being baited, the inexperienced English diplomat lost his poise and sent the secretary of state a long, detailed memorandum accusing Americans of violating the peace treaty on several occasions. Jefferson responded with a devastating critique of Hammond's memorandum and a vigorous set of counteraccusations. The American won the argument so conclusively as to mortify the Englishman; but winning arguments is scarcely the stuff of which diplomatic accommodations are made. Moreover, as he argued and assumed a posture of moral outrage, Jefferson supported the ongoing efforts of Madison and other Republicans to legislate an anti-British and pro-French set of mercantilistic commercial policies. As Hamilton said, had Jefferson and Madison had their way a war with Britain would have been provoked within six months. And yet, even as he took this hard line in his non-negotiations with Britain, Jefferson was telling the president that one defect of the Constitution was its failure to prohibit "standing armies." In short, Jefferson inverted Theodore Roosevelt's maxim: he spoke loudly and self-righteously and carried no stick at all.[11]

To Hamilton, Jefferson's policy seemed designed "to widen, not to heal, the breach between the two countries," and Hamilton perceived that it was vital that the breach be healed. From a purely strategic point of view the United States could not afford to have a powerful and hostile neighbor, but that was by no means the whole issue. Great Britain was the primary market for American exports and the primary supplier of necessary American imports. Until the United States should become self-sufficient, no amount of efforts, *à la* Jefferson and Madison, to use the power of government to force trade into artificial channels could change that commercial pattern. The military and economic factors being unchangeable, Hamilton believed the United States should negotiate toward demilitarization of the Canadian frontier and the removal of as many barriers to trade as possible.[12]

Having no official reason for dealing with Hammond, Hamilton could talk with him only informally, but such contact was adequate to win the confidence and friendship of the Englishman. Hamilton's formula was candor, goodwill, and good sense. Recriminations and arguments over which nation had violated the treaty first were avoided as fruitless, and he and Hammond, in a series of discussions, considered what ought to be the relations between the two countries. Certain points at issue, Hamilton suggested, should form no part of the negotiations; specifically, the questions of confiscations and slaves should be dropped since they could not be satisfactorily resolved, and the private debts could be collected through private suits in the federal courts. Certain other points Hamilton regarded as nonnegotiable; specifically, Britain must evacuate its military posts inside the United States, and it must abandon its plan, a favorite with the Grenville ministry, of creating a buffer Indian state between the United States and Canada. After shaking Hammond with the vehemence of his insistence on those points, however, Hamilton pleased and surprised him with the additional suggestion that fur traders from both nations should be allowed to move and trade freely on either side of the Canadian border. He went further, suggesting an audacious plan to secure the navigation of the Mississippi to both nations, which was nominally guaranteed them by treaty but was in fact denied them by Spain. Hamilton proposed that the United States cede to Britain a strip of land west of the Great Lakes, thus providing direct access to the Mississippi from Canada, in exchange for which Britain would join forces with the United States to seize and divide the Spanish territories on the Gulf. Simultaneously, Hamilton was urging a buildup of American military strength, and from time to time he dropped a hint to Hammond that the United States might seek a cozier relationship with France.[13]

None of these conversations amounted to negotiations, but they were sophisticated diplomacy all the same. They aimed at making formal negotiations possible by convincing the Englishman—who in turn would convince his superiors—that the United States would defend and advance its interests through firm and enterprising measures, but that it bore no ill will toward Britain despite the secretary of state's truculence. The time, however, was not yet ripe.

That was the way things stood until the winter of 1792–93, when developments in France suddenly changed everything.

Most Americans had applauded the French Revolution when it began in 1789; Hamilton said that it had filled him with the passions he had felt in 1775. His own ardor quickly cooled, for he foresaw that a demand for absolute liberty in France would lead instead to absolute tyranny, but not many Americans shared his viewpoint. Having convinced themslves that Louis XVI was a great champion of liberty because he supported American independence, Americans were enthusistic when, in the summer of 1790, Louis signed a constitution limiting his own power and providing a measure of representative government. Their illusions were shattered a year later when the king, disguised as a woman, was arrested in a wild attempt to flee the country. Thenceforth, Louis was prisoner in his own country, though he nominally continued to serve as the constitutional monarch. That turn of events divided Americans, the more conservative fearing and expecting that increasingly radical turns were to come, the more radical earnestly hoping so.[14]

France moved rapidly leftward, and toward war as well. The Girondists, a new party committed to republicanism, gained a powerful influence in the national assembly; their archrivals were the

Feuillants, led by Lafayette, who sought desperately to save the constitutional monarchy. Both parties believed that war would serve their ends, and they cooperated secretly to bring war about. On February 7, 1792, Prussia and Austria provided them an excuse by signing an alliance against France, and ten weeks later, on April 20, France declared war on Austria. During the next five months France was a shambles: its armies met repeated defeats, its officers joined other nobles in fleeing the country, its soldiers deserted in droves, and runaway inflation disrupted its economy. Order was retained in the capital only by resort to terror: the execution of more than a thousand political and criminal prisoners and imprisonment of many more accused enemies of the revolution. By that time— early September—Prussian and Austrian armies were closing in on Paris. The revolution, it seemed certain, had but a few days to live.[15]

Then came a miracle. On September 20, 1792, at the village of Valmy, a ragged army of 18,000 Frenchmen, ill-equipped and armed mainly with enthusiasm for liberty, took a stand at an indefensible spot against the powerful, machinelike Prussians, whom all Europe reckoned to be invincible; and the French held. The Prussians, stupefied, retreated. They did not know they had been in one of the most important battles in the history of the world, the battle that gave birth to the modern popular army, but they knew they had seen something awesome. The very next day the National Convention proclaimed France a republic. In the weeks that followed, the French withstood repeated attacks, and then their citizen armies seized the offensive and swept over the Austrian Netherlands. On November 19 the National Convention, intoxicated with freedom and power, issued a manifesto urging all the world's peoples to overthrow their rulers and promising support to those who thus embraced the cause of liberty.[16]

Few Americans could remain uninspired by this turn of events; most were ecstatic. Even Washington succumbed to the enthusiasm and decided it was time "to effect a stricter connection with France." He told Jefferson that, in view of American difficulties with Spain and Britain, "there was no nation on whom we could rely, at all times, but France; and that, if we did not prepare in time some support, in the event of rupture with Spain and England, we might be charged with a criminal negligence." Jefferson, delighted, recorded that that "was the very doctrine which had been my polar star, and I did not need the successes of the republican arms in France . . . to bring me to these sentiments."[17]

Hamilton's reaction was entirely different. Far from being a time for making "stricter connections" with France, he saw it as a time for maintaining the firmest neutrality. Otherwise, if the French Republic proved unstable, if France lost the war and the king were restored, the United States would have won itself the enmity of every crowned head in Europe. If France did develop a stable non-monarchical government, Hamilton predicted, it would not be a free one but a military dictatorship. And, whatever the course of French government, Hamilton assumed that the basic aims of France's foreign policy would remain the same. Inasmuch as these aims included the restoration and aggrandizement of the old French empire in America, Hamilton could see nothing but trouble for the United States in any actions that favored France.[18]

The French were soon to force the issue. On January 21, Louis XVI was beheaded. Eleven days later France declared war against Spain, Great Britain, and Holland. Between these two events, Citizen Edmond Genet was sent from Paris to enlist the United States in the cause of liberating the world. The Americans were not expected to join the French actively as belligerents, but Genet was instructed to propose a "national pact in which the two peoples would amalgamate their commercial and political interests and establish an intimate concert, which would promote the extension of the Empire of liberty, guarantee the sovereignty of all peoples, and punish the powers still retaining colonial systems by refusing to admit their ships to the harbors of the two contracting nations." In addition, Genet had three specific charges: to obtain sufficient food from America to sustain France while it fought, to use the United States as a base for privateering against Spanish and British shipping, and to employ Americans in the reconquest of Canada, Florida, and Louisiana. The Girondists assumed that the United States would be cooperative out of gratitude for French help during the American Revolution, out of interest in the crusade for republicanism, and out of obligation under the 1778 Franco-American treaties of commerce and alliance.[19]

These developments brought Washington, though not Jefferson, around to Hamilton's way of thinking. Washington's earlier position had been based upon the assumption that Britain and Spain were hostile toward one another as well as toward the United States, and that France would be a valuable ally as a makeweight between them. Now France had forced them into an alliance by making war on both, and Washington believed that to tie the United States to a politically unstable France in those circumstances would be suicidal. That was precisely Hamilton's view, for it squared with his belief that all parties to the conflict were concerned with national self-aggrandizement. Jefferson read European affairs ideologically and therefore differently: along with most other American Republicans, he saw the coalition against France as a monarchical design to destroy republicanism once and for all, and believed that if republican France were destroyed republican America would be next on the royal agenda.[20]

Hamilton was concerned with the Genet mission in two different official capacities. The first was as manager of the nation's finances. Genet's instructions included an order to seek economic aid in the form of advance installments on the American debt to France, payable in grain, and a request for an advance arrived before he did. There was a precedent for prepayment, for the United States had, on the urgent appeal of Genet's predecessor Jean Baptiste de Ternant, recently made advances for helping refugees from the slave insurrection in French Sainte Domingue (modern Haiti). The new request was discussed in a cabinet meeting late in February. Jefferson favored honoring it; Hamilton did not. He questioned the stability of the National Convention as the government of France and questioned France's ability to defeat its enemies. Should the allies against France succeed, they would almost certainly restore the Bourbons, who could legitimately maintain that payments by the United States to a band of usurpers constituted no payments at all. But there was another, more compelling reason for Hamilton's opposition to prepayment: the French themselves had undermined the ability of the United States to pay. A regular payment of interest and principal was to fall due on September 1, and Hamilton had counted on meeting it by floating a new loan in Holland; but French armies poured into Holland and totally, if temporarily, destroyed the money market there. Hamilton skillfully arranged to meet the payment by floating a loan of $800,000 from the Bank of the United States and by engaging in arbitrage through the purchase of bills of exchange, but he simply did not have the wherewithal for making sizable advances to France. Indeed (and ironically, in light of the Republicans' belief that the bank was under his personal control) it required all his arts of persuasion to induce the reluctant directors of the bank to make the necessary loan. [21]

Hamilton was also involved in the Genet affair as a member of the cabinet. Washington had begun the extraconstitutional practice of calling cabinet meetings—at which the three heads of departments and Attorney General Randolph discussed the full range of executive matters and made formal recommendations to the president— in 1792, largely as a device for trying to restore some harmony to the administration. In 1793 the president relied on cabinet meetings increasingly, for a different reason: he was genuinely torn in his attitudes. Intellectually he believed that Hamilton was right, but in his heart he hoped the French would succeed, and besides, he was not certain that Jefferson's argument was unsound. Immobilized, he opted for an uncharacteristic course: that decisions be made by majority vote of his advisers. [22]

As it happened, Washington was in Mount Vernon for the funeral of a nephew when news of the expansion of the war in Europe reached Philadelphia early in April. As soon as the president received the information, he arranged for a hasty return and fired off instructions to Jefferson to prepare a plan for preserving American neutrality. He also instructed Hamilton and Knox to have the matter "seriously thought of" by the time he arrived. When he got to Philadelphia, however, the secretary of state greeted him with nothing more tangible than a stack of routine correspondence. Secretary Henry Knox, to whose War Department the question of neutrality was rather of interest, had prepared a draft of instructions for some pending Indian negotiations. Only Hamilton moved as vigorously as Washington had. Without waiting for the president's orders, he had reacted to the news from Europe by inducing Jay to prepare a draft of a neutrality proclamation. He had also begun to sound out popular opinion regarding the war by writing to friends around the country, and had begun to sketch the first of a series of essays designed to convince the public of the importance of neutrality. When the instructions from Washington arrived, he drew up a list of thirteen questions to guide cabinet discussions. Washington submitted those questions to the cabinet as his own.[23]

The cabinet was divided. Jefferson argued that since only Congress could declare war, it alone could declare neutrality, and thus that a presidential proclamation of neutrality would be unconstitutional. The others agreed that a neutrality proclamation should be issued, and it was done. There was general agreement that Genet should be received, but Hamilton and Knox took the position, Jefferson and Randolph dissenting, that the reception should be accompanied by a statement that the United States reserved judgment on suspending the Franco-American treaties. Hamilton and Knox also argued that the treaties should in fact be suspended. Washington himself reserved judgment on their arguments.[24]

As Washington pondered the issue, Genet clouded it. Genet arrived in America on April 8, but he landed in Charleston rather than in the temporary national capital. With characteristic Girondin naïveté, enthusiasm, and audacity, the illustrious Citizen considered the president and cabinet relatively unimportant, since his mission was to the American people; and he proceeded overland, leisurely, northward, accompanied by huzzahs and enthusiastic receptions. Overwhelmingly and unmistakably the American people, or rather the southerners, were making known their sympathy for the French cause. There was more to their enthusiasm, however, than mere sentimentality, for Genet was passing out licenses to steal. South Carolina planters such as Alexander Moultrie, William Clay Snipes, and Isaac Huger (who owned more than 600 slaves among them) quickly discovered their fondness for French-style liberty, for they had plunged deeply into land speculations in the Mississippi territory, Moultrie with money embezzled from the state; and Genet was handing out commissions for raising an *Armée du Mississippi* and an *Armée des Florides*—which, if they succeeded, would yield richly to speculators. The Charleston merchant Alexander Gillon and the adventurer James O'Fallon, ardent Republicans who likewise had invested in the Yazoo Land Company of South Carolina, were among the first to accept military commissions from Genet. Recruitment of volunteers for an attack on Saint Augustine was begun, and soon a force of 1,600 had been raised. In Virginia Genet engaged the services of the old hero of western fighting, General George Rogers Clark, to head the expeditions on Louisiana and the Floridas. Meanwhile, he was also issuing licenses for plunder by sea, commissioning vessels as privateers. Such commissions entitled the bearer to lurk offshore, attack unarmed and unsuspecting British merchant ships, and haul them into American ports to be sold as prizes of war. Genet commissioned four privateers even before presenting his credentials in Charleston, and as he proceeded northward he commissioned others and helped in financing, arming, and equipping them. By the time he finally reached Philadelphia on May 16, privateers had already seized a number of British ships, one of which had been lying at anchor in Delaware Bay.[25]

Outrageous, presumptuous, and dangerous as Genet's doings were, preventing them was no simple matter, for the federal government's law enforcement machinery was but nominal, and no one could foresee how cooperative the state governors and judges would be. Nor was Jefferson helpful; though he acquiesced in the decision for neutrality, he sought to make American neutrality as advantageous to France as possible and regarded Hamilton's efforts on behalf of strict neutrality as "pro-English." Hamilton was quick to propose a solution to the enforcement problem—that the customs collectors, the only federal officers in the major ports, be authorized to report violations of neutrality to him. Jefferson denounced the proposal as a design to create a "corps of spies or informers against their fellow citizens, whose actions they are to watch in secret, inform against in secret to the Secretary of the Treasury." Republicans had spread rumors, in fact, that revenue officers were already "a corps, trained to the arts of spies," and Randolph confronted Hamilton with that accusation. Hamilton not only denied the canard but opened his letter books for Randolph's investigation, whereupon Randolph suggested that to scotch such rumors, customs collectors should be instructed to report violations of neutrality to the attorney general. Hamilton, who certainly needed no extra duties, readily agreed. Jefferson complained that that was a "hairsplitting" compromise.[26]

Even with the assistance of Treasury officials, Randolph had no easy time of it. The neutrality proclamation was based on the law of nations, not an act of Congress, and finding juries willing to convict on that basis was difficult. His problems became manifest when, late in May, a pair of Americans named Gideon Henfield and John Singletary were arrested in Philadelphia for having signed on board a French privateer in Charleston. In the absence of a federal law against recruiting and given the shaky footing of the law of nations, Randolph resorted to basing his prosecution mainly on the common-law offense of disturbing the peace. The jury acquitted the prisoners, and one of them promptly reenlisted on another privateer. Jefferson, for his part, had hoped Henfield would be acquitted and wanted to go so far as to express that wish officially to Genet.[27]

Preventing violations of American neutrality by French citizens was a more thorny problem. French privateers brought British prizes into American ports, where French consuls, acting on Genet's instructions, tried, condemned, and sold them. The Supreme Court ruled a year later that such procedures were illegal, but that was of no avail in the crisis of 1793; and the administration had no way in the meantime to prevent the French prize courts from functioning. Commissioning and equipping privateers in American ports, on the other hand, was a violation of American sovereignty as well as its neutrality, and the British minister protested vigorously. After considerable rancor in the cabinet, it was ordered that prizes taken in American territorial waters must be released, that the outfitting of privateers in American ports must cease, and that those previously fitted in the United States would be banned from the country. Hamilton argued that restitution should be made for the prizes already sold, but to no avail.[28]

The next two months were turbulent: in one stormy cabinet meeting after another, the administration made decisions designed to keep Genet in check, only to see them ignored by the exuberant Frenchman. On June 5 Genet was ordered to stop outfitting privateers; ten days later he began to refit as a privateer a captured British merchant vessel (*Little Sarah,* rechristened *La Petite Democrate*) under the very nose of the government in Philadelphia. On June 11 he was informed that Washington had declined his request for advance payments on the American debt to France; four days later he contrived a way to extort a prepayment, refusing to honor bills that his predecessor Ternant had issued against earlier American advances. Genet's contempt for Washington's authority was engendered, in no small measure, by association with Jefferson and some of his more radical friends in Philadelphia, from whom Genet derived the impression that the people overwhelmingly opposed the president's neutrality policy. So friendly was Jefferson that when a vitriolic series of attacks on Washington, signed "Veritas," appeared in Freneau's *National Gazette,* Genet assumed that Jefferson was the author. Even after Genet began to vow that he would take his case over Washington's head to the people, even after he wrote Jefferson what Hamilton called the "most offensive paper perhaps that was ever offered by a foreign minister to a friendly power with which he resided," even after Jefferson himself began to confide to intimates that Genet's rashness would seriously jeopardize the Republican cause if the public learned of it, Jefferson persisted in abetting Genet's designs. As late as July 6, for instance, the secretary of state facilitated Genet's efforts to recruit Americans for an attack upon Spanish Louisiana, contrary to the neutrality proclamation, the law of nations, and administration policy.[29]

Meanwhile, Hamilton had begun to act in a third capacity, this one unofficial: he took up his pen to rally popular support for neutrality. In seven essays, signed "Pacificus" and published in the newspapers between June 29 and July 27, Hamilton dismantled the arguments in favor of a pro-French policy. The first of the common objections against the neutrality proclamation, Jefferson's contention that the president lacked the constitutional authority to issue it, was easily disposed of. It was true, Hamilton said, that Congress alone had the power to declare war, but it was the president's duty to preserve peace unless and until Congress did declare war, for until then to enforce peace was to enforce the law. A second common objection, that the United States was bound to support France by the 1778 treaties of commerce and alliance, was more complex. Hamilton dissected the relevant features of the treaties carefully and analyzed them in terms of the law of nations; but his most telling point was that the alliance explicitly comprehended only a defensive war, whereas France was in fact the aggressor in the present conflict. A third pro-French argument was that the United States should support France out of gratitude for France's support during the War for Independence. Gratitude, said Hamilton, was no sound basis for relations among nations; the only sound bases were mutual interest and reciprocal advantage, guided by the "sacred and unequivocal" principles of faith and justice. Besides, France had supported the United States not from generosity but to serve its own interests; and if American gratitude were due anyone, it was Louis XVI, whom the French had executed. Finally, Hamilton dealt with those who had argued that the timing of the neutrality proclamation was bad, that it should have been issued when the war began in 1792 or not at all. There was a simple and obvious reason for the timing, Hamilton pointed out. As long as France had been at war only with Prussia and Austria, the United States was entirely unlikely to become involved. When France declared war against Britain, Holland, and Spain, however, the situation was fundamentally altered because of American commercial relations with those countries.[30]

In addition, Hamilton made two wise observations that no doubt upset Jefferson considerably. One concerned the National Convention's declarations that France would assist all peoples who rebelled against their rulers and would *"treat as enemies the people,* who *refusing* or *renouncing* liberty and equality *are desirous* of preserving their *Prince* and *privileged casts."* That revolutionary doctrine, Hamilton predicted, would serve as a cloak for conquest; "liberate" would become a euphemism for "subjugate." The other observation was equally perceptive. Foreign friendships and foreign attachments, he said, led to foreign influence, "The GRECIAN HORSE to a republic." It was most dangerous, he warned, when it was not overt, but "comes under the patronage of our passions, under the auspices of national prejudice and partiality."[31]

The Pacificus articles, which appeared first in the *Gazette of the United States* and were soon widely republished, began to have the effect that Hamilton hoped for. Frantically, Jefferson wrote to Madison, "For God's sake, my dear Sir, take up your pen, select the most striking heresies and cut him to pieces in the face of the public. There is nobody else who can & will enter the lists with him." Madison responded belatedly, reluctantly, and vainly.[32]

Hamilton's efforts were facilitated by external developments. In mid-July a French fleet arrived, escorting private vessels carrying 10,000 refugees from a fresh wave of bloodletting at the hands of black rebels in Sainte Domingue. The horror stories they told were enough to give pause to the most ardent of revolutionaries; Jefferson expressed a fear that blacks would seize the entire West Indies and, soon or late, the southern United States as well. In the wake of that news, information began to arrive from Paris that mass arrests and wholesale executions—20,000 Frenchmen would be beheaded before the Reign of Terror ran its course—were replacing every semblance of liberty in France. Concurrently with reports of the Terror came news of French perfidy in regard to American commerce. In February France, desperately in need of American foodstuffs, had opened its ports to American shipping on terms equal to those of French-owned vessels, and large numbers of American shippers had responded; but late in July Americans learned that the National Convention had, on May 9, passed a new decree under which scores of American ships were seized and their cargoes confiscated. The American mercantile community was thrown into confusion, and insurance rates soared.[33]

As the tide of popular opinion began to turn against France, dissatisfaction over the administration's inability to contain Genet grew apace. In fact, the administration, in addition to its intrinsic difficulties, had a crisis of will. The cabinet, as Jefferson put it, was divided against itself 2½ to 1½, Hamilton and Knox usually opposing Jefferson, Randolph swinging from one side to the other. Deadlocked, the cabinet resolved in mid-July to send a list of questions to the Supreme Court for an opinion. Hamilton had originally opposed that procedure on the ground that the issues were matters of state, not questions of law; but, presumably assuming that the Court, under Jay's influence, would break the deadlock in a satisfactory manner, he now not only acquiesced but wrote most of the questions actually submitted. The Court, however, refused on constitutional grounds to give an advisory opinion. A set of Rules Governing Belligerents was worked out by August 3, and it was agreed that France should be asked to recall Genet. But, despite Hamilton's vigorous protests, Jefferson had his way about the manner of Genet's removal. Hamilton wanted to issue a peremptory demand for Genet's recall and wanted him to be suspended in the meantime. Instead, the request was carefully worded so as to avoid offending France, and it was not even made public. That left Genet at large to engage in continued mischief.[34]

The time had come, Hamilton believed, when it was both possible and necessary that Genet be thoroughly discredited. To that end, he wrote a new series of articles exposing Genet's conduct in merciless detail and, simultaneously, warning that partisanship for France would involve the United States in war with Britain and Spain. In the first of nine essays signed "No Jacobin," published on July 31, Hamilton stunned the public by disclosing what Jefferson had been trying to keep secret, that Genet had *"threatened to appeal from the President of the United States to the People."* In subsequent numbers Hamilton shocked his readers again and again by revealing Genet's insulting attitude, his flouting of presidential authority, and his generally subversive behavior.[35]

Stimulated by these revelations—but not, so far as is known, with any active prodding by Hamilton—various groups of friends of the administration began to call public meetings to support neutrality. The first such meeting, convened in Boston by Hamilton's friend and sometime adviser, the merchant Stephen Higginson, was in fact held a week before Hamilton published the first of his No Jacobin essays. Twenty more public meetings were held in New England during August; all adopted resolutions supporting neutrality and urging vigorous punishment of violators. In New York more personal resolutions, inspired by Rufus King and John Jay, were adopted both by the Chamber of Commerce and by a large public meeting. They not only approved neutrality but also condemned foreign diplomats' efforts to deal with the nation rather than with the executive branch. A few days after the public meeting Jay and King published a signed statement, which many people inaccurately assumed was authorized by Washington, attesting to Genet's vow to appeal to the people. By the end of the month, meetings in New Jersey, Maryland, and Delaware had followed New York's lead.[36]

The most important and most widely publicized set of anti-Genet resolutions were adopted in Richmond on August 17, at a large public meeting organized by John Marshall. This foray into the heart of Jefferson country caught the Republican leaders unawares. Jefferson's two closest allies, Madison and Monroe, were visiting at Monroe's plantation when they heard of the Richmond meeting, and they improvised a counterattack, planning to promote the adoption of resolutions treating the minister's transgressions as minor indiscretions. They also proposed to denounce the anti-Genet resolutions as the product of "active zeal displayed by persons . . . of known Monarchical principles." As it happened, Madison had with him a letter from Jefferson warning that Genet would "sink the republican interest if they do not abandon him"; but that warning was written in a cipher code that Jefferson used because he thought Hamilton had spies in the post office, and Madison had neglected to bring the cipher with him. Accordingly, they drafted model resolutions that would have been highly embarrassing, except that a last-minute dispatch from Jefferson arrived, cautioning them about the gravity of Genet's offenses. Hastily, they modified their resolutions and added to them an affirmation of the principle that foreign diplomats must deal with the executive and a condemnation of appeals by diplomats to the people. That disclaimer so diluted their proposed resolutions as to render them ineffective; and besides, the Republicans proved unable to promote many meeetings.[37]

Hamilton, King, and Jay won the "war of the resolutions," but they were far from happy that the contest had started at all. As King wrote to Hamilton, the United States had "with great Trouble established a Constitution which vests competent powers in the hands of the Executive"; "it was never expected that the executive should sit with folded Arms, and that the Government should be carried on by Town Meetings, and those irregular measures, which disorganize the Society, destroy the salutary influence of regular Government, and render the Magistracy a mere pageant." That view was an echo of the sentiment Hamilton had expressed a year earlier, apropos of protests when the Clintonians stole the gubernatorial election from Jay. Advocates of the meetings justified their actions on the grounds that "democratic-republican" clubs, which seemed to spring up everywhere Genet went, had created the false impression that the people strongly favored a pro-French policy, and that the administration had simply been unable to keep Genet in check.[38]

But the precedent, Hamilton and his friends feared, was a dangerous one.

What dealt the death blow to the "French fever" was a far more virulent one of a different kind. An epidemic of yellow fever struck Philadelphia late in August of 1793, raged throughout September and October, killed almost 5,000 people, and paralyzed government. During the first week of September Hamilton himself was stricken with the disease, and Betsey got it three days later. The treatment confidently prescribed by the city's leading physician,

Benjamin Rush, was as lethal as the disease: Rush kept his patients on a near-starvation diet, drained them of blood, and subjected them to massive evacuations of the bowels. Few survived these tender ministrations. Fortunately for Hamilton, his boyhood friend Dr. Edward Stevens was in Philadelphia with a rational course of treatment, including full diet, cold baths, laudanum (opium), and cinchona bark (quinine). The Hamiltons were cured in five days.[39]

Total recovery, however, took longer. After a period of convalescence at the Schuyler home, Hamilton returned to Philadelphia in mid-October, only to be debilitated either by a relapse or by a new attack of a different fever. Consequently, it was November before he was back at his desk with strength intact. In the meantime, a number of important developments had taken place. Genet's various promotions had apparently collapsed, and he had been recalled. Freneau's *National Gazette,* financially marginal for some time, folded, and Freneau retired to New Jersey. Fenno's pro-administration *Gazette of the United States* almost folded as well, but Hamilton arranged loans and gifts from friends to keep it going. Jefferson, having had his fill of combat with Hamilton, having abandoned hope of moving the administration toward a pro-French stance, and having stayed on longer than he had intended anyway, announced his retirement as of December 31.[40]

All that was to the good; other developments were not. Before departing, Jefferson completed and submitted to the House a report on European restrictions against American commerce, arguing for the enactment of a mercantilistic system designed to force American trade away from Britain and toward France. Republicans seemingly had enough votes in the new House to pass Jefferson's proposals into law, and thus to accomplish what Jefferson had been unable to accomplish in the cabinet and in the forum of popular opinion.[41]

Serious as that prospect was, it was not all. The Republicans now had—or thought they had—proof, which they had lacked a year earlier, that Hamilton had illegally reallocated certain government funds without a presidential order. More ominously yet, even as Congress convened a new international crisis was brewing, and this one seemed certain to drag the United States into war with Great Britain.

The retirement Hamilton hoped for would have to wait.

XIII

Prime Minister

The rising tempest puts in act the soul,

Parts it may ravage, but preserves the whole.

The long and acrimonious struggle in the cabinet had taken its toll on everyone involved. Washington, daily regretting his decision not to retire after one term, was exhausted and somewhat addled, as he demonstrated in his choice of a new secretary of state. Jefferson had suggested Governor Thomas Johnson of Maryland, but Washington declared that Johnson, "from a want of familiarity with foreign affairs, would be in them like a fish out of water; everything would be new to him, and he awkward in everything." Whereupon Washington offered Johnson the job. When Johnson refused, the president offered it to Randolph, though he told Jefferson, "I do not know that he is fit for it." No sooner had Randolph accepted, however, than Washington started turning to him increasingly (and at times solely) for advice. Randolph had been sufficiently neutral in the partisan rivalry so that neither Hamilton nor Jefferson fully trusted him; and to Washington, smarting under charges of partisanship himself, that was a crucial asset. Nevertheless, Randolph was a second-rate figure. Moreover, he was involved in some financial dealings that threatened his personal independence. It is a measure of Washington's temporarily impaired judgment that he came for a while virtually to dote upon Randolph and to trust almost no one else.[1]

Hamilton, for his part, had almost lost sight of the grand goals for which he had labored; sick of public life, disgusted with politics, and still weak from his illness, he craved only to retire with honor, and he impatiently counted the days until the impending congressional inquiry would bestow that luxury upon him. His impatience turned to peevishness as Republicans in Congress delayed the inquiry and subjected him to harassment. In the House, when Hamilton's formal request for the investigation was presented, Giles introduced the appropriate resolutions but then moved that consideration be postponed until certain unrelated accusations against Hamilton, levied by Andrew Fraunces, could be fully examined. Fraunces, a clerk in the Treasury Department until Hamilton dismissed him for drunkenness and incompetence, had set up shop in New York as a broker of sorts. In that capacity he acquired (probably by fraudulent means) some old Board of Treasury warrants which, though they probably had already been paid, he nonetheless presented for redemption. Hamilton, suspecting fraud, refused. Angry, and egged on by James Reynolds's erstwhile partner Jacob Clingman (now working as an agent for John Beckley, the Republicans' chief political hatchet man), Fraunces lodged various charges that Hamilton had been involved in Duer's speculations. After a lengthy inquiry, the House rejected the accusations and adopted resolutions commending Hamilton for his diligence in preventing frauds, but the diversion delayed consideration of Giles's resolutions until February 24, 1794.[2]

In the meantime, Hamilton was being badgered by the Senate. Albert Gallatin, newly elected Republican senator from Pennsylvania, introduced in the upper chamber a series of resolutions calling for information on all Treasury operations since the beginning. These resolutions resulted in a series of demands for reports on trivial matters, consumed an inordinate amount of Hamilton's time, hampered the operations of the Treasury, and precluded the systematic investigation that Hamilton desired. In submitting the reports as they were demanded, Hamilton made no effort to conceal his irritation. Fortunately for him, it turned out that Gallatin had not been a citizen long enough to qualify constitutionally for his office, and Hamilton's tormentor was summarily unseated.[3]

The House investigation, when it finally got under way, was grueling. It was conducted by a committee of fifteen, one representative from each state; the members were overwhelmingly if not exclusively Republicans. For nearly three months the committee met every Tuesday and Thursday evening and every Saturday morning. Hamilton attended perhaps half the meetings to answer questions in person, and his written reports furnished a detailed account of

Treasury transactions and full descriptions of all his operating procedures. As he had hoped, there could be no charge that this investigation was lacking in deliberation or thoroughness.[4]

By then, however, Hamilton had stopped counting the days, for the pressure of external events had restored his sights to a grander plane. The survival of his financial system, and perhaps of the republic itself, had suddenly been threatened anew by the prospect of international war, and soon the system and the republic would be challenged by domestic insurrection as well. In these circumstances something far more important to Hamilton than his popular reputation came on trial. As always, he rose to the occasion—even though, this time, doing so required self-effacement and resulted in personal loss.

Hamilton's temporary myopia—his concern for the good opinion of petty scoundrels—was a form of battle fatigue, like that of a soldier too busy fighting to remember he is at war. But another reason for his preoccupation with the investigation was that everything else seemed under control. With Jefferson gone, Genet recalled, and Francomania abated, the only other problem demanding serious attention, apart from routine administrative matters, was the congressional debate on Jefferson's valedictory commercial proposals, in the form of seven resolutions moved by Madison on January 3. This debate raged for several weeks, and Hamilton had an active if indirect hand in the fray. The Republicans professed that their aims were nonpolitical, that the measures were designed simply to benefit American commerce, but Hamilton supplied the data to explode that claim. On January 13 William Loughton Smith, building his case upon a lengthy analysis prepared by Hamilton, delivered a powerful speech proving that American trade with Britain was far more advantageous than trade with France, and that the Republican policy of commercial restrictions against Britain would severely damage the United States. Smoked out, the Republicans now spoke "all French," as Fisher Ames put it, and openly avowed that Madison's resolutions were "war regulations" that would sacrifice American commerce "in order to reach the tender sides of our enemy."[5]

[287]

That much of the debate, ideological and partisan at base, was conducted more or less in a vacuum; but portentous substantive news from the outside world was already beginning to intrude. The first news came from Portugal. For years Portugal had been engaged in warfare against the pirates on the Barbary Coast of Africa and, with the aid of a British subsidy, had patrolled the Strait of Gibraltar, containing the pirates in the Mediterranean and often escorting American and other merchant ships safely through the most dangerous waters. But early in 1794 Americans learned that Britain, wishing to enlist the Portuguese navy in the fight against France, had negotiated and subsidized a truce between Portugal and the Algerines. The truce released the pirates into the Atlantic and freed them to prey upon American shipping—which they began to do, with all their accustomed savagery.[6]

Republicans responded by railing against England; Hamilton and his friends, perceiving that unleashing the pirates was only a by-product of British policy, not its aim, responded by proposing the creation of a navy to protect American shipping. In a caucus attended by three senators, four representatives, and Hamilton and Knox, it was agreed to propose the building of six 44-gun frigates, and appropriate resolutions were introduced in Congress. Madison, protesting that to build a navy was to court war with Britain, suggested that bribing the pirates would be a cheaper and safer tactic. Other Republicans managed to interpret the Algerian depredations as an argument in favor of commercial restrictions against Britain. Smith, Ames, and Theodore Sedgwick (all of whom had been present at the caucus) belittled those Republicans who believed the truce stemmed from British animus toward the United States, scoffed at them for being belligerent toward Britain but unwilling to defend American interests, and championed the Hamiltonian position that in times of peril the nation must negotiate for peace but prepare for war.[7]

Fresh news from the West Indies, however, convinced southerners—who needed little convincing—that the piracy not only reflected an anti-American British design but was a part of a barbaric overall strategy. Americans had known for some time that the Pitt ministry, instead of sending troops to aid its continental allies against France, had elected in 1793 to plunder French possessions in the West Indies. By late summer 7,000 British troops and much of the Royal Navy were engaged in the conquest of rich French sugar colonies in the Lesser Antilles and of the richest colony of them all, Sainte Domingue. The smaller islands fell readily, but Sainte Domingue, in chaos after the bloody slave insurrections of the preceding two years, was another story. In January 1794, Americans learned that the British were trying to subdue the colony by arming the greatest of the black rebel leaders, Toussaint L'Ouverture. Widespread massacres of whites soon followed. The mere fact of the British campaign imperiled American neutrality, for the Franco-American treaty of alliance of 1778 bound the United States to defend the French West Indies in the event of a British attack.[8]

The Washington administration had long insisted that the treaty was inapplicable because France was the offensive power, and thus Hamilton could hold that Britain's operations in Sainte Domingue were no concern of the United States. However, he could not slough off news from the Caribbean of a wholesale attack upon American shipping by the Royal Navy. On November 6, 1793, the British government had issued orders to naval commanders to seize all vessels, neutral or French, that were carrying produce to or from the French West Indies. The orders were kept secret until late in December, by which time the Caribbean was aswarm with American shipping sent to the area to profit from the recent opening of the islands. The seizures thus resulted in a rich harvest, more than 300 American vessels and their cargoes. The text of the order was published in Philadelphia on March 7, and reports of the seizures were published almost daily thereafter.[9]

War appeared certain, and Hamilton's preoccupation with self vanished. He sent Washington a memorandum proposing a series of measures for national defense—though, out of regard for the president's state of mind, he tactfully described his proposals as "some reveries which have occupied his imagination." "The pains taken to preserve peace," he wrote, "include a proportional responsibility that equal pains be taken to be prepared for war"; and he deferentially suggested that Washington might choose to consider "whether there ought not to be some executive impulse," since "many persons look to the President for the suggestion of measures corresponding with the exigency of Affairs." Washington did not so choose: he called no cabinet meetings on the subject, he made no proposals to Congress, and, in his correspondence during the next week or two, he showed greater concern for the affairs of his plantation than for affairs of state.[10]

A few years earlier, Washington's lethargy might have posed an unresolvable dilemma for Hamilton, but now he did not even pause: if Washington would not provide the requisite "executive impulse," Hamilton would. Two days after Hamilton wrote his memorandum, Theodore Sedgwick announced in the House that he would shortly present some resolutions regarding national defense. On the same day, March 10, the House passed the bill authorizing the establishment of an infant navy, and four of Hamilton's closest political friends, senators Rufus King of New York, Oliver Ellsworth of Connecticut, and George Cabot and Caleb Strong of Massachusetts, met to determine what advice they should give the president. On March 12 Sedgwick offered his resolutions, which proved to be virtually identical to Hamilton's proposals. Ellsworth called upon Washington the same day and suggested that the president appoint an envoy extraordinary to go to Great Britain and try to work out a peaceful solution to the problems between the two nations. Ellsworth mentioned Hamilton as "the character whose qualifications afforded a very commanding preference" for such a mission. There is no evidence that Hamilton had a hand in any of these efforts by his friends, but if he did not the coincidence of sentiments is remarkable.[11]

The president remained exasperatingly inert. When Ellsworth suggested a special envoy to England, Washington replied only that he doubted Hamilton's suitability for such a mission, since Hamilton "did not possess the general confidence of the Country." As to the idea of the mission itself, Washington apparently agreed with Randolph that appointing a special envoy would be improper until "congress shall have given nerve to our affairs." Yet he persisted in refusing to recommend preparations for defense—and without a nudge from him the Republicans who dominated the House, almost paranoid in their fear of "standing armies," were ill disposed to approve adequate measures.[12]

Then came news that made action imperative. Late in March it became known in Philadelphia that Lord Dorchester, governor of Canada, had delivered a remarkably incendiary address to the Indians six weeks earlier. Dorchester, rattled by reports that Genet's agents were working among French Canadians, concluded that an Anglo-American war was imminent, and he so informed delegates from the Six Nation Indians. In effect, he incited the Redmen to join the Redcoats in common cause against the United States. Since negotiations between the Indians and the United States had broken down, Dorchester's inflammatory speech made Indian warfare in the interior certain and pushed Britain and the United States to the brink of formal hostilities. Congress reacted by resolving to raise an army of 50,000 men and to place an embargo upon shipping—normally the last step before a declaration of war.*[13]

These developments forced Hamilton into an awkward position. He agreed upon the urgent necessity of both the preparations for war and the mission to seek peace, and he doubtless hoped to be the special envoy, for he was not confident that anyone else could succeed. His appropriateness for the assignment, however, had become the subject of heated controversy. King and others, including Washington's old and still-trusted friend Robert Morris, were urging that Hamilton be sent; Secretary of State Randolph's friend, Senator James Monroe, and his brother-in-law, Representative John Nicholas, wrote Washington strongly opposing any mission and bitterly protesting against Hamilton's nomination should an envoy be sent. Nicholas, in an especially vitriolic attack, charged that "more than half America have determined it to be unsafe to trust power in the hands of this person. . . . Did it never occur to you that the divisions of America might be ended by the sacrafice of this one man?"[14]

Moreover, House Republicans chose just this moment to execute a maneuver that drove Washington and Hamilton closer to a break than they had been since 1781. The maneuver arose from the committee investigating Hamilton's official conduct, which was continuing to meet despite the war crisis. Hamilton had testified that, from the outset, he had managed all moneys in the Treasury as a single fund, no matter what their source or their budgeted purpose. That practice was more convenient and flexible than the maintenance of a multiplicity of segregated funds, and Hamilton insisted that so long as all money was accounted for and was expended in

---

* The army never materialized, the immediate need for it being removed when negotiations proved successful.

accordance with congressional or presidential directives, it was entirely proper. Many members of the committee believed on the contrary that money received from a specific source and appropriated to a specific purpose should be kept separate; yet it could not be maintained that Hamilton had violated the law. At some point, however, the inquisitors renewed, with a twist, the charge that on one occasion Hamilton had expended funds without authority and contrary to congressional acts of August 4 and 12, 1790. Those statutes had given the secretary of the treasury blanket authority to negotiate foreign loans from time to time but required that the president approve each such loan. It was now charged that Hamilton had mixed and used the funds from two loans, to the advantage of the Bank of the United States, without first obtaining presidential authorization. Had that charge been provable, it would technically have constituted an unlawful misappropriation of funds and, given the political complexion of Congress, might well have led to Hamilton's impeachment. [15]

In fact Hamilton had received appropriate authorization, mostly verbal but partly written, and as he testified to the committee, he had one letter from Washington as verification. But the president was in no mood to get Hamilton off the hook by confirming his testimony—possibly because he had a resentful sense that Hamilton's measures were at the root of the bitter partisan controversy, as Nicholas's poisonous letter had charged; possibly because Washington resented Hamilton for planning to desert him. In any event, when Randolph told him of Hamilton's testimony, he exploded in a rage and vehemently denied that the letter of authorization existed. Hamilton's display of the letter only exacerbated the situation, for Washington was never keen upon admitting that he was wrong. Thus when the committee requested Hamilton to obtain further corroboration from the president, Washington, with singular ill grace, refused to supply it. Instead, he offered only a petulant written statement that Hamilton's documents "speak for themselves" and that the verbal authorizations were no doubt "substantially" as Hamilton had testified. Hamilton protested that the equivocal response would be interpreted as "proof that he does not think [Hamilton's] representation true"; but Washington would say no more. Gleefully, Madison reported to Jefferson that Washington's letter was "inexpressibly mortifying" to Hamilton and his friends. [16]

Mortified Hamilton may have been, but at that crucial juncture he could not afford to succumb to his emotions. War with Britain would destroy the Union: the attendant disruption of the revenues would dissolve the Union's most powerful cement, Hamilton's financial system, and the conflict would set the sections one against another, the states north and east of Pennsylvania opposing it and those to the south and west favoring it. Republicans in Congress, advocating actions that would make war certain and simultaneously opposing preparations for defense, seemingly cared not for the consequences. On the other hand, the British were taking steps that made the success of an extraordinary mission seem possible. Hammond assured Rufus King that Dorchester's rantings were unauthorized, and news arrived that the noxious Orders in Council of November 6 had been repealed and that the British ministry had so far relaxed its regulations as to permit virtually unchecked American trade with the French West Indies. Hamilton, having no alternative, swallowed his feelings and sat down to write one of the most important letters of his life.[17]

The letter was addressed to Washington; its purpose was to rouse the president out of his torpor, to convince him that only vigorous executive leadership could avert a national calamity. Out of passion on the part of some and rashness on the part of others, Hamilton pointed out, a majority in the House had lined up in support of two measures—to sequester private debts owed by Americans to British merchants, and to cut off all intercourse with Britain—which would dishonor the nation and plunge it into a war for which it was unprepared. Continued presidential passivity would amount to sanctioning that suicidal course. The only reasonable alternative was "preparation for war and negotiation unincumbered by measures which forbid the expectation of success." If Washington agreed with this judgment, it was *"urgent* for him to demonstrate that opinion as a preventive of wrong measures and future embarrassment." He should appoint a suitable envoy extraordinary to Great Britain and simultaneously recommend that Congress prepare for war but refrain from enacting proposals "contrary to the spirit of an attempt to adjust existing differences by Negotiation." In conclusion, Hamilton asked that his own name be dropped from consideration for the mission and urged that John Jay be appointed instead.[18]

Shortly after dawn the next day, Washington scribbled a terse

note to Jay: "At as early an hour this morning, as you can make convenient to yourself . . . I will expect to have the satisfaction of con-
versing with you on an interesting subject." That was Wednesday,
April 15. Jay was offered the appointment and, after a day of consultation with Hamilton and others, agreed to accept on condition that
the sequestration and nonintercourse bills not become law. On
Thursday Washington submitted Jay's name to the Senate. The following Monday, over vehement Republican opposition, the mission
and Jay's appointment were confirmed. The sequestration bill died
in the House, the nonintercourse bill in the Senate.[19]

Even though Jay would be the envoy, the mission was Hamilton's, and for the most part Hamilton's ideas prevailed in the preparation of Jay's instructions. Fortunately, Washington asked all cabinet members for suggestions, and Randolph proved to have no firm
ideas on the subject. Hamilton's full, vigorous, and decisive proposals—worked out in consultation with Jay and sometimes with
King, Cabot, and Ellsworth—therefore formed the heart of what became Jay's official orders. Jay was to insist upon indemnification for
seizures under the November Orders in Council, to press for a mutual agreement not to arm Indians against either party, to iron out
disputes arising from noncompliance with the peace treaty of 1783,
and to seek improved commercial relations with Britain. All this was
consistent with what Hamilton had long believed should form the
basis of an Anglo-American treaty. Randolph added to the formal instructions, however, a number of points with which Hamilton disagreed, particularly in regard to commercial affairs. Accordingly, in a
confidential supplementary letter to Jay, Hamilton urged that he not
be inflexible, since there was room for bargaining on both sides; and
if "truly beneficial" gains could be made in one area, other areas
could be "more laxly dealt with." As he phrased it in a note to Randolph, "We are still in the path of negotiation. Let us not plant it
with thorns."[20]

Hamilton's decisive leadership in regard to the special mission was misleading, for he was inwardly torn over whether to go
through with his proposed retirement. The urge to do so was powerful; working with Washington had become embarrassing and at
times nearly impossible. The problem was growing acute even as
preparations for sending Jay to London were being made. Because

of increased military expenditures and because the Dutch money market had again contracted, the Treasury faced a shortage of almost a million dollars by July 1. Congress authorized a new domestic loan in that amount, but Hamilton was not confident that the funds could be mobilized in time to meet principal payments on old Dutch debts falling due in June. As it happened, the United States had to its credit in Holland about $1.5 million, borrowed the preceding summer with the intention of moving the money to Philadelphia for sinking-fund purchases. Hamilton proposed the simple and obvious expedient of leaving much of that money in Amsterdam to cover the impending deficit there and using the proceeds of the new domestic loan to cover the ensuing shortage in the sinking fund. In the wake of the controversy over authorizations, however, Washington decided (upon Randolph's urging) that his previous authorization of a loan for the sinking fund was an irreversible appropriation, and he refused to sanction Hamilton's commonsense arrangements. Consequently, Hamilton could only follow the absurd and expensive course of exporting money to Europe and simultaneously importing money from Europe—which, given the uncertainties of oceanic shipping during wartime, was as risky as it was foolish. Working under such erratic conditions was vexing and painful, and not being trusted was doubly so.[21]

On the other hand, the moral pressures not to quit were powerful also. In March Hamilton's friend Henry Lee had chided him for proposing to join the cowardly "set" (meaning Jefferson) who persuaded the president "to stand at the helm & when the storm threatens desert the ship." How, Lee asked, could Hamilton "reconcile such pusillanimity to your feelings. . . . I did not for a moment believe it possible for *you* thus to act." That letter doubtless stung, especially because Hamilton knew there were things to be done that only he could do. Someone had to see to the building of the newly authorized frigates, and someone had to equip General Anthony Wayne and his troops for the impending Indian war, and Secretary of War Henry Knox was not competent to either task. Moreover, three crises were shaping up in the back country: Indian war was looming in Georgia, adventurers in Kentucky were arming for an attack on Spanish Louisiana, and ruffians in western Pennsylvania were moving toward armed insurrection in opposition to the excise tax.[22]

The day of decision came late in May, when the House committee completed its inquiry and submitted its final report. Despite the embarrassment over the authorizations, Hamilton was fully exonerated—for, as the Virginian William Heth observed, "The more you *probe,* examine, & investigate Hamiltons conduct; rely upon it, the *greater* he will appear." Indeed, except for the deletion of a few theoretical observations, the committee's report was a verbatim copy of written statements prepared by Hamilton and Wolcott. The path was cleared for a departure with honor; but Hamilton could not go through with it, despite his "impatient desire to relinquish a situation in which even a momentary stay," as he put it, was "opposed by the strongest personal & family reasons." Five days after the committee issued its report, Hamilton swallowed his pride again and withdrew his resignation.[23]

Washington accepted Hamilton's decision with cool formality, but warmth and affection soon set in, bringing the two men closer than they had ever been before. That was a development of immense significance. For more than three years Washington had attempted to steer an intermediate course between the positions held by Jefferson and Hamilton, and the effort had rendered the administration virtually impotent. When he embraced Hamilton anew in the summer of 1794, he became a genuinely Hamiltonian president—and Hamilton became, truly, the prime minister.[24]

In the spring it appeared that the summer's most serious domestic problems would erupt in the Southwest. In western Georgia, frontiersmen and speculators were encroaching upon Creek Indian lands, stirring up hostilities in Florida, talking of secession, and flirting with going over to the Spanish. In Kentucky, settlers were alternately arming to attack Louisiana under French auspices and declaring that, in the absence of effective federal protection against the Indians, they would secede and seek the protection of the British. Both situations were explosive, but the newly united and reenergized administration skillfully defused them. On Hamilton's suggestion, the governor of Georgia was induced to employ the state militia, at the federal government's expense, to rout the secessionists. The Kentuckians were managed with a combination of firmness and art. A presidential proclamation sternly forbade them to assemble for a filibustering expedition; and then, to channel rather than suppress the energies of those anxious to fight for local advantage, General Wayne was authorized to enlist 2,000 Kentucky volunteers for his Indian campaign in Ohio.[25]

But a grave and unexpected crisis arose in western Pennsylvania. In mythology the people of that area were sturdy yeoman farmers, working hard to carve a decent living out of the wilderness for themselves and their families but neglected when not oppressed by a plutocratic government on the seaboard. In reality most of them were—as the Frenchman Crèvecoeur described them—uncouth, drunken, lazy, brutal, wasteful, and contentious, "no better than carnivorous animals of a superior rank." Law was a stranger among them; clan and kin were all. They rarely worked, hard or otherwise; rather, like their Scotch-Irish ancestors, they provided for their necessities by maintaining herds of swine and cattle which roamed wild in the woods and were rounded up and driven to eastern markets once a year. Far from being oppressed by government, they ignored it; they rarely paid taxes or paid for the land they inhabited; any official who attempted to enforce the law among them did so at his mortal peril. And, contrary to another myth, they distilled little if any whiskey as a "cash crop" to be sold in the east. Rather, they distilled it in prodigious quantities and drank almost all of it themselves.[26]

Along with counterparts and kinsmen in the Carolinas and Kentucky, the Scotch-Irish in western Pennsylvania had resisted the 1791 excise tax on whiskey from the beginning—though home distilleries were exempt from the tax, though the tax was modest (about 7½ cents a gallon) and though, as Hamilton pointed out, the federal government paid out four or five times as much to them (for whiskey purchased as army rations) as it collected in taxes from them. In 1792 they became so violent in their treatment of revenue officers that Hamilton was afraid that force would be necessary to bring them into compliance with the law. A presidential proclamation, however, coupled with patience, persuasion, and a moderation of the collection and enforcement procedures, gradually pacified the area and brought most of the distillers into compliance with the law. In the spring of 1794, only 37 of the 1,200 or so distillers in the area were delinquent.[27]

But then a number of volatile new ingredients were added to the brew. One was directly related to the excise: United States District

Attorney William Rawle obtained and federal Marshal David Lenox was sent to serve subpoenas upon the thirty-seven delinquent distillers, requiring them to appear in the federal district court in Philadelphia. That was a dangerously provocative move. The expense and inconvenience of answering processes in Philadelphia had been a major complaint against the excise and, in fact, by the time Lenox set out to serve the papers the law had been changed to permit hearings in the nearby state courts. Issuing the subpoenas under the old law was legal and proper, for the violations had taken place under the old law a year earlier, but it evoked widespread anger in the west. Moreover, hostility toward that move was reinforced by local discontent with two other recent actions of the administration: the proclamation against the Kentucky filibusterers, with whom inhabitants of the area were in strong sympathy, and an order prohibiting settlement (pending the outcome of Wayne's expedition) of Presque Isle, which was hungrily coveted by western Pennsylvania speculators.[28]

Despite the intensity of feeling, drastic action might have been averted but for political developments inside the area. The local political balance had recently been altered, which inspired a new group of office-hungry demagogues to stir up agitation against the whiskey excise as a means of election to the Pennsylvania legislature. More dangerously, advocates of violent radicalism had just organized three democratic-republican societies. Such organizations, of which there were about three dozen in the country, now constituted the militant left wing of the Republican party. They swallowed whole the rantings of Philip Freneau and his successor in scurrility, Benjamin Franklin Bache. They truly believed that Hamilton was the head of a monarchical and plutocratic conspiracy, that the purpose of his financial system was to crush the people with taxes for the benefit of the rich, that ostensible preparations for national defense masked a design to reduce the people under military despotism, that the excise was levied because it was traditionally the favorite tax of tyrants. They called repeatedly for the people to rise in resistance against this sinister plot. To form such organizations among the lawless hotheads of western Pennsylvania was to throw fire into a powder keg.[29]

The explosion began in mid-July, when Marshal Lenox and the excise inspector, General John Neville, set out toward Mingo Creek, west of Pittsburgh—the location of the most violent of the demo-cratic-republican societies—to serve the last of Lenox's writs. At dawn on July 16 a party of about forty men, many of them armed, made an abortive attack on Neville's home. Repulsed with one killed, the gang gathered 500 additional men for a major assault, by which time Neville had brought in seventeen regular soldiers to defend his house. After an exchange of fire in which an insurgent leader was killed and some soldiers were wounded, the soldiers sur-rendered, and the rebels destroyed the residence. Neville and Lenox fled the area, which in the next few weeks was teeming with impas-sioned meetings, radical oratory, violent acts, and threats to oust all federal authority. A call was issued for the militia to rendezvous for an attack on the government fort in Pittsburgh. In response, five or six thousand men gathered to drill and to march on the town. In the meantime, armed bands beat and tarred and feathered excise of-ficers, forced them to resign, and destroyed the property of distillers who had complied with the law. On July 26 a band waylaid the post rider and robbed the mails. State and county officials, when they acted at all, supported the rebels.[30]

The administration moved quickly to organize the machinery for suppressing the rebellion. Under the militia act of 1792, the presi-dent was authorized to call out the militia only if a federal judge cer-tified that laws of the United States were being opposed "by combi-nations too powerful to be suppressed by the ordinary course of judicial proceedings." Documentary evidence of the insurrection was placed in the hands of Associate Justice James Wilson, who supplied the necessary certification on August 4. Meanwhile, on August 2 Washington convened the cabinet in a meeting with top officers of Pennsylvania. State officials were loath to act, despite the president's declaration that he intended to move forcibly against the rebels, and after the meeting Washington asked the cabinet members for written opinions on the most efficacious way to pro-ceed. The new attorney general, William Bradford, insisted upon armed intervention on the ground that "insurgency was high trea-son, a capital crime punishable by death." Randolph demurred from fear that such force would alienate the affections of the people at large; he counseled that further judicial proceedings be attempted first.[31]

Hamilton perceived the disturbances as a threat to national security. The robbery of the mails made it unsafe to send funds for provisioning and paying Wayne's troops, which could seriously jeopardize the offensive just then being mounted. Moreover, Congress had recently enacted additional internal taxes, and more would be necessary if Jay's mission failed and war cut off revenues from import duties. An example of successful resistance to internal taxes now would be a dangerous precedent. But there were even deeper matters at issue. The question, Hamilton said, "is plainly this—shall the majority govern or be governed? shall the nation rule, or be ruled? shall the general will prevail, or the will of a faction?" There were, he said, two species of government, one of force and the other of laws. "The first is the definition of despotism—the last, of liberty." If the laws are not respected, force "must be substituted; and where this becomes the ordinary instrument of government there is an end to liberty. Those, therefore, who preach doctrines, or set examples, which undermine or subvert the authority of the laws, lead us from freedom to slavery; they incapacitate us for a GOVERNMENT of LAWS, and consequently prepare the way for one of FORCE, for mankind MUST HAVE GOVERNMENT OF ONE SORT OR ANOTHER."[32]

What Hamilton proposed was a stratagem designed to preserve the authority of the laws: a display of force so powerful as to make the actual employment of force unnecessary. Specifically, he urged the mobilization of 12,000 militiamen, 6,000 from Pennsylvania and 2,000 apiece from New Jersey, Maryland, and Virginia, the troops to rendezvous six weeks hence, on September 10. In the meantime, according to law, the president should issue a proclamation "commanding the Insurgents to disperse and return peaceably to their respective abodes within a limited time." Whether force would have to be employed would "depend on circumstances as they shall arise," but Hamilton hoped and believed that the show of such imposing power would "deter from opposition, save the effusion of the blood of Citizens and secure the object to be accomplished."[33]

Washington followed all Hamilton's recommendations except one. The proclamation was issued on August 7, and Knox, on the president's instructions, wrote the governors of the four states "to take measures for calling forth the militia," a total of 12,950 men. That was Knox's last action in the drama, for the next day he requested a leave of absence to tend to some land speculations in

Maine. The request was granted; Hamilton became acting secretary of war and began making preparations for supplying the troops. He made preparations in another way as well: in accordance with his policy of keeping the public informed, he published (with Washington's approval) a long report on the insurrection that he had written for Washington on August 5.[34]

Hamilton's advice was not followed on a matter of timing, and events vindicated his judgment. It was agreed that Attorney General Bradford and two Pennsylvanians should be sent to try to persuade the insurgents to desist, and that amnesties would be granted if "satisfactory assurances" were given that the laws would "be no longer obstructed." Hamilton thought it would be fruitless to send commissioners to treat with the rebels until the militia force was assembled, but his opinion was not shared by the others, and Bradford set out immediately. When Bradford reached the scene, met with the co-commissioners, and conferred with leading residents of Pittsburgh, he concluded that there was no hope of enforcing the laws "but by the Physical strength of the Nation." The rebels' plan, Bradford reported to Washington, was to delay until cold weather made military operations impossible, which would give them "time to strengthen themselves—to circulate the manifesto they are preparing—to tamper with . . . Kentucky—to procure Ammunition and . . . seduce the well-affected." Negotiations were impossible, for "any man who would openly recommend obedience . . . would be in danger of assassination." This letter reached the president on August 23, by which time Philadelphia was rife with rumors (which had some substance) that the insurgents had determined to secede and were buying up arms and seeking British aid. Soon afterward insurgency erupted in western Maryland. Thus ended all hopes for successful negotiation without the backing of force.[35]

The climax came on with a rush. Militia troops began to be assembled early in September, and popular response to the call—contrary to Randolph's fears and Republican predictions—was enthusiastic. It seemed briefly that the mere calling of the militia would be adequate to the task and that the troops would not have to enter the disaffected area, for the commissioners now began to make some headway and induced many western Pennsylvanians to sign loyalty oaths. The more violent, however, became increasingly defiant, and by the 17th Washington had determined that if the resistance continued he would personally take command of the expedition. Hamilton asked to go along, for "in a government like ours, it cannot but have a good effect for the person who is understood to be the adviser or proposer of a measure, which involves danger to his fellow citizens, to partake in that danger." That was a painful step to take, for one of Hamilton's sons was desperately ill, and Betsey, pregnant, was ill herself. Nonetheless, on September 30 Hamilton set out with Washington to join the troops. Washington stayed with the force for three weeks, making sure everything was in order, then turned command over to Governor Henry Lee of Virginia and went back to Philadelphia. Hamilton stayed with the troops until the mission was completed on November 19. He learned on his way home that Betsey had had a miscarriage.[36]

The expedition had precisely the effect that Hamilton had hoped for and expected. In the face of the federal government's awesome display of strength and will, the insurrection vanished. Not a shot was fired in anger, yet two thousand rebels fled the area. A few score people were arrested and sufficiently ill treated so they would remember to behave themselves in future. Twenty were taken to Philadelphia and tried for treason; two were convicted despite the absence of witnesses that far from the scene. Washington pardoned both. The combination of strength and clemency had a salutary effect throughout the land: a wave of enthusiasm for the administration swept the country, and with few exceptions seditious and even libelous talk virtually ceased. The French minister reported to his superiors that checking "this local and precipitate eruption" prevented "a general explosion for some time prepared in the public mind."[37]

As a southern justice of the Supreme Court said, the skillful handling of the Whiskey Rebellion was "a lesson to Governments and People." The lesson was not lost on the voters, who restored supporters of the administration to control of both houses of Congress in that year's elections. Nor was Washington blind to the political effects of the episode. In his annual message to Congress (delivered the day Hamilton left Pittsburgh) he gave a history of the insurrection and placed a large share of the blame for it upon "self-constituted societies," meaning the democratic-republican clubs. That all but destroyed the organizations.[38]

This turn of events, together with news that Jay's mission prom-

ised success and that Wayne had crushed the Indians without en-
countering British opposition, made it safe for Hamilton to retire at
last. As he wrote to his sister-in-law, "All is well with the public. Our
insurrection is most happily terminated. Government has gained by
it reputation and strength, and our finances are in a most flourish-
ing condition. *Having contributed to place those of the Nation on a
good footing, I go to take a little care of my own; which need my
care not a little.*" On December 1, he formally and officially announced his resignation, effective January 31.[39]

The finances of the nation, however, were not on quite so
good a footing as Hamilton desired, and he devoted much of his
remaining time in office to improving them. Events of the last two
years had revealed to him some important weaknesses in the original system. The means for handling the foreign debt, for example,
were entirely unsatisfactory. The transactions were slow and uncertain, borrowing to pay maturing principal entailed periods of double
interest, and most importantly the vicissitudes of war could cut off
foreign money markets entirely. War interfered with domestic finance as well: it disrupted shipping and thereby imperiled the government's main source of revenue, duties upon tonnage and imports. Moreover, domestic politics compounded these problems and
engendered others. Even if hotheaded, partisan politicians did not
blunder the nation into a war, Republicans were ever disposed to restrict commerce as an instrument of foreign policy, and that would
play havoc with the revenues. Nor were Republicans averse to
direct impairment of public credit, as their recent advocacy of taxing interest on the public debt and of sequestering the holdings of
foreigners had shown.[40]

On the other hand, the time was propitious for remedying the
weaknesses, despite Republican dominance of the lame-duck session of the Third Congress. Thanks to the temporary internal taxes
and temporary increases in import and tonnage duties that had
been enacted during the British war crisis, revenues for 1795 promised to exceed expenditures by nearly a million dollars, even after
allowing for continuing Indian warfare and the expense of the small
navy. What was more, should the British Orders in Council of January 8, 1794, be implicitly or explicitly confirmed in the treaty Jay

was negotiating, the ensuing bonanza for American trade as a neutral carrier would send revenues soaring. If that happened, if the temporary taxes were made permanent, and if the proceeds were appropriated to the sinking fund, the public debt could be put in train to extinction, and American independence would be complete.[41]

For these reasons Hamilton submitted, on January 16, his valedictory Report on the Public Credit. He proposed that the unfunded domestic debt (about $1.5 million) be paid off, that the foreign debt be converted to a domestic debt, and that most of the temporary taxes be extended until the entire debt was retired. He proposed that Congress explicitly pledge never to tax interest on the public debt or to sequester the holdings of foreigners. Most importantly, he proposed that all revenues of the federal government, up to the amount necessary to retire the debt on a regular schedule in thirty years, be inviolably appropriated to the sinking fund.[42]

In general and in detail the report bore Hamilton's ingenious stamp, and several features were masterful. He proposed that as the debt was retired it be held in the Treasury rather than destroyed, which meant that the Treasury itself would collect and be enabled to divert to the sinking fund an increasing proportion of the fixed annual interest payments. By that means a principal of almost $80 million could be retired in less than thirty years at an annual cost of only $836,000. The modesty of the annual appropriation for principal payments, together with the setting of a minimum sum (which in normal times would be far exceeded) rather than a fixed amount, freed Hamilton's system of a weakness that characterized more rigid sinking-fund systems, notably that of Great Britain—namely, that in time of war the fund must be suspended. In the event of war, to be sure, it would be necessary to borrow anew. Moreover, in a popular government politicians would always be tempted to abuse public credit by overusing it, to court the electorate by spending now and saddling posterity with the burden of payment. But both difficulties would be surmounted if it were fixed as an invariable principle that, at the time of contracting any new debt, funds be established for paying the interest and reimbursing the principal within a determinate period.[43]

The capstone to the system was a provision for removing the sinking fund from politics. Republicans had cried for years against the perpetual nature of the original funding scheme. They had no grounds on which to oppose a systematic plan for retiring the debt, and politically they scarcely dared tamper with it in future. Furthermore, as Hamilton frankly said to the legislators, in a government as complex as that of the United States, once things were done, undoing them was extremely difficult. If Congress enacted his proposals, he could expect that his system would remain essentially intact for three more decades. After that long a time, he hoped, the habit of sound fiscal policy would be ingrained, and public credit would be rendered immortal.[44]

To Hamilton's chagrin, Congress refused to follow his recommendations in regard to old creditors who had not opted to fund their paper under the act of 1790; but otherwise it enacted his proposals almost *in toto*. By that time he was five weeks into retirement.[45]

And thus, after twenty years of service to his country, Hamilton laid down the mantle of power. He had just celebrated his thirty-seventh birthday.

XIV

Minister in Absentia

For modes of Faith let graceless zealots fight;

His can't be wrong whose life is in the right.

Shortly after Hamilton left office, his old friend James
McHenry wrote him a letter of congratulation and advice. Having
ensured his immortal frame, McHenry said, what remained for Hamilton to do was to seek private felicity "in the moderate pursuit of
your profession," in "objects that require no violent waste of spirits,"
and in "little plans that involve gentle exercise and which you can
drop or indulge in without injury to your family." Describing his
own life, McHenry said "I have built houses, I have cultivated fields,
I have planned gardens, I have planted trees, I have written little essays, I have made poetry once a year to please my wife, at times got
children and at all times thought myself happy. Why cannot you do
the same"?[1]

Such an idyllic life might have appealed to Hamilton in the abstract, but he could not have emulated McHenry's example, even
had the capacity for serenity been in him. He could scarcely afford
to pursue his profession moderately, for he left office with little
property, no income, and a large burden of personal debts. Beyond
the need to earn a livelihood, which alone required that he continue
to work hard, there was the impulsion to do so out of sheer psychic
momentum: when one has labored with such passionate intensity,
slowing down does not come easily. Nor could he, despite his firm
resolution to stay out of public life, suddenly stop caring what happened to his country. Finally, and most tellingly, it turned out that
the Washington administration simply could not function without
him.

All these pressures were illustrated in an episode that took place a few months after he resigned. During the spring and summer of 1795 a heated controversy developed over the treaty Jay had negotiated with Britain, and Hamilton plunged into the fray with his accustomed ardor, giving speeches, organizing petition campaigns, and debating with all and sundry. Feelings in New York were running so high that when supporters of the treaty encountered opponents, fist fights were apt to result; on one occasion, Hamilton was stoned by a mob when he attempted to speak in behalf of the treaty.[2]

On Saturday, July 18, Hamilton and several friends were strolling down Wall Street when they met Commodore James Nicholson, president of the erstwhile Democratic Society, and a group of his friends. Nicholson, Albert Gallatin's father-in-law, was a man whose politics stemmed from his pocketbook: like many another Francophile, he had reaped a fortune in trade with Revolutionary France and its colonies. Yet he had had the effrontery, a couple of weeks earlier, to spread a rumor that Hamilton had embezzled £100,000 from the Treasury and invested it in British government bonds. Though Hamilton was apparently unaware of Nicholson's role in circulating the rumor, friction was inevitable when the two groups met. State Assemblyman Josiah Ogden Hoffman, one of Hamilton's companions, soon fell into a vehement argument with Nicholson. To prevent violence, Hamilton attempted to intervene, whereupon Nicholson first insulted him and then snarled that Hamilton "would not pursue the affair for he had declined an interview [that is, a duel] upon a former occasion." No such affront to Hamilton's honor was acceptable, and Hamilton promptly challenged Nicholson to a duel—a challenge he put in writing two days later.[3]

A few minutes after this encounter the Hamilton group met another band of Republicans in front of Edward Livingston's house, and a rancorous argument started between Hoffman and Peter Livingston. When the argument grew personal, Edward Livingston and Rufus King tried to stop it by urging that "personal disputes" ought to be "settled elsewhere." Hamilton, his blood boiling, stepped forward and declared that "if the parties were to contend in a personal way, he was ready . . . to fight the whole 'Detestable faction' one by one." Maturin Livingston, arriving at just that moment, said "he was one of the party that he accepted the challenge &

would fight him in half an hour where he pleased." Hamilton replied that as soon as his affair with Nicholson was resolved, he would call on Livingston.[4]

The affair with Livingston went no further, inasmuch as the honor of neither party had been involved, but that with Nicholson was more serious. After a week of negotiations between principals and seconds, however, Nicholson submitted a satisfactory retraction and apology, and the duel was averted. During that week Hamilton made out his will and entrusted it to Troup; ironically, that document attested to the absurdity of Nicholson's charge of embezzlement. Apart from his bank account, containing about $1,800, Hamilton's only property of consequence was a tract of 5,450 acres of upstate land, barely worth what he still owed on the purchase. His other debts, including $1,000 he had received in retainers for legal work not yet done, came to something over $17,000. In sum, his personal expenses during his tenure as secretary had been approximately twice as great as his income—and yet he had fashioned a system that made his country wealthy.[5]

Sorely as Hamilton needed money, and eager as he was to work for it, he was scrupulous, even fastidious, about the way he obtained it. An example of his concern for propriety involved a proposal that promised to net him more than a million dollars. James Greenleaf, a New York merchant and financier, had acquired about $5 million in land and securities, against which he owed about $1.2 million. He asked Hamilton "to aid me with your name responsibility and talents in the liquidation of my Concerns and payment of my engagements." The fee would be a third of Greenleaf's net worth, "provided you will consent that the Mass shall remain undivided for Ten years & constitute the Capital of a Banking House to be established either in this City, or at Philadelphia in our joint Names and under your sole guidance and the profits divided between us in equal portions." Nothing illegal or unethical was involved, and had Hamilton accepted and the liquidation succeeded he would have become one of the richest men in America: all he had to do was sell his name. But as he said to Greenleaf, "though I discover nothing in the affair which an Individual differently circum-

stanced might not with propriety enter into—yet in my peculiar situation, viewed in all its public as well as personal relations, I think
myself bound to decline the overture."[6]

As revealing was his response to an offer made by his good friend
Robert Troup. Troup had been approached by Charles Williamson,
the British agent for a number of wealthy English investors, with a
proposal to buy several million acres of land in western New York.
He wanted Troup and Hamilton to provide "advice & assistance in
executing the plan," for which they would be handsomely rewarded
with shares in the venture. If Hamilton did not wish his name to be
connected with the operation, Troup added, "I will chearfully be
your Trustee." Hamilton weighed the proposition long and hard, for
there was no hint of impropriety in it, and he knew he could trust
Troup unreservedly. Yet he turned it down in the end, not wanting
to expose himself to charges that he was involved with British
speculators, "because there must be some *public fools* who sacrifice
private to public interest" and "because my *vanity* whispers I ought
to be one of those fools and ought to keep myself in a situation the
best calculated to render service." The stakes of the game to be
played, he added, "may be for nothing less than true liberty, property, order, religion and of course *heads.*" As to Troup's offer "to
stand between me and ostensibility," Hamilton thanked him but
said "it has been the rule of my life to do nothing for my own emolu-
ment *under cover*—what I would not promulge I would avoid. This
may be too great refinement. I know it is pride. But this pride makes
it part of my plan to *appear truly what I am.*"[7]

He carried his concern for proper appearances into his law practice, tending to undervalue his private services lest it be inferred
that he was capitalizing on his public services. He charged notoriously low fees. When a client sent a retainer that Hamilton
thought excessive, he promptly returned it. In a case involving an
enormous sum, Isaac Gouverneur made the mistake, in his letter
seeking to retain Hamilton, of enclosing correspondence with another lawyer in which Gouverneur had casually remarked, "Attorneys like to make the most of their bills of cost." Resenting that slur
on his profession, Hamilton declined Gouverneur's request and became principal counsel for his opponent, Lewis Le Guen. In the ensuing litigation, which dragged out for five years, Hamilton obtained for Le Guen a judgment of almost $120,000—probably the

largest sum that had ever been awarded in a personal damage suit in America. In gratitude, Le Guen wanted to pay Hamilton a generous fee, but Hamilton would accept only $1,500. By contrast, Aaron Burr, who participated as co-counsel with Hamilton for part of the litigation, demanded a fee several times as large.[8]

Despite Hamilton's self-imposed restrictions, the cases and the fees came pouring in. Nearly every major merchant and financier in New York City sought his services, as did hordes of smaller businessmen, land dealers, and craftsmen. He became counsel for the Holland Land Company, which was making huge land purchases in behalf of Dutch investors; for the United States Insurance Company, which was heavily involved in maritime litigation arising from the ongoing international wars; for the city of Albany and for the state of New York. His income quickly rose to twice what it had been as secretary, then to three and four times that sum.[9]

Hamilton's practice was not, however, simply a matter of making money: in large measure his activities as lawyer supplemented and implemented his design for American society. In many of his cases, he was associated with a small but rapidly growing group of lawyers and judges who were effecting a radical transformation of American law, and by that means effecting a transformation of society. Until the 1790s, private law in America (that governing transactions and relations among individuals in such legal actions as torts, contracts, damages, and the like) was static and rigged in favor of the status quo. It protected the interests of great landowners, slaveholders, possessors of inherited wealth and status—the oligarchical establishment Hamilton sought by his public measures to undermine. By virtue of its inflexibility and inapplicability, it discouraged and discriminated against merchants, traders, shippers, financiers, capitalistic manufacturers, and entrepreneurship and the developmental spirit in general; and people in those lines of endeavor tended to be antilegalistic and to operate according to their own rules outside the body of conventional law. But during the 1790s, partly because of wartime commercial opportunities and risks and partly because of the powerful institutional impetus provided by Hamilton's system of public credit, a new breed of aggressive entrepreneurs emerged and joined forces with a new breed of lawyers and judges. Through a subtle but profound alteration in legal philosophy, these lawyers and judges evolved an instrumental conception of the common law (paralleling that worked out in England by William Murray, First Lord Mansfield, a generation earlier), whereby the rules came to favor private economic development, whatever the pronouncements of politicians and legislators. That turn of events ensured the completion of Hamilton's revolution, no matter how successful his enemies might be in garnering votes.[10]

Fittingly for a movement that Hamilton was part of, the substantive transformation was made possible by changes in procedure. Historically, civil actions had been settled by the hallowed institution of trial by juries of laymen. In the late eighteenth century two procedural innovations, the awarding of new trials for verdicts "contrary to the weight of the evidence" and the expansion of the "special case" and "case reserved," relegated juries to the determination of facts and allowed judges, upon argument by contending lawyers, to settle questions of law. To have the facts thus stipulated, and to make the outcome of cases result from arguments between and before fellow professionals, were of enormous advantage to Hamilton. More importantly, this procedure made possible the conversion of mercantile custom into a recognized and regularized judge-made body of common-law precedent that would govern all transactions, including those between nonmerchants. The old theory of contract law, for example, wherein everything was assumed to have an objective value and a just price, was replaced by a new theory that made the market the determinant of value. Only by incorporating such changes into the law could a modern, dynamic market economy replace the static, fixed economy that had been rooted in feudalism.[11]

Hamilton had many contract cases, and some of the decisions he won and principles he established continued to be cited into the twentieth century. Perhaps his most important contribution to contract law, however, lay in a case that wrote new constitutional law. In 1795 the legislature of Georgia had sold to four companies, for a total of $500,000, no less than 35 million acres of land. A year later a rival group of politicians led by Hamilton's old opponent, Senator James Jackson, gained control of the legislature and, charging fraud in the original transaction, passed an act repealing the act of sale. Hamilton's political supporter, Senator James Gunn of Georgia, headed one of the companies, and another ally, Representative Robert Goodloe Harper of South Carolina, was counsel for the companies. They sought Hamilton's legal opinion on the controversy. Hamilton responded with an opinion that greatly expanded the contract clause of the Constitution. Article 1, section 10 of the Constitution prohibits states from "impairing the obligation of contracts," and it was generally assumed that the prohibition referred only to private contracts. Hamilton argued that the clause also applied to contracts between a state and individuals, that grants were in fact contracts, and therefore that Georgia's rescinding act was unconstitutional. Ultimately (in the case of *Fletcher* v. *Peck*) the Supreme Court ruled in accordance with Hamilton's opinion. When it did so, and when it handed down its decision in the Dartmouth College Case a few years later, the course of America's economic development—through franchises to private developers and through the market rather than through government subsidies and regulation—was firmly staked.[12]

The creation of a new law of contracts, of course, was not all there was to it: similar developments were necessary in regard to bills and notes, the negotiability of commercial paper, bankruptcy proceedings, creditor's rights, insurance, corporate privileges and obligations, and a host of other matters, and Hamilton was among the leaders in them all. He was especially influential, for instance, in the development of marine insurance law. Such marine insurance law as existed was of limited value because of a traditional distinction between ordinary and extraordinary risks. In the case of *Barnwell* v. *Church,* Hamilton posited an entirely new doctrine based upon actuarial conceptions. An underwriter attempted to avoid a claim for recovery on the ground that the insured vessel had latent defects that made it unseaworthy. Hamilton argued, conversely, that "the underwriter, in forming his calculation, considers the quantity of losses in proportion to the safe arrivals. On this datum he forms his estimate; seaworthiness must therefore be included. Of the number foundered at sea, many must have perished from latent defects" and thus "these must have constituted part of the risks calculated." If so, "latent defects are paid for, and premiums actually received for them by the underwriter." That line of thinking became the basis for fire and other casualty insurance law in the nineteenth century and as such provided one of the prerequisites for economic growth—a means of stabilizing business expectations.[13]

One of Hamilton's cases in an unrelated area was important for different reasons: it was the first time the Supreme Court passed upon the constitutionality of an act of Congress. Hamilton intended not to practice before the Supreme Court, for the action, the challenges, and the money were in state courts; and for the most part he abided by that intention. Just after he left the Treasury, however, the constitutionality of a federal tax on carriages, passed on his recommendation in 1794, was challenged by a group of Virginia Republicans, and Attorney General William Bradford asked Hamilton to plead the case as special counsel for the government. At issue was whether the carriage tax was a direct tax under the meaning of the Constitution. If so it would be void, since it did not accord with the constitutional mandate that direct taxes be apportioned by states on the basis of population. Hamilton argued brilliantly to the contrary, maintaining that the tax was actually an excise and need therefore merely be uniform throughout the United States; and the court so ruled. His three-hour argument, delivered before a packed gallery, was so powerful that many even among those "in the habit of reviling him" were swept away by "his eloquence, candour and law knowledge."[14]

Said Justice Joseph Story, many years later, "I have heard Samuel Dexter, John Marshall, and Chancellor Livingston say that Hamilton's reach of thought was so far beyond theirs that by his side they were schoolboys—rush tapers before the sun at noon day."[15]

B y the time the carriage-tax case was being argued, Hamilton had become far more to the administration than special legal counsel. His new role came about by degrees. At first he was cautious not to offer any unsolicited advice to Washington lest he appear "officious," and though he had some correspondence with others in the government he dealt extensively only with his own successor, Oliver Wolcott. Wolcott had a number of problems; though the Treasury was sound, it had troubles with liquidity. The money market in Europe continued to be closed. Credit in the United States also became tight for a variety of reasons, and the situation was aggravated by friction between the Bank of the United States and the Bank of New York. To make matters worse, Congress proved considerably more generous in making appropriations than in providing the necessary revenues. Wolcott was an excellent administrator, entirely capable of operating the nation's fiscal machinery in normal times, but he lacked Hamilton's imagination and finesse, and he repeatedly called upon his predecessor for advice. Busy as he was, Hamilton made time to aid Wolcott.[16]

Washington's first serious appeal to Hamilton was for advice concerning the treaty Jay had negotiated with England. Copies of the treaty arrived shortly after Congress adjourned in March of 1795, and Washington called the Senate into a special session to meet in June. Meanwhile, he kept the terms secret, which (as Hamilton predicted) fanned the fears and suspicions of Republican ideologues and their mercantile allies, those in trade with France and its colonies. By the time the Senate met, their propaganda campaign against ratification was intense. After a brief debate, the Senate struck out one objectionable article of the treaty and then ratified the remainder by the narrowest of constitutional margins, twenty votes to ten. Washington, however, hesitated to sign it in the face of what appeared to be widespread public opposition. No one in the cabinet was strong and wise enough to resolve Washington's dilemma for him, so he turned to his erstwhile secretary of the treasury.[17]

Hamilton's analysis was careful, thorough, and candid. He found acceptable the first ten articles of the treaty, those designed to settle permanently the mutual grievances between Britain and the United States. The British agreed to evacuate the northwest posts, and Indian traders from both nations were to be allowed to move freely between the United States and Canada—a significant step toward a goal Hamilton cherished, neutralizing the border. Boundaries, which had been the subject of some dispute, were to be settled cooperatively, that west of Lake Superior by a joint survey, that in Maine by a three-man commission. Claims for spoliations—the seizures of American vessels under the November 6, 1793, Orders in Council—were to be settled by a five-man commission, two from each nation and a fifth to be agreed upon by the first four, and Britain pledged to pay all valid claims. Two other permanent features were certain to incense American Republicans, though Hamilton regarded them as just. Each nation pledged not to confiscate the property of the citizens or subjects of the other in the event of war (contrary to a favorite Republican tactic); and debts from Americans to British merchants whose collection had been impeded by state law, in violation of the 1783 treaty, were to be appraised by a five-man commission and if found valid were to be paid (contrary to the interests of large numbers of Virginia planters). One source of complaint remained unsettled: the treaty was silent on the question of confiscated slaves, to Hamilton's satisfaction and to the outrage of southern Republicans.[18]

The last nineteen articles of the treaty were temporary; either party could revoke them two years after the end of the present war in Europe. Most merely clarified points of the law of nations, and Hamilton found them unexceptionable. Two of the articles, those opening the British East Indies to Americans and placing American trade with Britain on a "most favored nation" basis, were definitely advantageous to the United States. Article XII, concerning trade with the West Indies, had (properly, Hamilton believed) been rejected by the Senate. Hamilton objected to article XVIII, which broadened the definition of contraband and provided for seizure with compensation instead of confiscation in disputed cases; but he thought it was the best that could be obtained and did not warrant rejection of the whole treaty. Article XVII, permitting British seizure of French property on board American vessels, effectively waived the claim that "free ships make free goods," but it was in accordance with the laws of war, and the United States was in no position to enforce a different doctrine. All in all, Hamilton concluded, the treaty should be signed because it avoided war and fairly settled most points in dispute. It went without saying—though Hamilton said it later, when he published a lengthy defense—that the treaty was a considerable accomplishment for Jay, who had been dealing with a great maritime power that was fighting for its survival and who had represented a weak neutral that was giving aid and comfort to Britain's enemy.[19]

Hamilton followed his letter with a barrage of public essays defending the treaty. In a series of twenty-eight pieces (plus ten contributed by Rufus King), entitled "The Defence" and signed "Camillus," Hamilton reiterated at greater length and depth the analysis he had given Washington and went on to annihilate the arguments of opponents. In a letter to Madison, Jefferson attested to the effect: "Hamilton is really a colossus to the anti-republican party. Without numbers, he is an host within himself. They have got themselves into a defile, where they might be finished; but too much security on the republican part will give time to his talents and indefatigableness to extricate them."[20]

Washington substantially agreed with Hamilton, but then a new complication arose. Britain, facing a disastrous crop failure and widespread hunger after an abnormally wet spring, had issued new Orders in Council, authorizing the Royal Navy to seize American ships carrying provisions to France. The seized vessels were paid what the British regarded as a fair price for the cargoes, but the proceedings were a flagrant violation of American rights. Washington, on advice from Secretary of State Randolph, at first decided to withhold his signature from Jay's treaty until the "provisions order" was rescinded, but a consultation with the British minister indicated that that would be unavailing. Hamilton advised signing but instructing the American diplomat charged with delivering the signed treaty to withhold the exchange of ratifications until the noxious order were revoked; that method might be more likely to succeed. In any event, Hamilton insisted, the United States should never "give even an implied sanction" to the seizures, and if the order turned out to have been canceled by the time the ratifications were to be exchanged, the United States should still remonstrate strongly against the orders "as a protest against the principle."[21]

The matter was brought out of limbo by a bizarre episode and by Washington's somewhat irrational reaction to it. Only Hamilton and Randolph knew the tenor of Washington's thinking. The other three members of the cabinet—Wolcott, Secretary of War Timothy Pickering, and Attorney General Bradford—were eager that the treaty be ratified, the objectionable British provisions order notwithstanding, and, lacking information, they believed Washington's delay meant that Randolph had poisoned the president's mind against the treaty. They had long regarded Randolph's fence-straddling as pro-French; and toward the end of July, when Randolph finally told them, in Washington's absence, that the president intended to sign but was still weighing the attachment of conditions, their hostility and suspiciousness increased. At just that point they came across proof of Randolph's perfidy, or so it seemed: George Hammond gave Wolcott an intercepted dispatch in which the French minister, Fauchet, reported to his superiors that Randolph had sought a bribe from Fauchet to influence American policy. Washington, hastily summoned back to Philadelphia, was handed a translation of the dispatch; in anger and anguish, and with the prodding of the three cabinet members, he signed the treaty unconditionally.[22]

Washington's precipitate action put him in a bind that would soon make him almost totally dependent upon Hamilton. Randolph's resignation in disgrace left the administration without a secretary of state for three months while Washington made a futile search for a suitable successor. In the meantime, Pickering handled the routine affairs of the office, but he was not sufficiently neutral, able, or experienced to handle the vexing problem of the provisions order and the new negotiations necessary to implementing Jay's treaty. Desperately, and apologetically, Washington wrote Hamilton for the advice that should have come from a secretary of state. Hamilton's reply amounted to a draft of instructions for the acting minister to London, John Quincy Adams. As to the provisions order (which in fact was just then being repealed), Hamilton considered it only as part of something larger. It was indispensable, he said, that the United States make "a very serious though calm and measured remonstrance," to convey to the British ministry (whom he subsequently described as being "as great fools, or as great rascals, as our Jacobins") that it was not enough that they bear no malice toward the United States. They must also be told that they must take adequate steps to ensure that American citizens and American commerce would not be oppressed by the Royal Navy in future. As to the additional negotiations regarding Jay's treaty, Hamilton pointed out improvements young Adams might be able to obtain in three of the commercial articles, suggested that an attempt be made to improve the terms of article XVIII though the effort would probably fail, and urged that an agreement be sought in regard to British impressment of American seamen.[23]

In November, when as a last resort Washington made Pickering full-time secretary of state, Pickering himself began to turn to Hamilton for guidance. He did so tentatively and deferentially at first, for he had never been on intimate or even confidential terms with Hamilton, but Hamilton put him at his ease and began advising him freely. Hamilton, however, was never entirely at ease with Pickering. His reservations were partly personal: Pickering, though fiercely independent, idolized Hamilton and tended, once the relationship was established, to seek a too-intimate connection. He was also a zealot, sharing Hamilton's positions but carrying them to extremes, being excessively pro-British and excessively anti-French, inclined to capitulate to the one and antagonize the other. And, as Hamilton confided to Washington, though he was a "worthy man," he "has nevertheless something warm and angular in his temper & will require much a vigilant moderating eye." But he was all that was available.[24]

The sense of desperation that led Washington to turn to Pickering was evident in a remarkable letter he wrote to Hamilton on October 29. Pleading for help, he recited his difficulties in finding competent people: whereas six years earlier he had been inundated with requests for appointments, and the talent pool seemed bottomless, public life had grown so vile that no decent man now wanted any part of it. Washington had asked four men to serve as secretary of state, and all had turned him down. John Marshall had declined the attorney generalship, Edward Carrington had indicated he would not accept War if Pickering moved over to State, and there were rumors that John Rutledge—whom Washington had nominated to replace Jay in the chief justiceship, which Jay had vacated to become governor of New York—had lost his mind. Hamilton could only reply that no first-rate person was attainable. "A second rate must be taken with good dispositions & barely decent qualifications. . . . Tis a sad omen for the Government."[25]

Only Washington's dignity and integrity sustained him, and monumental as those qualities were, they were no substitutes for leadership. Unable to do so himself, he asked Hamilton to prepare his seventh annual message to Congress. When Hamilton agreed, Washington simply bundled up the relevant official documents and forwarded them to New York. Hamilton produced the address, and that set the pattern for Washington's final sixteen months in office. The president and his department heads sent Hamilton information, Hamilton decided what should be done, and they did it. Had someone read the correspondence with the names deleted, he might have assumed that Hamilton was the chief executive and the others his faithful subordinates.[26]

Hamilton's growing influence with the administration was counterbalanced by a loss of influence among his friends in Congress, but there was nothing contradictory in that development. Rather, the two phenomena, as well as the unwillingness of good men any longer to serve in government, were products of the same cause: the transformation of the Federalists into a political party. Previously the "friends of government," as Hamilton called them, had voted in Congress with some cohesion because they agreed upon a number of principles, because they shared various attitudes about policies that would most benefit the country, or because Hamilton used reason to persuade them to do so. They did not behave as a party: they never compromised the interests of the nation in behalf of the interests of the group; they did not vote for Hamilton's proposals when they disagreed with them; they did not resort to trickery, caucusing, or voting as a bloc. Above all, they did not think of themselves as a party. They used the words "party" or "faction" in contemptuous reference to Republicans, who had been evolving as a party since 1791. Now, however, in the winter of 1795–96, Federalists began to employ the kinds of tactics Republicans used, and as a result almost the entire Congress became polarized.[27]

Though some of the newly partisanized Federalists looked to Hamilton for leadership, and all assumed he would support them, it was simply not in him to play a party role, any more than it was in Washington. To be sure, Hamilton had sometimes campaigned vigorously for individual candidates, and he had helped coordinate the electoral votes for president and vice-president in 1788 and 1792, but his campaigns were for measures and men; he was incapable of subordinating his own judgment to that of a faction or party. Few Federalists ever understood this, and when they did they disregarded his counsel.[28]

His loss of influence in Congress soon became apparent. Early in 1796 Republicans in the House made a bold bid designed simultaneously to defeat Jay's treaty and to embarrass the administration, and thus improve their chances of capturing the presidency in the fall's elections. Under the guise of seeking information necessary to decide whether to appropriate the funds for implementing the treaty, they pushed through a resolution, proposed by Edward Livingston, requesting the president to submit all the papers relevant to Jay's mission. To Washington and Hamilton that was objectionable on both political and constitutional grounds, and Washington flatly refused. The Republicans then voted to withhold the appropriations. Congressional Federalists, resolved at last to fight fire with fire, determined to block the appropriations for implementing three other recently negotiated treaties which Republicans ardently approved—those with Spain, Algiers, and the Northwestern Indians. Hamilton urged his friends in Congress to disdain such tactics and to fight instead on constitutional grounds and in the arena of honest appeals to public opinion, for "the misconduct of the other party cannot justify in us an imitation of their principles. . . . Let us be *Right,* because to do right is intrinsically proper & I verily believe it is the best means of securing final success." He preferred to "let our adversaries have the whole glory of sacrificing the interests of the Nation." His plea was ignored.[29]

His pleas on another matter that came up a few weeks later were more fervid but equally vain. Congress, informed by Wolcott of the strain upon the Treasury, decided on the expedient of authorizing the sale of the government's stock in the Bank of the United States rather than increasing taxes. Hamilton was enraged, for the dividends on that stock had been inviolably pledged for the support of the sinking fund. Almost frantically, he tried to organize opposition to the measure, but again his efforts were futile.[30]

Another symptom of the new party spirit became manifest in late spring: Federalists became almost as extreme in their Anglophilia as Republicans were in their Francophilia. Relieved when the House finally voted the appropriations for Jay's treaty, doubly so when news arrived that the provisions order had been canceled, they gave a veritable hero's welcome to the new British minister, Robert Liston, when he showed up in May. Hamilton saw more clearly. The same ministry that sent Liston was still engaged in violating American commercial rights and was demanding that the United States sacrifice the advantages Anthony Wayne had won over the Indians in the Northwest. The British ministry was populated by fools, Hamilton wrote to Wolcott, and he warned that "it will be an error to be too tame with this overbearing Cabinet."[31]

These developments were troubling Hamilton deeply when he sat down that summer to write Washington's Farewell Address. Washington supplied him with an abstract of points that might be covered and with the draft of a farewell address Madison had penned for him four years earlier, to which the president had added a great deal. Both Washington and Hamilton were concerned that the address employ Washington's still-great prestige to heal the current afflictions in the body politic and, at the same time, convey a message to posterity. Washington's additions to Madison's draft, however, were ill calculated to achieve either goal, for they were infused with a bitter, self-pitying defense against Republican calumnies. In his own draft (which after minor changes by Washington became the final version), Hamilton discarded most of what Washington had written, used Madison's beginning and ending, and composed the heart of the address anew, though generally following Washington's suggested "points."[32]

The body of the Farewell Address tells Americans what they must embrace to be a happy people and what they must shun to realize their hopes for freedom, prosperity, and harmony. The affirmative part was relatively brief: Americans must cherish the Union (three paragraphs), adhere to the Constitution and the laws (three paragraphs), encourage religion and morality (two paragraphs), cultivate habits of frugality and industry (one paragraph), and support public credit (one paragraph). The remainder comprised a sober warning against evils which, if not checked, would destroy the Republic and tear the Union asunder: the spirit of party, especially when combined with sectional loyalty (nine paragraphs), and attachment, emotional or political, to the interests or ideologies of foreign nations (twelve paragraphs).[33]

Many assumed, then and later, that these observations were directed mainly at or against southern Republicans. In truth, the address was directed equally toward northern Federalists, toward whatever portion of the nation remained within the reach of reason. It was an eloquent plea, by two men who loved their country, for their fellow citizens to return to their senses.

Appeals to reason were growing daily less frequent and more futile, for—now that Washington was retiring—the first real presidential election was coming up. There was some support for Hamilton himself, especially in New England, to the consternation of John Adams; but as Hamilton had analyzed the situation a year earlier, there were only three serious contenders—Jay, Adams, and Jefferson. Hamilton would doubtless have preferred Jay, until the controversy over Jay's treaty eliminated the New Yorker, but he had no reservations about supporting Adams. He respected the vice-president and had worked cordially enough with him on a variety of occasions.[34]

His attitude gradually changed as a result of a new crisis, arising from France's reaction to Jay's treaty. French dissatisfaction with the treaty was to be expected, but no one in the administration knew what they would do about it. In fact the Directory at first considered declaring war against the United States, but James Monroe (who, to placate France, had been sent as minister to Paris when Jay went to England) dissuaded them from taking that action immediately. Among his other arguments, Monroe let drop the remark that if the United States were left alone, everything would be "satisfactorily arranged and perhaps within the course of the present year"—meaning upon the election of Jefferson as president. Before 1796 was over, the French had decided to take an active hand in seeing to Jefferson's election.[35]

That design was slow to come to light, however, and in the meantime France maintained an eerie silence, during which sinister rumors abounded. It was rumored, accurately, that French ships had begun preying upon American shipping in the Caribbean and the Mediterranean. It was reported, inaccurately, that a French privateer had captured an American vessel just off the coast of Delaware; it turned out that the vessel had recently been sold to British merchants. And Hamilton received from Gouverneur Morris a letter from London, reporting that France was dispatching a fleet and a new minister to America, in effect to issue an ultimatum demanding that the United States go to war on one side or the other. Hamilton forwarded Morris's letter to Washington, who fired back a request asking what he should do if the report were accurate. For himself, Washington said, "*my* answer wd. be short & decisive, to this effect. . . . We will not be dictated to by the Politics of any Nation under Heaven." Hamilton, in reply, counseled a more diplomatic course. Fortunately, Morris's report also turned out to be inaccurate.[36]

It was crucial, Hamilton believed, that the United States not overreact to rumors or to petty sources of friction; "we must not quarrel with France for *pins* and *needles*." The administration, he advised, ought to be conciliatory. When Pierre Adet, Fauchet's successor, protested at the behavior of the American consul in Hamburg,

Hamilton wrote McHenry (who had become secretary of war) that the consul should be removed forthwith. "Tis a case for temporising," he said, adding that the United States should reserve its firmness "for *great and necessary* occasions." Rufus King, doubtless at Hamilton's urging, wrote essentially the same advice to Pickering, and the consul was promptly dismissed. A week later, Hamilton was in Philadelphia, where Adet was surprised to see him exerting his efforts to calm the more bellicose Federalists.[37]

Already, however, the great and necessary occasion seemed to be taking shape. At the end of May Wolcott informed the president that three French agents, on orders from Adet, were moving from Pittsburgh through Kentucky and down the Mississippi, sounding out local Republicans and persuading them that in the event of a Franco-American war they should look to France as "their natural ally and protector." The agents were also instructed "to use all means in their power to promote the election of Mr. Jefferson." Albert Gallatin had apparently aided Adet in drawing up the orders.[38]

Wolcott was even more worried, as he informed Hamilton in mid-June, by the tenor of the editorials in Benjamin Bache's semiofficial Republican newspaper, the *Aurora*. Bache was suggesting that France had every right to respond to Jay's treaty by seizing American shipping on a larger scale than Britain had—as if to warn Americans that such a policy was coming. At just that moment Hamilton was learning from his client Le Guen that directives to begin a large-scale policy of seizures had been issued. He forwarded the news to Wolcott in Philadelphia and to Washington at Mount Vernon. He also suggested that Wolcott proceed "without delay" to finish the naval frigates—construction of which has been suspended upon the negotiation of the Algerian treaty—even if it were necessary to borrow the requisite funds from merchants "by secret movements."[39]

Then came another twist that seemingly tied tighter the machinations of the French government with those of American Republicans. Wolcott and Pickering somehow obtained a letter Monroe had written to Dr. George Logan of Philadelphia, clearly indicating that Monroe was furnishing Bache with confidential information for use in attacking the administration's foreign policy. Since Monroe's closest political friends were Jefferson, Madison, Burr, and Pierce Butler, the letter to Logan gave additional (and well-founded) credence to the charge Wolcott, Pickering, and McHenry dispatched to Washington: "A minister who has thus made the notorious enemies of the whole system of government his confidential correspondents in matters which affect that Government, cannot be relied on to do his duty to the latter." The suggestion was in fact superfluous; Hamilton had already advised Washington that it had become "urgent that the U States should have some faithful organ near the French Government to explain their real views and ascertain those of the French," and Washington had agreed that Monroe must be superseded. Hamilton also suggested that the new minister should be "at the same time a friend to the Government & understood to be *not unfriendly* to the French Revolution," and recommended Charles Cotesworth Pinckney of South Carolina. Pinckney was appointed to replace Monroe.[40]

After that flurry of activity, however, affairs grew so strangely quiet that Washington wrote Pickering toward the end of July that the threats Bache had published had been false alarms. In truth, Adet had warned his government not to create a crisis for the time being, lest Washington consent to serve a third term and thus prevent Republicans from capturing the presidency. Then, about the third week of August, Adet received definite authorization to intervene in the American election; he was to announce that diplomatic relations were suspended and that henceforth France would treat American vessels the way the United States had allowed the British to do under the provisions order. The timing was left to Adet. Before deciding when to make his move, he took a tour northward (on which he asked and received letters of introduction from Hamilton), ostensibly to see the countryside but actually to sound out New York and New England Republicans. He concluded that only fear of war would shake people in the port cities of New England, New York, and Philadelphia from their staunch support of Adams. He also concluded that he should delay his intervention until the eve of the elections, when Washington would have announced his retirement and published his Farewell Address.[41]

On October 31 Adet published in Bache's *Aurora* the first of four "campaign documents," a letter to Pickering announcing that henceforth the French navy would "treat the flag of neutrals in the same manner as they shall suffer it to be treated by the English." No genuine neutral could have cause to complain, Adet went on, for a nation was in fact acting as a belligerent "if, through weakness, partiality, or other motives, they should suffer the English to sport with their neutrality, and turn it to their advantage." That was the bombshell the administration had been dreading. Washington's reaction was to dash off a letter asking Hamilton for counsel.[42]

Hamilton's advice, sent after an evening's consultation with Jay, was cautious. The first notice given to Adet should be negative—that is, indicated "by the *personal conduct* of the President toward the Minister." Washington should receive Adet at his next formal levee "with a *dignified reserve,* holding an *exact medium* between an *offensive coldness* and *cordiality.* The *point* is a nice one to be hit, but no one will know better how to do it than the President." As to formal and positive notice, Jay thought it should be given through Pinckney; Hamilton was not convinced of the wisdom of that course. At all events, the reply should not be published. This advice came too late: by the time Hamilton's letter reached Washington, Pickering had, with Washington's approval, already published a spirited answer to Adet. Appalled, Hamilton wrote the president again. There must be no more of such "epigrammatical and *sharp*" communications from the United States, he warned. "The Card now to be played is perhaps the most delicate that has occurred in your administration. And nations like Individuals sometimes get into squabbles from the manner more than the matter of what passes between them. It is all important to us—first, if possible, to avoid rupture with France—secondly, if that cannot be, to evince to the People that there has been an unequivocal disposition to avoid it."[43]

On the day Hamilton wrote his second letter, the voters of Pennsylvania went to the polls and chose a slate of fourteen presidential electors, all pledged to Thomas Jefferson. During the next two weeks Adet published his other three campaign documents. One was an address to French citizens in the United States, ordering them to wear the tricolor cockade of the Revolution—a particularly ominous order, since a French fleet was reported on its way to New York. The second was an announcement that diplomatic relations were being suspended. The third was a review of French policy toward the United States, together with fulsome praise of Jefferson's adherence to pure republican principles.[44]

In these circumstances Hamilton made a political decision that would have fateful consequences. Earlier he had resolved to support Adams for president, without thinking deeply about it; now what seemed imperative was not so much electing Adams as keeping Jefferson out of the government. Federalists were generally agreed upon supporting Adams for president and Thomas Pinckney (Charles Cotesworth Pinckney's brother) for vice-president; but Hamilton feared that some New England electors, concerned that Pinckney might slip in ahead of Adams by virtue of southern votes, would waste their second ballots. That would make it possible for Jefferson to become vice-president or, worse, president. (The South Carolina electors voted last, and if the New England electors had failed to support Pinckney equally, the South Carolinians might waste all their second ballots or even cast them for Jefferson.) To prevent this, Hamilton wrote to influential New Englanders urging that Federalist electors cast their votes solidly for both Adams and Pinckney. He recognized the possibility that Pinckney might thereby end up as president, but he thought that unlikely as well as unimportant. What was crucial was to keep Jefferson out.[45]

Hamilton's political advice was disregarded. Eighteen of New England's thirty-nine electoral votes were wasted on candidates other than Pinckney, and South Carolina cast its votes equally for Pinckney and Jefferson—with the result that Adams became president by a margin of three votes and Jefferson became vice-president. Moreover, Hamilton's efforts to stop Jefferson were, by some (most importantly, by John and Abigail Adams), misinterpreted as a scheme to trick Federalists into electing Pinckney instead of Adams. That misunderstanding would bear bitter fruit.[46]

In the meantime, though France's actions had been timed to coincide with and therefore determine the presidential elections, they also constituted seriously warlike moves and required handling as such. Two additional developments toward year's end deepened the crisis. How belligerent France would be toward the United States depended in some measure upon how the French armies fared against the Austrians in northern Italy; under Napoleon, the French routed the Austrians, ensuring that their American policy would be bellicose indeed. The second development was a warning gesture: when Pinckney arrived in Paris in mid-December, the Directory announced that France would not acknowledge or receive a replacement for Monroe "until after the redress of the grievances demanded of the American Government."[47]

Hamilton's advice to the outgoing president was slow to evolve because of the press of legal business. He did find time to pen a number of newspaper essays defending the administration's French policy, thus preparing public opinion for war if it should come. Then, on January 19, 1797, upon learning that French depredations on American shipping were reaching wholesale proportions, he wrote Washington, "We seem to be where we were with G Britain when Mr Jay was sent there." He suggested that "the Policy then pursued with regard to England will be the proper one now in respect to France (viz) a solemn and final appeal to the Justice and interest of France & if this will not do, measures of self defence." The flaw in that approach, as Washington wrote, was that Pinckney had just been sent, and it would scarcely be appropriate to send a new special envoy on his heels. Brooding on the problem, Hamilton came up with a plan that he submitted to the president at the end of January. Instead of a special minister, he proposed, there should be appointed three *"Commissioners* Plenipotentiary & extraordinary." Pinckney should be one of the commissioners, some New England commercial man (he suggested former Senator George Cabot of Massachusetts) should be the second, and the third should be James Madison. Madison would have the confidence of France and of the Republican party, and the other two could keep him from causing mischief.[48]

It was too late in the day for Washington to act on the proposal— Adams succeeded him in office on March 4—but Hamilton persisted in pushing for a special commission as a last-ditch effort to avoid war. Adams did in fact follow much the course that Hamilton recommended; but he did so in spite of Hamilton's efforts, not because of them. For, as events were to demonstrate, when Washington left the presidency Hamilton lost his influence over the federal government. The new president was his own man, the Federalist party was its own party, and Hamilton was not doing the planning for either.

XV

The Adams Years:
1797–1801

But ask not, to what Doctors I apply?

Sworn to no master, of no Sect am I.

Had Hamilton known John Adams better, he no doubt would have opposed his election in 1796, openly and early. He did know the man was vain and eccentric personally and pedantic and dogmatic philosophically. He also knew Franklin's judgment of Adams: "he means well for his Country, is always an honest Man, often a wise one, but sometimes, and in some things, absolutely out of his senses." But Hamilton believed that Adams, for all his foibles, would not let his emotional problems impair the soundness of his judgment, and believed that the new president's political principles were essentially in accord with his own. On both counts he was gravely mistaken.[1]

Hamilton was warned by friends in Massachusetts that Adams bore him ill will, believing Hamilton had conspired against him in 1796. But the New Yorker had no idea of the intensity of Adams's feelings, nor did he know that deep inside the man lay an insecure and resentful heart. Convinced that his services for his country had been as great as any man's, Adams resented the lack of praise that had been his lot and envied the acclaim that had fallen upon Washington, Jefferson, and above all Hamilton. Yet his craving for recognition was so strong that he could respond with pathetic enthusiasm to the slightest hint of an overture from any of the three. Two such hints came, or seemed to come, from Hamilton, and the episodes are instructive. Facing a war crisis during the spring of 1798, Adams was approached by Federalist Congressman Robert Goodloe Harper with the suggestion that he make Hamilton secretary of war. It was natural (albeit mistaken) for Adams to suppose that Harper was tendering feelers from Hamilton himself, since the two had been intimate politically. Adams had told his wife that he would have nothing to do with Hamilton; and yet the notion that Hamilton would voluntarily serve as his subordinate so flattered him that he told Harper he would give Hamilton the position immediately if Hamilton indicated a definite willingness to serve. Hamilton said no, and that was that. A few months later, having suffered the humiliation of being forced to appoint Hamilton as the ranking major-general in the army, Adams was more hostile toward him than ever. But then Hamilton wrote him a letter (his first in five years to Adams) deferentially asking him, as a personal favor, to appoint Hamilton's nephew Philip Church as a captain so that Church might serve as Hamilton's aide-de-camp. So pleased was Adams at being in a position to do favors for Hamilton that he not only complied with the request but also, gratuitously, mentioned commissioning Hamilton's Scottish cousin as a lieutenant in the navy. When Hamilton sent an appropriate letter of appreciation, Adams did not let the matter die there: he wrote an unnecessary reply, containing an opening for Hamilton to continue the correspondence and extend it to matters of state. Surely, had Hamilton been willing to play the sycophant, and had he been the devious manipulator Adams had accused him of being, he could have played upon the president's vanity and led him anywhere.[2]

Or, rather, nearly anywhere. Greatly as Hamilton underrated Adams's personal animosity, greater yet was his underrating of the differences between Adams's political principles and his own. Hamilton had simply not paid much attention to what Adams thought. That was an easy enough oversight, since Adams tended to be a pompous bore—he lectured people, like Polonius prattling to Laertes—but it was also an unfortunate oversight. Hamilton knew Adams admired the British constitution, as Hamilton did; but had he listened to Adams's opinions, he would have learned that Adams's understanding of that constitution was Bolingbrokean, the antithesis of Hamilton's Walpolean view. Hamilton knew that Adams was outspoken in his hostility toward the French Revolution, as Hamilton was; but had he inquired he would have learned that Adams was also incapable of being neutral toward Britain, hating that nation passionately. Hamilton knew that Adams was as quick as he was to oppose encroachments upon American sovereignty; but had he plumbed Adams's attitudes further, he would have learned that Adams's viligance was mitigated by an unreasoning fear, shared with Bolingbroke and Jefferson, of standing armies. Finally, Hamilton knew that Adams had approved his funding and assumption plan and, in contrast to Jefferson, had been cooperative in the management of the sinking fund; but he did not know that Adams described Hamilton's understanding of money as "shallow and superficial," that Adams could rant against public debts in unison with Republicans and their English Oppositionist forebears, that Adams opposed the Bank of the United States as vehemently as Jefferson did, and that Adams embraced the agrarian ideal as ardently as did any Virginia Republican.[3]

None of these differences need have mattered, except that Hamilton soon felt the necessity of reentering public service, and John Adams was president of the United States. To be sure, Adams came to believe that Hamilton controlled both the cabinet (which Adams held over from the Washington administration) and the Federalist party in Congress, but unfortunately for Hamilton he was entirely mistaken. All three cabinet members did continue to ask Hamilton's advice from time to time, but only McHenry regularly followed it, within the limits of his competence; Wolcott disagreed with Hamilton on a matter of central importance, the need for an army; and Pickering, the real leader of the party, schemed his own extravagant schemes, in which he had a role picked out for Hamilton. As for Congress, Hamilton's Federalist friends solicited his advice in 1797 but largely disregarded it, and thereafter he ceased to offer his counsel.[4]

In the circumstances, it is scarcely cause for wonder that Adams's presidency provided the most frustrating period of Hamilton's life.

The Adams administration began with wild vacillation, first toward a dovish position and then toward its opposite extreme. In his inaugural address Adams spoke of his friendship for the French nation, and before and afterward he was seen much in the company of Vice-President Jefferson—to the surprise and delight of Republican partisans, and to the surprise and chagrin of Federalist partisans. Indeed, not only did the new president take up quarters in a Philadelphia boarding house (a marvelously homespun comedown from Washington's maintenance of an elegant household, and a suggestion that he viewed his office as a part-time pursuit), but it was the same boarding house in which the vice-president lived. In truth the coziness between Adams and Jefferson was deceptive: Adams was sounding out Jefferson, seeking to induce him or Madison to accept appointment as a special emissary to France, which was much like what Hamilton had wanted Washington to do, except that Hamilton had moderated his proposal with the suggestion that Jefferson or Madison be checked by co-commissioners. But Hamilton, knowing of the Adams-Jefferson liaison only what he read in the newspapers, thought Adams was trying to affect a rapprochement between "the *Lion* & and *Lamb*" and was correspondingly doubtful. "Sceptics like me," he wrote to King, now minister to London, "quietly look forward to the event—willing to hope but not prepared to believe."[5]

Rebuffed by Jefferson, and failing to recognize as Hamilton did that winning the support of Republicans was complementary rather than antithetical to resisting French encroachments, Adams veered sharply in the opposite direction. On March 25, 1797, having learned officially that the French Directory had refused to recognize Pinckney, he called for a special session of Congress to meet in mid-May. In the intervening weeks, he asked his cabinet officers for written opinions on how to handle the situation. The tenor of his questions to them (hardened by news that France, by a decree of March 2, had virtually declared naval war against the United States) suggested that he doubted the wisdom of further efforts at negotiation and proposed to take a tough line should further negotiations be attempted.[6]

Hamilton had already written several letters on the subject to Wolcott, Pickering, McHenry, and Senator Theodore Sedgwick; he wrote more now and wrote also to Federalist Representatives William Loughton Smith and Uriah Tracy. His suggestions to each were the same, though offered in lesser or greater detail. He insisted that the crisis with France should be handled just as the crisis with Britain had been in 1794—negotiate to avoid war and, to make the negotiations credible and to make the country ready in the event the negotiations failed, simultaneously prepare for defense. He repeated the proposal he had made to Washington, that the new effort to negotiate be entrusted to a politically balanced three-man commission.[7]

But there was a crucial difference between the way Hamilton approached the French crisis and the way he had approached the British: he would go further to avoid war with France than with Britain. Repeatedly he warned his friends that the United States had nothing to gain and much to lose from a war with France. In the first place, such a war would tear the Union apart unless French sympathizers in America were convinced that every effort short of abject humiliation—and Hamilton was willing to endure a goodly amount even of that—had been made to effect a reconciliation. (Hamilton was acutely conscious, and had been pointing out for some time, that the ease of France's conquests in Europe had derived in no small measure from the presence in the victimized nations of a strong pro-French party.) In the second place, though it was unlikely that France could invade the United States as long as Britain remained able and willing to fight her on the seas, it was possible that Americans might soon find themselves facing France alone. The First Coalition was rapidly coming apart: Spain had become France's ally, Prussia had made a separate peace, Austria was wavering, and Emperor Paul of Russia was apt to reverse the anti-French policy of his mother Catherine the Great. What was worse, Britain seemed on the verge of collapse, for its navy was in mutiny and its financial system was tottering on bankruptcy.[8]

To Smith and McHenry Hamilton was most specific. For the congressman, he spelled out the defense legislation that should be introduced. For the secretary of war, he specified the very tone that the proposed negotiators should employ. (Remonstrances against French spoliations of American shipping, for instance, "should be *mild* and *calm* without offensive epithects, but *serious* and depicting strongly the extent of the evil." They should be expressed in such a way as to suggest that the depredations were abuses of orders given by the Directory, but should notice that the orders "were so vague and indefinite in themselves as to be naturally liable to abuse." In asking reparations for the spoliations, the United States should be willing actually to bear some of the cost as an offset against gratuities from France during the American Revolution.)[9]

Hamilton's opinions met with a cool reception. Tracy was against initiating any new negotiations and in favor of preparation for war; he considered the whole idea of being conciliatory toward France as pandering to the South, and rather than go another step with that policy he would see the Union dismembered. Smith introduced most of Hamilton's proposals as a set of resolutions in the House but explicitly said he did not pledge himself to support them all. Wolcott and Pickering opposed the idea of a commission and doubly opposed including a Republican on it. Wolcott disagreed with Hamilton about the necessary taxes to be raised for defense, and Pickering advocated a great deal of bellicose action. Against Hamilton's strong objections, for instance, he wanted to arm American merchantmen to cruise as privateers against French shipping. Only McHenry followed Hamilton's line; he submitted Hamilton's letters almost verbatim to Adams as his own opinion.[10]

Adams, for his part, unknowingly pursued a course much like the one Hamilton recommended. He proposed measures for defense, he spoke in moderate and measured terms, and, over the protests of Wolcott and Pickering, he appointed a three-man commission that included the Francophile Elbridge Gerry. "I like very well the course of Executive Conduct," Hamilton wrote. He did not like the behavior of the House, which was long on *"hard words"* and short on proper action. *"Real firmness,"* he said, "is good for every thing— *Strut* is good for nothing."[11]

Hamilton paid scant attention to the activities of the special session of Congress, however, for he became preoccupied with a pressing personal matter. Toward the end of June a notoriously scurrilous journalist, James T. Callender, published the fifth of eight pamphlets collectively entitled *The History of the United States for 1796; Including a Variety of Interesting Particulars Relative to the Federal Government Previous to That Period.* Among the "interesting particulars" was a reiteration of the old charge that Hamilton had used James Reynolds as an agent in private speculations. Hamilton would scarcely have given the pamphlet any notice except that it was supported by certain of the documents with which Monroe, Venable, and Muhlenberg had confronted him on December 15, 1792, and which he had explained with his account of his relationship with Maria and James Reynolds. Left unchallenged, the documents Callender published were damaging. Accordingly, Hamilton solicited from the three men confirmation that they had been "perfectly satisfied" and had found "nothing in the transaction which ought to affect my character as a public Officer or lessen the public Confidence in my Integrity." Expecting that their confirmation would be readily forthcoming, and apparently intending to publish their letters, he sent a brief piece to John Fenno's *Gazette of the United States,* saying all he intended to say in reply to Callender: that Reynolds's charges had been a "contrivance" to avoid prison and that the three congressmen had seen all the evidence and regarded it as conclusive proof of the falsity of the accusation.[12]

By the time Hamilton wrote to Fenno, however, Callender had published another pamphlet in his series, together with new documents that cast serious doubts on Hamilton's explanation. One of these was a memorandum of the three congressmen, written a day after their meeting with Hamilton, saying, "We left him under an impression our suspicions were removed." Another was a memorandum of an interview Monroe had subsequently had with Reynolds's cohort Jacob Clingman, in which Clingman said Maria Reynolds denied having had an affair with Hamilton, charging that Hamilton had fabricated the story to cover his speculations with her husband. Hamilton considered rebutting Clingman's testimony with the commonsense argument that, had he been knave enough to have speculated in Treasury paper, he would certainly not have been fool enough to have dealt with clods like Clingman and Reynolds when he had ample connections with clever and well-heeled operators. But such a course would have left the congressmen's memorandum unexplained.[13]

Accordingly, he pressed for the confirmation from Venable, Muhlenberg, and Monroe. The first two complied fully, but Monroe complied only in part. Monroe was hostile toward Hamilton for helping to bring about his recall as minister to France. Moreover, Hamilton hinted in a letter to him that Monroe had violated his pledge of secrecy by furnishing the documents Callender had published—

which, according to Monroe, was an unfair slur, since it had apparently been John Beckley who leaked the documents. In any event, Monroe was willing to say he had been satisfied with Hamilton's original explanation but was unwilling to say he had not believed Clingman's subsequent claim. Several heated confrontations and the exchange of a number of letters almost led to a duel between the two, but Monroe remained adamant: he would not give Hamilton the statement he sought.[14]

That posed a painful dilemma for Hamilton. He believed it was imperative that there be no room for doubt among fair-minded men that he had administered the Treasury with absolute propriety. In his eyes, not only his reputation but the integrity of his financial system and of the public credit itself were at stake. What was more, if the crisis with France led to war, he intended to be available for service to the country, doubtless in a military capacity. To preserve his availability, he had forsaken opportunities for personal fortune, and the destruction of his reputation could be fatal to his intentions. But he could see no way to defend himself except by publishing a full disclosure of the affair with the supporting written documents. The pain such a publication would give to Betsey and his children was almost too much to contemplate, and almost too much to ask them to bear.

But Hamilton was Hamilton, and the only course he could pursue was to jeopardize his private felicity, including the felicity of those he dearly loved, for the sake of service to his country. On August 25, 1797, he published a lengthy pamphlet called, innocuously enough, *Observations on Certain Documents Contained in No. V & VI of "The History of the United States for the Year 1796," In Which the Charge of Speculation Against Alexander Hamilton, Late Secretary of the Treasury, is Fully Refuted. Written by Himself.* "The charge against me," he wrote, "is a connection with one James Reynolds for purposes of improper pecuniary speculation. My real crime is an amorous connection with his wife." There followed a lurid and detailed description of his affair with Maria Reynolds.[15]

The Republican press had great sport with Hamilton for a year and more after the publication of the Reynolds Pamphlet, and Hamilton's friends believed he had gone to unnecessary, perhaps absurd, lengths to protect his public reputation. But the pamphlet accomplished its purpose: Hamilton remained available for service.

Betsey, of course, forgave him. She never forgave Monroe.

During the next few months there was no way of knowing whether Hamilton's availability was relevant, for there followed another long, strange absence of news from France. Reports of seizures of American shipping continued to filter in, but not a word came from the special commission to Paris, on which all seemed to depend. Congress met in November, and though its proceedings were marked by acrimony, tension, and physical violence between members, nothing constructive was done or even seriously attempted: all was waiting. No one in government asked Hamilton for advice, and he volunteered none.

Finally, on January 24, 1798, President Adams, deciding that no news was bad news, addressed a set of inquiries to his department heads. Assuming that the mission failed, the president asked, what should the United States do now? Most importantly, he asked whether he should recommend a declaration of war and whether the United States should seek an alliance with Britain. Adams himself leaned toward the former action but away from the latter. Pickering leaned toward both war and an alliance. Wolcott, cautious as usual, considered the costs and doubted whether either course was desirable. McHenry was another matter. A man of good heart and modest talents, he was in over his head and he knew it. He was not a "tool" of Hamilton's, as he would be accused of being, but he was proud to be a friend of Hamilton's, for he recognized greatness when he saw it. In the present circumstances, he turned automatically to his friend.[16]

Hamilton's answer was carefully considered. He opposed both a declaration of war ("a mitigated hostility leaves still a door open to negotiation") and an alliance with England ("mutual interest will command as much from her as Treaty," and "Twill be best not to be entangled"). But since France was in fact waging maritime war against the United States and since Hamilton believed an invasion sufficiently likely that not to prepare for it would be foolhardy, he urged strong countermeasures. On the seas, he recommended, the United States should fight back. He would permit the arming of merchant vessels, build as fast as possible twenty sloops of war, and rush to completion the three frigates that remained unfinished. All these vessels should be authorized to capture any vessels that attacked them and any French privateers they found hovering along the coast; but they should not be permitted to attack unarmed shipping, nor should an embargo be declared, except if formal war came. In addition, the president should be authorized, in the event of formal war, to acquire ten ships of the line by whatever means he saw fit. Hamilton believed that these could be purchased or borrowed from Britain, and suggested that provisional negotiations toward that end should be begun forthwith. As to land defenses. Hamilton urged that an army of 20,000 men, at least 2,000 of them cavalry, be organized at once, and that provision be made for an additional force of 30,000 in case of formal war. If war with Spain came as well, the United States should seize Spanish Florida and Louisiana, the obvious sites from which France would invade and known objects of French intrigue since 1793. Moreover, the United States should look to a joint project with Britain to liberate South America, since Spain's treasures from that source fueled the French war machine. Finally, a matter of "the most precious importance," the president should proclaim a day of "fasting humiliation & prayer."[17]

Three weeks after Hamilton's letter reached McHenry, news finally came from Paris, and it was disastrous. The American commissioners had never been officially received; instead, they had been engaged in fruitless unofficial talks with three of Foreign Minister Talleyrand's agents (identified in the diplomatic correspondence as X, Y, and Z), who demanded a bribe of 1.2 million *livres* (about $250,000) for the privilege of being officially received by Talleyrand. It was made clear to the Americans that when they did see the minister, they would be informed that the United States must pay France $6 million in tribute lest the depredations on the seas continue. To emphasize its position, France issued a new decree declaring lawful prize all neutral vessels containing any English-made products whatever—which meant virtually all American ships, for some of their equipment was almost invariably of British manufacture. Upon receiving this news Adams drafted a message calling for war, then declined to send it; but when the correspondence was made public, a wave of rage swept the country. In the ensuing months the nation was in a frenzy for war and for repressing French agents and sympathizers in the United States. As the war fever mounted, President Adams found himself a popular hero, and each successive petition or resolution of support made him more bellicose and more popular than the last.[18]

Hamilton was later accused of attempting to fan the hysteria into war so as to satisfy a long-frustrated craving for military glory. In fact his was one of the few voices of moderation in the land. In the spring and early summer—when Congress was passing a host of war measures and the Alien and Sedition Acts, when bands of citizens were arming and drilling in the streets, when the president was talking ever more belligerently and fortifying his own home—Hamilton was practicing law. He was so busy that he could not find time to answer McHenry's plea for suggestions regarding the management of the naval force. He did find time to write one letter to Senator Theodore Sedgwick and a few to Pickering, reiterating in briefer form his earlier advice to McHenry, and to pen seven newspaper articles calling for a spirit of resistance to France but not going beyond the position he had recommended. He assumed (and friends in Congress led him to believe) that he would be asked to command the army if one were created, but he could not afford to reenter public service unless the emergency became far more acute than it was. He turned down an offer of a Senate seat when one of the New York senators resigned, and he refused Harper's feeler offer regarding the War Department. As to giving advice, he wrote nothing further to congressmen, despite Wolcott's plea that he do so.[19]

Of the few recommendations he did make, three are most revealing. He suggested that an American frigate be dispatched to South Carolina to attack a man-of-war that was harassing American shipping—a *British* man-of-war. Second, he wrote to Pickering that a pending alien act should not be "cruel or violent"; afterward, he told Sedgwick that the alien act as passed "seems to me deficient in precautions against abuse and for the security of Citizens." Third, he wrote to Wolcott that a sedition bill pending before the Senate be dropped as "highly exceptionable & such as more than any thing else may endanger civil war." And he went on: "Let us not establish a tyranny. Energy is a very different thing from violence. If we make no false step we shall be essentially united; but if we push things to an extreme we shall then give to faction *body* & solidarity."[20]

Hamilton was also accused, later, of conspiring to obtain control of the newly created army, in defiance of the president's wishes. What actually happened was more complex and, on Hamilton's part, more honorable. At the outset, Hamilton indicated to Washington that he would serve only "if I am invited *to a station in which the service I may render may be proportioned to the sacrifice I am to make*"—meaning the enormous loss of income that would be involved. Assuming that Washington would be called from retirement to be commander-in-chief, Hamilton said that "the place in which I should hope to be most useful is that of Inspector General with a command in the line." As inspector general he would bear administrative responsibility for the actual organization of the army.[21]

By mid-July, Washington had reluctantly accepted Adams's appointment as commander-in-chief, but with two conditions: that the principal officers "shall be such as I can place confidence in," and that he would not be called into the field until the "urgency of circumstances" made that indispensable. Reluctant to take on the duty at all unless he could rely on Hamilton "as a Coadjutor, and assistant in the turmoils I have consented to encounter," Washington chose Hamilton as inspector general. Hamilton would have the rank of major general, above the two other major generals Washington selected, Charles C. Pinckney and Henry Knox. Adams submitted Washington's choices to the Senate, and the appointments were promptly confirmed.[22]

Confusion and misunderstanding surrounded the appointments, however, and they engendered considerable acrimony. Pickering and McHenry had gone to lengths to convince Washington that Hamilton should be the ranking major general. Washington knew Hamilton was the best qualified of the three, but he had had a mild reservation. If there were to be an invasion, it almost certainly would be in the South. Thus it would be important to have a southerner as one of the major generals, and Washington was not sure that Pinckney would accept the commission if he were outranked by Hamilton, his junior during the Revolutionary War. Hamilton thought (accurately) that Pinckney would not object to being ranked below himself, and as for Knox—who during the Revolution had outranked both of them—Hamilton was willing, though not eager, to be ranked beneath him. But he informed Washington that "if the Gentlemen concerned are dissatisfied & the service likely to suffer by the preference given to me—I stand ready to submit our relative pretensions to an impartial decision and to wave the preference. It shall never be said, with any color of truth, that my ambition or interest has stood in the way of the public good."[23]

President Adams was not similarly inhibited. He had rushed Washington's appointment to the Senate without consulting anyone and without obtaining Washington's approval, out of fear that pressure to make Hamilton commander-in-chief would be irresistible. When that plan backfired as a consequence of Washington's conditions and stated preferences, Adams had to submit Hamilton's name to the Senate as the ranking major general and thus as the active head of the army. His hostility was aggravated when the Senate overwhelmingly refused to confirm the appointment of his son-in-law William S. Smith as a brigadier general, on the ground that Smith's private business dealings had been disreputable if not fraudulent. Back home in Massachusetts, Adams's pique increased even more when Knox carped at being ranked below Hamilton; and he and Knox hit upon an obscure (and in fact inapplicable) congressional regulation of 1780 as a means of attempting to reverse the order of seniority.[24]

Hamilton himself inadvertently brought the issue to a head. The law establishing the army provided that officers would remain inactive "until called into actual service," which would have been personally advantageous to Hamilton, since full-time service would cost him £4,000 a year in legal fees. As a public matter, however, it was not at all satisfactory, for if McHenry had to make do without Hamilton's help, it would take forever to organize the army. Accordingly, Hamilton suggested that he be called to active duty right away, and McHenry wrote the president for permission to activate both Hamilton and Knox. Adams refused to do so unless the rank order were reversed, and he added, intemperately, "you may depend upon it, the five New England States will not patiently submit to the humiliation that has been meditated for them." In a follow-up letter Adams angrily threatened to lower Hamilton to sixth in command and, blustering, said "the power & authority is in the President. . . . I foresee it will come to me at last, after much altercation & exasperation of passions & I shall then determine it exactly as I should now—Knox, Pinckney & Hamilton. There has been too much intrigue in this business both with General Washington & me. If I shall ultimately be the dupe of it, I am much mistaken in myself."[25]

The president would soon have to eat his words. Knox refused to serve except as the ranking major general; and Hamilton, after seeing Adams's letters to McHenry, refused to serve except on the basis of Washington's original rankings. (Privately, however, he told Troup he would serve even as Washington's aide-de-camp if the need arose.) Wolcott then wrote Adams a long, calmly reasoned letter pointing out that Knox's claim of a legal right to the top rank was spurious, and urging that since Washington had stated his preference, Adams should accede to Washington's wishes. That letter was unavailing, but another was more effective. Washington, informed of the situation by Pickering and McHenry, wrote Adams a proper but cold letter, suggesting in effect that if Washington could not have Hamilton then Adams could not have Washington. Adams, whose envy and fear of Washington matched his envy and fear of Hamilton, capitulated.[26]

And John Adams suddenly lost all his enthusiasm for the war with France. Eleven days later he began to talk of a new peace mission: this from a man who, in June, had boldly declared, "I will never send another minister to France without assurances that he will be received, respected, and honored as the representative of a great, free, powerful, and independent nation."[27]

In the circumstances, Hamilton's task was impossible. His specific duty was to implement an act of July 16, 1798, providing for the raising of twelve regiments of infantry and six troops of dragoons—about 12,500 officers and men in all. He was fourth in the chain of command under Washington, McHenry, and ultimately President Adams. Washington was essentially inactive, McHenry was cooperative but incompetent, and Adams was hostile (though, characteristically, it was several months before Hamilton even began to suspect that Adams would allow personal feelings to influence his conduct of national policy and that he would covertly obstruct the execution of an Act of Congress). Outwardly Adams wore a cooperative demeanor—"to extend and invigorate . . . our measures of defense . . . is our true policy," he told Congress in December—but inwardly he was determined to sabotage what he had suddenly come to perceive as a sinister plot to saddle America under the tyranny of a military despotism. Having delayed the appointment of the senior officers by more than three months, he employed dilatory tactics to delay the appointment of the remaining officers for another three months.[28]

When the officer corps had been substantially completed, other problems arose. McHenry's two chief civilian subordinates, Purveyor of Public Supplies Tench Francis and Superintendent of Military Stores Samuel Hodgdon, were utter bunglers; and yet it was politically impossible to replace them, for Francis was related by marriage to the wealthy and powerful Willing and Bingham families of Philadelphia, and Hodgdon was a close friend and erstwhile business partner of Timothy Pickering. Their failure to procure uniforms held up recruiting for several more months, and after recruiting began, equipment and supplies failed to materialize, despite adequate funds. Hamilton wailed that the problem was as acute as it had been during the darkest hours of the Revolution.[29]

But the most important obstacle to Hamilton's efforts to organize the army was Adams's erratic diplomacy. In early February 1799, Adams followed a hawkish line by appointing ministers to negotiate treaties of "amity and commerce" with Russia and Portugal, both of which had just declared war against France. He followed those steps on February 16 (in what proved to be a crucial decision, encouraged by Hamilton through Pickering) by sending Hamilton's boyhood friend Edward Stevens to Sainte Domingue to try to open trade relations with the leaders of the black revolution in France's richest colony. Yet two days later, without having discussed the subject with anyone, he suddenly nominated William Vans Murray, the American minister in Holland, to be minister plenipotentiary to France. Federalist leaders in the Senate were stunned at this latest of "the wild & irregular starts of a vain, jealous, and half frantic mind." Hamilton, in fact, said that the mission "must go into effect," for he wanted to continue exploring every avenue to an honorable peace; but Murray was too young and inexperienced "for so immensely important" an undertaking, and Hamilton urged that it be entrusted to a commission of three. The senators forced Adams to do just that. Then Adams—contrary to his later claim that Hamilton, the cabinet, and Federalist senators delayed the mission with their "insidious and dark intrigues"—held up the departure of the commissioners for six months by insisting, quite properly, that they not go until France provide written assurances that they would be respectfully received.[30]

This fits-and-starts diplomatic style confused the general population, cast clouds of doubt on the reality of the war threat, and thereby greatly increased the already great difficulties of recruiting soldiers for the new army. Recruits came in trickles, and those who did show up were by and large a scurvy and unmanageable rabble. Hamilton worked with his usual energy (which, since he found it necessary to continue devoting much of his time to his law practice, almost broke his health), and he brought his great administrative gifts to bear, but it was all an exercise in futility. In the fall of 1799, fifteen months after the passage of the act establishing the army, less than half the authorized complement of troops had been enlisted. Still Hamilton labored on, trying desperately to create an army out of nothing and against insurmountable odds.[31]

He did so for two broad categories of reasons. The first concerned the long-range security of the United States. His goal was to keep the country independent of Europe at a time when isolation from Europe was impossible and Europe was in a state of almost perpetual war. (France and Britain were at war with one another during twenty-five of the forty-seven years of Hamilton's life.) Given those circumstances, it could "never be wise to vary our measures of security with the continually varying aspect of European affairs. . . . Standing, as it were, in the midst of falling empires, it should be our aim to assume a station and attitude which will preserve us from being overwhelmed in their ruins." In practice, that meant the United States should do what Hamilton and Washington had been advocating since 1783 and especially since 1793—"organize all our resources" for a standing military establishment "and put them in a state of preparation for prompt action." Though it should always be "the policy of our Government to cultivate peace," the best way to guarantee peace in a warring world was to be prepared to fight and to negotiate from strength to avoid the necessity of fighting.[32]

There were two flaws in that approach: no one believed the country could afford a genuinely adequate full-time military force, and repeated experience had shown that the American people had an irrational fear of anything resembling a permanent military establishment. But the war hysteria of 1798 created a temporary opportunity for getting around that fear, and Hamilton, in consultation with Washington and Pinckney, worked out a plan for simultaneously overcoming both the prejudice and the problem of cost: the idea of an expandable army. Under this plan, the "new army" of 12,500 men (which, miniscule in comparison with what European powers were raising, could scarcely be regarded by reasonable men as an insupportable burden or a threat to civilian liberties) would become the permanent core of American defense. It would be supplemented by a "provisional army" of 38,000 men, whose commissioned and noncommissioned officers would be appointed and trained in advance, so that mobilization of the privates, volunteer or drafted, could be accomplished in short order. Given a standing army of 12,500 that was expandable to 50,000 within sixty days or so, and given a comparable naval establishment, the United States would have a credible military potential that would enable it, in the crises certain to come, to negotiate for honorable neutrality and probably obtain it. Such was Hamilton's plan for peace.[33]

The other set of reasons for Hamilton's determined efforts against the odds had to do with the immediate situation, domestically and internationally. In regard to the domestic scene, he had urged every measure of caution lest the country be divided during a war with France. At the height of the war fever it had appeared that all Americans except the most radical southern Republicans were united in support of the government, but that illusion soon evanesced. Late in 1798 the Virginia and Kentucky legislatures adopted resolutions, authored by Madison and Jefferson, defying several of the internal security measures passed by Congress during the summer. Early in 1799 a friend of Hamilton's on the scene informed him that the Virginia legislature was preparing for armed resistance to federal authority and had, toward that end, bought up 5,000 stands of arms and raised taxes for other military measures. That report was buttressed by reports that Congressman John Nicholas, a dedicated Republican and fiery opponent of the war measures of 1798, had broken with the party because he was not willing to support a movement to destroy the Union. St. George Tucker, one of Virginia's leading Republican legal theorists, had taken the opposite position, declaring that 100,000 Americans, himself among them, would join forces with the French if an invasion came. And, early in 1799, an actual if trivial insurrection did break out in eastern Pennsylvania.[34]

Hamilton's prescription for coping with the prospect of civil war was the same as for international war: moderation and conciliation combined with a show of force. With a regular army of 12,500, he would simply march southward and "put Virginia to the Test of resistance." He had no doubt as to what would happen if that were done: the Virginia "rebels" of 1799 would vanish as surely as had the whiskey rebels of 1794, and not a shot would have to be fired. As he said to McHenry in regard to the new uprising in Pennsylvania, "Whenever the Government appears in arms it ought to appear like a *Hercules,* and inspire respect by the display of strength . . . to awe the disaffected."[35]

Internationally, the uses to which Hamilton's army might be put had undergone a radical transformation in recent months. Horatio Nelson's sinking of the French fleet at the Battle of the Nile in August 1798, followed by the formation of the Second Coalition in December, meant that in 1799 the French Republic was in mortal peril. Invasion of the United States was therefore out of the question, temporarily; but Hamilton was aware that France had not abandoned its plan to reestablish its empire in North America, and that obtaining the Floridas and Louisiana from Spain was an integral part of that design. French possession of those territories would pose an intolerable security risk for the United States. Accordingly, Hamilton saw it as only logical that the United States army, with naval protection from Britain, should seize the areas while France was in an exposed condition—and possibly, with the support of Spanish colonial rebels, increase the long-term security of the United States by liberating Spanish America. The British were willing to cooperate without requiring an alliance, and during 1798 and early 1799 Rufus King, as American minister in London, worked out most of the details.[36]

That dream—or rather, that hard-nosed and realistic plan in the interest of national security—was soon to be destroyed. In September 1799, appropriate assurances having arrived from France that an American minister or commission would be respectfully received, Timothy Pickering was at work preparing the instructions for the commission that had been appointed in February. Adams was at home in Braintree, Massachusetts, where he habitually stayed except during the four or five months a year that Congress was in session, when he received a disturbing letter from Benjamin Stoddert, secretary of the newly created Navy Department. If a peace mission were sent without Adams's being present, Stoddert said, "artful designing men"—meaning Republicans—would exploit the fact to jeopardize Adams's chances for reelection. After brooding a week or two on the implications of Stoddert's letter,

Adams reluctantly decided to go to Trenton (where the government had temporarily moved because of another yellow fever epidemic in Philadelphia) and discuss the subject with his cabinet. When he left Braintree in early October, however, he was not at all sure the mission should be sent at that juncture, for signs from Europe portended the imminent collapse of the French Directory—the surest sign being that Talleyrand, who never backed a loser, had resigned as foreign secretary.[37]

Coincidentally, Hamilton was in Trenton when Adams arrived, having gone there for a conference with McHenry and General James Wilkinson to work out final instructions for Wilkinson's deployment of the small "old army" on the frontier. Adams could not see Hamilton's unexpected presence in that light. Instead, in the words of a nineteenth-century Federalist historian, "Again had HAMILTON risen up like a spectre in his path. To meet *him,* the intriguer, there, with his coadjutors, Pickering, Wolcott, and McHenry . . . had roused the lurking demon of suspicion in his breast, and from that moment he was ungovernable. He had nearly been the victim of a plot, but the chief actor had too soon discovered himself." So reacting, Adams ordered Pickering to deliver the instructions to the envoys and to ask them to sail for France within two weeks.[38]

Hamilton pleaded with the president in vain to suspend the mission—a spectacle Adams maliciously enjoyed. Hamilton insisted that the Directory was about to topple; it did, less than a month later, in the coup d'état that brought Napoleon to power. He argued that Britain would retaliate by resuming its attacks upon American shipping; it did, within a matter of months, inflicting enormous damages on American commerce. Most of all, Hamilton, like many of his friends, feared French diplomacy more than he feared French arms; this fear, too, proved justified, for the mission resulted in a brilliant diplomatic triumph for France. When the agreement ending the quasi-war was finally reached, the United States had been removed as one of France's antagonists, had resumed the carrying of vital goods to France, and had sacrificed the valid spoliation claims of its citizens in the amount of $12 million. In exchange, it received nothing except a cessation of the hostilities that France had momentarily lost the capacity to sustain. Furthermore, in a secret agreement signed the same day the American agreement was signed (though dated a day later), France obtained Florida and Louisiana from Spain. Finally, when it suited France's purposes to do so, the French resumed their piratical policies regarding American shipping. In sum, Hamilton was right on all counts. But it is one thing to be right. It is more efficacious to be president.[39]

The sending of the mission doomed the army, and during the next session of Congress it was abolished. Hamilton, the alleged militarist, worked diligently and effectively to disband it in an orderly fashion.

Though the outcome of the new negotiations was not known until early in 1801, the rashness of Adams's decision left Federalist leaders in a perplexing political situation. None among them could support Adams with good conscience in the election of 1800; yet if they did not it seemed certain that Jefferson would become president. The problem of the election, moreover, was compounded by a pair of circumstances. On the one hand, Adams had gained a considerable measure of popularity—though scarcely as much as the conquest of Louisiana and the Floridas might have won him— because the general impression among ordinary voters was that his vigorous stand in 1798 made possible peace in 1799–1800. On the other hand, popularity among the voters was of small and rapidly declining importance. In 1796, two-fifths of the presidential electors had been chosen not by the voters but by the state legislatures; and in 1800 partisans on both sides in most states sought to manipulate the election laws to their own advantage, with the result that five states made their elections less democratic and nearly two-thirds of the electors would be chosen by legislatures. Since voters chose their legislators for reasons other than concern with the presidency, the presidential election of 1800 would therefore reflect the will of politicians, not the will of the people.[40]

The problem was brought home in the spring of 1800. Aaron Burr, having previously united the leaders of the rival Republican factions in New York through a devious scheme that fattened their purses, now employed an artful stratagem to gain control of the state's electoral votes. Party strength outside the city was about evenly balanced, and in 1799 Federalists had swept the city. In 1800, after Federalists announced their slate of legislative candidates in the city (a list appropriately undistinguished, considering the offices being sought), Burr induced a host of big-name figures—including ex-Governor George Clinton, Judge Brokholst Livingston, and General Horatio Gates—to allow their names to be used as candidates, though none had any intention of actually serving in such a mediocre station. Burr's slate won handily, giving Republicans control of the legislature for purposes of choosing presidential electors. Federalists everywhere were dismayed, for if the other states ran true to form, Burr's success would give the presidency to the Republicans.[41]

Hamilton had a ready solution to the problem. Burr, as Hamilton saw it, had stolen the election by a trick; all that was necessary to defeat the trick was to place the choice of electors in the hands of the people. Several months would elapse before the new legislature convened, and if the outgoing, Federalist-dominated legislature were called into special session, it could change the election law and provide for popular elections of electors by district. If that were done, Federalists would win at least half the state's twelve electoral votes and retain the presidency. Unfortunately for Hamilton, Governor Jay declined to go along with the suggestion, and thus New York was lost.*[42]

Adams, for his part, worsened the situation by his reaction to the New York elections. Stewing over his plight, he convinced himself that the Federalist defeat in New York had been a Machiavellian plot engineered *by Hamilton* to prevent his reelection. In retaliation for the imagined injury, he decided to demand the resignation of the "traitors" in his cabinet, McHenry and Pickering. That he chose not to fire Wolcott—who fiercely opposed his reelection and was, despite being against an army, much closer to Hamilton than was the staunchly independent Pickering—is a mark of the breakdown of his faculties. In the interview in which he dismissed McHenry, he ranted and raved and revealed an almost total loss of contact with reality. And thus was a good man, who had served his country well, tragically consumed by his basest passions.[43]

---

* Hamilton's proposal was not just an ad hoc electioneering trick: two years later he proposed a constitutional amendment that would provide for the popular election of presidential electors by districts. "Draft of a Resolution for the Legislature of New York for the Amendment of the Constitution of the United States," January 29, 1802, in Syrett, ed., *Papers,* 25:512–13.

Hamilton was not sympathetic. Upon reading McHenry's transcript of the interview, he said "the man is more mad than I ever thought him and I shall soon be led to say as wicked as he is mad." But he did not succumb to anger toward Adams. Instead, he worked out his hostilities by pleading his law cases with especial vehemence and became coolly calculating in regard to the presidency. He decided that the only chance for a favorable outcome of the election was to adopt the strategy he had urged in 1796—trying to persuade Federalist electors to support Adams and Pinckney equally—but with two exceptions. This time he would support Charles Cotesworth Pinckney rather than his brother Thomas, and his openly avowed aim would be to make Pinckney president and return Adams to the vice-presidency. In the immediate wake of Burr's triumph, such an approach seemed futile, but then occurred a development that promised to compensate for the loss of New York. Pennsylvania, whose fifteen electoral votes had gone Republican in 1796, was caught in a legislative deadlock over the election law for the year, and by early summer it appeared virtually certain that the state would choose no electors. If that should happen, Federalists would recoup their New York losses and emerge with a net gain of three electoral votes.[44]

The key to the success of Hamilton's plan was New England, whose electors in 1796 had wasted eighteen second ballots. In an attempt to persuade New England Federalists to support his campaign, he made an extended tour through the region in June of 1800, talking to Federalists high and low, leaders and followers. He was perfectly candid with them all ("You know," commented Fisher Ames, "he is the most frank of men."), and he won a goodly number of converts. Adams was popular among rank-and-file Federalists in Massachusetts, however, and his supporters were industriously cultivating his image as the courageous independent whose firmness and diplomatic skill had saved the nation from a calamitous war. When Hamilton returned to New York on June 30, it therefore seemed that New England, though solidly Federalist, would waste at least a handful of its second votes.[45]

To prevent that eventuality, Hamilton decided upon two tactics. The first was to induce Federalists in the middle states to declare to their Yankee co-partisans that if New England refused to support Pinckney, they would refuse to support Adams. To some extent that tactic was employed, and to some extent it was successful. The second was to write to a few of the more discreet of Adams's supporters and try to dissuade them by giving them a full exposé of his conduct. The more Hamilton considered this notion the better he liked it, especially after an episode that took place in August. Having been told a number of times that Adams had repeatedly accused him of being the head of a "British faction," which Hamilton regarded as tantamount to a charge of treason, he wrote a cold letter to the president asking him to confirm or deny the statement. When Adams refused to answer, a touch of malice entered Hamilton's calculations, which heretofore had been purely political.[46]

From these roots stemmed an idea as brilliant as it was bizarre. Hamilton began to compose a long, full, and devastating account of Adams's erratic and capricious course as president, written in the form of a letter to be printed as a pamphlet and circulated to Federalist leaders. When completed in October, it ran more than fifty printed pages. The first forty-nine were a critical review of Adams's career, the next three a defense of Hamilton against Adams's "British faction" charge. The last three paragraphs were a surprising twist, to say the least: "Yet with this opinion of Mr. ADAMS, I have finally resolved not to advise the withholding from him a single vote," but to urge that all Federalist electors vote equally for Adams and Pinckney.[47]

By one means or another, the pamphlet went into general circulation, to the bewilderment and consternation of Federalists and the unmitigated delight of Republicans. Hamilton's performance was denounced by his friends as calculated to destroy the Federalist party; and yet, to the extent that it influenced the election at all, it came extremely close to accomplishing its goal. Hamilton's aim was to elect Pinckney president. To achieve that, it was necessary to hold New England solid for both Federalists and to induce South Carolina electors to vote only for Pinckney without actually asking them to do so. For whatever reason, the New Englanders did what he wanted: thirty-eight of the thirty-nine electors in the area voted for both Adams and Pinckney. To turn South Carolina against Adams, Hamilton in his pamphlet called attention to a harsh letter Adams had written about the Pinckney brothers in 1792. Unfortunately for Hamilton's plan, General Pinckney himself apparently insisted that the electors vote for both Federalists or none at all;

whether for that reason or because of certain of Burr's manipulations, South Carolina's eight electoral votes went for Jefferson and Burr. One other thing went wrong. At the last minute the Pennsylvania legislature reached a compromise and, instead of casting no electoral votes, gave eight to the Republicans and seven to the Federalists. The end result was that Jefferson and Burr got seventy-three votes apiece, Adams received sixty-five, and Pinckney got sixty-four.[48]

Myriad explanations for the Federalist defeat have been offered. In actuality almost all the votes from almost every state in 1800 were just what they had been in 1796. The main differences were in New England, where Hamilton's influence altered the casting of second ballots, and in New York and possibly South Carolina, where Burr's influence won both sets of ballots. Two extremely shrewd politicians had locked horns, and Burr had won.[49]

They would meet in one more contest, four years later.

The election, of course, was not yet over. Since Jefferson and Burr had tied, the choice was thrown into the House of Representatives. Federalists held a majority there, but the Constitution specified that the voting be by state delegations, each state having one vote; and on that basis Republicans had eight votes, Federalists had six, and two states were evenly split. Federalists caucused and decided to support Burr, figuring that a few wayward Republicans could be won over if they held firm, and that Burr as president would subsequently support them as they had supported him. Hamilton, fiercely opposing that course, wrote a torrent of letters to dissuade friends in Congress from following it. For all his flaws, Hamilton wrote, Jefferson had a "temporizing rather than a violent" character, and thus was unlikely to go to extremes in undoing Federalist measures. Hamilton would "add to this that there is no fair reason to suppose him capable of being corrupted." Burr, by contrast, was driven only by lust for power: "He is sanguine enough to hope every thing—daring enough to attempt every thing—wicked enough to scruple nothing." Hamilton's position was not personal. "If there be a man in the world I ought to hate," said he, "it is Jefferson. With *Burr* I have always been personally well. But the public good must be paramount to every private consideration."[50]

The Federalists rejected Hamilton's pleas, and for thirty-five ballots they kept the issue deadlocked. But then Hamilton's efforts bore fruit: James Bayard of Delaware, his state's only Representative, to whom Hamilton had repeatedly appealed, announced that he was changing his vote. On the thirty-sixth ballot Jefferson was elected president of the United States.[51]

There was a postscript. In April Hamilton campaigned vigorously for his brother-in-law Stephen Van Rensselaer, Federalist candidate for governor of New York. Robert Troup described the popular reception to his ward-by-ward speeches: "At one of the polls General Hamilton, with impunity by the populace, was repeatedly called a thief; and at another poll with the same impunity he was called a rascal, villain, and every thing else that is in famous in society! What a commentary is this on republican virtue!"[52] "He assures me that nothing short of a general convulsion will again call him into public life."[53]

Epilogue

What's Fame? a fancied life in others' breath,

A thing beyond us, even before our death.

Some time since, Hamilton had decided to take up the life of a country gentleman—or at least that of a commuter—and in 1800 he had begun to purchase land in upper Manhattan, about eight miles north of the city. He plunged into the project with apparent gusto, plunging rather deeply into debt as well. Plans for a house were completed in June of 1801, construction was soon under way, and the family occupied the premises in August of 1802, though the main house was not completed until the following winter. Hamilton christened his home the Grange, after the ancestral Hamilton estate in Ayrshire. He divided his time between the country place and a small house he retained in the city.[1]

Meanwhile, though his career in government was over, he continued to voice his thoughts on matters of public policy, and as a medium he founded a newspaper, the *New-York Evening Post*. Along with Troup and several other friends, Hamilton provided the necessary financial backing, and he engaged William Coleman, an able and experienced journalist, to edit the paper. It was Hamilton's personal organ: Coleman regularly interviewed Hamilton, usually late in the evening, took shorthand notes, and used the notes to fill his columns with political news and editorial comments. The paper began publishing on November 16, 1801.[2]

The *Evening Post* had just been established when personal tragedy struck. On Friday, November 20, Hamilton's son Philip, in his twentieth year and freshly graduated from Columbia, became involved in an altercation with a Republican lawyer named George Eacker. Philip and a friend named Price instigated the trouble,

[355]

Eacker proved to be intransigent, and negotiations to avoid duels were fruitless. Hamilton, learning of the affair, "commanded his Son, when on the ground, to reserve his *fire* 'till after Mr E, had shot and then to discharge his pistol in the air." Price's duel was fought on Sunday without harm to either party. Philip's duel was fought on Monday. The two men fired almost simultaneously, Philip into the air, Eacker into Philip's right side above the hip. After twenty-four hours of agony, with his father lying, weeping, on one side of the bed with him and with his mother on the other, Philip died.[3]

Hamilton never completely recovered from the loss. Philip, he said, had been "the eldest and *brightest* hope of my family," and as Troup wrote to King, Hamilton had "formed high expectations of his future greatness." After a week or two Hamilton had composed himself enough to be "able again to attend to business; but his countenance," Troup added, was "strongly stamped with grief." It was four months before Hamilton could bring himself to answer the letters of condolence he had received.[4]

By that time everything he cherished seemed to be coming to an end, for the Jeffersonian Republicans, in full control of the government, were trying to cripple the federal judiciary, scrap the navy, and destroy all he had labored to build. Late in February of 1802, in a letter to Gouverneur Morris, he revealed the depth of his depression. "Mine is an odd destiny," he wrote. "Perhaps no man in the UStates has sacrificed or done more for the present Constitution than myself—and contrary to all my anticipations of its fate . . . I am still labouring to prop the frail and worthless fabric. Yet I have the murmurs of its friends no less than the curses of its foes for my rewards. What can I do better than withdraw from the Scene? Every day proves to me more and more that this American world was not made for me."[5]

He sought consolation in religion. His youthful faith had never entirely departed him, and the overt atheism of the French Revolution had rekindled his sense of the importance of religion. Now, in the wake of Philip's death, he became as devout as he had been as a protégé of the Reverend Hugh Knox. In the spring of 1802 he went so far as to propose the formation of a political party to be known as the Christian Constitutional Society. An appeal to the "good passions" of the religious impulse, he believed, would be intrinsically desirable and might help overcome the advantage that Republicans had gained by appealing to the "vicious" passions. To act as a party and to appeal to the passions at all, rather than relying "on the rectitude and utility" of public measures, would be a compromise of Hamiltonian principles, but Hamilton thought it warranted by circumstances. Besides, he had always tried to combine what was right with what was expedient, allowing some give or take one with the other, and this proposal—which got nowhere—was in keeping with that practice.[6]

It was, however, an act of near desperation, and despair was not in Hamilton. He slowly regained his wonted hopefulness: the Grange helped, as a diversion; his law practice helped too, and not just as a diversion. The ongoing revolution in American law, of which he was a central part, would in the long run more than offset the political revolution Jefferson was effecting. By 1803 his interest in public affairs was as lively as ever, his confidence in his own political acuity as pronounced as ever.

The sharpness of his thinking, as well as its consistency, was illustrated in the affair of Louisiana. Shortly after Jefferson was inaugurated, Hamilton learned from a friend in Paris of Spain's retrocession of Louisiana to France, and he so informed Madison, who had become secretary of state. The administration took no steps until 1802. In the fall of that year the Spanish Intendent of New Orleans, in anticipation of France's expected reoccupancy of the city, closed the port to American vessels, violating implicit American treaty rights and portending a grave threat to national security. Jefferson was as alarmed by that ominous turn of events as Hamilton was, but his reaction was the opposite. Jefferson's first impulse was to try to protect the United States by seeking an alliance with Great Britain. What he did instead was send James Monroe to France in an effort to buy New Orleans from Napoleon.[7]

Hamilton, as he analyzed the situation in the *Evening Post*, approached the matter differently. He said there were only two reasonable ways to proceed. "First, to negotiate, and endeavor to purchase; and if this fails, to go to war. Secondly, to seize at once on the Floridas and New Orleans, and then negotiate." He considered the latter course much the better, both because it was more likely to succeed and because it would be less expensive. (The purchase, when consummated, seemed a bargain, but the terms contained hidden costs that greatly increased the actual price, and added nearly 20 percent to the public debt. A military expedition would have been far cheaper.) When the purchase was made, however—in keeping with his insistence upon responsibility in opposition—Hamilton was almost alone among critics of the administration who applauded the transaction.[8]

The severity of less restrained Federalist newspapers led to one of Hamilton's last and most celebrated lawsuits. Harry Croswell, editor of a small upstate newspaper, *The Wasp,* charged that Jefferson had paid J. T. Callender (the notorious pamphleteer who had written the attack that provoked Hamilton's publication of the Reynolds Pamphlet in 1797) "for calling Washington a traitor, a robber, and a perjurer—For calling Adams, a hoary headed incendiary; and for most grossly slandering the private characters of men, who, he well knew were virtuous." The charge against Jefferson was true; but the Jeffersonians, who had stoutly defended freedom of the press when in the opposition, thought a "few wholesome prosecutions" were in order to muffle their own critics. The Jeffersonian attorney general of New York, Ambrose Spencer, brought proceedings against Croswell for libel. On conviction, he appealed, and Hamilton became his counsel in the arguments before the state supreme court.[9]

The key point at issue was that the judge in the trial had refused to admit testimony regarding the truth of the statement as defense. The English common-law doctrine, to which Republicans interestingly adhered, held that truth was not a defense. Hamilton and his co-counsel scored heavily by showing that the common-law doctrine itself was questionable, having originated in the odious Star Chamber as a departure from older law. But Hamilton was particularly concerned with the suitability of the doctrine in a republic. Libel, he said, was "a slanderous or ridiculous writing, picture or sign, with a malicious or mischievous design or intent, towards government, magistrates, or individuals." Intent was crucial, and truth was relevant to determining intent. Truth was therefore a defense, though not an absolute one. Truth could be used "wantonly; if for the purpose of disturbing the peace of families; if for relating that which does not appertain to official conduct, so far we say the doctrine of our opponents is correct. . . . But that the truth cannot be material in any respect, is contrary to the nature of things. No tribunal, no codes, no systems can repeal or impair this law of God, for by his eternal laws it is inherent in the nature of things. . . . It is evident that if you cannot apply this mitigated doctrine for which I speak, to the cases of libels here, you must for ever remain ignorant of what your rulers do. I never can think this ought to be; I never did think the truth was a crime; I am glad the day is come in which it is to be decided; for my soul has ever abhorred the thought, that a free man dared not speak the truth."[10]

The court was divided, and so the verdict was not reversed. But Hamilton's eloquent plea bore fruit. Virtually all the members of both houses of the state legislature came to hear his argument, and a bill was forthwith introduced declaring Hamilton's position the law of the state. It was formally enacted the next year. In time it was embraced throughout the American Republic and formed the legal foundation, firmer than the First Amendment, for the ideal of a free and responsible press.[11]

Before the New York statute became law, Hamilton was dead.

Northern Federalists, convinced that Jefferson and the Republicans would destroy everything they held dear, had regarded the Louisiana Purchase as the last straw: it fundamentally altered the constitutional compact and promised to ensure perpetually the rule of the southern slavocracy. Under the leadership of Timothy Pickering, New England Federalists decided that the only way to save the Union was to leave it—to secede and form a separate country of which New York would become a part. New York was essential to the scheme, and Federalists, who had been flirting with Vice-President Burr for some time (over Hamilton's vehement protests), agreed to support Burr for governor of New York in 1804 as a means to that end. At first there were two candidates: the regular Republican or Clintonian candidate, John Lansing, and the dissenting Republican candidate, Aaron Burr. Hamilton tried to induce Rufus King to run as a Federalist, but King refused, so Hamilton campaigned for Lansing. When Lansing suddenly and without explanation withdrew, the regulars nominated Morgan Lewis in his place. Hamilton continued to exert his efforts to persuade Federalists not to vote for Burr. His effectiveness is unknown, but Lewis won by a margin of about 8,000 out of 53,000 votes.[12]

That was late in April of 1804. On June 18, Burr sent William Van Ness to Hamilton with a note demanding an explanation for remarks Hamilton was alleged to have made. One Charles D. Cooper claimed to have heard Hamilton say that he "looked upon Mr. Burr to be a dangerous man, and one who ought not to be trusted with the reins of government." Burr did not take offense at that statement, but at one which followed: "I could detail to you a still more despicable opinion which General HAMILTON has expressed of Mr. BURR."[13]

Certain mysteries surrounded the ensuing negotiations, then and later. It was a part of the *code duello* that injuries requiring explanation or apology must be specifically stated. Hamilton protested to Burr that the statement in question was too vague to confirm or deny, since it could refer to anything Hamilton might have said over the course of fifteen years of political rivalry; but Burr insisted upon an answer. What inspired Burr is unknown. It could have been sheer animosity born of Hamilton's having repeatedly thwarted his ambition—which is what Hamilton thought. But, according to the code, political enmity alone was not sufficient to provoke a duel; the injury must be personal, and despite the intensity of their political opposition, Hamilton and Burr had always got along personally. Moreover, nothing Hamilton could have said in 1804, politically or personally, could have been worse than what many others had said. Besides, Burr was normally amiable to the point of irresponsibility; his very lack of serious principle was among the characteristics Hamilton regarded as most dangerous about him politically. Again, the code forbade issuing a challenge out of malice, and Burr held to the code as strictly as Hamilton did.

For his part, Hamilton abhorred dueling, doubly since the death of Philip, but when negotiations broke down he accepted the challenge and went through with it. One of his stated reasons was that, given the prejudices of the country, he would be regarded as a coward if he declined the "interview," and that would end all prospects of public service in future. A second stated reason was his belief that he would have to face Burr sooner or later: Burr's ambition, he was convinced, was boundless, and Hamilton knew he must always try to prevent Burr from obtaining any position of real power. And there was still a third, unstated consideration. The dueling ground was not a killing ground; it was an arena in which gentlemen proved their honor by facing with courage the possibility of death, whether by accident or by the baseness of one's opponent. Men of honor fired and deliberately missed, though they might try to miss closely. That is what Eacker and Price had done in their duel: each had fired four times and missed, after which they shook hands, each having obtained "satisfaction" that the other was a gentleman. Hamilton intended to do this in his interview with Burr. It was possible that Burr would do the same; for one could be unprincipled in politics and immoral in private life, and yet comport oneself among gentlemen as a man of honor.[14]

The meeting was delayed for various reasons until July 11. Hamilton went calmly about his business, made out his will, wrote two farewell letters to his wife, and was noticeably gay on social occasions. That was the way gentlemen behaved. On the morning of July 11 he and his second, accompanied by a physician, met Burr and his second at a secluded spot in Weehawken, New Jersey, near where Philip had fallen. By accident or design, Burr's shot struck Hamilton in the right side and passed through his liver. Hamilton was taken back to the city, where he survived in intense pain for thirty-six hours. He pleaded with the Episcopal bishop, Benjamin Moore, to administer the last sacraments, but Moore declined on the ground that Hamilton had never been confirmed as a member of the church and, possibly, because he had been felled in a duel. After a second call Moore relented. Hamilton repented his sins, forgave Burr, and committed his soul to his Maker. About two o'clock in the afternoon of July 12, his Maker took him.

That was not the end of the story. As Troup had often predicted, it was necessary for Hamilton's friends and admirers to pay his debts and save his widow and family from penury.[15] But that was not the end of the story, either, nor is it important. What is important is that the revolution Hamilton had set in train proved immune to the attacks of his enemies, and thus the United States was spared the fate of every other republic that was established on the American continents. Instead, it became what Hamilton dared dream it might become—the richest, most powerful and freest nation in the history of the world.

The realization of that miracle was, to be sure, resisted. The Jeffersonians labored for a dozen years to tear down what Hamilton had built, only to blunder their way into a war and thereby to discover the necessity of putting it back together again. A generation later the Jeffersonians' heirs, the Jacksonian Democrats, tore it down again, with a peculiar result. In the absence of an effective national government, it became possible for each state to make its own rules of the game. Those in the South adopted Jeffersonian rules, and their society continued to rest upon the mystique of the land, upon slavery, and upon the exercise of force without the impartial restraint of law. Those elsewhere adopted Hamiltonian rules, and their society rested upon the market, free labor, contractual relationships, and law. The Civil War brought the triumph of the Hamiltonian way, leaving Jefferson's beloved South a wretched and accursed backwater. The rest of the nation moved on toward greatness.

For a long time, Hamilton's country was appropriately grateful to him: for nearly a century and a half, his Fame seemed secure. Partly his memory was kept alive by the efforts of his family, who strove diligently to safeguard the place in history he had earned. Partly he got his deserts because most of American history was written by New England Yankees who, except for descendants of John Adams, almost uniformly idolized him. For many decades after the Civil War his niche in the pantheon of American demigods was beneath only Washington's, if indeed it was not at Washington's right hand.[16]

But the American nation reached the peak of its greatness in the middle of the twentieth century: after that time it became increasingly Jeffersonian, governed by coercion and the party spirit, its people progressively more dependent and less self-reliant, its decline candy-coated with rhetoric of liberty and equality and justice for all: and with that decline Hamilton's Fame declined apace.

Though he would have cried for his country, perhaps he would have been content that his Fame lasted as long as it did. To return to the words of Hume, "It is a sufficient incitement to human endeavours, that such a government would flourish for many ages; without pretending to bestow, on any work of man, that immortality, which the Almighty seems to have refused to his own productions."

Betsey outlived Hamilton by half a century. When she had long since been a widow, James Monroe, who had long since completed his presidency, came to call upon her. She entered the parlor to receive him. "Monroe rose. She stood in the middle of the room facing him. She did not ask him to sit down. He bowed, and addressing her formally, made her rather a set speech—that it was many years since they had met, that the lapse of time brought its softening influences, that they both were nearing the grave, when past differences could be forgiven and forgotten." Betsey, still standing, looked at him and replied, "Mr. Monroe, if you have come to tell me that you repent, that you are sorry, *very* sorry, for the misrepresentations and the slanders, and the stories you circulated against my dear husband, if you have come to say this, I understand it. But, otherwise, no lapse of time, no nearness to the grave, makes any difference."[17]

It would become the American people to consider that as a parable.

Notes

I—Young Man Hamilton

1. This couplet, like those opening each chapter of this book, is from Alexander Pope, who obviously influenced Hamilton's world view and doubtless was his favorite poet. That Hamilton read Pope as a youth is evident from a poem he wrote in 1772 entitled "The Soul ascending into Bliss, In humble imitation of Popes Dying Christian to his Soul" (Harold C. Syrett and others, eds., *The Papers of Alexander Hamilton* [25 vols. to date, New York, 1961–], 1:38). That Hamilton reread Pope while in the army is suggested by an entry in his paybook, 1777, ibid., 1:396. Hamilton was not given to quoting poets in his public writings, and in fact quoted none besides Pope, but he quoted Pope in one of his earliest such pieces and in at least three of his mature writings: "The Farmer Refuted," February 23, 1775; "The Defence No. 17," September 22, 1795; "The Stand No. 2," April 4, 1798, and "The Examination No. 10," January 19, 1802, ibid., 1:83, 19:292, 21:390, and 25:511. He also on occasion quoted Pope in his personal correspondence; see, for example, Hamilton to Elizabeth Schuyler, October 27, 1780, and to Catherine Greene, September 3, 1793, ibid., 2:493, 15:319. Friends, sharing his fondness for Pope, sometimes quoted Pope in letters to Hamilton; see, for example, the letters from Philip Schuyler, August 6, 1798, from George Cabot, November 29, 1800, and from Fisher Ames, December 1800, ibid., 22:57, 25:248, 25:284. The editors of the *Hamilton Papers* do not always identify Pope as the poet being quoted. The unidentified source in the letter to Elizabeth Schuyler, for instance, is lines 75 and 76 of Pope's "Eloisa to Abelard."

2. The observations in the first half of this paragraph are developed more fully in chapter 4. Those concerning Hamilton's vision for America are developed in chapters 6ff.

3. That this was an accurate, if somewhat exaggerated, view of American society—despite twentieth-century notions to the contrary—is developed more fully in chapter 6 and succeeding chapters. That this was Hamilton's perception of it is evident in many of his writings, for instance in Hamilton to John Laurens, September 11, 1779, and June 30, 1780 (from which the quotations are taken), Syrett, ed., *Papers*, 2:167, 347. His analysis of the main props of American provincialism, as summarized here, is in his speech of June 18, 1787, ibid., 4:188–90. For his judgment that Americans "labour less now than any civilized nation of Europe," see Hamilton to Robert Morris, April 30, 1781, ibid., 2:635.

4. See chapters 6–10.

5. Hamilton to Edward Stevens, November 11, 1769; "The Farmer Refuted," February 23, 1775; Hamilton to Catherine Livingston, May 1777, to Susanna Livingston, March 18, 1779, to John Laurens, April 1779, to Elizabeth Schuyler, August 1780; Constitutional Convention, remarks of June 26, 1787; Hamilton to Robert Troup, April 13, 1795, in Syrett, ed., *Papers*, 1:4, 157, 259, 2:22–23, 34–35, 399, 4:218, 18:329.

6. Except for a few additional facts unearthed by Broadus Mitchell in the preparation of his *Alexander Hamilton*, vol. 1, *Youth to Maturity, 1755–1788* (New York, 1957), and for two letters written by Hamilton when he was in his forties, practically all the documentation concerning Hamilton's background and childhood is contained in three sources. The first is Gertrude Atherton, "The Hunt for Hamilton's Mother," in *The North American Review*, 175:229–42 (June 1902), an account of that biographer's researches in the West Indies. The second, the fruit of years of researchers in St. Croix, is H. U. Ramsing, "Alexander Hamilton og Hans Mødrene Slaegt. Tidsbilleder fra Dansk Vest-Indiens Barndom," in *Personalhistorisk Tidsskrift* (Copenhagen, 1939). A translation of this article by Solvejg Vahl, a microfilm of an original typescript belonging to Broadus Mitchell, is available in the New York Public Library; I have used that version, and my page references are to it. The third source is Harold Larson, "Alexander Hamilton: The Fact and Fiction of His Early Years," in *William and Mary Quarterly*, 9:139–51 (April 1952); Larson's work, based mainly on Atherton's and Ramsing's with some additional data of his own, is a thorough, scholarly effort to separate what is documentable regarding Hamilton's parentage and early life from the misstatements that had become generally accepted. In my judgment, Larson is a bit harsh in dismissing the claims of Hamilton's son, John Church Hamilton (*Life of Alexander Hamilton*, vol. 1, New York, 1834); for, though the son did put a gloss on Hamilton's parentage, it must be assumed that what he reported was based in large measure on what his father had told him and is therefore important as an indication of what Hamilton remembered and believed about his parents. See also Hamilton's letters to William Hamilton (his father's older brother and Laird of Grange, Ayrshire, Scotland), May 2, 1797, and to William Jackson, August 26, 1800, in Syrett, ed., *Papers*, 21:77–80, 25:88–90. The second of these letters is quite revealing and has, as far as I am aware, never been used by a biographer before.

The editors of the *Hamilton Papers* correctly spell Rachel's maiden name "Faucett" in vol. 1 but switch to the spelling "Fawcett" in vol. 3.

The specific data in the present paragraph are from Ramsing, 1–5, 8, 14; Larson, 141–43; Atherton, 230; and Syrett, ed., *Papers*, 25:89.

7. Hamilton to Jackson, August 26, 1800, ibid., 25:89; Ramsing, "Hamilton," 6–7.

8. Most historians now give January 11, 1755, as Hamilton's birthday, despite Hamilton's own statement attesting to 1757 and his son's unequivocal statement that Hamilton was born January 11, 1757 (*Life of Hamilton*, 1:1). The only document supporting 1755 is one written by the clerk of probate after Rachel's death; he gives Hamilton's age in 1768 as thirteen. Since Hamilton was not present at the probate hearing, and since the clerk did not even spell Rachel's name correctly (he spelled it "Lewine"), it seems reasonable to assume that he was in error about Hamilton's age.

Notes

On the other hand, Hamilton himself spelled the name "Lavine" in his letter to Jackson in 1800, cited in note 3 above. For the pros and cons of this inconsequential controversy, see Mitchell, *Hamilton,* 1:11–13, and Robert Hendrickson, *Hamilton I (1757–1789)* (New York, 1976), 1–4. One bit of tangential evidence not used by Mitchell or Hendrickson strikes me as additional support for 1757. In 1798 Hamilton described himself to James McHenry as "a man past 40"; Hamilton to McHenry, December 16, 1798, in Syrett, ed., *Papers,* 22:369. The trauma of the decade turnover in one's age—when one reaches 30, 40, 50—normally lasts a year or two, after which one is accustomed to being in one's forties, or whatever. If Hamilton was born in 1757, he was still 41 when he wrote to McHenry, and the language seems appropriate; had he been born in 1755, he would have had nearly four years to adjust to the decade change, and seems more likely to have used some such phrase as "a man in his forties."

My statement regarding the illegal marriage of James and Rachel is based upon Hamilton's own statement that "a marriage between them ensued," in Hamilton to Jackson, August 26, 1800, ibid., 25:89–90; as for the trip to St. Croix in 1765, the terms of the divorce (1759), and James Hamilton's departure early in 1766, see Ramsing, "Hamilton," 15, and Larson, "Fact and Fiction," 141–42.

Two recent biographers, Hendrickson, *Hamilton I,* 1–19, and James Thomas Flexner, *The Young Hamilton: A Biography* (Boston, 1978), have built interpretations of Hamilton's psyche on the basis of a depiction of Rachel as a sexually promiscuous woman, a portrait drawn from a misreading of the 1759 divorce decree. In 1750, when Lavien had Rachel jailed, he did not list adultery among her alleged "errors," and as Larson points out (p. 143), her misconduct "consisted simply in refusing to live with her husband, for had there been a third party he would undoubtedly have been named by Lavien." In his petition for a divorce in 1759, Lavien did charge Rachel with "whoring" and with having "begotten several illegitimate children," and the charges were technically accurate, for she had been living out of wedlock with James Hamilton for nine years. But that is a far cry from "whoring" in any wanton sense of the term.

Flexner's book is extremely provocative, and I am indebted to it, for reading it forced me to rethink and reexamine the whole subject. But upon checking it against the available documents, I have concluded that his interpretation cannot be reconciled with the sources. In attempting, for instance, to justify the suggestion that Rachel deserted James rather than the reverse (pp. 25–26), Flexner says that "when Rachel, no longer banned from St. Croix, succeeded in getting under the wing of her rich relatives she saw no further reason to tolerate the paramour who had failed to make her life financially 'eligible.'" Flexner is leaving out of account the following facts: (1) that Rachel's "banishment" ended in 1759, though she did not go to St. Croix (with James Hamilton and their children) until 1765; (2) that her family had been well off earlier but in 1764 had suffered losses that virtually wiped them out, and deteriorated further in 1765 (see Ramsing, 18–19, 21–22); (3) that she had, when James left her, lived with him for nearly sixteen years as a common-law wife (not a "paramour"), and (4) that there is no evidence that she was ever unfaithful to James. Flexner goes on to assert that "the fear of a comparable fate"—that is, desertion by his wife—"haunted Alexander." He bases this on a letter Hamilton wrote his fiancée, Elizabeth Schuyler, in 1780 (not, as Flexner mistakenly says, 1790). In context, Hamilton was asking "Betsey," a very rich young lady, to examine her heart to make sure she would be able to bear the strained economic circumstances under which he expected them to live. After expressing his "diffidence" of a *"female* heart," which Flexner reads as an indication of fear of the inconstancy of women, Hamilton goes on to say (what Flexner leaves out) that men are even less reliable and to describe the female sex in terms that only one who genuinely admired them could use. See Hamilton to Elizabeth Schuyler, August 1780, September 3, 1780, in Syrett, ed., *Papers,* 2:397–400, 418–20.

9. Ramsing, "Hamilton," 23, 24; Larson, "Fact and Fiction," 145; Hamilton, *Life of Hamilton,* 1:3. Flexner, *Young Hamilton,* 29, 34, asserts that Hamilton kept the books and handled Rachel's business affairs; he cites Ramsing, 23, which says no such thing. That Rachel was a methodical businesswoman and good manager should not be surprising; her mother was also, and careful attention to strict business practices was in the Huguenot tradition.

10. Ramsing, "Hamilton," 23–29; Syrett, ed., *Papers,* 1:4–5, note 1; Larson, "Fact and Fiction," 144–47.

11. See Hamilton's correspondence with Cruger and others, October 1771 to May 1772, in Syrett, ed., *Papers,* 1:8–31; see also Mitchell, *Hamilton,* 1:15–28.

12. Hamilton to Edward Stevens, November 11, 1769, in Syrett, ed., *Papers,* 1:4–5.

13. The quotations regarding the meaning of "contemn" are from Webster's *Unabridged Dictionary,* 3d ed., 614, under "despise." I have generally been guided in ascertaining eighteenth-century usage, however, by the *Oxford English Dictionary.* Sensitivity to the differences between modern and eighteenth-century usages is, I believe, indispensable to an understanding of the eighteenth century. For a rare and excellent example of such sensitivity, see Garry Wills, *Inventing America: Jefferson's Declaration of Independence* (Garden City, N.Y., 1978).

14. An excellent account of Knox and his influence upon Hamilton is Broadus Mitchell, "The Man Who Discovered Hamilton," in *Proceedings of the New Jersey Historical Society,* 69:88–114 (April 1951).

15. Ibid.; Cedric B. Cowing, *The Great Awakening and the American Revolution: Colonial Thought in the 18th Century* (Chicago, 1971); John E. Pomfret, *Colonial New Jersey: A History* (New York, 1973), 218–37; Sydney E. Ahlstrom, *A Religious History of the American People* (New Haven, 1972), 265–79, 353–56; Roger Jerome Fechner, "The Moral Philosophy of John Witherspoon and the Scottish-American Enlightenment" (Ph.D. thesis, University of Iowa, 1974).

16. See, for example, Owen S. Ireland, "The Ethnic-Religious Dimension of Pennsylvania Politics, 1778–1779," in *William and Mary Quarterly,* 30:423–48 (July 1973); and Dorothy Rita Dillon, *The New York Triumvirate: A Study of the Legal and Political Careers of William Livingston, John Morin Scott, William Smith, Jr.* (New York, 1949), especially 31–53. See also Mitchell, "Man Who Discovered Hamilton," 89, 111. In emphasizing the ethnic-religious dimension to the revolutionary divisions in the middle colonies I do not mean to suggest that the polarization was absolute. The Anglican ministry was overwhelmingly Tory, but the laity was split, only leaning toward Toryism. John Jay himself, for instance, was Anglican.

Notes

17. Mitchell, *Hamilton,* 1:42–43.

18. Nathan Schachner, ed., "Alexander Hamilton Viewed by His Friends: The Narratives of Robert Troup and Hercules Mulligan," in *William and Mary Quarterly,* 4:209 (April 1947).

19. Ibid. (Troup), 212–13; Mitchell, *Hamilton,* 1:52–56.

20. Mitchell, *Hamilton,* 1:57–73; the tracts are in Syrett, ed., *Papers,* 1:45–78, 81–165. They are considered at more length in chapter two.

21. Schachner, ed., "Narratives" (Mulligan), 210, (Troup), 218–19.

22. Ibid. (Mulligan), 211, (Troup), 219; Mitchell, *Hamilton,* 1:75.

23. The quotations are from "The Farmer Refuted," February 23, 1775, in Syrett, ed., *Papers,* 1:156–57. For an example of Hamilton's recognition and rewarding of merit, see Hamilton to the Convention of Representatives of the State of New York, August 12, 1776, ibid., 1:187. Detailed accounts of Hamilton's military career are to be found in Mitchell, *Hamilton;* Hendrickson, *Hamilton I;* and, less reliably, Flexner, *Young Hamilton.* To illustrate his thesis that "a feeling of humiliation, of shame," the legacy of his childhood, was predominant among Hamilton's passions (p. 5), Flexner writes (p. 106), "He could only regard his first military engagement as a humiliating failure" because several of his cannon burst, killing six and wounding four or five. As documentation for Hamilton's feelings (p. 471), Flexner cites Syrett, ed., *Papers,* 1:188, 190 and *Calendar of Historical Manuscripts, Relating to the War of the Revolution, in the office of the Secretary of State, Albany, New York* (Albany, 1868), 1:501, 631. The documents in Syrett are mere certifications that William Douglass, a matross in Hamilton's company, had lost his arm and was entitled to compensation as provided by a resolution of Congress. One of the documents in the *Calendar* is a duplicate of the one in Syrett, 1:190, and the other is a petition by Douglass. None of the documents bears a relation to Flexner's interpretation.

24. The quotation regarding dependency and the data regarding the two offers from other generals are from Hamilton to Philip Schuyler, February 18, 1781, in Syrett, ed., *Papers,* 2:565–66. Regarding the nature and extent of Hamilton's services to Washington, see the works of Mitchell and Hendrickson cited in note 23.

25. See the letters between Hamilton and the various persons mentioned in the paragraph, in Syrett, ed., *Papers,* vol. 2. For an example of the continued loyalty to former comrades despite political opposition, see the Promissory Note from William Grayson, October 1, 1789, ibid., 5:414. Grayson was a leading Virginia anti-Federalist who happened to be in New York and in need of cash; because they had been fellow officers, Hamilton lent him $200. For an example regarding Von Steuben, see page 249. The deep friendship for Laurens might have had interesting later political consequences, but unfortunately Laurens was killed in a minor skirmish after the war was, for practical purposes, over.

26. Regarding Hamilton's physical appearance, see Harry MacNeill Bland and Virginia W. Northcott, "The Life Portraits of Alexander Hamilton," in *William and Mary Quarterly,* 12:187–98 (April 1955). His charm for women is evident in various documents scattered through Syrett, ed., *Papers,* vols. 1 and 2.

27. Hamilton to Laurens, April 1779, ibid., 2:34–38.

28. Hamilton to Catherine Livingston and Elizabeth Schuyler, January–February 1780, to Elizabeth Schuyler, March 17, June–October, July 2–4, 6, 20, 31,

August 8, 31, August, September 3, 6, 1780, Registry of Marriage, December 14, 1780, ibid., 2:262, 285–87, 350, 350–52, 353, 361–62, 370–71, 374–75, 387–89, 397–99, 418–20, 422–23, 521.

29. Hamilton to Elizabeth Schuyler, September 25, 1780, ibid., 2:441–42. In the *Hamilton Papers*, 2:442, "forfeited" is rendered "forfieted."

30. Hendrickson, in *Hamilton II (1789–1804)* (New York, 1977), *passim*, maintains—unconvincingly, in my judgment—that Hamilton was adulterously involved with Angelica Schuyler Church. On the one documented extramarital affair in Hamilton's life, see chapters 11, 12, and 15.

31. Publius Letters I, II, III, October 16, 26, November 16, 1778, in Syrett, ed., *Papers,* 1:562–63, 567–70, 580–82. The quotations are at 580–81.

32. Robert Troup's account of the personal side of Hamilton's mission to Gates is in Schachner, ed., "Narratives," 222–25. Related data are in Syrett, ed., *Papers,* vol. 1, *passim*. Regarding the "Conway Cabal," see Edmund Cody Burnett, *The Continental Congress* (New York, 1941), 279–97.

33. See Hamilton to George Clinton, December 22, 1777 in Syrett, ed., *Papers,* 1:368; and Mitchell, *Hamilton,* 1:140ff. Hamilton's arrival at Valley Forge is dated on the basis of his expense account for the mission, January 20, 1778, in Syrett, ed., *Papers,* 1:412–13.

34. Howard Swiggett, *The Extraordinary Mr. Morris* (Garden City, N.Y., 1952), 50 and *passim*. For a sampling of Morris's political ideas, see Morris to Hamilton, May 16, 1777, in Syrett, ed., *Papers,* 1:253–54; for his skepticism and wit, see Morris to Hamilton, January 27, 1784, ibid., 3:498–503; for Hamilton's imitative response, see Hamilton to Morris, February 21, 1784, ibid., 3:512–14.

35. Hamilton to Clinton, February 13, 1778, ibid., 1:425–28.

36. The wholesale expropriations and similar lawless government actions are documented in Forrest McDonald, "The Taking Issue: The Fifth Amendment in Historical Perspective" (1976, available at the Institute for Humane Studies, Menlo Park, California). For examples of what is said here, see the Brown and Arnold Papers in the John Carter Brown Library, Providence; Robert A. East, *Business Enterprise in the American Revolutionary Era* (New York, 1938); Merrill Jensen, *The Articles of Confederation: An Interpretation of the Social-Constitutional History of the American Revolution, 1774–1781* (Madison, 1940); Hamilton to Clinton, March 12, 1778, and to ———, December 1779–March 1780, in Syrett, ed., *Papers,* 1:439–40, 2:241. The other quotations are from Hamilton to Laurens, May 22, 1779, and Nathanael Greene to Hamilton, January 10, 1781, ibid., 2:53, 529. On the fiat government of rival oligarchs in North Carolina and Virginia, the best account I have seen is in an as yet unfinished manuscript of a book by Professor James R. Morrill of the University of Louisville. See also the same author's *The Practice and Politics of Fiat Finance: North Carolina in the Confederation, 1783–1789* (Chapel Hill, 1969) for an account of the continuation of such practices after the war.

37. Mitchell, *Hamilton,* 1:165–70; John Brooks to Hamilton, July 4, 1779, in Syrett, ed., *Papers,* 2:91, and the correspondence with William Henley, Francis Dana, and William Gordon in the same volume; Hamilton to Laurens, September 11, 1779, and January 8, 1780, ibid., 2:168–69, 255.

38. The concept of war as described here is developed at some length in Forrest

Notes

McDonald, "Eighteenth-Century Warfare as a Cultural Ritual," paper presented at the General Wilburt S. Brown Conference on Military History, Tuscaloosa, Alabama, February 1976. Blackstone's comment is in Sir William Blackstone, *Commentaries on the Laws of England* (12th ed., 4 vols., London, 1793–95), 1:406.

39. Hamilton to John Jay, March 14, 1779, to Laurens, June 30, September 12, 16, 1780, in Syrett, ed., *Papers,* 2:17–18, 347–48, 426–28, 431–32.

40. Hamilton to Laurens, September 11, 1779, January 8, June 30, September 12, 1780, ibid., 2:167, 255, 347, 428.

41. The following account is derived from Hamilton to Elizabeth Schuyler, October 2, 1780, and to John Laurens, October 11, 1780, in Syrett, ed., *Papers,* 2:448–49, 460–70.

42. Hamilton to Philip Schuyler, February 18, 1781, ibid., 563–68.

43. Ibid., 566–67, and Hamilton to James McHenry, February 18, 1781, ibid., 569. Hamilton's remarks about the absence of friendship in the relationship are generally true but not entirely so. One can infer much on this score from the complimentary closings on letters. Among gentlemen, minor variations even in the conventional formal closing—"I have the honor, sir, to be your most humble obedient servant"—signified important shades of differences in relationships. The term "affectionately" was used sparingly, for it indicated shared intimacy. That Washington had stronger personal feelings for Hamilton than were reciprocated is indicated by Washington's use of the affectionate closing even after Hamilton's resignation; see Washington to Hamilton, March 7, 1781, ibid., 583. In all the years prior to the resignation, Hamilton used the affectionate closing in a letter to Washington only once, on March 17, 1780; ibid., 288. Later, the relationship did become personally more intimate, and the complimentary expressions reflected the increased closeness of the two men.

Ellen Shapiro McDonald has catalogued the variations in complimentary closings in Hamilton's incoming and outgoing correspondence for the period 1768 to 1800. Her findings constitute an index to the vicissitudes of Hamilton's personal relations.

44. A good account of Hamilton at Yorktown is Broadus Mitchell's, in *Hamilton,* 1:250–61. Hamilton's own brief summary of the action is in his report to Lafayette, October 15, 1781, in Syrett, ed., *Papers,* 2:679–81.

II—Education in the Political Arts

1. Hamilton to _____, December 1779–March 1780, and "The Continentalist" No. I (July 12, 1781), in Syrett, ed., *Papers,* 2:242, 650. In regard to Hamilton's own "utopian speculations," compare his 1775 estimate of the relative strength of Britain and America, in "The Farmer Refuted" (ibid., 1:155–60) with his experienced and realistic comments in "The Continentalist" No. III, August 9, 1781, ibid., 2:663–64.

2. The quotations are from "A Full Vindication" and "The Farmer Refuted," ibid., 1:144–45, 94, 75–76, and 50, in that order. On the Oppositionist mentality, see Isaac Kramnick, *Bolingbroke and His Circle: The Politics of Nostalgia in the Age of*

Walpole (Cambridge, Mass., 1968), and Bernard Bailyn, *The Ideological Origins of the American Revolution* (Cambridge, Mass., 1967). A forthcoming book by Rodger Parker, The Gospel of Opposition, promises to be the definitive work on the subject. See also Forrest McDonald, "A Founding Father's Library," in *Literature of Liberty*, 1:4–15 (January-March 1978), and chapter 10, where the Oppositionist origins of the resistance to Hamilton's financial measures are considered more fully.

3. See, for example, Charles Louis de Secondat Montesquieu, *The Spirit of the Laws* (New York, 1949 ed.); John Locke, *Two Treatises of Civil Government* (W. S. Carpenter edition, New York, 1924); Henry St. John, First Viscount Bolingbroke, *A Dissertation upon Parties* (London, 1744); J. R. Pole, *Political Representation in England and the Origins of the American Republic* (New York, 1966), 405–23 and *passim.* The quotation is from Merrill D. Peterson, *Adams and Jefferson: A Revolutionary Dialogue* (Athens, Ga., 1976), 100. The democratic branch in this scheme of things was not really democratic even in a representative sense, for members of the Commons were required to own large freehold estates, and only holders of real property were allowed to vote. Comparable property qualifications were established in the colonies. The reason for the property restrictions on voting, according to Blackstone, was to exclude persons of "so mean a situation that they are esteemed to have no will of their own." If the poor and dependent could vote, Blackstone explained, artful or wealthy men would have a larger influence in elections "than is consistent with general liberty." Another compelling consideration was the belief that, as the Methodist theologian John Wesley put it, "The greater the share the people have in government, the less liberty, civil or religious, does a nation enjoy." Statutes of England, 8 Henry VI, ch. 7, and 10 Henry VI, ch. 2; Pole, *Political Representation,* 25, 31, 397–98; Blackstone, *Commentaries,* 1:171–76; Chilton Williamson, *American Suffrage: From Property to Democracy, 1760–1860* (Princeton, 1960), 12–15.

4. The classical study of the subject is Charles H. McIlwaine, *The American Revolution: A Constitutional Interpretation* (New York, 1924). For contemporary statements of the American view, see John Dickinson, *Essay on the Constitutional Power of Great Britain over the Colonies in America* (Philadelphia, 1774) and James Wilson, *Considerations on the Nature and Extent of the Legislative Authority of the British Parliament* (Philadelphia, 1774). Blackstone's definition of sovereignty is in the *Commentaries,* 1:46–47, 49.

5. "The Farmer Refuted," in Syrett, ed., *Papers,* 1:98–99, 103 and note. The position that John Dickinson and the First Continental Congress held was in practice not different from Hamilton's; what was novel about Hamilton's argument was the theoretical notion of the Crown in a plurality of capacities.

6. Locke, *Two Treatises of Civil Government.* For an excellent analysis of Locke's influence in America, see Wills, *Inventing America,* 169–75.

7. "The Farmer Refuted," in Syrett, ed., *Papers,* 1:136. Hamilton's use of the term "municipal law" was based upon Blackstone's *Commentaries,* 1:44, wherein the term is defined as a "rule of civil conduct prescribed by the supreme power in a state, commanding what is right and prohibiting what is wrong"; it applies not merely to a *"municipium* or free town" but to "any one state or nation, which is governed by the same laws and customs."

Jefferson's tract was *A Summary View of the Rights of British America,* 1774, in

Notes

Julian P. Boyd, and others, eds., *The Papers of Thomas Jefferson* (19 vols. to 1791, Princeton, 1950–1974), 1:121—37; Adams's was the *Novanglus Essays*, 1775, in George A. Peek, Jr., ed., *The Political Writings of John Adams: Representative Selections* (New York, 1954), 29–79; Wilson's was *Considerations on the Nature and Extent of the Legislative Authority of the British Parliament*, 1774.

8. "A Full Vindication," in Syrett, ed., *Papers*, 1:47; "The Farmer Refuted," ibid., 1:100, 105.

9. Gouverneur Morris to Hamilton, May 16, 1777, Hamilton to Morris, May 19, 1777, ibid., 1:253–55. It should be noted that Hamilton qualified "the people" in "The Farmer Refuted" by quoting and endorsing Blackstone on the reasons for a limited suffrage. See ibid., 1:106 and note 3, above.

10. Hamilton to Jay, November 26, 1775, in Syrett, ed., *Papers*, 1:176–77.

11. "A Full Vindication" and "The Farmer Refuted," ibid., 68, 134–35, 151 note. Hamilton intended to write an essay examining "the justice and policy" of the Boston Tea Party (1:134 note) but never got around to doing so—which probably reflects his mixed feelings on the subject.

12. Hamilton to Jay, March 14, 1779, ibid., 2:17–19. Historians have sometimes asserted that Hamilton, despite his activities in behalf of emancipation, did personally own slaves, though his family stoutly denied it. John C. Miller, for instance, in *Alexander Hamilton and the Growth of the New Nation* (New York, 1964), 122 note, says that Hamilton "held slaves throughout his life." As authority for the statement, Miller cites Nathan Schachner, *Alexander Hamilton* (New York, 1946), 183. Schachner's documentation, in turn, consists of a single reference to a purchase of a slave woman and child by Hamilton on May 29, 1797. But that transaction, as the document clearly indicates (it is published in Syrett, ed., *Papers*, 21:110–11), was not a purchase Hamilton made in his own behalf, but only as agent and attorney for John B. Church.

The editors of the *Hamilton Papers*, in a footnote to a letter Hamilton wrote George Clinton on May 22, 1781 (2:643), say that "this sentence provides one of the few pieces of extant evidence that either H or his wife owned slaves." The sentence referred to reads, in full and with no explanatory context, "I expect by Col Hay's return to receive a sufficient sum to pay the value of the woman Mrs H had of Mrs. Clinton." That could conceivably be a reference to the purchase of a slave; but given Hamilton's limited means at the time, and given that the reference to Lt. Col. Udny Hay, deputy quartermaster general, could concern only Hamilton's back pay, much less than enough to buy a slave, it is far more likely that Betsey, in keeping with common practice at the time, had merely hired a servant employed by or belonging to Mrs. Clinton.

13. For Hamilton's gross misjudgment of the relative strengths and weaknesses of the two countries, see "The Farmer Refuted," ibid., 1:155–60.

14. Pay Book of the State Company of Artillery, 1777, ibid., 1:373–411. The quotes are at 391 and 390, respectively.

15. For full titles of the works of Beawes and Price and evidence that Hamilton had studied them, see Hamilton to Timothy Pickering, April 20, 1781, ibid., 2:595–96 and note. Hamilton demonstrably had read Smith's *Wealth of Nations* by 1790, but I believe it unlikely that he had read it before 1782. In "The Continentalist"

No. V (April 18, 1782), in Syrett, ed., *Papers*, 3:75–82, Hamilton argued against the Smithean idea that trade must regulate itself but cited only David Hume; I assume that if he had read *Wealth of Nations* he would have cited that work. It does seem likely that he had read Smith's *Theory of Moral Sentiments*. As for Hume, the quotations are from Hamilton's Western Lands Brief, 1786, in Julius Goebel, ed., *The Law Practice of Alexander Hamilton: Documents and Commentary* (2 vols. to date, New York, 1964, 1969), 1:616–17. Documentation of Hamilton's indebtedness to Hume follows in the text and notes below.

It is to be observed that one of Hume's major philosophical contributions lay in divorcing morality from a foundation in natural law—which, before Hume, had rested upon a presumed divine foundation—and placing it instead upon a foundation in utility. Hume was a doubter and Hamilton was a Christian, but Hamilton could readily accept the Humean point of view: precisely because Hamilton was a believer as well as a Humean, he was able to perceive that the Christian religion could be socially useful as well as true. See the discussion of Vattel in chapter three.

16. "The Farmer Refuted," in Syrett, ed., *Papers*, 1:94–95.

17. Thomas Hill Green and Thomas Hodge Grose, eds., *David Hume: The Philosophical Works* (4 vols., 1964 reprint of 1886 London edition), 3:117–22 (*Essays Moral, Political, and Literary*, vol. I, part I, essay VI, "On the Independency of Parliament.")

18. Ibid., 2:195, 214–15 (*A Treatise of Human Nature*, book II, "Of the Passions," part III, sections III and IX). Hamilton encountered variations of the theory of the passions in Pope's essays and doubtless in his other readings as well. He might, for instance, have read Rene Descartes' *Treatise on the Passions* (1659), though it seems unlikely that he would have wasted his time on such fanciful theorizing. Descartes believed that the passions were directly connected to parts of the body—that fear was connected with the legs, for example, which impelled one to flee from danger (Anthony, Earl of Shaftesbury, *Characteristics of Men, Manners, Opinions, Times* [Indianapolis, 1964 edition of the 1711 two-volume edition, ed. by John M. Robertson], 1:191). Apparently Hamilton did read Shaftesbury; see Pay Book, in Syrett, ed., *Papers*, 1:396.

It is often assumed or asserted—for example, by Mitchell, *Hamilton*, 1:385–87—that Hamilton was greatly influenced by Thomas Hobbes, whose work *The Leviathan* contains, among other things, a dissertation on the passions. Though Hamilton referred to Hobbes in "The Farmer Refuted," there is no evidence that he ever read him, and the misrepresentation of Hobbes's views in that early work suggests that he had not. Moreover, anyone familiar with both Hamilton and Hobbes must realize that the former did not have the temperament to wade through the work of the latter. Hobbes's influence upon Blackstone and Hume accounts for such resemblance as there is between their thinking.

Flexner, in *Young Hamilton*, 5 and elsewhere, uses the word "passion" in a modern sense, which gives a misleading impression.

19. Green and Grose, eds., *Hume's Works*, 2:264 (*Treatise of Human Nature*, book III, part II, section II); Adam Smith, *The Theory of Moral Sentiments* (reprint of the Dugald Stewart edition, New York, 1966), 80. An elegantly printed new edition of the latter work is the Liberty Classics edition, with introduction by E. G. West (Indi-

Notes

anapolis, 1976). For an example of Hamilton's use of the concept, see his speech in the Constitutional Convention on June 22, 1787, in Syrett, ed., *Papers*, 4:216–17.

20. Gerald Stourzh, *Alexander Hamilton and the Idea of Republican Government* (Stanford, 1970), 101; Douglass Adair, "Fame and the Founding Fathers," in Edmund P. Willis, ed., *Fame and The Founding Fathers* (Bethlehem, Pa., 1967), 35 note. See also Richard Wheeler Crosby, "Alexander Hamilton's Political Principles: Natural Rights, Democracy, and the Good Regime" (Ph.D. thesis, Cornell University, 1970). Regarding Pope, see note 1, chapter 1.

21. The quotations are from Hamilton's Pay Book, in Syrett, ed., *Papers*, 1:395–96, and from Hamilton to Laurens, January 8, September 12, 1780, ibid., 2:255, 428. Regarding Shaftesbury, see, for example, his *Characteristics*, 1:268–77.

22. This theme runs throughout Hamilton's essays entitled "The Continentalist," July 12, 19, August 9, 30, 1781, April 18, July 4, 1782, in Syrett, ed., *Papers*, 2:649–52, 654–57, 660–65, 669–74, 3:75–82, 99–106.

23. E. James Ferguson, *The Power of the Purse: A History of American Public Finance, 1776–1790* (Chapel Hill, 1961), 25–47.

24. Hamilton to _____, December 1779–March 1780, in Syrett, ed., *Papers*, 2:236–51. The editors, ibid., 2:234–36, give the history of efforts to determine precisely when this letter was written, and to whom. Miller, *Hamilton*, 52, argues that the addressee was Schuyler, and though there is no direct evidence to support that argument, I believe Schuyler is the only person who fits all the known indirect evidence.

25. Hamilton to Duane, September 3, 1780, in Syrett, ed., *Papers*, 2:400–418.

26. Worthington C. Ford and others, eds., *Journals of the Continental Congress, 1774–1789* (34 vols., Washington, 1904–1937), 19:102–3, 110, 112–13, 290–99, 432–33 (February, March 1781).

27. Hamilton to Robert Morris, April 30, 1781, in Syrett, ed., *Papers*, 2:604–35; Ferguson, *Power of the Purse*, 136.

28. Hamilton to Morris, April 30, 1781, to Laurens, September 12, 1780, in Syrett, ed., *Papers*, 2:629–30, 427.

29. Hamilton to Morris, April 30, 1781, ibid., 2:618, 619, 632, 635. On the mixture of good and evil, compare Shaftesbury, *Characteristics*, 1:257ff., 289ff. See also Alexander Pope's *Essay on Man*, Epistle II.

30. See note 22. Hamilton wrote two more essays in the series, published April 18 and July 4, 1782. These additional essays, in my judgment, are far more sophisticated than the first four and reflect the influence of Hamilton's legal studies.

31. "The Continentalist" No. II, July 19, 1781, in Syrett, ed., *Papers*, 2:654–55. Regarding the influence of Hume's moral philosophy, subtle indications pop up frequently in Hamilton's writing. In "The Continentalist" No. III, for instance, in this sentence: "But as these evils are at a little distance, we may perhaps be insensible and short sighted enough to disregard them" (ibid., 2:661). Hume, in his explorations of the human psyche, devotes a great deal of attention to the effects of distance and proximity upon the strength of impressions and judgments.

32. Morris to Hamilton, April 15, May 2, June 4, Hamilton to Morris, May 18, June 17, 1782, in Syrett, ed., *Papers*, 3:72–74, 86–87, 89–91, 93–94. New York's quota of continental requisitions for 1782 was set by Congress at $373,598; *Journals*

of Congress, 21:1089–91. The commission, at one-fourth of 1 percent, would have been $933.99. Hendrickson, *Hamilton I,* 360, misquotes Morris's letter of May 2, making it read "one fourth of the monies you receive" instead of "one fourth pr Cent on the monies you receive"; one fourth would have given Hamilton a fantastic commission in excess of $90,000. On the same page, Hendrickson says Morris was fifty-nine years old—he was forty-nine—and refers to New York as "one of the wealthiest states," which was far from the case.

33. Resolutions of the New York Legislature, July 20, 22, 1782, in Syrett, ed., *Papers,* 3:110–13, 117. The evidence for Hamilton's authorship of the resolutions is strong but not conclusive; ibid., 3:110 note.

34. Clarence L. Ver Steeg, *Robert Morris, Revolutionary Financier* (Philadelphia, 1954), 126; *Providence Gazette,* January 1782, to February 1783; Proceedings of the General Assembly, November 1782, in Rhode Island Archives, Providence; David Howell to Welcome Arnold, November 17, 1782, in Edmund C. Burnett, ed., *Letters of Members of the Continental Congress* (8 vols., Washington, 1921–1936), 6:542–43; Burnett, *Continental Congress,* 533; *Journals of Congress,* 23:769ff. (December 6, 1782). The following account is drawn largely, with corrections, from the more detailed version in Forrest McDonald, *E Pluribus Unum: The Formation of the American Republic, 1776–1790* (Boston, 1965), 17–32.

35. Ver Steeg, *Robert Morris,* 78–96, 105, 126–29; Ferguson, *Power of the Purse,* 117–24; *New York Packet,* October 24, 1782; Philadelphia *Pennsylvania Packet,* July 6, September 5, 24, 1782; Philadelphia *Independent Gazetteer,* September 14, 1782; Hamilton to the Public Creditors of the State of New York, September 30, 1782, in Syrett, ed., *Papers,* 3:171–77.

36. Ver Steeg, *Robert Morris,* 165; Washington to Hamilton, March 12, 1783, in Syrett, ed., *Papers,* 3:287.

37. Burnett, *Continental Congress,* 553ff.; Madison's minutes, January 6, 1783, in *Journals of Congress,* 25:846. One faction of officers thought that the states were a more likely source of payment; see Benjamin Lincoln to Henry Knox, December 3, and Knox to Lincoln, December 20, 1782, in Henry Knox Papers, Massachusetts Historical Society, Boston.

38. Hamilton to Clinton, January 12, 1783, to Washington, March 17, 25, 1783, in Syrett, ed., *Papers,* 3:240, 292–93, 306; Gouverneur Morris to John Jay, January 1, 1783, in Jared Sparks, ed., *Life of Gouverneur Morris* (3 vols., Boston, 1832), 1:249; Alexander McDougall to Knox, January 9, 1783, in Knox Papers, Massachusetts Historical Society; Charles Page Smith, *James Wilson: Founding Father, 1742–1798* (Chapel Hill, 1956), 179–83; Arthur Lee to Samuel Adams, January 29, 1783, in Burnett, ed., *Letters of Members of Congress,* 7:27–28, and to James Warren, February 19, 1783, in Massachusetts Historical Society, *Warren-Adams Letters, 1778–1814,* 2:190 (Boston, 1925); Ver Steeg, *Robert Morris,* 176.

39. Madison's minutes, January 24, 25, 28, 29, February throughout, 1783, in *Journals of Congress,* 25:862–66, 870–85; Hamilton to Washington, February 7, Madison to Edmund Randolph, February 13, 18, 25, Hugh Williamson to James Iredell, February 17, Arthur Lee to James Warren, February 19, 1783, all in Burnett, ed., *Letters of Members of Congress,* 7:33, 44, 46, 49, 51, 57; Burnett, *Continental Congress,* 556–61; Ver Steeg, *Robert Morris,* 170–71.

Notes

40. G. Morris to Knox, February 7, McDougall and Ogden to Knox, February 8, 1783, in Knox Papers, Massachusetts Historical Society; John Armstrong, Jr., to Horatio Gates, April 29, 1783, in Burnett, ed., *Letters of Members of Congress,* 7:155 note; G. Morris to Nathanael Greene, February 15, 1783, in Sparks, ed., *Gouverneur Morris,* 2:250–51; Hamilton to Washington, February 13, and Washington to Hamilton, March 4, 1783, in Syrett, ed., *Papers,* 3:254, 277; Ver Steeg, *Robert Morris,* 172.

41. Washington to Hamilton, March 4, 12, 1783, in Syrett, ed., *Papers,* 3:277, 286; list of security holders in *Pennsylvania Packet,* July 6, 1782. The two mutinous addresses are published in *Journals of Congress,* 24:294–98.

42. Washington to President of Congress, April 18, 1783, in John C. Fitzpatrick, ed., *Writings of George Washington* (39 vols., Washington, 1931–1944), 26:330–34; Burnett, *Continental Congress,* 563–66, 567–69; see also Hamilton to Washington, March 17, 25, and Hamilton's report in Congress, March 21, 1783, in Syrett, ed., *Papers,* 3:290, 301, 305, 307.

43. McDonald, *E Pluribus Unum,* 29–32. Hamilton voted against the final package but nonetheless urged Governor Clinton to support its ratification. Hamilton to Clinton, May 14, 1783, in Syrett, ed., *Papers,* 3:354–56.

44. "The Defence of the Funding System," July 1795, ibid., 19:41 and note.

III—Education in the Legal Arts

1. The first quotation is from "Publius Letter, III," November 16, 1778, in Syrett, ed., *Papers,* 1:581; the others are from Hamilton's Practice Manual (1782), manuscript pages 42, 49, 50, 119, 161, in Goebel, ed., *Law Practice,* 1:81, 83, 109, 128.

2. The quotation is from Blackstone, *Commentaries,* 1:44.

3. Goebel, ed., *Law Practice,* 1:47; Mitchell, *Hamilton,* 1:269. Philip was born January 22, 1782; Hamilton, *Intimate Life,* 210.

4. Goebel, ed., *Law Practice,* 1:47–48, and Mitchell, *Hamilton,* 1:269 take Hamilton's sprinkling of references to legal authorities to mean that he had studied more deeply in the law than I believe he actually had—as Hamilton no doubt intended his readers should. For the references, see "The Farmer Refuted," in Syrett, ed., *Papers,* 1:86, 87, 88, 91, 106, 108, 143, 144. To appreciate their superficiality, one must read the sources thoroughly and compare them with Hamilton's polemic.

5. Syrett, ed., *Papers,* 3:122, 189; Goebel, ed., *Law Practice,* 1:1–35, 47. Some time during the next year Hamilton qualified separately to practice before the court of chancery as both solicitor and counsel.

6. The contents of Duane's library are implicit in the references Hamilton made in his Practice Manual; Goebel, ed., *Law Practice,* 1:55–135. Regarding New York law and practice, see the editors' essay, "The Law and the Judicial Scene," ibid., 1:1–35.

7. Ibid., 1:37–54.

8. James Kent to Simeon Baldwin, July 18, 1786, ibid., 1:50.

9. Duane's decision in *Rutgers* v. *Waddington,* 1784, ibid., 1:401; Hamilton

cited all four authorities in his brief in the case, but drew most heavily upon Vattel. He never cited Wolff, who in fact influenced Vattel greatly; Wolff himself had drawn heavily on Leibnitz. That Hamilton had not read Vattel before 1782 is inferred from the fact that in none of the extant Hamilton documents, public or private, is Vattel mentioned before that date. The first references are in Hamilton's Practice Manual; they become frequent in his public writings thereafter.

10. There are many editions of Emmerich de Vattel, *The Law of Nations, or, Principles of the Law of Nature, Applied to the Conduct and Affairs of Nations and Sovereigns*; I have used the 1817 Philadelphia edition, which is reprinted from the last London edition, 1797. Since pagination varies, Vattel is customarily cited by book, chapter, and paragraph numbers; the quotation is from Preliminaries, para. 3, pp. xli–xlii of my edition.

11. Ibid., Preliminaries, para. 6n, pp. xliii–xliv. For an analysis of a different strain of the eighteenth-century preoccupation with happiness, see Wills, *Inventing America*, 149–64.

12. Ibid., book 1, ch. 4, "Of the Sovereign, his Obligations, and his Rights," paras. 38–55, pp. 12–23. Regarding the services of the Founding Fathers despite their personal weaknesses, see McDonald, *E Pluribus Unum, passim*. Hamilton's appeals to the better public side—the reason and virtue—of his contemporaries is repeatedly documented in the chapters that follow.

13. Vattel, *Law of Nations*, book 1, chs. 6, 8, 11, 14, 20, pp. 33–34, 37–40, 87, 109–16; "The Continentalist, No. V," April 18, 1782, in Syrett, ed., *Papers*, 3:76–77. Hamilton's reasoning in this essay is strikingly similar to Vattel's.

14. Vattel, *Law of Nations*, book 1, ch. 11, paras. 110–24, pp. 47–55. Regarding Hamilton's rearing of his children, see "Rules For Mr. Philip Hamilton," in Hamilton, *Intimate Life*, 215, and the following pages.

15. Vattel, *Law of Nations*, book 1, chs. 14–15, paras. 177–91, pp. 87–93.

16. Ibid., book 1, ch. 4, paras. 53–54, pp. 21–23, ch. 13, paras. 163–64, pp. 78–79; Hamilton's sixth brief in *Rutgers* v. *Waddington*, in Goebel, ed., *Law Practice*, 1:362–92. Coke's pronouncement was in Dr. Bonham's Case, wherein he expressly declared that if an act of Parliament contradicted the common law, "the common law will controul it and adjudge such act to be void" (*The Reports of Sir Edward Coke* [11 parts, London, 1658], 8:118a [1610]). Compare Blackstone, *Commentaries*, 1:242. Coke's abandonment of this position is documented by Louis B. Boudin in "Lord Coke and the American Doctrine of Judicial Power," *New York University Law Review*, 6:223 (March 1929). Hamilton cited Dr. Bonham's Case in his brief, along with many references to Vattel; Goebel, ed., *Law Practice*, 1:357, 358, 382. Regarding Montesquieu, see *Federalist*, number 78, in Syrett, ed., *Papers*, 4:657.

17. The myth of Blackstone's omnipotent influence in America has been carefully dissected by Dennis Nolan in "Sir William Blackstone and the New Republic: A Study of Intellectual Impact," *The Political Science Reviewer*, 6:283–324 (fall 1976). I believe that Stourzh, in his not unflawed but generally excellent study, *Hamilton and the Idea of Republican Government*, 9–36, misinterprets and overstates Blackstone's influence upon Hamilton. Even Broadus Mitchell, in his thorough and careful *Hamilton*, 1:268, describes Hamilton's legal education as consisting of "mainly Blackstone, surely."

Notes

18. Blackstone, *Commentaries*, 3:48, 248, 261, 413, 416, 421, xxxii; Goebel, ed., *Law Practice*, 1:72, 101–3 and notes.

19. Blackstone, *Commentaries*, 1:38–62 *passim*, 63–91 *passim* but especially pp. 41, 85, 89, 91, and 161–62, 4:67; "The Farmer Refuted," in Syrett, ed., *Papers*, 1:87. For a brilliant article on the subject of this paragraph see Paul Lucas, *"Ex Parte Sir William Blackstone, 'Plagarist': A Note on Blackstone and the Natural Law,"* in *The American Journal of Legal History*, 7:142–58 (1963).

20. Blackstone, *Commentaries*, 1:57–58, 70–71, 91.

21. For a felicitous introduction to Blackstone, see Daniel J. Boorstin's *The Mysterious Science of the Law: An Essay on Blackstone's COMMENTARIES . . .* (Cambridge, Mass., 1941). There is, however, no substitute for the original, though I would recommend that the interested reader skip the dull opening lecture, "On the Study of the Law."

22. Blackstone, *Commentaries*, 1:244–46.

23. Ibid., 1:62.

24. The quotations are ibid., 1:124 and 2:2. It should be observed that Blackstone used "absolute rights" to mean such internal rights as freedom of conscience, and "relative rights" to include all those in relation to other people.

25. Ibid., 1:125–26.

26. Hamilton's brief in *Rutgers* v. *Waddington*, in Goebel, ed., *Law Practice*, 1:374–78; "Letters of Phocion," January, April 1784, in Syrett, ed., *Papers*, 3:489, 544–45; Smith, *James Wilson*, 152. Hamilton's implicit argument for a division of sovereignty in "The Continentalist" No. II, July 19, 1781, is not nearly so convincing or sophisticated as in his "Letters of Phocion," which provide numerous examples of the influence of both Vattel and Blackstone.

27. Blackstone, *Commentaries*, 1:51; Hamilton's Draft of a Constitution, September 17, 1787, in Syrett, ed., *Papers*, 4:265–67; *Federalist* No. 78, May 28, 1788, ibid., 4:655–63.

28. Mitchell, *Hamilton*, 1:203, 333, 346–47.

29. Hamilton, *Intimate Life*, 198; Donald Roper, "Elite of the New York Bar as Seen from the Bench: James Kent's Necrologies," *New York Historical Society Quarterly*, 56:203 (July 1972); Troup to John Mason, March 22, 1810, in Schachner, ed., "Narratives," *William and Mary Quarterly*, 4:215–16. Troup, in his original document, rendered the word "propound" as "profound."

30. Goebel, ed., *Law Practice*, 1:3–5, and the documents contained throughout the volume.

31. Ibid., 1:3; see also the account of *Rutgers* v. *Waddington*.

32. *Laws of New York*, Third Session, Chapter 25 (October 22, 1779), and Sixth Session, Chapter 1 (July 12, 1782), and Sixth Session, Chapter 31 (March 17, 1783).

33. Ibid.; Goebel, ed., *Law Practice*, 1:200–202, 287, 297; Hamilton, John Laurance, Morgan Lewis, and Richard Varick to the President of Congress (Thomas Mifflin), December 10, 1783, in Syrett, ed., *Papers*, 3:478–79.

34. For sources on the facts of the case, see Goebel, ed., *Law Practice*, 1:289, note 17.

35. Ibid., 1:289–90 and Hamilton's Brief No. 1, pp. 338–39; Vattel, *Law of Nations*, book 2, ch. 7; book 3, ch. 9; and book 4, ch. 3.

36. Goebel, ed., *Law Practice,* 1:320–28; "Letters of Phocion," January, April 1784, in Syrett, ed., *Papers,* 3:483–97, 530–38.

37. The following account of the trial is based upon my own study of the extant documents of the case, as published in Goebel, ed., *Law Practice,* 1:317–31, 338–419, but I have followed fairly closely the editors' analysis of Hamilton's tactics, ibid., 1:298–306.

38. Ibid., 1:418.

39. The quotations are from "The Continentalist" I and II, in Syrett, ed., *Papers,* 2:649, 656. It has been charged that Hamilton advocated government by the "rich and well-born," but there is no substance to the charge. See Thomas P. Govan, "The Rich, the Well-born, and Alexander Hamilton," in *Mississippi Valley Historical Review,* 36:675–80 (March 1950).

IV—*Completion of an Education*

1. Hamilton to Washington, April 8, 1783, to Robert Morris, April 30, 1781, in Syrett, ed., *Papers,* 3:318, 321, and 2:605.

2. E. Wilder Spaulding, *His Excellency George Clinton, Critic of the Constitution* (New York, 1938), *passim;* Mitchell, *Hamilton,* 1:140; Alfred F. Young, *The Democratic Republicans of New York: The Origins, 1763–1797* (Chapel Hill, 1967), 29; Hamilton to Clinton, February 13, 1778, and Hamilton to Robert Morris, August 13, 1782, in Syrett, ed., *Papers,* 1:428, 3:137–38; see also the correspondence between Hamilton and Clinton throughout vols. 1–3 of Hamilton's *Papers.*

3. E. Wilder Spaulding, *New York in the Critical Period, 1783–1789* (New York, 1932), ch. 6; Young, *Democratic Republicans,* 66–67; A. C. Flick, *Loyalism in New York during the American Revolution* (New York, 1901).

4. Hamilton to Clinton, June 1, 1783, to Duane, August 5, 1783, and to Robert R. Livingston, August 13, 1783, in Syrett, ed., *Papers,* 3:367–72, 430, 431. The figure 35,000 is from Young, *Democratic Republicans,* 66; according to the report of the British Commissary General, as cited in Goebel, ed., *Law Practice,* 1:216, the number was 29,000.

5. For an excellent portrayal of Livingston that captures the spirit of the manor-lord aristocracy better than any other work I know, see George Dangerfield, *Chancellor Robert R. Livingston of New York, 1746–1813* (New York, 1960).

6. Regarding Hamilton's failure to comprehend the New York aristocracy—whereas all native New Yorkers did—see his remarks in the state's ratifying convention, June 21, 1788, in Syrett, ed., *Papers,* 5:41–42, and Dangerfield's perceptive analysis of those remarks in *Livingston,* 226–27.

7. Ibid., 177–79, 200; Livingston to Hamilton, August 30, 1783, in Syrett, ed., *Papers,* 3:434–35; Livingston to Jay, January 25, 1784, in Henry P. Johnston, ed., *The Correspondence and Public Papers of John Jay, 1763–1826* (4 vols., New York, 1890–1893), 3:108. Syrett, ed., *Papers,* 3:435 renders "tranquility" as "tranquilily."

Notes

8. Harry B. Yoshpe, *The Disposition of Loyalist Estates in the Southern District of the State of New York* (New York, 1939), *passim;* Dangerfield, *Livingston,* 200–201. Regarding Livingston's financial embarrassment, see Livingston to Hamilton, June 5, 1783, and Hamilton to Livingston, July 23, August 13, 1783, in Syrett, ed., *Papers,* 3:375, 414–15, 431–32.

9. Dangerfield, *Livingston,* 200–201; Young, *Democratic Republicans,* 30.

10. Dangerfield, *Livingston,* 201–3; Henry W. Domett, *A History of the Bank of New York, 1784–1884* (New York, 1884), 4–10; Hamilton to Church, March 10, 1784, in Syrett, ed., *Papers,* 3:520–23; *New York Packet,* February 12 and subsequent issues, 1784.

11. Church to Hamilton, February 7, 1784, Hamilton to Church, March 10, 1784, Church to Hamilton, May 2, June 15, 1784, in Syrett, ed., *Papers,* 3:507–8 and note, 520–23, 558–59, 565; John D. R. Platt, "Jeremiah Wadsworth: Federalist Entrepreneur" (Ph.D. thesis, Columbia University, 1955), 47–68.

12. McDonald, *E Pluribus Unum,* 42–43 and notes 15–19 cited therein. For an example of Hamilton's inquiries regarding the practical details of banking, see Hamilton to Gouverneur Morris, March 21, April 7, 1784, in Syrett, ed., *Papers,* 3:523–24, 529.

13. Dangerfield, *Livingston,* 215.

14. Hamilton to Robert Livingston, Jr., April 25, 1785, in Syrett, ed., *Papers,* 3:608–9. The New Englanders to whom Hamilton specifically referred were Matthew Adgate and Jacob Ford (mistakenly identified by Syrett as Matthew Ford and Jacob Adgate); he said they made "tools of the Yates" faction in the legislature and "now governed" the state. He was quite wrong on both counts—whether inadvertently or deliberately, it is impossible to say. A comparison of the votes of Adgate and Ford with other legislators, as recorded in *Journal of the Assembly of the State of New York,* January 1785, Session, reveals that (1) they were in the minority a large percentage of the time and (2) they did not vote consistently on the same side as the three members of the Yates family in the Assembly. Incidentally, Syrett mistakenly identifies the members to whom Hamilton refers as Abraham and Robert Yates. Neither of these men was in the legislature; Christopher Yates, C. P. Yates, and Peter W. Yates were.

15. Robert Livingston, Jr., to Hamilton, June 13, 1785, in Syrett, ed., *Papers,* 3:614–16. Regarding the chancellor's vindictiveness toward Duane, see Dangerfield, *Livingston,* 217–18; his growing coolness toward Jay—who had married the daughter of Hamilton's early sponsor William Livingston, younger brother of the manor lord—is described at pages 237–41.

16. McDonald, *E Pluribus Unum,* 43–47; John Chaloner to Jeremiah Wadsworth, February 14, 1784, in Wadsworth Papers, Connecticut Historical Society; Gouverneur Morris to Hamilton, January 27, 1784, and Chaloner to Hamilton, February 12, 1784, in Syrett, ed., *Papers,* 3:498–503, 509–10; Philadelphia *Pennsylvania Packet,* June 17, July 31, August 7, 1783, January–February 1784.

17. Ver Steeg, *Robert Morris,* 193; Chaloner to Hamilton, March 25, 1784, William Seton to Hamilton, March 27, 1784, and Chaloner to Hamilton, May 26, 1784, in Syrett, ed., *Papers,* 3:524–25, 526–27, 561–62; Chaloner to Church and Wadsworth, March 25, 1784, in Wadsworth Papers; *Minutes of the General Assem-*

bly of Pennsylvania (published in Philadelphia by sessions, 1781–1790), March 31, April 1, 1784; Philadelphia *Pennsylvania Journal,* May 15, 19, 1784; *Pennsylvania Packet,* May 20, 1784.

18. *Pennsylvania Packet,* October 6, 9, 13, 1784, March 2, 12, 29, 31, April 1, 1785; *Freeman's Journal,* January 19, February 2, 9, March 2, 1785; *Pennsylvania Journal,* February 19, 23, 1785; Philadelphia *Evening Herald,* September 7, 1785; *Minutes of the General Assembly of Pennsylvania,* December 4, 24, 1784, February 3, 1785; James T. Mitchell and Henry Flanders, comps., *The Statutes at Large of Pennsylvania from 1682 to 1801* (17 vols., Harrisburg, 1896–1908), 11:454–86, 560–72; McDonald, *E Pluribus Unum,* 49–51.

19. *Evening Herald,* March 8, 1785, April 5, May 6, 1786; *Pennsylvania Packet,* March 31, April 1, 1785; and the manuscript volumes entitled New Loan Certificates, in the Public Records Division of the Pennsylvania Historical and Museum Commission, Harrisburg.

20. *Pennsylvania Packet,* February 3, 1784; *Evening Herald,* May 3, 1786; Pieter Johan Van Berckel to Thomas Willing, in Stockholders Minutes, Bank of North America, January 9, 1786, in Historical Society of Pennsylvania; Hamilton to Wadsworth, October 29, 1785, in Syrett, ed., *Papers,* 3:625–27. The Journal of the Council of Censors, vol. 2, August 27, 1784, in Public Records Division, Pennsylvania Historical and Museum Commission, contains the ruling referred to in the text. It concerned the constitutionality of the University of Pennsylvania Act of 1779; the council gave a clear and carefully reasoned explication of the principle that popular assemblies can revoke charters at will. James Wilson argued the contrary in *Considerations on the Bank of North America,* a pamphlet published in summer 1785, but the Council of Censors more nearly represented the attitude of the Pennsylvania courts.

21. McDonald, *E Pluribus Unum,* 53–55; Wadsworth to Hamilton, November 11, 1785, in Syrett, ed., *Papers,* 3:633–34.

22. Ibid.; Platt, "Jeremiah Wadsworth," 152, note 2.

23. Van Berckel, Edgar, Fleming, Denning, and Hamilton to Wadsworth, January 3, 1786, Wadsworth to Hamilton, January 9, 1786, in Syrett, ed., *Papers,* 3:643–46; Willing to Wilson, June 10, 1784, and Wilson to Willing, July 29, 1784, in Minutes and Letter Book of the Bank of North America, and Stockholders Minutes, January 9, 1786, in Historical Society of Pennsylvania.

24. Jacques Necker, *A Treatise on the Administration of the Finances of France* (translated by Thomas Mortimer, 3 vols., London, 1785); the quotation is at 1:cxlvi–cxlvii. Since the work was published late in 1785 and Hamilton was familiar enough with it to cite it in February 1787 and to paraphrase it in June, his reading of the work clearly took place while the events described in the narrative here were happening. Necker's influence upon Hamilton has been underrated by historians. Hamilton frequently referred to Necker (e.g., as "a great and good man," to Lafayette, October 6, 1789; as "the celebrated Mr. Neckar," in the New York Assembly, February 17, 1787; and as "the able Minister," in his Report on the Mint, January 28, 1791; Syrett, ed., *Papers,* 5:425, 4:95, 7:593). The editors of the *Hamilton Papers* cite three instances in Hamilton's Report on the Public Credit, January 9, 1790, in which Hamilton's thinking parallels Necker's (ibid., 6:66, 71, 76–77); and there are others. In

Notes

regard to Hamilton's Report on Manufactures, December 5, 1791, which in my judgment is the capstone to his entire program, those editors say that a study of the report "clearly reveals the influence of Jacques Necker on Hamilton's thinking. . . . It is difficult to overlook the fact that the general conclusions of the Report are closer to those of Necker than to those of [Adam] Smith" (ibid., 10:8–9). The general influences, I believe, were even more profound, as will be visible to students of Hamilton who read Necker thoroughly and carefully.

25. Adair, "Fame and the founding Fathers," 38–39, 42, 45 note.

26. Stourzh, *Hamilton and the Idea of Republican Government*, 99; Syrett, ed., *Papers*, 4:613, 21:78.

27. Dugald Stewart's introduction to Smith, *Theory of Moral Sentiments*, xxxix; Douglass Adair, "A Note on Certain of Alexander Hamilton's Pseudonyms," in *William and Mary Quarterly*, 12:284, 285 (April 1955). Adair's article, however, contains some important misstatements about Hamilton, which are corrected in Thomas P. Govan, "Alexander Hamilton and Julius Caesar: A Note on the Use of Historical Evidence," in *William and Mary Quarterly*, 32:475–80 (July 1975).

28. Adair, "Hamilton's Pseudonyms," 283; Syrett, ed., *Papers*, 1:580, 4:613.

29. Green and Grose, eds., *Hume's Works*, 3:493 (*Essays Moral, Political, and Literary*, vol. I, part II, essay XVI).

30. Burnett, *Continental Congress*, 540–46; Spaulding, *George Clinton*, 142–48; *Journal of the Assembly*, March 2, April 22, October 18, 1784, and Clinton's messages to the legislature, recorded therein, January 21, October 18, 1784, January 18, 1786; Clinton to Ezra L'Hommedieu, August 23, 1783, Hamilton to Clinton, October 3, 1783, Hamilton to Robert Livingston, Jr., April 25, 1785, and Hamilton to William Duer, May 14, 1785, in Syrett, ed., *Papers*, 3:436 note, 464–69, 608–9, 610–11; Summary Report of the Committee on the Treasury, January 16, 1788, published in the *New York Journal*, January 31, 1788. Information regarding New York's commerce is from commodity prices as quoted in the New York *Daily Advertiser* throughout 1785 and from my tabulations of ship movements, 1784–1790, as recorded in New York newspapers and the *London Daily Universal Register*. See also Samuel Duff McCoy, "The Port of New York (1783–1789): Lost Island of Sailing Ships," in *New York History*, 17:379–90 (October 1936), and Newburyport *Essex Journal and New Hampshire Packet*, February 21, 1789.

31. The legislative program can be traced in *Laws of the State of New York Passed at the Sessions of the Legislature* (3 vols., Albany, 1886–1887), vol. 2.

32. The act is chapter 40 of the Acts of 1786, ibid., 2:253ff.

33. *New York Journal*, January 31, 1788; *Daily Advertiser*, March 31, 1787, February 2, 5, May 5, 1788; *New York Packet*, February 16, March 13, 1786; and see especially "Gustavus" in *New York Packet*, April 13, 1786, and the remarks of Assemblyman John Taylor as quoted in the *Daily Advertiser*, March 22, 1787.

34. McDonald, *E Pluribus Unum*, 61 and note 56, p. 256.

35. *Journal of the Assembly*, April 13, 1786, and the sources cited in note 33, above.

36. For Rhode Island's actions, see Forrest McDonald, *We The People: The Economic Origins of the Constitution* (Chicago, 1958), 326–38; for those of Maryland, Virginia, and North Carolina, see Ferguson, *Power of the Purse*, 182, 230, 233; and

for Virginia and North Carolina see also the manuscript by James Morrill, cited in chapter one, note 36.

37. *New York Packet,* April 17, May 1, 1786; *Journal of the Assembly,* April 20, 1786; Hamilton's commission dated May 5, 1786, in Syrett, ed., *Papers,* 3:665–66. That Troup, Duer, and Schuyler engineered Hamilton's appointment is inferred.

38. McDonald, *E Pluribus Unum,* 139–41 and the sources cited thereto.

39. Hamilton to Elizabeth Hamilton, September 8, 1786, Thomas Cushing and others to Hamilton and Benson, September 10, 1786, "Annapolis Convention. Address of the Annapolis Convention," September 14, 1786, in Syrett, ed., *Papers,* 3:684, 685, 686–90; Thomas A. Emmet, *Annapolis Convention held in 1786 with the Report of the Proceedings Represented to the States by President John Dickinson* (New York, 1891).

40. Necker, *Finances of France,* 1:cxxiv; Rufus King to James Bowdoin, September 17, King to John Adams, October 2, James Monroe to Madison, October 2, and Henry Lee to St. George Tucker, October 20, 1786, in Burnett, ed., *Letters of Members of Congress,* 8:468–69, 475–76, 489–90; *Journals of Congress,* September 20, 1786; Burnett, *Continental Congress,* 668–71, 673.

41. The legislature had, in 1786, commissioned Richard Varick and Samuel Jones to revise the state's statutes; *Laws of New York,* 1786, chapter 35. For Hamilton's contributions to the enactment of the revised laws, see *Journal of the Assembly,* January Session, 1787, and his various "Remarks" in the assembly, as reported in Syrett, ed., *Papers,* vol. 4.

42. *Journal of the Assembly,* February 15, 17, 18, 22, 1786; *Journal of the Senate of the State of New York,* March 29, 1786; *Daily Advertiser,* February 27, 1787.

43. Speech of February 15, 1787, in Syrett, ed., *Papers,* 4:71–92; see also "Leo" in *Daily Advertiser,* February 27, 1787. Rhode Island's paper money had not yet reached the full extent of its depreciation when Hamilton gave his speech.

44. Ibid., February 26, 27, 1787; *Journal of the Assembly,* February 15, 1787. The quotation is from Thomas C. Cochran, *New York in the Confederation: An Economic Study* (Philadelphia, 1932).

45. McDonald, *E Pluribus Unum,* 145–54, and the sources cited thereto.

46. *Journal of the Assembly,* March 6, April 16, 1787; *Daily Advertiser,* March 8, 1787; *Journal of the Senate,* April 18, 1787.

V—*Constitutional Revolution*

1. For an excellent analysis of Hume's thinking in these matters, see Duncan Forbes, *Hume's Philosophical Politics* (Cambridge, England, 1975), 66ff., 83ff., 311ff., and *passim.* The quotation is from Green and Grose, eds., *Hume's Works,* 3:456 (*Essays,* vol. I, part II, essay XII). For examples of Hamilton's adherence to the first of these Humean propositions, see Syrett, ed., *Papers,* 4:276, 554. Regarding the second, see Hamilton's speeches of June 18 and June 26, 1787, where he argues that distinctions between the rich and the poor arise "in every community where industry is encouraged"—not simply "every community"—and where there is liberty (ibid.,

Notes

4:192, 218). Regarding the third, see the enumeration of sources of allegience in his June 18 speech, none of which is a contractual obligation (ibid., 4:188–89).

2. Max Farrand, ed., *Records of the Federal Convention of 1787* (4 vols., New Haven, 1937), 1:147; Syrett, ed., *Papers*, 4:191, 221. Compare Vattel, *Law of Nations*, book 1, chs. 6, 8, 11, 14, pp. 33–34, 37–40, 47, 87.

3. James Steuart, *An Inquiry into the Principles of Political Oeconomy* (2 vols., London, 1767), 1:504; for evidence that Hamilton read and was influenced by Steuart, see Syrett, ed., *Papers*, 7:462–63. For Hamilton's remarks, see his speech of June 26, 1787, ibid., 4:218. See also Gottfried Dietze, "Hamilton's Concept of Free Government," in *New York History*, 38:351–67 (October 1957).

4. Speech of June 22, 1787, in Syrett, ed., *Papers*, 4:216–17 and note (Yates's minutes); speech of June 26, 1787, ibid., 4:218–19; Green and Grose, eds., *Hume's Works*, 3:120–21 (*Essays*, vol. I, part I, essay VI). The idea in the last sentence in this paragraph is developed at length in chapters 6–10.

5. Syrett, ed., *Papers*, 4:184, 216–17, 276. See also *Federalist* number 68, ibid., 4:589.

6. There are several versions, or notes or scraps of versions, of Hamilton's June 18 speech, including his own notes on which the speech was based and the abridgments of it recorded by four listeners, Madison, Robert Yates, John Lansing, and Rufus King. Scholars have uniformly based their analyses mainly upon Madison, who is ordinarily the most reliable reporter of the debates in the convention. In this instance, however, primary reliance upon Madison is in my judgment unsound; Madison not only missed some points, in at least one instance he garbled Hamilton's argument (see note 12). Moreover, Hamilton's observations are considerably amplified by comments he made in the *Federalist* papers, numbers 6, 15, 16, 17, 22, 27. The following analysis is guided by Hamilton's notes, tempered by the notes of the witnesses, and informed by further reference to the *Federalist* papers. The reference to Hume in the above paragraph, incidentally, is to be found in *Federalist* number 85.

7. Farrand, ed., *Records of the Federal Convention*, 1:145.

8. Ibid., 1:81–85, 146 (June 2, 6, 1787).

9. Speech of June 26, 1787, and Hamilton to Washington, July 3, 1787, in Syrett, ed., *Papers*, 4:218, 224. I have quoted these remarks in reverse order. Both seem to me to be explanations of Hamilton's reasons for his behavior at this stage of the convention.

10. The quotation is from Hamilton's notes, ibid., 4:179. Hamilton elaborated and explained his position in regard to the states in remarks the next day, ibid., 4:211 and note (Madison's and Yates's notes).

11. Ibid., 4:180–81 (Hamilton's notes). Though Hamilton's analysis is his own, it bears a considerable resemblance to Hume's. See Green and Grose, eds., *Hume's Works*, 2:313–28 (*A Treatise of Human Nature*, book III, part II, sections IX and X) and 3:109–13 (*Essays*, vol. I, part I, essay IV). In his outline Hamilton had another category, "Necessity," which he listed third, but in his speech this was apparently subsumed under his second category, "Opinion of Utility & necessity."

12. Syrett, ed., *Papers*, 4:180 (Hamilton's notes), 188–89 (Madison's), 197 (Yates's), 202–3 (Lansing's). Madison garbled his account a bit at this point. He

placed the figure "2" before the words "the love of power," indicating that that was Hamilton's second principle; Hamilton's own notes and the logic of the argument make it clear that "the love of power" was part of his first category. Madison's notes make sense if the figure "2" is dropped down five sentences, to the sentence beginning "It may be remarked."

13. Ibid., 4:180 (Hamilton), 189 (Madison).

14. Ibid., 4:180 (Hamilton), 189 (Madison). For a fuller exposition of this point, see Hamilton's remarks in the New York Assembly, February 15, 1787, ibid., 4:82–83.

15. Ibid., 4:189 (Madison), 205–6 (King). For Hamilton's fuller development of the point, see *Federalist* number 15, especially ibid., at 359–62.

16. Ibid., 4:189 (Madison), 197 (Yates). Interestingly, Hume also had put in a demurrer to his comment, much in the language that Hamilton employed; Green and Grose, eds., *Hume's Works,* 3:121 note (*Essays,* vol. I, part I, essay VI).

17. Syrett, ed., *Papers,* 4:192–93 (Madison). For the use of the term "imbecility," see Hamilton's speech in the New York Assembly, February 15, 1787, ibid., 4:82; it occurs again in several of the *Federalist* papers. During this phase of his speech, Hamilton cited Necker's remark that the British system was the only one "which unites public strength with individual security" (ibid., 4:192). The original is in Necker, *Finances of France,* 1:60.

18. The quotation is in Syrett, ed., *Papers,* 4:194 (Madison); the essential point of the paragraph is developed below. The nonideological character of Hamilton's proposals are made abundantly clear if they are read in conjunction with his essays in *The Federalist.*

19. Syrett, ed., *Papers,* 4:185 (Hamilton), 192 (Madison).

20. Hamilton offered a rough outline of a proposed constitution along with his June 18 speech; at the end of the convention he gave Madison a more detailed version of what he would have considered ideal. The property qualification regarding the Senate is in the second version. Regarding his efforts to make the House more democratic, see the manhood suffrage feature in his speech of September 8, 1787, ibid., 4:244, and in his Draft of a Constitution, September 17, 1787, ibid., 4:254.

21. Ibid., 4:208. In the second version (p. 259) Hamilton included a large property qualification for electors. For a clearer understanding of Hamilton's conception of the executive branch, see *The Federalist,* numbers 69–77.

22. Ibid., 4:193–94.

23. The Johnson quotation is from Yates's notes, in Farrand, ed., *Records of the Federal Convention,* 1:363. The proceedings after Hamilton's speech can be traced in that volume, *passim.* My own version of the politics of the compromise on representation is in *E Pluribus Unum,* 162–73.

24. Syrett, ed., *Papers,* 4:223–34, *passim.* Regarding Lansing's and Yates's misrepresentations, see Govan, "The Rich, the Well-born, and Alexander Hamilton," in *Mississippi Valley Historical Review,* 36:675–80.

25. Hamilton to King, August 20, 28, 1787, in Syrett, ed., *Papers,* 4:235, 238.

26. Ibid., 4:243–48; the quotation is at 253.

27. Farrand, ed., *Records of the Federal Convention,* 2:645. See also Morris to W. H. Wells, February 24, 1815, ibid., 3:421–22.

Notes

28. The bibliography of commentary upon *The Federalist* is enormous. The best of the studies that are relevant here include Alpheus Thomas Mason's "The Federalist—A Split Personality," in *American Historical Review*, 57:625–43 (April 1952); Maynard Smith, "Reason, Passion, and Political Freedom in *The Federalist*," in *The Journal of Politics*, 22:525–44 (August 1960); and Gottfried Dietze, "Hamilton's Federalist—Treatise for Free Government," in *Cornell Law Quarterly*, 42:307–28, 501–18 (spring and summer 1957).

29. The authorship of several of the numbers was in dispute for many years; for a history of the controversy, see the Introductory Note in Syrett, ed., *Papers*, 4:287–301. The most important single work of scholarship in resolving the dispute was Edward Gaylord Bourne's "The Authorship of the Federalist," in *American Historical Review*, 2:443–60 (April 1897); see also the exchange between Bourne and Paul Leicester Ford in the July 1897 issue, pp. 675–87. More or less the definitive word on the subject was Douglass Adair's "The Authorship of the Disputed Federalist Papers," in *William and Mary Quarterly*, 1:97–122, 235–64 (April and July 1944). See also Frederick Mosteller and David L. Wallace, *Inference and Disputed Authorship: The Federalist* (Reading, Mass., 1964), a quantitative analysis that confirms Adair's analysis except for concluding that number 55 could have been Hamilton's. I have followed Adair with one partial exception and one definite exception. I have assigned numbers 18–20 to Madison, whereas they were in a sense co-authored: Hamilton planned and perhaps composed a rough draft of them, but when he learned that Madison had done extensive research on the subject he turned his manuscript over to Madison to revise or, more probably, write anew.

My one total difference with the Bourne-Adair assignments is in regard to number 63: they assign the essay to Madison, but I believe it virtually certain that Hamilton wrote it. Bourne's case (which Adair regards as conclusive) rests exclusively upon internal evidence, upon a comparison of quotations from number 63 against other of Madison's writings. As Ford said in his critique of Bourne's article, that method can be challenged on the ground that enough ideas were common currency that in some instances it would be possible to "prove," by such "internal evidence," that an anti-Federalist had written the disputed *Federalist* papers. More specifically, Bourne's "evidence" is not only unconvincing, it is misused. (1) Bourne quotes an early passage in number 63, concerning "a sense of national character," and sets it against an extract from Madison's notes concerning motives restraining a majority from injustice, as follows: "Secondly. Respect for character. However strong this motive may be in individuals, it is considered as very insufficient to restrain them from injustice." Clearly, Madison is talking about a different thing from "national character"—which was not often a major preoccupation with him and was always a preoccupation with Hamilton, and had to do with such things as the reputation, honor, and glory of the nation. (2) Bourne quotes the reference in number 63 to essay number 10, and cites Madison on the same subject in number 10. But the remainder of the paragraph in 63 is a demurrer or qualification to the generalizations made in 10; as was indicated in the text above, Hamilton had definite reservations about Madison's theory as expressed in number 10. (3) Bourne quotes from number 63 the very Hamiltonian sentiment that "liberty may be endangered by the abuses of liberty, as well as by the abuses of power," and that the former are more dangerous in the

United States than the latter. This is not a Madisonian sentiment; Bourne sets against it a quotation from a letter Madison later wrote to Mazzei, regarding the extent of liberty that is compatible with the purposes of society. That is quite a different thing. (4) The remaining comparative quotations are minor historical references that were available to both Madison and Hamilton; and the uses of them in 63 and in Bourne's quotations from Madison are sometimes subtly different. (5) It is argued in number 63 that the smaller the representative body the more responsible and better suited it is for public trust; this is a Hamiltonian sentiment and is directly contrary to what Madison says in number 55, in Syrett, ed., *Papers*, 4:516. (6) The whole tone as well as the style of this essay is Hamiltonian in that it argues for the safety of lodging powers in an aristocratic body and for the desirability of appearing to foreigners to have a "wise and honorable policy."

30. For the most part, the following analysis is supported by that of Alpheus T. Mason, cited in note 28, but it rests upon its own merits and its own documentation. Mason does not call attention to the differences between Hamilton's and Madison's conceptions of federalism and republicanism, as delineated in the two following paragraphs.

31. Madison's analysis of federalism as described here is in number 39, as published in the Modern Library Edition of *The Federalist* (New York, 1937), 245–50. Hamilton's views are most clearly set forth in his Opinion on the Constitutionality of the Bank, 1791, in Syrett, ed., *Papers*, 8:98—though, as indicated, he had expressed that position earlier, in his 1784 "Phocian" essays.

32. The quotation is from Hamilton to Edward Carrington, May 26, 1792, ibid., 11:443; see also Hamilton's remark in the Constitutional Convention at note 18. For Madison's definition of a republic, see *The Federalist*, 59, 243 (numbers 10, 39).

33. The quotations are ibid., 339, 299, and Syrett, ed., *Papers*, 4:702 (numbers 51, 45, and 83), and 19:9. Madison's best essays, in my judgment, are numbers 10, 51, and 52; Hamilton's best are those on the executive and the judiciary, plus 25, 35, 36, and 84.

34. The references to Madison's statements in this paragraph are from *The Federalist*, 303, 292–94, 268, and 295, in that order; references to Hamilton's are from Syrett, ed., *Papers*, 4:415, 465–68, 412, 417, 476, and 655–63, in that order.

35. *The Federalist*, 337 (number 51), 361 (number 55); Farrand, ed., *Records of the Federal Convention*, 1:584.

36. Syrett, ed., *Papers*, 4:614, 562, 634 (numbers 72, 63, 76); and Hamilton's speech in the New York ratifying convention, June 27, 1788, ibid., 5:95. There is a typographical error (a "the" for a "to") in the *Hamilton Papers* at 4:614; see *The Federalist*, 471. Compare Hamilton's thinking as summarized here with Hume's in Green and Grose, eds., *Hume's Works*, 2:315 (*Treatise of Human Nature*, vol. II, book III, part II, section IX).

37. The conjecture is based upon some hard evidence and is relevant to the future relations between the two men. Hamilton's self-confidence should be abundantly clear by now. Madison's lack of it, despite his great abilities, was based upon the fact that he was an epileptic—or, more properly, was a victim of epileptiform hysteria. For evidence of the malady, see Irving Brant, *James Madison* (6 vols., Indianapolis, 1941–1961), and Ralph L. Ketcham, *James Madison: A Biography* (New

York, 1971). For an appraisal of the effects of the malady on Madison's makeup, see Forrest McDonald, *The Presidency of George Washington* (Lawrence, Kansas, 1974), 80–81.

38. Third Speech of June 28, 1788, in Syrett, ed., *Papers*, 5:125.

39. For Hamilton's analysis, see "Conjectures about the New Constitution," September 17–30, 1787, ibid., 4:275–77. He included noneconomic as well as economic considerations in his forecast. For a historical analysis of the economics of ratification, see McDonald, *We The People*, 111–399.

40. On Hamilton's role in framing the rules, see the debates of September 10 in Farrand, ed., *Records of the Federal Convention*, 2:559–63. The convention had decided earlier that ratification should be by the conventions of nine states; added, at the suggestion of Hamilton and others, was a procedure that obtained the consent of both Congress and the state legislatures and thus added legitimacy to the innovation.

41. For a fuller account of ratification, see McDonald, *E Pluribus Unum*, 209–35, and for details of Hamilton's role in it see Mitchell, *Hamilton*, 1:414–65.

VI—Hamiltonianism

1. The quotations are from Henry S. Commager, *The Empire of Reason: How Europe Imagined and America Realized the Enlightenment* (Garden City, N.Y., 1977), 114, 122.

2. The authoritative work on the franchise is Williamson, *American Suffrage: From Property to Democracy;* but see also Pole, *Political Representation.* The estimate of the vote on the Constitution is my own and is based upon tabulation of all the known returns as reported in newspapers and upon estimates and extrapolations where the vote is not known.

3. These observations are based upon study of the several state constitutions, as published in Francis Newton Thorpe, comp., *The Federal and State Constitutions, Colonial Charters, and Other Organic Laws* (7 vols., Washington, 1909).

4. There is no adequate general study of the local oligarchies, but the flavor may be sampled in such works as Jackson Turner Main, *The Social Structure of Revolutionary America* (Princeton, 1965); Richard J. Purcell, *Connecticut in Transition, 1775–1818* (Washington, 1918); Walter R. Fee, *The Transition from Aristocracy to Democracy in New Jersey, 1789–1829* (Somerville, N.J., 1933); Charles Sydnor, *Gentlemen Freeholders: Political Practices in Washington's Virginia* (Chapel Hill, 1952); Dangerfield, *Livingston;* Leonard Woods Labaree, *Conservatism in Early American History* (Ithaca, N.Y., 1948); and William Cullen Dennis II, "A Federalist Persuasion: The American Ideal of the Connecticut Federalists" (Ph.D. thesis, Yale, 1971). See also the perceptive chapters, "Anti-Virginia and Antislavery" and "Images of the Social Order" in Linda K. Kerber, *Federalists in Dissent: Imagery and Ideology in Jeffersonian America* (Ithaca, N.Y., 1970), 23–66, 173–215. Regarding the Virginians, see Jackson T. Main, "The One Hundred," in *William and Mary Quarterly*, 11:354–84 (July 1954) and compare the names in Main's lists with those in Labaree, *Conservatism*, 6–10.

5. The bibliography on American attitudes toward land is huge; for a discussion of the ideology that accompanied it, see chapter ten. Regarding the land laws, see Lawrence M. Friedman, *A History of American Law* (New York, 1973), 51–57, 202–17. Regarding the distribution of landholding, see Main, *Social Structure, passim,* and the same author's "The Distribution of Property in Post-Revolutionary Virginia," in *Mississippi Valley Historical Review,* 41:241–58 (September 1954). My generalizations on the subject, however, are derived from my own study of the extant manuscript tax records of the period.

6. Regarding confiscated property see, for example, Yoshpe, *Disposition of Loyalist Estates;* regarding mortgage law, see Robert H. Skilton, "Developments in Mortgage Law and Practice," in *Temple Law Quarterly,* 17:315–84 (August 1943); for the South Carolina legislation of 1786, see McDonald, *We The People,* 206–12.

7. Morton J. Horwitz, *The Transformation of American Law, 1780–1860* (Cambridge, Mass., and London, England, 1977), 160–81. The English quotation is from John Powell's *Essay upon the Laws of Contracts and Agreements,* 1790, as cited by Horwitz, 160. The Henry quotation is from Jackson Turner Main, *The Antifederalists: Critics of the Constitution, 1781–1788* (Chapel Hill, 1961), 166.

8. For the Rutledge episode, see Charleston *Gazette of the State of South Carolina,* April 1, 29, 1784; for the Madison episode, see Brant, *Madison,* 3:233–34; for the Adams quotation, see Wills, *Inventing America,* 35; for the episode in New York, see Young, *Democratic Republicans,* 476–77; for the Fisher Ames quotation, see Seth Ames, ed., *Works of Fisher Ames. With a Selection from His Speeches and Correspondence* (2 vols., Boston, 1854), 1:103. Young gives the misleading impression that Hamilton was sympathetic to the alderman and contemptuous of the Irishmen; for corrective information, see Hamilton to Rufus King, May 4, 1796, and editor's note to Certificate on Robert Lenox, January 11, 1796, in Syrett, ed., *Papers,* 20:35–36, 158.

9. The quotation is from Hamilton to Robert Morris, April 30, 1781, ibid., 2:635. Hamilton's mature writings are riddled with remarks which confirm that his perception of American society was along the lines roughly sketched here and that he proposed to change that society in a fundamental way. For example, in the excise law he proposed in 1789, he suggested that the preamble justify taxing liquor "as well to discourage the excessive use of those Spirits, and promote Agriculture, as to provide for the support of the Public Credit, and for the Common Defence and General Welfare." In his 1790 Report on the Bank he offered as a major advantage of augmenting the supply of currency that doing so "generates employment" and "animates and expands labor and industry." In his 1791 Report on Manufactures, virtually a frontal attack on the agrarian ideal, he came closest to stating the implications of his whole program—as, for instance, when he said that "to cherish and stimulate the activity of the human mind, by multiplying the objects of enterprise, is not among the least considerable of the expedients, by which the wealth of a nation may be promoted. Even things in themselves not positively advantageous, sometimes become so, by their tendency to provoke exertion. Every new scene, which is opened to the busy nature of man to rouse and exert itself, is the addition of a new energy to the general stock of effort (ibid., 6:138, 7:317, 10:256). As for the last sentence in the paragraph, see the responses to the inquiries Hamilton sent in regard to the preparation of his Report on

Notes

Manufactures, ibid., vol. 9, *passim.* Regarding the Scotch-Irish herdsmen, see Forrest McDonald and Grady McWhiney, "The Antebellum Southern Herdsman: A Reinterpretation," in *Journal of Southern History,* 41:147–66 (May 1975).

10. Blackstone, *Commentaries,* 4:154–59; Friedman, *History of American Law,* 66–68, 232–35; Michael Kammen, *Colonial New York, A History* (New York, 1975), 56–57, 189; Sydney V. James, *Colonial Rhode Island: A History* (New York, 1975), 157; William B. Weeden, *Economic and Social History of New England, 1620–1789* (2 vols., New York, 1890), 1:99, 118–19, 132, 178, 189, 200, 406, 2:524–26; Richard L. Bushman, *From Puritan to Yankee: Character and the Social Order in Connecticut, 1690–1765* (New York, 1970), 113; Lewis Cecil Gray, *History of Agriculture in the Southern United States to 1860* (2 vols., Peter Smith edition, Gloucester, Mass., 1958), 1:103, 163, 2:583.

11. These and the following interpetive observations are documented in chapters seven to ten.

12. Hamilton to Theodore Sedgwick, October 9, November 9, 1788, January 29, 1789, Sedgwick to Hamilton, October 16, November 2, Hamilton to Madison, November 23, 1788, Hamilton to James Wilson, January 25, 1789, Jeremiah Wadsworth to Hamilton, February 5–28, 1789, in Syrett, ed., *Papers,* 5:225, 226, 228, 230–31, 235–37, 247–49, 250–51, 252. The electoral college system was changed to the modern basis by the Twelfth Amendment, adopted after Jefferson and Burr tied in the presidential election of 1800–1801.

13. Hamilton to Washington, August 13, September, November 18, 1788, Washington to Hamilton, August 28, October 3, November 6, 1788, ibid., 5:201–2, 206–8, 220–22, 222–24, 230, 233. Interestingly, Washington broke the ice of formality that had prevailed since 1781 by using the word "affectionately" in the complimentary closing to his letter of November 6; Hamilton responded in kind on November 18.

14. James Thomas Flexner, *George Washington and the New Nation, (1783–1793)* (Boston, 1969), 160–61, 213–14; John C. Fitzpatrick, ed., *The Diaries of George Washington, 1748–1799,* vol. 4, 1789–1799 (Boston, 1925), *passim;* Brant, *Madison,* 3:242–43, 282–83; Washington to Jay, June 1789, in Johnston, ed., *Correspondence of Jay,* 3:369; Hamilton to Washington, May 5, 1789, Washington to Hamilton, May 5, September 25, 1789, in Syrett, ed., *Papers,* 5:335–37, 409.

15. Flexner, *Washington and the New Nation,* 195–96; Fitzpatrick, ed., *Washington Papers,* 30:319–21; Hamilton to Washington, May 5, 1789, in Syrett, ed., *Papers,* 5:335–37 and 335 note; McDonald, *Presidency of Washington,* 25–26, 29–30; Edgar S. Maclay, ed., *Journal of William Maclay United States Senator from Pennsylvania, 1789–1791* (New York, 1890).

16. For a fuller exposition of the dual nature of the presidency, see Forrest McDonald, "A Mirror for Presidents," in *Commentary,* 62:34–41 (December 1976). Hamilton's most extensive comments on the presidency are in his June 18, 1787 speech in the Constitutional Convention and *Federalist* numbers 67–77, all cited earlier; these should be read in connection with his letter to Washington, May 5, 1789, and his frequent observation that appearances are as important as realities. The British system as described here had evolved under the first two Hanoverian kings, George I and George II (1714–1760). George III attempted to become an ex-

ception to it and temporarily succeeded, with calamitous results; afterward it was restored.

17. These remnants of monarchical practices can be traced in newspapers from 1783 to 1789 and in the elaborate exchange of opening messages between governors and legislators, in emulation of British practice, as recorded in the legislative journals of the several states. There is no systematic study of monarchical rituals in the United States, as far as I am aware, but two studies of the colonies on the eve of the revolution offer a good introduction to such practices: Robert Dennis Fiala's "George III in the Pennsylvania Press: A Study in Changing Opinions, 1760–1776" (Ph.D. thesis, Wayne State University, 1967); and William David Liddle, "A Patriot King, or None: American Public Attitudes towards George III and the British Monarchy, 1754–1776" (Ph.D. thesis, Claremont Graduate School, 1970).

18. For examples of Hamilton's conception of his role, see Hamilton to Edward Carrington, May 26, 1792, where he refers to "my administration," and "The Defence of the Funding System," July 1795, where he refers to himself in the third person as "The Minister"; Syrett, ed., *Papers*, 11:427, 19:3–4.

19. Flexner, *Washington and the New Nation*, 191; James D. Richardson, ed., *A Compilation of the Messages and Papers of the Presidents, 1789–1897*, vol. 1, 1789–1817 (Washington, 1896), 51–54.

20. Ketcham, *Madison*, 286–88; Brant, *Madison*, 3:281–85; Dangerfield, *Livingston*, 243–46.

21. Schachner, ed., "Narratives" (Troup), *William and Mary Quarterly*, 4:220; Mitchell, *Hamilton*, 1:21–22; Brant, *Madison*, 281; Adams to Hamilton, July 21, 1789, and "Cash Book," entry dated July 20, 1789, in Syrett, ed., *Papers*, 5:363–64 and 3:57. Another consideration in Hamilton's acceptance of Adams's son may have been one of propriety: he could not have declined on the ground that he expected to be appointed soon to an office that had not yet been created. On the other hand, one imagines that he could have thought of some reasonable excuse.

22. The conditions Hamilton required are partly explicit and partly implicit in his letter to Carrington, cited in note 17. As to having a foot in the door of Congress, Hamilton told Carrington that if the power to make direct reports were removed, he would have been forced to resign (Syrett, ed., *Papers*, 11:432–33). On Washington's administrative procedures, see Jefferson to his own department heads, November 6, 1801, in Paul Leicester Ford, ed., *The Writings of Thomas Jefferson* (10 vols., New York, 1892–1899), 8:99–101.

23. Thomas Hart Benton, ed., *Abridgment of the Debates of Congress, from 1789 to 1856* (New York, 1857), 1:85–86 (May 19, 1789).

24. Ibid., 1:86–90 (May 19, 1789). Regarding Jackson, see Wayne to Hamilton, April 6, 1789, in Syrett, ed., *Papers*, 5:316; regarding Gerry, see George Athan Billias, *Elbridge Gerry: Founding Father and Republican Statesman* (New York, 1976); regarding Smith, see George C. Rogers, Jr., *Evolution of a Federalist: William Loughton Smith of Charleston, 1758–1812* (Columbia, S.C., 1962).

25. Benton, ed., *Abridgment of Debates*, 1:102–3 (June 16, 1789); *The Federalist*, number 77, April 2, 1788, in Syrett, ed., *Papers*, 4:638–39.

26. Benton, ed., *Abridgment of Debates*, 1:102–8 (June 16, 1789); William L. Smith to Edward Rutledge, June 21, 1789, in George C. Rogers, Jr., ed., "The Letters

Notes

of William Loughton Smith to Edward Rutledge," *South Carolina Historical Magazine,* 69:8 (January 1968).

27. Benton, ed., *Abridgment of Debates,* 1:90–91 (May 20, 1789). For examples of republicans' semihysterical fear of and hostility toward Morris, see Billias, *Gerry,* 118; *Acts and Resolves of Massachusetts,* 1782–1783 (Boston, 1890), 796–98; Arthur Lee to Samuel Adams, March 5, 1783, Arthur Lee to James Warren, March 12, 1783, A Member of Congress to _____, May 1783, Stephen Higginson to Samuel Adams, May 20, 1783, Arthur Lee to James Warren, September 17, 1783, and Samuel Osgood to John Adams, December 7, 1783, in Burnett, ed., *Letters of Members of Congress,* 7:67–68, 77–78, 156, 166–69, 299–300, 378–88.

28. Benton, ed., *Abridgment of Debates,* 1:92–94 (May 20, 1789).

29. Ibid., 1:109, 111–12 (June 25, 1789).

30. Ibid., 1:109, 112 (June 25, 1789).

31. *The Laws of the United States of America* (Philadelphia, 1796), 1:36–40; Broadus Mitchell, *Alexander Hamilton,* vol. 2, *The National Adventure, 1788–1804* (New York, 1962), 20–21.

32. Syrett, ed., *Papers,* 5:365–72.

33. Fitzpatrick, ed., *Diaries of Washington,* vol. 4, *passim;* Syrett, ed., *Papers,* 6:497. Jefferson's description is in Jefferson to his own heads of departments, November 6, 1801, in Ford, ed., *Writings of Jefferson,* 8:99–101. For examples of Hamilton's routine compliance with Washington's administrative system, see Hamilton to Washington, June 26, 1790 (two letters), and Tobias Lear to Hamilton, June 29, 1790, in Syrett, ed., *Papers,* 6:472–74. See also Lynton K. Caldwell, *The Administrative Theories of Hamilton & Jefferson: Their Contribution to Thought on Public Administration* (Chicago, 1944); and Leonard D. White, *The Federalists: A Study in Administrative History* (New York, 1948).

34. Conversation with Comte de Moustier, September 13, 1789, Hamilton to Lafayette, October 6, 1789, Hamilton to William Short, October 7, 1789, in Syrett, ed., *Papers,* 5:366–68, 425–26, 429–30. See also the documents on 5:428.

35. Conversation with George Beckwith, October 1789, ibid., 5:482–90.

36. Hamilton to Washington, July 8, July 15, 1790, Conversations with George Beckwith, August 7–12, 1790, ibid., 6:484–86, 493–96, 546–49, 550–51; Fitzpatrick, ed., *Diaries of Washington,* 4:143 (July 14, 1790). Julian P. Boyd, in an editorial note to *The Papers of Thomas Jefferson,* 17:35–108, and subsequently in a book called *Number 7, Alexander Hamilton's Secret Attempts to Control American Foreign Policy* (Princeton, 1964), attacks Hamilton for improper interference in foreign affairs, deceit, and duplicity. For an effective critique of *Number 7,* see Gilbert L. Lycan, *Alexander Hamilton & American Foreign Policy: A Design for Greatness* (Norman, Oklahoma, 1970), 122–23; for a balanced account of these matters, see Helene Vivan Johnson, "Alexander Hamilton and the British Orientation of American Foreign Policy, 1783–1803" (Ph.D. thesis, University of Southern California, 1963), especially chs. 2 and 5. See also chapter twelve.

37. Necker, *Finances of France,* xxx–xxxii, xxxiv–xxxv, xxxvii, xxxviii, xl–xli, lxxv.

38. Ibid., lxxxiii, lxxxvi, lxxxviii, xcv, ciii.

39. Lee to Hamilton, November 16, 1789, in Syrett, ed., *Papers,* 5:517. Interest-

ingly, had Hamilton provided the information Lee sought and had Lee invested on the strength of it, the Virginian would not have done as well as if he had selected securities at random. Lee asked specifically about "indents," certificates issued in lieu of interest on continental securities. Hamilton proposed that these be funded on the same basis as certificates of principal, but Congress voted to fund them at only half the interest rate of regular securities. Interestingly, too, Richard Bland Lee was one of the principal opponents of Hamilton's proposal to assume the state debts but changed his vote after a deal involving Madison and Jefferson, and also involving a land speculation scheme in which Henry Lee and Madison were interested. See chapter VIII.

40. Hamilton to Lee, December 1, 1789, ibid., 6:1.

41. The loans included one of $2,000 to William Duer, made on July 29, 1789, one of $2,000 to Arthur St. Clair on September 25, 1789, and one to William Grayson of $200 on October 10, 1789; ibid., 5:364, 400, 414. Regarding Hamilton's debts in 1795, see Mitchell, *Hamilton*, 2:377; regarding the forsaken bonuses see ibid., 2:549.

42. Ibid., 2:39–40; Morris to Hamilton, November 13, 1789, Hamilton to Brockholst Livingston, March 30, 1790, Livingston to Hamilton, April 4, 1790, Morris to Hamilton, April 4, 1790, in Syrett, ed., *Papers,* 5:513–15, 6:329–30, 347–48, 348–49; William Constable to Robert Morris, November 16, 1789, in William Constable Papers, New York Public Library.

43. Hamilton to Duer, April 4–7, 1790, in Syrett, ed., *Papers,* 6:346–47; Mitchell, *Hamilton,* 2:156–57.

44. See Treasury Department Circulars to Collectors of the Customs, September 14, 22, October 1, 2, 3, 6, 10, 14, 15, 20, 31, November 25, 30, 1789, in Syrett, ed., *Papers,* 5:373, 394–95, 415–16, 419–21, 422, 427, 434–35, 444–46, 446–47, 454–56, 478, 559, 575–78. The circular of October 2, 1789, is especially revealing, as is Hamilton to Benjamin Lincoln, November 20, 1789, ibid., 5:530.

45. The first questionnaire was enclosed in a Treasury Department Circular to the Collectors of the Customs, October 15, 1789; later, questionnaires requested information on distilleries, manufacturing, and other subjects. Among the more informative responses to the first inquiry were Stephen Higginson to Hamilton, October 27, 1789, ———— to Hamilton, October 1789, John Fitzgerald to Hamilton, October 1789, William Bingham to Hamilton, November 25, 1789 (enclosure), Tench Coxe to Hamilton, November 30, 1789, ibid., 5:446–47, 466–71, 479–81, 554–57, 569–70.

46. Benton, ed., *Abridgment of Debates,* 1:24–45, 48–51, 53–64, 69–84 (April 9–24, May 5, 7–9, 11–16, 1789); Ketcham, *Madison,* 280–82; Brant, *Madison,* 3:246–54; Conversation with George Beckwith, October 1789, in Syrett, ed., *Papers,* 5:488. Madison's biographers cited here are, of course, sympathetic to him.

47. Benton, ed., *Abridgment of Debates,* 1:48–51, 53–56 (May 5, 7, 1789); Stephen Higginson to Hamilton, October 27, 1789, in Syrett, ed., *Papers,* 5:466–71.

48. Otho H. Williams to Hamilton, October 23, 26, 1789, ibid., 5:459, 462.

49. Ibid., 5:412 note 2.

Notes

VII—The Financial Dilemma

1. Ferguson, *Power of the Purse,* 203–4.

2. Ibid., 205–7; Hugh Williamson to Alexander Martin, September 30, 1784, editor's note at Rufus King to Elbridge Gerry, March 24, 1785, and Nathan Dane to Jacob Wales, January 31, 1786, in Burnett, ed., *Letters of Members of Congress,* 7:595, 8:71 note, 294–97.

3. Ferguson, *Power of The Purse,* 209–19.

4. Report Relative to a Provision for the Support of Public Credit, January 9, 1790, Schedule B, in Syrett, ed., *Papers,* 6:112–13.

5. Ibid., 6:107, 137.

6. Conversation with Comte de Moustier, September 13, 1789, Hamilton to Lafayette, October 6, 1789, Hamilton to William Short, October 7, 1789, Short to Hamilton, November 30, 1789, ibid., 5:366–68, 425–26, 429–30, 570–74.

7. Willinks, Van Staphorsts, and Hubbard to Hamilton, January 25, 1790, Short to Hamilton, January 28–31, 1790, Gouverneur Morris to Hamilton, January 31, 1790, ibid., 6:211–18, 227–32, 234–39.

8. Report on the Public Credit, January 9, 1790; Hamilton to Willinks, Van Staphorsts, and Hubbard, April 7, 1790, ibid. 6:87, 98, 358–59.

9. Ferguson, *Power of the Purse,* chs. 2, 3, 4, 9, *passim;* Report on the Public Credit, Schedule C, in Syrett, ed., *Papers,* 6:114–15.

10. Ibid.; Ferguson, *Power of the Purse,* 181–83, 226–28.

11. Ibid., 230–34; Report on the Public Credit, Schedule E, in Syrett, ed., *Papers,* 6:118–25; Richard P. McCormick, *Experiment in Independence* (New Brunswick, N.J., 1950), 171–78, 197–204; *New York Journal,* January 31, February 7, 21, 1788; Mitchell and Flanders, comps., *Statutes of Pennsylvania,* 11:454–86, 560–72. See also chapter four, notes 18 and 33.

12. McDonald, *We The People,* 326–38, for a detailed account of the Rhode Island scheme; Adelaide L. Fries, "North Carolina Certificates of the Revolutionary War Period," in *North Carolina Historical Review,* 9:229–42 (July 1932); Ferguson, *Power of the Purse,* 222; Report on the Public Credit, Schedule E, in Syrett, ed., *Papers,* 6:119.

13. Ibid., 6:100–101, 109. See also Stephen Higginson to Hamilton, November 11, 1789, and William Bingham to Hamilton, November 25, 1789, ibid., 5:508, 549. The constitutional restriction on direct taxes is in article I, section 9.

14. The actual distribution of support for and opposition to Hamilton's proposals is analyzed in chapter eight.

15. For a thorough analysis of the excise problem, see William D. Barber, " 'Among the Most *Techy Articles of Civil Police'*: Federal Taxation and the Adoption of the Whiskey Excise," in *William and Mary Quarterly,* 25:58–84 (January 1968).

16. The best general account of American commercial patterns during the period is in Curtis P. Nettels, *The Emergence of a National Economy, 1775–1815* (New York, 1962). Valuable information is contained in *American State Papers: Documents, Legislative and Executive, of the Congress of the United States* (38 vols., Washington, 1832–1861), *Commerce* and *Finance,* and in Hamilton's correspon-

dence with advisers and with customs collectors. I have studied the subject through contemporary newspapers and customs records in the South Carolina Department of Archives, the Virginia State Library, the Maryland Hall of Records, the Historical Society of Pennsylvania, the Rhode Island Archives, the Essex Institute, and the National Archives.

17. Debates of April 9, 1789, especially the remarks of Congressmen Fitzsimons and Hartley of Pennsylvania, in Benton, ed., *Abridgment of Debates*, 1:24–25; Young, *Democratic Republicans*, 100; Report on the Subject of Manufactures, December 5, 1791, in Syrett, ed., *Papers*, 10:1–340.

18. Brant, *Madison*, 3:251–54; Ketcham, *Madison*, 280–82. Both accounts are favorable to Madison, though Ketcham objectively quotes opposite points of view. This subject was virtually an obsession with Jefferson. See Jefferson to Jay, May 27, 1786, in Jared Sparks, ed., *The Diplomatic Correspondence of the United States* (5 vols., Washington, 1832–1833), 3:57–63. Boyd, ed., *Jefferson Papers*, editorial note to Report on the Fisheries, 19:140–72, is quite misleading. See also chapters twelve and thirteen. For an account of the Virginians' misreading of the nature of the tobacco trade in the 1780s, see McDonald, *E Pluribus Unum*, 75–76 and notes 20–21, p. 261.

19. A clear contemporary account of the reasons that American trade fell into Britain's orbit instead of France's is contained in Charles Maurice Talleyrand-Perigord, *Memoir Concerning the Commercial Relations of the United States with England* (Boston, 1809). See also View of the Commercial Regulations of France and Great Britain in Reference to the United States, 1792–1793, in Syrett, ed., *Papers*, 13:395–436; Nettels, *Emergence of a National Economy*.

20. Report on the Public Credit, in Syrett, ed., *Papers*, 6:71–72.

21. My observations are based upon lengthy study of the Records of the Loan of 1790 in the National Archives. Ferguson, *Power of the Purse*, ch. 12, "Speculation in the Public Debt," contains much valuable information, but Professor Ferguson ignores the complexities of speculation, especially various bear operations; he assumes that everyone in the market must have been betting on the rise, and a one-time at that. For more detailed information on the activities of the Boston and Providence merchant-speculators, see McDonald, *E Pluribus Unum*, 125–26, 131–32, and the notes cited thereto.

22. On land speculation in general, see for example Aaron M. Sakolski, *The Great American Land Bubble* (New York, 1932); Paul Demund Evans, *The Holland Land Company* (Buffalo, 1924); Jensen, *Articles of Confederation;* Beverly W. Bond, ed., *The Correspondence of John Cleves Symmes* (New York, 1926); *American State Papers: Public Lands;* Smith, *James Wilson*, 159–68, 382–86; C. Peter Magrath, *Yazoo, Law and Politics in the New Republic: The Case of Fletcher v. Peck* (Providence, 1966); Joseph Stancliffe Davis, *Essays in the Earlier History of American Corporations* (2 vols., Cambridge, 1917); Ellis Paxson Oberholtzer, *Robert Morris: Patriot and Financier* (New York, 1903); William G. Sumner, *The Financier and the Finances of the American Revolution* (2 vols., New York, 1892). As to the specific speculations mentioned here, for Washington see his will as published in Jared Sparks, *The Life of George Washington* (Boston, 1842), appendix IX; for Knox see North Callahan, *Henry Knox: George Washington's General* (New York, 1968),

Notes

282–83, 292–94; for Madison see Ketcham, *Madison,* 146–48; for Hamilton see the Papers of the Ohio Company, Marietta College Library, Marietta, Ohio.

23. Charles Wilson, *Anglo-Dutch Commerce & Finance in the Eighteenth Century* (Cambridge, England, 1941), 189–91 and *passim;* Simon Schama, *Patriots and Liberators: Revolution in the Netherlands, 1780–1813* (New York, 1977), 24–63. See also Hendrik Willem Van Loon, *The Fall of the Dutch Republic* (Boston, 1924).

24. The principal extant sources on the activities of American speculators and agents involved in marketing securities with Dutch investors are the William Constable Papers, New York Public Library; the Andrew Craigie Papers, American Antiquarian Society; the Matthew Ridley Papers, Massachusetts Historical Society; the Robert Morris and Gouverneur Morris Papers, Library of Congress; and the Records of the Loan of 1790, National Archives. These papers are quoted extensively in Mitchell, *Hamilton,* 2:154–67, and Ferguson, *Power of the Purse,* 254–72; the contracts between Parker and Stadnitski are discussed by Ferguson on page 262, and subsequent Dutch purchases are briefly described at 262–64. Unfortunately, neither Mitchell nor Ferguson presents his materials chronologically, with the result that events between early 1788 and 1790 are often blurred, as if the positions of such active speculators were constant instead of continuously changing. Both authors ignore the role of speculators and of Dutch investors in establishing the market, and neither takes short operations into account—oversights which considerably impair the value of the data they present.

25. Constable to Gouverneur Morris, November 14, 1789, to Alexander Ellice, November 18, 1789, and to Robert Morris, October 30, November 22, December 17, 1789, in Constable Papers, New York Public Library; Report on the Public Credit, January 9, 1790, in Syrett, ed., *Papers,* 6:69–70. On the flukish commercial boom, see Thomas Willing to Hamilton, March 12, 1790, Higginson to Hamilton, May 20, 1790, and Tench Coxe to Hamilton, July 10, 1790, ibid., 6:301, 424–25, 491.

26. Constable to Gouverneur Morris, November 9, December 1, 1789, to Robert Morris, December 1, 17, 1789, in Constable Papers, New York Public Library; Craigie to Parker, November 14, 1789, in Craigie Papers, American Antiquarian Society. Ferguson's reading of Constable's remarks on the interest on state securities, in *Power of the Purse,* 271, does not quite square with either Constable's letters or Hamilton's reports. It has been alleged that another of Hamilton's friends, William Duer, used inside information to buy up certain special certificates of soldiers at great profit to himself, but the charge rests on the testimony of Jacob Clingman, a man of questionable veracity, and was explicitly denied by Oliver Wolcott, Jr. (deposition of Jacob Clingman, December 13, 1792, deposition of Oliver Wolcott, Jr., July 12, 1797, in Syrett, ed., *Papers,* 21:275, 280). On the other hand, Duer was clearly engaged with Constable in a plan to buy up North Carolina and South Carolina securities; see the agreement between the two, December 23, 1789, reproduced in Brant, *Madison,* illustration facing 3:281. Yet that very document suggests that both men figured the state securities would remain low, which in turn suggests that neither had any precise knowledge of what Hamilton would propose in his report seventeen days later—or that if they did, they grossly misguessed the effect the report would have.

27. The Defence of the Funding System, July 1795, in Syrett, ed., *Papers,* 19:40,

41. In the quoted passages, Hamilton was referring specifically to the assumption of state debts, but the remarks apply equally to funding the continental debts.

28. Higginson to Hamilton, November 11, 1789, ibid., 5:510–11; regarding congressional attitudes toward repudiation, funding, scaling, and assumption, see chapter eight.

29. For examples of arguments for discrimination, see *The American Museum,* May 1787; Boston *Independent Chronicle,* April 15, 1790; Philadelphia *Freeman's Journal,* January 20, 27, 1790; Philadelphia *Independent Gazetteer,* February 20, 1790. The most sophisticated advocate of discrimination was Madison, for whose position see chapter eight. For Hamilton's anticipation and refutation of discrimination, see Report on the Public Credit, in Syrett, ed., *Papers,* 6:73–78.

30. Bingham to Hamilton, November 25, 1789, ibid., 5:538–54, especially 543–44. These suggestions should be compared with Hamilton's Report on the Public Credit, in which a scaling of interest forms a crucial part of the proposed operation; again, see chapter eight.

31. For Hamilton's analysis of the pros and cons of assumption, see The Defence of the Funding System, July 1795, ibid., 19:8–46.

32. There is a large bibliography on the English financial system, the opposition to it, and the impact of the Oppositionist ideology in America. The best work on the system itself is P. G. M. Dickson, *The Financial Revolution in England: A Study in the Development of Public Credit, 1688–1756* (London, 1967). On the Opposition, see Caroline Robbins, *The Eighteenth-Century Commonwealthman: Studies in the Transmission, Development, and Circumstance of English Liberal Thought from the Restoration of Charles II until the War with the Thirteen Colonies* (Cambridge, Mass., 1959); Kramnick, *Bolingbroke and His Circle;* and Rodger D. Parker, "The Gospel of Opposition: A Study in Eighteenth Century Anglo-American Ideology" (Ph.D. thesis, Wayne State University, 1975). On the influence of the ideology in America, see Parker's work; Bailyn, *Ideological Origins,* and Richard Buel, *Securing the Revolution: Ideology in American Politics, 1789–1815* (Ithaca, 1972). Far better than Buel is Lance Banning, *The Jeffersonian Persuasion: Evolution of a Party Ideology* (Ithaca and London, 1978). See also M. E. Bradford's Introduction to *John Taylor, Arator; Being a Series of Agricultural Essays, Practical and Political: In Sixty-Four Numbers* (Indianapolis, 1977); and chapter ten.

33. The most thorough analysis of the sources of Hamilton's thinking on the subject is in the editor's introductory note to the first Report on Public Credit, in Syrett, ed., *Papers,* 6:51–65. That essay contains much useful information, but it strains to suggest influences that did not exist—for example, in suggesting that Thomas Hobbes might have been an influence simply because Hobbes held that contracts were binding in natural law, despite the crucial fact that Hamilton's thinking in regard to contracts was post-Mansfield, whereas Hobbes's contractual thinking was of the older school. Moreover, it underestimates the influence of Necker. Almost no one who has dealt with the subject has examined the *operations* of the British system closely to determine what parallels there were in Hamilton's system. The only exception I know of is Donald F. Swanson's excellent monograph, *The Origins of Hamilton's Fiscal Policies* (Gainesville, Fla., 1963).

34. Sparks, ed., *Gouverneur Morris,* 10–19; Philip Schuyler Papers, Box 38,

Notes

New York Public Library; Benjamin Walker to Hamilton, September 15, 1789, John Witherspoon to Hamilton, October 26, 1789, Higginson to Hamilton, November 11, 1789, Madison to Hamilton, November 19, 1789, Bingham to Hamilton, November 25, 1789, Samuel Osgood to Hamilton, November 28, 1789, Oliver Wolcott, Jr., to Hamilton, November 29, 1789, in Syrett, ed., *Papers,* 5:373–76, 464–65, 507–11, 525–27, 538–54, 563, 564–68.

35. Introductory Note, ibid., 6:52–56.

36. Green and Grose, eds., *Hume's Works,* 3:360–74 (*Essays,* vol. I, part II, essay IX); Adam Smith, *An Inquiry into the Nature and Causes of the Wealth of Nations* (New York, Modern Library edition, 1937), book V, ch. 3; Malachy Postlethwayt, *The Universal Dictionary of Trade and Commerce* . . . (2 vols., London, 1757), *passim;* Swanson, *Origins of Hamilton's Fiscal Policies,* 22–33. The last is a careful analysis and devastating critique of Dr. Price's plan for a sinking fund that would mechanically retire the public debts—which was quite different from the sinking fund Hamilton would propose.

VIII—Funding and Assumption

1. Report Relative to a Provision for the Support of Public Credit, January 9, 1790, in Syrett, ed., *Papers,* 6:68.

2. Ibid., 6:97.

3. Most of the judgments discussed in this paragraph are implicit or explicit in all Hamilton's political writings from 1787 onward. The belief that the contract, broadly defined, is the foundation of morality—as opposed to the more conventional contemporary belief that morality derived from natural law—was one Hamilton acquired from Hume. For a good analysis of the significance of Hume's thinking in this respect, see Forbes, *Hume's Philosophical Politics,* 77–80 and *passim.* See also the analysis of the emerging new view of contracts, chapter XV.

4. Report on Public Credit, in Syrett, ed., *Papers,* 6:70–72.

5. The editors of the *Hamilton Papers* fail to understand the principle of funding debts; when citing the statute which provided for funding and assumption, "An Act making provision for the Debt of the United States," they invariably insert in parentheses the words "payment of the" before the word "Debt," though the statute (following Hamilton's proposals) made no provision for payment. See, for examples, ibid., 6:570 note 2, 581 note 3, 589 note 1.

6. Ibid., 6:73–78.

7. Ibid., 6:78–81.

8. Ibid., 6:81–84, 111. Compare Wolcott to Hamilton, November 29, 1789, ibid., 5:564–68.

9. Ibid., 6:84–85.

10. Ibid., 6:84–88, 99.

11. Ibid., 6:88–90. For a fuller explication of these points, see Fisher Ames's speech in the House of Representatives, as recorded in *Annals of Congress* (vols. 1

and 2, Washington, 1834), 2:1489–91 (March 13, 1790). The pagination of the edition of the *Annals of Congress* in the University of Alabama Library is different from the pagination in most editions; here, citations are given by dates as well as pages to reconcile this difference.

12. Report on the Public Credit, in Syrett, ed., *Papers*, 6:90–97.

13. Ibid., 6:97–99.

14. Ibid., 6:99–105, 138.

15. Ibid., 6:97, 106–8. On the British sinking fund, see Swanson, *Origins of Hamilton's Fiscal Policies*, 22–33.

16. *Annals of Congress,* 1:1043–45, 1056 (January 9, 14, 1790); New York *Gazette of the United States,* January 20, 23, February throughout, 1790; Philadelphia *Pennsylvania Packet,* January 18, 19, 1790, for summary reports, January 26 following for the entire report and January 26 for an advertisement of the report in pamphlet form; Boston *Independent Chronicle,* January 28, 1790; Philadelphia *Independent Gazetteer,* January 30, 1790; *The Salem Gazette,* February 2, 1790.

17. *Gazette of the United States,* February 27, March 3, 1790; New York *Daily Advertiser,* February 3, 5, March 4, 12, 1790; *Pennsylvania Packet,* February 8, 9, 16, 1790; *Massachusetts Centinel,* April 10, 1790; *Salem Gazette,* February 23, 1790; William Heth to Hamilton, February 21, 1790, in Syrett, ed., *Papers,* 6:274–75; Christopher Gore to Rufus King, January 24, July 25, 1790, in Charles R. King, ed., *The Life and Correspondence of Rufus King,* 1:385–86, 392 (New York, 1894); Andrew Craigie to Daniel Parker, February 4, 21, 1790, in Craigie Papers, American Antiquarian Society; Billias, *Gerry,* 240. For an analysis of the faction in the Senate that insisted on 6 percent, see Kenneth Russell Bowling, "Politics in the First Congress, 1789–1791" (Ph.D. thesis, University of Wisconsin, 1968), 224–25, 228. As late as 1795, holders of $1,561,175 of old 6 percent continental securities had refused to subscribe to the loan of 1790 (Report on a Plan for the Further Support of Public Credit, January 16, 1795, in Syrett, ed., *Papers,* 18:80).

18. Philadelphia *Freeman's Journal,* March 10, 1790; *Pennsylvania Packet,* March 18, 1790; *Gazette of the United States,* February 24, 1790; Constable to James Seagrove, January 17, 1790, to Alexander Ellice, February 2, 1790, and to Gouverneur Morris, January 28, July 30, 1790, in Constable Papers, New York Public Library; Craigie to Samuel Rogers, January 17, August 18, 1790, in Craigie Papers, American Antiquarian Society; Thomas Willing to Hamilton, February 24, 1790, in Syrett, ed., *Papers,* 6:278–79; Thomas Jefferson to George Washington, May 3, 1790, enclosing dispatches from Europe, in Boyd, ed., *Jefferson Papers,* 16:410.

19. Public reaction has been surveyed in various newspapers. For examples of arguments pro and con, in addition to the papers cited in note 17, see Boston *Independent Chronicle,* April 15, 22, 1790; Philadelphia *Freeman's Journal,* January 20, 27, 1790; Philadelphia *Independent Gazetteer,* February 6, 20, 27, March 6, April 10, 1790; *Pennsylvania Gazette,* March 10, 1790; *New York Journal,* January 21, 1790; *Massachusetts Centinel,* February 10, 1790; *Gazette of the United States,* February 23, 1790. The only subject that consumed more newspaper space than the funding system during these months was the spectacular European demand for American foodstuffs.

Notes

20. Maclay, ed., *Maclay Journal, passim;* Rogers, *Evolution of a Federalist,* 168–69; Anne King Gregorie, *Thomas Sumter* (Columbia, S.C., 1931); Magrath, *Yazoo,* 8–12; William Omer Foster, *James Jackson: Duellist and Militant Statesman, 1757–1806* (Athens, Ga., 1960); Lilla M. Hawes, ed., "Miscellaneous Papers of James Jackson, 1781–1798," in *Georgia Historical Quarterly,* 37:152–56 (June 1953); Ames, ed., *Works of Ames,* 1:87.

21. William Henry Egle, ed., *Pennsylvania Archives,* 3d series (vols. 24–26, Harrisburg, 1897–1899), 24:100, 25:167, 168, 177, 180, 234, 241, 634, 26:272, 273, 275, 604, 606; Maclay, ed., *Journal,* 335–36; William C. Pool, "An Economic Interpretation of the Federal Constitution in North Carolina," in *North Carolina Historical Review,* 27:136, 304, 446, 455 (April, July, October 1950); Charles A. Beard, *An Economic Interpretation of the Constitution of the United States* (New York, 1913), 277; Young, *Democratic Republicans,* 65 note, 234 note; Carl S. Driver, *John Sevier: Pioneer of the Old Southwest* (Chapel Hill, 1932), *passim;* William H. Masterson, *William Blount* (Baton Rouge, La., 1954), *passim;* Magrath, *Yazoo,* 3–11. The data cited here reflect only a brief sampling of the speculations in state lands by antiassumptionists; doubtless a deeper probe would reveal far more.

22. Madison's principal biographers argue unconvincingly that his motives were humanitarian, though Ketcham admits that tactical and local considerations were important; Brant, *Madison,* 3:300; Ketcham, *Madison,* 311–12. More convincing are Bowling, "First Congress," 208–11, and Ferguson, *Power of the Purse,* 298ff. My own analysis is inferred from Bowling, Ferguson, and study of Madison's tactics in the *Annals of Congress,* together with study of Virginia sources. None of these four authors takes into account the information in the following paragraph. Regarding tobacco prices, another crucial element none of the above authors takes into account, see *Gazette of the United States,* May 6, August 13, September 2, 1789, June 16, 1790, and Gray, *History of Agriculture in the Southern United States,* 2:605.

23. Madison's Potomac speculations, which Brant overlooks and Ketcham mentions only in passing (*Madison,* 148), are described and thoroughly documented in the Editorial Note, "Locating the Federal District," in Boyd, ed., *Jefferson Papers,* 19:9–16. Madison was able to raise only £100 or £200 toward his one-quarter share in the venture but hoped to finance the rest from loans in Europe through the influence of Jefferson. Ultimately, though he succeeded in locating the capital on the Potomac, he failed to obtain the backing necessary to profit from his operations.

24. Security holdings are derived mainly from Records of the Loan of 1790, National Archives. For Gerry's, vol. 279, accounts 582 and 795, vol. 282, folios 324 and 931, vol. 283, folio 1, vol. 284, folio 6, vol. 622, folio 142, and vol. 630, folio 60; for Sherman's, vol. 495, folio 28; for Wadsworth's, vol. 491, folio 1023, vol. 495, folios 6, 24, 34, 63, and 134, and vol. 498, folios 13, 19, 27, 83, 143, and 147; for Boudinot's, Ferguson, *Power of the Purse,* 284; for Clymer's, vol. 631, folio 158; for Smith's, Rogers, *Evolution of a Federalist,* 203; for Bland's, vols. 1114, 1115; for Burke's, Alexander S. Salley, ed., *Stub Entries to Indents Issued in Payment of Claims against South Carolina Growing out of the Revolution, Books Y–Z* (Columbia, S.C., 1927), 106, 125; for Gilman's, vol. 249, folio 32; for Gale's, vols. 72 and 73, folios 17 in each; for White's, vol. 1113, folio 43; for Sumter's, Salley, ed., *Stub Entries . . . Books L–N* (Columbia, S.C., 1910), 307, *Book X* (Columbia, S.C., 1925), part 1, p.

51; for Baldwin's, vols. 495–97, folios 135–36 in each. Sedgwick did own $1,680 face value of continental securities.

25. For Langdon's securities, Records of the Loan of 1790, National Archives, vol. 249, folio 35, vol. 242, folio 4, vol. 495, folio 128; for Strong's, vol. 280, account 1284; for Ellsworth's, McDonald, *We The People,* 47 and 47 note; for King's, vol. 22, folio 14, vol. 25, folio 60, vol. 32, folio 14; for Schuyler's, Beard, *Economic Interpretation of the Constitution,* 270–71; for Morris's, New Loan Certificates, vol. B, accounts 8237, 11673–676, 11690, and vol. C, page 11, manuscripts in the Public Records Division of the Pennsylvania Historical Commission, Harrisburg; for Izard's, vol. 1258, folio 27, vol. 1259, folio 8; for those of Maclay, Lee, and Johnston, Charles A. Beard, *Economic Origins of Jeffersonian Democracy* (New York, 1915), 180; for Few's, vol. 1313, folio 25, vol. 1305, folio 16. In the text of *We The People,* 47, I mistakenly said that Ellsworth's holdings were of continental securities; they were in fact state securities, as note 25 on that page indicates.

26. Benton, ed., *Abridgment of Debates,* 1:190–211 (February 8–12, 1790).

27. Ibid., 1:198–201, 205–7, 211–28 (February 10–11, 15–19, 22); Mitchell, *Hamilton,* 2:578. For evidence that Hamilton's supporters were aware of the need for funding and assumption in relation to foreign investors, see Fisher Ames's speech of March 13, in *Annals of Congress,* 2:1489–91.

28. Again, Madison's motives as described here are inferred from his actions, as recorded in *Annals of Congress.* See also his resolutions of April 26, 1783; Madison to Jefferson, February 14, 1790, in Boyd, ed., *Jefferson Papers,* 16:183–84; the remarks of Sedgwick and Lawrence in Benton, ed., *Abridgment of Debates,* 1:212–15 (February 15, 1790); Ferguson, *Power of the Purse,* 300–301.

29. Records of the Loan of 1790, in the National Archives: vol. 1243, folios 7–144, and vol. 1244, accounts 79 and 86 (Subscription Registers, North Carolina Assumed Debt), and vol. 1258 (Journal of the Assumed Debt, South Carolina), *passim;* Whitney K. Bates, "Northern Speculators and Southern State Debts: 1790," in *William and Mary Quarterly,* 19:32 (January 1962); Rogers, *Evolution of a Federalist,* 202–3 (I have not included the South Carolina debt acquired by Leroy and Bayard of New York, of a face value of $395,386; that was purchased over a longer period of time, in behalf of the Dutch financier Theophile Cazenove); William Constable to G. Cottringer, February 13, 1790, and to Benjamin Harrison, February 13, 1790, in Constable Papers, New York Public Library; *Gazette of the United States,* May 22, 1790. The enormous profits New Yorkers and Philadelphians made by buying state securities in the Carolinas would scarcely have been possible had Congress acted swiftly upon Hamilton's recommendations. Significantly, those who purportedly had or thought they had "inside information" from Hamilton—and whose papers have been most used by historians to support the charge that Hamilton was helping speculators—lost money by acting on the basis of what they thought they understood from Hamilton; see Craigie to Samuel Rogers, August 28, 1790, in Craigie Papers, American Antiquarian Society, and Constable to Gouverneur Morris, July 30, 1790, in Constable Papers, New York Public Library.

30. The quotation is from Peters to Jefferson, June 20, 1790, in Boyd, ed., *Jefferson Papers,* 16:539. Peters was referring to the related fight over the capital, but his observations are equally applicable to the fight over assumption.

Notes

31. The best account of the shifting alignments in regard to assumption is Bowling, "First Congress," 211–21, though Bowling makes no effort to correlate positions with individual security holdings. Ferguson, *Power of the Purse,* 317–18 and 318 note says that Fitzsimons, Carroll, and Boudinot became ready to drop assumption to save funding. Fitzsimons held over $8,000 in continentals but no state securities, Carroll had only $226 in continentals and no state securities, and Boudinot held $12,000 in state securities but three times as much in continentals. According to Bowling, in "Dinner at Jefferson's: A Note on Jacob E. Cooke's 'The Compromise of 1790,'" in *William and Mary Quarterly,* 28:637 (October 1971), Ferguson is obviously mistaken about Carroll, who was opposed to assumption. Thomas Sumter, though the holder of $1,625 in state securities and under instructions from the South Carolina legislature to support assumption (*Pennsylvania Packet,* March 18, 1790), refused to do so (William L. Smith to Edward Rutledge, July 25, 1790, in George C. Rogers, Jr., ed., "The Letters of William Loughton Smith to Edward Rutledge," in *South Carolina Historical Magazine,* 69:123 [April 1968]). It scarcely seems coincidental that Sumter had also purchased 114,820 acres of western lands, payable in state securities (Gregorie, *Sumter,* 216). See also note 21.

32. Madison's motion, February 24, is in *Annals of Congress,* 2:1388; White's amendment is ibid., 2:1393–94 (February 25), rejection of White's amendment is ibid., 2:1426 (February 26); passage of Madison's motion is ibid., 2:1459 (March 2); the debate on these various matters is ibid., 2:1374–1459 (February 24–26, March 1–2). Regarding the board's report, see Smith to Rutledge, August 8, 1790, in Rogers, ed., "Letters of Smith to Rutledge," 135–36; Ferguson, *Power of the Purse,* 310. Ferguson's account of these matters is somewhat garbled and confusing, since he narrates the events out of the sequence in which they happened. See also note 31.

33. *Annals of Congress,* 2:1446, 1456; the vote on White's motion was a 25–25 tie, broken by the Speaker who voted in favor of it. For Hamilton's report, see Syrett, ed., *Papers,* 6:286–89 (March 4, 1790).

34. *Annals of Congress,* 2:1466–98 (March 9–13, 1790), and the summary of the resolves at 2:1529 (March 29). For the size of the majority, see Williamson's remarks, 2:1530 (March 29).

35. Ibid., 2:1530–31 (March 29, 1790). Hugh Williamson of North Carolina arrived on March 19 and John Ashe on March 24.

36. Ibid., 2:1528–1685 (March 29–June 2, 1790). Timothy Bloodworth of North Carolina arrived April 6, ibid., 2:1572; Theodorick Bland died on June 1. Regarding the change of votes by New Jersey's Thomas Sinnickson and James Schureman, see Smith to Rutledge, June 14, 1790, in Rogers, ed., "Letters of Smith to Rutledge," 117; for a reconstruction of the unrecorded vote on April 12 and a table of changes from then until July 24, see Bowling, "Dinner at Jefferson's," 635–38.

37. For examples of Maclay's virtually paranoid fear of Hamilton's "tools," see Maclay, ed., *Journal,* 252, 275, 290. The view was apparently widespread: when Hamilton proposed a deal to Morris and later was obliged to report that he could not induce his New England supporters to go along with it, Morris (according to Maclay) did not believe him; ibid., 292–93. The most conclusive evidence of Hamilton's lack of power is that he was unable to "deliver" the votes of the two New York senators, his intimate friend King and his father-in-law Schuyler; see King, ed., *King,*

1:384–85; Bowling, "First Congress," 190–92, 223–25; *Annals of Congress,* 1:985–86, 995–98, 1000, 1002 (Senate votes on the capital, June 8, 28, 29, 30, July 1, 1790).

38. For examples of attitudes toward "corrupt bargains," see the correspondence of King and Ames; Maclay, ed., *Maclay Journal;* Billias, *Gerry;* Buel, *Securing the Revolution;* James M. Banner, Jr., *To The Hartford Convention: The Federalists and the Origins of Party Politics in Massachusetts, 1789–1815* (New York, 1970). For Lee's comment, see Bowling, "First Congress," 178; for the vote on the capital, see *Annals of Congress,* 2:1680 (May 31, 1790), which should be compared with the final vote, ibid., 2:1737 (July 9, 1790). Every representative who voted against the Delaware on May 31 voted for the Potomac on July 9, except Ames and Grout of Massachusetts and Gilman of New Hampshire; all who favored the Delaware on May 31 voted against the Potomac on July 9, except Stone of Maryland and Coles, Lee, and Madison of Virginia. That advocates of the Potomac could thus have carried the vote in the House in May is not taken into account by any historians who have studied the compromises of 1790.

39. Smith to Rutledge, June 14, 1790, in Rogers, ed., "Letters of Smith to Rutledge," 117; Ames to Thomas Dwight, June 11, 1790, in Ames, ed., *Works of Ames,* 1:79–81. Compare the votes of Ames, Grout, and Gilman as cited in note 38.

40. Morris's central role in bringing about the compromises of 1790 has long been overlooked by historians, though Maclay's *Journal,* used by generations of historians, makes that role abundantly evident if not always clear. For examples of the oversight, see Brant, *Madison,* 3:313–18, Ketcham, *Madison,* 308–10, and Mitchell, *Hamilton,* 2:79–84. Bowling's excellent account in "First Congress," chs. 6 and 7, was the first to put Morris's part back in perspective.

41. Jefferson wrote, presumably in 1792, an account of his role in the compromises of 1790, which with revisions he repeated on two subsequent occasions (Boyd, ed., *Jefferson Papers,* 17:205–8). Even Jefferson's most sympathetic biographer, Dumas Malone, in *Jefferson and the Rights of Man* (Boston, 1951), 299–306, expresses some doubts about the accuracy of Jefferson's account. Ferguson, *Power of the Purse,* 319–20, Bowling, "First Congress," chs. 6 and 7, Bowling's "Dinner at Jefferson's" (cited in note 31 above), and Jacob E. Cooke, "The Compromise of 1790," in *William and Mary Quarterly,* 27:523–45 (October 1970) among them demolish Jefferson's claim to have been passive, innocent, and disinterested. They also point out many (though by no means all) of the discrepancies, errors, and contradictions in Jefferson's account, and actually (though none goes quite so far as to say it) reveal him as a wily manipulator. The 1792 account is bitter, self-serving, self-contradictory, and in conflict with the evidence in Jefferson's own correspondence in 1790. Boyd's partisan editorial note on the 1792 document, in *Jefferson Papers,* 17:163–83, is rendered obsolete by the researches of Ferguson, Bowling, and Cooke.

For Jefferson's attitudes in 1790 as quoted here, see Jefferson to Thomas Mann Randolph, Jr., June 20, 1790, to Francis Eppes, July 4, 1790, and to Monroe, June 20, July 11, 1790, ibid., 16:540, 598, 537, and 17:25. For earlier evolution of Jefferson's attitudes, see Jefferson to Randolph, April 18, 1790, to Henry Lee, April 26, 1790, to Randolph, May 30, 1790, to George Mason, June 13, 1790, to Richard Peters, June 13, 1790, ibid., 16:351, 385–86, 449–50, 493, 494.

Notes

42. Maclay, ed., *Journal*, 294 (June 15); Bowling, "First Congress," 182ff. That Washington had a hand in the negotiations and that Jefferson was acting as his emissary is charged in Maclay, ed., *Journal*, 312; Bowling, "First Congress," 194–99, demonstrates the president's active interest in the subject. See also chapter nine. Interestingly, on the day Jefferson approached Morris, Washington was writing a Virginia friend that, despite the unpopularity of assumption in Virginia, assumption "under *proper* restrictions, and scrutiny into Accounts," was both important and just (Washington to David Stuart, June 15, 1790, in Fitzpatrick, ed., *Writings of Washington*, 31:52–53).

43. The most explicit evidence that the agreement was as set forth here is contained in King, ed., *King*, 1:384–85; and Smith to Rutledge, July 25, August 8, 1790, in Rogers, ed., "Letters of Smith to Rutledge," 125–26, 132, 135–36. Tangential or inferential evidence is abundant; see for example Ames to Thomas Dwight, June 27, 1790, in Ames, ed., *Works of Ames*, 1:83–85, and, most particularly, *Annals of Congress* from June 28 in the Senate to July 29 in the House. Cooke, in "The Compromise of 1790," 541–42, argues that only the financial aspects were involved in the bargaining over the assumption, and that these were not settled at the dinner at Jefferson's. Bowling, in "Dinner at Jefferson's," 629–40, rebuts Cooke's argument, but not as effectively as he might have done had he fully exploited the evidence in his doctoral thesis. The Cooke-Bowling exchange obscures the existence of two separate but interlocked compromises, each of which involved both houses of Congress. Once that is understood, the purpose of the interlocking—to cover a "corrupt" financial deal with an acceptable nonfinancial deal—becomes visible. So, too, does the great service Jefferson performed for the nation as well as his state by his diplomacy in 1790, despite his recanting two years later. Jefferson's claim in his 1792 document (Boyd, ed., *Jefferson Papers*, 17:205–6), that he initiated the dinner meeting only after Hamilton pleaded with him for help, does not square with the active role Jefferson was actually playing in 1790. Regarding the work of the commissioners in settling the state accounts, see The Defence of the Funding System, July 1795, in Syrett, ed., *Papers*, 19:37–38. It is clear from that document that Hamilton looked the other way while the commissioners made the "thousand compromises of principle" that were necessary to completing the terms of the compromises of 1790.

44. For Jefferson's satisfaction that Virginia had obtained "justice" in the assumption and settlement package—though he candidly admitted that some other states, unrepresented by such adroit bargainers, had not—see Jefferson to Eppes, July 25, to George Gilmer, July 25, to John Harvie, Jr., July 25, to Thomas Mann Randolph, Jr., July 25, and to Thomas Mann Randolph, July 25, 1790, in Boyd, ed., *Jefferson Papers*, 17:266–67, 269–70, 270–71, 274, 275–76. For evidence that Virginia received far more than "justice," see note 46.

45. Bowling, "First Congress," 224–25, 227–29; Rogers, *Evolution of a Federalist*, 197, citing Smith to Rutledge, July 14, 17, 1790. Smith, in writing to Rutledge on July 25, put Schuyler in the 4 percent camp (*South Carolina Historical Magazine*, 69:126). Briefly, the plan was to work as follows. Subscribers of the principal of the Continental debt, $29,384,000, would receive $19,589,333 in 6 percents and $9,794,667 in deferred sixes, face value. If interest fell to 4 percent in a decade, those securities would appreciate to 150 percent of their face value, a total of $44,076,000. Subscribers of back interest on the old debt would receive $13,030,000 in 3 percents,

which would be worth $9,772,500 on the market when interest rates reached 4 percent. The combined market value of all three kinds of securities—given the limited redeemability feature—would thus be $53,848,500. This, together with the interest paid during the decade ($15,662,600), would total $69,511,100. Subtracting the original capital investment (old principal and arrears of interest combined) of $42,414,000, the yield to subscribers would be $27,097,100—63 percent, or 6.3 percent a year. Calculations on the assumed state debts are different because 6 percent interest was compounded into the principal for one year, but over the course of the decade the yield (again assuming that interest fell to 4 percent) would be an average of 6.6 percent per annum; for the last nine years it would be almost exactly 6 percent.

According to Maclay (*Journal,* 335–36), Morris was not contented with the compromise but agreed to it because "half a loaf is better than no bread." Regarding the limitation on the redeemability of the 6 percents, see Hamilton's "Report on a Plan for the Further Support of Public Credit," January 16, 1795, in Syrett, ed., *Papers,* 18:67. Though I have seen no documentary evidence to this effect, it seems certain that the House version of the bill had increased the amount that could be redeemed or even dropped the restriction altogether, and that reduction or restoration was central to the compromise.

46. *Annals of Congress,* 1:998–99, 1002 (Senate, June 29, July 1, 1790), 2:1737 (July 9, 1790); King, ed., *King,* 1:384–85; Smith to Rutledge, July 25, 1790, in Rogers, ed., "Letters from Smith to Rutledge," 125–26.

47. Bowling, "First Congress," 226–27; Bowling, "Dinner at Jefferson's," 635–38; *Annals of Congress,* 2:1740–58 (July 16–29, 1790); vols. 72 and 73, folios 17 in each, and vol. 1113, folio 43, in Records of the Loan of 1790, National Archives; Maclay, ed., *Maclay Journal,* 336. Incidentally, five of the six Maryland congressmen were defeated for reelection in 1790, in an angry reaction against the failure to obtain the capital for Baltimore, and Washington provided federal apppointments for three of the four who remained politically active—Carroll, Gale, and William Smith (Bowling, "First Congress," 197).

48. Smith to Rutledge, June 28, July 4, August 8, 1790, in Rogers, ed., "Letters of Smith to Rutledge," 119–20, 121, 135–36; Ferguson, *Power of the Purse,* 322–24. See also The Defence of the Funding System, July 1795, in Syrett, ed., *Papers,* 19:37–38. Ferguson mistakenly makes the extension of time part of the Madison-Jefferson-Hamilton bargain.

49. *United States Statutes at Large,* 1:178–79 (August 5, 1790); 138–44 (August 4, 1790); 186–87 (August 12, 1790); and 180–82 (August 10, 1790).

50. "Address to the Public Creditors," September 1, 1790, in Syrett, ed., *Papers,* 7:1–5.

IX—The Mint, the Excise, and the Bank

1. The rise in value is estimated on the basis of newspaper quotations of security prices. Such quotations were rare until the spring of 1790, fairly common for some months thereafter, and regular after that. Prices are also quoted in the correspondence of William Constable and Andrew Craigie.

Notes

2. Regarding the popularity of funding and of the administration, and regarding the euphoric national mood, see *Gazette of the United States, Massachusetts Centinel,* Boston *Columbian Centinel, Providence Gazette and Country Journal, Pennsylvania Packet, Federal Gazette,* and *Charleston Evening Gazette,* August–December 1790. At various times in December, these and other newspapers reported the erection of a new monument in Boston which recited all the heroic episodes of the Revolution—battles, the Declaration of Independence, and so on—concluding with the funding of the public debts. See also John Wheelock to Hamilton, August 27, 1790, and Samuel Paterson to Hamilton, September 30, 1790, in Syrett, ed., *Papers,* 6:573–74, 7:81; Mitchell, *Hamilton,* 2:152–53.

3. Ames to Thomas Dwight, December 23, 1790, in Ames, ed., *Works of Ames,* 1:90; Maclay, ed., *Journal,* 352–55 (December 18–24, 1790); Report on a Plan for the Further Support of Public Credit, January 16, 1795, in Syrett, ed., *Papers,* 18:80.

4. Duer to Hamilton, January 19, 1791, Troup to Hamilton, January 19, 1791, James Tillary to Hamilton, January 1791, ibid., 7:442–44, 445, 614–16; Dangerfield, *Livingston,* 254–59; Young, *Democratic Republicans,* 187–92. The members of the first Senate had drawn lots to establish the constitutional rotation by which the terms of one-third of the senators expire every two years; Schuyler drew a two-year term. Burr, of course, was elected for a six-year term.

5. *Journal of the House of Delegates of the Commonwealth of Virginia,* 1790, November 3, 5, pp. 35–36, 38; Hamilton to Jay, November 13, 1790, in Syrett, ed., *Papers,* 7:149–50.

6. Jefferson to Gouverneur Morris, November 26, 1790, in Boyd, ed., *Jefferson Papers,* 18:82; Jefferson to Washington, April 24, 1791, in Andrew A. Lipscomb and Albert Ellery Bergh, eds., *The Writings of Thomas Jefferson* (20 vols., Washington, 1903–1904), 8:185; Magrath, *Yazoo,* 4. It seems reasonable to assume that Jefferson passed these bits of gossip along to Hamilton; he delighted in telling such stories about his enemies, and at this time, as will be seen, he and Hamilton were on friendly terms. Whether Jefferson's account is true is another matter. I found no record of Henry's funding of Georgia certificates in the Treasury records in the National Archives; but that is not conclusive evidence against the validity of Jefferson's charge, of course, since Henry could have operated through nominees or bought and sold the securities privately.

7. Jefferson to Hamilton, November 24, December 29, 1790, January 1, 1791, January 24, 1791, in Syrett, ed., *Papers,* 7:163–64, 389–90, 408, 451; Hamilton to Jefferson, January 11, 13, 1791, ibid., 7:423–24, 425–26; Conversation with George Beckwith, January 19–20, 1791, ibid., 7:440–42; Election to American Philosophical Society, ibid., 8:29. Madison made no recorded comment adverse to the bank between January of 1790, when Hamilton first mentioned that he would recommend it, and late January or early February of 1791, and made no efforts to organize an opposition despite the length of the warning he had. As to the excise, he had actually suggested one to Hamilton (Madison to Hamilton, November 19, 1789, ibid., 5:525). Jefferson first mentioned the bank and the excise, casually, in a letter to his son-in-law, expressing no opposition to the one and saying the other was supported on "Moral, as well as fiscal reasons"; he mentioned both subjects again in a letter to William Short a few days later, saying that the excise was unpopular in the South but again expressing neither opposition to nor reservations about the bank (Jefferson to

Thomas Mann Randolph, Jr., January 11, 1791, and to William Short, January 23, 1791, in Boyd, ed., *Jefferson Papers,* 18:489, 596). He first expressed reservations about the bank in early February—the timing, as will be shown, is significant—and even then he only indicated that such financial measures were being passed too fast for public opinion and declined to declare "whether these measures be right or wrong, abstractly" (to George Mason, February 4, 1791, and to Nicholas Lewis, February 9, 1791, ibid., 19:241–42, 263).

Boyd, ibid., 18:563–64 and note, properly corrects the editors of the *Hamilton Papers* and assigns January 11 to the letter dated January 1 in those papers, cited above. Boyd's interpretation of the exchange of January 11–13, however, in *Jefferson Papers,* 18:542–43, misrepresents Hamilton's position and is not sustained by the documents on which Boyd is commenting. In fact, Hamilton was in such an accommodating mood that he viewed without concern the prospect that Congress would pass a "navigation act" restricting British vessels in the American trade; see the conversation with Beckwith cited above.

8. Regarding Hamilton's conferring with Morris and Fitzsimons, see Hamilton to Robert Morris, November 9, 1790, in Syrett, ed., *Papers,* 7:146. The subject of the remainder of the paragraph is developed at length in chapter ten.

9. The several drafts of each of the reports are ibid., 7:210–36, 236–342, and 462–607. The reports on the bank and the mint are preceded there by lengthy editorial essays, concerned mainly with the sources of Hamilton's thinking on these subjects.

10. Hamilton's original idea of monetizing the debt directly and using the bank for purposes of the sinking fund is clear from his first Report on the Public Credit, ibid., 6:70, 106–8. His administrative decision is indicated in his letter to Nathaniel Appleton, commissioner of the United States loan office in Massachusetts, September 30, 1790, ibid., 7:80.

11. Report on a National Bank, in Syrett, ed., *Papers,* 7:334.

12. Some of the observations made here are explicit in the report, ibid., 7:338–39; the others are implicit.

13. Hamilton's insistence upon management of the bank for private profit is ibid., 7:331; an example of his overt use of the Bank of England's example to justify features of his own proposals is ibid., 7:339. For the original scholarly article comparing the two charters to show the similarities, see Charles F. Dunbar, "Some Precedents Followed by Alexander Hamilton," in O. M. W. Sprague, ed., *Economic Essays* (New York, 1904), 91–93. For an excellent analysis of Hamilton's use of the symbols of English fiscal orthodoxy, see Swanson, *Origins of Hamilton's Fiscal Policies,* especially at 73–87. Necker's influence upon Hamilton's thinking regarding the bank, though important, has been overlooked by historians; Necker is mentioned only in passing, for example, in the long introductory note in the *Hamilton Papers,* 7:236–56. Necker had, in creating the Caisse d'Escompte (Bank of Discount) in Paris, followed the English example closely but had experienced serious difficulties because public ministers could not resist the urge to make sound banking practice secondary to short-range reasons of state. He concluded that unless a nation's public debt were put on a footing as permanent and stable as that of England, the one-to-one relationship between it and the bank's capital would be unsound, and he cau-

Notes

tiously urged a departure from the English model; Necker, *Finances of France,* 3:348–51. Hamilton, operating under still different circumstances and not trusting politicians to act in the public interest, went the whole way, for he was convinced that he could trust businessmen to act in their own interest—which, given a proper organization of the bank, would be in the public interest.

14. Report on the Bank, in Syrett, ed., *Papers,* 7:326–28, 334–37.

15. Further Report on the Public Credit, ibid., 7:226.

16. In his first draft of the Report, Hamilton estimated a $975,000 yield and thus a surplus of nearly $150,000, and in a schedule annexed to the final report he made the same estimate; but in the body of the final draft he estimated a yield of $875,000 and a surplus of just under $50,000 (ibid., 7:213, 225, 227–28).

17. Ibid., 7:230; Necker, *Finances of France,* 1:lxxiii–lxxiv. The limitation upon the collectors' power of search did not preclude their obtaining a warrant permitting searches in other areas under special circumstances. Jefferson believed these features of Hamilton's recommendations ridded the excise of "the odious method of collection" (Jefferson to Thomas Mann Randolph, Jr., January 11, 1791, in Boyd, ed., *Jefferson Papers,* 18:489).

18. Syrett, ed., *Papers,* 7:228–30. Some of Hamilton's remarks are confusing unless it is remembered that, in discussing details of the proposed law, he is referring to his recommended bill of a year earlier, for which see ibid., 6:138–81.

19. Ibid., 7:231–35.

20. Ibid., 7:570–607, especially at 601.

21. Benton, ed., *Abridgment of Debates,* 1:262–67, 270–72 (January 5, 6, 21, 27, 1791); Bowling, "First Congress," 237–39, 338; Barber, "Adoption of the Whiskey Excise," in *William and Mary Quarterly,* 25:77–79; Paul S. Boyer, "Borrowed Rhetoric: The Massachusetts Excise Controversy of 1754," ibid., 21:328–51 (July 1964).

22. Maclay, ed., *Journal,* 368–74 (January 10–20, 1791); Bowling, "First Congress," 231–34; Report on the Bank, in Syrett, ed., *Papers,* 7:329–30.

23. Maclay, ed., *Journal,* 381–82, 385–90 (January 27–31, February 5–12, 1791); Barber, "Adoption of the Whiskey Excise," 79–80; Boyd, ed., *Jefferson Papers,* 19:37–38.

24. Theodore Sedgwick to Mrs. Sedgwick, December 26, 1790, quoted in Bowling, "First Congress," 234; Editorial Note on Locating the Federal District, in Boyd, ed., *Jefferson Papers,* 19:3–58; Jefferson to Washington, April 10, 1791, in Lipscomb and Bergh, eds., *Writings of Jefferson,* 8:165; Washington to William Deakins, Jr., and Benjamin Stoddert, April 1, 1791, in Fitzpatrick, ed., *Writings of Washington,* 31:263. The Pennsylvania Senate voted to postpone the appropriations bill. Regarding Jefferson's early indifference, see note 7.

25. Joseph Jones to James Monroe, January 27, 1791, and William L. Smith, *Politics of a Certain Party* (1792), quoted in Bowling, "First Congress," 233–34, 235; John Rutledge to William Short, March 30, 1791, in Boyd, ed., *Jefferson Papers,* 19:39, note 111; Ames to Thomas Dwight, February 7, 1791, and to George Richards Minot, February 17, 1791, in Ames, ed., *Works of Ames,* 1:94–96.

26. Benton, ed., *Abridgment of Debates,* 1:274–78, 306–8 (February 2, 8, 1791). The Constitutional Convention had in fact rejected a motion—made by Madison himself—regarding the power to create corporations, but the issue was muddled,

since some delegates thought Congress would have the power anyway and did not want to stir unnecessary opposition by making the grant explicit. See Farrand, ed., *Records of the Federal Convention*, 2:615–16 (Madison's Journal, September 14, 1787).

27. Brant, *Madison*, 3:331–32; Madison to Jefferson, February 14, 1790, in Boyd, ed., *Jefferson Papers*, 16:184. See also chapters six and eight.

28. Benton, ed., *Abridgment of Debates*, 1:278–96 (February 3–7, 1791); Bourne to Zephaniah Andrews, February 3, 1791, quoted in Bowling, "First Congress," 235; Ames to Minot, February 17, 1791, in Ames, ed., *Works of Ames*, 1:95–96; Theophile Cazenove to his princpals, February 5, 1791, in Boyd, ed., *Jefferson Papers*, 19:281, and the editor's note, ibid., 19:3–58.

29. Washington to Hamilton, February 16, 1791, in Syrett, ed., *Papers*, 8:50–51. Jefferson's opinion is in Boyd, ed., *Jefferson Papers*, 19:275–80. For evidence of Jefferson's endorsement of loose construction on other occasions, see the editor's note, ibid., 19:281, and Malone, *Jefferson and the Rights of Man*, 346–47. Jefferson's opinion is, in my judgment, so superficial and so desultory that it is difficult to believe that he took the matter seriously. Interestingly, he closed his opinion by saying that if Washington had doubts, "if the pro and the con hang so even as to balance his judgment, a just respect for the wisdom of the legislature" should induce him to approve the bill.

30. Bowling, "First Congress," 195–96; Bowling, "The Bank Bill, the Capital City, and President Washington," in *Capital Studies*, vol. 1 (1972); Washington to Arthur Young, December 5, 1791, December 12, 1793, in Fitzpatrick, ed., *Writings of Washington*, 31:438, 33:175–76; Boyd, ed., *Jefferson Papers*, editorial note at 19:26, 30, 47–49, 281. Boyd, ibid., 50–58, speculates that Washington's motivation was partisan politics, an effort abetted by Jefferson to weaken antinationalism in Virginia by winning favor with Washington's powerful neighbor and erstwhile friend, the anti-Federalist George Mason.

31. Theodore Sedgwick to Ephraim Williams, January 24, 1791, as quoted in Richard E. Welch, Jr., *Theodore Sedgwick, Federalist: A Political Portrait* (Middletown, Conn., 1965), 104; Madison to Washington, November 20, 1789, in Boyd, ed., *Jefferson Papers*, 19:15–16; Jefferson to Washington, March 27, 1791, in Lipscomb and Bergh, eds., *Writings of Jefferson*, 8:155; Washington to Deakins and Stoddert, April 1, 1791, and to the Commissioners of the District of Columbia, April 3, 1791, in Fitzpatrick, ed., *Writings of Washington*, 31:262–64; Washington to Hamilton, February 16, 1791, in Syrett, ed., *Papers*, 8:50; Maclay, ed., *Journal*, 373–75, 395–97 (January 19, 20, February 16–18, 1791).

32. Ibid., 396–98 (February 18, 23, 1791).

33. Ibid., 398–99 (February 23, 1791); Hamilton to Washington, February 21, 23, Washington to Hamilton, February 23, Hamilton to Washington, February 23, 1791, in Syrett, ed., *Papers*, 8:57–58, 62, 134, 135; Boyd, ed., *Jefferson Papers*, 19:37–38.

34. Opinion of the Constitutionality of an Act to Establish a Bank, February 23, 1791, in Syrett, ed., *Papers*, 8:98.

35. Ibid., 8:99.

36. Ibid., 8:99–101.

37. Ibid., 8:101–7.
38. Ibid., 8:107.
39. Ibid., 8:107–19.
40. Ibid., 8:120. Hamilton was most alert in reminding Washington that the territorial governments were corporations, quite as municipalities and banks were. The first English corporate charter, in fact, was that granted by William the Conqueror for the governance of the City of London; use of corporations for commercial purposes did not come along in England until the sixteenth century.
41. Ibid., 8:120–21.
42. Ibid., 8:121.
43. Ibid., 8:122.
44. Ibid., 8:123–24.
45. Ibid., 8:127–33.
46. Ibid., 8:129–34.
47. Hamilton to Washington, February 24, 1791 (two letters), ibid., 8:142–43.
48. Maclay, ed., *Journal,* 400–401 (February 25, 1791); Boyd, ed., *Jefferson Papers,* 19:37–40.

X—*Triumph and Trouble*

1. Ames to _____, enclosed in Ames to George Richards Minot, November 30, 1791, in Ames, ed., *Works of Ames,* 1:103–4. Nathaniel Gorham informed Hamilton that the "spirit of industry" of which Ames was so proud had only developed in Massachusetts during the last twenty years, and other correspondents made it clear that many Connecticut farmers still lacked it; Gorham to Hamilton, October 13, 1791, Peter Colt to John Chester, July 21, 1791, and Elisha Colt to John Chester, August 20, 1791, in Syrett, ed., *Papers,* 9:371, 323, 325. That Ames's description of southerners is applicable to Jefferson is clearly implicit in Dumas Malone's multivolume biography of Jefferson. For a good description of the Virginia oligarchy on the eve of the Revolution, see Sydnor, *Gentlemen Freeholders;* for an account of the way Virginians perverted law to write off their private debts, see Isaac S. Harrell, *Loyalism in Virginia: Chapters in the Economic History of the Revolution* (Durham, N.C., 1926); for an analysis showing North Carolina's disdain for the lawful obligation of contracts, see Morrill, *Practice and Politics of Fiat Finance;* for an example of similar disdain among South Carolina planters, see McDonald, *We The People,* 210–12.

2. Regarding the presidential succession bill, see Ames to Thomas Dwight, January 24, 1791, February 23, 1792, in Ames, ed., *Works of Ames,* 1:93, 114; Bowling, "First Congress," 266–67. See also Hamilton to Edward Carrington, May 26, 1792, in Syrett, ed., *Papers,* 11:441. Jefferson's distrust of men to whom achievement came easily is strikingly evident in his hostility toward, and envy of, Patrick Henry and John Marshall.

3. Washington to Hamilton, Jefferson, and Knox, April 4, 1791, and Adams to Hamilton, April 9, 1791, in Syrett, ed., *Papers,* 8:242–43, 258. That Hamilton was unaware of having alienated Jefferson on the occasion about to be described is evi-

dent from his sending to Madison a draft of his Report on Manufactures, with a suggestion that Madison, Jefferson, and Hamilton have a friendly discussion of it (Hamilton to Madison, November 24, 1791, ibid., 9:528).

4. Franklin B. Sawvel, ed., *The ANAS of Thomas Jefferson* (New York, 1970), 36–37; Hamilton's speech of June 22, 1787, in Syrett, ed., *Papers,* 4:216–17 (Yates's minutes); Green and Grose, eds., *Hume's Works,* 3:120–21 (*Essays,* vol. I, part I, essay VI).

5. For bibliography on the Oppositionists and their influence in America, see chapter seven, note 32.

6. Kramnick, *Bolingbroke and His Circle, passim.* I have paraphrased here the longer description of Bolingbroke's ideology in Forrest McDonald, *The Presidency of Thomas Jefferson* (Lawrence, Kansas, 1976), 18–22, which is based upon the works referred to in note 5.

7. Sawvel, ed., *Anas of Jefferson,* 35, 37. Regarding the notion that the Revolution had been fought to prevent the spread of Walpolean corruption to America, see Bailyn, *Ideological Origins,* and Parker, "Gospel of Opposition."

8. Sawvel, ed., *Anas of Jefferson,* 35, 37, 43–45, 113–14, and *passim.* For Hamilton's account of the break, see Hamilton to Edward Carrington, May 26, 1792, in Syrett, ed., *Papers,* 11:426–45. Regarding Hamilton's attitude toward parties, see Stourzh, *Hamilton and the Idea of Republican Government,* 110–20, and chapters fourteen and fifteen. For English and American attitudes toward parties in general, see Richard Hofstadter, *The Idea of a Party System: The Rise of Legitimate Opposition in the United States, 1780–1840* (Berkeley and Los Angeles, 1969), 1–73. Hofstadter's understanding of Hamilton, however, is derivative and flawed.

9. On the Bolingbrokean strategy, see Kramnick, *Bolingbroke and His Circle;* on the Jeffersonians' implementation of it, see chapter eleven, and Noble E. Cunningham, Jr., *The Jeffersonian Republicans: The Formation of Party Organization, 1789–1801* (Chapel Hill, 1957). The Ames quoatation is from Ames to George Richards Minot, May 3, 1792, in Ames, ed., *Works of Ames,* 1:118–19.

10. Troup to Hamilton, June 15, 1791, Nathaniel Hazard to Hamilton, November 25, 1791, in Syrett, ed., *Papers,* 8:478–79, 9:534. Malone, *Jefferson,* 2:359–63, emphasizes the pleasurable and "scientific" aspects of Jefferson's and Madison's trip and belittles the political aspects, but he cannot refute Troup's firsthand account. Moreover, the connections between the Virginians and the New Yorkers were many, varied, and strong; see Young, *Democratic Republicans,* 194–201, and, for example, Jefferson to Robert R. Livingston, February 4, 1791, and Livingston to Jefferson, February 20, 1791, in Boyd, ed., *Jefferson Papers,* 19:240–41, 295–96. See also Ketcham, *Madison,* 323, 332.

11. Treasury Department Circular to the Captains of the Revenue Cutters, June 4, 1791, in Syrett, ed., *Papers,* 8:426–33; the quotation is at page 432. Hamilton had employed Oppositionist rhetoric in his 1775 pamphlet, "The Farmer Refuted," but it seems clear that the influence of Bolingbroke upon him was almost nil.

12. Hamilton to Washington, April 17, 1791, ibid., 8:291–94; Mitchell, *Hamilton,* 2:357–59; White, *Federalists,* 116–27.

13. William Lowder for the Board of Assessors of the Town of Boston to Hamilton, July 14, 1791, Hamilton to the Board of Assessors, July 27, 1791, in Syrett, ed.,

Papers, 8:549–50, 580–81; William Skinner to Hamilton, July 22, 1791, Hamilton to Skinner, August 12, 1791, to James Taylor and Abishai Thomas, November 3, 1791, ibid., 8:565–69, 9:32–33, 456; Treasury Department Circular to Commissioners of Loans, November 1, 1790, ibid., 7:134–35; Hamilton to Jabez Bowen, August 20, 1791, to Theodore Foster, September 1, 1791, ibid., 9:80, 153–57; Catharine Greene to Hamilton, January 26, 1791, Hamilton to Catharine Greene, March 8, 1791, Report on the Petition of Catharine Greene, December 26, 1791, ibid., 7:457–58, 8:165–66, 10:406–68.

14. Hamilton to Washington, April 17, 1791, to William Heth, June 23, 1791, Jefferson to Hamilton, June 25, 1791, Heth to Hamilton, July 2, 1791, Hamilton to Welcome Arnold, July 22, 1791, Jeremiah Olney to Hamilton, July 29, 1791, Hamilton to Olney, October 7, 1791, ibid., 8:292–94, 499–501, 503, 523–26, 564, 584–86, 9:295–96; Jefferson to William Carmichael, March 17, 1791, in Boyd, ed., *Jefferson Papers,* 19:575; White, *Federalists,* 129, 143–44.

15. Circular to the Collectors of the Customs, December 18, 1790, Hamilton to William Heth, June 23, 1791, in Syrett, ed., *Papers,* 7:368–72, 8:500; for a sample of a general circular, see that to customs collectors, November 30, 1789, and for a specific one see that of March 5, 1791, ibid., 5:575–78, 8:162–63. See also Hamilton's correspondence with William Heth, Benjamin Lincoln, Jeremiah Olney, William Ellery, and Otho H. Williams.

16. Circular to the Collectors of the Customs, September 22, 1789, Hamilton to Sharp Delany, February 8, 1791, Nathaniel Appleton to Hamilton, March 16, 1791 (two letters), Appleton to Hamilton, May 15, 1791, Circular to the Collectors of the Customs, June 1, 1791, ibid., 5:394–95, 8:14, 191–93, 341–42, 409; Bray Hammond, *Banks and Politics in America from the Revolution to the Civil War* (Princeton, 1957), 125.

17. Hamilton to Lincoln, February 1, 1791, Lincoln to Hamilton, February 25, 1791, Meeting of Commissioners of the Sinking Fund, August 15, 1791, Hamilton to Seton, August 15, 16, 1791, Seton to Hamilton, August 18, 1791, in Syrett, ed., *Papers,* 8:1–2, 144, 9:67–69, 71–72, 77.

18. Short to Hamilton, July 26, 27, 1791, Hamilton to Willinks, Van Staphorsts, and Hubbard, October 3, 1791, February 14, 1792, ibid., 8:577–78, 581–82, 9:274, 11:33–34 and notes.

19. See the correspondence between Hamilton and Short throughout 1790–92, and especially the letters of September 1, 1790, May 9, 1791, and February 14, 1792, ibid., 7:6–13, 8:335–36 and notes, and 11:32. For a more detailed account, see Mitchell, *Hamilton,* 2:123–34.

20. Hamilton to Rufus King, August 17, 1791, and to James Brown, John Graham, and George Pickett, August 27, 1791, in Syrett, ed., *Papers,* 9:75–76, 113–14.

21. Report on the Bank, December 13, 1790, Hamilton to President and Directors of the Massachusetts Bank, May 30, 1791, and to the President and Directors of the Bank of New York, May 30, 1791, ibid., 7:334, 8:396, 397, and the act quoted at 397 note; James O. Wettereau, "The Branches of the First Bank of the United States," in *Journal of Economic History,* 2:71–72 (supplement, 1942); Rogers, *Evolution of a Federalist,* 219.

22. Miller, *Hamilton,* 268; James O. Wettereau, "New Light on the First Bank of

the United States," in *Pennsylvania Magazine of History and Biography*, 61:273–75 (July 1937); King to Hamilton, August 15, 1791, in Syrett, ed., *Papers*, 9:59–61; Jefferson to Edward Rutledge, August 25, 1791, quoted in Rogers, *Evolution of a Federalist*, 226–27.

23. King to Hamilton, August 15, 1791, Meeting of the Commissioners of the Sinking Fund, August 15, 1791, Hamilton to Seton, August 15, 16, 1791, to William Duer, August 17, 1791, to King, August 17, 1791, Seton to Hamilton, August 18, 1791, in Syrett, ed., *Papers*, 9:60–61 and note, 67–68, 68–69, 71–72, 74–75, 75–76, 77; Wettereau, "New Light," 275.

24. Report on the Bank, in Syrett, ed., *Papers*, 7:329–30; Ames to Hamilton, August 15, 1791, ibid., 9:55–59; Hamilton to Seton, November 25, 1791, ibid., 9:538–39; Wettereau, "Branches of the First Bank," 71–75; Rogers, *Evolution of a Federalist*, 225–26, 230 note 1; Christopher Gore to Rufus King, August 7, 1791, in King, ed., *King*, 1:400–401. See also Stuart Bruchey, "Alexander Hamilton and the State Banks, 1789 to 1795," in *William and Mary Quarterly*, 27:347–78 (July 1970).

25. Wettereau, "Branches of the First Bank," 74–75; Young, *Democratic Republicans*, 218; Ames to Dwight, March 8, 1792, in Ames, ed., *Works of Ames*, 1:115; Gore to King, August 7, 1791, in King, ed., *King*, 1:400–401; Ames to Hamilton, July 31, 1791, August 15, 1791, September 8, 1791, in Syrett, ed., *Papers*, 8:589–91, 9:55–59, 187–88.

26. Gore to King, August 7, 1791, in King, ed., *King*, 1:400–401; Paul Goodman, *The Democratic-Republicans of Massachusetts: Politics in a Young Republic* (Cambridge, Mass., 1964), 37–42; Davis, *Corporations*, 2:65–79.

27. Young, *Democratic Republicans*, 169–86; Ferguson, *Power of the Purse*, 331–32; chapter four.

28. Young, *Democratic Republicans*, 216, 245–50; Ferguson, *Power of the Purse*, 332.

29. Young, *Democratic Republicans*, 218, 233–43.

30. Ibid., 215–20; Hamilton to Nicholas Low, December 21, 1791, in Syrett, ed., *Papers*, 10:398–400.

31. Blair McClenachan et al. to Hamilton, March 16, 1791, John Nicholson to Hamilton, March 23, April 19, 1791, Hamilton to Thomas Forrest, John Nicholson, and Others, Public Creditors, May 27, 1791, Thomas Mifflin to Hamilton, June 2, 1791, and John Donnaldson to Mifflin, June 1, 1791, ibid., 8:193–97, 211–12, 298–99, 392–93, 410, 410–11 and note; Ferguson, *Power of the Purse*, 331–32.

32. Hamilton to King, July 8, 1791, and to Elizabeth Hamilton, July 27, 1791, in Syrett, ed., *Papers*, 8:532, 581.

33. Editors' Note and Draft and Printed Versions of the "Reynolds Pamphlet," August 25, 1797, ibid., 21:123, 226, 250. Regarding Hamilton's reputation for benevolence, see the appeal from Sarah Mumford, a boardinghouse keeper whose husband was an unemployed veteran, September 24, 1792, ibid., 12:423. As to Maria's family connections, Young, *Democratic Republicans*, 47, makes it clear that, though Gilbert Livingston was not of the manor-lord aristocracy, he was decidedly of the gentry—as were the families of Maria's parents, Richard Lewis and Susannah Van Der Burgh Lewis.

34. "Reynolds Pamphlet," in Syrett, ed., *Papers*, 21:226–27, 250–51. Though

Notes

Hamilton himself said only that his first encounter with Maria Reynolds was "some time in the summer of the year 1791," historians have generally concluded that the affair began shortly *before* rather than shortly *after* Betsey left Philadelphia; see, for example, Mitchell, *Hamilton,* 2:400, and Hendrickson, *Hamilton II,* 118. I do not agree with that conclusion, partly because I believe it would have been out of character for Hamilton, and partly for two more precise reasons. First, in the handwritten draft of his account of the affair (which, together with the slightly different printed version thereof, constitutes the only documentary evidence on the subject), Hamilton wrote that "She was shewn into the parlour where I went to her." It seems unlikely that Hamilton would have received a lady privately in the parlour had Betsey been at home. Secondly, the conclusion that Betsey was still in Philadelphia rests upon Hamilton's phrasing, in the printed version, that he "attended her into a room apart from the family." That language would seem to indicate conclusively that Betsey and the children were in the house at the time—but only to a modern reader. The word "family," in the eighteenth century, was most commonly used to mean the servants in a household or the retinue of a high official; Washington's wartime staff, for example, was referred to as his family, as in Hamilton's letter to Schuyler, February 18, 1781, in Syrett, ed., *Papers,* 2:563, "I am no longer a member of the General's family." This reading of Hamilton's use of the word in the Reynolds Pamphlet is borne out by the language he used two paragraphs later (ibid., 21:251). He said the assignations took place mainly at his home, "Mrs. Hamilton with her children"—not the family, but Betsey and her children—"being absent on a visit to her father."

35. Hamilton to Elizabeth Hamilton, August 2, 9, 10, 21, September 4, 1791, ibid., 9:7, 24, 25–26, 87, 172. Compare the tone and language of these letters with that of letters written to Betsey earlier, May 1786–April 1788, September 8, 1786, May 28, 1789, September 11, 15, 1790, ibid., 3:673, 684, 5:342–43, 7:33, 35.

36. Hamilton's fourth son, John Church Hamilton, was born August 22, 1792 (Hamilton, *Intimate Life,* 210).

37. Readers who know the phenomenon through experience or firsthand observation will readily understand what Hamilton was going through simply by reading the Reynolds Pamphlet. Others may gain an insight by studying the biographies of such of the great romantic poets as Shelley and Byron, who repeatedly experienced forbidden passions; or by considering the long-time relationship between Lord Admiral Horatio Nelson and Emma Hamilton; or by reading any of a number of the novels and short stories of Somerset Maugham.

38. "Reynolds Pamphlet," in Syrett, ed., *Papers,* 21:251. The editorial appendix, "The First Conflict in the Cabinet," in Boyd, ed., *Jefferson Papers,* 18:611–88, contains valuable information on the pay claims and other subjects, but it garbles the facts in a partisan effort to prove that Hamilton's account of the Reynolds affair was a lie to cover dishonest activity as secretary.

39. For a clear statement of these aims, see Report on Manufactures (Hamilton's Final Version, December 5, 1791), ibid., 10:295–96.

40. Prospectus of the Society for Establishing Useful Manufactures, August 1791, and Report on Manufactures, ibid., 9:145–47, 10:266. Regarding Coxe's role in the preparation of the report, see Jacob E. Cooke, *Tench Coxe and the Early Republic* (Chapel Hill, 1978), 182–89, and the same author's "Tench Coxe, Alex-

ander Hamilton, and the Encouragement of American Manufactures," in *William and Mary Quarterly*, 32:369–92 (July 1975).

41. Prospectus, in Syrett, ed., *Papers*, 9:146. Regarding the Bank of New York, see, for example, Hamilton to Seton, May 25, 1792, ibid., 11:424–25.

42. Miller, *Hamilton*, 300–301; Mitchell, *Hamilton*, 2:181ff.; Davis, *Corporations*, 1:349–89.

43. Mitchell, *Hamilton*, 2:193.

44. For an introduction to the physiocrats, see the editor's essay in Gilbert Chinard, ed., *The Correspondence of Jefferson and Du Pont de Nemours* (Baltimore, 1931), ix-cxxiii. That American farmers knew little of their own operations is clear in the letters Hamilton received, in answer to his inquiries, from Richard Peters, Edward Carrington, John Chester, and John Beale Bordley, in Syrett, ed., *Papers*, 9:114–18, 299–304, 318–63, 490–93.

45. Report on Manufactures, ibid., 10:245, 246–48, 253, 280.

46. Ibid., 10:262–64; Necker, *Finances of France*, 2:192.

47. Report on Manufactures, in Syrett, ed., *Papers*, 10:266–67.

48. Ibid., 10:255–56.

49. Hamilton develops these several points ibid., 10:317, 340, 295, 308, 312, 309, and 293–95, in that order.

50. Ibid., 10:282, 295, 290.

51. Ibid., 10:296–311, 338–40. Hamilton had doubts about the constitutionality of internal improvements at federal expense, and later proposed a constitutional amendment to authorize them.

XI—Attack and Counterattack

1. The quotation is from Hamilton to Laurens, October 11, 1780, in Syrett, ed., *Papers*, 2:467.

2. Davis, *Corporations*, 2:22–23; Ferguson, *Power of the Purse*, 222. The statement regarding debts to foreign creditors is derived from Jefferson to Madison, June 4, 1792, in Lipscomb and Bergh, eds., *Writings of Jefferson*, 8:366. According to Rogers, *Evolution of a Federalist*, 250–53, there were also some old debts outstanding in Charleston, mainly claims against the estates of deceased persons. Charleston, however, was thriving along with the rest of the country (ibid., 233–35). Regarding the relief of state tax burdens, see The Defence of the Funding System, July 1795, in Syrett, ed., *Papers*, 19:14–23.

3. Entries of April 12, May 7, June 3, 4, 1791, in Fitzpatrick, ed., *Diaries of Washington*, 4:159, 174, 192, 196. The quotes are from 196.

4. An excellent summary of the state of the press, partisan and otherwise, is in the appendix to Douglas Southall Freeman, *George Washington: A Biography*, Vol. 6: *Patriot and President* (New York, 1954), 395–413.

5. Cunningham, *Jeffersonian Republicans*, 13–19 and note 54; Ketcham, *Madison*, 326–27; debates of December 26, 1791, in *Annals of Congress*, 3:284–86; Lewis Leary, *That Rascal Freneau: A Study in Literary Failure* (New Brunswick,

Notes

N.J., 1941), 86–197; Jacob Axelrad, *Philip Freneau: Champion of Democracy* (Austin, 1967), 197–208.

6. *National Gazette,* October 31, 1791, to February 20, 1792, especially issues of November 3, 21, December 8, 15, 19, 1791; Leary, *That Rascal Freneau,* 197–99. Ketcham, *Madison,* 328–30, summarizes Madison's essays—overstating, I believe, the tone of animosity. In *The Presidency of Washington,* 93, I mistakenly said that the attacks on Hamilton began in the "very first issue," whereas in actuality they began late in February.

7. *National Gazette:* "British Government," January 30, 1792, "Government of the United States," February 6, 1792, and "Spirit of Governments," February 20, 1792, all by Madison; anonymous article on speculation, February 27, 1792; "A Farmer," March 1, 26, 1792; "Brutus No. 1," March 15 and subsequent numbers; March 19, April 5, 1792; and every issue thereafter.

8. *Annals of Congress,* 3:167–91, 199–204, 229ff., 284–86, 289–90, 362–401 (Debates of November 10–18, 21ff., December 6, 26, 27, 28, 1791, February 3–9, 1792); appendix compilation of roll-call votes in Cunningham, *Jeffersonian Republicans,* 267–72; Ames to Minot, December 23, 1791, to Thomas Dwight, February 23, 1792, to Minot, March 8, 1792, in Ames, ed., *Works of Ames,* 1:108, 113–14, 114–15; Freeman, *Washington,* 6:343–48.

9. Entries of July 10, October 1, 1792, March 2, 23, 1793, in Sawvel, ed., *Anas,* 85, 90–91, 113–15, and, for example, Jefferson to Washington, May 23, 1792, and to Lafayette, June 16, 1792, in Lipscomb and Bergh, eds., *Writings of Jefferson,* 8:344–45, 380–81. The "paper men" not on Jefferson's list were William Findley, who acquired nearly $6,000 in public securities (Records of the Loan of 1790, National Archives, vol. 624, folio 40, vol. 631, folio 223); John Francis Mercer, who acquired more than $7,000 in securities (ibid., vol. 945, folio 72); Alexander White, who held $1,619 in certificates of the Virginia debt (ibid., vol. 1113, folio 43); Abraham Baldwin, who had acquired about $2,500 in securities and nine shares of stock in the Bank of New York (ibid., vols. 495–97, folios 135–36 in each, and Domett, *Bank of New York,* 133); Anthony Wayne, who had acquired $3,600 in securities (New Loan Certificates, vol. A, accounts 739–42, in Public Records Division, Pennsylvania Historical and Museum Commission, Harrisburg); and Thomas Tudor Tucker (Beard, *Economic Origins,* 192). Comparisons of votes are tabulated from the appendix in Cunningham, *Jeffersonian Republicans,* 267–72. Hamilton's definition of republicanism is to be found, among other places, in Hamilton to Edward Carrington, May 26, 1792, and in "Catullus No. III," the source of the quotation, in Syrett, ed., *Papers,* 11:443 and 12:505. Slaveholdings are recorded in the several volumes by state entitled *Heads of Families in the Census of 1790.* The slaveholding New York anti-Federalists were Thomas Tredwell and Cornelius Schoonmaker, each of whom owned twelve slaves (*Heads of Families: New York,* 165, 183).

10. Entry of February 28, 1792, in Sawvel, ed., *Anas,* 50–51; White, *Federalists,* 176–77 and note. The Post Office bill became law on February 20, 1792.

11. Entry of February 29, 1792, in Sawvel, ed., *Anas,* 54–56.

12. "Reynolds Pamphlet," in Syrett, ed., *Papers,* 21:251–52.

13. Ibid., 21:253–54; James Reynolds to Hamilton, December 15, 17, 1791, Maria Reynolds to Hamilton, December 15, 1791, Hamilton to _____, December

18, 1791, Receipts from James Reynolds dated December 22, 1791, and January 3, 1792, ibid., 10:376–77, 387–88, 378–79, 389–90, 401, 503.

14. "Reynolds Pamphlet," ibid., 21:254–55; James Reynolds to Hamilton, January 17, 1792, Maria Reynolds to Hamilton (three letters), January 23—March 18, 1792, James Reynolds to Hamilton, March 24, 1792, Maria Reynolds to Hamilton, March 24, 1792, James Reynolds to Hamilton, April 3, 7, 17, 23, May 2, 1792, Maria Reynolds to Hamilton, June 2, 1792, James Reynolds to Hamilton, June 3–22, 23, 24, August 24, 30, 1792, ibid., 10:519–20, 557–59, 11:175–76, 176–77, 222, 254, 297, 330, 354, 481, 482, 553–54, 558, 12:271, 291.

15. Davis, *Corporations,* 1:278–80, 283; Young, *Democratic Republicans,* 220–21; William Seton to Hamilton, January 22, 1792, in Syrett, ed., *Papers,* 10:528–30. Part of the reason for Duer's frenzied activity was that he was in strained circumstances because of losses suffered in a land operation, the Scioto Company.

16. Hamilton to Seton, January 18, 1792, Seton to Hamilton, January 22, 1792, Hamilton to Seton, January 24, 1792, ibid., 10:525, 528–30, 562–63.

17. This is my reading of the evidence in Young, *Democratic Republicans,* 221; Mitchell, *Hamilton,* 2:171; and Davis, *Corporations,* 1:281–82. Young says the Duer group was "alarmed" by the proposed new bank; this is true, but only regarding the prospect that the bank would actually materialize, since the promotion had been initiated by them. Mitchell, pointing out that Duer secretly sold short 100 shares of stock in the Bank of New York on the day before the syndicate bought 110 shares, says Duer's plan was to break the market four months hence. That does not ring true, for it was contrary to Duer's nature; the short sale was doubtless partly a hedge and partly a product of Duer's growing insanity. Davis' contention—supported by contemporary observations—that a corner was contemplated is the only explanation that makes sense and squares with the known facts.

18. Davis, *Corporations,* 1:281, 284–85, is a well-documented account of these events. See also, for fuller quotations of security prices than Davis had available, "Market Prices of Public Stocks," in Hamilton's Report on the State of the Treasury, February 19, 1793, in Syrett, ed., *Papers,* 14:121–27. Troup's reference to Duer's insanity is in Troup to Hamilton, March 19, 1792, ibid., 11:156. This was written after Duer's failure and before his imprisonment. It could be nothing more than an exaggerated way of saying that Duer was extremely distraught over his failure; but Troup was not given to hyperbole, and the contrast between Duer's behavior during his last great speculation and his earlier behavior leads me to conclude that he was, at the end, in a euphoric mania, to say the least.

19. Davis, *Corporations,* 1:283, wherein these events are interpreted somewhat differently; Dangerfield, *Livingston,* 246; Young, *Democratic Republicans,* 222–23; Seton to Hamilton, February 6, 1792, James Tillary to Hamilton, March 6, 1792, Hamilton to William Short, April 16, 1792, in Syrett, ed., *Papers,* 11:17–18, 110, 289–91. Miller, *Hamilton,* 305, says that the Livingstons precipitated the collapse by cornering "all the gold and silver in New York," then drawing their specie from the banks. That may be true, but it seems unlikely; Miller cites no evidence, and I have been unable to find any.

20. Hamilton to Seton, February 10, 1792, in Syrett, ed., *Papers,* 11:27–28; see also Seton to Hamilton, February 6, 1792, ibid., 11:17–18. The quotation about Duer is from Davis, *Corporations,* 1:285.

Notes

21. Duer to Hamilton, March 12, 1792, and Hamilton to Duer, March 14, 1792, in Syrett, ed., *Papers,* 11:126–27, 131–32; Davis, *Corporations,* 1:289–92.

22. Troup to Hamilton, March 19, 1792, Schuyler to Hamilton, March 25, 1792, in Syrett, ed., *Papers,* 11:155–58, 186–90; Davis, *Corporations,* 1:295–305.

23. Hamilton to the President and Directors of the Bank of the United States, March 17, 1792, to Seton, March 19, 1792, Seton to Hamilton, March 21, 1792, Hamilton to Nathaniel Appleton, March 22, 1792, to Seton, March 25, 1792, Seton to Hamilton, March 26, 1792, Hamilton to Otho H. Williams, March 29, 1792, to Philip Livingston, April 2, 1792, to Seton, April 12, 1792, in Syrett, ed., *Papers,* 11:151–52, 154–55, 163–64, 166–68, 190–92, 194–95, 206, 218, 272–73.

24. Jefferson to T. M. Randolph, quoted in Davis, *Corporations,* 1:305–6; Jefferson to William Short, March 18, 1792, in Lipscomb and Bergh, eds., *Writings of Jefferson,* 8:317; Malone, *Jefferson,* 2:434–36, which approves of Jefferson's attitudes as it approves nearly everything Jefferson said and did; *National Gazette* throughout March and April, for example April 19, 1792; Hamilton to John Adams, March 20, 1792, to Jefferson, March 20, 1792, John Adams to Jay, March 21, 1792, Jay to Hamilton, March 23, 1792, Philip Livingston to Hamilton, March 24, 1792, Meeting of the Commissioners of the Sinking Fund, March 26, 1792, Jay to the Commissioners of the Sinking Fund, March 31, 1792, Meeting of the Commissioners of the Sinking Fund, April 4, 1792, Seton to Hamilton, April 9, 11, 1792, Hamilton to the President and Directors of the Bank of New York, April 12, 1792, to Seton, April 12, 1792, to the Governor and Directors of the Society for Establishing Useful Manufactures, April 14, 1792, Seton to Hamilton, April 16, 1792, Hamilton to Seton, May 10, 25, 1792, in Syrett, ed., *Papers,* 11:158, 159, 159–60, 172–73, 174–75, 193, 214–16, 224, 257–58, 263–64, 266, 272–73, 280–81, 288–89, 384, 424–25. For a complete record of sinking-fund purchases during the period, see ibid., 14:59–64, 114–17.

25. Seton to Hamilton, May 28, 1792, ibid., 11:453–54 and note. Interestingly, Steuben's debt was to the celebrated author of *Letters from an American Farmer,* J. Hector St. John Crèvecoeur.

26. *Annals of Congress,* 3:437–52 (March 8, 1792); Hamilton to Edward Carrington, May 26, 1792, in Syrett, ed., *Papers,* 11:432–33.

27. *Annals of Congress,* 3:489–94, 590–92 (March 27, May 2–4, 1792); White, *Federalists,* 148–50; Hamilton to Carrington, May 26, 1792, in Syrett, ed., *Papers,* 11:434 and note; *Gazette of the United States,* May 5, 1792.

28. Cunningham, *Jeffersonian Republicans,* 33–49; Young, *Democratic Republicans,* 324–41. Regarding Washington's continuing indecision, see entry of October 1, 1792, in Sawvel, ed., *Anas,* 88.

29. Jefferson to Washington, May 23, 1792, in Lipscomb and Bergh, eds., *Writings of Jefferson,* 8:341–49. The letter is couched as an appeal for Washington to serve a second term, most of the charges are cast as a report on popular opinion, and Hamilton is not mentioned by name; but the sense of it is clearly as reported here.

30. Entry of July 10, 1792, in Sawvel, ed., *Anas,* 83–86. See also the interview of October 1, 1792, ibid., 88–92.

31. Washington to Hamilton, July 29, 1792, in Syrett, ed., *Papers,* 12:129–34; compare Jefferson to Washington, May 23, 1792, in Lipscomb and Bergh, eds., *Writings of Jefferson,* 8:341–49. Compare also the complimentary closings of Washington's peacemaking letters to Jefferson and Hamilton, August 23 and 26, 1792, in

Fitzpatrick, ed., *Writings of Washington,* 32:132 and 134. Regarding the earlier exchange concerning the Bank, see Hamilton to Washington, March 27, 1791, Washington to Hamilton, April 4, 1791, in Syrett, ed., *Papers,* 8:217–23, 241–42.

32. Hamilton to Washington, August 18, 1792, ibid., 12:228–58. The quotations and specific points cited are at 228–29, 238, 249, 257.

33. Ibid., 12:252.

34. The unpublished pieces were entitled "The Vindication," numbers I–IV, ibid., 11:461–78. Hamilton's reaction on coming to realize the hostility of Madison and Jefferson is best seen in Hamilton to Edward Carrington, May 26, 1792, ibid., 11:426–45. Dumas Malone, in *Jefferson,* 2:472–73, characterizes Hamilton's public attacks as "recklessly abusive" and says that "he showed his worst taste when he wrote as SCOURGE." In fact, Hamilton did not write as "Scourge," the author was William Loughton Smith; see editorial note in Syrett, ed., *Papers,* 12:411–12. Malone compounds the error by citing another piece which he identifies as having been written by Smith, whom he characterizes as a "partisan of Hamilton's who wrote just like him."

35. Hamilton's defensive pieces were "Anti-Defamer," August 19, "Civis," September 5, "Amicus," September 11, "Civis to Mercator," September 11, and "Fact," I and II, September 11, October 16, 1792, in Syrett, ed., *Papers,* 12:259, 320–27, 354–56, 357–61, 361–65, 570–71. The quote is at 354.

36. The revelations are given here in the order in which the events occurred, not in the order in which Hamilton presented them. They are to be found, together with Hamilton's rebuttals of attempts to deny them, in "T.L.," I–III, July 25, 28, August 11, 1792, ibid., 12:107, 123–24, 193–94; "An American," I–III, August 4, 11, 18, 1792, ibid., 12:157–64, 188–93, 224; "Catullus," I–VI, September 15, 19, 29, October 17, November 24, December 22, 1792, ibid., 12:379–85, 393–401, 498–506, 578–87, 13:229–31, 348–56; "Metellus," October 24, 1792, ibid., 12:613–17; "A Plain Honest Man," October 30–November 17, 1792, ibid., 12:633–34. The quotation is 12:193–94. Malone, *Jefferson,* 2:470–73, castigates Hamilton for "irresponsible" journalism, but as indicated in note 34 above, Malone attributes writings to Hamilton inaccurately; and as for the charges Hamilton did make, if one will read carefully his articles cited here, and compare them with Malone's own coverage of the events in the first two volumes of his biography of Jefferson, one will find Hamilton's charges confirmed—though, of course, Malone puts a better face on Jefferson's doings than Hamilton did. See also Mitchell, *Hamilton,* 2:207–16.

37. Hamilton to John Adams, June 25, to Edward Carrington, July 25, to Coxe, September 1, to Washington, September 1, to Jay, September 3, 1792, Draft of September 7, 1792, Jay to Hamilton, September 8, 1792, Edmund Randolph to Hamilton, September 8, 1792, Hamilton to Washington, September 8, 9, 1792, Washington to Hamilton (two letters), September 17, 1792, Hamilton to Washington, September 22, 1792, King to Hamilton, September 27, 1792, George Clymer to Hamilton, September 28, October 4, 10, 1792, Hamilton to John Steele, October 15, 1792, Coxe to Hamilton, October 19, 1792, in Syrett, ed., *Papers,* 11:559–60 and note, 12:83–85, 305–10, 311–13, 316–17, 330–31 and note, 334–35, 336–40, 341, 344–47, 390–92, 412–15, 493–94, 495, 497, 517–22, 540–42, 567, 592–602. See also Marshall Smelser, "The Federalist Period as an Age of Passion," in *American Quar-*

Notes

terly, 10:391–419 (winter 1958); the same author's "The Jacobin Phrenzy: The Menace of Monarchy, Plutocracy, and Anglophilia, 1789–1798," in *The Review of Politics*, 21:239–58 (January 1959); the same author's "The Jacobin Phrenzy: Federalism and the Menace of Liberty, Equality, and Fraternity," ibid., 13:457–82 (October 1951); and John R. Howe, Jr., "Republican Thought and the Political Violence of the 1790s," in *American Quarterly*, 19:147–65 (summer 1967).

38. Malone, *Jefferson*, 2:158, 183; Boyd, ed., *Jefferson Papers*, 16:146ff.; entry of December 30, 1792, in Sawvel, ed., *Anas*, 102; Jefferson to William S. Smith, 1787, and to William Short, 1793, as quoted in Saul K. Padover, ed., *Thomas Jefferson on Democracy* (New York, 1939), 20–21.

39. Jefferson's "Explanation" and entries of September 30 and October 1, 1792, in Sawvel, ed., *Anas*, 40, 86–92; "Mirabeau," in *National Gazette*, December 12, 1792; Freeman, *Washington*, 412–13; Jefferson to Madison, October 1, 1792, in Syrett, ed., *Papers*, 12:85 note.

40. Young, *Democratic Republicans*, 304–23; Hamilton to King, June 28, July 25, 1792, in Syrett, ed., *Papers*, 11:588–89, 12:99–101.

41. Washington to Jefferson, August 23 and to Hamilton, August 26, 1792, in Fitzpatrick, ed., *Writings of Washington*, 32:128–32, 132–35; Hamilton to Washington, September 9, 1792, in Syrett, ed., *Papers*, 12:347–50; Jefferson to Washington, September 9, 1792, in Lipscomb and Bergh, eds., *Writings of Jefferson*, 8:394–408.

42. Hamilton to _____, September 26, to Charles Cotesworth Pinckney, October 10, to John Steele, October 15, 1792, in Syrett, ed., *Papers*, 12:480, 543–45, 567–69. An account of the election state-by-state is in McDonald, *Presidency of Washington*, 96–108; see also Cunningham, *Jeffersonian Republicans*, 33–50; Ketcham, *Madison*, 334–36; Young, *Democratic Republicans*, 324–41. Malone's portrayal of Hamilton as the "commander" of the Federalist campaign, in *Jefferson*, 2:418–85, is unsubstantiated by the evidence he cites and any I know of. On the outcome, see also Jefferson to Thomas Mann Randolph, Jr., November 16, 1792, in Lipscomb and Bergh, eds., *Writings of Jefferson*, 8:439–40.

43. Ames to Dwight, December 5, 31, 1792, January 1793, February 6, 1793, to Minot, February 20, 1793, in Ames, ed., *Works of Ames*, 1:124–29; Cunningham, *Jeffersonian Republicans*, 52–53; Jefferson to Randolph, November 16, 1792, in Lipscomb and Bergh, eds., *Writings of Jefferson*, 8:439–40.

44. A good brief account of all this is in the editorial note to an unfound letter from Reynolds to Hamilton, November 13–15, 1792, in Syrett, ed., *Papers*, 13:115–16. The editors do, however, make a minor error, dating Hamilton's Reynolds Pamphlet "August 31, 1797" three times and "August 31, 1791" once, whereas the actual date was August 25, 1797; ibid., 21:215. Documentation of this paragraph is ibid., 21:267–75.

45. "Reynolds Pamphlet," ibid., 21:257–58. See also Hamilton to Monroe, Muhlenberg, and Venable, December 17, and Monroe to Hamilton, December 20, 1792, ibid., 13:330, 344.

46. The sources cited in note 45, and entry of December 17, 1792, in Sawvel, ed., *Anas*, 100.

47. Report on the Redemption of the Public Debt, November 30, 1792, and Report on Foreign Loans, January 4, 1793, Syrett, ed., *Papers*, 13:261–75, 451–66.

48. The material in this paragraph is fully documented in the editorial note, ibid., 13:532–41. Mitchell, *Hamilton*, 2:249–52, has a copious account of the charges and their lack of substance.

49. Reports of February 4, 5 (two reports), 13, 13–14, 14, 19, 1793, in Syrett, ed., *Papers*, 13:542–79, 14:2–6, 17–26, 26–67, 68–79, 93–133.

50. Debates of February 28, March 1, 1793, in Benton, ed., *Abridgment of Debates*, 1:418–40. Regarding Jefferson's authorship of the resolutions, see Cunningham, *Jeffersonian Republicans*, 52, citing the Ford edition of Jefferson's *Writings*, 6:168–71.

XII—The Duel with Jefferson

1. James Monroe, *An Examination of the Late Proceedings in Congress Respecting the Official Conduct of the Secretary of the Treasury* (Philadelphia, 1793); *National Gazette*, March 9, 16, 23, 27, 1793; Edward Carrington to Hamilton, March 26, 1793, and William L. Smith to Hamilton, April 24, 1793, in Syrett, ed., *Papers*, 14:247–48, 341. It was long thought that the pamphlet was written by John Taylor of Caroline, another slaveowning Virginia senator, who soon emerged as the leading theoretical spokesman of Bolingbrokean agrarianism in America. Monroe's authorship has recently been established; see Edmund Berkeley and Dorothy Smith Berkeley, " 'The Piece Left Behind': Monroe's Authorship of a Political Pamphlet Revealed," in *Virginia Magazine of History and Biography*, 75:174–80 (April 1967).

2. Hamilton to Jonathan Trumbull, February 20, 25, 1793, John Bard to Hamilton, March 4, 1793, William Seton to Hamilton, March 5, 1793, David Ross to Hamilton, March 13, 1793, Hamilton to William Short, March 15, 1793, Gulian Verplanck to Hamilton, March 17, 1793, Jonathan Ogden to Hamilton, March 18, 1793, Elisha Boudinot to Hamilton, March 26, 1793, Edward Carrington to Hamilton, March 26, 1793, James McHenry to Hamilton, April 14, 1793, William L. Smith to Hamilton, April 24, 1793, John Steele to Hamilton, April 30, 1793, in Syrett, ed., *Papers*, 14:134–35, 151–53, 186–87, 192, 200–201, 206–7, 209, 213, 245–46, 247–48, 316–17, 338–41, 358–60.

3. Hamilton to Washington, June 21, 1793, ibid., 15:13.

4. Hamilton's superior knowledge of Europe and his superior judgment and skill are evident from a dispassionate comparative study of his correspondence with that of Jefferson during the period. This was also the judgment of the most astute and successful diplomat of the epoch, Talleyrand himself. See Talleyrand, *Étude sur la république*, 192, as quoted in Hamilton, *Intimate Life*, 255. The most thorough study of Hamilton as diplomat is Lycan, *Hamilton and Foreign Policy;* see also Johnson, "Hamilton and the British Orientation of American Foreign Policy." An interpretation unfavorable to Hamilton is Albert H. Bowman, "Jefferson, Hamilton and American Foreign Policy," in *Political Science Quarterly*, 71:18–41 (1956).

5. For a good brief summary of Jefferson's attitude toward France and the French Revolution, see Peterson, *Adams and Jefferson*, 46–60. For examples of that attitude in Jefferson's own words, see Jefferson to Short, January 3, 1793, in Lips-

comb and Bergh, eds., *Writings of Jefferson,* 9:9–13, and entries of December 27, 30, 1792, in Sawvel, ed., *Anas of Jefferson,* 100–103. The Hamilton quotation is from Hamilton to Carrington, May 26, 1792, in Syrett, ed., *Papers,* 11:439.

6. For examples of Hamilton's dispassionate approach and his attitude toward war, see Hamilton to Washington, September 15, 1790, "Pacificus No. VI," July 17, 1793, and Hamilton to Washington, April 14, 1794, ibid., 7:49–52, 15:100–106, and 16:266–79.

7. See the sources cited in note 6; Hamilton to James McHenry, April 29, 1797, and to Wolcott, June 6, 1797, ibid., 21:61–68, 98–100; see also Lycan, *Hamilton and Foreign Policy,* and Johnson, "Hamilton and the British Orientation of American Foreign Policy," *passim.*

8. Jefferson to Gouverneur Morris, August 12, 1790, Washington to Members of the Cabinet, August 27, 1790, Jefferson to Washington, August 28, 1790, and Jefferson to Thomas Mann Randolph, Jr., August 29, 1790, in Boyd, ed., *Jefferson Papers,* 17:127–28, 128–30, 473–74. Boyd's editorial note at 130 is contrary not only to the evidence in the *Hamilton Papers* but also to the opening paragraph of the document on which Boyd is commenting. For the general background of the Spanish-British crisis of 1790, see William Ray Manning, "The Nootka Sound Controversy," in American Historical Association *Annual Report for 1904* (Washington, 1905). See also Lycan, *Hamilton and Foreign Policy,* 120–31. Washington also requested opinions from Jay and Adams.

9. Hamilton to Washington, September 15, 1790, in Syrett, ed., *Papers,* 7:36–57. The quotations are at 47, 52–53.

10. For background to Anglo-American differences, see A. L. Burt, *The United States, Great Britain, and British North America from the Revolution to the Establishment of Peace after the War of 1812* (New York, 1961), 1–105; Samuel Flagg Bemis, *Jay's Treaty: A Study in Commerce and Diplomacy* (New Haven, 1962), 2–49, 434–37; Frederick A. Ogg, "Jay's Treaty and the Slavery Interests of the United States," in American Historical Association *Annual Report for 1901* (Washington, 1902), 1:275–98.

11. Hammond to Jefferson, March 5, 1792, Jefferson to Hammond, May 29, 1792, in Walter Lourie and others, eds., *American State Papers, Foreign Relations* (6 vols., Washington, 1832–1856), 1:191–200, 201–37; Jefferson to Washington, September 9, 1792, in Lipscomb and Bergh, eds., *Writings of Jefferson,* 8:400; Hamilton to Carrington, May 26, 1792, in Syrett, ed., *Papers,* 11:439; Lycan, *Hamilton and Foreign Policy,* 197–99. In reporting the exchange to his superior, Hammond put the best possible face on it and said, among other things, that Hamilton told him he lamented "the intemperate violence of his colleague" and assured Hammond that Jefferson's letter did not represent a "faithful exposition of the sentiments of this government" ("Conversation with George Hammond, May 29–June 2, 1792," in Syrett, ed., *Papers,* 11:454). Many scholars have severely criticized Hamilton on that account; Dumas Malone, for instance, in *Jefferson and the Rights of Man,* 419, says, "One would have to search far in American history to find a more flagrant example of interference by one high officer of the government with the policy of another which was clearly official policy, and the attempt to defeat it by secret intrigue with the representative of another country." Yet, as Malone himself points out, Hammond's re-

port contains a goodly number of misstatements and overstatements; and there is no reason to assume that his reporting of what Hamilton said was any more accurate than the rest of his letter. In any event, efforts to soothe the ruffled feathers of a representative of a country with which the United States was at peace can scarcely be called "secret intrigue" to defeat "official policy."

12. "View of the Commercial Regulations of France and Great Britain in Reference to the United States," 1792–1793, and editor's introduction to the same, in Syrett, ed., *Papers*, 13:395–436; Lycan, *Hamilton and Foreign Policy*, 198; Samuel Flagg Bemis, "Alexander Hamilton and the Limitation of Armaments," in *The Pacific Review*, 2:587–602 (March 1922).

13. Conversations with George Hammond, December 15–16, 1791, January 1–8, January 2–9, March 31, April 30–July 3, May 28–29, May 29–June 2, July 1–2, November 15–December 3, November 22, December 15–28, 1792, in Syrett, ed., *Papers*, 10:373–76, 493–96, 498–99, 11:212–14, 347–48, 446–49, 454–55, 12:1–3, 13:147–48, 213–15, 326–28, 410; entry of October 31, 1792, in Sawvel, ed., *Anas of Jefferson*, 92–95. See also the excellent analyses of these conversations in Lycan, *Hamilton and Foreign Policy*, 194–205, and Johnson, "Hamilton and the British Orientation of American Foreign Policy," 88–112.

14. Regarding Hamilton's evolving attitude toward the French Revolution, see Miller, *Hamilton*, 363; Hamilton to Lafayette, October 6, 1789, and Hamilton to Washington, September 15, 1790, in Syrett, ed., *Papers*, 5:425–26, 7:50–51; and Lycan, *Hamilton and Foreign Policy*, 132–45. Regarding American reactions in general, Charles D. Hazen, *Contemporary American Opinion of the French Revolution* (Baltimore, 1897) is a survey.

15. The best general account of the French Revolution is Georges Lefebvre, *The French Revolution from its Origins to 1793* (2 vols., New York, 1962, 1964).

16. Interestingly, about a month before Valmy, France conferred honorary citizenship upon a handful of people distinguished for antimonarchical and republican achievements. Three Americans were so honored: Washington, Madison, and Hamilton. Jean Marie Roland to Hamilton, October 10, 1792, in Syrett, ed., *Papers*, 12:545–46; Harry Ammon, *The Genet Mission* (New York, 1973), 19–20.

17. Ibid., 41; Entry of December 27, 1792, in Sawvel, ed., *Anas of Jefferson*, 100–102.

18. Editor's note to Cabinet Meeting of April 19, 1793, in Syrett, ed., *Papers*, 14:329. See also Hamilton's "Pacificus" letters, cited in note 30, below.

19. Ammon, *Genet Mission*, 25–28; Alexander DeConde, *Entangling Alliance: Politics & Diplomacy under George Washington* (Durham, N.C., 1958), 198–200.

20. Washington's earlier thinking is explicit in Jefferson's account of the conversation of December 27, 1792, in Sawvel, ed., *Anas of Jefferson*, 100–101; his new attitude is implicit in his letters to Hamilton and Jefferson on April 12, 1793, in Fitzpatrick, ed., *Writings of Washington*, 32:415–16. His conviction that internal instability would doom revolutionary France is expressed in Washington to Henry Lee, May 6, 1793, ibid., 32:450. Jefferson's attitude is implicit in much of his correspondence during the period; see, for example, Jefferson to William Short, January 3, and to Madison, May 19, June 2, 1793, in Lipscomb and Bergh, eds., *Writings of Jefferson*, 9:9–13, 96–98, 105–7.

Notes

21. Entries of November 1792, and May 7, 1793, in Sawvel, ed., *Anas of Jefferson*, 95, 121; editor's note, Tobias Lear to Hamilton, February 8, 1793, Cabinet Meeting of February 25, 1793, Willinks, Van Staphorsts, and Hubbard to Hamilton, February 26, 1793. Hamilton to Willinks, Van Staphorsts, and Hubbard, March 15, 1793, Hamilton to Washington, March 18, 1793, Washington to Hamilton, March 21, 1793, William Short to Hamilton, March 22, 1793 and enclosures, Hamilton to the President and Directors of the Bank of the United States, March 26, April 1, 1793, Hamilton to King, April 2, 1793, Willinks, Van Staphorsts, and Hubbard to Hamilton, April 4, 1793, William Bingham to Hamilton, April 9, 1793, Hamilton to Bingham, April 10, 1793, Hamilton to Thomas Willing, April 10–May 31, 1793, Willinks, Van Staphorsts, and Hubbard to Hamilton, May 1, 1793, Hamilton to King, May 2, 1793, Short to Hamilton, May 11, 1793, Agreement with . . . Bank of the United States, May 31, 1793, Washington to Hamilton, June 3, 1793, Draft of a Report on the French Debt, June 5, 1793, Hamilton to Washington, June 8, 15, 1793, Willinks, Van Staphorsts, and Hubbard to Hamilton, July 1, 1793, Hamilton to Willinks, Van Staphorsts, and Hubbard, August 12, 1793, Willinks, Van Staphorsts, and Hubbard to Hamilton, October 15, December 1, 1793, in Syrett, ed., *Papers*, 14:16–17, 141–42, 166–67, 207–8, 218–23, 226–27, 235–38, 245, 271–72, 274–76, 280–82, 296, 301, 307, 364–67, 397, 432–37, 500–501, 514–16, 518–21, 523–25, 550–53, 15:47–49, 231–32, 362–63, 433–34.

22. All known records of Hamilton's participation in the cabinet meetings are published ibid.; Jefferson's *Anas* contain notes on many of the discussions. See also John J. Reardon, *Edmund Randolph: A Biography* (New York, 1974), 220–38.

23. Washington to Gouverneur Morris, March 25, to David Stuart, April 9, to Jefferson, April 12, to Hamilton, April 12, and to Knox, April 12, 1793, in Fitzpatrick, ed., *Writings of Washington*, 32:402–3, 414, 415–16, 416, 417; "For the Gazette of the United States," March–April 1793, Hamilton to Jay, April 9, 1793 (two letters), Jay to Hamilton, April 11, 1793, Washington to Hamilton, Jefferson, Knox, and Randolph, April 18, 1793, and Carrington to Hamilton, April 26, 1793, in Syrett, ed., *Papers*, 14:267–69, 297–98, 299–300, 307–10, 326–27, 346–52; entry of April 18, 1793, in Sawvel, ed., *Anas of Jefferson*, 118–19.

24. Entries of April 18, May 7, 1793, in Sawvel, ed., *Anas of Jefferson*, 118–21; *American State Papers: Foreign Relations*, 1:140; Cabinet Meeting, April 19, 1793, and Hamilton and Knox to Washington, May 2, 1793, in Syrett, ed., *Papers*, 14:328–29, 367–96.

25. Ammon, *Genet Mission*, 44–53; DeConde, *Entangling Alliance*, 197–203; Rogers, *Evolution of a Federalist*, 254–56; slaveholdings from *Census of 1790, Heads of Families, South Carolina;* Charleston *City Gazette and Daily Advertiser*, April 16, 19, 20, 25, 27, May 2, 4, June 1, 6, 1793.

26. Jefferson to Monroe, May 5, to Randolph, May 8, to Madison, May 13, 1793, in Lipscomb and Bergh, eds., *Writings of Jefferson*, 9:75–78, 81–84, 87–89; Randolph to Jefferson, May 9, 1793, in Syrett, ed., *Papers*, note at 14:413–14.

27. Reardon, *Randolph*, 231–32; Jefferson to Hamilton, June 1, 1793, and editor's note thereto, in Syrett, ed., *Papers*, 14:508–10.

28. Hamilton to Washington, May 15, 1793, and editor's introductory note thereto, Treasury Department Circular to the Collectors of the Customs, May 30,

1793, Hamilton to King, June 15, 1793, ibid., 14:451–60, 499, 547–49; Charles Warren, *The Supreme Court in United States History* (2 vols., Boston, 1922, 1926), 1:105–17; entry of May 20, 1793, in Sawvel, ed., *Anas of Jefferson*, 122–23.

29. Ammon, *Genet Mission*, 74, 80–86; DeConde, *Entangling Alliance*, 217–22, 236–48; Jefferson to Monroe, June 28, 1793, in Lipscomb and Bergh, eds., *Writings of Jefferson*, 9:144–46; Entries of July 5, 8, 10, 15, 23, 26, in Sawvel, ed., *Anas of Jefferson*, 129–46, 148–53; Conversation with George Hammond, June 10–July 6, 1793, Jefferson to Genet, June 23, 1793, Cabinet Meeting of July 8, 1793, "Reasons for the Opinion of the Secretary of the Treasury and the Secretary at War Respecting the Brigantine *Little Sarah*," July 8, 1793, in Syrett, ed., *Papers*, 14:525–28, 15:17, 70–73, 74–79, and the notes thereto.

Two observations in this paragraph require further comment. Regarding the prepayment, Genet had the funds, provided by the Treasury, with which to honor Ternant's bills. When he refused to honor them, Hamilton felt obliged—to Jefferson's surprise—to honor the bills out of Treasury funds, leaving Genet with the original funds to spend as he pleased. Regarding Jefferson's aid to Genet on July 6, that entailed providing cover for a mission to the interior by the French agent André Michaux, which Jefferson willingly did with a letter of introduction to Governor Isaac Shelby of Kentucky. Genet's and Jefferson's accounts of the episode differ in an important detail: Jefferson maintained that he approved Michaux's mission but disapproved recruiting Americans for an attack on Louisiana, whereas Genet maintained that Jefferson cooperated even in that aspect of the venture. Ammon, *Genet Mission*, 84–85, asserts that Jefferson's account "is undoubtedly accurate"; I see no reason for trusting either account over the other. In any event, the fact remains that Jefferson covertly assisted Genet and thereby violated American neutrality.

30. "Pacificus," I–VII, June 29, July 3, 6, 10, 13–17, 27, 1793, in Syrett, ed., *Papers*, 15:33–43, 55–63, 65–69, 82–86, 90–95, 100–106, 130–35. The quotation is at 15:84.

31. "Pacificus," II, VI, ibid., 15:59–62, 106.

32. Mitchell, *Hamilton*, 2:233–35; George Cabot to King, August 2, Christopher Gore to King, August 4, 1793, in King, ed., *King*, 1:489, 490; Malone, *Jefferson*, 3:110–13.

33. Jefferson to Monroe, July 14, 1793, in Lipscomb and Bergh, eds., *Writings of Jefferson*, 9:165; King to Hamilton, August 3, 1793, in Syrett, ed., *Papers*, 15:172–74 and note; Ammon, *Genet Mission*, 121–23, 156–57; DeConde, *Entangling Alliance*, 400–402. Reports of the Terror began to be published in early June. See, for example, Charleston *City Gazette and Daily Advertiser*, June 7, 1793. That newspaper, by the way, carefully suppressed news of the slave uprising in Haiti, lest local slaves be infected with the spirit, but the awareness and fear of it is evident between the lines; see, for example, issues of June 15, 19, 27, 1793.

34. Hamilton to Washington, May 15, 1793, Cabinet Meetings of July 12, 18, 29–30, August 3, 1793, in Syrett, ed., *Papers*, 14:459, 15:87–88, 110–16, 139–42, 168–69 and the notes thereto; entries of July 23, 29, 30, August 1, 2, 3, 20, 23, 1793, in Sawvel, ed., *Anas of Jefferson*, 148–51, 153–61, 166–72; Ammon, *Genet Mission*, 99–104; Warren, *Supreme Court*, 1:108–12; Reardon, *Randolph*, 234–38.

35. "No Jacobin," I–IX, July 31, August 5, 8, 10, 14, 16, 23, 26, 28, 1793, in

Syrett, ed., *Papers*, 15:145–51, 184–91, 203–7, 224–28, 243–46, 249–50, 268–70, 281–84, 304–6. The quotation is at 15:145.

36. Boston *Independent Chronicle*, July 25, 1793; Higginson to Hamilton, July 26, 1793, King to Hamilton, August 3, 1793, Hamilton to King, August 13, 1793, in Syrett, ed., *Papers*, 15:127–29, 172–74, 233–41; New York *Daily Advertiser*, August 7, 8, 1793; Ammon, *Genet Mission*, 132–35. Ammon suggests tht Hamilton was the moving spirit behind these meetings, but support for that opinion is lacking. For instance, he says that Jay and King published their expose in hopes of provoking Genet "into making a public denial, which would enable them to confound him by producing Hamilton's circumstantial account"; but Hamilton's "circumstantial account" was written on August 13, the day after King's and Jay's statement was published in the New York *Diary* and five days after the public meeting which adopted the anti-Genet resolutions. Again, Ammon suggests (135–36) that Hamilton was behind the Richmond meeting of August 17, discussed in the following paragraph, saying that Hamilton's "point of contact" was Edward Carrington; but in fact Hamilton had not corresponded with Carrington since June 15 (Carrington had replied on July 2), and then not about a public meeting.

37. Ammon, *Genet Mission*, 136–41; the quotations are at 137 and 138.

38. The quotations are from King to Hamilton, August 3, 1793, in Syrett, ed., *Papers*, 15:173. See also Hamilton to King, July 25, 1792, ibid., 12:99–100.

39. For fuller accounts, see J. H. Powell, *Bring Out Your Dead: The Great Plague of Yellow Fever in Philadelphia in 1793* (Philadelphia, 1949); Mitchell, Hamilton, 2:281–86; Miller, *Hamilton*, 379–83. Rush has been regarded as the hero of the epidemic, which is possible only if one disregards the first premise of humane medicine: "Physician, do no harm."

40. Miller, *Hamilton*, 382–83; Axelrad, *Freneau*, 262–66; Fenno to Hamilton, November 9, 1793, Hamilton to King, November 11, 1793, to John Kean, November 29, 1793, in Syrett, ed., *Papers*, 15:393–94, 395–96, 418; Jefferson to Washington, December 31, 1793, in Lipscomb and Bergh, eds., *Writings of Jefferson*, 9:278–79.

41. Jefferson's report is in *American State Papers: Foreign Relations*, 1:300–304.

XIII—Prime Minister

1. Entry of August 6, 1793, in Sawvel, ed., *Anas of Jefferson*, 164–65; James Thomas Flexner, *George Washington: Anguish and Farewell (1793–1799)* (Boston, 1972), 104–11; Randolph to Hamilton, April 3, 1793, and William Bell to Hamilton, June 2, 1793, in Syrett, ed., *Papers*, 14:278–79 and note, 511; Reardon, *Randolph*, 220–83 *passim*. Flexner, at page 108, maintains that Washington chose Randolph as secretary of state because "the well of brilliant 'founding fathers' had been emptied to the bottom," but there were many better qualified men available—Ellsworth and King, for instance. It seems certain that the most appealing thing about Randolph was, to Washington, his apparent nonpartisanship.

2. These matters are thoroughly analyzed and documented in the editor's intro-

ductory notes for Andrew G. Fraunces to Hamilton, May 16, 1793, and Hamilton to Frederick A. C. Muhlenberg, December 16, 1793, in Syrett, ed., *Papers*, 14:460–70, 15:460–65.

3. Hamilton to John Adams, February 6, 22, 1794, and editorial notes thereto, ibid., 16:9–12, 47–49, and the introductory note for Hamilton to Muhlenberg, December 16, 1793, ibid., 15:461.

4. An excellent brief summary is contained in the editor's introductory note for Hamilton to Muhlenberg, December 16, 1793, ibid., 15:460–65. Hamilton's written reports to the committee are sprinkled through volumes 15 and 16.

5. Benton, ed., *Abridgment of Debates*, 1:458–59, 464–73 (January 3, 13–16, 1794); "View of the Commercial Regulations of France and Great Britain in Reference to the United States," 1792–1793, in Syrett, ed., *Papers*, 13:395–436; Rogers, *Evolution of a Federalist*, 260–61; Ketcham, *Madison*, 350–51; Ames to Timothy Dwight, January 17, 1794, to Christopher Gore, January 28, 1794, in Ames, ed., *Works of Ames*, 1:133–34.

6. Willinks, Van Staphorsts, and Hubbard to Hamilton, November 18, 1793, Jefferson to Hamilton, December 12, 1793, in Syrett, ed., *Papers*, 15:400–401, 456–57; *American State Papers: Foreign Relations*, 1:295–300.

7. Knox to Hamilton, April 21, 1794, and the editor's notes thereto, in Syrett, ed., *Papers*, 16:304–8; *Annals of Congress*, 4:153–55, 163–65, 432–37, 438–41 (January 2, 7, February 6, 7, 1794). A brief minute of the caucus, partly in Hamilton's handwriting, is in the Charleston Library Society; it is printed in Syrett, ed., *Papers*, 16:307–8.

8. Charles Callan Tansill, *The United States and Santo Domingo, 1798–1873: A Chapter in Caribbean Diplomacy* (Gloucester, Mass., 1967), 9–12; C. L. R. James, *The Black Jacobins: Toussaint L'Ouverture and the San Domingo Revolution* (New York, 1963), 146, 148, 151, 200; Syrett, ed., *Papers*, 14:298 note.

9. Bemis, *Jay's Treaty*, 214–16; *Gazette of the United States*, March 7, 1794, and subsequent issues; *Augusta Chronicle and Gazette of the State of Georgia*, March 29, 1794; *Hartford Gazette*, March 24, 1794. For press coverage, see Donald H. Stewart, *The Opposition Press of the Federalist Period* (Albany, New York, 1969), 179ff.

10. Hamilton to Washington, March 8, 1794, in Syrett, ed., *Papers*, 16:130–36 (the quotes are at 136); Washington's letters to William Pearce and others, March 9–23, 1794, in Fitzpatrick, ed., *Writings of Washington*, 33:287–304. There was a cabinet meeting on March 10, but the subject was filibustering expeditions being mounted in Kentucky for attacks on Louisiana.

11. *Annals of Congress*, 4:484–98 (March 10, 1794); see also the editor's notes for Hamilton to Washington, March 8 and April 14, 1794, in Syrett, ed., *Papers*, 16:130–34, 261–63, which provide full documentation for the data in this paragraph.

12. Randolph to Washington, April 6, 1794, ibid., 16:261–62; memorandum of March 12, 1794, in King, ed., *King*, 1:518.

13. Bemis, *Jay's Treaty*, 239–40, 267–68; Burt, *United States, Great Britain, and British North America*, 133–35.

14. King's notes, March 10–May 6, 1794, Nicholas to Washington, April 6, 1794, in Syrett, ed., *Papers*, 16:262–63.

Notes

15. Hamilton's position is stated in his "Report on Rules and Modes of Proceeding with Regard to the Collection, Keeping, and Disbursement of Public Moneys, and Accounting for the Same," March 4, 1794, ibid., 16:106–17; Republican opposition is indicated in the editor's notes thereto. See also the sources cited in note 16.

16. Hamilton to Washington, April 10, 14, 1791, Washington to Hamilton, May 7, 1791, Hamilton to the Select Committee, March 24, 1794, Randolph to Wahington, March 23, 1794, "Report on . . . Moneys Borrowed Abroad . . . as to the Point of Authority," April 1, 1794, Randolph to Washington, April 1, 1794, Abraham Baldwin to Hamilton, April 5, 1794, Washington to Hamilton, April 8, 1794, Madison to Jefferson, April 14, 1794, Randolph to Madison, July 9, August 8, 1811, Hamilton to Washington, April 8, 1794, ibid., 8:270–71, 288–89, 330, 16:193, 195, 231–32, 233, 241, 249–53 (the quotes are at 249, 251, and 249 note, respectively); Reardon, *Randolph,* 260–61.

17. Much of the material in this paragraph is derived or inferred from the letter cited in note 18; see also King's memoranda of March 27 and April 7 (1794), in King, ed., *King,* 1:518, 523–25.

18. Hamilton to Washington, April 14, 1794, in Syrett, ed., *Papers,* 16:261–79. The quotations are at 278.

19. Washington to Jay, April 15, 1794, in Fitzpatrick, ed., *Writings of Washington,* 33:329; King's memoranda of April 14–20, 1794, in King, ed., *King,* 1:520–22; editor's notes 22 and 23 for Hamilton to Washington, April 14, 1794, in Syrett, ed., *Papers,* 16:272–73.

20. Hamilton to Washington, April 23, 1794, to Randolph, April 27, 1794, "Suggestions for a Commercial Treaty," April–May 1794, Hamilton to Jay, May 6, 1794, ibid., 16:319–28, 346–47, 357–60, 381–85, and the notes thereto. The quotations are at 382 and 347, respectively. Jay's official instructions are in note 13 of Hamilton's letter to Washington of April 23, ibid., 18:323–28. Samuel Flagg Bemis's account of the sending of Jay, in the classic work *Jay's Treaty,* 272–75, 289–98, contains a number of errors. Bemis says, for instance, that "Hamilton now—after the resignation of Jefferson—[completely] dominated all matters of greater importance in the Department of State, as well as in the Treasury, and, in fact, in the War Department" (p. 273). This was true by July or August but far from true in April. Bemis also says, inaccurately, that Hamilton "expressly acquiesced in the Rule of the War of 1756."

21. Hamilton to Thomas Willing, March 3, 1794, to Washington, March 21, 1794, Washington to Hamilton, March 22, 1794, Hamilton to Washington, April 21, 1794, Washington to Hamilton, April 22, 1794, Hamilton to Washington, April 23, 1794, Washington to Hamilton, April 24, 1794, Hamilton to Washington, April 25, 1794, Washington to Hamilton, April 27, 1794, Hamilton to Washington, April 28, 1794, in Syrett, ed., *Papers,* 16:105–6, 190–91, 192, 308, 313, 328–29, 334–35, 340–43, 349–50, 352.

22. Lee to Hamilton, March 6, 1794, Cabinet Meetings of March 10, 18–19, 1794, Randolph to Bradford, Hamilton, and Knox, July 11, 1794, ibid., 16:121–22, 136–40, 162–63, 588–90. The key fact in regard to the frigates was that the legislation authorizing them provided that construction would cease when a treaty were signed with the Algerines. Speed was therefore imperative. Some of the ships were

built in time; the rest were not completed until the quasi-war with France, 1798–1800. See Knox to Hamilton, April 21, May 12, June 25, 1794, Hamilton to Thomas Mifflin, September 18, 1794, Tench Coxe to Hamilton, October 22, December 25, 1794, ibid., 16:304–8, 406–7, 526, 17:247–48, 339–40, 466–75. Wayne's expedition, the Kentucky problem, and the insurrection in western Pennsylvania are discussed below.

23. Editor's introductory note for Hamilton to Muhlenberg, December 16, 1793, Hamilton to Washington, May 27, 1794, Heth to Hamilton, July 6, 1794, ibid., 15:464–65, 16:434–35, 570.

24. Washington to Hamilton, May 29, 1794, ibid., 16:441–42. The thaw was signaled when, on July 2 and 11, Washington closed letters to Hamilton with the phrase, "Your Affectionate"—the first time he had done so in nine months.

25. Cabinet Meetings of March 10 and 18–19, May 13, 1794, Randolph to Bradford, Hamilton, and Knox, July 11, 1794, Washington to Hamilton, July 11, 1794, Hamilton to Washington, July 13, 1794, Hamilton to Governor George Mathews, September 25, 1794, ibid., 16:136–40, 162–63, 407–8, 588–90, 591–92, 600–602, 17:270–75. The editorial notes to these several documents give many important details regarding the handling of the situations in Georgia and Kentucky. See also *Augusta Chronicle and Gazette of the State of Georgia,* April 12, May 17, 1794, and throughout the summer.

26. Jacob E. Cooke, "The Whiskey Insurrection: A Re-evaluation," in *Pennsylvania History,* 30:316–46 (July 1963), dispels many of the myths about the whiskey rebels, though he refers to them as "Scotch and Irish" (p. 320), whereas actually the Scotch-Irish were a single distinct ethnic group, being descended from Scots Presbyterians who had settled the Ulster Plantations of northern Ireland in the seventeenth century. See James G. Leyburn, *The Scotch-Irish: A Social History* (Chapel Hill, 1962), Archibald R. B. Haldane, *The Drove Roads of Scotland* (London, 1952), and Gerhard Herm, *The Celts: The People who Came out of the Darkness* (London, 1976). See also J. Hector St. John Crèvecoeur, *Letters from an American Farmer* (New York, 1961), 52; Francois A. Michaux, *Travels to the West of the Alleghany Mountains* (Paris, 1804); and McDonald and McWhiney, "The Antebellum Southern Herdsman," in *Journal of Southern History.* The generalizations about southerners in this last-named article apply equally to western Pennsylvanians in the eighteenth century. The myth that whiskey was the frontiersmen's "cash crop" has been uncritically repeated by virtually every historian (Cooke excepted) who has dealt with the subject; see, for example, Leland D. Baldwin, *Whiskey Rebels: The Story of a Frontier Uprising* (Pittsburgh, 1939), 10, 25–28. The source of the notion was apparently Henry M. Brackenridge, son of one of the participants, who in a book written sixty-four years later even provided prices: he claimed that whiskey sold for fifty cents a gallon in the west and brought a dollar in the east, and that the iron and salt for which it was exchanged cost fifteen to twenty cents a pound and five dollars a bushel, respectively (quoted by Cooke at 329–30). I have studied the "prices current" lists in Philadelphia newspapers for the 1780s and 1790s and have never seen whiskey listed, even though almost every other conceivable commodity was. Incidentally, pig iron sold at a penny a pound, salt at forty to fifty cents a bushel. A resolution by the inhabitants of the town of Fayette, published in the *Pittsburgh Gazette,* October

Notes

4, 1794 (quoted by Cooke, p. 330, note 32) declares that the locals felt the tax as consumers but makes no mention of selling whiskey to the outside world.

27. "Report on the Difficulties in the Execution of the Act Laying Duties on Distilled Spirits," March 5, 1792, Hamilton to Tench Coxe, September 1, 1792, to Washington, September 1, 1792, to Jay, September 3, 1792, "Draft of a Proclamation Concerning Opposition to the Excise Law," September 7, 1792, Randolph to Hamilton, September 8, 1792, Hamilton to Washington, September 9, 1792, Hamilton to Washington, August 5, 1794, in Syrett, ed., *Papers*, 11:77–106, 12:305–10, 311–12, 316–17, 330–31, 336–40, 344–46, 17:24–48; *Pennsylvania Archives*, Second Series, 4:41, 288; Cooke, "Whiskey Insurrection," 328, 331–32; Baldwin, *Whiskey Rebels*, 100–101, 111, 285–86. Baldwin (p. 111) places the number of subpoenas issued against delinquent distillers in 1794 at 61; Cooke (p. 328) sets it at 37. Cooke (p. 319, note 3) takes issue with Baldwin's estimate of the number of stills in the four western counties of Pennsylvania, which is based largely on a documentary record of 1798 showing 1,357 stills at that date (Baldwin, 285–86); but, though Cooke's refutation of Baldwin is generally excellent, it is unconvincing on that point. Richard H. Kohn, in "The Washington Administration's Decision to Crush the Whiskey Rebellion," *Journal of American History*, 59:570 (December 1972), asserts that Hamilton was "eager" to use force in 1792. That is based mainly on a distortion of Hamilton's language in his letter to Washington of September 1, 1792, and it overlooks the fact that one of Hamilton's express reasons for advocating a proclamation (to Washington, September 9, 1792, in Syrett, ed., *Papers*, 12:345) was that it might "prevent the necessity of ulterior coertion." Curiously, Kohn (p. 571) interprets Washington as having a moderating influence upon a trigger-happy Hamilton because the president said that force should be used only as a "dernier resort"; and yet he fails to mention that in the letter in which Hamilton allegedly expressed his eagerness to employ force, Hamilton himself said that force was to be used only as a "last resort." Kohn's article appears in essentially the same form in his book, *Eagle and Sword: The Federalists and the Creation of the Military Establishment in America, 1783–1802* (New York, 1975), 157–70.

28. Hamilton has often been accused of seeking the subpoenas in a deliberate effort to provoke resistance so he could crush it with force; see Baldwin, *Whiskey Rebels*, 110–12. Uncritically following Baldwin, I repeated that charge myself in *The Presidency of Washington*, 145–46. As Cooke points out, however ("Whiskey Insurrection," 326–28), the source of the charge was William Findley, one of Hamilton's inveterate political enemies; there is absolutely no evidence to support it; and in the absence of evidence it must be assumed that the subpoenas were issued, as the law provided, by the federal district judge on application of the federal district attorney. Regarding the other complaints, see ibid., 334–35, and Baldwin, *Whiskey Rebels*, 73, 108–9.

29. Cooke, "Whiskey Insurrection," 336–42; Baldwin, *Whiskey Rebels*, 92–98; Eugene Perry Link, *Democratic-Republican Societies, 1790–1800* (New York, 1942), 145–48 and *passim*. The position of the western Pennsylvania democratic-republicans was strikingly reminiscent of the position Hamilton himself had held in 1775.

30. Deposition of Francis Mentges, August 1, 1794, Hamilton to Washington,

August 5, 1794, in Syrett, ed., *Papers,* 17:2–6, 49–58, and notes thereto; *Pennsylvania Archives,* Second Series, 4:78–79; Baldwin, *Whiskey Rebels,* 113–55; Neville to Tench Coxe, July 18, 1794, cited in Kohn, "Washington Administration's Decision," 572 (note 25).

31. Hamilton to Coxe, August 1, 1794, Deposition of Francis Mentges, August 1, 1794, Conference Concerning the Insurrection in Western Pennsylvania, August 2, 1794, Randolph to Washington, August 5, 1794, Hamilton to Washington, August 2, 1794, Hamilton and Knox to Washington, August 5, 1794, Hamilton to Washington, August 5, 1794, in Syrett, ed., *Papers,* 17:1, 2–6, 9–14, 10 note, 15–19, 21, 24–58; Cooke, "Whiskey Insurrection," 324–25.

32. Hamilton to Washington, August 2, 21 (first letter), 1794, "Tully" numbers II and III, in Syrett, ed., *Papers,* 17:18, 123–24, 148, 160.

33. Hamilton to Washington, August 2, 1794, ibid., 17:15–19; the quotations are at 19 and 18, respectively. Baldwin, *Whiskey Rebels,* 112, quotes William Findley as saying that Hamilton believed "a government could never be considered as established, till its power was put to the test by a trial of its military force." Kohn, "Washington Administration's Decision," 583 (note 73) gives almost the same quotation but attributes it to Randolph and only speculates that Randolph "may have" been quoting Hamilton. Both authors ignore Hamilton's primary goal, to avoid the use of force. In addition, in the note cited and in note 72 on pages 582–83, Kohn employs strained reasoning and speculation to make Hamilton out as trigger-happy. Ironically, in his concluding paragraph (p. 584), Kohn applauds the decision and concedes that "it defused the crisis and prevented bloodshed."

34. "Proclamation," August 7, 1794, in Fitzpatrick, ed., *Writings of Washington,* 33:457–61; Washington to Hamilton, August 12, 1794, Hamilton to Washington, August 16, 1794, Hamilton to Abraham Hunt, August 17, 1794, Knox to the governors of New Jersey, Pennsylvania, Maryland, and Virginia, August 7, 1794, in Syrett, ed., *Papers,* 17:88–89, 101, 102–3, and 103 note; *Dunlap and Claypoole's American Daily Advertiser,* August 21, 1794. Kohn, "Washington Administration's Decision," 576, in asserting that between August 7 and August 24 "the administration did not make any serious military preparations for an expedition," overlooks Knox's letters and Hamilton's letter to Hunt. In note 38 on the same page, Kohn mistakenly says that Washington asked Hamilton to prepare the report on August 6, whereas it was actually written on August 5.

35. The instructions to the commissioners are in Syrett, ed., *Papers,* 17:22–24; Hamilton's demurrer is at the bottom of the draft; Bradford's report is as quoted by Kohn, "Washington Administration's Decision," 577–78. According to Kohn, 578 and notes 49 and 50 thereon, the British minister George Hammond was called upon by two representatives of the rebels, proposing some kind of alliance with the Crown, and Pennsylvania Chief Justice Thomas McKean confirmed the rumors of overtures to the British in a letter to the state's attorney general. There were some negotiations between the commissioners and the rebels a few days later, but these broke down and reconfirmed Bradford's opinion. Regarding western Maryland, see Hamilton to Thomas Sim Lee, September 6, 1794, and Lee to Hamilton, September 12, 13, 1794, in Syrett, ed., *Papers,* 17:201–2, 225–27, 231–33, and the notes thereto.

36. Hamilton to Henry Lee, August 25, 1794 (two letters), to Thomas Sim Lee,

August 29, 1794 (two letters), Thomas Sim Lee to Hamilton, September 4, 1794, Hamilton to Thomas Mifflin, September 9, 1794, Hamilton to Thomas Sim Lee, September 10, 1794, Hamilton to King, September 17, 1794, Hamilton to Thomas Sim Lee, September 17, 18, 1794, Hamilton to Samuel Smith, September 19, 1794, Hamilton to Washington, September 19, 1794, Hamilton to King, September 22, 1794, ibid., 17:142–45, 161–63, 196–98, 210–11, 218–19, 241–42, 242–43, 246–47, 254, 254–55, 258–59; entry of September 30, 1794, in Fitzpatrick, ed., *Diaries of Washington*, 4:209; Kohn, "Washington Administration's Decision," 579–82. In regard to the family illnesses and Betsey's miscarriage, see Hamilton to Washington, July 11, 1794, Washington to Hamilton the same day, Hamilton to Washington, July 23, 1794, Hamilton to Elizabeth Hamilton, July 31, August 2, 8, 12 (two letters), 17, 21, October 20, 1794, and Knox to Hamilton, November 24, 1794, in Syrett, ed., *Papers*, 16:591–92, 615–16, 627–28, 17:14–15, 78, 84, 85, 101–2, 121, 330–31, 392.

    37. Baldwin, *Whiskey Rebels*, 220–72; J. Fauchet to Commissioner of Foreign Relations, October 31, 1794, in Reardon, *Randolph*, 371. The principal exception to the applause for the administration was Benjamin Bache's *General Advertiser*, which attacked Hamilton viciously for his part in putting down the insurrection; Philadelphia *General Advertiser*, November 8, 9, 1794; Washington to Hamilton, November 5, 1794, and Hamilton to Washington, November 11, 1794, in Syrett, ed., *Papers*, 17:357–58, 366–67. In his letter to Washington, Hamilton shrugged off Bache's attack, saying, "It is long since I have learnt to hold popular opinion of no value." He added that his reward for public service would be in "the esteem of the discerning and in internal consciousness of zealous endeavours for the public good." Kohn, "Washington Administration's Decision," 583–84, echoing a sentiment held by many historians, quotes the first part of Hamilton's statement as if Hamilton proposed to govern without regard to public opinion. ("The President," Kohn comments, "knew he could not govern on such principles.") Hamilton was, in actuality, ever concerned with public opinion in relation to government, as his repeated efforts to inform and influence that opinion attest; after all, his voluminous writings as Publius, Americus, Tully, Camillus, and others represented an enormous expenditure of energy toward that end. What he obviously meant in the quoted passage, read in context, was simply that he no longer cared what the opposition thought of him personally and that he had no desire to be "popular"; and even on that score he was partly indulging in bravado.

    38. Kohn, "Washington Administration's Decision," 584, quoting Justice James Iredell; Sixth Annual Address to Congress, November 19, 1794, in Fitzpatrick, ed., *Writings of Washington*, 34:28–35. It is the consensus of most historians that Washington's position was unfair, since some members of the Philadelphia and Baltimore societies had voluntarily served with the force that suppressed the rebellion; see, for example, William Miller, "The Democratic Societies and the Whiskey Insurrection," in *Pennsylvania Magazine of History and Biography*, 62:324–49 (July 1938). On the other hand, their vitriolic attacks upon the administration and upon Washington himself had earned them no right to expect favors from him. Only a handful of the societies survived after a few more months; Link, *Democratic-Republican Societies*, 200–203.

    39. Hamilton to Muhlenberg, December 1, 1794, to Washington, December 1,

1794, to Angelica Church, December 8, 1794, in Syrett, ed., *Papers,* 17:405, 413, 428–29.

40. Most of these weaknesses have been discussed in the context of Hamilton's coping with them, above. He summarized them in his Report on a Plan for the Further Support of Public Credit, January 16, 1795, ibid., 18:46–148.

41. Ibid., 18:81–82, 145–48. Actually, as a result of Jay's Treaty and related British commercial policies, American trade was so booming within a year that revenues were $2 million more than Hamilton estimated.

42. The proposals are cast in the form of ten "propositions," ibid., 18:85–92, followed by a series of "remarks" explaining each, ibid., 18:92–115.

43. Ibid., especially at 18:104–9. An excellent summary and analysis of the plan is Swanson's *Origins of Hamilton's Fiscal Policies,* 67–72. It is to be observed that, had Congress followed Hamilton's principle in modern times, the essentially uncontrolled inflation of the public debt since World War II would have been avoided.

44. Syrett, ed., *Papers,* especially at 18:94–95. Regarding the Republicans' embarrassment, see the introductory note at 18:48; Ames to George Richards Minot, January 20, 1795, in Ames, *Works of Ames,* 1:164–65.

45. Syrett, ed., *Papers,* 18:48–56; Hamilton to Theodore Sedgwick, February 18, 1795, to King, February 21, 1795, ibid., 18:277–81.

XIV—Minister in Absentia

1. McHenry to Hamilton, February 17, 1795, in Syrett, ed., *Papers,* 18:275.

2. A good account of the raucous fight over Jay's treaty is Young, *Democratic Republicans,* 445–67. The stoning episode is discussed at page 451.

3. Ibid., 248–49, 354, 356, 359, 414, 449–54, 458–59; Hamilton to Nicholson, July 20, 1795, and the note thereto, in Syrett, ed., *Papers,* 18:471–72; Milton Halsey Thomas, "Alexander Hamilton's Unfought Duel of 1795," in *Pennsylvania Magazine of History and Biography,* 78:342–52 (July 1954).

4. Edward Livingston to Margaret Beekman Livingston, July 20, 1795, quoted fully in Dangerfield, *Livingston,* 272–73, and at length in Syrett, ed., *Papers,* 20:42, note 2. See also Hamilton to Maturin Livingston, January 18, 21, 1796, and Livingston to Hamilton, January 20, 1796, ibid., 20:41, 44–45.

5. The negotiations are in seven letters exchanged between Nicholson and Hamilton, July 20–22, 1795, and "Drafts of Apology Required from James Nicholson," July 25–26, ibid., 18:472–74, 489–91, 501–3. Regarding Hamilton's bank account, see Hamilton to Thomas Willing, June 3, 1795, ibid., 18:358–59; for the will, see Hamilton to Troup, July 25, 1795, ibid., 18:503–7. Figures in the will are sometimes expressed in pounds and sometimes in dollars; I have converted them all into dollars on the basis of New York currency, in which a pound was equivalent to $2.50.

6. Greenleaf to Hamilton, July 27, 1796, and Hamilton to Greenleaf, July 30, 1796, ibid., 20:261–62, 264. Greenleaf subsequently went broke; whether Hamilton could have saved him is unknowable, but the association with Hamilton's name would surely have improved Greenleaf's ability to raise money.

Notes

7. Troup to Hamilton, March 31, 1795, and Hamilton to Troup, April 13, 1795, ibid., 18:309–11, 328–29.

8. James Watson to Hamilton, May 27, 1796, Le Guen to Hamilton, May 1, 1800, ibid., 20:199–200, 24:438–40; Hamilton, *Intimate Life,* 169 note; Goebel, ed., *Law Practice,* 2:48–164; Hendrickson, *Hamilton II,* 562–63, 566.

9. For Hamilton's practice in general, see Goebel, ed., *Law Practice,* vol. 2, *passim;* for a sampling of his early clientele, see Walter Livingston to Hamilton, January 29, 1795, Richard Peters to Hamilton, February 18, 1795, Hamilton to Walter Livingston, March 18, 1795, to Robert Morris, March 18, 1795, Richard Peters to Hamilton, March 24, 1795, Hamilton to Moses Brown, April 2, 1795, to Tjerck C. De-Witt, April 2, 1795, Horace and Seth Johnson and Company to Hamilton, April 9, 1795, Hamilton to James Watson, April 20, 1795, Gerrit Boom to Hamilton, May 6, 1795, Troup to Hamilton, May 11, 1795, Jacob Cuyler to Hamilton, June 1, 1795, Hamilton to Abraham Yates, Jr., June 12, 1795, to John Thurston and Company, and Thurston's reply, July 10, 1795, Nathaniel Ruggles to Hamilton, July 12, 1795, Hamilton to Troup, July 25, 1795, in Syrett, ed., *Papers,* 18:205–6, 277, 294, 295–301, 304, 313–14, 314, 315–16, 333, 337, 340–44, 355–56, 373, 455–56, 461, 507; see also Hamilton, *Intimate Life,* 156–76. Mitchell, *Hamilton,* 2:548, says that during the last few years of his life, Hamilton's income was $12,000 to $14,000 annually. In a letter to McHenry, July 30, 1798 (Syrett, ed., *Papers,* 22:42), Hamilton said his professional income was "three to four thousand pounds a year," but the kind of currency was not indicated. If Hamilton meant New York currency, as seems probable, that came to $7,500 to $10,000; if he meant sterling, the dollar equivalent was $13,320 to $17,760. On December 16, 1798 (ibid., 22:368) he said he could "moderately estimate" his practice at £4,000 a year.

10. These matters are brilliantly analyzed in Horwitz, *Transformation of American Law,* 1–30 and *passim.* See also Goebel, ed., *Law Practice,* 2:1–45. Goebel's essay, "The Role of Counsel" (1–28) contains valuable technical data but, unfortunately, is written in legalese that is difficult to follow. His essay, "The Economy in Hamilton's New York" (29–45), also contains valuable information but it is not always accurate. In notes 4 and 9, pages 30 and 31, for instance, he misrepresents what I had to say about New York's economy in an earlier work, *E Pluribus Unum.*

11. Goebel, ed., *Law Practice,* 2:14–26; Horwitz, *Transformation of American Law,* 141–43, 160–81. The quotation is from John Powell's *Essay upon the Laws of Contracts and Agreements* (1790), as quoted ibid., 160.

12. Magrath, *Yazoo,* 6–23, 149–50; Hamilton to James Greenleaf, October 9, 1795, and to Wolcott, May–August 1796, in Syrett, ed., *Papers,* 19:309–11 and notes, 20:211 and notes; Horwitz, *Transformation of American Law, passim.*

13. Ibid., 233–34; Goebel, ed., *Law Practice,* 2:569. There are four minor differences of transcription between the Horwitz and Goebel versions of this passage. I have followed Goebel.

14. Mitchell, *Hamilton,* 2:380–82; Henry Cabot Lodge, ed., *The Works of Alexander Hamilton,* vol. VIII (New York, 1903), 378–83; Warren, *Supreme Court,* 1:146–49 (the quote is at 149 note). The case was *Hylton* v. *U.S.,* 3 Dallas 171–84 (1796).

15. Warren, *Supreme Court,* 1:149 note.

16. See the following exchanges: Hamilton to Wolcott, April 10, June 13, 1795, from Wolcott, June 18, 1795, to Wolcott, June 22, 1795, from Wolcott, July 10, 28, September 26, 1795, to Wolcott, October 3, 1795, in Syrett, ed., *Papers,* 18:316–28, 376, 379–82, 384–86, 456–59, 509, 19:294–95, 296–97.

17. Washington to Hamilton, July 3, 1795, ibid., 18:398–400; see also Hamilton to Wolcott, June 26, 30, 1795, ibid., 18:388–89, 392–93. Despite the secrecy, Hamilton himself had seen the treaty before it was published; Hamilton to King, June 11, 1795, ibid., 18:370–71. Regarding the ultimate publication of the treaty, see ibid., 18:389–92, note 2. For a thorough survey of Republican propaganda against the treaty, see Stewart, *Opposition Press,* 195–235.

18. Hamilton to Washington, July 9–11, 1795, in Syrett, ed., *Papers,* 18:404–31.

19. Hamilton to Washington, July 9–11, 1795, ibid., 18:432–54. Regarding article XVII and the principle of "free ships, free goods," see also Hamilton to Washington, September 4, 1795, ibid., 19:235. Hamilton's public defense of the treaty is discussed in the following paragraph. That Hamilton was disappointed in the treaty and convinced he could have done better is strongly hinted in Angelica Church to Hamilton, February 19, 1796, and Hamilton to Angelica Church, June 19–20, 25, 1796, ibid., 20:56, 233, 235–36. Jefferson claimed that Hamilton told Talleyrand the treaty was "execrable" and that Jay was "an old woman for making it"; Bemis, *Jay's Treaty,* 371–72 note 27; but Jefferson had no way of knowing such a thing.

20. For the history of the Camillus essays, see the introductory note to "The Defence No. I," in Syrett, ed., *Papers,* 18:475–79; the essays ran from July 22, 1795, to January 9, 1796. Jefferson's comment is in Jefferson to Madison, September 21, 1795, in Lipscomb and Bergh, eds., *Writings of Jefferson,* 9:309–11.

21. Washington to Hamilton, July 7, 1795 and note 3 thereto, Washington to Hamilton, July 29, 1795, Hamilton to Wolcott, August 10, 1795, Randolph to Hamilton, August 16, 1795, Washington to Hamilton, August 31, 1795, in Syrett, ed., *Papers,* 18:402–3, 524–25, 19:111–12, 149–53, 204–6 (quotes at 112); Bradford Perkins, *The First Rapprochement: England and the United States, 1795–1805* (Berkeley and Los Angeles, 1967), 34–36; Reardon, *Randolph,* 299–303.

22. The most careful account of this episode is ibid., 301–2. The crucial documents necessary to understanding what happened, apart from Fauchet's dispatches themselves (printed in translation, ibid., 368–80), are Washington to Randolph, July 22, 1795, in Fitzpatrick, ed., *Writings of Washington,* 34:243–46, indicating that the president had not informed the other cabinet officers of his thinking and instructing Randolph to inform them; and Wolcott to Hamilton, July 30, 1795, in Syrett, ed., *Papers,* 18:526–32, in which Wolcott's anxiety for the treaty and his belittling of the importance of the British provisions order are made clear. Hamilton had not, at that point, told Wolcott of his own belief that the order was of vital importance; that came in Hamilton's letter to Wolcott of August 10, 1795, ibid., 19:111–13. See also the editorial notes to that letter, and Randolph to Hamilton, August 16, 1795, and the accompanying notes and enclosures, ibid., 19:149–53.

23. Washington to Hamilton, August 31, 1795, Hamilton to Washington, September 4, 1795, to Wolcott, April 20, 1796, ibid., 19:204–7, 232–36, 20:128. The provisions order was canceled by an order of September 9, 1795; Perkins, *First Rapprochement,* 195, note 25.

Notes

24. Pickering to Hamilton, November 17, 1795, Hamilton to Washington, November 5, 1796, to Wolcott, November 22, 1796, in Syrett, ed., *Papers,* 19:435–41, 20:374, 413–15. On July 16, 1796, Pickering closed a letter to Hamilton "respectfully & affectionately yours," which was taking improper liberties. Hamilton put him in his place at once, closing his next letter to Pickering (July 21, 1796) "respectfully & truly"; ibid., 20:257, 261. Pickering did not essay such intimacy again, even though Hamilton invited him to do so with his own affectionate closing, March 29, 1797, ibid., 20:557. See also Pickering to Hamilton, August 22, 1798, ibid., 22:156–57.

25. Washington to Hamilton, October 29, 1795 (second letter), Hamilton to Washington, November 5, 1795, ibid., 19:355–63, 395–97. Regarding Rutledge, see Wolcott to Hamilton, July 28, 1795 (first letter), and note 3 thereto, and Hamilton to King, December 14, 1795, ibid., 18:509–12, 19:484–85.

26. Washington to Hamilton, October 29, November 10, 16, 28, 1795, "Draft of George Washington's Seventh Annual Address to Congress," November 28–December 7, 1795, ibid., 19:359–63, 400, 431, 459–60, 460–67. Washington used Hamilton's draft almost without change; Richardson, ed., *Messages and Papers of the Presidents,* 1:182–86.

27. On American attitudes toward parties in general, see Hofstadter, *The Idea of a Party System.* For characteristic Federalist attitudes toward party and the Republicans as a party, see Fisher Ames to George Richards Minot, May 3, 1792, to Thomas Dwight, January 1793, to Christopher Gore, December 17, 1794, in Ames, ed., *Works of Ames,* 1:118–19, 126–27, 156–57, and ibid., 2:118; William Loughton Smith to Hamilton, April 24, 1793, in Syrett, ed., *Papers,* 14:338–41. Voting patterns and the changed attitudes in 1795–96 have been traced in *Annals of Congress.* As to the employment of partisan tactics in 1795–96, see note 29. Mary P. Ryan, in "Party Formation in the United States Congress, 1789–1796: A Quantitative Approach," in *William and Mary Quarterly,* 28:523–42 (July 1971), and H. James Henderson, "Quantitative Approaches to Party Formation in the United States Congress: A Comment," ibid., 30:307–24 (April 1973), have demonstrated that voting blocs existed in Congress from the beginning. It is viewing history out of context, however, to see such blocs as parties in the sense indicated here.

28. Hamilton's clearest statement of his opposition to parties is in his draft of Washington's Farewell Address, July 30, 1796, in Syrett, ed., *Papers,* 20:273–80. More about the misunderstandings between Hamilton and the Federalist party is discussed in chapter fifteen.

29. Hamilton to King, April 15, 1796, ibid., 20:114–15. See also Hamilton to William Loughton Smith, March 10, 1796, for his advice on how to refute Madison's defense of the Livingston resolution; and Hamilton to King, April 18, 20, 23, 24, 1796, for his efforts to mobilize public opinion; ibid., 20:72–74, 123, 126–28, 135–36, 136–37. For an example of Washington's antipathy to party, see Washington to Jefferson, July 6, 1796, in Fitzpatrick, ed., *Writings of Washington,* 35:118–20.

30. Hamilton to Wolcott, May 30, 1796, to Washington, June 1, 1796, in Syrett, ed., *Papers,* 20:204–5, 214–15.

31. Perkins, *First Rapprochement,* 44–45; Hamilton to Wolcott, April 20, 1796, in Syrett, ed., *Papers,* 20:128–31 (quote at 130).

32. Hamilton to Washington, May 10, 1796, Washington to Hamilton, May 15,

1796, Hamilton to Washington, July 30, 1796, Washington to Hamilton, August 10, 1796, Hamilton to Washington, August 10, 1796, ibid., 20:169–83, 264–88, 292–93, 293–303.

33. Hamilton to Washington, July 30, 1796, ibid., 20:265–88.

34. Page Smith, *John Adams* (2 vols., New York, 1962), 2:897; "The Defence No. I," July 22, 1795, in Syrett, ed., *Papers,* 18:482.

35. Samuel Flagg Bemis, "Washington's Farewell Address: A Foreign Policy of Independence," in *American Historical Review,* 39:258 (January 1934).

36. Gouverneur Morris to Hamilton, March 4, 1796, Hamilton to Washington, May 5, 1796, Washington to Hamilton, May 8, 1796, Hamilton to Washington, May 20, 1796, Wolcott to Hamilton, June 14, 17, 1796 and notes thereto, in Syrett, ed., *Papers,* 20:59–62, 161, 162–66, 190–95, 220–22, 230–33 (quote at 164).

37. Hamilton to McHenry, June 1, 1796, Adet to Pickering, May 31, 1796, Pickering to John Parish, June 2, 1796, ibid., 20:212–14 and note; King to Pickering, June 1, 1796, in King, ed., *King,* 2:63; Stephen G. Kurtz, *The Presidency of John Adams: The Collapse of Federalism, 1795–1800* (Philadelphia, 1957), 124.

38. Ibid., 117–19; Lycan, *Hamilton and Foreign Policy,* 276–77.

39. Wolcott to Hamilton, June 14, 1796, Hamilton to Wolcott, June 15, 1796, to Washington, June 16, 1796, to Wolcott, June 16, 1796, Wolcott to Hamilton, June 17, 1796, in Syrett, ed., *Papers,* 20:220–28, 230–33 and notes.

40. Wolcott, Pickering, and McHenry to Washington, July 2, 1796, in Fitzpatrick, ed., *Writings of Washington,* 35:123–24 note 47; Hamilton to Wolcott, June 15, 1796, to Washington, June 16, 1796, Washington to Hamilton, June 26, 1796, Hamilton to Washington, July 5, 1796, in Syrett, ed., *Papers,* 20:223–24, 225–26, 237–40, 246–48 (quotes at 226 and 246); Kurtz, *Presidency of Adams,* 118–21.

41. Ibid., 83, 125–27. Kurtz speculates that Adet received his instructions at the end of August, but since he was already in New York on his way northward by August 25, I assume he received them a few days earlier. See Adet to Hamilton, August 25, 1796, Hamilton to Stephen Van Rensselaer, August 25, 1796, in Syrett, ed., *Papers,* 20:304–5 and notes, 307.

42. Philadelphia *Aurora. General Advertiser,* October 31, 1796; Hamilton to Wolcott, November 1, 1796, Adet to Pickering, October 27, 1796, Washington to Hamilton, November 2, 1796, in Syrett, ed., *Papers,* 20:361, 361–62 note, 362–66.

43. Washington to Hamilton, November 3, 1796, Hamilton to Washington, November 4, 5, 1796, ibid., 20:366–67, 372–73, 374–75. See also Hamilton to Washington, November 11, 1796, ibid., 20:389–90.

44. Kurtz, *Presidency of Adams,* 128; Hamilton to Washington, November 5, 1796, Wolcott to Hamilton, November 17, 1796, in Syrett, ed., *Papers,* 20:374–75, 398–400.

45. It was assumed by some at the time and has been almost universally assumed by historians (myself included) that Hamilton was throughout 1796 engaged in a conspiracy to dump Adams and elect Pinckney. Except for one passing comment (in a letter to Elias Boudinot, July 7, 1796, ibid., 20:248), however, there is no evidence that Hamilton did any campaigning whatsoever until November 8—upon hearing from Wolcott that Pennsylvania, in the wake of Adet's first publication, had gone Republican. Nor is there any evidence in the *Hamilton Papers* that Hamilton

sought to slip Pinckney in ahead of Adams. Robert Troup said, in a letter to Rufus King written two years later, that in 1796 Hamilton "publickly gave out his wishes that Pinckney should be elected President" (Troup to King, November 16, 1798, in King, ed., *King,* 2:466). But Troup's memory was faulty: in a letter to King written just after the election, on January 28, 1797, he made it clear that the interpretation given here is accurate. The "antifederal party," he said, was attempting to woo Adams by "endeavoring to raise an opinion that Hamilton and his friends wished to bring Pinckney forward in preference to him," but the truth was that "we judged it the soundest policy to take a double chance" by supporting Adams and Pinckney equally. (ibid., 2:135). Theodore Sedgwick, writing to King on March 12, 1797, said the same thing (ibid., 2:156–57). Hamilton clarified this point in his "Letter from Alexander Hamilton, Concerning the Public Conduct and Character of John Adams, Esq. President of the United States," October 24, 1800, in Syrett, ed., *Papers,* 25:194–95. Pinckney's election to the presidency, he said, "would not have been disagreeable to me," and he so indicated "in the circles of my confidential friends." He specifically mentioned his brother-in-law, Stephen Van Rensselaer, and Troup. But the "primary object," he said, was to "exclude" Jefferson, and "if chance should decide in favor of Mr. PINCKNEY, it probably would not be a misfortune." For Hamilton's activities as described above, see Hamilton to _____, November 8, 1796, to Jeremiah Wadsworth, November 8, December 1, 1796, and "Federal Republican," December 12, 1796, ibid., 20:376–77, 377–78, 418–19, 439–42. See also Stephen Higginson to Hamilton, December 9, 1796, and Hamilton to King, December 16, 1796, ibid., 20:437–38, 444–46.

46. Stephen Higginson to Hamilton, January 12, 1797, ibid., 20:465–66.

47. King to Hamilton, November 30, 1796, February 6, 1797, and the notes thereto, ibid., 20:415–17, 505–8. King had, at Hamilton's urging to Washington, become minister to England.

48. Hamilton to Washington, January 19, 1797, Washington to Hamilton, January 22, 1797, Hamilton to Washington, January 25–31, 1797, ibid., 20:469–71, 476–77, 480–82 (quote at 470). Kurtz, *Presidency of Adams,* 116, mistakenly dates the first of these letters January 19, 1796. The newspaper pieces were "The Answer," December 8, 1796, and "The Warning," January 27, February 7, 21, 27, March 13, 27, 1797, in Syrett, ed., *Papers,* 20:421–34, 490–95, 509–12, 517–20, 524–27, 539–42, 551–56.

XV—The Adams Years

1. The quotation is from Franklin to Robert R. Livingston, July 22, 1783, in Syrett, ed., *Papers,* 25:3 note 5.

2. Harper to Hamilton, April 27, 1798, Hamilton to Adams, August 24, Adams to Hamilton, September 3, Hamilton to Adams, October 20, Adams to Hamilton, October 29, 1798, ibid., 21:449, 22:161, 172, 206–7, 217. Hamilton had asked Navy Secretary Benjamin Stoddert for assistance in obtaining a commission for his cousin Robert Hamilton; Adams reminded Hamilton of his signing of the commission,

suggesting that Hamilton had also sought that as a personal favor of the president, which he had not. See Hamilton to Stoddert, August 8, 21, Stoddert to Hamilton, August 24, Hamilton to Stoddert, August 29, September 3, 1798, ibid., 22:60–61, 152, 162, 168–69, 173. Regarding Adams's character, see Peter Shaw's excellent *The Character of John Adams* (Chapel Hill, 1976).

3. Regarding Adams's pomposity and verbosity, see Maclay, ed., *Journal, passim.* Regarding the qualifications to his admiration of the British constitution, see Sawvel, ed., *Anas of Jefferson,* 36–37. Regarding the remaining statements in this paragraph, see Smith, *Adams,* 2:875; John R. Howe, Jr., *The Changing Political Thought of John Adams* (Princeton, 1966), 200, 204, 222; Zoltán Haraszti, *John Adams & the Prophets of Progress* (Cambridge, Mass., 1952), 37; Kohn, *Eagle and Sword,* 173, 243; Manning J. Dauer, *The Adams Federalists* (Baltimore, 1953), 35–77; Adams to Abigail Adams, January 9, 1793, in Charles Francis Adams, ed., *Familiar Letters of John Adams and His Wife Abigail Adams* (2 vols., Boston, 1875), 2:138; Adams to Jefferson, May 11, 1794, in Lester J. Cappon, ed., *The Adams-Jefferson Letters* (2 vols., Chapel Hill, 1959), 1:255; Adams to McHenry, July 27, 1799, in Charles Francis Adams, ed., *The Works of John Adams, Second President of the United States: With a Life of the Author, Notes and Illustrations* (10 vols., Boston, 1850–1856), 9:4–5. On Adams as president, the most recent work is Ralph Adams Brown, *The Presidency of John Adams* (Lawrence, Kansas, 1975).

4. Historians have almost uniformly shared Adams's belief that Hamilton was running the government behind the scenes, even though their own evidence indicates the contrary. See, for instance, Dauer, *Adams Federalists;* Kurtz, *Presidency of Adams;* Howe, *Thought of Adams;* Alexander DeConde, *The Quasi-War: The Politics and Diplomacy of the Undeclared War with France, 1797–1801* (New York, 1966). At times even the editors of the *Hamilton Papers* seem to follow that line. Instances of straining or ignoring the evidence will be cited in the notes that follow.

5. The best account of Adams's overtures to Jefferson is in Kurtz, *Presidency of Adams,* 222, 228–30; see also DeConde, *Quasi-War,* 13–17, and Dauer, *Adams Federalists,* 124–26. Jefferson and Adams left their own accounts; Sawvel, ed., *Anas of Jefferson,* 184–85 (entry of March 2, 1797), and Adams, ed., *Works of Adams,* 1:508. Hamilton's remarks are from Hamilton to King, February 15, 1797, in Syrett, ed., *Papers,* 20:515–16.

6. Adams's questions to the cabinet are printed as an enclosure in McHenry to Hamilton, April 14, 1797, ibid., 21:48–49 note. Dauer, *Adams Federalists,* 127, mistakenly says Pickering sent a copy of the questions to Hamilton; only McHenry did ·so.

7. Hamilton to Sedgwick, January 20, February 26, to Pickering, March 22, 29, to Wolcott, March 30, to McHenry, March, to Smith, April 5, 1797, in Syrett, ed., *Papers,* 20:473–75, 521–23, 545–46, 556–57, 567–68, 574–75, 21:20–21. See also Tracy to Hamilton, April 6, 1797, ibid., 21:24–26.

8. See the letters cited in note 7 and Hamilton to Pickering, April 1, to Wolcott, April 5, to Smith, April 10, and to McHenry, April 29, 1797, ibid., 21:7, 22–23, 29–41, 61–68. Britain later saved its financial system by suspending specie payments and relying entirely on its paper money. Hamilton mistakenly thought that would be fatal; Gouverneur Morris believed Britain could hold out for a few years. See Hamil-

Notes

ton to Morris, January 10, 1801, and Morris to Hamilton, January 16, 1801, ibid., 25:307, 326.

9. Hamilton to Smith, April 10, to McHenry, April 29, 1797 and April 1797, ibid., 21:29–41, 61–68, 72–75. The quotations are at 66, the suggestion regarding reparations is at 41.

10. Hamilton to Pickering, March 22, Pickering to Hamilton, March 26, Wolcott to Hamilton, March 31, Tracy to Hamilton, April 6, Hamilton to Smith, April 10, to McHenry, April 29, Pickering to Hamilton, April 29, 1797, ibid., 20:545–46, 548–49, 569–74, 21:24–26, 29–41 and note 12, p. 38, 61–68, 68–71.

11. Adams's message of May 16, 1797, in Richardson, ed., *Messages and Papers*, 1:233–39; Smith, *Adams*, 2:929–35; Dauer, *Adams Federalists*, 128–30; Hamilton to Wolcott, June 6, 1797, in Syrett, ed., *Papers*, 21:99.

12. The background to this episode is fully treated in the admirable introductory note for Wolcott to Hamilton, July 3, 1797, ibid., 21:121–44. The quotations are from Hamilton to Monroe, July 5, 1797, ibid., 21:146–48. The statement to Fenno, July 6, was published in the *Gazette of the United States* of July 8. The concluding sentence in this letter—"It is my intention shortly to place the subject more precisely before the public"—I interpret to mean that he intended to publish Monroe's, Venable's, and Muhlenberg's explicit confirmation of his statement, since it follows immediately a statement of their acceptance of his explanation. DeConde, *Quasi-War*, 33, says that Callender's pamphlet was an exposé of Hamilton's affair with Maria Reynolds, whereas in actuality the exposure of the affair was Hamilton's defense against Callender's charges of peculation.

13. Introductory Note, in Syrett, ed., *Papers*, 21:135–36 and notes 50 and 51. As for the commonsense approach see Hamilton to Fenno, July 17–22, 1797, ibid., 21:167–68.

14. Hamilton to Monroe, July 5, 8, Venable to Hamilton, July 9, Hamilton to Monroe, July 10, Monroe to Hamilton, July 10, Muhlenberg to Hamilton, July 10, Venable to Hamilton, July 10, "David Gelston's Account of an Interview between Alexander Hamilton and James Monroe," July 11, John B. Church to Hamilton, July 13, Monroe to Hamilton, July 16, Monroe and Muhlenberg to Hamilton, July 17, Hamilton to Monroe and Muhlenberg, July 17, to Monroe, July 17, Monroe to Hamilton, July 17, Hamilton to Monroe and Monroe to Hamilton, July 18, Hamilton to Monroe, July 20, Monroe to Hamilton, July 21, Hamilton to Monroe, July 22, William Jackson to Hamilton, July 24, 25, Monroe to Hamilton, July 25, Hamilton to Monroe, July 28, Jackson to Hamilton, July 31, Monroe to Hamilton, July 31, Hamilton to Monroe, August 4, Jackson to Hamilton, August 5, Monroe to Hamilton, August 6, Jackson to Hamilton, August 7 (two letters), McHenry to Hamilton, August 7, Hamilton to Monroe, August 9, Jackson to Hamilton, August 11, Certificate by Monroe, August 16, 1797, ibid., 21:146–48, 152, 153–54, 157, 158–64, 166, 168–75, 176–77, 178–87, 192–93, 200–201, 204–9, 211. See also Introductory Note, ibid., 21:137–38.

15. Hamilton's rough draft of the pamphlet is ibid., 21:215–38, the printed version 238–84. The quotation is at 243.

16. McHenry to Hamilton, January 26, 1798, enclosing Adams to McHenry, Pickering, Wolcott, and Attorney General Charles Lee, January 24, 1798; ibid., 21:339–41. See also Pickering to Hamilton, March 25, 1798, ibid., 21:378, wherein

Pickering says that "provisional orders should be sent to Mr. King" regarding "a treaty offensive & defensive."

17. Hamilton to McHenry, January 27–February 11, 1798, ibid., 21:341–46. The quotes are at 342, 345, 346.

18. Relevant documents are in Hamilton to Pickering, March 23, 1798, note 1, and "The Stand No. V," April 16, 1798, ibid., 21:368–70, note 28, pp. 428–31; secondary accounts include William Stinchcombe, "The Diplomacy of the WXYZ Affair," in *William and Mary Quarterly*, 34:590–617 (October 1977); Smith, *Adams*, 2:952–65; Kohn, *Eagle and Sword*, 210–18; DeConde, *Quasi-War*, 66–108. The last is a good example of the kind of scholarship that has marked study of Hamilton's role in the Adams presidency. At page 67, DeConde says that Pickering "sent Hamilton a detailed summary of the [XYZ] dispatches. Hamilton replied, 'I am delighted with their contents.' " DeConde cites letters from Hamilton to Pickering dated March 17, 25, and 27, 1798 (page 399, note 65). There is no letter of March 25 to Pickering. That of March 27 contains the passage DeConde quotes but reveals that DeConde has altered the meaning by quoting it out of context. In context, Hamilton wrote, "I have this moment received your two favours of the 25th. I am delighted with their contents." Clearly, Hamilton's use of the relative pronoun "their" refers to Pickering's two letters of the 25th, which contain not merely a summary of the XYZ affair but a report on government measures being taken—and does not refer to the contents of the XYZ dispatches.

Hamilton was much upset at the growing bellicosity of Adams's replies to petitioners. See, for example, Hamilton to Wolcott, June 5, 1798, in Syrett, ed., *Papers*, 21:485–88 and note 1, 487–88.

19. McHenry to Hamilton, February 12, Hamilton to McHenry, February 20, to Sedgwick, March 1–15, to Pickering, March 17, 23, 27, "The Stand" Nos. I–VII, March 30, April 4, 7, 12, 16, 19, 21, Hamilton to King, March, Jay to Hamilton, April 19 (two letters), Hamilton to Jay, April 24, Harper to Hamilton, April 27, Hamilton to King, May 1, Wolcott to Hamilton, May 18, Hamilton to Washington, July 29–August 1, 1798, ibid., 21:351–52, 357, 361–63, 364–66, 368, 379–80, 381–87, 390–96, 402–8, 412–18, 418–32, 434–40, 441–47, 389–90, 433–34, 447, 449, 454–55, 465, 22:36–37.

20. Hamilton to Pickering, June 7, 8, to Wolcott, June 29, 1798, to Sedgwick, February 2, 1799, ibid., 21:494–95, 500–501, 522, 22:453. The quotes are at 21:495, 22:453, and 21:522, respectively. Hamilton also told Wolcott he objected to a statement of the president's that was "intemperate" and had too much "violent spirit," and he urged Washington to make a southern tour to help promote national unification; to Wolcott, June 5, to Washington, May 19, 1798, ibid., 21:485, 466–68. Kurtz, in *Presidency of Adams*, 314–17, quotes the "let us not establish a tyranny" statement but argues that it "is not an accurate or honest summary" of Hamilton's position (p. 316). He cites as evidence a letter that Hamilton wrote Jonathan Dayton (October–November 1799, published in Syrett, ed., *Papers*, 23:599–604), and concludes from that letter that Hamilton was espousing a "reactionary program" of repression based upon the use of "his military machine" (p. 317). In actuality the letter is a broad program of suggestions to render the national government more energetic, popular, and convenient, largely through constitutional amendments; the only "repression" Ham-

Notes

ilton advocated was the deportation of several "Renegade Aliens" who were conducting some of "the most incendiary presses" in the country "in open contempt and defiance of the laws" (23:604). For a contrary view—which I find unconvincing—see James Morton Smith, "Alexander Hamilton, the Alien Law, and Seditious Libels," in *The Review of Politics,* 16:305–33 (July 1954). See also note 10 of the epilogue.

21. Hamilton to Washington, June 2, 1798, in Syrett, ed., *Papers,* 21:479. Recent historians have uniformly misread this letter as if Hamilton were angling or conspiring for a military command he ardently desired out of long suppressed hunger for military glory; see the works of Kurtz, Dauer, and Kohn, cited above, and the editorial comment in the *Hamilton Papers,* 22:5. That Hamilton, as an adolescent and in his early manhood, craved military glory is indisputable. That he was similarly motivated as a mature, forty-one-year-old father of a large family is an idea unsupported by evidence. Every extant document of Hamilton's for 1798 attests that he was reluctant to reenter military service, that he preferred not to make the sacrifice if doing so was avoidable, that he bent every effort to make it avoidable, and that he finally reentered out of an intense sense of public duty.

22. Washington to Hamilton, July 14, McHenry to Hamilton, July 25, 1798, ibid., 22:17–21, 29–33. The quotes are at 18. The editors' introduction to Washington's letter (22:4–17) contains a history of and a great deal of information about the dispute over command in 1798; but the editors' contention that Hamilton "supported . . . at every step in their campaign" (22:5) a conspiracy of the cabinet members to make Hamilton first in command behind Washington is contradicted by the very evidence they cite. That Pickering was so conspiring, and that McHenry cooperated with him, is abundantly documented; but Hamilton's own letters indicate (1) that Hamilton preferred not to serve at all and (2) that he was perfectly willing, though not eager, to accept a lower position. See the following two paragraphs. On the other hand, Hamilton strongly resented Adams's efforts, *after* appointing him first among the major generals, to then reduce him by surreptitious means to the third position. See "Letter from Alexander Hamilton, Concerning the Public Conduct and Character of John Adams, Esq. President of the United States," October 24, 1800, ibid., 25:228–29. But that is an entirely different matter.

23. Pickering to Hamilton, July 16, Hamilton to Pickering, July 17, to Washington, July 29–August 1, 1798, ibid., 22:22–23, 24, 36–40.

24. Smith, *Adams,* 2:972–74; Kurtz, *Presidency of Adams,* 325–26; Pickering to King, August 29, 1798, in King, ed., *King,* 2:404; Adams to McHenry, August 29, and Wolcott to Adams, September 17, 1798, in Syrett, ed., *Papers,* 22:8, 10–14.

25. Hamilton to Washington, July 29–August 1, to McHenry, July 30, to Wolcott, August 6, Wolcott to Hamilton, August 9, McHenry to Hamilton, August 10, 1798, ibid., 22:38–39, 41–42, 58–59, 64–65, 66–68. The Adams quotations are from Adams to McHenry, August 14, 29, 1798, ibid., 22:7, 9.

26. McHenry to Hamilton, September 6, Hamilton to McHenry, September 8, Wolcott to Adams, September 17, Washington to Adams, September 25, Adams to Washington, October 9, 1798, ibid., 22:176, 177, 10–14, 14–15, 15; Troup to King, October 2, 1798, in King, ed., *King,* 2:430.

27. Adams's talk of a new peace mission was in the form of a feeler suggestion to his secretary of state (Adams to Pickering, October 20, 1798, in Adams, ed., *Works of*

Adams, 8:609). The quotation is from Adams's message to Congress, June 21, 1798, in Richardson, ed., *Messages and Papers,* 1:266.

28. Hamilton's first intimations of his suspicions about Adams are in his letter to McHenry, December 26, 1798, McHenry's reply on December 28, 1798, and Hamilton to Washington, February 16, 1799, in Syrett, ed., *Papers,* 22:392, 397, 483. The Adams quote is from his message to Congress, December 8, 1798, in Richardson, ed., *Messages and Papers,* 1:272. His perception of the plot is clear from Adams to McHenry, July 27, 1799, in Adams, ed., *Works of Adams,* 9:4–5, wherein he said, "All the declamations, as well as demonstrations [of the dangers of standing armies, debts, and taxes], of Trenchard and Gordon, Bolingbroke, Barnard and Walpole, Hume, Burgh and Burke, rush upon my memory and frighten me out of my wits." On the delay in appointing officers, see Kohn, *Eagle and Sword,* 244–45. Kohn somewhat overrates the importance of political doctrine and somewhat underrates Adams's opposition to Hamilton's army in accounting for the delays, but he makes Adams's actions in causing the delays quite clear.

29. Wolcott to Hamilton, April 1, Hamilton to McHenry, June 14, McHenry to Hamilton, June 15, Hamilton to McHenry, August 19, 1799, in Syrett, ed., *Papers,* 23:1–2, 186–87, 190, 325–28 and note.

30. Pickering to Hamilton, February 9, Hamilton to Pickering, February 9, Sedgwick to Hamilton, February 19, Pickering to Hamilton, February 20, Hamilton to Pickering, February 21, to Sedwick, February 21, Sedgwick to Hamilton, February 22, Pickering to Hamilton, February 25, 1799, ibid., 22:473–74, 475, 487–90, 491 and note, 492–93, 494–95, 500–503 and note. The quote regarding Adams is from Sedgwick's letter of February 22 (ibid., 494) and that of Hamilton regarding the mission is from his letter of February 21 (ibid., 493). On the subject of the delay of the mission, see Jacob E. Cooke, "Country above Party: John Adams and the 1799 Mission to France," in Edmund P. Willis, ed., *Fame and the Founding Fathers* (Bethlehem, Pa., 1967), 66–67. This article, a work of thorough and careful scholarship, dispels many of the clichés and errors regarding Adams's presidency and Hamilton's role in it. See also Stephen G. Kurtz, "The French Mission of 1799–1800: Concluding Chapter in the Statecraft of John Adams," in *Political Science Quarterly,* 80:543–57 (December 1965), a careful and courageous article in which the author not only adds to his previous work but also corrects it and points where he had been wrong—as, for instance, in the matter of the delay of the mission (pp. 552–53 and note 24). Kurtz does not, however, accept all of Cooke's findings and corrections; see Kurtz's comments, printed at the end of Cooke's article (pp. 78–79).

31. The nightmare of trying to organize the army can be traced in vols. 22–24 of the *Hamilton Papers;* a good, though strangely biased and sometimes inaccurate account is Kohn, *Eagle and Sword,* 239–55.

32. Hamilton's philosophy on this subject runs through all his comments on military matters for a period of twenty years and more. A good succinct summary is in Washington to McHenry, first of three letters dated December 13, 1798, all of which Hamilton wrote, in Syrett, ed., *Papers,* 22:341–53. The quotations cited here are at 345.

33. Hamilton to William Loughton Smith, April 10, to Pickering, May 11, 1797, Washington to McHenry, December 13, Hamilton to James Gunn, December 22,

Notes

1798, Hamilton to McHenry, January 14, 1799, ibid., 21:39–40, 83–84, 22:344–46, 388–90, 416–17. The editorial note to the letter to Gunn (22:383–88) contains a summary of the legislation regarding the raising of the various regular and provisional armies, but is of no help in understanding what Hamilton was about.

34. William Heth to Hamilton, January 18, 1799, ibid., 22:422–24; Kurtz, *Presidency of Adams*, 354, 338–39; Kohn, *Eagle and Sword*, 216; Dice Robins Anderson, *William Branch Giles: A Study in the Politics of Virginia and the Nation from 1790 to 1830* (Gloucester, Mass., 1965), 69–70. The John Nicholas who defected may not have been the congressman; see Dumas Malone, *Jefferson and the Ordeal of Liberty* (Boston, 1962), 416 note. Malone argues that the militant measures did not contemplate armed resistance, and the editors of the *Hamilton Papers* (22:424 note 6) say that no resolution regarding arms was adopted by the Virginia legislature. So to say is to overlook the statutes cited by Kurtz (p. 354) and to disregard the later statements of the eminent Virginia Republicans William B. Giles and John Randolph of Roanoke, who said that Virginia's military measures of early 1799 were taken to enable the state "to resist by force the encroachments of the then administration upon her indisputable rights"; Anderson, *Giles,* 70, and Henry Adams, *John Randolph* (Boston, 1883), 28.

35. Hamilton to Sedgwick, February 2, and to McHenry, March 18, 1799, in Syrett, ed., *Papers,* 22:452–53, 552–53. Hamilton's letter to Sedgwick is often cited in support of the charge that Hamilton wanted to provoke a rebellion in Virginia, whereas his aim was obviously to prevent one through intimidation.

36. For the evolution of this plan, see Francisco Miranda to Hamilton, April 1, 1797, Hamilton to McHenry, January 27–February 11, Miranda to Hamilton, February 7, April 6–June 7, "The Stand" No. IV, April 12, King to Hamilton, June 8, July 31, Miranda to Hamilton, August 17, Hamilton to King, August 22, to Miranda, August 22, King to Hamilton, September 23, October 20, Hamilton to James Gunn, December 22, 1798, King to Hamilton, January 21, Hamilton to Harrison Gray Otis, January 26, 1799, ibid., 21:1–6, 345, 348–49, 399–402, 414, 499, 22:44, 78–79, 154–55, 155–56, 187–88, 207–8, 389, 426, 440–42; King to Pickering, April 6, August 17, October 20, to McHenry, December 8, to Charles Cotesworth Pinckney, December 10, 1798, in King, ed., *King,* 2:304–6, 392–94, 453–54, 483, 486–87.

37. Cooke, "Country above Party," 67–68 and notes; Stoddert to Adams, August 29, Adams to Stoddert, September 4, Stoddert to Adams, September 13, Adams to Pickering, September 16, 21, to Oliver Ellsworth, September 22, 1799, in Adams, ed., *Works of Adams,* 9:18–19, 19–20, 25–29, 30, 33, 35.

38. Hamilton to Adams, September 7, to Washington, September 9, Washington to Hamilton, September 15, Hamilton to Washington, September 23, to McHenry, October 6, 12, McHenry to Hamilton, October 16, 1799, "Letter from Alexander Hamilton," October 24, 1800, in Syrett, ed., *Papers,* 23:393–95, 402–7, 417–20, 468–69, 510, 515–22, 534–37, 25:221; Cooke, "Country above Party," 69–70; George Gibbs, *Memoirs of the Administrations of Washington and John Adams, Edited from the Papers of Oliver Wolcott* (2 vols., New York 1846), 2:276.

39. Cooke, "Country above Party," 71–77, thoroughly documents most of what is said in this paragraph. Adams's account of Hamilton's arguments, penned in 1809, is in Syrett, ed., *Papers,* 23:546–47.

40. Regarding Adams's popularity, see Kurtz, *Presidency of Adams,* 389–402. For the shifting legislation and election laws in 1800, see the introductory note for Hamilton to Sedgwick, May 4, 1800, in Syrett, ed., *Papers,* 24:444–52.

41. For a summary of Burr's tactics and the election of 1800 in New York, see Cunningham, *Jeffersonian Republicans,* 176–85. Burr's scheme for pulling dissident Republicans together had been the formation of the Manhattan Company, ostensibly for a waterworks but actually for a bank with an extremely liberal charter; see Beatrice G. Reubens, "Burr, Hamilton and the Manhattan Company," in *Political Science Quarterly,* 72:578–607 and 73:100–125 (December 1957 and March 1958).

42. Hamilton to Jay, May 7, 1800, in Syrett, ed., *Papers,* 24:464–67. Hamilton has been uniformly condemned for this proposal, even by his most sympathetic biographers; see, for example, Mitchell, *Hamilton,* 2:467–68. Mitchell says "Hamilton was here scheming to set aside the manifest will of the people." Left out of account was that (1) the city elections did not represent the will of the people in the presidential election except indirectly; (2) that Hamilton's proposal was designed to make the election directly reflect the will of the people in regard to the presidency; and (3) that most states considered changing their election laws to make them less democratic in 1800 and that five states, *including Republican Virginia,* actually did so. Hamilton's proposal thus violated none of the acceptable political conventions of the time.

43. McHenry to Adams, May 31, 1800 (a transcript of the conversation in which Adams forced McHenry to resign), in Syrett, ed., *Papers,* 24:552–65. See also McHenry to John McHenry, Jr., May 20, 1800, ibid., 24:507–12. Regarding Wolcott's attitude, see, for example, Wolcott to Hamilton, July 7, September 3, 1800, ibid., 25:15–16, 104–11. Kurtz, *Presidency of Adams,* 393–95, maintains that Adams's firing of Pickering and McHenry was, in part, a carefully calculated plan to run for reelection as an independent, which in fact is what Wolcott believed. But Kurtz leaves out of consideration the powerful element of irrationality that McHenry's transcript reveals. Kurtz is also mistaken in his analysis of the makeup of the split Federalist party, describing one wing as "loyal to Hamilton," the other as loyal to Adams. In fact, the split was between the *Pickering faction* and that supporting Adams, as Kurtz's own evidence attests.

44. The quotation is from Hamilton to McHenry, June 6, 1800, in Syrett, ed., *Papers,* 24:573. Regarding the situation in Pennsylvania, see the editors' notes ibid., 24:449–50. On Hamilton's unusual vehemence in the courtroom, see Goebel, *Law Practice,* 2:86, 88.

45. Introductory note for Hamilton to Benjamin Stoddert, June 6, 1800, Hamilton to Wolcott, July 1, 1800, in Syrett, ed., *Papers,* 24:574–85, 25:4; the quotation is from Ames to King (to William Payne), July 15, 1800, in King, ed., *King,* 3:275–76.

46. Hamilton to Charles Carroll of Carrollton, July 1, to Wolcott, July 1, to Adams, August 1, to Wolcott, August 3, to McHenry, August 27, to Adams, October 1, 1800, in Syrett, ed., *Papers,* 25:1–2, 4–5, 51, 54–55, 97, 125–26. For evidence that the threat of withholding outside votes was effective in holding New England in line, compare Ames to Hamilton, August 26, 1800, with Ames to Hamilton, December 1800, ibid., 25:86–88, 283–85.

47. "Letter from Alexander Hamilton," October 24, 1800, and the introductory note thereto, ibid., 25:169–234. The quote is at 233.

Notes

48. The revelations regarding Adams's attitude toward the Pinckneys is in "Letter from Alexander Hamilton," October 24, 1800, ibid., 25:198–204. For the effect in South Carolina, see Bushrod Washington to Wolcott, November 1, 1800, ibid., 25:249–50 note 7, and the introductory note for Hamilton to Sedgwick, May 4, 1800, ibid., 24:451–52. See that same note at 450 for the compromise settlement in Pennsylvania. As to Burr's machinations in South Carolina, he had arranged the marriage of his daughter to Joseph Allston, a prominent member of the South Carolina aristocracy, and through that connection had worked assiduously to promote the Jefferson-Burr ticket.

49. State-by-state electoral votes in the 1800 election are in the introductory note for Hamilton to Sedgwick, May 4, 1800, ibid., 24:452; compare those with the 1796 results, as reported in Kurtz, *Presidency of Adams,* 412–14.

50. For Hamilton's efforts see, among others, Hamilton to Sedgwick, December 22, to Otis, December 23, to Gouverneur Morris, December 24, to James A. Bayard, December 27, to James Ross, December 29, to Wolcott, December 16, 1800, to John Rutledge, Jr., January 4, to Bayard, January 16, 1801, in Syrett, ed., *Papers,* 25:269–70, 271, 271–72, 275–77, 280–81, 257, 293–98, 319–24. The quotes are at 320, 272, and 275, respectively. Hamilton did make one concession to expediency: he suggested that Federalists try to use their bargaining position to obtain assurance that Jefferson would support the existing fiscal system, the navy, and the policy of neutrality, and that he would retain existing officeholders except those in the "Great Departments."

51. Hamilton to Wolcott, December 16, 1800, note 1, and Bayard to Hamilton, March 8, 1801, ibid., 25:258–59, 344–45.

52. Troup to King, May 27, 1801, ibid., 25:376–78 (quote at 378, note 6).

53. Troup to King, August 8, 1801, in King, ed., *King,* 3:496.

Epilogue

1. For details on the building of the Grange, see the introductory note for Philip Schuyler to Hamilton, July 17, 1800, in Syrett, ed., *Papers,* 25:38–41.

2. Ibid., 25:450–51 note 7; Hamilton, *Intimate Life,* 71–72; Allan Nevins, *The Evening Post: A Century of Journalism* (New York, 1922), 9–34 and *passim.*

3. Contemporary accounts of the duels are republished in "The Duels between ———— Price and Philip Hamilton, and George I. Eacker," in *The Historical Magazine,* 2:193–204 (October 1867). Some details were disputed; probably the most nearly accurate account was that in *The Evening Post* of November 28, 1801, reprinted ibid., 2:197–200. The quotation is from a letter from Philip's college classmate Thomas W. Rathbone to his sister Eunice Rathbone, ibid., 2:203.

4. Hamilton to John Dickinson, March 29, 1802, and to Benjamin Rush on the same day, in Syrett, ed., *Papers,* 25:583–84 (quote at 583); Troup to King, December 5, 1801, in King, ed., *King,* 4:27–28.

5. Hamilton to Morris, February 29, 1802, in Syrett, ed., *Papers,* 25:544. Regarding Jeffersonian policies, see McDonald, *Presidency of Jefferson, passim.*

6. Douglass Adair and Marvin Harvey, "Was Alexander Hamilton a Christian Statesman?" in *William and Mary Quarterly,* 12:308–29 (April 1955), is the fullest examination of the subject, but unfortunately the article contains numerous errors, is strongly biased against Hamilton, and is written from the perspective of modern Arminian Christianity, which is inappropriate to a historical examination of Hamilton's religious beliefs. Regarding the Christian Constitutional Society, see Hamilton to James A. Bayard, April 16–21, 1802, and Bayard to Hamilton, April 25, 1802, in Syrett, ed., *Papers,* 25:605–10, 613 (quotes at 606).

7. William Constable to Hamilton, March 23, 1801, Hamilton to Madison, May 20, 1801, Madison to Hamilton, May 26, 1801, ibid., 25:372–73, 385, 386; McDonald, *Presidency of Jefferson,* 62–69. Pinckney's treaty had guaranteed the United States the right of deposit at New Orleans for only three years, but practice had extended the privilege, and the United States had a reasonable claim that it was of indefinite duration.

8. "Hamilton on the Louisiana Purchase: A Newly Identified Editorial from the New-York Evening Post," in *William and Mary Quarterly,* 12:268–81 (April 1955). The quote is at 271. The editorial comment to this piece is misleading concerning Hamilton and the presidency of John Adams. Regarding the actual cost of Louisiana, see McDonald, *Presidency of Jefferson,* 69–70.

9. Goebel, ed., *Law Practice,* 1:775–806. Mitchell, *Hamilton,* 2:503, following Hamilton, *Intimate Life,* 177, gets the offending quotation wrong, misidentifies Charles Holt, editor of Croswell's rival Republican newspaper, *The Bee,* as John Holt, and mistakenly says Holt wrote for the *Evening Post.* For documentation of other errors in historians' accounts of the case, see Goebel, ed., *Law Practice,* 1:775, note 1, page 776, note 6, page 783, note 32, and pages 790–93, note 58. Besides the quoted passage, Croswell was indicted for another and similar article, critical of Jefferson, which had appeared a few weeks earlier; ibid., 1:776–77 and note 8. Regarding Jefferson and freedom of the press, see Leonard W. Levy, *Jefferson and Civil Liberties: The Darker Side* (New York, 1973), 42–69.

10. Goebel, ed., *Law Practice,* 1:813, 820–21, and 822 for the quoted passages, and for the Star Chamber argument, 795–97. Hamilton's championship of freedom of the press has sometimes been denigrated on the ground that in 1799 he had actuated the attorney general to prosecute a printer for having printed libelous statements about himself. But Hamilton's position was consistent: he sought in that trial to testify as to the truth of the statements (which were untrue), but he was not permitted to do so (ibid., 1:784 note 37).

11. Ibid., 1:796, 844–48.

12. For an account of the history of and historical controversy over this subject, see Mitchell, *Hamilton,* 2:518–27; for the relevant documents, see Henry Adams, ed., *Documents Relating to New-England Federalism, 1800–1815* (Boston, 1877).

13. The account of the duel which follows is derived from study of the pertinent documents, all of which are published in Harold C. Syrett and Jean G. Cooke, eds., *Interview in Weehawken: The Burr-Hamilton Duel as Told in the Original Documents* (Middletown, Conn., 1960). Though I disagree with the introductory essay written by Willard M. Wallace in several particulars, I have tried to recite here only what is generally agreed upon, except for additional comments about the *code duello.*

Notes

See also Merrill Lindsay, "Pistols Shed Light on Famed Duel," in *Smithsonian* (November 1976), 94–98.

14. Should Burr kill Hamilton in the duel, it would prove to the world that Burr was not a man of honor; thereby Hamilton would be sacrificing his life to end Burr's political career forever.

15. For details see Josephine Mayer and Robert A. East, "The Settlement of Alexander Hamilton's Debts: A Footnote to History," in *New York History,* 18:378–85 (October 1937); Mitchell, *Hamilton,* 2:547–53.

16. The history of Hamilton's public image is admirably traced in a book-length manuscript by Professor Lynn H. Parsons of the State University of New York, Brockport. Professor Parsons kindly allowed me to read the manuscript.

17. Hamilton, *Intimate Life,* 116–17.

Index

Index

Index

Index

Index

Index

Index

Index

Index

Index

Index

Index

Index

Index

Waddington, Benjamin, 65

Waddington, Joshua, 65, 66, 68

Wadsworth, Jeremiah, 77, 80, 82, 83, 176, 224

Walker, Benjamin, 160, 232, 244

Walpole, Robert, 126, 155, 215, 223, 330, 444

war, 20–24, 265, 266–67, 270–73, 279, 287, 288–91, 303, 323

War Department, 129, 154, 218, 250, 274, 339, 429

War for Independence, 14–25

Warville, Jean Pierre Brissot de, 146

Washington, George, 6, 20, 71, 114, 123, 137, 154, 165, 175, 184, 205, 217, 238, 239, 258, 328, 332, 358, 362; as administrator, 99, 125, 134–35; appointments, 99, 127–29, 133, 318–19; army career, 14–15, 18–19, 23–25, 45–47, 339–42, 344; and cabinet feud, 242–43, 250–53, 257, 285; and capital location, 175, 183–84, 202–4, 209, 210, 406; and foreign relations, 266–67, 271–78, 293–94, 314–19, 324–26; personal qualities, 124–126, 183, 204, 322; personal relations with Hamilton, 14–15, 23–24, 124, 252–53, 264, 289–93, 295–96, 340, 371, 429; presidency, conception of, 127; and Whiskey Rebellion, 299–302

Wasp (newspaper), 358

Wayne, Anthony, 130, 295, 297, 300, 303, 321

Webster, Daniel, 63

Weehawken, N.J., 361

Wesley, John, 372

West Indies, 150, 197, 268, 279, 288–89, 293

Whig school of political thought, *see* Oppositionists

whiskey, 150, 196, 297

Whiskey Rebellion, 86, 255–56, 297–303, 346, 430, 431

whiskey tax, 150, 196, 239, 255–56

White, Alexander, 176, 179, 186

Wilcox, William, 66

Wilkinson, James, 347

Williams, Otho H., 141

Williamson, Charles, 310

Williamson, Hugh, 46, 174

Willing, Thomas, 79–80, 83

Willing family, 343

Willinks, Van Staphorsts, and Hubbard, 146, 172, 221

Wilson, James, 32, 45, 46, 61, 83, 95–96, 105, 299, 382

Witherspoon, John, 12, 160

Wolcott, Oliver, Jr., 133, 160, 167, 218, 247, 258, 314–15, 321, 324–25, 331, 332, 334, 342, 347, 397

Wolff, Christian, 53, 378

work ethic, 3–4, 42, 121, 122, 165, 212, 213, 216, 233–36, 365

X, Y, Z affair, 338, 442

Yates, Robert, 93–94, 106, 381, 385

Yates family, 381

Yazoo Land Company of South Carolina, 275

yellow fever, 227–28, 282–83, 347

Yorktown, battle of, 25